Professional .NET Framework

Jeff Gabriel

Denise Gosnell

Jeffrey Hasan

Kevin Hoffman

Christian Holm

Ed Musters

Jan Narkiewicz

Jonothon Ortiz

John Schenken

Thiru Thangarathinam

Scott Wylie

Wrox Press Ltd. ®

Professional .NET Framework

Published by Wrox Press Ltd,
Arden House, 1102 Warwick Road, Acocks Green,
Birmingham, B27 6BH, UK
Printed in the United States
ISBN 1-861005-56-3

Trademark Acknowledgements

Wrox has endeavored to provide trademark information about all the companies and products mentioned in this book by the appropriate use of capitals. However, Wrox cannot guarantee the accuracy of this information.

Credits

Authors
Jeff Gabriel
Denise Gosnell
Jeffrey Hasan
Kevin Hoffman
Christian Holm
Ed Musters
Jan Narkiewicz
Jonothon Ortiz
John Schenken
Thiru Thangarathinam
Scott Wylie

Additional Material
Kent Tegels

Category Manager
Steve Farncombe
Kirsty Reade

Technical Architect
Sarah Drew

Technical Editors
Claire Brittle
Daniel Kent

Author Agents
Avril Corbin
Laura Jones

Project Administrators
Louise Carr
Cathy Succamore

Production Manager
Simon Hardware

Technical Reviewers
Martin Beaulieu
Maxime Bombardier
Navin Coutinho
Edgardo D'Andrea
Slavomir Furman
John Godfrey
Vic Honnaya
Ajoy Krishnamoorthy
Don Lee
Hal Levy
Juan T Llibre
Phil Powers-DeGeorge
Matthew Rabinowitz
Rachelle Reese
Juan Rovirosa
Larry Schoeneman
David Schultz
Marc Simkin
Adrian Sloan
Andrew Stopford
Rick Tempestini
John Timney

Production Project Coordinator
Paul Grove

Layout and Figures
Paul Grove

Cover
Dawn Chellingworth

Index
John Collin

Proof Reader
Agnes Wiggers

About the Authors

Jeff Gabriel

Jeff is currently Lead Architect for Active Technologies Group, Inc. where he works on e-commerce web sites for some of the companies that are still profitable after the bubble burst. Jeff has been studying and working with .NET since before beta 1 arrived, and worked with Microsoft in their .NET Enterprise Early Adopters program. When not writing or reviewing for Wrox, Jeff uses his spare time to hang out with his wife and kids and read other people's technical books and articles.

Of course, I would like to thank my lovely wife and wonderful children for giving me up for a while to finish work on this book. I also appreciate the opportunities and training given by Bill and Sara from Microsoft, and the great folks of eNationwide. Finally, Wrox's editors and reviewers deserve all the credit for making my work end up better than I could make it alone.

Denise Gosnell

Denise Gosnell is a consultant in the Microsoft Consulting Services Public Sector Practice at Microsoft (dgosnell@microsoft.com). Denise has a unique background in both law and technology and uses her background to help federal, state, and local governments implement hi-tech solutions.

She received a bachelor's degree in Computer Science – Business (summa cum laude) from Anderson University and a Doctor of Jurisprudence from Indiana University School of Law in Indianapolis. Denise is an attorney licensed to practice law in Indiana and is an active member of the Indiana and Indianapolis Bar Associations. Her legal areas of expertise are intellectual property law and real estate law. Denise is also a Microsoft Certified Solution Developer.

Denise has worked in the computer industry since 1994 in a variety of roles ranging from Systems Engineer, Programmer, IS Manager, and Senior Consultant. Denise is also an avid writer, and has co-authored the following books: *MSDE Bible* (IDG Books – Dec 2000) and *Professional SQL Server 2000 XML* (Wrox Press – June 2001).

When Denise isn't working, writing, or studying, she and her husband Jake enjoy traveling around the globe to interesting places such as Russia, China, and Poland.

To my husband Jake for his continued support of my writing and professional efforts.

Jeffrey Hasan

Jeffrey Hasan is a technical architect specializing in Microsoft technology at LiveMarket, Inc., an e-business solutions provider in Orange County, California. He has extensive experience developing N-Tier applications with Visual Studio, SQL Server, Internet Information Server, Commerce Server, and BizTalk Server. He has written numerous articles on application development, and is a contributing author to several books by Wrox Press. He holds an M.S. degree from Duke University and is a Microsoft Certified Professional Developer. Jeff is a chronic traveler and an avid music fan, although he has yet to figure out how to combine the two. His passport has most recently been stamped in Costa Rica, Mexico, Pakistan, Sweden, the UK, and a smattering of places in between. E-mail Jeff at: JHasan85@hotmail.com.

Kevin Hoffman

I'm currently employed as a Software Engineer and "Web Product Line Manager" for a company that provides software and services for total chemical management. I've been programming since I was 10 when my grandfather gave me a VIC-20 he had salvaged and repaired. I've written applications in everything from Assembly and Scheme to Pascal, C++, VB, Python, PHP, Java, Delphi and my new favorite toy, C#. My interests include programming, movies (only the good ones, though), and science fiction/fantasy books.

I would like to dedicate my work on this book to the memory of my grandfather, to my wife, Connie, for all her patience and support and without whom I would have neither the confidence nor the patience for technical writing, and to my daughter Alia.

I would like to acknowledge the editors at Wrox for all their hard work in putting this great book together.

Christian Holm

Christian started his writing career in mid-2000, writing articles for AspHeute.com, which has grown to the largest German-centric developer platform for Active Server Pages and .NET related technology. His focus shifted away from ASP to .NET when he was introduced to Microsoft's .NET vision shortly after it was introduced to the public at the PDC 2000 in Orlando.

Since that time he eagerly adapted the rich features of the .NET technology for his business and additionally revealed the attained .NET experience to the developers reading his articles on AspHeute.com. Despite his close to 24-by-7 job he tries hard to finish his study of Mechanical Engineering.

Ed Musters

Ed Musters is the Chief Technology Officer for Systemgroup Inc., where his role is to evangelize the Microsoft Technology Platform. He specializes in architecting demanding transactional applications that must scale to thousands of users. Ed lives with his wife and three sons in Toronto, Canada. Ed holds a Bachelor of Mathematics degree from the University of Waterloo, specializing in Statistics and Computer Science.

Jan Narkiewicz

Jan D. Narkiewicz is Chief Technical Officer at Software Pronto, Inc (jann@softwarepronto.com). Jan began his career as a Microsoft developer thanks to basketball star, Michael Jordan. In the early 90's Jan noticed that no matter what happened during a game, Michael Jordan's team won. Similarly, no matter what happened in technology, Microsoft always won (then again this strategy is ten years old and may need some revamping). Clearly there was a bandwagon to be jumped upon. Over the years Jan managed to work on an e-mail system that resided on 17 million desktops, helped automate factories that make blue jeans you have in your closet (trust me you own this brand) and kept the skies over the Emirate of Abu Dhabi safe from enemy aircraft. All this was achieved using technology such as COM/DCOM, COM+, C++, VB, C#, ADO, SQL Server, Oracle, DB2, ASP.NET, ADO.NET, Java, Linux and XML. In his spare time Jan is Academic Coordinator for the Windows curriculum at U.C. Berkeley Extension, teaches at U.C. Santa Cruz Extension, writes for ASP Today and occasionally plays some football (a.k.a. soccer).

Jonothon Ortiz

Jonothon Ortiz is a Christian who works with Youth at the Bread of Life mission in Plant City, FL. He is also the Vice President of Xnext, Inc. in Winter Haven, FL. Somehow during the course of his obviously busy life he found time to marry his wife, Carla Ortiz, and they are currently living within the central Florida area.

At Xnext, Inc. Jonothon handles all of the administrative duties of a Vice President plus handles personnel and the programming department. He has experience programming with various low-to-high level languages, including Assembly, C/C++, Ruby, Perl/CGI, ASP, and Visual Basic within the .NET platform. Jonothon is happy to be working within Xnext, Inc. and sees immense growth in the future of the company.

I would like to thank my wife, Carla Ortiz, my grandparents Lydia & Luis Gonzalez (I wish you were here to see this grandpa!) <rach>, my mother Belgica Gonzalez, my second parent set of Eduardo & Anna Argüelles, my sister Gigi Ortiz, my new brother Lucas Argüelles & his wife, Sarah, my new cousin Elizabeth Caballero, my boss, Richard Young, co-worker Joe Boyd, BJ K., Jim K., Douglas H., Richard L, Nathalie L., Ryan S., Josh, Chris, blindeyesopen, and the Lauze family, and online friends MauriAnne, AmyCrow, Heidanseek, Cynnapede, MbCash 218, and Soulfrost.

A VERY special thanks to Ms. Barto, Mr. Stephen Mayer, Mr. & Mrs. Grey, and the rest of the staff during my time at Hernando Christian Academy for all their support. Thanks for being the first teachers I ever had who knew what I was capable of.

Finally, and most importantly, Jesus Christ – I wouldn't be here without him.

John Schenken

John Schenken is an SDET/Lead at Viair Inc., a mobile applications management and services delivery platform provider for wireless carriers. John earned his Computer Science degree at Texas A&M University, along with a minor in Genetics. Prior to moving to Viair, John worked at Microsoft as an SDET on Visual InterDev, Windows NT Option Pack, Microsoft Script Debugger for IIS, Visual Basic, and the .NET Frameworks team. He currently develops in Java, VB.NET, VBScript, or C# code depending on the application being developed. John has previously authored chapters for Introducing .NET, ASP 3.0 Programmers Reference, Professional ASP 3.0, and Professional CDO Programming.

I would like to take this chance to thank my dad, Carl, for all of his support and encouragement. I would also like to dedicate this book to the memory of my grandparents Ruth & Carl, as well as to my grandparents Sid & Big John for all they have done. Many of my accomplishments would not have been realized without the support of my family.

Thiru Thangarathinam

Thiru works as a Consultant at Spherion Technology Architects, an international technology consulting company, in Phoenix, Arizona. He is an MCSD. During the last two years, he has been developing Distributed N-Tier architecture solutions for various companies using the latest technologies, such as VB, ASP, XML, XSL, COM+ and SQL Server. When not sitting in front of his computer and writing .NET code, Thiru can be seen chatting with his family, listening to tamil songs, and of course reading books. He can be reached via e-mail at ThiruThangarathinam@spherion.com.

I would like to dedicate this book to my father who has been a source of motivation and inspiration for me all along. I am sure when he gets to know about this writing venture of mine, he will be the happiest person in the world, as I will be, on seeing his reaction. Also special thanks to my friends Sridhar and Laxminarayana for their constant support and encouragement throughout this project.

Scott Wylie

Scott Wylie, MCSD, is a senior consultant working for Magenic Technologies (http://www.magenic.com) in San Mateo, California, although his home will always be, Vancouver, British Columbia, Canada. Scott knew his life would never be the same when his mother, a schoolteacher, borrowed an Apple II+ from work to use over the Christmas break in 1977.

Scott has been working with Microsoft products since the days of DOS. He began his career as a developer with the release of Visual Basic 3.0 and has continued working with VB with each subsequent release. Scott has always felt that he was different when it comes to development, preferring to focus on process first and coding second. When Scott isn't working he spends almost all his free time living and breathing auto racing (Gilles Villeneuve is a god!). His greatest personal accomplishment to date is graduating from Skip Barber Racing School at Laguna Seca Raceway in California.

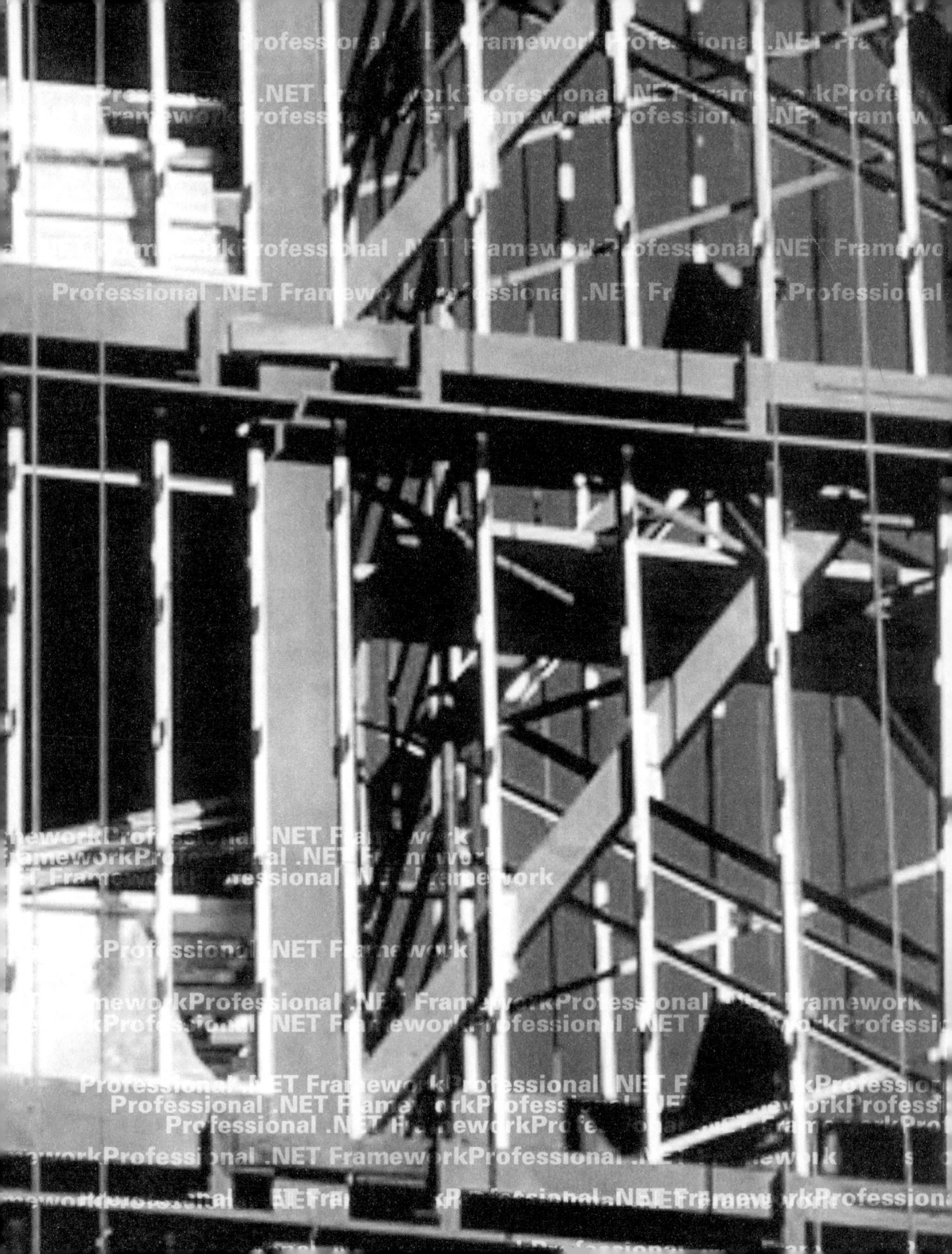
Professional .NET Framework

Table of Contents

Table of Contents

Table of Contents

Table of Contents

Table of Contents

Table of Contents

Table of Contents

Introduction

Those of us who are Microsoft developers can't help but notice that .NET has received a fair amount of visibility over the last year. .NET really is a product for developers, providing a great foundation for building all types of applications. .NET has huge scope, presenting us with a wealth of new technologies and techniques. The sheer number of new possibilities may seem daunting at first, but ultimately it will make our lives as developers much easier.

This book aims to introduce and explain the key features of the .NET framework – the multi-language application execution environment that underpins the .NET philosophy. We will look at how we can best leverage its functionality to create the next generation of applications.

What Does This Book Cover?

This book was written with the Beta 2 version of the .NET Framework in mind. This release is almost feature complete, and stable enough for developers to begin learning about and using the new technology as well as deploying live sites. While we can't guarantee that the final release version will be identical, you can be sure that almost all of the concepts, examples, and explanations we provide are accurate within the timeframe of the first full version of .NET.

In this book, we attempt to explain just what the .NET Framework is all about, how you can use it, and what you can use it for. We start in **Chapter 1** with a look at the aims of .NET, placing it firmly within the context of its predecessors to see exactly why .NET is such a change and why we should be getting excited about the opportunities that it affords.

Chapter 2 moves on to look at the constituent parts of the .NET Framework, such as the Common Language Runtime, Common Type System, and maps out the 'big picture' we should all keep in mind. **Chapter 3** continues this by delving more into the Common Language Runtime and the Stack, explaining more about what it is, managed and unmanaged code, and object types.

Chapter 4 discusses the advantages and disadvantages of the Common Language Runtime, explaining more deeply the Common Language System and the Microsoft Intermediate Language. This is further examined in **Chapter 5**, where we move on to runtime hosts, and how the Code Manager controls the execution process.

Now that we have a general idea of the .NET Framework and what it contains, **Chapter 6** delves into the specifics of the System namespace, in particular the classes defined within, the functionality they contain, and how best to use them to exploit their full capability.

With .NET, we should be looking at building solid code for business logic and data, with only a thin presentation layer differentiating between a Windows and a Web application. **Chapter 7** looks at this in detail, including an extended example showing exactly this concept.

Chapter 8 moves on to look at controls and components: how COM controls can be used in .NET and how .NET components can be used in COM. This chapter looks at building components for both Windows and Web applications, and looks also at the concept of transactions.

Chapter 9 changes tack a little and concentrates on the data that we will be using in .NET and, more specifically, how to access that data. We look at ADO.NET, which is not merely the .NET version of ADO, and also look at XML, as well as the relevant namespaces they utilize.

With the continued success of the Internet, Web Services are becoming more important. **Chapter 10** looks at the high-level business factors behind Web Services, as well as the related technology to bring them to force, such as SOAP, DISCO, WDSL, and UDDI. Related to this is the idea of .NET Remoting – the way in which inter-process communication is handled – obviously of great importance when dealing with distributed systems. Remoting is covered in **Chapter 11**.

As .NET is so new, and so many people are trying to learn how to use it to its best advantage, **Chapter 12** covers some best practices in .NET, such as coding standards, what documentation to provide to ensure that everyone is at the same level, and even when to avoid .NET if there is a better way of doing something.

Building a .NET application from scratch is all well and good, but with a product so new, it is maybe best to take an existing application and move it to .NET. With this in mind, the book ends with **Chapter 13**, which covers migration to .NET. Here you will find discussion about the three 'rules' of migrating – reduce, reuse, recycle – and what tools there are to use in migrating your application to .NET.

We then have a series of case studies which demonstrate .NET from a real application perspective, and really let you sink your teeth into the framework and its classes.

Who Is This Book For?

This is a book aimed at intermediate to advanced level programmers, sitting alongside *Professional ASP.NET* or *Professional C#* as a practical guide to the .NET framework itself and a guide to *leveraging* the scalability, reusability, and functionality in developing new applications, and working with old ones, in the most efficient and effective way. This book should place .NET in a meaningful context and help developers make the transition by providing a thorough, yet relevant example-led approach to understanding and working with the constituent parts of the framework. It will drill down to a level that scopes specific classes in detail, yet retain a focus on imparting information that developers *need* because it is practical, relevant, and useful.

What You Need To Use This Book

To run the samples in this book you need to have the following:

- ❑ Windows 2000, Windows XP, or Windows NT 4.0.

- ❑ Beta 2 release of the .NET Framework SDK. This can be downloaded from http://msdn.microsoft.com/downloads/default.asp?url=/downloads/sample.asp?url=/msdn-files/027/000/976/msdncompositedoc.xml&frame=true.

- ❑ Beta 2 release of Visual Studio.NET. Although this isn't strictly necessary, as you can compile and run the examples in this book from the console, if you prefer a GUI, you can find information about how to obtain Visual Studio.NET Beta 2 at http://msdn.microsoft.com/vstudio/nextgen/getbeta.asp. If you decide to obtain this, it already includes the .NET Framework, so a further download is not necessary.

This book has not been written with any specific language in mind: examples are provided in Visual Basic.NET and C#, the new .NET language. For more information about these specific languages, consult *Professional VB.NET*, Wrox Press, ISBN 1861004974, or *Beginning C#*, Wrox Press, ISBN 1861004982.

Conventions

We've used a number of different styles of text and layout in this book to help differentiate between the different kinds of information. Here are examples of the styles we used and an explanation of what they mean.

Code has several fonts. If it's a word that we're talking about in the text – for example, when discussing a For...Next loop, it's in this font. If it's a block of code that can be typed as a program and run, then it's also in a gray box:

```
<?xml version 1.0?>
```

Sometimes we'll see code in a mixture of styles, like this:

```
<?xml version 1.0?>
<Invoice>
   <part>
      <name>Widget</name>
      <price>$10.00</price>
   </part>
</invoice>
```

In cases like this, the code with a white background is code we are already familiar with; the line highlighted in gray is a new addition to the code since we last looked at it.

In addition, if a line of VB.NET code is too long to fit on a page, it will include a continuation character. '_', at the end of a line, with the code on the next line indented to show that it should continue unbroken, as follows:

```
Public Class ShippingService
    Inherits System.Web.Services.WebService

    <WebMethod()> Public Function CalculateShippingCost(ByVal dblWeight as _
                 double, ByVal strShippingMethod as String) As Double

    Dim dblHandlingCost as Double
    Dim dblShippingCost as Double
```

C# and XML compile to the next end of statement, and so code carrying over to another line will not cause any problems in compiling– for this reason, you will not see continuation characters in C# or XML code, although the following lines of code may be indented to show that ideally the code belongs on one line.

There are occasions in this book that you will type code at a command line; in many cases you can just copy what you see. However, sometimes the line of code may carry on to the next line, due to the width of the page: in this case, we have included a continuation character, '⅂', at the end of the line, showing that the line should be entered continuously and unbroken, as follows:

```
csc /out:SimpleLibrary1.dll /t:library SimpleClass1.cs ⅂
        /r:System.Runtime.Remoting.dll
csc /out:SimpleClient.exe /t:exe Class1.cs /r:System.Runtime.Remoting.dll ⅂
        /r:SimpleLibrary1.dll
```

Advice, hints, and background information comes in this type of font.

Important pieces of information come in boxes like this.

Bullets appear indented, with each new bullet marked as follows:

❑ **Important Words** are in a bold type font.

❑ Words that appear on the screen, or in menus like the File or Window, are in a similar font to the one you would see on a Windows desktop.

❑ Keys that you press on the keyboard like *Ctrl* and *Enter*, are in italics.

Customer Support

We always value hearing from our readers, and we want to know what you think about this book: what you liked, what you didn't like, and what you think we can do better next time. You can send us your comments, either by returning the reply card in the back of the book, or by e-mail to feedback@wrox.com. Please be sure to mention the book title in your message.

How to Download the Sample Code for the Book

When you log on to the Wrox site, http://www.wrox.com/, simply locate the title through our Search facility or by using one of the title lists. Click on Download in the Code column, or on Download Code on the book's detail page.

The files that are available for download from our site have been archived using WinZip. When you have saved the attachments to a folder on your hard-drive, you need to extract the files using a de-compression program such as WinZip or PKUnzip. When you extract the files, the code is usually extracted into chapter folders. When you start the extraction process, ensure your software (WinZip, PKUnzip, etc.) is set to extract to Use Folder Names.

Errata

We've made every effort to make sure that there are no errors in the text or in the code. However, no one is perfect and mistakes do occur. If you find an error in one of our books, like a spelling mistake or a faulty piece of code, we would be very grateful for feedback. By sending in errata you may save another reader hours of frustration, and of course, you will be helping us provide even higher quality information. Simply e-mail the information to support@wrox.com, your information will be checked and if correct, posted to the errata page for that title, or used in subsequent editions of the book.

To find errata on the web site, log on to http://www.wrox.com/, and simply locate the title through our Advanced Search or title list. Click on the Book Errata link, which is below the cover graphic on the book's detail page.

E-mail Support

If you wish to directly query a problem in the book page with an expert who knows the book in detail then e-mail support@wrox.com, with the title of the book and the last four numbers of the ISBN in the subject field of the e-mail. A typical e-mail should include the following things:

- ❑ The **name, last four digits of the ISBN,** and **page number** of the problem in the Subject field.
- ❑ Your **name, contact information,** and the **problem** in the body of the message.

We **won't** send you junk mail. We need the details to save your time and ours. When you send an e-mail message, it will go through the following chain of support:

- ❑ Customer Support – Your message is delivered to our customer support staff, who are the first people to read it. They have files on most frequently asked questions and will answer anything general about the book or the web site immediately.
- ❑ Editorial – Deeper queries are forwarded to the technical editor responsible for that book. They have experience with the programming language or particular product, and are able to answer detailed technical questions on the subject. Once an issue has been resolved, the editor can post the errata to the web site.

❑ The Authors – Finally, in the unlikely event that the editor cannot answer your problem, he or she will forward the request to the author. We do try to protect the author from any distractions to their writing; however, we are quite happy to forward specific requests to them. All Wrox authors help with the support on their books. They will e-mail the customer and the editor with their response, and again all readers should benefit.

The Wrox Support process can only offer support to issues that are directly pertinent to the content of our published title. Support for questions that fall outside the scope of normal book support, is provided via the community lists of our http://p2p.wrox.com/ forum.

p2p.wrox.com

For author and peer discussion join the P2P mailing lists. Our unique system provides **programmer to programmer**™ contact on mailing lists, forums, and newsgroups, all **in addition** to our one-to-one e-mail support system. Be confident that your query is being examined by the many Wrox authors and other industry experts who are present on our mailing lists. At p2p.wrox.com you will find a number of different lists that will help you, not only while you read this book, but also as you develop your own applications.

To subscribe to a mailing list just follow these steps:

1. Go to http://p2p.wrox.com/.

2. Choose the appropriate category from the left menu bar.

3. Click on the mailing list you wish to join.

4. Follow the instructions to subscribe and fill in your e-mail address and password.

5. Reply to the confirmation e-mail you receive.

6. Use the subscription manager to join more lists and set your e-mail preferences.

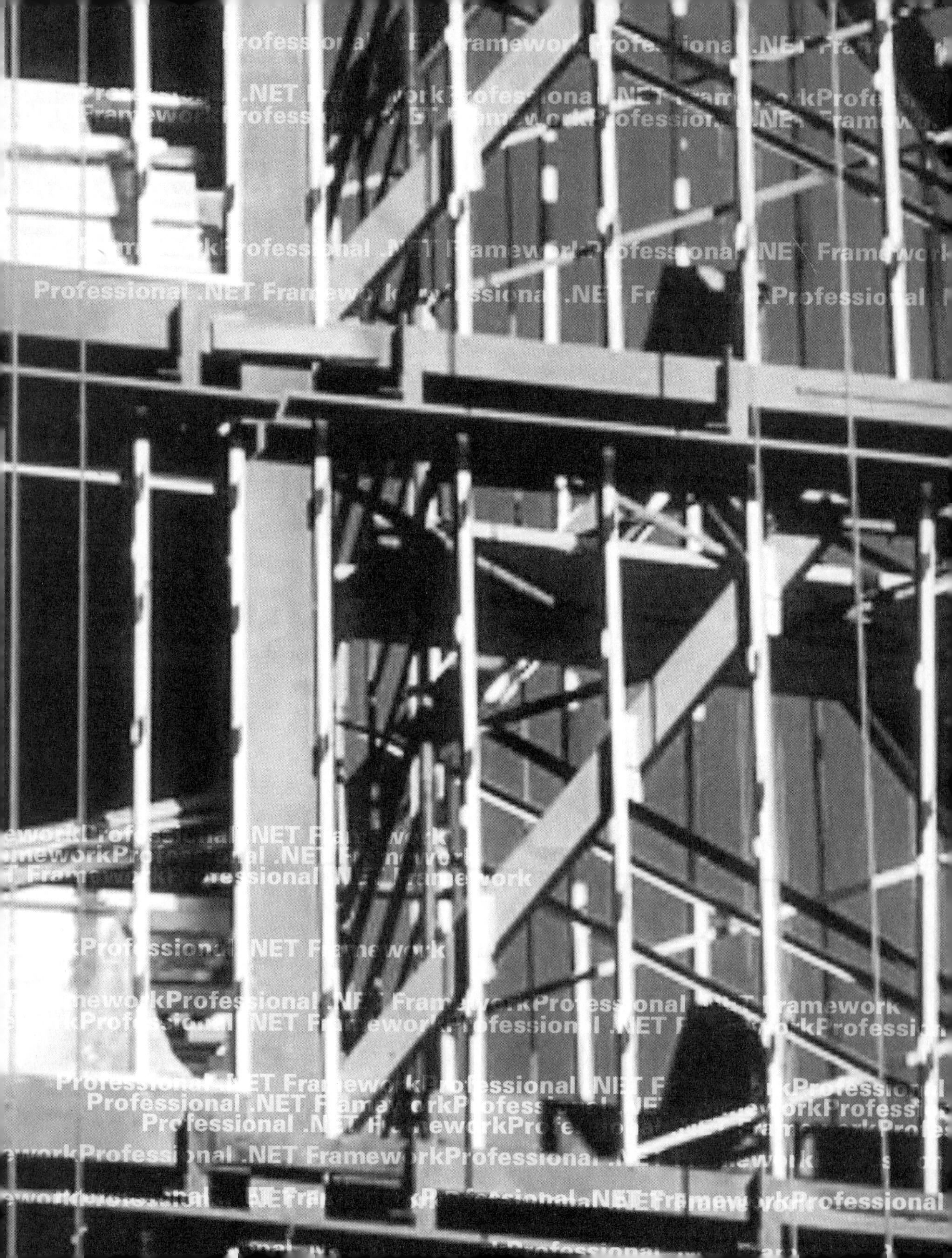
Professional .NET Framework

1

.NET in Context

The .NET initiative encompasses a suite of tools and technologies that represent Microsoft's next - generation platform for Windows and Internet development. For developers, Microsoft seeks, with .NET, to simplify application development and deployment (especially for Internet applications), and to promote web services as the best way to design and deploy distributed applications.

Microsoft has redesigned the Windows development platform into the new .NET Framework, which encompasses the execution platform, updated languages, and a large number of extensible class libraries. Those readers who are familiar with the original Microsoft Foundation Classes paradigm will likely recognize elements of MFC in the .NET Framework, because, like MFC, the Framework encapsulates system functionality into a set of classes and interfaces that are easy to use and easy to extend into custom classes.

Unlike MFC, the Framework provides a complete environment for executing code in a type-safe manner and the other important feature is that the Framework Classes are more highly available than MFC, because developers may use the same set of classes from multiple languages; including VB.NET, C#.NET, and C++.NET. MFC was restricted to C++.

Microsoft is also pitching the business benefits of the .NET Framework to non-technical, business consumers. They are promoting the concept of "software as a service", where software becomes a set of distributed services that you can access from a variety of platforms, from PCs to handheld devices. The thrust of this concept is web services and .NET is conceived as the platform for delivering them. These are highly distributed components that respond to requests over the Internet using the Simple Object Access Protocol (SOAP), which is a protocol for delivering XML over HTTP.

The vision behind web services is that they will change the way that applications are designed and deployed. Applications built with .NET may be made up of distributed web services components that collaborate together to provide a set of services. Microsoft is touting the benefits by saying that .NET applications will collaborate more easily, and will be easily accessible from a variety of devices, from the desktop PC to handheld PDAs. These are common concerns for business consumers who often cannot access their information in the same way from different devices.

The HailStorm initiative represents the consumer side of the .NET initiative. With HailStorm, Microsoft is promoting on-demand consumer services that are available on centralized servers, and available from any device. The services would be available to consumers for a monthly subscription fee. From a technical perspective, HailStorm services are consumer-oriented web services that may leverage a base set of services provided by Microsoft, including authentication and messaging. These are services that are common to consumer-oriented, distributed applications. Microsoft's approach is to make these services available to developers, and allow them to focus on specialized functionality. Of course, Microsoft's intentions are not entirely altruistic. They are hoping to generate significant revenue by charging a monthly subscription fee for consumers to access centralized services such as on-demand authentication from whichever device they happen to be using. For developers, Microsoft is hoping to engage the independent software vendor (ISV) community into developing web services, much as the ISVs embraced ActiveX Component technology several years ago.

Many developers welcome the release of a major new technology, especially one that promises to make application development easier. But with this anticipation comes the natural trepidation that leads to questions such as "What problem does this new platform fix?", "How do I use it?", and "What was wrong with what we had before?". The aim of this chapter is to address these concerns, by explaining the wider goals of .NET and how it evolved from previous development platforms in response to today's software development challenges.

We will discuss:

❑ What the .NET initiative encompasses: a new development platform; a managed execution environment; a choice of new application types, including web services

❑ How .NET is designed to address limitations with developing and deploying COM-based applications

❑ What .NET has to offer us

The Vision and Goals of .NET

The vision behind the .NET Framework is to provide a feature-rich application development platform and a managed, protected execution environment. The .NET Framework is intended to provide an environment that simplifies the development, deployment, and execution of distributed applications. This is the vision as it relates to developers: you and me. And, of course, on the consumer side, Microsoft is presenting .NET as the platform for XML Web Services, which they envision will enable applications to collaborate and to exchange data more easily. In the broadest sense, the .NET initiative represents Microsoft's realignment and total focus on Internet-enabled, distributed application technology.

The goals of .NET are to:

❑ Provide a new development platform for Internet and distributed applications

❑ Simplify application development and deployment

❑ Provide a platform for building web services

❑ Improve interoperability and integration between systems and applications

❑ Enable "universal access" of applications from any device

We will discuss each of these points in great detail in this chapter. But first, there is a history that led up to the .NET initiative, and the story is one of developing a new platform to meet the challenges of creating applications for today's Internet-enabled world. So let's dig deeper into the .NET initiative, in the context of the challenges that today's developers and software consumers face.

What Are Today's Challenges?

Developers today are faced with a "patchwork quilt" of tools and technologies for building Internet applications. Microsoft has made a significant push over the last several years towards making Internet development easier. The Windows 2000 platform today provides a powerful set of services that support Internet development, including Internet Information Services (IIS) and Component Services (COM+).

However, the Windows API is not easy to program with, largely because it does not provide a consistent, object-oriented hook into the operating system. The API model is plagued by inconsistencies and bugs that make it difficult to call some of the functions, particularly for Visual Basic developers, who don't always have access to the same data types that Windows API functions require. Developers often get around this problem by substituting analogous data types into the function calls, which may make their application unstable. C++ developers are slightly better off, because they have access to the Microsoft Foundation Classes, which do provide object-oriented wrappers to Windows API functions. The basic challenge here is that Windows system functionality is not exposed as a uniform, consistent programming model to developers using different languages.

Consider the following Windows API function, `CreateWindowEx`, which creates a new window, and returns the handle:

```
HWND CreateWindowEx(
    DWORD dwExStyle,        // extended window style
    LPCTSTR lpClassName,    // registered class name
    LPCTSTR lpWindowName,   // window name
    DWORD dwStyle,          // window style
    int x,                  // horizontal position of window
    int y,                  // vertical position of window
    int nWidth,             // window width
    int nHeight,            // window height
    HWND hWndParent,        // handle to parent or owner window
    HMENU hMenu,            // menu handle or child identifier
    HINSTANCE hInstance,    // handle to application instance
    LPVOID lpParam          // window-creation data
);
```

Now look at the function declaration for creating a new window in .NET, using C#:

```
public virtual void CreateHandle(
    CreateParams cp
);
```

The `CreateParams` class represents the properties of the new window. Its members include: `Caption`, `ExStyle`, `Height`, `Width`, `X`, `Y`, and `Parent`. This is just a single example, but it illustrates how .NET encapsulates familiar Windows API functions inside object-oriented wrappers. And the best part is that these base classes are uniformly available across all .NET-compliant languages, including VB.NET, C#, and Managed C++.

Another of today's challenges includes limited toolset support for working with XML, which is becoming a critical technology for data exchange in Internet and distributed applications. XML is text-based, portable, and based on industry standards. It promotes data sharing and interoperability between applications that can communicate using the common language of XML. Yet current Microsoft support for working with XML is really quite limited, although you could point to specific examples such as SQL Server 2000 (which can generate both raw and formatted XML from stored procedures); in addition, Microsoft provides an object-oriented implementation of the Document Object Model. But while it is true that there are a number of XML tools and capabilities available today, they are not designed to work together, and they don't plug into Visual Studio's integrated development environment. VS.NET, on the other hand, provides an integrated XML Data Designer.

As professional developers, we are primarily concerned with the challenges that are directly facing us. However, some mention must be made of another important audience for the .NET initiative, namely, the business consumers of software applications. This audience works with data all the time, and needs to be able to share information between applications and across different devices. Consumers today have a lot of technology to work with. There are, for example, database-driven web applications to store information, and spreadsheet applications to crunch that information. But how do you get the web application to talk to the spreadsheet application? If you're lucky, the web application will provide an export utility to the spreadsheet application. If you're unlucky, you could find yourself pulling the numbers up on your browser, and typing them by hand into a new spreadsheet. This is a simple, and perhaps very obvious example, but it illustrates how getting different technologies to work together can be a difficult and frustrating challenge. Difficult, that is, unless the applications are designed to work together, and can collaborate seamlessly. The implications to businesses are staggering in terms of productivity loss and efficiency loss. Every hour that you spend struggling to get information from one device to another is an hour that you could instead have been focusing on the real business task at hand.

Let's consider where we are today in terms of our technology's ability to collaborate:

❑ **Multiple, Disparate Systems** – business data is often spread across multiple systems, sometimes running on multiple operating systems. For example, employee data may be stored in PeopleSoft running on Unix, while application data is stored in Oracle running on Windows. It is difficult to pull all of the data together into a unified view. Business users need to view multiple data sets together in order to make intelligent business decisions.

❑ **Limited Device Support** – e-mail and messaging are the current killer applications over remote, wireless networks. Data is still designed to be very device-specific. Synchronization is today's answer for getting devices to collaborate. For example, your e-mail and messaging service may be an account on your corporate Microsoft Exchange Server, but you find yourself accessing your e-mail more from your wireless PDA than from your desktop PC (PDAs are a large family of hand-held devices that includes wireless phones, messaging devices, and even the delivery tablets that are used by mail services such as UPS). Today, you may have to periodically synchronize your PDA's copy of your e-mail using a docking station attached to your desktop PC (Blackberry/RIM users are at an advantage here, because their devices receive e-mail directly).

❑ **Limited Applications** – we are beginning to see other kinds of applications available on these devices, such as news services and stock quote services. However, the kinds of application we can access over wireless is still very limited compared to what we can get from a local, desktop PC that is wired into the Internet. We need a new development platform that makes it easier to develop the next generation of wireless applications. Furthermore, we need a new platform that makes it easier to develop applications that are used by multiple clients.

Before you reach over to toss your PDA into the nearest waste-basket, read on, because there may well be a bright future for this device, as well as for many of the other limitations that we find ourselves with today. For those readers who feel more skeptical about the vision of .NET, let me say that visions are valuable, because they focus us on a journey in a new direction. There will be practical challenges to working with .NET, because it is an immature technology that will require a steep learning curve. But developers are never ones to shy away from a challenge!

> *.NET has been designed primarily with Windows-based Internet and distributed applications in mind. Other kinds of development, such as games and drivers, may or may not recognize the same benefits from .NET.*

Now let's take a look at how .NET addresses the challenges that we have just described.

How .NET Addresses Today's Challenges

Clearly, business users today are faced with a lot of technology, but a limited ability to get at their data in a meaningful, productive way. Like it or not, the venerable old desktop PC (or laptop) is still your best choice for accessing both your data and a rich set of applications. As we've already said, the .NET platform attempts to address these deficiencies by enabling the creation of highly distributed applications that are easily accessible from any device. .NET provides a unified set of tools and technologies for building applications that are based on collaborative web services. We've already touched briefly on the problematic areas for programmers that .NET may present, but here we're going to focus more deeply on how it will address them.

So, first of all, what are the benefits of .NET?

Simplify Application Development

There are several limitations with current development tools and technologies that reduce developer productivity. Development should become easier because the .NET Framework provides a new set of tools, including a large set of object-oriented, extensible, system-level classes. The .NET Framework brings the power of the operating system much closer to the developer, through a rich set of classes and services that are more easily accessible than any previous Windows-based set of APIs. Developers will be able to spend less time on getting to the functionality they need, and more time building software.

The .NET Framework simplifies development in the long term. In the short term, many developers can expect to face a steep learning curve, as they explore what the .NET Framework offers, and how to work with the new system of classes. For Visual Basic developers especially, .NET programming is more complex and more abstract than Visual Basic 6.0 programming. In particular, Visual Basic lets you get away with shortcuts that .NET will not, for example, allowing weak typing of variables using the `Variant` and `Object` keyword.

Simplify Application Deployment

Application deployments are subject to the familiar headaches of "DLL Hell" that arise when component registrations get corrupted, or type library versions get mixed up. The .NET Framework overcomes these deployment limitations by making components self-describing through meta data, so removing the need for GUID-based registration.

XML Everywhere

The .NET Framework introduces XML into every aspect of software development on this new platform. XML is the common communication technology in .NET. It is used as the basis for a number of XML-based grammars that describe information in the .NET Framework. A **grammar** refers to a collection of fixed XML tags that combine to describe a specific object or entity. For example, XML is the basis for data streaming and persistence in ADO.NET. Disconnected data sharing is easier than before, because ADO.NET natively serializes to XML, which is easy to share between distributed components, or tiers within a distributed application. XML is also the basis for UDDI and WSDL, which document and publish information about web services. We will explore the role of XML in .NET further in a dedicated section later in the chapter.

So, XML provides a unified system for sharing data within the .NET Framework, and between components built using .NET. The prominent role of XML makes web services possible, and also makes it easier to share data across disconnected components. This may in turn change the way that developers think about designing and building their applications. XML will become as integral to .NET development, and as essential to developers, as ActiveX controls are to putting together a form-based application. It will also help to overcome the limitations of current development tools and technologies for building distributed applications.

Universal Data Access

This catchphrase sounds suspiciously like the one behind OLE DB, and Microsoft's vision of a data access technology for all data sources, beyond the traditional relational database source. However, in the case of .NET, universal data access means that ability to access data anytime, from anywhere, regardless of what device you have at hand. Business users care first and foremost about their data. Applications are simply useful containers for displaying data. Applications today can almost be an impediment to data access, if you need to use them on different devices. Microsoft Access may work beautifully on a desktop PC, but try using it on a hand-held PDA, and you're in for a much more awkward user experience. (This example is for illustrative purposes only, and does not reflect a specific problem with Access!).

With .NET, traditional applications can be rewritten as Web Services that deliver data as XML over HTTP, using the open standard called Simple Object Access Protocol (SOAP). This is a very flexible way to exchange data, because XML does not dictate how it is displayed. XML's only role is to provide an efficient way of organizing the data. Web services deliver the data, and leave it up to the consumer to interpret it. So, the same set of raw XML data is delivered automatically to several different devices. Each device in turn transforms the XML into a presentation that is best suited to the device.

Web Services: Collaboration over the Internet

Microsoft's .NET initiative provides the tools and technology for creating and implementing XML Web Services. We said right at the start of the chapter that, with .NET, Microsoft is promoting the concept of "software as a service". This concept states that software should be highly available, easily accessible and support collaboration. The Internet is the great enabler of this vision, because it provides a TCP/IP based global communication network that is available around the clock.

Web Services are a natural step towards harnessing the distributed power of the Internet. .NET has been designed to ensure that all types of services can participate in collaborative applications. In this context, an application is no longer a tightly integrated set of components: instead, it is made up of loosely-coupled, distributed Web Services that interoperate using XML and HTTP. According to the .NET vision, every Internet-enabled device is a potential platform for hosting web services. The only prerequisite to this collaborative effort is that both the provider and the consumer interoperate using the same protocols.

Developers can code Web Services in any language that they choose (proprietary or otherwise), and their component may interact with any consumer that can work with XML, on any operating system. And by their distributed nature, Web Services are available to respond to any device that is hooked into the Internet. Thus, Web Services enable universal data access because they communicate with XML, and are highly available. In a nutshell, Web Services return the focus to the data, and away from a specific site or application.

The Building Blocks of .NET

How do you put .NET to work for you? Microsoft is putting together a dizzying array of resources that enable you to deliver a .NET solution. This includes the full suite of support products: everything from Visual Studio .NET (the development environment) to Windows 2000 and Windows XP (the operating systems that host .NET solutions, which will move on to Windows.NET in the future). Collectively, these resources are known as the .NET Building Blocks.

The Building Blocks of .NET are:

- ❑ The .NET Framework
- ❑ .NET Enterprise Servers
- ❑ .NET Building Block Services
- ❑ Visual Studio.NET

Let's discuss each of these in turn.

The .NET Framework

For developers, Microsoft provides the new .NET Framework, which is a set of system services, classes, and data types that enhance developer productivity, and give easier access to the deep set of functionality provided by Windows. The .NET Framework enhances developer productivity, because it handles many of the low-level plumbing details that are required for components to work together, and to scale. It handles memory management as well, and introduces a high level of thread safety, so that errant components cannot easily crash an application. The .NET Framework allows developers to concentrate on building functionality, instead of worrying about management details.

The .NET Framework is shown in the figure below:

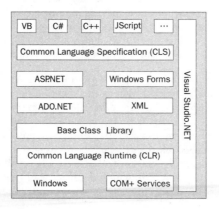

The .NET Framework is a layered system of classes and services that starts with the operating system services, and moves up through a set of system-level classes (the Base Class Library), and abstracted classes (for example, ASP.NET).

The .NET Framework constituent parts are:

❑ **Common Language Runtime** – a rich runtime environment that handles important runtime tasks for the developer, including memory management and garbage collection. Built around the Common Type System, and defines a common type system for all languages.

❑ **Base Class Library** – a rich set of functional base classes that may be inherited and extended by other classes in the Framework. For example, System.Object provides base object functionality that all classes in the Framework inherit. System.IO provides serialization to and from different input/output devices, such as files and streams.

❑ **Extended Class Libraries** – class libraries that are focused on one aspect of development. These classes are extended from the Base Class Library, and are designed to make it easier and faster to develop a specific type of application. For example, ASP.NET includes classes that are focused on developing Web Services. Other examples include ADO.NET (for data access), XML.NET (to parse and manipulate docs), and Windows Forms (the successor to VB forms).

❑ **Common Language Specification** – defines requirements for .NET languages, by specifying a set of rules that .NET-compliant languages must follow. One of these rules is that the language must adhere to a common type system.

❑ **Multiple Programming Languages** – VB.NET, C++.NET, and C#.NET are just some of the many languages that are available for coding in .NET. The .NET Framework provides one platform and a unified programming model for several languages. Java is conspicuously absent from the .NET family of languages, probably due to the licensing dispute between Sun Microsystems and Microsoft.

❑ **Visual Studio.NET** – an integrated development environment for coding with the .NET Framework. The diagram shows VS.NET spanning the entire .NET Framework because it provides tools that access each part of the Framework.

❑ **Windows and COM+ Services** – these are technically not part of the .NET Framework, but they are a requirement for today's .NET Framework SDK.

The .NET Framework provides greater access to the Windows system functionality, using a set of object-oriented classes that encapsulate the Windows API. The Framework provides base classes that can be used as they are, or easily extended and abstracted into custom classes. The System-level classes provide the lowest level functionality. The Extended class libraries, such as ASP.NET, are simply an abstracted set of classes that are designed for a specific kind of application. ASP.NET, for example, is essentially just a set of classes that have been abstracted in a way that is useful for web developers. You can directly use the Base classes and ignore the specialized ASP.NET classes if you want to. You can also leverage both the ASP.NET classes and the Base classes at the same time.

Of course, the .NET Framework is more than just a programming API. It includes the Common Language Runtime (CLR), which provides a managed execution environment, and a suite of runtime services that free the developer up from having to handle them manually. For example, the CLR manages garbage collection automatically, which means that developers no longer need to set object references to nothing. This of course breaks a fundamental convention for COM components, which recommends that you set all unused object references to nothing so that COM+ can more efficiently manage resources. Code that runs under the control of the CLR is called **managed code**. The CLR is built around a Common Type System (CTS), which defines a standard set of data types for .NET languages. So, managed code conforms to the CTS and runs under the control of the CLR.

The purpose of this brief overview is to introduce you to the basic structure and common terminology of the .NET Framework. Chapter 2 delves into each part of the .NET Framework in further detail before we reach the drill-down, which will come in the chapters that follow. Learning the .NET Framework is the key to developing applications on the Windows platform over the next several years. Once you have learned the fundamentals of the Framework, it will become much easier to learn how to architect and build robust web services and distributed applications.

To summarize, the important concepts behind the .NET Framework are:

❑   Built on a common set of Framework classes.

❑   Provides a Common Type System, that is the cornerstone of a unified programming model for all .NET-compliant languages.

❑   Provides a Common Language Runtime that provides runtime services for components and applications.

❑   Provides extended class libraries for ASP.NET, ADO.NET, XML.NET, and Windows Forms.

❑   Visual Studio.NET is an integrated development environment for the .NET Framework.

The .NET Framework is the first major building block of .NET. Obviously, the focus of this book is on the .NET Framework, but we will be looking at other aspects of the .NET initiative in order to round out the picture. With that said, in the next section we will take a quick look at the second building block of .NET, which are the **.NET Enterprise Servers**.

The .NET Enterprise Servers

Microsoft is orienting all of their recent and upcoming technology around .NET. To this end, they have identified a suite of products called **.NET Enterprise Servers**, which are server-based applications that Web-enable enterprise systems. These include applications that you may already be using, but did not realize were part of the .NET initiative. Examples of .NET Enterprise Servers include:

❑   **Windows 2000 Advanced Server** – operating system that provides a platform for .NET server software, as well as custom .NET applications, once the .NET Framework is installed. Windows 2000 Advanced Server is Microsoft's recommended platform for developing enterprise-level applications, but you do have other options, namely, the other Microsoft operating systems, such as Windows 2000 Professional, and the new Windows XP.

❑   **Application Center 2000** – provides management support for applications, to improve their scalability and availability.

❑   **SQL Server 2000** – provides Database support, including data storage, analysis and indexing.

❑   **Exchange Server 2000** – provides real-time communication services, including e-mail.

❑   **Host Integration Server 2000** – provides integration with legacy host systems.

❑   **Internet Security and Acceleration Server** – manages Internet connectivity, including firewall management.

❑   **Commerce Server 2000** – enables development of e-commerce sites.

❑   **BizTalk Server 2000** – facilitates business-to-business communications and enables data translation between applications, and automates business processes.

❏   There are other .NET Enterprise Servers that you may encounter in the course of your work, but this list highlights the most common ones.

How .NET Enterprise Servers Benefit the Web-Enabled Enterprise

The .NET initiative aims to enable solutions that address common business concerns, such as application availability across a broad range of devices, and the ability for applications to collaborate more easily. Business applications are most effective when they can be accessed from different devices over the Internet. The trend today is to web-enable the enterprise, whether to create an Intranet, Extranet, or public Internet presence. To further understand the significance of the .NET Enterprise Server suite of products, consider the challenges that an IT Manager faces when evaluating how to web-enable their enterprise:

❏   It is expensive and difficult to replace existing network infrastructure. New technology must work with existing infrastructure investments.

❏   New technology must continue to support the system-level demands of existing applications on the enterprise.

❏   The Internet brings with it scalability demands that may be much greater than previously required.

❏   Enterprise-level systems have demanding reliability and performance requirements that cannot be compromised by technology upgrades.

Clearly, the web-enabled enterprise has high scalability demands, and strict service-level agreements for uptime and availability. Businesses cannot redesign their infrastructure without incurring high expenses and heavy productivity losses. This is where .NET Enterprise Servers become important. At a simplified level, .NET Enterprise Servers are any Microsoft server-based application that is interoperable using existing, open Web standards, such as XML, HTML, and HTTP. These protocols and languages operate over existing infrastructure, and are designed to meet the scalability demands of the Internet. Microsoft is hoping to convince businesses that they can transform their enterprise by installing .NET Enterprise server software that leverages their existing infrastructure.

Many of the .NET Enterprise Server products are already familiar to you, and had product lifecycles that were initiated prior to the .NET initiative, so it's important to realize that, to some degree, Microsoft is simply putting a new spin on its products. SQL Server 2000, for example, was released well before .NET. It was not built on .NET, rather, it was designed to be interoperable with .NET. What is significant is that Microsoft is now tailoring their product roadmaps for these server products around the .NET initiative. Collaboration is a key aspect of the initiative, and the .NET Enterprise Servers are designed to collaborate seamlessly. This is why .NET Enterprise Servers are an integral building block in the .NET initiative: give businesses the software that will run their enterprise, and in the process make them players in a .NET world.

There are future .NET Enterprise servers in development, including a future release of Microsoft's Windows Operating System, code-named Blackcomb, which has an estimated release date of 2003. Blackcomb is expected to be the first fully .NET-enabled OS; meaning that it will have the .NET Framework embedded directly into the OS. There is some confusion about the future lines of Microsoft's OS, which we should address here. First, Windows.NET will be the server line for the recently released Windows XP (64-bit platform) OS. Windows XP itself will have two flavors: Home User and Professional.

We can load .NET today in several ways. The easiest way is by installing Visual Studio.NET, which will install both the .NET Framework SDK as well as the Visual Studio.NET integrated development environment. Alternatively, you can download just the .NET Framework SDK, which contains the Common Language Runtime and the class libraries, as well as a toolset for developing .NET applications – you do not have to use Visual Studio.NET for developing .NET applications. Microsoft has designed the .NET Framework to be compatible with a number of operating systems. Application development with the .NET Framework is restricted to Windows XP, Windows 2000 Professional and Advanced Server, and Windows NT. They have also provided a redistributable package that enables .NET applications to run additionally on Windows Millenium and Windows 98.

The .NET Enterprise Servers make up the second major building block of .NET. The third building block is made up of the so-called **.NET Building Block Services**, which are the topic of the next section.

.NET Building Block Services

As we have discussed already, the vision of .NET for developers is to simplify application development. Earlier, we discussed how the .NET Framework simplifies programming, but in addition, developers need to spend less time handling details of plumbing and administration, and more time creating a functional software product. Specifically, Microsoft wants to make it easier for developers to create Web Services, since these are key to the .NET initiative and its business ramifications.

To this end, Microsoft is embarking on an effort to create so-called building block services that developers can leverage to simplify the administration of Web Services. One example is authentication services, which are critical for most applications. Building block services save developers' time, just as ActiveX controls today save developers' time in building form-based Windows applications. Why build, for example, a fancy database display grid from scratch, when you can purchase one cheaply from a third-party vendor? Microsoft's core building block services will unify key Windows operating system functions, and allow developers to focus on the higher-level details of their application and beyond. There is a key difference though, between .NET building blocks and ActiveX controls: the building blocks are Web Services themselves, so they can operate as stand-alone components, or in collaboration with other components. As Web Services, they are programmable, and can be easily called from a custom application. In contrast, ActiveX controls must be included within a Windows application at design time, and compiled directly into the runtime executable.

The .NET building block services will include:

- ❑ **Authentication** – builds on Microsoft's Passport and Windows authentication technologies. Enables developers to authenticate a user behind-the-scenes, and give them access to private content without bothering them to log in manually every time they access a new application. This authentication service will be available in the future operating system, code-named Blackcomb.

- ❑ **Notification and Messaging** – provides integrated messaging capabilities for any device, including instant messaging and e-mail.

- ❑ **Directory and Search** – directory search services, akin to "white pages" and "yellow pages" lookups, for locating people and finding information.

- ❑ **Calendar** – much more than an applet-like pop-up calendar. This service provides time management and scheduling services for your application (this is not the same as the server-side `Calendar` control in ASP.NET).

- ❑ **XML Store** – provides an addressable location on the Internet for storing data. The data is stored as XML, and is delivered using SOAP. This takes data replication and synchronization to the next level. XML data stores provide you with a single data store that can be accessed by all of your devices.

HailStorm

HailStorm is the code-name for Microsoft's initiative to create .NET Building Block Services. It is also a key part of their future strategy for generating revenue from subscription-based web services. HailStorm aims to provide a core set of services that can be implemented in fee-based web services. These core services include basic services such as authentication and messaging, which most web services applications will need. It also includes specialized services, such as auction services, which would provide personalized access to online auctions. Microsoft is partnering with several key companies, such as American Express and eBay, to develop these services.

In the future, Microsoft envisions that people will pay for the ability to access information and services from any device. As an example, your e-mail lists, documents, and digital photos would be stored for you on a centralized server. You would be able to access this information from any device, your desktop PC to your PDA. This information would be accessible to you from a set of web services that would authenticate you, and then deliver the information that you requested in an XML stream to your device. You would have to pay for the privilege of receiving the information, but Microsoft reckons that consumers will find this a service worth paying for. Another example would be a messaging-based application, such as an auction service that alerts you to the outcome of the auction. You would access an auction service, place your bid, and then wait for a message to be streamed to you whenever there is an update on the auction. You would, of course, be able to receive updates from any of your devices, and not worry about missing a message, because it would be queued and waiting until you next sign on, from wherever that may be.

What does this mean for developers? For now, it largely means wait-and-see, because the core services envisioned in HailStorm are still several months away from completion. Keep in mind the distinction between HailStorm and web services in general. HailStorm is largely a business strategy that Microsoft is undertaking in cooperation with selected partners. It remains to be seen whether people will embrace things like centralized authentication, or the idea of paying for the privilege of accessing personal information from any device. Web services, on the other hand, represent a new way of developing and accessing software on the Internet. As a developer, you should learn as much as you can about developing and using web services, because they are a viable new direction in software development. As for HailStorm, its viability will become clear over time, and we should not worry about it in the short term.

You can read more about HailStorm on Microsoft's web site, at
http://www.microsoft.com/NET/hailstorm.asp

The .NET Building Block Services make up the third major building block of .NET. The fourth building block is the .NET integrated development environment, Visual Studio.NET, which we will now move on to look at.

Visual Studio.NET

Visual Studio.NET is actually the first new product for the .NET initiative, and certainly one of the more significant ones, because it enables developers to build the next generation of solutions, most notably XML Web Services. Visual Studio.NET is the newest version of Microsoft's development toolkit for creating .NET solutions. It is designed to promote Rapid Application Development (RAD), just like earlier versions of the product. As we discussed earlier, you are not required to use Visual Studio.NET for developing .NET applications. The .NET Framework SDK actually provides everything that you need. However, you will miss out on many of the benefits that Visual Studio.NET provides: an integrated development environment, and tight integration with the .NET Framework. Visual Studio.NET supports multiple programming languages, including Visual Basic, Visual C++, and C#. In fact, you can even mix and match class files from different languages within the same project. Visual Studio.NET supports cross-language debugging, which allows you to step through mixed-language files within the same project.

The key features of Visual Studio.NET are:

- ❑   Full integration with the .NET Framework
- ❑   Integrated development environment
- ❑   Mixed-language development, including cross-language debugging
- ❑   RAD features for applications development
- ❑   Visual Designers for XML, HTML and Data
- ❑   Expanded debugging across projects, including stored procedures

More information about Visual Studio.NET can be found at
http://msdn.microsoft.com/vstudio/nextgen/default.asp

Overview of .NET Applications

Now that we've reviewed the reason behind the .NET initiative, we are now in a position to discuss what kinds of applications you can build with the .NET Framework.

The .NET Framework enables you to build any kind of application that you want. The focus of this chapter so far has been on .NET's capabilities for building Internet and distributed applications, but .NET is certainly not limited to just these types.

Earlier in this chapter we identified current areas in application programming under Windows DNA that still pose problems for developers. That said, Windows DNA is still relevant in .NET, because it is primarily an architectural model for distributed applications that still applies. Now, the choice comes down to whether you will build your distributed application using .NET versus COM+. If, ultimately, you are going to buy into the advantages of .NET, then .NET will be your preferred solution. It is also interesting to consider that you could build your components in .NET, and then generate COM type libraries for them, for use in COM+.

The underlying technology of the .NET Framework may have changed considerably from Windows DNA and COM+; however, what do not change are the demands on the developer. You still need to architect solutions that are scalable and secure. These goals have not changed from Windows DNA to .NET, but the .NET Framework provides developers with new tools and technology that make it easier to build applications that meet these exacting standards. In order to help you make a better decision about how to build your future solutions, let's consider the variety of applications that you can build with .NET.

There are several types of applications that you can build with .NET:

- ❑   **Windows Forms Applications**
- ❑   **Windows Forms Controls**
- ❑   **Windows Service Applications**
- ❑   **ASP.NET Web Applications**
- ❑   **Web Services**

Let's discuss each of these briefly:

Windows Forms Applications

Windows Form Applications are the newest generation of the traditional Windows-based applications that provide a form-based user interface and an n-Tier, partitioned architecture. Windows Forms are objects that are derived from the .NET Framework, so they consist of an extensible set of classes. These classes may be used as they are, or may be extended by the developer. For example, the framework provides a `Form` class with a standard set of attributes. When you create your own form, it may inherit directly from the .NET `Form` class, or it may inherit from another custom form.

Of course, forms are not very useful unless they hold controls that the user can interact with. The .NET Framework provides Windows controls that can be dropped onto Windows Forms to create your user interface. Windows Forms also support menus, including context menus that display frequently-used menu commands (you should be used to seeing these in Microsoft Office 2000). Just as with Visual Studio 6.0, you may choose to write code directly behind the Windows controls. This is appropriate for validation logic only. Major business logic should be encapsulated in separate .NET components that are called from the form-based application. Remember, the .NET Framework does not eliminate the need for good application design, nor does it really change what we consider good design today.

Windows Forms provide the following useful features:

❑ **A new Forms architecture** – an object-oriented set of classes, including the base `Form` class. Custom forms may inherit directly from the base `Form` class.

❑ **The Control Object Model** – a set of Windows controls for the user interface.

❑ **A new Event Model** – A set of events, based on delegates, which are similar to callbacks. Delegates allow you to develop more complex, responsive event handlers.

Form-based development was fairly painless with Visual Basic 6.0, although there were some behaviors that could only be accomplished through direct Windows API calls. For example, there was no standard property for making a specific form stay on top. Instead, the developer had to grab the form's window handle, and pass it into a Windows API function. Now with .NET, Windows Forms are more functional than ever before. If you still require additional functionality, you need only make a call to a System-level class.

Keep in mind that COM objects are still fully supported in .NET. We will discuss the interoperability between COM and .NET in more detail later in this chapter. For now, suffice to say that .NET provides utilities for importing COM libraries into .NET, and vice versa (generating COM type libraries for .NET components). Visual Studio.NET provides a graphical interface for selecting a COM library that is registered on your machine, and generating the assembly meta data information that is required to use the COM library in your .NET applications.

Windows Forms Controls

Windows Form Controls are the successors to ActiveX controls. They are reusable components that provide a user interface and are responsive to user events. They are compiled into a Windows Forms application, for example, in a `Form` container, and they run on the client-side. The .NET Framework provides a namespace called `System.Windows.Forms.Control`, which provides the base classes that all Windows Forms controls inherit from. This includes the classes that provide the control with its user interface and its event-programming model. Like ActiveX controls, Windows Forms Controls typically extend and add to other controls. Of course, you may also author a Windows Forms Control that is a complete original, although even these controls derive their basic attributes from the `System.Windows.Forms.Control` class, as all controls must do.

Windows Service Applications

Windows Service applications were formerly known as NT Services. They are executables that run in independent Windows sessions with no user interaction. Windows Service Applications provide the functionality for a large number of important Windows 2000 services, as well as a number of applications, including Microsoft SQL Server 2000 and Microsoft Commerce Server 2000. I counted upwards of 85 different services on my Windows 2000 machine. Microsoft developers will be most familiar with the following services:

- ❏ **Distributed Transaction Coordinator** – coordinates transactions that are distributed across two or more databases, message queues, file systems, or other transaction-protected resource managers.

- ❏ **IIS Admin Service** – allows administration of Web and FTP services through the Internet Information Services snap-in.

- ❏ **Simple Mail Transport Protocol (SMTP)** – transports electronic mail across the network.

- ❏ **Task Scheduler** – enables a program to run at a designated time.

- ❏ **Windows Installer** – installs, repairs, and removes software according to instructions contained in .MSI files.

- ❏ **World Wide Web Publishing Service** – provides web connectivity and administration through the Internet Information Services snap-in.

Windows Service applications may provide functionality that is available to all users on a server. Optionally, a service may be designed to run in the security context of a specific user. Services are typically long-running tasks that may run all the time, or that may be scheduled to run at specific times. Services may be stopped, started, paused, and resumed. They may start up automatically, when the server reboots, or may require manual startup. Services are administered via the Services Control Manager on the server. Finally, just like any other application, a Windows service may have dependencies on one or more other Windows services.

Windows Service applications have special requirements that make them unlike standard application executables. In particular, Windows Services must be compiled with a set of resources that allow, for example, the Services Control Manager to recognize and administer your custom Windows Service. Visual Studio .NET provides a special application installer that you include in your project as a dedicated application installer class. This class instantiates objects that are used to install and configure your Windows Service application.

Windows Service applications also share similarities to regular applications. For example, they respond to lifecycle events, just as forms and classes respond to initialization and termination events. Windows Service applications respond to events such as starting and stopping, using associated procedures like OnStart and OnStop, which contain the appropriate processing logic. Of course, one significant difference with Windows Service applications is that they do not have a user interface.

NT Services were previously difficult to write and deploy using Visual Studio 6.0, especially using Visual Basic. Now, with Visual Studio.NET, the Installer provides much of the plumbing for you, and Windows Services are now easy to write, as they should be.

ASP.NET Web Applications

ASP.NET is the next-generation platform for developing Web applications. ASP.NET has moved leaps and bounds beyond the simple, interpreted ASP scripting engine that ships with IIS. ASP.NET is now a compiled, object-oriented development environment, where you develop using languages such as Visual Basic and C#. In addition, ASP.NET leverages the same powerful .NET Framework classes and services that are available to any other development environment within the Framework.

ASP.NET provides the following two programming models:

❑ **Web Forms** – these are analogous to Windows Forms, and even provide Web Controls that can be dropped on to the form to provide a user interface, and to automate common functions such as input validation. Web forms support an event-driven programming model that mimics the functionality of client-side script.

❑ **Web Services** – these are remote application components that receive and respond to requests using open standard protocols, namely, RPC calls over HTTP using XML (combined into SOAP envelopes).

ASP.NET provides a number of advantages to Web application developers:

A Compiled, .NET Development Environment

ASP.NET applications leverage all the benefits of the .NET Framework, including extensible classes, a common type system, and a common language runtime. ASP.NET applications may be authored using a .NET framework language such as Visual Basic or C#. ASP.NET applications are compiled code, unlike today's ASP scripts, which are interpreted. The ASP scripting languages, such as VBScript and JavaScript, are limited in that they must offload significant business logic to COM components. ASP.NET code may also, by design, offload business logic to outside components, but this is not required, because ASP.NET applications are written with first-class .NET languages, and are executed as managed code under the control of the CLR. Developers will recognize significant performance benefits from migrating their code from ASP to ASP.NET.

Powerful Server Controls

Remember all of the tasks that drove you crazy in ASP, because there was no easy way to handle them without extensive scripting? For example, it was difficult to persist submitted form information for display back to the user, if you redirected the user back to the form to correct an input error. Typically, you would write dozens of lines of JavaScript validation code to prevent input errors from happening. Or, you would pass the user input values back to the original page via URL arguments. Or, heaven forbid, you would persist the user input values to a scripting dictionary stored in a Session variable. With ASP.NET all of these workarounds go away, because new server controls such as the textbox will automatically persist user input after a redirect back to the original form.

Automatic Caching

ASP.NET provides caching, to improve web site performance, and to deliver pages more rapidly. There are two types of cache:

❑ Output cache – saves completely rendered pages.

❑ Fragment cache – stores part of a rendered page.

ASP.NET caching is very flexible, and provides classes that allow applications and request handlers alike to access and manipulate the cache.

State Management Services

The Web is intrinsically stateless, that is, information is not persisted between page requests. However, ASP.NET provides state management services that will manage state across HTTP requests. This capability is greatly expanded from what was offered with traditional ASP. Session state management in ASP applications had several limitations. First, ASP session state is tied to the process that the ASP application runs in. Should anything happen to that process and it terminates, then the session state will be lost. Second, ASP applications cannot share session state across servers in server farms.

ASP.NET provides the following state management features:

❑   Application State – specific to an application instance.

❑   Session State – specific to a session, and stored in a distinct process. Can be configured for a specific machine, and used on a web farm.

❑   User State – similar to session state, except that it is persisted even after the user's session is over. It is useful for storing user preferences and personalization settings.

ASP.NET session state is process independent and, optionally, cookie independent. In addition, ASP.NET session state may be shared across all servers in a server farm, by pointing all of the servers to a common server that is responsible for managing the session state.

Backwards Compatibility with ASP

In general, Microsoft designed Visual Studio.NET to allow developers to leverage their existing technical skills. ASP.NET is no exception, and your ASP skills are still valuable to you as an ASP.NET developer. ASP.NET applications peacefully co-exist on the same server with ASP applications, because they use different file extensions, and are "interpreted" differently at run-time. Specifically, at run-time, the .NET Common Language Runtime compiles ASP.NET applications, while the ASP engine interprets ASP applications. ASP.NET and ASP applications will not share session information with each other, so there is no risk that they will interfere with each other. For performance reasons it is to your advantage to migrate your ASP scripts to ASP.NET. This will be a significant effort if your ASP scripts contain lots of business logic in script, instead of in COM components. This is because ASP.NET applications contain managed code, while ASP scripts contain weakly-typed, unmanaged code.

Web Services

ASP.NET and the .NET Framework together provide classes and services (such as automatic SOAP support) for building Web Services components. Web services are a large and important topic, so this section will be divided into two parts. First, we will provide a brief overview of what Web Services are. Second, we will look at how ASP.NET enables you to build Web Services.

Web Services Overview

Web Services are distributed business components that may function as stand-alone components, or in collaboration with other web services, in order to provide an application service. From a business standpoint, Web Services are particularly important for meeting the exacting demands of today's business users. For business users, the value of their enterprise is directly measured by its availability (for example, uptime) and its ability to enable data sharing, application integration and collaboration. Business users demand richly functional software that is accessible remotely, and available 24/7. Information and data are the currency of the enterprise, and users get quickly frustrated if they have to struggle to access and manipulate their data remotely. Collaboration is difficult today, because many applications do not exchange data well, especially between devices.

Web services, by their nature, facilitate collaboration and integration, because they combine to form loosely-coupled, distributed applications. They work together, but are not necessarily packaged together. Most importantly, they are built on open Internet standards, which means that they are accessible by anyone who communicates using standard Internet protocols. This open standard foundation is supposed to allow a range of different devices to access the same applications, because each device is free to interpret the XML data stream in the manner best suited to that device.

Today it is difficult for one application to adequately service multiple devices, usually because applications are typically designed for one kind of device. Spreadsheet applications, for example, are designed for desktop or laptop PCs with sizable screens; spreadsheets are not as easily accommodated by the displays on wireless phones and handheld PDAs. Even putting presentation issues aside, most applications are not currently designed to stream their data as presentation-neutral XML. In summary, web services aim to promote collaborative, integrated applications that transcend device boundaries.

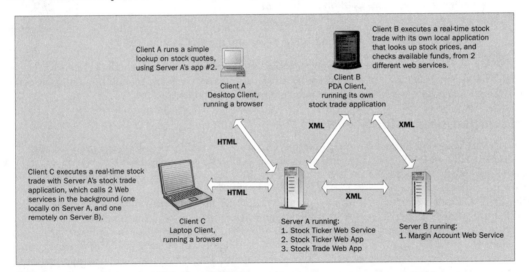

The figure above provides an interesting illustration of Web Services architecture. Server A runs a Stock Ticker web service, while Server B runs a Margin Account web service. Server A also runs two standard web applications: a stock ticker lookup application, and a stock trade application, both of which are accessible via a standard browser. There are three clients, each of whom issue different requests:

❑ Client A is an old desktop PC that runs a browser. Client A does simple stock ticker lookups using Server A's web application, just like doing a stock ticker lookup at Yahoo. Client A never interacts with web services directly. In fact, Client A receives a simple HTML stream, instead of an XML document from the stock ticker web application. This is an example of a server-side transformation that occurs to provide the most suitable output to the client.

❑ Client B is a PDA that runs a snazzy custom stock trading application. Client B just needs to know current stock prices, and the funds that are available in their margin account for purchasing stocks. Client B uses two separate web services, one on Server A, and one on Server B. Client B's local application collects the information from the user for the trade, and then invokes the web services on Servers A and B to actually execute the trade.

❑ Client C is a laptop that runs a browser. Client C executes a stock trade using Server A's browser-based stock trade application, which uses web services in the backend. Client C never interacts with web services directly.

This simple example illustrates the power of Web Services: they are flexible and highly available, and work in collaboration, even though they may be deployed across several separate servers. The Internet opens the door to a new application architecture consisting of web services that collaborate across the Internet to service client requests: .NET is the technology that allows us to build web services.

ASP.NET and Web Services

ASP.NET provides high-level, abstracted classes for developing web services. It hides the low-level specifications and protocols, such as HTTP and SOAP, which saves you from having to construct the protocol calls manually. If you are so inclined then you can bypass ASP.NET, and call the System-level classes directly, but this would be missing out on a major productivity advantage. Web services can be invoked using HTTP POST, HTTP GET, or SOAP requests, although SOAP requests are preferred, because they provide the most flexibility for specifying requests and receiving responses.

The important technical aspects of web services are:

❑ Web services are based on open standards.

❑ ASP.NET provides high-level, abstracted classes for developing web services.

❑ The ASP.NET framework makes it easier to develop them, because it hides the low-level specifications and protocols, such as HTTP and SOAP.

❑ Web Services are very flexible; they are compiled as .asmx files. They may reference a managed class, or they may define their own classes. Public methods in the web service are marked with a <WebMethod> attribute. This enables them to be called by sending HTTP requests directly to the URL of the .asmx file. ASP automatically generates the SCL (Service Control List), based on the web services meta data.

❑ Web services can be invoked using HTTP POST, GET, or SOAP.

❑ The .NET Framework can generate a strongly-typed proxy file to use the web service just like other managed code.

❑ The .NET Framework provides an easy-to-use application model for building web services, and handles the plumbing for deploying them.

Web Services are very easy to create from standard class modules. They are compiled as special files with a .asmx extension. Web service methods may reference an existing managed class, or they may define their own classes. Public methods in the web service are marked with a <WebMethod()> attribute. This enables the Web Services method to be invoked by sending HTTP requests directly to the URL of the .asmx file. The .NET Framework actually generates a Service Control List (SCL) directly from the Web Services meta data.

Here is an example of a simple web services function that returns an ADO DataSet.

```
Public Function <WebMethod()> GetOrders() As DataSet
End Function
```

The <WebMethod()> tag accepts parameters of its own that allow you to specify whether the method uses session state, and whether it operates in a transactional mode, as in:

```
Public Function <WebMethod(False, TransactionMode.RequiresNew)> UpdateOrder ( _
    ByVal OrderID As String, _
    ByVal Status As String) As Boolean
End Function
```

Obviously, there is a lot more to developing web services than this simple example would suggest. But the purpose of these code snippets is to illustrate the simplicity of the programming interface for a web service.

Web Services: the Vision versus the Reality

We have discussed the vision behind Web services, but as developers we are very much concerned with the reality. It is difficult to comment about the challenges of implementing the vision, because this is still a prerelease technology. Developers have a number of important concerns about web services that still need to be addressed before they fully embrace the technology. One concern is security, namely, how secure is the data stream that web services transmit, and how well do web services protect against unauthorized requests. Another big concern is around the Web Services Description Language (WSDL), which provides such a detailed level of information about a web service that developers are concerned that it will be very easy to reverse-engineer their code.

Microsoft is clearly hoping for strong developer acceptance of web services technology, from both Microsoft-oriented developers, as well as other developers who embrace the open standards foundation of web services. They are even hoping to promote web services development on non-Windows platforms. Interestingly, web services exchange information using XML-based vocabularies, but they operate on Microsoft windows operating systems, which makes them an interesting blend of proprietary software and open standards. Of course in the future, Microsoft hopes that a wider development community will embrace Web Services.

XML and .NET

XML is pervasive in .NET. Microsoft's web site states unequivocally that ".NET is Microsoft's platform for XML Web Services". Microsoft has embraced XML fully in .NET, using it to revolutionize the way in which components and applications communicate with each other. All parts of the .NET Framework use XML as their native data representation format.

The .NET Framework is built on a number of industry-standard XML technologies, including:

- ❑ DOM Level 2 Core
- ❑ XPath 1.0
- ❑ XSLT 1.0
- ❑ XML Schemas (XSD)
- ❑ XML 1.0 Namespaces Recommendation
- ❑ Simple Object Access Protocol (SOAP)

Developers may still use the MSXML 3.0 COM library in .NET, using .NET's COM Interop services, which will provide a wrapper for .NET to use this COM component. However, there is no advantage in doing so, unless you need to support an older implementation of XSLT, or if your code uses an XML structure that does not conform to industry standards. Given that XML is such an integral part of .NET, Microsoft has provided a rich set of APIs for working with XML. These APIs are collectively known as the .NET Framework XML Classes. Microsoft has been criticized in the past for incorporating non-standard XML implementations into its technology, such as ADO's implementation of the "XML Recordset". This issue has largely gone away in .NET, because the XML implementations are all industry-standard, or are part of an industry consortium that is still in the process of being ratified by the W3C. Arguably, there are still certain .NET XML implementations that could be considered non-proprietary, such as the XML Schema Document (XSD) format. However, these "non-proprietary" implementations are by far the exception in .NET.

The .NET Framework XML Classes

The .NET Framework XML classes are tightly coupled with .NET's Managed Data Provider (ADO.NET). Data can be quite varied in nature, from following a traditional relational model, to following a less traditional hierarchical model, such as a corporate organization chart, for example. Now, with XML, there is a common format for describing data, and with ADO.NET, there is a unified programming model for accessing all types of data (OLE DB was actually Microsoft's first initiative towards providing unified data access, and it was very successful, although it lacked the ability to describe data consistently as industry-standard XML, because XML was not a standard at the time that OLE DB was first developed).

There are two abstract classes that are the core classes of the .NET Framework XML Classes. They are:

❑ XmlReader – provides a fast, read-only, forward cursor for processing an XML document stream.

❑ XmlWriter – provides an interface for producing industry-standard document streams, that conform to the W3C's XML 1.0 Namespaces Recommendation.

The .NET Framework XML classes are all found under the System.Xml namespace. Specifically, the XmlReader and XmlWriter classes are found directly under the System.Xml namespace. Other classes are found within child namespaces, such as the XSLT classes, which are found under System.Xml.Xsl, and the XPath classes, which are found under System.Xml.XPath. Your application can access all of the XML classes using a single reference to the parent System.Xml namespace, as in this C# code snippet:

```
Using System.Xml;
```

The .NET Framework XML Classes add a document streamlining capability that is a significant advantage over MSXML 3.0. The XMLReader class does not rely on using an expensive, in-memory cache, as does the Document Object Model (DOM), provided by MSXML 3.0. The XMLWriter class ensures that your XML documents will conform closely to current industry standards. MSXML 3.0 did not provide the same level of constraint over your XML documents.

.NET Framework XML Classes versus the SAX API

There are currently two main APIs for accessing XML programmatically: the **Simple API for XML (SAX API)** and the **Document Object Model (DOM)**. At the simplest level, the DOM provides an in-memory representation of an XML document, while the SAX API provides streaming access to an XML document. SAX became extremely popular with developers, despite never being ratified by the W3C. Microsoft incorporated SAX wrapper functions into the MSXML 3.0 library, so developers currently have access to both the SAX API and the DOM API from the same COM library.

The SAX API is the lightweight alternative to the DOM, because it requires fewer resources for accessing XML documents, particularly as the documents get very large. The DOM is inefficient for accessing XML, especially for large documents, because it has to load up the document in a resource-expensive, in-memory cache. You can work around this by just loading up a document fragment, but this requires you to have a prior knowledge about the structure and contents of the XML document. In other words, you may not always know which part you need, until you have walked through the entire document.

While the DOM made for an inferior alternative to SAX, it did have the advantage of being easier to use. The SAX API is not very easy to use, because it employs a complex set of interfaces that push the document stream into the consuming application. The .NET Framework XML classes use a more intuitive set of interfaces that allow a consumer application to easily pull an XML document stream in. The .NET Framework XML classes implement richer streaming document functionality than the SAX API currently provides. In particular, the `XmlReader` class allows a consumer to be very selective with how they pull the document in. For example, a consumer can specify not to expand certain nodes. On the other hand, the SAX API is not so selective: it pushes the entire document stream out to the user. The workaround to this is that users are forced to create a state machine to track specific XML tags, which increases the programming complexity.

Benefits of XML as the .NET Lingua Franca

It seems almost unnecessary to describe the benefits of using XML in .NET, because XML has gained such widespread acceptance. However, it's all part of telling a compelling story, so here it goes.

- ❑ XML is an open standard, defined by the W3C
- ❑ XML provides a Universal Data Format
- ❑ XML is self-describing and lightweight
- ❑ XML enables collaboration

There are some readers who are not currently using XML in their applications, because they have yet to see a benefit from this technology. It is therefore fair for those readers to question why XML's incorporation into .NET is such a great thing. I would point out that XML is a text-based, extensible system of organizing information that may be used as the basis for any number of organizational systems. In .NET, **XML-based grammars** are set up to organize and describe all sorts of important information, from assembly meta data to describing web services interfaces. An XML-based grammar is simply a specific collection of XML tags (including elements and attributes) that combine to provide a way of describing and organizing a specific kind of information.

There is another benefit to having XML underpin the .NET Framework, namely, faster industry acceptance of .NET by different vendors. Microsoft has long been criticized for focusing on its proprietary software and for not embracing accepted industry standards. With .NET, Microsoft is still providing a lot of proprietary software, but it is built on open XML standards.

XML allows .NET components, namely Web Services, to potentially communicate with any component on any platform, as long as it subscribes to the same XML standards, and can communicate over HTTP and SOAP. There will always be critics who will contend that Microsoft did not go far enough. And it is unlikely that Web Services will seamlessly integrate with other vendor's offerings, at least in the initial release of .NET. However, it is all a good first step, and an important recognition by Microsoft that open standards represent shared values and a spirit of collaboration. Of course, the less altruistic viewpoint is that Microsoft needed to embrace an industry standard to forward its own product goals, and improve its product suite's abilities to collaborate, both internally and externally. Regardless of the viewpoint, in the end result, it is everyone who benefits.

XML-Based Grammars in the .NET Framework

We've talked about how the .NET Framework embraces industry-standard XML specifications, but this is only half the story. The .NET Framework actually supports a series of **XML-based grammars** that provide a way to organize and describe information both within the .NET Framework, and to outside consumers of .NET components. Most of the XML grammars were developed in partnership between major industry players, including Microsoft, IBM, and Ariba.

The XML grammars in the .NET Framework include:

❑ **Web Simple Description Language (WSDL)** – an XML-based grammar for describing network services over the Internet. WSDL allows outside consumers to gather the information they need to communicate with your web service.

Read the WSDL specification at http://www.w3.org/TR/wsdl.

❑ **Simple Object Access Protocol (SOAP)** – the SOAP specification defines how to send XML over HTTP. Requests and responses to and from Web Services are formatted and passed via SOAP envelopes. SOAP 2.0 complies with the WSDL specification.

Read more about SOAP at http://msdn.microsoft.com/xml/general/soapspec.asp.

❑ **Universal Description, Discovery and Integration (UDDI)** – the UDDI enables developers to publish information about their Web Services on the Internet. UDDI also enables consumers to locate and use web services on the Internet. UDDI is powerful because businesses can publish detailed information about both their product offerings and their company. Consumers can learn in great detail about available web services, and their suitability for the business. Microsoft publishes a UDDI SDK that enables developers to build UDDI capability programmatically into their applications.

Read about UDDI on MSDN at http://msdn.microsoft.com/library/techart/progguide.htm.

❑ **Template Definition Language (TDL)** – used to render enterprise templates in Visual Studio.NET. Enterprise templates are reusable sets of classes and code that allow you to jump-start your development effort.

The specifications for each of these grammars are complicated, but the .NET Framework does a good job of hiding the complexity from developers. ASP.NET, in particular, hides all of the lower-level SOAP calls and remote procedure calls that are required for Web Services.

Interoperability between .NET and COM+

It should be no surprise that .NET provides good COM interoperability support. COM is an established technology with an enormous developer base, and there have been years of development time invested in COM applications around the world. In fact, early releases of .NET will be very reliant on COM components for certain core functionality, such as OLE DB data access. .NET is dependent on COM in particular because .NET currently runs on Windows 2000, which itself uses COM components for a range of functionality.

What are the differences between COM components and .NET components? There are several important differences, including:

❑ COM components have separate type-library files. .NET components are self-referencing using an assembly manifest.

❑ COM components are interface-based. .NET components communicate directly, rather than through intermediate interface queries.

❑ COM components must be registered with GUID entries in the registry. .NET components do not require any manual registration.

❑ COM components may only be registered one version at a time (if it preserves binary compatibility). .NET components may exist side-by-side, with multiple versions of the same component.

COM components may be used in .NET projects once the .NET Framework generates a wrapper for the COM type library that makes it look like a .NET assembly. Specifically, the .NET Framework provides a set of **InterOp services** that support interoperability between COM and .NET. This includes a utility that you can run manually to convert COM type libraries to assembly wrappers. The assembly wrapper includes a manifest that fully describes the component's interface using meta data. With Visual Studio.NET, this task is made even easier, because VS.NET allows you to set a reference to a COM component from the Project | Add References menu. This provides an Add Reference pop-up window with one tab for .NET assemblies and system classes, and another tab for COM components. The COM tab provides a list of available, registered COM components for you to choose from. Once you select a component, VS.NET will generate the assembly wrapper for you, and then show the reference in the Solution Explorer.

Nothing comes for free, in particular if you want to leverage existing COM components in your .NET projects. To do this, you need to ensure that your COM components follow good programming practices; otherwise you may create instabilities in the parent .NET project. These rules include:

❑ Use types that are common to both COM and .NET

❑ Use data types that are supported by COM automation

❑ Clean up all resources

❑ Do not use method names that are in use by the .NET System.Object class, which is an important root class

❑ Always use the Binary Compatibility setting

There will likely be performance implications from using COM components in .NET projects. COM components require extra marshalling calls that will slow performance. .NET components will generally respond faster than COM components anyway, because they are not hindered by an intermediate interface-based plumbing layer between components. By all means, leverage COM components as needed, but before doing so you should think through whether there is another alternative; namely, would it be better to migrate the COM code over to .NET, or does .NET provide a system class that performs the same function?

Competing Platforms: How does .NET Measure Up?

The Java Enterprise development platform is a competitor to .NET. Like .NET, J2EE provides a set of technologies, from programming languages, to execution, to object request brokers, which provide a framework for enterprise-level application development. .NET applications currently run only on Windows, whereas J2EE applications will run on any machine that provides a Java Virtual Machine. One fairly obvious but interesting difference is that J2EE provides a single language, Java, whereas .NET provides multiple supported languages, including VB.NET, C# .NET and C++ .NET.

> The .NET vs. J2EE comparison table below was adapted from an article by Jim Farley, entitled: *Microsoft.NET vs. J2EE: How do they stack up?* (November 2000). Find this article at: http://www.javasoft.com/features/2000/11/dotnetvsms.html.

The table below provides feature-specific comparisons between .NET and J2EE:

.NET Feature	J2EE Feature	Differentiators
C# language	Java language	C# and Java both derive from C and C++. Both languages provide similar syntax, though C# adds meta data tags.
		C# is compiled by the Common Language Runtime (CLR) into Intermediate Language (IL) byte code. C# is run using either Just-In-Time (JIT) byte code, or is compiled directly to native code.
		Java runs on any platform with the Java VM.
		C# (and other .NET languages) currently only run on Microsoft Windows where .NET is installed.
.NET Framework Classes	Java core API	.NET will include classes that integrate XML and SOAP directly into a .NET application.
		The Java core API provides classes for XML, but does not provide them for SOAP.

Table continued on following page

.NET Feature	J2EE Feature	Differentiators
SOAP-based Web Services and ADO.NET	Java XML Libraries, JavaBeans, JDBC, etc.	ADO.NET is built on SOAP messaging support, which allows for the exchange of XML between remote objects or tiers in an N-tier application. ADO.NET does not provide an alternative protocol.
		EJB and JDBC require the developer to implement the messaging protocol. They do not assume SOAP, but they do operate on top of HTTP.
Active Server Pages.NET (ASP.NET)	Java Server Pages (JSP)	Similar: ASP.NET uses any .NET supported language, and is compiled into native code by the CLR (rather than interpreted, like ASP).
		JSP uses compiled byte code that is written in Java.
Common Language Runtime (CLR)	Java VM and CORBA	The .NET CLR supports multiple programming languages, as long as they conform to the Common Language Specification (CLS).
		Java byte codes run on any machine with a Java VM. CORBA (an object request broker), allows code in multiple languages to access the same set of objects, as long as they are on a platform with an object request broker installed. CORBA is not as tightly integrated to J2EE, as are the constituent parts of the .NET Framework.
WinForms and WebForms	Java Swing and AWT (Abstract Windowing Toolkit)	The .NET Framework provides common controls for use across both Windows Forms and WebForms, but they can only be used in the Visual Studio Integrated Development Environment (IDE).
		The Swing toolkit provides common user-interface controls for selected Java IDEs.
.NET Components	Enterprise Java Beans (EJB)	Both .NET components and EJBs may be compiled as native code, although in both cases there is an intermediate compilation step. .NET components are compiled to IL (Intermediate Language), and EJBs are compiled to Java bytecode.
		COM components may be imported and used in .NET. Also, .NET components may be exported for use in COM+.

.NET Feature	J2EE Feature	Differentiators
Interoperability/ Remoting (DCOM/SOAP)	Interoperability/ Remoting (RMI/IIOP)	.NET uses DCOM (Microsoft proprietary) and SOAP (open standard). J2EE uses RMI/IIOP (Remote Method Invocation over Internet InterOrb Protocol), which is based on the CORBA protocol.

There are several commercial products that use the J2EE, framework. This includes:

- BEA WebLogic
- IBM WebSphere
- Oracle iAS
- Open Source (for example Apache, Tomcat)
- IPlanet Application Server

Why should you use .NET over J2EE?

.NET provides several distinct advantages over J2EE, which, in my opinion, make it the preferred platform for developing enterprise applications. These are:

- .NET provides multiple languages that leverage the same class framework. J2EE provides just a single language, Java. Ultimately, many .NET developers may determine that only certain .NET languages, such as C#, provide the best programming benefits. But they still have a choice in programming languages, which makes it easier for developers of different backgrounds to start programming in .NET.

- .NET takes a big step towards addressing the "open source" argument that J2EE/Java proponents have used for so long, namely, that J2EE and Java are built on open standards, and therefore serve a wider development community. .NET is built on, and tightly integrated with, standards such as XML, HTTP, and SOAP. J2EE does not implement SOAP, whereas .NET does. This is surprising given the J2EE "open-standard" philosophy, and the fact that SOAP is a well-established standard.

- .NET components have built-in XML support for tasks such as messaging, and interface exporting. J2EE components (Enterprise Java Beans) do not.

- .NET holds much more promise for interoperability than does J2EE, because .NET uses XML and SOAP. The SOAP protocol enables interoperability between vendors on different platforms. The J2EE IIOP protocol does not enable interoperability among all of the current J2EE vendors, much less non-J2EE vendors.

> Roger Sessions' excellent web site provides whitepapers and slides that discuss .NET and J2EE in great detail, and compares these technologies. Visit his web site at: http://www.objectwatch.com.

I am not aware of any benchmark tests that compare .NET to J2EE, but these should be available soon after .NET is released. Only time will tell how well .NET measures up to meeting key goals for enterprise application developers, such as application scalability and availability. Clearly, Microsoft has designed .NET to go head-to-head against platforms like J2EE. There are currently still significant differences between the two platforms, but it will be interesting to see what evolves in the future. Microsoft is obviously hoping for widespread acceptance of .NET, and Web Services in particular.

Summary

In this chapter we've discussed what .NET is, and what its main goals are. We spent some time considering the limitations of current development tools with Windows DNA and how .NET has been specifically devised to address these difficulties that programmers face.

To summarize, .NET has been designed to:

- ❑ Simplify application development and deployment
- ❑ Enhance developer productivity with a rich functional set of classes
- ❑ Provide a platform for developing distributed Internet applications and XML Web Services
- ❑ Support multiple development languages in a common framework
- ❑ Support COM interoperability with .NET
- ❑ Provide a robust, secure execution environment

The .NET initiative holds a lot of exciting potential. It promises to change the way in which we develop software, by providing a new development framework and a new set of development tools. Specifically, the .NET initiative aims to provide a platform for rapidly building distributed Internet applications and web services.

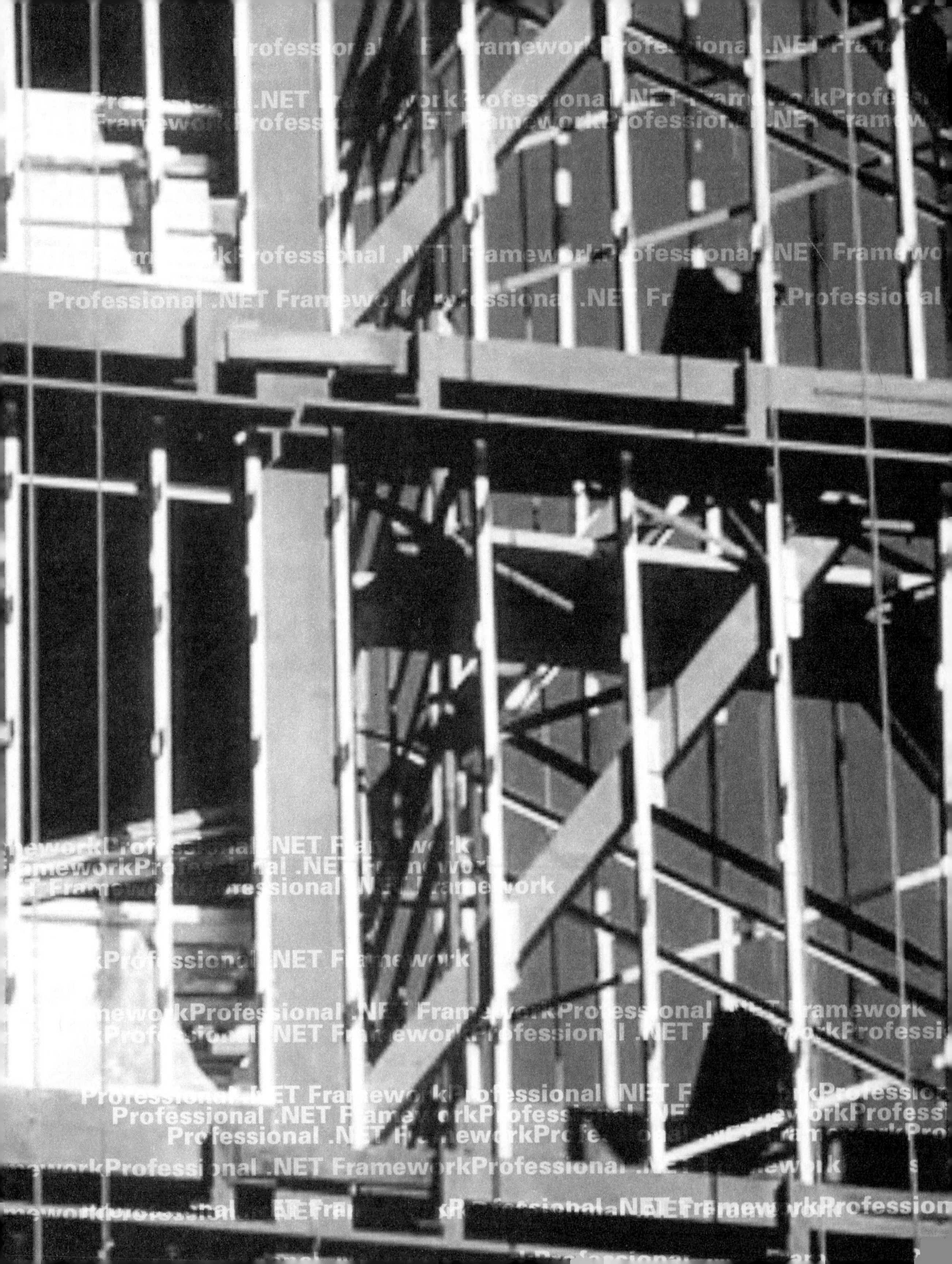
Professional .NET Framework

2

Overview of the .NET Framework

The .NET Framework provides the technical underpinnings of the .NET initiative. Broadly speaking, the Framework is the set of types, classes, services and tools that combine to form the new .NET platform. From the developer's perspective, the .NET Framework *is* .NET. However, this is only partially true. As we discussed in the previous chapter, the .NET initiative that Microsoft envisions actually encompasses a set of business goals and deliverables including XML Web Services, HailStorm, and a new generation of collaborative software that extends Microsoft's existing .NET servers. Taken from this perspective, the .NET Framework simply provides the core technical features and the development platform that enables .NET to deliver on these business goals. As developers, architects and programmers, we are interested in the technical side of .NET. So in this chapter, we will focus on .NET as a development Framework.

In the previous chapter we looked at how the design of the .NET platform was motivated largely by the need to overcome the limitations of developing applications with Windows DNA, particularly distributed Internet applications. In particular, Microsoft realized that they needed to empower developers with a new set of technologies, including a unified development framework, which would allow them to focus less on plumbing details, and more on solving business problems. Internet applications, in particular, require a lot of work on the plumbing details, such as generating XML packets for SOAP calls. With .NET, Microsoft is attempting to make these and other details an intrinsic part of the platform, and easy to use. In this chapter we will extend the discussion of how .NET evolved. This will provide you with a clearer understanding of .NET, within the context of what Windows DNA currently provides and its present limitations.

To recap, this chapter will cover the following:

- ❑ An introduction to the design goals of the .NET Framework

- ❑ An overview of the structure and features of the .NET Framework

- ❑ A discussion of how the .NET Framework addresses limitations with Windows DNA development

The discussions in this chapter extend from Chapter 1, so I would recommend that you read Chapter 1 before diving into Chapter 2! This chapter should prepare you well for the deep technical discussions that are provided in subsequent chapters of this book.

Highlights of the .NET Framework

The .NET Framework is made up of layered, constituent parts that provide the services, classes and tools that work together to provide the new .NET development platform. The figure below presents a high-level schematic of the .NET Framework:

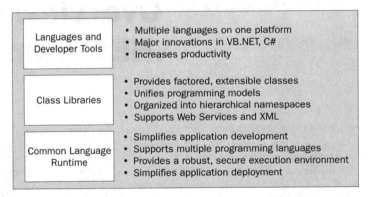

The high-level layers of the .NET Framework are:

- ❑ **Common Language Runtime** – provides a reliable, secure execution environment, and supports multiple programming languages.

- ❑ **Class Libraries** – provides a set of factored, extensible classes that are used across all .NET-compliant languages.

- ❑ **Language and Developer Tools** – familiar languages such as C++, VB and JavaScript are overhauled in .NET, and their feature sets are greatly extended. The Framework includes the new C# language, which follows in the tradition of C++, but is greatly simplified and oriented towards .NET development. C++ itself has evolved into managed C++. Visual Studio.NET provides an integrated development environment for .NET.

The .NET Framework is layered into increasingly abstracted levels of functionality. At the base of the Framework you find the Common Language Runtime, which provides the core managed execution environment that runs all .NET assembly code (a .NET **assembly** is a compiled component or executable). Next come the Class Libraries, which abstract system-level functionality into a set of extensible classes that you can implement in your application code. At the top of the Framework sit the .NET languages and developer tools. The .NET languages conform to rules that are outlined by the Common Language Runtime, so that they can be managed properly in the execution environment.

The Common Language Runtime

The Common Language Runtime (CLR) provides a runtime execution environment for .NET applications. Code that runs under the control of the CLR is called **managed code**, because the CLR defines the rules that the code's development language must conform to. Specifically, the CLR works with two other Framework services to define the rules for .NET languages. These are:

❑ **Common Type System (CTS)** – defines standard reference and value types that are supported in the .NET Framework.

❑ **Common Language Specification (CLS)** – defines rules that a development language must comply with, in order to be managed by the .NET Framework.

The Common Language Runtime (CLR) is an advanced runtime engine that provides the highest level of type safety, code verification and exception handling. Managed code is more stable in a large part because it conforms to a strict set of rules that the CLR understands and can interpret at a high confidence level. The CLR is not restricted to working with just managed code. It will also work with unmanaged code, such as COM components, via .NET's COM InterOp services, which generates .NET wrappers for unmanaged COM components.

Briefly, the CLR provides the following features:

❑ It manages running code by verifying type safety, providing memory management, garbage collection, and exception handling.

❑ It provides a Common Type System that promotes type safety, and therefore more stable code.

❑ It provides access to system resources, including the Windows API and COM InterOp services.

❑ It provides cross-language support, including unified exception handling and debugging across languages.

We will discuss the CLR, the CTS, and the CLS in more detail later in this chapter.

Class Libraries

C/C++ programmers are familiar with Microsoft Foundation Classes (MFC) and the Active Template Library (ATL). Visual Basic developers do not have access to a similarly sophisticated OO class system, nor does Visual Basic support all of the object-oriented features that are required for such a class system. The .NET Framework classes are similar in concept to MFC, namely, they provide developers with access to a wide range of system services without having to do a lot of coding. The Framework classes are organized into **namespaces**, which organize classes into a hierarchical structure of related groups. For example, the System.Data namespace contains a set of classes that provide data access functionality. For an overview of namespaces, look at Appendix A.

Framework classes save developers time and effort, because they provide an excellent level of encapsulation support for Windows system functionality. MFC/ATL developers are used to working with a well-developed class framework, but it is arguably not as intuitive as the .NET Framework classes, especially for developers from non-C++ backgrounds. Let's illustrate the benefit of the Framework classes using the simple example of a Button control on a Windows Form. The Button control in the .NET Framework is encapsulated within the System.Windows.Forms.Button class, which in turn inherits and implements a number of system-level classes, including:

- ❑ System.Object – every class in the .NET Framework inherits from System.Object. It enables object references to conform to type safety rules, among other things.

- ❑ System.ComponentModel.Component – this is the base class for all components in the System.Windows.Forms namespace.

- ❑ System.Windows.Forms.Control – this class implements the functionality that is required for classes that display visually to the user. This includes functionality for interpreting user interaction from a keyboard or pointing device.

- ❑ System.Windows.Forms.ButtonBase – implements the basic functionality that is common to Button controls.

This is a lot of work for creating a simple Button control, and not something that you would want to go through every time you needed a Button for your application. So you feel a lot of relief knowing that to get a Button control, all you have to do is to create an instance of the System.Windows.Forms.Button class. This is a trivial example, but the same concept holds for any of the classes that you regularly use in the .NET Framework. The fact is that Framework classes save developers lots of time, effort and coding, by encapsulating the required services into a single, easy-to-reference class.

Let's look at another example to illustrate the point. Here are two code listings that create a new Windows Form:

Windows API code:

```
HWND hwndMain = CreateWindowEx(0, "MainWClass", "Main Window",
    WS_OVERLAPPEDWINDOW | WS_HSCROLL | WS_VSCROLL,
    CW_USEDEFAULT, CW_USEDEFAULT,
    CW_USEDEFAULT, CW_USEDEFAULT,
    (HWND)NULL, (HMENU)NULL, hInstance, NULL);
ShowWindow(hwndMain, SW_SHOWDEFAULT);
UpdateWindow(hwndMain);
```

.NET code:

```
Form form = new Form();
form.Text = "Main Window";
form.Show();
```

The .NET Framework provides classes at different levels of abstraction. At the lowest level, the Base Class Library provides a rich set of base classes that give you easy access to Windows API functionality. These classes may be abstracted and extended by your own custom classes. At a higher level, .NET provides a set of abstracted classes that are targeted to specific areas of software development. For example, ASP.NET provides classes to write Web Services, while ADO.NET provides classes for data access. These abstracted classes are simply extended from the Base Class Library, so if you are resourceful enough, you could create Web Services without ASP.NET, and instead access the Base Class Library directly. Of course, you would lose out on the productivity benefits that ASP.NET provides for developing Web Services. For developers, productivity is what .NET is all about.

This section presented a very simplified view of the .NET Framework. It was intended to introduce you just to the highlights of the .NET Framework, so that you begin to form a picture of what the Framework is composed of. In the next section we will extend our discussion from Chapter 1 on how the .NET Framework addresses limitations within the current development platform.

The .NET Evolution

As we discussed in Chapter 1, the .NET Framework was designed to address the limitations of the current DNA model, frequently experienced by programmers, and to eliminate them, or improve the situation. We identified in broad terms that the limitations are with development, deployment, and interoperability (the ability of components and applications to communicate and collaborate). Just to recap, at a high level, these limitations include:

- Development Issues

  - Windows DNA does not provide a unified set of classes for developers. They are forced to use the Windows API for some functionality.

  - Too many choices for where to place application logic. Each choice has relative disadvantages. ASP applications, for example, are weakly-typed, interpreted code. Windows DNA does not provide a unified programming framework.

  - Code is unmanaged, and does not provide type safety.

- Deployment Issues

  - Applications are difficult to deploy, mainly because COM components have separate type library files and require GUID entries in the Windows Registry.

- Interoperability Issues

  - Applications do not natively serialize to XML.

  - Windows DNA is suitable for tightly coupled applications. This does not suit the highly distributed nature of the Internet.

The basic message here is that while Windows DNA was a good architectural model, it did not provide a unified set of tools, nor did it make it easy to create interoperable applications. The .NET Framework addresses these limitations by providing a powerful, unified set of tools for creating highly distributed, interoperable applications. So, the .NET Framework improves the technology. Many of the architectural concepts behind Windows DNA are still valid in a .NET world, but the toolsets are not.

The specific benefits of the .NET Framework are:

- DLL "Heaven" not "DLL Hell"
- Component integration replaces interfaces
- Simplified deployment
- Improved resource management
- Multiple language integration
- Unified, extensible Class Library
- Structured exception handling

Let's look at these benefits of the .NET Framework, and contrast them against what we have today:

DLL Heaven

The most overused phrase in reference to Windows DNA COM development has to be "DLL Hell". However, the expression is very appropriate, because registering DLLs is every developer's greatest source of headaches and frustration. Currently, COM components are tracked with a unique identifier, or GUID, that must be entered in the registry in order to run. In addition, the DLL must be registered in a dedicated package for Component Services to manage it. Component references are dependent on the GUID, so DLLs are only effective if their GUID is preserved and if it is entered correctly in the Registry. This situation is not easy to maintain. Subsequent recompilations of a DLL may break a GUID, and all of the dependencies on that DLL. Sometimes, a developer has no choice but to break compatibility if a component's interface needs to change. If this happens then the developer must carefully recompile every dependent DLL, to preserve the dependency order, and to prevent ugly type library mismatch errors from arising at execution time. Most experienced developers are careful about cascading GUID changes through an application, but they have usually gained that experience through a lot of difficult "DLL Hell" situations.

In .NET, this problem goes away, because .NET components are compiled with **meta data** that fully describes the component, including its interface, supported types, and any custom information that the developer has added. Meta data makes components self-describing so they do not require external type libraries or Registry entries. Multiple versions of the same .NET component can exist side-by-side on the same system, without ill effects, and you do not need to worry about having multiple versions of the same component conflicting with each other in the Registry. .NET applications will automatically load up the version of the DLL that they were built, tested and compiled with. Alternatively, you can edit the Application Configuration file to specify that different DLL versions be used. This file is generated along with the application executable at compile-time, and is discussed later in the chapter.

Component Integration Replaces Interfaces

COM components communicate with each other via an intermediate COM+ plumbing layer. COM components must be queried before use, to determine what interface they provide, which adds an additional layer between the calling component and the receiving component. COM components rely on HRESULT codes to specify the result of an interaction. These are hexadecimal codes that are typically not raised to the application user unless an unhandled exception occurs during execution. Added to this complexity is the requirement that COM components must be properly entered into the Registry in order to be recognized. COM components will not respond properly if these Registry entries are incorrect or get corrupted. Sometimes this problem is missed at compile time, and not recognized until execution time, at which point the application may become unstable or crash.

These problems go away in .NET because .NET components are self-referencing using meta data, and do not require Registry entries. In addition, .NET components do not require special plumbing to manage calls between components. All of the familiar COM+ constructs such as IUnknown(), IDispatch(), AddRef(), and HRESULT simply do not exist for .NET components. Instead, the Common Language Runtime interprets the meta data to manage interactions between components. In .NET, a request to a component goes directly to the component instead of through an intermediate interface query, or a Registry lookup, which reduces the complexity of component interactions .NET applications use an **Application Configuration File** to document the locations of dependency assemblies. The application configuration file is an XML file that can be edited to point at alternative versions of assemblies if required. This is how .NET executables know which assemblies to use, in the absence of a centralized registration mechanism.

Deployment

Windows DNA applications are difficult to deploy, mainly because COM components have separate type library files and GUID entries in the Windows Registry. COM components are not self-referencing, which is why they need entries in the Registry. Also, COM components do not directly provide their own type library information, which is why they require a separate type library file. A typical Windows DNA installation involves deploying a large number of files, and setting a lot of registry entries. The Windows Installer does a good job of managing installations, but this Registry-based installation system involves a higher level of complexity than should really be necessary.

.NET greatly simplifies deployments, because .NET components are self-referencing, and do not require either separate type library files, or Registry entries. .NET components track their own meta data, which fully describes the component. DLLs written in .NET are typically deployed using a simple command-line XCOPY procedure call, and may be uninstalled using a simple command-line DEL *.*. Of course, you should still use an installer program for complicated deployments, because it is always difficult to track every component and file that makes up an application.

Resource Management

COM components are very susceptible to memory leaks if the developer does not properly manage resources inside the components. A memory leak occurs when a resource manager does not release memory space that is allocated to references (usually object references), such that the object reference count continues to climb, and existing references are not released. **Resources** refer to anything from object references to database connections. Currently, object references must be explicitly de-referenced; otherwise the Component Services manager is at risk of holding on to the reference, and generating a memory leak. Although the COM+ manager is very efficient at managing the activation and deactivation of resources, it is not foolproof.

In .NET, the Common Language Runtime (CLR) automatically manages all resources for you, including memory management and garbage collection. The CLR tracks the amount of memory that resources use, and actively cycles through the resources at frequent intervals to refresh the memory usage, and to prevent any particular resource from being retained in memory indefinitely. .NET languages continue to support keywords for de-referencing an object (for example, the Nothing keyword in Visual Basic), but these keywords only serve as an early notification to the CLR that the resource is no longer needed. Unlike in COM+, this keyword does not garbage collect the resource. The CLR will automatically handle this for you. In theory you do not need to set any of your object references to Nothing, although it remains good programming practice to use this keyword for indicating when the code listing is done using an object reference. The key point here is that in .NET, the Nothing keyword only *indicates* to the GC that the object reference may be garbage collected. The GC will not actually release the reference until it determines that this is necessary.

Language Integration

Windows DNA development languages are not created equal. For example, Visual Basic provides limited native functionality compared to Visual C++, because it does not support the same high level of object-oriented features or the same set of data types (this is alleviated to some degree by the huge market of custom controls and components that have been developed by third-party vendors). Different languages also use their own compilers, which each provide different levels of type safety and execution services.

.NET supports a common language model that manages code for multiple languages. .NET languages must conform to rules that are defined by the Common Language Specification (CLS) and the Common Type System (CTS). The CTS is especially important, because it defines a common type system for all .NET languages. This reduces the discrepancy in data types between languages, which can make inter-language operation difficult to impossible, if the two languages do not "speak" the same data types. The CLS essentially provides instructions to each language's compiler as to how to prepare the code for management by the Common Language Runtime (CLR).

The figure below shows how languages integrate:

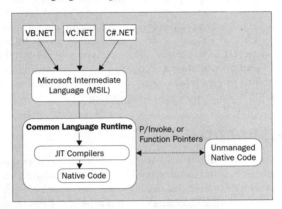

The Common Language Runtime will manage code for any language that conforms to the CLS and the CTS. .NET code is compiled in a two-step process whereby the code is first converted into a language-neutral, generalized instruction set called **Microsoft Intermediate Language** (IL). Next, the Just-In-Time (JIT) compiler works with the IL instruction set to convert the code into native code that is then executed by the CLR. .NET code is compiled into **assemblies**, which are similar to dynamic link libraries (DLLs), except that they hold meta data, and are self-describing, as we will discuss later in this chapter. You can mix-and-match language files within the same project in Visual Studio.NET. For example, you could write some of the class files in C# and others in VB.NET, and then have the Common Language Runtime manage the compiled project.

The CLR will also work with so-called **unmanaged** native code, such as COM components. There are a number of mechanisms available for the CLR to do this. The strictest and safest method is the **COM Interoperability service** (COM Interop), which generates a .NET wrapper for the COM component, and uses the Platform Invoke, or **P/Invoke mechanism** for making calls out to the COM component via the wrapper. This mechanism works both ways, from .NET to COM, and from COM to .NET. COM type libraries can be converted to meta data, and imported into .NET projects. The reverse can also happen: .NET assemblies can be exported to COM type libraries. The P/Invoke mechanism will automatically marshal a number of data types, although most data types will be converted during the process of importing the COM type library. In most cases this conversion will not cause a problem, but before using COM Interop you need to check the data types in your COM object, and verify that they can be seamlessly imported over to .NET.

> For a list of data type conversions that occur during a COM type library import
> into .NET, see the MSDN article: *Marshaling COM Types to the .NET Framework*,
> available in the .NET Framework SDK at:
> http://msdn.microsoft.com/library/default.asp?url=/library/en-us/cpguidnf/
> html/cpconmarshalingcomtypestonetframework.asp.

Unified, Extensible Class Library

Windows DNA does not provide a consistent way to access system functionality and services. In this era of Rapid Application Development (RAD), the main purpose of a development platform is to encapsulate system functionality into extensible, reusable classes that are powerful and easy to use. These classes save developers the time and effort of having to access the system functionality directly at the API level. Unfortunately, this is what developers frequently have to do. Visual Basic, for example, provides consistently good encapsulation of Windows Forms related classes, but it provides very uneven encapsulation of more abstract functionality. Visual Basic developers have grown used to adding direct Windows API calls to their code to get at certain functionality. In some cases, the Windows API function requires a data type that is not supported by Visual Basic. In this case, the API function is simply not available for use in the application, and the developer is forced to find a workaround.

Visual Basic developers lack a unified class framework that encapsulates system functionality. In fact, the language is designed to hide these low-level structures from the developer. Compounding this problem is the fact that Visual Basic does not support the true object-oriented features that are necessary to work with a unified, extensible class framework. Visual C++ developers are in a better position, because they have available to them a framework of system classes, encapsulated in the Microsoft Foundation Classes (MFC). Yet most developers will tell you that MFC is difficult to work with.

Another restriction with COM components (written in Visual Basic) is that they lack the ability to support implementation inheritance; instead, they support interface inheritance and delegation. For example, if Component A inherits from Component B, then every method on Component A needs to wrap a call to a method on Component B. Delegation means that Component B actually gets instanced inside Component A. Thus, COM+ libraries cannot be easily extended without creating unwieldy code that ends up being a poor substitute for true inheritance.

Finally, COM component libraries also lack the organization that is found in the .NET Class Framework. COM+ libraries cannot be grouped into logical sets of components, nor do they support sophisticated hierarchies of classes that can be referenced as branches of a root class. The .NET Framework, on the other hand, allows you to compile logically related classes into a hierarchical namespace. Classes in the .NET Framework appear more organized, and are easier to locate than COM+ libraries.

So what developers really need is a unified class system that is easy to use. The .NET Class Framework provides the following:

❑ **Unified programming model** – The Framework provides hundreds of classes, interfaces, types and structures, grouped into a hierarchical system of namespaces that contain logically related classes. For example, `System.Data.SqlClient.SqlConnection` refers to a `SqlConnection` class, which is located in the `System.Data.SqlClient` namespace.

❑ **Full object-oriented programming (OOP) support** – Framework classes may be inherited in custom classes and customized by overriding specific methods. A .NET class may inherit from only one other class, but it may implement multiple interfaces. .NET classes also support method overloading, which allows another class to override an inherited method as many times as needed, so long as at least one interface member is different in the method call. For example, the `DataSet` object in the `System.Data` namespace has several versions of the `ReadXML()` method. One version accepts a `System.IO.Stream` object as the argument, while another version accepts a file name (as `String`) as the argument. Method overloading simplifies the Class Framework by limiting the number of unique methods that you have to create for variations on the same function.

❑ **Cross-language interoperability** – the Framework classes are not language-specific. They may be used from any .NET-compliant language.

The .NET Framework Class Library provides a managed alternative to existing COM+ libraries and Windows API functions for accessing system-level functions. The Class Library is not a replacement for the current Windows API, but it does provide a useful set of wrappers that make it easier to access these functions. As a developer, you still have a choice as to in which method you prefer to use for accessing system-level functions. The biggest advantage of the Class Library is that it provides the same programming model for all .NET-compliant languages, which allows developers to pick the language they are most comfortable with, without having to worry about functionality trade-offs.

Exception Handling

In Windows DNA, error codes were not consistent. They could be any of the following:

❑ HRESULT codes

❑ Win32 error codes

❑ Custom Exception Codes

In .NET, raised errors are handled consistently. All errors are reported as exceptions only, and they can be isolated in the application using dedicated exception classes. All exceptions in .NET derive from the System.Exception class, which provides a large number of error properties, including:

❑ Message – returns a string containing a description of the exception.

❑ Source – returns the name of the application or class that generated the exception.

❑ StackTrace – returns the call stack that led up to the exception being thrown, and contains the method and line number where the exception occurred.

❑ HRESULT – returned for a COM Interop exception, and contains the COM HRESULT value.

Interestingly, the base Exception class does not provide a Number property. However, derived exception classes do provide this property in a manner that is specific to the exception class. For example, the SqlException class provides a Number property that corresponds to an entry in the master.dbo.sysmessages table.

The .NET Framework provides several specialized exception classes that relate to specific service areas. These include:

❑ System.Exception – the base class for all runtime exceptions. Derived classes include the OutOfMemoryException class and the InvalidOperationException class.

❑ ArgumentException – the base class for all exceptions due to arguments that are passed to procedure calls. Derived classes include the ArgumentNullException class and the ArgumentOutOfRangeException class.

❑ CoreException – the base class for all fatal runtime exceptions. Derived classes include the NullReferenceException class.

All of these exception classes are located in the System namespace; however, other namespaces also contain exception classes. For example, the System.Data.SqlClient namespace contains the SqlException class, for representing data access errors that are specific to the SQL Server managed provider.

For example, here's code that catches two kinds of exceptions in a data access procedure:

```vb
Imports System.Data
Imports System.Data.SqlClient

Dim sqlConn As SqlConnection
Dim sqlCmd As SqlCommand
Dim sqlAdapt As SqlDataAdapter
Dim rowDataSet As New DataSet()

Try
    ' Create a new connection object
    sqlConn = New SqlConnection(SQL_CONNECTION)

    ' Create a new command object
    sqlCmd = New SqlCommand()

    ' Specify the command to be executed
    With sqlCmd
        .Connection = sqlConn
        .CommandType = CommandType.Text
        '.CommandText = SQL_SUPPLIERS
        ' Use this line to raise an exception:
        .CommandText = "select * from SUPPLIERS2"
    End With

    ' Open the connection
    sqlConn.Open()

    ' Open a DataAdapter object, using the command object
    sqlAdapt = New SqlDataAdapter(sqlCmd)

    ' Populate the DataSet from the DataAdapter
    Call sqlAdapt.Fill(rowDataSet, "Suppliers")

Catch errSql As System.Data.SqlClient.SqlException
    Dim colErrors As SqlErrorCollection = errSql.Errors
    Dim i As Integer
    For i = 0 To colErrors.Count
        Console.WriteLine("Error #" & errSql.Number & "[" & errSql.Source & _
        "] " & errSql.Message & ControlChars.CrLf & _
        "Raised from stack trace: " & errSql.StackTrace)
    Next

Catch errArg As System.ArgumentNullException
    Console.WriteLine("[" & errArg.Source & "] Error: " & _
        errArg.Message & ControlChars.CrLf & "Raised from stack trace: " & _
        errArg.StackTrace)

Finally

    sqlConn.Close()

End Try
```

Note that the `SqlException` class exposes a collection of errors, which you must loop through. The `ArgumentException` class, on the other hand, does not provide an `Errors` collection, or error numbers. This code sample forces an exception by selecting records from the non-existent SUPPLIERS2 table. The exception that would be written out to the console is shown below:

```
Error #208[SQL Server Managed Provider] Invalid object name 'SUPPLIERS2'.
Raised from stack trace:
at System.Data.SqlClient.SqlCommand.ExecuteReader(CommandBehavior cmdBehavior,
RunBehavior runBehavior, Boolean returnStream)
at
System.Data.SqlClient.SqlCommand.System.Data.IDbCommand.ExecuteReader(CommandBehav
ior behavior)
at System.Data.Common.DbDataAdapter.Fill(Object data, Int32 startRecord, Int32
maxRecords, String srcTable, IDbCommand command, CommandBehavior behavior)
at System.Data.Common.DbDataAdapter.Fill(DataSet dataSet, Int32 startRecord, Int32
maxRecords, String srcTable, IDbCommand command, CommandBehavior behavior)
at System.Data.Common.DbDataAdapter.Fill(DataSet dataSet, String srcTable)
at TestADONetChap2.Form1.ListSuppliers() in C:\Documents and Settings\jhasan\My
Documents\Visual Studio Projects\TestADONetChap2\Form1.vb:line 456
```

The .NET Framework's new structured handling system is a welcome change from the unstructured system that we currently have with languages such as Visual Basic. Structured error handling will make applications more stable, but the downside is that you will now have to write a lot more code to handle exceptions than you used to.

Does Windows DNA Still Apply in .NET?

Windows DNA is essentially an application architecture model that describes how to develop applications using multiple tiers for each of the application services (user interface, business and database). Windows DNA goes a step further by recommending specific technologies for each of the layers. For example, in a distributed Internet application, Windows DNA recommends using ASP scripts for the user interface tier, and COM+ business objects in the business tier. So, Windows DNA provides a dual message of architecture and technology. The architecture message still applies in .NET, but the technology message has changed somewhat with the introduction of new .NET technologies.

Component-based development is still the recommended approach in .NET. Instead of writing your components in COM+, you will now be writing them in a .NET-compliant language, such as C#.NET. With .NET, you now have more powerful ways to marshal disconnected data sets between tiers. This is one example where the basic architecture issues have not changed, but the technology has: Windows DNA always advocated passing lightweight, or disconnected recordsets to the user tier in an Internet application, but the ADO technology never effectively delivered this capability. With .NET, you now have that effective capability, via ADO.NET.

.NET also provides new ways to program the different tiers. For example, in the user interface tier, you can now develop with Web Forms (for Internet applications) and Windows Forms (for desktop applications). Web services, which are new with .NET, are distributed components that provide a public interface over the Internet, and can communicate directly with Web clients. Web services are another example of a new technology for an existing application tier (in this case, the business tier).

Finally, Windows DNA applications have always been difficult to deploy, because they involve so many different kinds of files, including COM+ DLLs, which must be registered correctly in order to work. With .NET, assemblies now hold manifests that fully describe the components in the assembly. .NET simplifies deployments, and eliminates a lot of the headaches that the Registry used to cause. .NET deployments have their own share of headaches, in particular, when you have too many side-by-side versions of the same assembly on a server. These versions will not interfere with each other directly, but you need to be careful not to get confused between them.

So, through Chapter 1, and the first half of this Chapter, we have taken an aerial overview of the .NET Framework's feature set, and have looked at how .NET is intended to overcome current development and deployment limitations. For the remainder of this chapter we will discuss the design goals of the .NET Framework, followed by a more technical drilldown into the Framework's architecture. Subsequent chapters in this book cover each part of the Framework in great detail. We will limit our discussion to overviews of each constituent part, and where necessary, a discussion of the concepts and theories behind the feature.

Design Goals of the .NET Framework

As we are, by now, well aware, the .NET Framework is designed to make software development more productive, especially Internet development. The .NET Framework provides this through a set of rich, integrated classes and services that are built around a common type system. The .NET Framework supports a unified programming model, one where all .NET languages access the same set of classes and services. This effectively removes language as a limiting factor to what your software development team can accomplish. In .NET, VB.NET, C# and C++ are all managed languages, and have access to the same set of classes and services. In fact, Visual Studio.NET allows you to mix languages within a project. Class files written in C# may be part of the same project as VB.NET class files. (Of course, it is not clear what the design advantages of this approach are!) So now your development team can stop worrying about what languages every one knows, and instead focus on what they do best: building software.

The design goals of the .NET Framework are:

- **Simplify Software Development**

  - Provide rich functional base classes that are extensible and easier to access than standard Windows API calls

  - Support XML Web Services Development, for example, ASP.NET provides native support for the Simple Object Access Protocol (SOAP)

- **Unify Programming Models**

  - All .NET languages must provide the same set of .NET Framework classes and services, as outlined in the Common Language Specification. .NET languages must be interoperable.

- **Leverage standard Web protocols**

  - Deep XML Support.

  - XML-based grammars are used throughout .NET, for example, SOAP, WSDL (Web Services Description Language – for describing network and web services over the Internet) and the `Web.config` file in ASP.NET applications.

❑   **Simplify Code Deployment and Maintenance**

    ❑   Eliminate "DLL Hell"

    ❑   Simplify deployment and versioning of components

    ❑   Provide richer compilers and runtime support

Finally, the .NET Framework simplifies application deployments. Gone are registry entries and separate type library files for compiled components. Also gone are the marshaling calls that are associated with interface-oriented COM components. The .NET Framework has eliminated much of the plumbing that is required for COM components. .NET components are truly object oriented, and intrinsically contain meta data information that describes their type library information. The meta data is used by different services across the .NET Framework. For example, the new Common Language Runtime reads the meta data during compilation, and uses it to generate the compilation bits. .NET (private) assemblies may now be installed through a simple copy operation, and run directly from the folder where they reside. .NET shared assemblies may be installed using the same simple copy operation, but in a location that is accessible to multiple applications. Complicated installations that involve the registry are now a thing of the past. Simplified application deployment for Microsoft technology has arrived!

The .NET Framework Architecture

In Chapter 1 we were introduced to the following architecture of the .NET Framework:

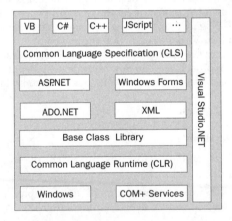

There are many components to the .NET Framework, and it is hard to absorb all at once. The .NET Framework provides a set of layered classes and services that start at the operating system level and increase in functionality through a set of base and abstracted classes all the way up to a set of managed, .NET-compliant languages.

At a high level, the .NET Framework components are:

❑   **Common Language Runtime** – a rich runtime environment that handles important runtime tasks for the developer, including memory management and garbage collection. Built around the Common Type System that defines a common set of data types for all .NET-compliant languages.

❑   **Base Class Library** – rich set of functional base classes that may be encapsulated and extended in custom classes, or used directly.

❑ **Extended Class Libraries** – abstracted classes that are focused on one aspect of development: ASP.NET (for Web Services), ADO.NET (for data access), XML (to parse and manipulate docs), and Windows Forms (for Windows-based applications).

❑ **Common Language Specification** – defines requirements for .NET-compliant languages.

❑ **Multiple Programming Languages** – VB.NET, C++, and C# are just some of the approximately 25 languages that are available for coding in .NET. The .NET Framework provides one platform for many languages, including non-Microsoft languages such as COBOL, Perl, and SmallTalk.

❑ **Visual Studio.NET** – an integrated development environment for coding with the .NET Framework, and increasing developer productivity.

If you are a developer, then you are very likely to be interested in the Class Framework, which is the set of classes that you actually code with. The .NET Framework provides much more than an API, however, so before we get to talking about .NET's rich class framework, we need to step back and introduce the underlying systems that enable the .NET Framework to achieve its design goals. These are:

❑ Common Type System

❑ Meta data

❑ Common Language Specification

❑ Common Language Runtime

The developers in the audience will need to bear with more systems-level information than they are used to, but hang in there! This discussion aims to enhance your understanding of the .NET Framework and the areas that will be explored in detail in chapters throughout the book.

The Common Type System

The Common Type System (CTS) defines standard, object-oriented data types and value types that are supported by all .NET programming languages. The CTS standards are what allow .NET to provide a unified programming model, and to support multiple languages. A common type system is the first prerequisite to allowing languages to interoperate. This is easy to understand, if you consider that languages can only interoperate if they are based on the same system of types. In the past, type discrepancies have caused many interoperability problems, particularly for Visual Basic developers. For example, some Windows API functions accept input data types that may exist in Visual C++, but not in Visual Basic. This forces the developer to approximate the data type, and call the API function with the closest type that they can declare. This can have undesirable consequences, such as stability problems that cause the calling application to crash. Some API functions are completely inaccessible to Visual Basic as a result.

So, a common type system is an important new feature in the .NET Framework. The CTS must support a range of languages, some of which are object-oriented, and some of which are not. Much has been made of the fact that COBOL is now a first-class .NET language. COBOL is a procedural language, not an object-oriented one. Yet the CTS supports it. How is this accomplished?

For a list of all Third Party .NET Resources, including links on non-Microsoft, .NET-support languages such as COBOL and Perl, visit:
http://msdn.microsoft.com/net/thirdparty/default.asp#lang.

Type Systems Defined

In object-oriented programming, a **type** is something that holds a value and supports an interface for describing the type. When most non-C++ programmers think of data types, they think only of values. However, in .NET, all types are object-oriented (and value types may be converted into reference types using a boxing conversion). This means that, in addition to storing values, they also exhibit a behavior that is defined by their interface. Types are reliable, because you can expect them to behave in a certain way.

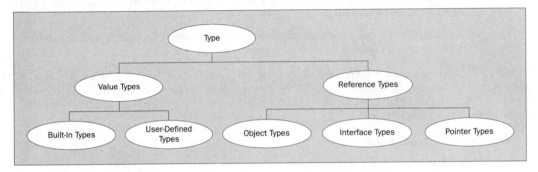

The Common Type System provides two main types:

❏ Value Types

❏ Reference Types

Value types are simple data types that roughly correspond to simple bit patterns like integers and floats. In .NET, a value type derives from the System.Object namespace, and supports an interface that provides information about the kind of data that is stored, as well as the data value. Value types are useful for representing simple data types, and any non-object user-defined type, including enumerations.

Reference types are also derived from the System.Object namespace, and may hold object references derived from classes. Reference types are self-typing, which means that they describe their own interface. This is not so different from the object references that we already use today. Object references are obviously very specific to the type of object you are assigning. Once the reference is assigned, you expect to query the object reference according to what its interface provides.

Value types are known as **exact types**, which means that they fully describe the value they hold. Value types support methods that collectively describe the type. These methods are provided courtesy of the System.Object namespace. The methods are:

❏ GetType – returns a Type object that fully describes the type.

❏ GetHashCode – returns a signed, 32-bit integer hash code that is unique to the object type. Two objects of the same type will have the same hash code.

❏ Equals – this method accepts an object reference and matches its type against the underlying system type. This method returns a Boolean value of true if the object reference type matches the underlying system type. For example:

```
Public Shared Sub Main()
    Dim objA As New System.Boolean()
    Dim objB As New System.Single()
    ' This statement writes 'false'
    Console.WriteLine(objA.Equals(objB).ToString())
End Sub
```

The Common Type System actually broadens the definition of reference types beyond traditional object references. Abstract classes (interfaces) and pointers are also tracked as types.

There are three kinds of Reference Type:

❑   **Object Types** – self-describing references to classes. The Object Type stores all kinds of classes, including abstract classes, custom (user-created) classes, and built-in system classes.

❑   **Interface Types** – stores references to interfaces.

❑   **Pointer Types** – stores references to pointers.

Primitive Types

Primitive types are supported directly by the compiler (specifically, the Virtual Execution System (VES), which is described later in the chapter), and are located in the root System namespace. The table below shows a selection of the most common primitive types.

Name in MSIL assembler (CTS)	CLS Type?	Name in class library	Description
Bool	Yes	System.Boolean	True/false value
Char	Yes	System.Char	Unicode 16-bit char.
class System.Object	Yes	System.Object	Object or boxed value type
class System.String	Yes	System.String	Unicode string
float32	Yes	System.Single	IEEE 32-bit float
float64	Yes	System.Double	IEEE 64-bit float
int8	No	System.SByte	Signed 8-bit integer
int16	Yes	System.Int16	Signed 16-bit integer
Typedref	No	System.TypedReference	Pointer plus runtime type
unsigned int8	Yes	System.Byte	Unsigned 8-bit integer
unsigned int16	No	System.UInt16	Unsigned 16-bit integer

Type Safety

The Common Type System promotes type safety, which in turn improves code stability. In .NET, type safety means that type definitions are completely known, and cannot be compromised. ASP developers, especially, will appreciate the benefits of this, because ASP does not support strongly-typed variables. This creates a number of problems, such as:

❑   You try to reference an object, thinking it's one thing, but it's another, so the object does not support the method you are trying to call.

❑   You try to equate one object to another, and the assignment fails.

The Common Type System ensures that object references are strongly typed. For example, when you set an object reference, you are guaranteeing that:

❑   The reference can be identified by type. In .NET, the object being referenced tracks its own type information, and the runtime compiler enforces it.

❑   You can only invoke the methods that are appropriate to the type. The runtime compiler will not compile code that tries to reference a non-existent method, or a method that cannot be viewed in the current context (for example, a private method that cannot be viewed by a subclass).

Keep in mind that type safety does not mean that you can't still write bad objects whose methods don't work properly. You still can, but the difference is that you can't compound the problem by having reference type issues as well. Late-bound code is still allowed in .NET, but references will still, at a minimum, inherit from System.Object, which guarantees a certain base interface. Currently, in Visual Basic, the TypeName() function checks and returns the reference type for a variable. Visual Basic developers are used to putting this check inside their code, to prevent them from accidentally treating a variable as the wrong type. This can lead to very ugly runtime errors, and can crash an application. With type safety, this manual step is unnecessary, because the compiler won't let you get as far as compiling "type unsafe" code. Type safety in .NET is all about guaranteeing the capabilities and availability of a reference type.

The CTS is the core system service that allows .NET to support multiple languages and unified programming models. The Common Type System is designed to resolve interoperability problems between languages that arise due to incompatible data types.

Meta Data

Meta data is organized information that the Common Language Runtime uses to provide compile-time and runtime services, including:

❑   Loading of Class Files

❑   Memory Management

❑   Debugging

❑   Object Browsing

❑   MSIL Translation to Native Code (described later in the chapter)

Meta data is analogous to the type library files that are generated for COM components. A COM+ type library describes the classes that a component exposes, which in turn facilitates OLE Automation. The COM component type library file is separate from the actual compiled DLL file. Here is where the similarities end, because unlike COM+ type libraries, meta data is stored as part of the actual .NET component source code.

.NET components are self-describing, because the meta data is stored as part of the compiled component (known in .NET as an **assembly**). Combine this with the fact that .NET components do not require Windows Registry entries, and you can immediately appreciate why deployments are so much easier in .NET.

The figure below illustrates different Meta Data consumers:

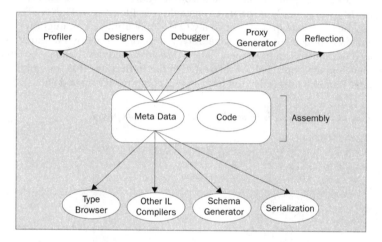

What's in Meta Data?

We've used the analogy that meta data is like a COM+ type library. However, in reality, meta data contains much more information than COM+ type libraries. Meta data is a structured description of the code in an assembly. Meta data contains:

- ❑ Description of the assembly (the deployment unit)
  - ❑ Identity: Name, Version and Culture
  - ❑ Dependencies (other assemblies)
  - ❑ Security permissions that the assembly requires to run
- ❑ Description of the Types
  - ❑ Base classes and interfaces
- ❑ Custom attributes
  - ❑ Defined by the User
  - ❑ Defined by the Compiler
  - ❑ Defined by the Framework

Meta data is language-independent. .NET supported languages access the same meta data, and can interpret it the same way. Recall that Visual Studio.NET allows you to mix and match source code files from different languages within the same project. This is possible thanks to meta data, which supplies the compiler with all the information that it needs to execute the component.

Meta data may also store custom attributes, some of which may be language-specific. For example, C++ header information may be stored in meta data. This information is ignored, unless you are loading the component files into C++.

Exporting and Emitting Meta Data

The compiler generates a component's meta data from its source code. Meta data is stored with the compiled component in a read-only Portable Executable (PE) file format. The .NET Framework provides APIs for exporting the meta data to XML, or to a COM+ type library. You might want to generate an export file if you need to document a .NET assembly, but there is arguably not much that the average developer will need to do with exported meta data. More advanced developers who are writing compilers, or creating new development tools, will be interested in the **Reflection** APIs for emitting meta data. The Common Language Runtime uses reflection to browse a component's meta data.

We'll be looking at Reflection APIs in much further detail in Chapter 4.

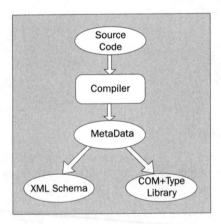

The `System` and `System.Reflection` namespaces provide APIs that allow you to do the same thing manually.

The Common Language Specification

The Common Language Specification (CLS) defines conventions that languages must support in order to be interoperable within .NET. The CLS defines rules that range from naming conventions for interface members, to rules governing method overloading. Consistency in data types is another important step for supporting interoperation between languages. The Common Type System provides this consistency. The Common Language Specification is in fact a subset of the Common Type System.

In order to provide interoperation, a CLS-compliant language must obey the following conventions:

❑ Public identifiers are case-sensitive. .

❑ Languages must be able to resolve identifiers that are equivalent to their keywords.

❑ Stricter overloading rules: a given method name may refer to any number of methods, as long as each one differs in the number of parameters, or argument types.

❑ Properties and events must follow strict naming rules.

❑ All pointers must be managed, and references must be typed; otherwise, they cannot be verified.

This is by no means a comprehensive list. There are close to forty conventions that CLS-compliant languages must obey, so we're highlighting only the most important conventions here. For many application developers, any more detail about the CLS would prove more confusing than helpful. You can consult the .NET Framework SDK documentation for specific details on the CLS.

Remember, the purpose of the .NET framework is to define standards that make it easier to write robust, secure and reusable code. The .NET framework extends this concept by allowing any language to participate in the framework, so long as it conforms to the specifications embodied by the Common Type System and the Common Language Specification.

The Common Language Runtime

The Common Language Runtime (CLR) provides a rich level of support that simplifies application development and provides for better code reuse. The CLR provides a broad set of runtime services, including compilation, garbage collection and memory management. In addition, the CLR lays out common type systems that are used throughout the framework. This enables convergence between languages and programming models, because all .NET languages access the same set of type systems and base classes.

The CLR is built around the Common Type System (CTS), which defines standard, object-oriented data types that are used across all .NET programming languages. It is the CTS that enables .NET to support a unified programming model, and to support multiple languages. In order to qualify as a .NET language, a programming language must conform to the Common Language Specification (CLS). And, as we've already discussed in this chapter, the CLS is a subset of the CTS.

Code that runs under the control of the Common Language Runtime is called **managed code**. The term refers to code that provides the CLR with the information it needs to run the code, and which is automatically cleaned up by the Garbage Collector. Unmanaged code, such as COM components, may also run under the CLR via COM InterOp Services, which generates a .NET wrapper for the unmanaged component. Managed code may also call unmanaged resources, such as file devices; which works fine, although you may need to add specific cleanup code to ensure that the resource is properly cleaned up by the Garbage Collector.

Managed code allows the CLR to do the following:

❑ Read meta data that describes the component interfaces and types

❑ Walk the code stack

❑ Handle Exceptions

❑ Retrieve security information

In the next section we'll move on to look at the design goals of the Common Language Runtime.

Design Goals of the CLR

The design goals of the Common Language Runtime are:

- ❏ Simplify Development
  - ❏ Define standards that promote code reuse
  - ❏ Provide a broad range of services, including memory management and garbage collection
- ❏ Simplify Application Deployment
  - ❏ Components use meta data instead of registration
  - ❏ Support side-by-side, multiple component versions
  - ❏ Command-line deployment (XCOPY) and uninstall (DEL)
- ❏ Support Development Languages
  - ❏ Provide rich base classes for developer tools and languages
- ❏ Support Multiple Languages
  - ❏ Define common type systems that are used by all .NET languages
- ❏ Enable Convergence of Programming Models
  - ❏ Build languages and tools on a common framework. For example, ASP.NET, VB.NET, and C# have access to the same base classes.

Let's discuss the Common Language Runtime in more detail, and see how it accomplishes these design goals.

Overview of the CLR

The architecture of the Common Language Runtime is shown in the figure below:

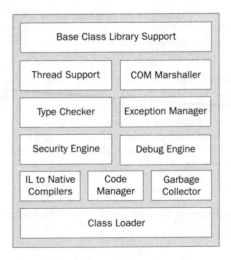

So, as we know, the CLR is designed to provide a robust and secure environment for executing managed code. It is built around the Common Type System, which guarantees type safety.

The CLR provides a number of runtime support services using the Virtual Execution System (VES). The Virtual Execution System is responsible for implementing and enforcing the Common Type System. The VES is designed to run managed code, that is, code that supports the CTS. The execution engine uses meta data information to understand the structure of the components.

The specific components of the VES are:

- ❏ Class Loader (Load managed code)
- ❏ Microsoft Intermediate Language (MSIL)
- ❏ MSIL-to-Native code conversion
- ❏ Verification of Type safety, according to CTS
- ❏ Stack Walker (services based on stack heap)
- ❏ Memory Management and Garbage Collection
- ❏ Profiling and Debugging
- ❏ Co-Instance Execution
- ❏ Unmanaged Code

Chapters 3, 4, and 5 will review each of these components in great detail. For now, we will take just a brief look at some of these components.

Class Loader

The Class Loader is responsible for loading classes into memory and preparing them for execution. The Class Loader works with the information provided in the component's meta data, which includes the name of the assembly, version information, and reference type information. The Class Loader provides important integrity checks on code before it is compiled and executed. Most importantly, it runs checks to ensure type safety, which greatly improves code stability at runtime. In summary, the Class Loader promotes type safety and efficient memory management.

Microsoft Intermediate Language (MSIL)

MSIL is a generalized instruction set that can be interpreted by a wide range of compilers from different programming languages. MSIL is generated by the VES, as it walks through the code stack. MSIL is referred to as a compiler-intermediate language because it is not fully compiled binary code. Instead, it is similar to byte code which must be converted into native code prior to execution. The Common Language Runtime delegates the task of creating binary code from MSIL to platform-specific compilers.

MSIL-to-Native Code Compilation

MSIL code must be converted to native code before it is deployed and executed on a target machine. The Common Language Runtime delegates this task to native compilers. There are two classes of compilers:

- ❏ **Just-In-Time (JIT) Compilers** – an optimized compiler that analyzes MSIL and converts it to native code as needed. JIT compilers take into account that some assembly code may not be executed all the time, and therefore does not need to be available as native code all the time.

❑ **Traditional Compilers** – the assembly is entirely converted to native code and loaded as a single instruction set. Traditional compilers are less optimized than JIT compilers, because they must compile an entire assembly all at once, rather than the parts that are needed at a given time.

Type Safety Verification using CTS

When code is compiled, its type safety must be verified, to prevent ugly runtime errors, or application crashes. The discussion until now has implied that type safety is guaranteed in code written for the .NET Framework. In reality, type safety is *enforced* rather than guaranteed. Type safety becomes especially important when code is compiled. Type safety must be verified, and it is done so in a collaborative effort between the Common Language Runtime's Code Loader and the Virtual Execution System. Together, they run type safety algorithms that check for consistency and alert the compiler to problems, if they are found. Plus, type safety is also maintained at runtime.

Stack Walker

The Common Language Runtime must be able to trace the stack heap of managed code at runtime. The CLR accomplishes this using an API called the **Code Manager**. Each source language may interpret the call stack in a different way. Each compiler supports the Code Manager API in order to account for these differences.

The Code Manager supports the following services:

❑ Garbage Collection

❑ Exceptions

❑ Security

❑ Debugging and Profiling

Several of these services are already listed in this section as services provided by the Common Language Runtime. They are in fact provided by the CLR, which works with the Code Manager APIs to account for different compilers.

Memory Management and Garbage Collection

The Common Language Runtime allocates and manages memory for reference types using the **managed heap**. The managed heap is a reserved chunk of memory that can be dynamically subdivided and allocated into smaller regions. The CLR allocates reference types to the managed heap and controls access such that only managed code can access the managed heap. Managed code is designed to work with references types. This ensures that the code references remain type safe.

As new references are created, the CLR continues to allocate them to a new subdivision of the managed heap. The following schematic figure shows the managed heap and garbage collection at work in one scenario:

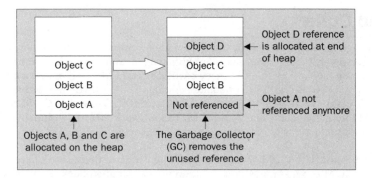

Now at some point you would expect the CLR to run out of space for allocating further references. This does not happen, because the Garbage Collector (GC) is continuously checking the managed heap and removing unused references. The CLR tracks information about a running application, including reference counts. The GC works with the CLR to determine which references are actively being used by a running application, and which may be released. So the CLR manages the heap, and the GC keeps it clean. The interesting aspect to this system is that the managed object itself plays no role in managing or tracking its lifecycle. This is very different in COM+, where the object is responsible for tracking the number of references, then destroying itself once the reference count hits zero. In .NET, the GC is entirely responsible for releasing objects, and typically you will not need to override automatic garbage collection with explicit calls to release references.

.NET does provide destructors for explicitly releasing object references, namely, the `Dispose()` and `Close()` methods, which are primarily intended for use with unmanaged code and resources. The `System.Object` class also supports a `Finalize()` method, which facilitates garbage collection for code that wraps unmanaged resources, including COM objects. You can populate this method with code that explicitly handles cleanup tasks for unmanaged resources. This method is called by the GC prior to releasing the object reference, and helps ensure that an object reference is fully cleaned up prior to being released. This method call should only be used in circumstances where the GC will have difficulty in managing resources. The `Finalize()` method may have a detrimental effect on performance relative to managed code, because the GC maintains a dedicated finalization queue for all components that invoke this method.

The main advantage of the managed heap and Garbage Collection is that in most scenarios there is no opportunity for memory leaks to crop up. The GC is designed to efficiently remove unused references, which are the cause of memory leaks.

Version and Co-instance Execution

The .NET Framework removes the need to have the complicated plumbing that was associated with COM components. Assemblies can be deployed through a simple copy operation to the installation directory. .NET allows multiple versions of the same assembly to exist side-by-side in the same directory. It even supports them running in the same process, although this would not have much value. The application executable uses an Application Configuration XML file to document the locations of the assemblies that the executable binds to. You can edit this file to bind the executable to alternative versions or locations of the assemblies. The application configuration file is typically located in the same directory as the application executable, and is created when you compile an application. This configuration file is not required, and by default the application executable will attempt to bind to assemblies that are located in the same directory.

Unmanaged Code

The Common Language Runtime is designed to provide a robust and secure environment for executing managed code. However, COM components are unmanaged, and cannot be run directly by the CLR (although they can be invoked by the CLR, as we will discuss below). To understand why this is so, remember that the CLR works with intermediate compiled code (MSIL), not native code directly. The CLR relies on JIT compilers to generate native code from MSIL. However, COM components are already compiled into native code, and so the CLR cannot work directly with them. Clearly, another mechanism is required, to allow COM components to interoperate with .NET components.

Backwards compatibility with COM components is a big concern, because we have so many years of investment in our COM code. (And Microsoft has in no way stepped back from COM, given that COM+ 1.5 is scheduled for release). To address this issue, the .NET Framework does indeed provide us with a way to call COM components from .NET applications. The .NET Framework provides the COM InterOperability service (COM Interop) that does the following:

❑ Provides the TlbImp.exe utility to convert COM type libraries into meta data, which can be imported into .NET. This allows COM components to be invoked from .NET.

❑ Provides the RegAsm.exe utility to generate COM type libraries for .NET assemblies. This allows .NET components to be invoked from COM+.

❑ Uses the P/Invoke mechanism for making function calls and marshaling data types.

COM InterOp will marshal many data types between COM+ and .NET, but there isn't a one-to-one equivalence, so if you are thinking about using a COM component in .NET, you should first scan through the COM+ code, and verify that all of the data types have equivalents in .NET. You can find data type reference tables in the Visual Studio Online Help.

COM components are still very important in .NET. For example, the OleDb Managed Provider operates using COM InterOp and existing OLE DB Providers that are written in COM+. You do not need to worry about losing your investment in COM+ technology. There will be a performance price for calling COM components instead of .NET components. As .NET gains acceptance, you may want to consider migration strategies for your existing COM+ code base. It will be up to you to decide whether the cost of migrating the code will pay off in terms of application performance and stability. Microsoft provides high-level migration roadmaps that start you thinking about how to convert specific kinds of code, such as data access code. I recommend that you allow yourself a lot of time to work with .NET and to get comfortable with it before you even start thinking about migrating your existing code. Chapter 13 describes .NET migration issues in more detail.

The .NET Class Framework

The .NET Class Framework provides developers with object-oriented, extensible classes, interfaces and types for accessing system functionality. The Class Framework is organized into hierarchical libraries of classes that may be used consistently across any .NET-compliant language. The Class Framework overcomes significant limitations with previous Windows and COM+ APIs, including:

- ❏ **COM+ libraries are poorly organized** – COM components provide a limited level of organization to classes, in that a single component will contain classes that serve a common purpose. However, COM lacks an easy way to group similar COM components. For example, two different COM components may both be related to data access, but there is no easy way to structurally link them as a unified API. COM does provide a feature called **component categories**, which allows you to define meta data information for a component. The meta data is stored in the registry, and can be queried via a special interface in the COM component category manager. But this is not as convenient or intuitive as having a namespace that compiles related COM components together.

- ❏ **COM+ libraries are not easy to extend** – COM+ libraries do not support implementation inheritance, and so other libraries cannot effectively extend them. COM+ libraries do support a form of inheritance called interface inheritance, which allows one class to delegate tasks to members in another class, but this has limited applications.

- ❏ **No unified class libraries** – In Windows DNA, each language provides its own class library. This lack of consistency means that a different class in each language must accomplish the same task, even though each class may wrap the same Windows API function. In addition, different languages support different data types. Visual C++, for example, supports a broader range of data types than Visual Basic. This inconsistency creates unnecessary inequality between languages that code against the same operating system.

- ❏ **Incomplete Windows API encapsulation** – The Windows API is not completely encapsulated within object-oriented wrappers, which means that there is no consistent way to access the full range of Windows system functionality. Some functionality may be accessed via COM components, while other functionality may be accessed via direct calls to Windows API functions.

The .NET Class Framework overcomes these limitations in the following ways:

- ❏ **Namespaces** – Classes, Interfaces and Types are organized into hierarchical structures called namespaces, which group related classes, and keep groups of classes distinct. For example, the `System.XML` namespace contains structures that relate to XML manipulation, while the `System.Drawing` namespace contains classes related to generating shapes. These are distinct and separate groups of classes, which is clearly reflected by the Namespace. Classes are referenced using an intuitive, hierarchical dot syntax notation that clearly indicates the class's position within the Class Framework.

- ❏ **Unified Programming Framework** – .NET provides a Common Type System that standardizes data types across the Framework, which puts all languages on an equal footing in terms of what data types they can communicate with. There are some differences between languages, but in general they are all able to access the same classes. The .NET Class Framework may be accessed equally from any .NET-compliant language (note that the Windows API may still be accessed from .NET, which does not yet provide 100% coverage of the Windows API, although it does provide far more coverage than was previously available).

- ❏ **Object-Oriented**– the Class Framework provides extensible classes that may be manipulated using standard object-oriented operations, including inheritance, method overriding, and polymorphism. Everything is a first-class construct in .NET, including data types, which brings a high level of consistency to accessing structures in .NET (.NET provides a boxing conversion that will convert even primitive data types (`boolean`, `integer`, `char`, etc.) into object-oriented reference types).

The figure below shows the organization of the .NET Framework Class Library, at a high level:

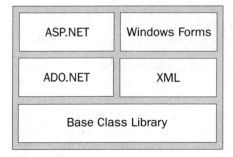

The System namespace is the root namespace for all other namespaces in the .NET Framework. The System namespace contains other namespaces and classes, and most importantly, the data types that are used across all .NET-compliant languages. The Base Class Library contains foundation classes, interfaces and types for the .NET Framework within a set of namespaces. This means that they are commonly used and inherited by classes in other namespaces within the Framework.

The important classes in the System namespace are:

❑ System.Object – all classes in the .NET Framework inherit this class. This class ensures that every Framework class implements a basic standard interface.

❑ System.Exception – contains classes that standardize Exception handling.

The features in the figure above translate to namespaces in the class library:

❑ ADO.NET provides the System.Data namespace for data access classes.

❑ ASP.NET provides the System.Web namespace for ASP.NET code, including Controls, and classes that support Web Services.

❑ XML.NET provides the System.Xml namespace for XML classes. It contains other namespaces, such as XPath, XSLT and Serialization namespaces.

❑ Windows Forms provides the System.Windows.Forms namespace for classes that support Windows Forms controls and functionality.

The figure below shows the organization of the .NET Framework Class Library at a more detailed level:

System.Web				System.Windows		
Services		**UI**		**Design**	**Component Model**	
Description		HTML Controls				
Discovery		Web Controls				
Protocols				**System.Drawing**		
Caching		Security		Drawing2D	Printing	
Configuration		Session State		Imaging	Text	

System.Data			System.XML		
ADO	SQL		XSLT	Serialization	
Design	SQL Types		XPath		

System			
Globalization	Resources	Threading	Serialization
Configuration	Net	ServiceProcess	Interop Services
Diagnostics	Reflection	Text	Remoting
Globalization	Resources	Threading	Serialization

The .NET Class Framework provides object-oriented access to a broad range of functionality, including direct system functionality, as well as specialized functionality. An example of system functionality would be thread management. An example of specialized functionality would be classes devoted to Web Services, including protocol support and discovery services. Broadly speaking, the Class Framework encapsulates the following functionality:

- Data access
- Thread management
- Interoperability with unmanaged code (for example, COM components)
- Network protocol support
- XML support
- Web Services support
- Windows Forms support
- Access to assembly meta data

More about the Class Framework and namespaces can be found in Appendix A.

Summary

We've taken a whirlwind tour of the .NET Framework in this chapter, and have discussed how .NET provides a number of benefits over current programming models. We introduced the benefits of .NET in the context of Windows DNA, and discussed how .NET addresses some significant limitations with today's development platform. The .NET Framework does not invalidate the n-Tier architectural model of Windows DNA; however, it does provide more effective ways to develop and deploy n-Tier, distributed applications. Ultimately, the .NET initiative is about freeing developers from having to worry about plumbing details and instead be able to concentrate on solving business problems through building applications. In addition, .NET provides access to system resources behind a unified programming framework that may be accessed from several different development languages. This serves to simplify application development by reducing inconsistencies between different languages, and to bring the same level of system functionality to a wider developer audience.

The .NET Framework provides the following features and benefits:

- A Common Language Specification (CLS) that defines rules for .NET compliant languages. This enables multiple-language support for the same Base Class Library, including Visual Basic.NET, C#.NET, and Visual C++.NET.

- A Common Language Runtime (CLR) that provides a robust, secure execution environment. Provides type-safe execution and garbage collection.

- A unified Type System, where all types inherit from System.Object, and all character data is in Unicode – no more variants.

- A rich, extensible Base Class Library that encapsulates system-level services and functionality in an object-oriented framework.

- Classes are organized into hierarchical namespaces.

- Simplified deployment using assemblies, which are compiled with a manifest that fully describes the components in the assembly – no more type libraries, or DLL registration.

- Support for standard Internet protocols, including XML, HTTP, SOAP, HTTP, XSLT.

- Deep XML integration, for data serialization and disconnected data access.

- ASP.NET classes for developing Web Services.

This concludes our overview of the .NET Framework. In the coming chapters we will drill into different aspects of the Framework in greater detail, starting with the Common Language Runtime, which is covered in Chapter 3.

3

Memory Management under the CLR

The **Common Language Runtime** (CLR) is the .NET Framework's run-time environment. When a Windows developer hears the term "runtime" they often think in a language-specific manner. (For example, the VB-runtime or the Java-runtime). This normally means language-specific support for memory management, debugging, and error handling. Remember that the 'C' in CLR stands for "Common" and .NET is not language specific.

The CLR (amongst other things) manages the execution of code. Such code is, not surprisingly, **called managed code**. Managed code gains the use of CLR services such as memory management, common error handling, debugging, cross-language support, versioning, deployment, security, and profiling.

The .NET SDK provides a set of compilers (C#, VB, JScript, and C++) that generate binaries that **target** the CLR. Other vendors are developing compilers for other languages that will also take advantage of the CLR. Such compilers include Java, Perl, Tcl, and Python, to name a few.

This chapter will expand on the various features of the Common Language Runtime including:

- ❑ Passing data by reference (data on the managed heap) and by value (stack resident data).
- ❑ Exploring the .NET managed heap and how it compares to legacy heaps.
- ❑ Managed versus unmanaged code.
- ❑ Safe versus un-safe code.

❑ The memory manager and garbage collection (GC). Within the context of garbage collection the `Finalize` method will be introduced and also the `try/finally` construct. Also pertinent to GC is the discussion of weak references, resurrection, and programmatically controlling GC.

❑ Architectural aspects of the managed heap will be discussed including per-thread arenas as a separate large memory heap. Both of these features are performance enhancements.

Details of the Common Runtime System

A key feature of the CLR is that it manages the lifetime of objects from creation to release. Such an object is referred to as a managed object. When a managed object is created the CLR ensures the object is placed in memory upon creation and cleaned-up when no longer in use. This management means that developers can forgo programming memory-specific clean up code. For C/C++ developers working with managed code this means no more `free` and no more `delete`. For all developers, the CLR will ensure that there are no more memory leaks. In the past, huge numbers of person-hours were spent tracking down such leaks.

The CLR provides a set of primitive types specified in the `System` namespace. These types include `Byte`, `Char`, `Decimal`, `Double`, `Int16`, `Int32`, `Int64`, `UInt16`, `UInt32`, and `UInt64`. Even more intricate types are provided via other classes in the `System` namespace: enumerations (class, `Enum`), strings (class, `String`), and arrays (class, `Array`). Managed applications do not necessarily need to explicitly declare the types found in the `System` namespace. This is because each language used to implement a managed application supports its own primitive types that are mapped to types within the CLR. For example, in C#, the `Array` class is intrinsically supported, as we see in the following code:

```
int [] justAFriendlyArray = new int[4] {1, 2, 3, 4};
```

Actually the phrase, "as we see in the following code" was not accurate. We don't see the `Array` class, because C# supports an intrinsic array type that happens to be (under the covers) a CLR `Array` from the `System` namespace. The `System` namespace is common to the .NET Framework, rather than being common to C# or any particular programming language. In VB.NET we also do not see the `System` namespace's `Array` class, because VB.NET intrinsically implements arrays such as:

```
Dim justANiceArray As Integer() = New Integer() {1, 2, 3, 4}
Dim justAHappyArray As Integer() = {1, 2, 3, 4}
```

Having all languages utilize the same fundamental types allows applications in multiple languages to communicate seamlessly with each other. Before .NET and the CLR, a language such as C++ utilized MFC strings (class, `CString`), STL strings (class, `string`), and arrays of characters representing strings. Visual Basic utilized a different string format, which in C++ was represented as a data type of `BSTR` or by using helper classes such as `_bstr_t` or `CComBSTR`. There was nothing more unpleasant than continually mapping a `CString` to a `BSTR`, or a `BSTR` to an STL `string`. In the span of a single paragraph, five different pre-.NET string formats were discussed and this was with respect to only two languages: C++ and Visual Basic. Moving back and forth between the string types of other languages used to be a daunting task.

The .NET Framework's data types do more than just provide data of the same format across multiple languages. Yes, the data types are a unified format, but the data types are also allocated from a memory standpoint in the same manner. Structures, for example, regardless of language, are allocated on the stack, while classes are always allocated on the heap. The heap in question is a heap common to all managed applications, not surprisingly called the **Managed Heap**. There are certain exceptions to these rules; it is possible to create a structure that resides in the managed heap. For the overwhelming majority of data types used, the memory allocation used is consistent.

Developing with cross-language heaps was certainly inconvenient before .NET and the Managed Heap. Special interfaces (such as `IMalloc`) and system functions were provided to support the dynamic allocation of cross-language types (for example, `SafeArrayCreate`, `SysAllocString`, and `CoTaskMemAlloc`). For C and C++ developers, data was often created using the heap provided by the C/C++ Runtime. Such a heap is referred to as a native heap (native to the language). This data had to then be reallocated when the data was passed to a VB application or a web page written in JScript. Even in a project created with the same version of Visual C++, different C++ heaps could be encountered. A single application containing two or three DLL's could end up with several versions of different C++ heaps (static library single threaded, static library multithreaded and multithreaded DLL).

Under .NET there are no such data format and dynamic memory allocation issues. To demonstrate this, consider the following C# code, which passes a string and an array to a method, `PleasePassMeSomeIntrinsicTypes`:

```
using System;

// This is the namespace for the class library in which the
// VB implemented class, AClassImplementedInVB, resides.
using WXAVBClassLibrary;

namespace WXLangInterop01
{
    class WXAccessOtherLang
    {
        static void Main(string[] args)
        {
            string strStuff = "Hello world!";
            int [] justAFriendlyArray = new int[4] {1, 2, 3, 4};
            AClassImplementedInVB someClass = new AClassImplementedInVB();

            someClass.PleasePassMeSomeIntrinsicTypes(ref strStuff,
                                              justAFriendlyArray);
        }
    }
}
```

The method, `PleasePassMeSomeIntrinsicTypes`, called by our C# snippet, calls into the following VB.NET code.

```
Public Sub PleasePassMeSomeIntrinsicTypes(ByRef str As String, _
                                     ByVal ray As Integer())

    Dim i As Integer

    Console.Out.WriteLine(str)
```

```
    For Each i In ray
        Console.Out.WriteLine("Ray contains: {0}", i)
    Next
End Sub
```

Notice that there was no extra code indicating that a C# string was being passed to a VB String. The reason that no extra code was required is that each language's string was in actuality a String from the System namespace. Representation and allocation were identical.

The value of the parameter, str, was passed into the Visual Basic method ByRef. This means that the following line of code could be added to the method, PleasePassMeSomeIntrinsicTypes:

```
str = "Likely this will cause memory be deallocated and" & _
      "new memory to be allocated"
```

The beauty of the previous line of code is that the CLR will free the original contents of the variable str, and allocate new memory to hold the longer string just assigned. There is no special code required in VB or C# in order to handle this potential de-allocation and subsequent allocation. This is because str is a managed type (an instance of the String class, from the System namespace).

Certain parts of the previous examples were glossed over. It does not show how the C# console application references the VB.NET class library. This was done using Visual Studio .NET's **Project** menu, the **Add Reference** menu item. A significant line of code in the C# code has not been addressed, namely, using WXAVBClassLibrary;. This code specifies that the C# code can use all elements with the VB.NET class library's namespace. If this line had not been specified then all elements within the class library's namespace would have to be fully qualified.

The example shown was C# to VB.NET. Skeptics will then wonder, what about VB.NET to C#, or managed C++ to VB.NET, or C# to managed C++? What about Active Perl to TCL and then having Active Perl call VB.NET? As long as the languages are managed, there is no issue with cross-language interoperability. It just works.

The common data format and common allocation scheme is just part of the services provided by the CLR. In future chapters other features will be described, such as how objects are self-describing and how it is possible to compile code once, and deploy it across any operating system and CPU combination that supports the CLR.

Data Storage: By Reference or By Value

A well-known Windows instructor is famous for saying: "Heaps grow. Stacks don't." The idea behind this saying is that a thread in Windows is associated with a region of memory (the stack). This thread's stack is limited to a certain maximum size (default stack size of 1 MB). Remember we are talking about the stack associated with a Windows thread and not the stack limits of a .NET application.

Heaps, unlike threads, have the ability to grow. This includes Windows heaps, C-Runtime heaps, and the .NET Managed Heap. An ideal environment (the CLR) would allocate memory for variables by default on the heap, rather than on the stack. Maybe the term "ideal environment" is a bit presumptuous, but the concept is that it is safer to use a heap rather than a stack. The infrastructure of the environment should encourage heap versus stack alocation. Ultimaty what will be demonstrated is that working with .NET simplifies development by encouraging safer/cleaner styles of memory management.

In this ideal environment, an array of 100,000 bytes would not consume 100,000 bytes of precious (limited) stack space, but would, by default, be created in the ever-expandable heap. The stack would contain a reference to this array. It would not be practical to store simple types (Boolean, char, integer, float) by reference (on the heap), but instead it would make more sense to store such data types by value (on the stack). More complicated data types (arrays and classes) would be stored on the heap and be referenced by a parameter on the stack.

To demonstrate this let's jump ahead and implement a structure and a class in VB.NET. We will learn more later on in the chapter about the fact that classes in VB.NET (keyword, Class) are references to a value stored in the Managed Heap and structures (keyword, Structure) are contained on the stack. To demonstrate "Heaps grow. Stacks don't", consider the following VB.NET structure and class:

```
Structure LotOBytesByValue
    Dim a, b, c, d, e, f, g, h, i, j, k, l, m, n, _
        o, p, q, r, s, t, u, v, w, x, y, z As Int64
End Structure

Class LotOBytesByReference
    Dim a, b, c, d, e, f, g, h, i, j, k, l, m, n, _
        o, p, q, r, s, t, u, v, w, x, y, z As Int64
End Class
```

The structure, LotOBytesByValue, and the class, LotOBytesByReference, contain twenty-six (data members a to z) eight-byte data members, each of type Int64. The data associated with this class and this structure takes up at least 208 (8 * 26) bytes.

To show how structures are passed by value and classes by reference, we implement two recursive subroutines designed to use all available memory in the stack: BlowOutByValue and BlowOutByReference:

```
Dim blowoutCountByValue As Integer

Sub BlowOutByValue(ByVal lotOBytes As LotOBytesByValue)
    blowoutCountByValue = blowoutCountByValue + 1
    BlowOutByValue(lotOBytes)
End Sub

Dim blowoutCountByRef As Integer

Sub BlowOutByReference(ByVal lotOBytes As LotOBytesByReference)
    blowoutCountByRef = blowoutCountByRef + 1
    BlowOutByReference(lotOBytes)
End Sub
```

Notice that both subroutines call themselves infinitely. Once the memory on the stack is exhausted an exception will be raised by the CLR (exception of type StackOverflowException, from the System namespace). Each time the BlowOutByValue subroutine is called, a data member, blowoutCountByValue, is incremented.

The value of blowoutCountByValue indicates the number of times the BlowOutByValue subroutine was called before space on the stack ran out and the exception, StackOverflowException, was raised. The BlowOutByRef data member is called each time the BlowOutByReference subroutine is called.

The value of blowoutCountByRef indicates the number of times the BlowOutByReference subroutine was called before space on the stack ran out and the exception, StackOverflowException, was raised.

The parameter to subroutine, BlowOutByValue, is a structure:

```
ByVal lotOBytes As LotOBytesByValue
```

This parameter is passed ByVal, which means that the value, lotOBytes, cannot change; however, if this parameter is a reference type, its contents can change. The parameter, lotOBytes, is therefore a structure and not a reference type. The contents of this parameter cannot change since it is passed ByVal and is a type stored by value. Do not confuse the fact that the parameter modifier, ByVal, is used and it just so happens that the LotOBytesByValue data type is a structure and hence passed by value.

The parameter to subroutine, BlowOutByReference, takes the following parameter of type, Class:

```
ByVal lotOBytes As LotOBytesByReference
```

This parameter is passed ByVal, which means that the value of the data cannot change in the subroutine. The underlying value is the memory location where lotOBytes is stored, as opposed to the contents of this parameter. The contents of lotOBytes can change, even though the parameter is specified as ByVal. This parameter is of data type class and that dictates that it is passed by reference. The parameter modifier, ByVal, does not affect the fact that a class is passed by reference and not by value.

The subroutine, Main, calls both subroutine BlowOutByValue and BlowOutByReference within in a Try/Catch region (analogous to try/catch in C# and C++). This Try/Catch region ensures that the exception, StackOverflowException, is handled gracefully. The code associated with the Main subroutine is as follows:

```vbnet
Sub Main()
   Try
      Dim lotOBytesStruct As LotOBytesByValue

      blowoutCount = 0
      BlowOutByValue(lotOBytesStruct)
   Catch ex As Exception
      Console.Out.WriteLine( _
         "BlowOutByValue made to to blowoutCount: {0}", blowoutCount)
         Console.Out.WriteLine(ex.ToString())
   End Try


   Try
      Dim lotOBytesClass As LotOBytesByReference

      blowoutCount = 0
      lotOBytesClass = New LotOBytesByReference()
      BlowOutByReference(lotOBytesClass)
   Catch ex As Exception
      Console.Out.WriteLine( _
         "BlowOutByReference made to to blowoutCount: {0}", blowoutCount)
```

```
            Console.Out.WriteLine(ex.ToString())
        End Try

        Console.Out.WriteLine("Done!")
    End Sub
```

The output from this code is as follows:

BlowOutByValue made it to blowoutCount: 4788
System.StackOverflowException: Exception of type System.StackOverflowException was thrown.
BlowOutByReference made it to blowoutCount: 64643
System.StackOverflowException: Exception of type System.StackOverflowException was thrown.

Remember that the default stack size of a Win32 thread is 1 MB keeping this in mind, the subroutine `BlowOutByValue` was called 4,788 times. Using the Visual Studio.NET's Debug Menu, the **Windows** submenu, and the **Call Stack** menu item, we can see how expensive each call to `BlowOutByValue` is.

Each call to `BlowOutByValue` consumes 0xe0 bytes (224 bytes). Recall that our structure, `LotOBytesByValue`, is at least 208 bytes in size, so an additional 16 bytes is required per call. A stack overflow exception was raised after 4788 * 224 = 1,072,512 bytes were placed on the stack.

The subroutine, `BlowOutByReference`, was called 64,643 times. Each time this subroutine was called, 16 bytes of the stack were consumed. This was determined using the **Call Stack** window. This 16 bytes was composed of a reference to an instance of the class `LotOBytesByReference`, and additional information tracked each time the subroutine was called. This resulted in a stack overflow exception after 64,643 references to `LotOBytesByReference` were placed on the stack. The number of bytes placed on the stack is 64,643 * 16 = 1,034,288.

Blowing out the stack using a structure (by value) or a class (by reference) demonstrates the limitation of per-stack data, namely that stacks do not grow beyond their initial limit. The following code snippet demonstrates 100,000 instances of the `LotOBytesByValue` structure, and 100,000 instances of the `LotOBytesByReference` class being allocated using the Managed Heap.

```
    Dim lotOBytesStruct(100000) As LotOBytesByValue
    Dim lotOBytesClass(100000) As LotOBytesByReference
    Dim byteByRef As LotOBytesByReference
    Dim i As Integer

    For i = 1 To 100000
        lotOBytesClass(i - 1) = New LotOBytesByReference()
    Next

    Console.Out.WriteLine("Now that is a heap: {0}", GC.GetTotalMemory(False))
```

The final line of the previous code snippet used the `GetTotalMemory` shared method from the `GC` class (where `GC` is the class that manages garbage collection). This class will be reviewed in detail towards the end of this chapter; suffice it to say that the `GetTotalMemory` method retrieved the total memory of the managed heap. The output from the previous code snippet is:

Now that is a heap: 42845612

The exact size will vary a bit depending on whether garbage collection has taken place for previously allocated data, but we can see that the Managed Heap grows to over 42 MB, which is dramatically larger than the default stack size of 1 MB. The Managed Heap is accessible to all threads and is bound by the limitations placed on it by the machine (physical memory and disk swap file size).

The point to emphasize is that the most common complex data type in VB.NET (a class) is created on the Managed Heap. The same is true for a C# class. Each of these languages recognizes the fundamental tenet that "Heaps grow. Stacks don't".

By Reference and By Value in VB.NET and C#

Our ideal language, working in conjunction with our ideal environment (the CLR), would create, by default, reference data for data such as classes, arrays, and strings. Simpler types (built-in types) such as numeric data types would be stored by default on the stack. Our ideal language is actually a plural – C# and VB.NET. Why not the plethora of other languages supported by .NET? VB.NET and C# are designed from the ground up to encourage seamless support for .NET. Other languages (especially C++) are not as elegant with respect to supporting .NET.

Support for By Reference and By Value in VB.NET and C# is broken down as follows:

❑ Primitive Data Types – passed by value. In C# the fundamental types include: `bool`, `byte`, `char`, `decimal`, `double`, `float`, `int`, `long`, `sbyte`, `short`, `uint`, `ulong`, and `ushort`. In VB.NET the basic types include all numeric data types, `Boolean`, `Char`, and `Date`.

❑ Enumerations – passed by value. In C# enumerations are declared using enum, and in VB.NET they are declared using the keyword `Enum`. An enumeration is passed by value, because their underlying types are `int`, `long`, `sbyte`, `short`, `uint`, `ulong`, and `ushort` in C# and `Byte`, `Integer`, `Long`, and `Short` in VB.NET.

❑ Structures – (such as the `Point` structure found in `System.Drawing`) are passed by value. Structures contain data members and expose properties, methods, and indexers. Structures are stored by value (on the stack). In VB.NET the `Structure` keyword specifies a structure while in C# the `struct` keyword is used. It is important to only use structures for data that is not excessive in size. Structures use up space on the stack so when faced with a large number of data members, a class makes more sense than a structure.

❑ Arrays – passed by reference and stored in the Managed Heap. Ultimately each language-specific array is actually the `Array` class from the `System` namespace.

❑ Strings – passed by reference (`string` in C# and `String` in VB.NET) and stored in the Managed Heap. Ultimately each language-specific string type is actually the `String` class from the `System` namespace.

❑ Classes, Delegates, and Interfaces - passed by reference. Classes, for example, make up the vast majority of the data types provided by the .NET Framework. Classes contain data members and are stored by reference (on the Managed Heap). Classes also expose properties, fields, methods, and constructors. In VB.NET, the `Class` keyword specifies a class, while in C# the `class` keyword specifies a class.

By Reference and By Value in C++

C++ as a language was designed with specific notions of by value and by reference long before the conception of .NET. By default, structures (specified by the keyword `struct`) and classes (specified by the keyword `class`) in C++ are passed by value. Passing parameters by pointer and reference is possible, but is not the default behavior. Actually, structures and classes can be created on the stack, or they can be created on the C-runtime heap using the `new` operator. The problem is not so much the `new` operator, but what happens if the corresponding `delete` operator is not called (a memory leak) and subsequently the class's destructor is not called.

C++ projects can use managed extensions and hence can work and play well with the CLR. Using the Visual Studio .NET IDE, the managed extensions for a C++ project are enabled using the Projects | menu, the Properties menu item. It is important to remember that the contents of Visual Studio .NET menus are context specific. The Properties menu item is only visible if the project is selected in Class View or the Solution Explorer window. From the Property Pages dialog, select the Configuration Properties; under this category select General, and then set Use Managed Extensions to Yes. The following figure shows this in Visual Studio.NET:

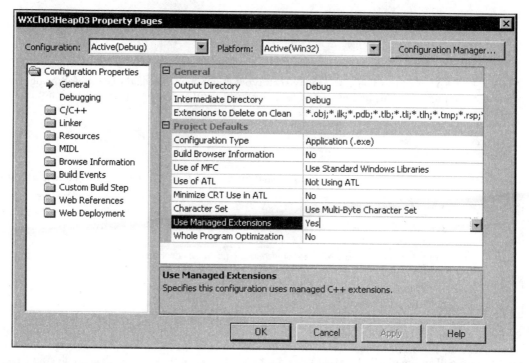

The aforementioned setting is equivalent to specifying the /clr option of the C++ compiler, `vc.exe`. Actually, Use Managed Extensions is set to Yes when a C++ a project is initially created specifying that a managed project should be created.

In order to develop managed code (code that runs under the CLR), C++ had to be extended to conform to the CLR's notations of by value and by reference. The extensions to C++ that support managed development include `__gc`. Prefixing a class, structure, interface, array, pointer, or the new operator with `__gc` causes the pointer type operation to work in conjunction with the Managed Heap. This means that it is subject to garbage collection, hence the `__gc` prefix. This extension is used as follows:

```
__gc class-specifier
__gc struct-specifier
__gc interface-specifier
__gc array-specifier
__gc pointer-specifier
__gc new
```

The following examples of a structure, class, and an array are all found in the managed heap due to the __gc prefix:

```
__gc struct InManagedHeap
{
    int abc;
};

__gc class AlsoInManagedHeap
{
    int abc;
};

int *p = __gc new int[10];
AlsoInTheCPPHeap *p1 = new AlsoInTheCPPHeap();
InManagedHeap *p2 = new InManagedHeap();
```

When __gc is specified it is illegal to specify such types "by value". For example, the following would result in a compilation error, because mustBeAPointer01 and mustBeAPointer02 are not specified as pointers:

```
InManagedHeap mustBeAPointer01;
AlsoInManagedHeap mustBeAPointer02;
```

The specific compilation errors generated by Visual Studio .NET due to the previous code is as follows:

!		✔	Description
			Click here to add a new task
!	📚	☐	error C3149: 'InManagedHeap' : illegal use of managed type 'InManagedHeap'; did you forget a '*'?
!	📚	☐	error C2262: 'mustBeAPointer01' : cannot be destroyed
!	📚	☐	error C3149: 'AlsoInManagedHeap' : illegal use of managed type 'AlsoInManagedHeap'; did you forget a '*'?
!	📚	☐	error C2262: 'mustBeAPointer02' : cannot be destroyed

Task List - 4 Build Error tasks shown (filtered)

Prefixing a class, structure, interface, array, pointer, or the new operator with __nogc causes the pointer type operation to work in conjunction with C++'s native heap. This is optional; if the prefix __gc isn't used, _nogc will automatically be assumed and then it will not be subject to garbage collection. This extension is used as follows:

```
__nogc class-specifier
__nogc struct-specifier
__nogc interface-specifier
__nogc array-specifier
__nogc pointer-specifier
__nogc new
```

The following instances (pCRTHeap01 and pCRTHeap02) are contained in the C-Runtime head due to the __nogc prefix and the lack of __gc prefix respectively:

```
__nogc struct InTheCPPHeap
{
    int abc;
};

// __nogc  is the default so also contained in CPP heap
struct AlsoInTheCPPHeap
{
    int abc;
};

InTheCPPHeap *pCRTHeap01 = new InTheCPPHeap;
AlsoInTheCPPHeap *pCRTHeap02 = new AlsoInTheCPPHeap;
```

Prefixing a class or structure by __value cause instances of this type to be stored by value on the stack. Arrays and pointers can also be stored by value. For arrays and pointer the __nogc C++ extension is used to specify storing by value. Specifying store-by-value is achieved as follows for a variety of data types:

```
__value class-specifier
__value struct-specifier
__nogc array-specifier
__nogc pointer-specifier
```

The following code demonstrates a structure stored on the stack because it is prefixed by __value:

```
__value struct StoredByValue
{
    int abc;
};

StoredByValue onTheStack;
```

Compared to VB and C#, the method C++ uses to support 'by value' and 'by reference' is much more complicated. Breaking the process down by intrinsic types, C++ handling of managed/unmanaged and by-value/by-reference can be thought of as follows:

❑ Primitive Data Types – instances of primitive data types such as long, int, float, double, char, and wchar_t are stored by value. Since they are stored by value, they are therefore not part of the Managed Heap.

❑ Structures – structures can be managed (__gc), not managed (__nogc), or by-value (__value).

❑ Classes and Arrays – like structures, variables of type class or of type arrays are managed, not managed, and by-value depending on the C++ managed extension specified (__gc, __nogc, and __value respectively).

❑ Strings – managed strings are specified using the `String` class exposed by the `System` namespace. In C++ string literals could be ANSI (for example, `"I am ANSI"`) or Unicode (`L"I am Unicode"`) depending on whether or not an `L` prefix was used before the string literal. The `S` prefix is placed before strings in C++ that are explicitly of type `System.String` (`S"I am System.String"`). The `S` prefix can only be specified with string literals associated with the managed string class, `String`. The `S` results in better performance than a string literal with no prefix or a string literal prefixed by `L`. When specifying a string literal for a variable of type `System.String` it is permissible to specify no string prefix, the `L` prefix, or the `S` prefix. A demonstration of this is as follows where variable `song3` will be more optimally allocated because of the `S` prefix:

```
String *song1 = "Boys Don't Cry";
String *song2 = L"Love Cats";
String *song3 = S"Just like Heaven";
```

Several dozen more pages could be written on developing managed applications using C++. What you should take away from this section is that it is more difficult to develop managed applications in C++ when compared to either VB.NET or C#. C++ is a fantastic language, but it was not originally developed for the managed environment.

Managed Heap Organization

Before we talk about the organization of the CLR's Managed Heap, consider the following C# code snippet:

```
long lLast = 0;

for (int i = 0; i < 5; i++)
{
    byte [] sixteenBytes = new byte [16];

    unsafe
    {
        fixed (byte *b = sixteenBytes)
        {
            Console.Out.WriteLine("Memory address 0x{0:X}, 0x{1:X}", (int)b,
                                  (lLast == 0) ? 0 : (int)b - lLast);

            lLast = (int)b;
        }
    }
}
```

The C# code allocates an array (an object) of sixteen bytes, `sixteenBytes`, using the `new` operator. The address of this array is displayed and then the array goes out of scope. By going out of scope, this object has begun its journey from being active to being cleaned up. We deliberately used the term "begun its journey" because the array, or an object of any type, is not cleaned up immediately. Demonstrating this is the output generated by the application, `WXCh03Heap01`, which is as follows (memory address followed by bytes until next object):

Memory address 0xB919EC, 0x0
Memory address 0xB93A3C, 0x2050
Memory address 0xB93C10, 0x1D4
Memory address 0xB93DDC, 0x1CC
Memory address 0xB93FA8, 0x1CC

Notice that each time a new value is assigned to the array, sixteenBytes, it is given a new and different memory address (0xB919EC followed by 0xB93A3C followed by 0xB93C10, etc.). Each instance of the sixteenBytes array is assigned a different address, even though an array of the same type and size was just freed from the heap. Wouldn't it make sense to keep reusing the memory slot at address 0xB919EC? To answer this, a bit more exploration is needed.

The Managed Heap at this time looks as follows:

```
Managed Heap
                        lower memory addresses


                        0xB919EC (marked for cleanup)
                        0xB93A3C (marked for cleanup)
                        0xB93C10 (marked for cleanup)
                        0xB93DDC (marked for cleanup)
                        0xB93FA8 (marked for cleanup)
                        0xB94174 NextFreeOffset



                        higher memory addresses
```

Our diagram representing the Managed Heap did stretch the truth a bit in one respect: certain objects were labeled as "marked for cleanup", but a better term for such objects would have been "un-referenced objects" or "orphaned objects." Basically, an object is only valid if it is still referenced by the application. Un-referenced objects are, by default, "marked for cleanup".

Our experiment (the C# code snippet) revealed that each new object (array) created by the managed heap is added at the memory location specified by the value of NextFreeOffset. Adding new objects at the offset specified by NextFreeOffset is quite an efficient process, because adding a new object simply returns a pointer and increments the value of the NextFreeOffset pointer. There is no costly traversal of the free space linked list. This scheme works great up until a system runs out of memory. When this limit is reached, the CLR must institute Garbage Collection (GC) in order to clean up unused memory. The GC process will be addressed in a section further on in this chapter but the basic concept is: to clean up all unused objects in the managed heap and to move all used objects down in the heap (compacting such objects). Yes, the physical storage location of reference objects changes.

To repeat, "the physical storage location of reference objects changes!" When writing code managed by the CLR, pointers are not being used; references are being used. When a variable is moved due to GC, the developer and the application code have no idea that the location of the object has changed. This concept is a descendent of the days of Win16 where developers played a big role in managing fixed and movable memory. To demonstrate this, let's focus on a subset of our code:

```
unsafe
{
    fixed (byte *b = sixteenBytes)
    {
        Console.Out.WriteLine("Memory address 0x{0:X}, 0x{1:X}", (int)b,
                        (lLast == 0) ? 0 : (int)b - lLast);
        lLast = (int)b;
    }
}
```

The C# keyword, unsafe, identified that our application was about to embark on an unsafe series of tasks (run in an unsafe context). In an unsafe context it is possible to do great evil to the memory space of an application. Unsafe operations are rarely required under managed development and are, by default, disabled. In order to even use the unsafe keyword in C#, the following steps had to be taken in Visual Studio .NET: select the Project | Properties menu item; under Configuration Properties select Build; from the build properties set Allow unsafe code blocks to True. Performing these steps in Visual Studio are equivalent to specifying the /unsafe C# compiler option. VB.NET does not support unsafe code blocks.

In the previous code snippet, the unsafe tasks performed included taking the address of data member sixteenBytes (for example, b = sixteenBytes). This operation is unsafe because it involves direct access to a pointer. Before we could actually view the address of sixteenBytes we also had to specify the fixed keyword in order to fix (pin) the address in memory. Remember that garbage collection will potentially move objects and hence change the underlying address referred to by the reference. The fixed keyword prevents the object from being relocated by garbage collection, while the statement following the fixed keyword is executed. The fixed keyword can only be used while executing in an unsafe context (as specified by the unsafe keyword). The fixed keyword should not be used to permanently lock a variable into a fixed location in memory. Using the fixed keyword in this manner will cause the managed heap to behave non-optimally and would likely cause the heap to become fragmented.

Managed, Unmanaged, and Unsafe

Thus far, some strange jargon has been bantered about, specifically the words **unsafe** and **unmanaged**. These words do not mean the same thing. To understand unmanaged, write a C++ or VB application using Visual Studio 6.0. When you run this code it is not managed by the CLR (because there is no CLR associated with code developed with Visual Studio 6.0). When C++ developers move to Visual Studio .NET, some will choose to write managed code using extensions to the C++ language, while other developers will continue to write unmanaged code. Unmanaged code is harder to write (more prone to errors), but can take greater advantage of lower-level operating system constructs.

Managed code is simply code that runs under the CLR with its common types, error handling, debugging, and memory management. Even managed code can be unsafe and being unsafe is more than just pointer specific. For example, the following C# code is managed (run under the CLR) but unsafe:

```
unsafe
{
    Console.Out.WriteLine("DateTime size in bytes: {0}", sizeof(DateTime));
    Console.Out.WriteLine("short size in bytes: {0}", sizeof(short));
    Console.Out.WriteLine("int size in bytes: {0}", sizeof(int));
    Console.Out.WriteLine("long size in bytes: {0}", sizeof(long));
}
```

The previous code sample using the C# sizeof keyword will only compile if placed in an unsafe block. The sizeof keyword determines the size of a type that is passed by value (a structure or basic type). But why is this unsafe? To answer this, consider the code sizeof(DateTime). At present the DateTime structure is eight bytes. In some future version of .NET this structure could be twelve bytes. This would mean that all the code compiled with the present version of .NET (when the structure was eight bytes) would be invalid. Unsafe in this context does not refer to present tense behavior but is a warning of what might take place. The reason why unsafe code has to be explicitly enabled is to encourage developers to use good (safe) coding practices.

The following code snippet demonstrates how a pointer (a variable specified using '*') taking the pointer of a variable (using the & operator) and the fixed keyword are all required to be placed in a region of code marked as unsafe:

```
DateTime ifYouHaveTheTimeCanIHaveADate;
DateTime [] playingTheField = new DateTime [10];

unsafe
{
    DateTime *pDateTime = &ifYouHaveTheTimeCanIHaveADate;
    fixed(DateTime *pTooManyDates = playingTheField)
    {
    }
}
```

Taking the pointer of a value type such as the DateTime structure is unsafe, because this data is placed on the stack. If this value goes out of scope, the stack location being pointed to could change; this would result in unpredictable behavior. Unpredictable in this case likely means, "the variable is long gone". This unpredictable behavior is why the previous piece of code is required to run in an unsafe context. A single DateTime structure is not contained in the Managed Heap and hence this variable will never move due to garbage collection. The following code is contained in the managed heap:

```
DateTime [] playingTheField = new DateTime [10];
```

The previous array contains a type, DateTime, that is not a reference type, but the array itself is a reference type and contained in the Managed Heap. The value of the array, playingTheField, can change due to garbage collection and hence this pointer must be fixed (pinned) using the fixed keyword so that it does not move if garbage collection takes place. If we had not specified the fixed region the following code would have resulted in a compilation error:

```
DateTime *pToManyDates = playingTheField;
```

It is possible to allocate data on the stack using C#'s stackalloc keyword. Reasons for performing this unsafe practice might include allocating thread-specific dynamic memory at run-time. The following code uses C#'s stackalloc keyword to allocate data on the stack, rather than on the Managed Heap:

```
unsafe
{
    byte *pBuffer = stackalloc byte[256];
}
```

In the previous code snippet we allocated an array of bytes, or more specifically an array of a by-value type. The keyword, stackalloc, cannot be used to create reference types. Using stackalloc is unsafe, because if pBuffer went out of scope, the contents of the stack would be unknown and would hence lead to unpredictable behavior.

C#: an Unsafe Example

The friendly confines of a safe and managed application are where the vast majority of development will take place, but there are reasons to delve into the land of unsafe code. One classic situation is where code exists that works and this code performs a rather unique task that may or may not be exposed by the .NET Framework. For example, on an NTFS volume, a single file can contain multiple data streams. NTFS is the native file system of Windows NT, Windows 2000, and Windows XP. An example of the multiple data streams supported by NTFS is as follows:

❑ `LegitimateBusiness.txt` – default data stream, which is what is seen in Windows Explorer.

❑ `LegitimateBusiness.txt:InterstateTrucking` – alternative data stream containing the business's data pertaining to interstate trucking.

❑ `LegitimateBusiness.txt:LocalPolitics` – alternative data stream containing the business's data pertaining to its interest in local politics.

Developers familiar with NTFS data streams recognize that the way to traverse each stream is to use `CreateFile` in conjunction with the tape backup functions `BackupRead` and `BackupSeek`. Is there a way to traverse each data stream using the .NET Framework? Rather than performing a wholesale rewrite of working code, it may be faster to simply port existing code to C#, even if this port is unsafe.

The following section of code is used to create a file, `LegitimateBusiness.txt` (the default data stream), and its alternative data streams, `InterstateTrucking` and `LocalPolitics`. This section of code uses the namespace `System.Runtime.InteropServices` in order to allow C# to access Win32 functions. This namespace is part of the .NET framework and hence languages such as VB.NET can use this mechanism to access Win32 functions. The code that creates our file and its alternative data streams is as follows:

```
using System;
using System.Runtime.InteropServices;

namespace WXCSharpUnmanaged01
{
   class WXShowUnsafe
   {
      [DllImport("KERNEL32.DLL", EntryPoint="GetLastError",
         SetLastError=true,
         CharSet=CharSet.Unicode, ExactSpelling=true,
         CallingConvention=CallingConvention.StdCall)]
      static extern int GetLastError();

      [DllImport("KERNEL32.DLL", EntryPoint="CreateFileW",
         SetLastError=true,
         CharSet=CharSet.Unicode, ExactSpelling=true,
         CallingConvention=CallingConvention.StdCall)]
      static extern unsafe uint CreateFile(
         string lpFileName,
         uint dwDesiredAccess,
         uint dwShareMode,
         void *pSecData,
         uint dwCreationDisposition,
         uint dwFlagsAndAttributes,
```

```csharp
                    uint hTemplateFile);

    [DllImport("KERNEL32.DLL", EntryPoint="CloseHandle",
        SetLastError=true,
        CharSet=CharSet.Unicode, ExactSpelling=true,
        CallingConvention=CallingConvention.StdCall)]
    static extern unsafe int CloseHandle(uint hHandle);

    // ToDo: Setup Win32's BackupRead and BackupSeek to traverse
    // the data as a single stream
    const uint GENERIC_WRITE =       0x40000000;

    const uint CREATE_ALWAYS      = 2;

    const uint WIN32_TRUE =          1;
    const uint WIN32_FALSE =         0;
    const uint INVALID_HANDLE_VALUE = 0xFFFFFFFF;
    const int ERROR_SUCCESS = 0;

    static string [] fileNames = new string []
        {"LegitimateBusiness.txt",
         "LegitimateBusiness.txt:InterstateTrucking",
         "LegitimateBusiness.txt:LocalPolitics"};

    static unsafe int WXSetupFiles()
    {
        uint handle;

        foreach (string fileName in fileNames)
        {
            handle = CreateFile(fileName,
                    GENERIC_WRITE,
                    0,
                    null,
                    CREATE_ALWAYS,
                    0,
                    0);
            if (handle == INVALID_HANDLE_VALUE)
            {
                return GetLastError();
            }

            if (WIN32_FALSE == CloseHandle(handle))
            {
                return GetLastError();
            }
        }

        return ERROR_SUCCESS;
    }
}
}
```

Each Win32 function called from our example is specified as an external method to our class, WXShowUnsafe, and is declared using the attribute DllImport (found in the namespace System.Runtime.InteropServices) in order to map from a legacy DLL to our managed application. An example of this is the following code that allows access to Win32's CreateFile function:

```
[DllImport("KERNEL32.DLL", EntryPoint="CreateFileW",
    SetLastError=true, CharSet=CharSet.Unicode, ExactSpelling=true,
    CallingConvention=CallingConvention.StdCall)]
static extern unsafe uint CreateFile(string lpFileName,
    uint dwDesiredAccess, uint dwShareMode, void *pSecData,
    uint dwCreationDisposition, uint dwFlagsAndAttributes,
    uint hTemplateFile);
```

Each flag (such as CreateFile's GENERIC_WRITE) and enumeration value used by our Win32 functions declared in our class so they can be passed to the appropriate Win32 function:

```
const uint GENERIC_WRITE =      0x40000000;
const uint CREATE_ALWAYS =      2;
```

At this stage each Win32 function can be called from within an unsafe region of code. In our code example, the WXSetupFiles method is declared to be unsafe (using the unsafe keyword):

```
static unsafe int WXSetupFiles()
```

All code in the body of the method WXSetupFiles can use unsafe constructs (such as passing a null pointer to CreateFile):

```
handle = CreateFile(fileName, GENERIC_WRITE, 0, null,
                    CREATE_ALWAYS, 0, 0);
```

What remains to be implemented is using Win32's WriteFile to write data to the file, LegitimateBusiness.txt, including its alternative data streams (InterstateTrucking and LocalPolitics). Code still to be implemented also includes using BackupRead and BackupSeek to traverse the contents of the file, LegitimateBusiness.txt, as a single stream of data.

C++: Managed and Unmanaged

C# was designed to comprehend managed, unmanaged, safe, and unsafe. The knowledge that pointers were useful at times, but unsafe, was built directly into the language. There is no way to easily retrofit C++ in order to suddenly view pointers as unsafe.

The C++ exposed by Visual Studio .NET contains two pragma directives that control whether C++ is managed or unmanaged. These pragma directives are valid when the C++ compiler's command-line option, /clr, is specified. The pragma directives that specify managed and unmanaged code are as follows:

❑ #pragma managed – functions and methods following this pragma are managed by the CLR. The variables in this section may or may not be part of the managed heap. This pragma works with C++, so managed versus unmanaged heap depends on the prefixes __gc, __nogc, and __value.

❑   #pragma unmanaged – functions and methods following this pragma are not managed by the CLR and are considered to be native. By native we mean that they use the features exposed by the C-Runtime (the language-specific runtime of C++). The prefixes __gc, __nogc, and __value are moot since the code is unmanaged.

An example of using #pragma unmanaged to call cout and #pragma managed to call Console::WriteLine is as follows:

```
#using <mscorlib.dll>
using namespace System;
#include <iostream>
using namespace std;

class ShowPragmas
{
public:
#pragma unmanaged
    static void HelloUnmanagedWorld()
    {
        cout << "Hello, unmanaged world" << endl;
    }
#pragma managed
    static void HelloManagedWorld()
    {
        Console::WriteLine(S"Hello managed world");
    }

};
#pragma managed

// This is the entry point for this application
#ifdef _UNICODE
int wmain(void)
#else
int main(void)
#endif
{
    ShowPragmas::HelloUnmanagedWorld();
    ShowPragmas::HelloManagedWorld();
    return 0;
}
```

Notice in the previous code that #pragma unmanaged comes before cout is called:

```
#pragma unmanaged
    static void HelloUnmanagedWorld()
    {
        cout << "Hello, unmanaged world" << endl;
    }
```

Correspondingly, when #pragma managed is specified the code uses Console::WriteLine to perform output:

```
#pragma managed
    static void HelloManagedWorld()
    {
        Console::WriteLine(S"Hello managed world");
    }
```

Garbage Collection (GC)

As mentioned previously, Garbage Collection (GC) is triggered when the Managed Heap runs out of space. GC can also be triggered programmatically using the System namespace's GC class. In order to understand how the garbage collection process is implemented, we need to understand some concepts related to the behavior of data.

To demonstrate this, consider an application that initially loads configuration information from SQL Server. The configuration information received is a set of objects of type WXNameInfo, WXUpperBound, and WXLowerBound. (These are not real objects, but are used for our example). In the process of retrieving these configuration objects, a dozen or so objects are created that access SQL Server and format the data. Once the configuration information is retrieved, these data retrieval objects are released. We can make some observations about these objects:

❑ Retrieving the configuration objects is a snapshot in time of our application and its data.

❑ During this time period, the objects (configuration and data retrieval) are highly dependent on each other. These objects would benefit from a performance standpoint if they were created in proximity to each other in memory. A scheme that uses linear allocation, such as that used by the Managed Heap and its NextFreeOffset pointer, would be highly advantageous. A scheme such as a doubly-linked list of free space will most likely over time not yield any proximity-related performance improvements due to fragmentation of the free space.

❑ During this time window there is a high likelihood that any newly created object will be marked for cleanup. Any object that is not cleaned up, during this execution window is less likely to be cleaned up during subsequent phases of execution. While loading up our configuration information, the objects used to access the data and format the data will be created and then will go out of scope. The configuration information (WXNameInfo, WXUpperBound, and WXLowerBound) will exist after this setup phase and will be accessed throughout the life of our program. Ultimately, it will be cleaned up, but at each phase of execution the following is true: the newer the object, the greater the likelihood that it will be cleaned up; the older the object, the smaller the likelihood that it will be cleaned up. A function tends to use numerous local variables with a short lifetime and tends to return a smaller number of results that may have a longer lifetime within the application.

The garbage collection scheme implemented by the CLR is based on these common-sense assumptions that have been backed by empirical data. To better understand how the CLR implements GC, the concept of a generation needs to be introduced. Generations allow the proximity of data to be more efficiently managed and allow better performance in allocating memory across multiple threads (more on this later).

We will call all objects created during the setup of our configuration information, Generation 0. After GC is run, all objects that are not cleaned up from this first generation (Generation 0) will be called Generation 1. All objects created after the first running of GC, but before the next running of GC, will be called Generation 0. Each time GC is run, the generation number of each object will be incremented. The maximum GC Generation currently supported is 2. This value was determined by calling the MaxGeneration property of the garbage collection class, GC.

An example of how GC takes advantage of each object's generation is as follows:

```
Managed Heap (before GC)

 data access object (to be cleaned up)
 WXNameInfo
 data access object (to be cleaned up)
 data configuration object (to be cleaned up)
 WXUpperBound                                  Generation 0
 WXLowerBound
 data access object (to be cleaned up)
 data configuration object (to be cleaned up)
 data configuration object (to be cleaned up)


Managed Heap (after GC)

 WXNameInfo
 WXUpperBound                                  Generation 1
 WXLowerBound
                                               Generation 0
                                               (no objects yet)
```

Notice that, after garbage collection, the WXNameInfo, WXUpperBound, and WXLowerBound are in close proximity to each other. This is a contrived example since we only have three objects. The idea on a larger scale is that older objects are in close proximity to each other, which will have a tendency to improve application performance.

On a machine containing more than one CPU, the region of the managed heap associated with Generation 0 is divided into arenas. There is one arena associated with each active thread in an application. Each thread allocates memory from its own arena. This means that there is no need to synchronize memory allocations between multiple threads. Recall that C++ uses a doubly-linked list: every thread had to lock this list in order to perform a memory allocation or de-allocation. This could become quite a serialization bottleneck.

Garbage Collection Algorithm

The basic premise of garbage collection is to look for objects that are not being used by an application. To be more technical, objects that are not referenced by code within the application can be cleaned up. During the cleanup process:

❑ An object's Finalize method is called. The Finalize method is written by the developer and provides object-specific cleanup code. The memory associated with the object is reclaimed. The trick to garbage collection is to determine which objects are not referenced. To determine this, the garbage collection algorithm traverses active objects within an application. To determine what objects are active (referenced) the following rules are used:

❑ All objects contained on a thread's stack are referenced, as are the objects they contain.

❑ All global objects and the objects they contain are referenced. Static objects are also considered to be global and are hence part of this root.

❑   All objects referred to by the CPU's registers are referenced, as are the objects they contain.

Simply knowing where to start is not enough. In order to traverse an object, the garbage collection algorithm must know the type of object it is traversing. Remember that each object within the CLR provides its own meta data. This meta data is what the garbage collection algorithm uses to traverse an object and all the objects it contains. Both the object and the objects contained by the object are added to the graph of active objects.

When the garbage collection processes an object, it makes sure that the object has not already been added to the referenced list (the graph). An object that was already traversed (an object in the reference list) is skipped. It is more efficient to skip an object that is already referenced. This also prevents infinite loops. If such objects were not skipped, a set of objects implementing a circular queue would prove "infinitely" dangerous.

Once every referenced object has been added to the graph, the garbage collection algorithm begins to walk up the managed heap (from bottom to top). Regions in the heap that contained non-referenced objects are discarded and referenced objects are moved down in the heap. This clusters referenced objects and places objects that we created near each other in time near each other in memory. An invalid pointer now refers to each object that is moved down the heap. The garbage collection algorithm must retraverse the active roots and update the pointers contained in each reference to an object that has been moved.

The final step is to reset the next object pointer. This is the point at which the next object (the first object in the newest Generation 0 will be placed) is allocated and it is placed at the next free offset above the compacted region.

Finalize

Between the time that an object goes out of scope and its memory is cleaned up, the garbage collection algorithm calls the object's Finalize method. Not every object exposes a Finalize method and, frankly, not every object should expose a Finalize method. A file object should expose a Finalize method to ensure the file is closed. A class that contains a list of favorite DVDs might use no shared resources. The list of DVDs is just memory that will be cleaned up by GC. There is no need to specify a Finalize method, because managed memory is never explicitly cleaned up programmatically.

A Finalize is similar to a C++ destructor. In unmanaged C++, the destructor of an object is called when the object goes out of scope (for a by-value object) or when delete is called (for an object allocated on the C-Runtime heap).

A Finalize method in C# looks like a C++ destructor, but don't be fooled. Finalize is not necessarily called as soon as the object goes out of scope. In the following snippet of code, ~WXSingThatFinalize() is the Finalize method that is called when garbage collection cleans up an instance of WXSingThatFinalize:

```
class WXSingThatFinalize
{
    ~WXSingThatFinalize()
    {
        StreamWriter lastGasp;

        lastGasp = File.CreateText("ForYourEyesOnly.log");
```

```
        lastGasp.WriteLine("In finalize: WXSingThatFinalize()");
        lastGasp.Flush();
        lastGasp.Close();
    }
}
```

The code is straightforward. When the object is garbage collected, it creates a file (ForYourEyesOnly.log) and writes text to this file. Actually the previous code snippet was compiled as:

```
class WXSingThatFinalize
{
    protected override void Finalize()
    {
        ... // code affiliated with Finalize() here
        base.Finalize();
    }
}
```

The class name prefixed by the tilde ('~') is just shorthand for the Finalize method. The compiler knows to call the Finalize method of the base class after the code associated with the current object's Finalize is executed. By specifying a Finalize method, it is possible for a VB.NET class to also take advantage of the guaranteed cleanup associated with Finalize. An example of the WXSingThatFinalize class implemented using VB is as follows:

```
Class WXSingThatFinalize

    Protected Overrides Sub Finalize()
        Dim lastGasp As StreamWriter

        lastGasp = File.CreateText("ForYourEyesOnly.log")
        lastGasp.WriteLine("In finalize: WXSingThatFinalize()")
        lastGasp.Flush()
        lastGasp.Close()
    End Sub
End Class
```

In our previous code snippet demonstrating the Finalize of the WXSingThatFinalize class, it is not a matter of *if* the file, ForYourEyesOnly.log, will be written to, but *when*. In theory, the object could go out of scope (be un-referenced) and four years later garbage collection would be run. During garbage collection, the Finalize would finally be called. Four years is a bit of an exaggeration, but what if GC took four hours, minutes, or seconds before it was triggered? How long is too long depends completely on the resource that the Finalize must clean up. What if our class locked a file and then unlocked the file in the Finalize method? What if our class began a database transaction (an expensive operation) and committed the transaction in the Finalize? In the latter two examples, the cost of the Finalize could be significant. An expensive resource could remain in use for an indefinite amount of time.

Be aware that Finalize adds overhead to the allocation of an object. When an object containing a Finalize method is created using new, a copy of the object must be placed in the finalization queue maintained by garbage collection. Specifying a Finalize method also adds overhead to object cleanup. This overhead at cleanup is intuitive since the Finalize method contains code that must be cleaned up. The CLR does not specify the order in which the Finalize methods of different objects are called. Consider the object, WXGamble, which contains a data member (an inner object), WXSomeFile. What happens if the Finalize for WXGamble attempts to write to its data member, WXSomeFile? The results of this operation are unpredictable.

The Finalize method may be called from a thread that is different to the thread that initially created the object. For this reason, the Finalize method should make no assumptions with respect to the thread in which it executes.

Finalize and Application Cleanup

A final question remains: do all Finalize methods get cleaned up before an application cleans up its virtual memory? Basically, would the CLR bother to call Finalize or simply just de-commit and release the virtual memory associated with the Managed Heap? As of Beta 2 of the .NET Framework, the CLR guarantees to call the Finalize method for those objects that expose a Finalize method.

In Beta 1 of .NET, the behavior of the Managed Heap was to release memory with no guarantee that Finalize would be called. Beta 1 provided the RequestFinalizeOnShutdown method of the GC class. This method changed the default behavior of garbage collection to ensure that Finalize was called for each object at application shutdown. As of Beta 2, GC no longer contains the RequestFinalizeOnShutdown method, and garbage collection guarantees to call each object's Finalize method.

Try and Finally

Although useful, Finalize does affect performance (increased cleanup overhead). Finalize can have adverse effects if the object for which Finalize is running attempts to access any of its own data members. What if the Finalize method attempts to clean up data members that have already been cleaned up? C#, VB.NET, and C++ each offer an alternative that helps ensure that cleanup takes place: the try/finally construct. The idea is that code is placed inside a try region (a protected region). The cleanup code for the protected region is placed in a finally region. No matter what mechanism is used to leave the try (protect) region, the code in the finally region is guaranteed to execute. An C# example of this follows where we open a file handle using WXShowUnsafe's CreateFile method and we ensure that this file handle is cleaned up using a finally region containing WXShowUnsafe's CloseHandle method:

```
uint handle = 0;

try
{
    unsafe
    {
        handle = WXShowUnsafe.CreateFile("PleaseMakeSureIAmClosed.txt",
            GENERIC_WRITE, 0, null, CREATE_ALWAYS, 0, 0);
    }
}

finally
{
    if ((handle != 0) &&
        (handle != WXShowUnsafe.INVALID_HANDLE_VALUE))
    {
        WXShowUnsafe.CloseHandle(handle);
        handle = 0;
    }
}
```

VB.NET supports the exact same mechanism of using a protect region and a cleanup region as follows:

```
Try
    ' Projected region
Finally
    ' Cleanup region
End Try
```

It is also possible to exploit a protected region (a `try` region) and a cleanup region (a `finally` region) using C++. The C++ mechanisms that support this are the extensions to the C++ language, `__try` and `__finally`:

```
__try
{
    // protected region
}
__finally
{
    // cleanup code
}
```

Weak References

Thus far, a graph has been presented of all objects referenced by an application. All objects not in this graph of "strong references" are subject to cleanup. What is a strong reference? It is just a reference to an object. There is though a special type of reference referred to as a weak reference. Such objects are not part of the garbage collection generated graph of referenced objects. This is because the application only maintains a weak reference to the object, rather than a strong reference.

Why would an application want to maintain strong (regular) references to some objects, but weak references to other objects? Consider an application that performs a set of web queries. These queries are used by an application and then are set to be weak references. If the same query is executed again, a weak reference can be made a strong reference, thus restoring (resurrecting) the data. There is a chance though that garbage collection has run. If this is the case then the results of the web queries (the weakly referenced objects) will have been cleaned up. The application will detect this and subsequently have to rebuild the objects. Although potentially a performance gain, weakly-referenced objects are clearly the exception rather than the norm.

Weakly-referenced objects are created using the `WeakReference` class. The object to be weakly referenced is associated with an instance of a `WeakReference` class. All instances of the object are then set to null or nothing. To demonstrate this, consider the following VB.NET code:

```
Dim okayToGC As WeakReference
Dim someString As String

someString = "This data can be garbage collected"
okayToGC = New WeakReference(someString)
someString = Nothing
```

The string, someString, in the previous code snippet is an object (all .NET strings are objects). This string is assigned a value and is then associated with an instance of a WeakReference, okayToGC. The string is associated with the WeakReference instance through the constructor of this object. After the value of the string is associated with the instance of the WeakReference, the string is set to nothing. With no strong reference remaining to the object, it is now a weak reference.

The WeakReference class exposes another constructor, as follows:

```
' VB.NET
Public Sub New(ByVal target As Object, ByVal trackResurrection As Boolean)

// C#
public WeakReference(object target, bool trackResurrection);
```

The first parameter is the object to which a weak reference is to be created. The second parameter is of type Boolean and is set to true if the weakly-referenced object is to be a long weak reference. This parameter can also be set to false if the weakly-referenced object is to be a short weak reference. A short weak-referenced object cannot be resurrected after its Finalize method has been called. A long weak-referenced object can be resurrected after its Finalize method has been called. Unfortunately, the results of this are "unpredictable" so the documentation does not recommend that you do this.

An object that contains a specific system resource should not be treated as a long weak reference. For example, if the object contained an open file handle, resurrection after Finalization would likely cause a failure. If the object just contained memory and no system resource, it might be possible to reap a benefit from specifying a long weak reference. Clearly a developer should have a strong motivation before setting the second of the WeakReference constructors to true.

The WeakReference class exposes a property of type Boolean, TrackResurrection. When TrackResurrection is true then the reference to the object is a long weak reference. When TrackResurrection is false then the reference to the object is a short weak reference.

The Target property of the WeakReference instance, okayToGC, contains the weak reference to the string. If the Target property is nothing (null in C#) then the string has been GC'd. If the Target property is not nothing then the string (the object) can be resurrected by creating a strong reference to the object. Creating a strong reference is as simple as: differentStringSameData = okayToGC.Target. The following code uses the Target property to create a strong reference to an object. If the object has been GC'd then the data is re-allocated:

```
Dim differentStringSameData As String

differentStringSameData = okayToGC.Target
If differentStringSameData = Nothing Then
    ' string was GC'd so re-allocate the data
    differentStringSameData = "This data can be garbage collected"
    okayToGC.Target = differentStringSameData
End If
```

The WeakReference object also exposes the IsAlive property. If this property is true then the object contained in Target has not been GC'd. If IsAlive is false then the object contained in Target has been cleaned up and the value of Target is nothing in VB.NET and null in C#/C++.

The System.GC class

The System namespace exposes the GC class in order to programmatically control garbage collection. The GC class exposes one property, MaxGeneration, which is defined as follows:

```
'[Visual Basic.NET]
Public Shared ReadOnly Property MaxGeneration As Integer
```

```
//[C#]
public static int MaxGeneration {get;}
```

Accessing the MaxGeneration property returns an integer corresponding to the current maximum generation support (the greatest generation supported by the Managed Heap). Notice that the MaxGeneration property is static in C# and Shared in VB. This means that in order to call this property it is not necessary to create an object of type GC.

Each method exposed by GC is also static in C# and Shared in VB. This means that an instance of a GC object is not created in order to call any of these methods. The methods associated with the GC object are:

❑ Collect – this method initiates garbage collection for all objects (if no parameters are specified for Collect) or for all objects in generation zero through maxGeneration (if the integer parameter, maxGeneration, is specified).

❑ GetGeneration – given an object (passed as either type Object or WeakReference) this method returns the generation associated with the object. An Object cannot be garbage collected because the caller maintains a strong reference to the object, while a WeakReference is an object that can be garbage collected because the caller has a weak reference to the object.

❑ GetTotalMemory – this method retrieves the number of bytes allocated by the managed heap. This number is more a best guess rather than an exact number. A single parameter, forceFullCollection, of type Boolean, is provided to this method. If this parameter is True then GetTotalMemory delays returning, thus giving garbage collection a chance to complete and for objects to be finalized.

❑ WaitForPendingFinalizers – suspends the current thread until the thread processing the finalization queue completes processing.

❑ KeepAlive – this method ensures that an object will not be garbage collected from the start of a function up until KeepAlive is called. There is no typo in that previous sentence. An object is marked as ineligible for garbage collection from the start of a routine until KeepAlive is called. This method is used to ensure that when a managed object is referenced from unmanaged code it is not inadvertently cleaned up by garbage collection.

❑ SuppressFinalize – for the specified object, suppressing this object's Finalize. This means that the Finalize method will not be called when garbage collection cleans up the object. An example of this method is provided in the next section.

❑ ReRegisterForFinalize – specifies that the object passed as a parameter will once again have its Finalize method called. An example using ReRegisterForFinalize is shown in a subsequent section of this chapter.

Developers should resist the temptation to directly control garbage collection using the GC class's Collect methods. Microsoft has invested a huge number of person-hours to ensure that garbage collection is handled in an efficient and practical manner. A developer does have intimate knowledge of their own application's behavior, but careful thought should be given before using GC's Collect to somehow improve application performance.

The following code snippet creats an object, someBaseData. It then retrieves this object's generation using GC.GetGeneration, saving this base-line generation in the variable baseLineGeneration. A different object, someBigData, is then created and set to null repeatedly until garbage collection takes place. We know garbage collection has occurred when GC.GetGeneration shows that our original object's generation has been incremented. Using the GC class's GetTotalMemory method, the size of the heap before and after garbage collection is determined.

```
byte [] someBaseData = new byte[1];
byte [] someBigData = null;
int baseLineGeneration = GC.GetGeneration(someBaseData);
int currentGeneration = 0;
long lTotalMemoryBefore = 0, lTotalMemoryAfter = 0;

while (true)
{
    currentGeneration = GC.GetGeneration(someBaseData);
    // Check if generation has been incremented
    if (baseLineGeneration != currentGeneration)
    {
        break;
    }

    lTotalMemoryBefore = GC.GetTotalMemory(false);
    someBigData = new byte[1000];
}

lTotalMemoryAfter = GC.GetTotalMemory(false);
Console.Out.WriteLine("Starting Generation: {0}, Ending Generation {1}",
                    baseLineGeneration,
                    currentGeneration);

Console.Out.WriteLine("Ending Generation for someBigData: {0}, " +
                    "Before Bytes: {1}, After Bytes: {2}",
                    GC.GetGeneration(someBigData),
                    lTotalMemoryBefore,
                    lTotalMemoryAfter);
```

The output from this code snippet is as follows:

Starting Generation: 0, Ending Generation 1
Ending Generation for someBigData: 0, Before Bytes: 166468, After Bytes: 13696

The variable, someBigData, that was allocated and then set to null repeatedly, is always found in GC generation 0. The allocation that triggers GC, someBigData = new byte[1000];, does not actually occur until after garbage collection completed. This is because space was made for this object by garbage collection. The space was available after GC had completed.

After GC has been run, the original object, someBaseData, is in generation 1 (generation 0 that was incremented after garbage collection) and the variable, someBigData, is in the new generation, generation 0. It is difficult to ascertain the significance of the total number of bytes at which garbage collection was triggered. This threshold is specific to the exact implementation of the garbage collection algorithm.

SuppressFinalize Example

Thus far, the advice surrounding garbage collection has been to "leave it alone unless you know it is broken". The SuppressFinalize method of the GC class is an excellent way to, at the very least, increase the performance of garbage collection. In order to demonstrate the SuppressFinalize method we will reintroduce the WXShowUnsafe class. Recall that WXShowUnsafe exposed a set of Win32 functions (CreateFile, CloseHandle and GetLastError). Our rationale for doing this was because we were (allegedly) porting existing code that utilized NTFS alternate data streams.

In order to demonstrate a practical use of SuppressFinalize we extended WXShowUnsafe to contain:

- ❑ A data member, fileHandle, which corresponds to the Win32 file handle.

- ❑ A constructor that opens a file using Win32's CreateFile. Remember that CreateFile can take a null value for one parameter; because of this, CreateFile must be called in an unsafe context (setup using the unsafe keyword).

- ❑ A close method that calls CloseHandle on the Win32 file handle.

- ❑ Finalize (alias ~WXShowUnsafe) that ensures Close is called. The purpose of Finalize is to ensure that, in the event of a programmer error, the file is not left open.

The new code associated with WXShowUnsafe is as follows:

```
class WXShowUnsafe
{
   // Previously shown portion of WXShowUnsafe containing
   // CreateFile, CloseHandle and GetLastError would go here

   uint fileHandle;

   public WXShowUnsafe(string fileName)
   {
      unsafe // required because we pass "null"
      {
         fileHandle = CreateFile(fileName, GENERIC_WRITE, 0, null,
               CREATE_ALWAYS, 0, 0);
      }

      if (fileHandle == INVALID_HANDLE_VALUE)
      {
         fileHandle = 0;
      }
   }

   ~WXShowUnsafe()
   {
      Close();
   }
```

```
    public void Close()
    {
        if (fileHandle > 0)
        {
            fileHandle = 0;
            CloseHandle(fileHandle);
            GC.SuppressFinalize(this);
        }
    }
}
```

Notice in the Close method that after the fileHandle instance is closed (using CloseHandle), the SuppressFinalize method of GC is called as follows:

```
GC.SuppressFinalize(this);
```

This call to SuppressFinalize means that Finalize will not be called for this class, because this (the current object) is specified as the object for which not to call Finalize. The reason for this is that there was no programmer error so the Finalize was not needed. Programmer error would be evident if Close was not called and hence the Finalize would be called during garbage collection, which would subsequently ensure that the file handle was closed. Clearly, an astute programmer would use a try/finally to ensure the Close method was called.

ReRegisterForFinalize Example

A demonstration of the ReRegisterForFinalize method is as follows, where the Finalize method of the WXTheCat class ensures that each instance survives garbage collection nine times:

```
class WXTheCat
{
    int numLives;

    public WXTheCat()
    {
        numLives = 9;
    }

    ~WXTheCat()
    {
        if (numLives > 0)
        {
            Console.Out.WriteLine("In Finalize: {0} ", numLives);
            numLives --;
            GC.ReRegisterForFinalize(this);
        }
    }
}
```

The reason why WXTheCat survives nine garbage collections is because it maintains a counter (data member, numLives). Each time the Finalize method is called (~WXTheCat) the value of numLives is decreased and the GC.ReRegisterForFinalize method is called. The GC.ReRegisterForFinalize method is called provided numLives is greater than zero.

Yes, the previous code snippet was making a bad pun about cats having nine lives. So why would an object need to survive garbage collection? One reason is to launch an object that monitors the garbage collection process or an object that needs to be called periodically. The garbage collection process in a sense acts as a heart beat. An object can stay dormant until it is triggered during garbage collection when its `Finalize` method is called. The `GC.ReRegisterForFinalize` method will keep this object alive indefinitely, so make sure that a mechanism exists that will turn this process off when the application terminates. If this process is not turned off, the application can loop indefinitely without terminating. Each time the application thinks it is all done, because garbage collection was run one final time, there is miraculously one more object to cleanup. One of the most practical uses of `GC.ReRegisterForFinalize` would be as a profiling device for determining how garbage collection affects a particular application.

Actually, the `Finalize` method presented is seriously flawed. When an instance of `WXTheCat` is created and the application immediately exits, it is possible to generate the following output when run from a console window:

```
D:\wrox\ProfNetFramework >wxcsharpunmanaged01.exe
In Finalize: 9
In Finalize: 8

Unhandled Exception: System.ObjectDisposedException: Cannot access a closed Stream.
   at System.IO.__Error.StreamIsClosed()
   at System.IO.BufferedStream.Write(Byte[] array, Int32 offset, Int32 count)
   at System.IO.StreamWriter.Flush(Boolean flushStream, Boolean flushEncoder)
   at System.IO.StreamWriter.Write(Char[] buffer, Int32 index, Int32 count)
   at System.IO.TextWriter.WriteLine(String value)
   at System.IO.TextWriter.WriteLine(String format, Object arg0)
   at System.IO.SyncTextWriter.WriteLine(String format, Object arg0)
   at WXCSharpUnmanaged01.WXTheCat.Finalize()
```

Notice that the `WXTheCat` instance survived two calls to its `Finalize` during garbage collection (In Finalize: 9 and In Finalize: 8) before an exception was generated. The `WXTheCat` instance was using `Console.Out` in order to display output. The garbage collecting process cleaned the object referred to by `Console.Out`. The lesson here is not to rely on any member objects, because there is no guaranteed order with respect to how objects are finalized.

Large Memory Heap

Our discussion of how the Managed Heap is organized is not complete. The Managed Heap stores large objects (objects greater than 20K in size) in a separate section of the Managed Heap. Developers are not required to take special action when creating large objects, because such objects are placed in this alternative store behind the scenes.

The reason why the Large Object Heap exists within the Managed Heap is straightforward: copying large blocks of data (blocks greater than 20K) is expensive. It is more efficient to leave such blocks in place rather than subjecting such objects to garbage collection. The size of 20K is not an arbitrary size: on an x86 machine (a machine with an x86 CPU) Windows uses a virtual page size of 4K (4096 bytes). The total number of virtual pages available to the operating system is dependent on the amount of physical memory (RAM) and the size of the swap file (disk). Virtual pages are:

❑ Reserved – a range of page addresses is reserved, but not backed by physical memory.

❑ Committed – a range of pages addresses is backed by physical memory. A committed page may be contained in memory (RAM), but may also be swapped out to disk (the swap file).

Virtual memory is typically not used programmatically by applications, because virtual memory is allocated in chunks of 4096 bytes at a time. Only certain applications can take advantage of such coarse dynamic memory allocation. For typical objects of 10 to 500 bytes, a minimum allocation of 4096 bytes would be wasteful. When dealing with large objects (size greater than 20K), 4096 bytes is not a coarse granularity. For this reason, it is more efficient for the managed heap to use a specific pool of committed and reserved pages of virtual memory than it is to move objects that are composed of several virtual pages.

Summary

There are a large number of advantages in developing code that executes within the Common Language Runtime. Clearly, C# and VB.NET have been designed from the ground up to work within the confines of this environment. It takes a greater development effort to work in C++ with the .NET Framework.

The environment encourages good programmatic style through its default behavior; for instance, creating most large objects on the managed heap and passing such objects to methods by reference. At the same time there is a large amount of flexibility. It is possible to create structures on the managed heap or place arrays on the stack.

Developers feeling confined by the limitations of managed code can still develop unmanaged code using .NET. Entire unmanaged C++ projects can be developed, or specific pragmas can be used to jump between managed and unmanaged code. Safe and unsafe code can also be developed within Visual Studio .NET using both C# and C++. C# can even access pointers and directly call intrinsic Win32 functions. The key to the environment is that most of the time it is better to "play it safe." When needed (typically not the norm), the most intricate features of the operating system can be exploited.

A great deal of control can be exerted over the garbage collection process, but this is not normally necessary. Hopefully, the way CLR handles memory, and the way this memory management is integrated into managed code (C#, VB and C++), will convince you that garbage collection is an efficient process and should only be tinkered with if absolutely necessary.

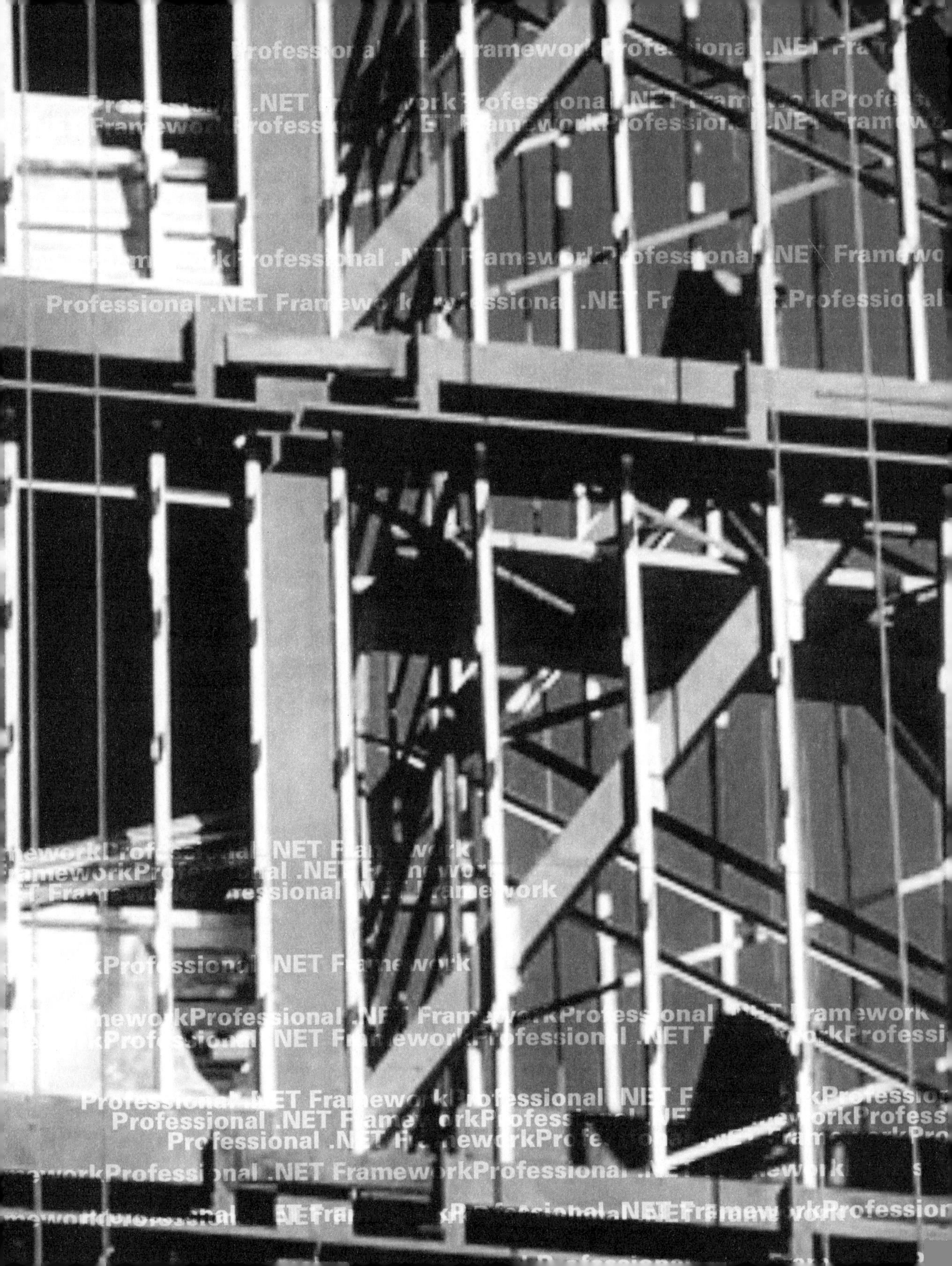
Professional .NET Framework

Working with the Runtime

In this chapter, we will look at why the Common Language Runtime (CLR) is such an important part of the .NET framework and also the various elements that are part of the .NET framework runtime. Then we will take a look at various elements such as assemblies, modules and types. We will also see what the Reflection API is and then how to use Reflection API to examine the meta data at runtime. Finally we will see how versioning and deployment is implemented in the .NET framework.

We will cover all aspects of the Common Language Runtime (CLR) in detail. Specifically, we will:

- ❑ Understand in general terms the various elements that form part of the .NET framework
- ❑ Discuss the advantages and disadvantages of the CLR
- ❑ Discuss the role of MSIL in the .NET framework
- ❑ Develop a clear understanding of how the Common Type System (CTS) enables Cross Language Programming
- ❑ Understand how meta data is an evolution of IDL and how it avoids DLL hell
- ❑ Use Reflection API to read meta data from an assembly
- ❑ Understand how the CLR uses the process called probing to identify static and Dynamic assemblies
- ❑ Discuss how the versioning scheme works in the .NET framework.

What is MSIL?

Microsoft Intermediate Language (MSIL) can be defined as CPU-independent instructions set into which .NET applications are compiled. It contains instructions for loading, storing and initializing objects. When we compile our C# application or any application written in a CLS compliant language, the application is compiled into MSIL. When the CLR executes the application, a Just-In-Time (JIT) compiler converts the MSIL into native CPU instructions that the machine can understand.

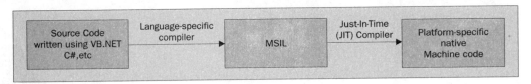

MSIL makes cross-language integration possible in conjunction with meta data and the common type system. We will see what a common type system is in the later part of the chapter. For the purpose of this conversation we will understand that the Common Type System is the core of the .NET framework that provides cross-language integration by supporting the types and operations found in most of the .NET programming languages.

What is a Portable Executable (PE) file

When we compile our application, along with MSIL, the compiler also generates meta data that is simply a collection of information about your application. This meta data is persisted in binary form in the Portable Executable File. Microsoft has designed PE file format for use in all of their Win32-based systems. Let us see the role of a portable executable file in the execution of a .NET program.

- ❑ You write source code in any .NET language.

- ❑ Then compile the source code using a .NET language specific compiler.

- ❑ The compiler outputs the MSIL code and a manifest into a read-only part of the EXE that has a standard PE (Win32 Portable Executable) header.

- ❑ When you execute the application, the operating system loads the PE and all the other dependent dynamic libraries.

- ❑ Then the operating system tries to start the execution of the MSIL code that was placed in the PE. Since MSIL code is not in machine-executable format, it cannot be executed directly. The CLR then compiles the MSIL into native code using the Just-In-Time compiler as it continues to execute the MSIL code.

CLR – Common Language Runtime

At the core of the .NET platform is the CLR, which is responsible for managing the execution of code that is targeted towards the .NET platform. The code that requires the CLR at run-time in order to execute is referred to as managed code. The managed code relies on the core set of services (which we will see in a moment) that CLR provides.

Advantages of the CLR

The CLR provides a host of benefits to the managed code like cross-language integration, enhanced security, versioning and deployment support, debugging and profiler services, memory management through garbage collection. Let us look at each of these benefits in detail.

Cross-Language Integration

The CLR allows managed code written in one language to seamlessly integrate with code written in another language. This is made possible through the CLS, which defines a set of rules that every language in the .NET framework has to abide by. The list of possible cross-language integration capabilities includes inheritance, exception handling and marshalling. For example, we can define an interface in COBOL and implement it in languages like VB.NET and C#. This is made possible because of the intermediate IL, which ensures that all the languages, even though they have different features, are treated the same once they are compiled into IL code.

Enhanced Security

Today we can get code into our machine not only through a setup application executed by us, but also from the internet via a web page or an e-mail. Recent experiences have shown that this can be harmful to our system. So how does .NET answer this threat?

The solution .NET provides is code access security, which allows us to control access to protected resources and operations. Code is trusted to varying degrees, depending on its identity and where it comes from. Some of the features of code access security are:

❑   Allows administrators to define security policies that assign specific permissions to defined groups of code.

❑   Code can demand that the caller must have specific permissions to execute it.

❑   Code can request the permissions it requires to run and the permissions that would be useful, as well as explicitly state which permission it must never have.

Versioning and Deployment Support

CLR supports side-by-side execution of multiple versions of the same component, even within the same process. Applications produced in the .NET framework can be installed into the system using a simple XCOPY with zero-impact install to the system. XCOPY means just copying the files to the bin directory of the application and the application will start picking up the changes immediately. This is possible because compilers in the .NET framework embed identifiers or meta data into compiled modules and the CLR uses this information to load the appropriate version of the assemblies. The identifiers contain all the information required to load and run modules, and also to locate all the other modules referenced by the assembly. In the later part of this chapter, we will see with examples how versioning and deployment works in the .NET framework.

Debugging and Profiler services

The CLR provides the necessary features to allow the developer to debug and profile managed code. Once we attach an executing .NET program to the debugger, we can perform operations such as walking through the stack of a section of managed code, examining its dependencies, interrogating the objects and much more. These features are available to all applications, regardless of the language in which they were written.

Garbage Collection

In unmanaged code, memory leaks can occur very often. A memory leak is caused by the condition when memory allocated by an application is not freed after it is no longer referenced by the application. Applications written using programming languages like C++, which provide the developers with the ability to allocate memory on the heap, are vulnerable to memory leaks. However, in managed code, the Garbage Collector (GC) is responsible for cleaning up all the objects that are no longer referenced by the application. Whenever memory is allocated for a managed code application, the memory is always associated with the object. Since GC takes care of collecting these objects when they are no longer referenced by the application, it is not possible for managed code to experience memory leaks. However there might be times the objects, if not disposed properly, could still stay in the memory and consume resources. In those cases, we need to ensure that we handle the deallocation of resources and memory ourselves by invoking the dispose method and performing the cleanup operation that is required.

Generally, the GC uses a process called elimination to identify the objects that need to be cleaned up. At runtime, GC accomplishes this elimination process by making use of the information that the CLR maintains about a running application. The GC first gets a list of root objects that are directly referenced by the application. The GC then finds a list of the objects that are referenced by the root objects. Once the GC identifies all the objects that are directly or indirectly referenced by the application, the GC is free to clean up all remaining objects on the managed heap. The garbage collector may be automatically invoked by the CLR, or sometimes it may be explicitly invoked by an application.

Rich Object Models and Class Libraries

The CLR furnishes a rich set of object models and class libraries that expose a wealth of functionality for performing operations such as accessing a relational database, input and output operations, dealing with XML data, capability to inspect meta data and so on. Since all the object models are at the runtime level, we can easily design tools to work across all the languages that target the CLR. The core namespace in the .NET framework that encapsulates most of the functionality is the `System` namespace.

What is an Assembly?

For .NET to live up to the bill that it is going to revolutionize the future of computing, it has to have all the possible innovative features implemented in its framework.

One of those innovations is the way the applications are executed and versioned that goes a long way in eliminating the infamous DLL Hell problem. Microsoft has tried to address this problem by introducing what is known as an assembly, which is the unit of deployment of a .NET application.

Assemblies are extensively used in .NET applications. An assembly is a primary building block of a .NET application. It represents a logical collection of one or more EXE or DLLs that contain an application's code and resources. It is also the unit of deployment for a .NET application. It is the assembly that provides the formal structure for visibility and versioning in the runtime. Assemblies also contain a manifest, which is a meta data description of the code and resources inside the assembly. Since the manifest contains all the information about the assembly, they are responsible for the self-describing nature of the assembly. Before we go on to look at the different types of assemblies and the advantages, let us look at the structure of an assembly.

Structure of an Assembly

An assembly has the following general structure.

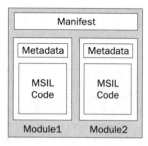

As you can see, it consists of four elements.

❑ Assembly Meta Data or Manifest

❑ Type data or Meta Data that describes the Types

❑ Module

❑ Set of resources

Out of these elements, manifest must be present in every assembly and all the other elements, like types and resources, are optional and required to give the assembly meaningful functionality.

Manifest

It is the manifest that makes an assembly "self-describing". It contains the following information:

❑ Identity – it is made up of the following parts: a name, a version number, an optional locale and a digital signature (if the assembly is to be shared across multiple applications).

❑ File list – a manifest includes a list of all the files that make up the assembly. A manifest also contains the following information for every file that is part of the assembly: its name and a cryptographic hash of its contents at the time of manifest creation. This hash is verified at runtime to ensure that the deployment unit is consistent and not tampered with. Dependencies between assemblies are stored in the calling assembly's manifest. The dependency information includes a version number that is used at runtime to load the correct version of the dependency.

❑ Types and resources – this consists of a list of types exposed by the assembly and the resources. It also consists of information about whether these types are visible to other assemblies and are private to this application.

❑ Security Permissions – assemblies are the unit at which code access security permissions are applied. Permission requests for an assembly can be classified into three groups:

    ❑ Minimum required permissions for the assembly to run.

    ❑ Those that are desirable but the assembly will still have some functionality even if they are not granted.

    ❑ This includes the list of permissions that the assembly must never be granted.

Module

A module is either a DLL or an EXE in the Windows PE executable format. The compiled code in the module is in Microsoft Intermediate Language (MSIL). It is important to realize that even though the assemblies use the extension .dll that the old styles also use, assemblies are completely different and they represent a radical change in the way they are deployed and versioned.

Type

A type is a combination of data and methods that work on that data. It consists of properties, fields, and methods. Fields are more like public variables and they can be accessed directly. Properties are similar to fields except that we can associate a set of statements to be executed when the properties are accessed. Methods are actions or behaviors of the type.

How Assembly enables XCOPY Deployment and Zero Impact Install

One of the primary goals of the .NET framework is to simplify deployment by making possible what is known as XCOPY deployment. Before we see how .NET enables XCOPY deployment, let us see what XCOPY deployment is. Prior to .NET, installing a component requires copying the component to appropriate directories, making appropriate registry entries, and so on. However, now in .NET, to install the component all we have to do is copy the assembly into the bin directory of the client application and the application will start using it right away because of the self-describing nature of the assembly. It is also called "zero-impact install" since we are not impacting the machine by way of configuring the registry entries and configuring the component. This zero impact install also makes it possible to uninstall a component without impacting the system in any manner. All that is required to completely uninstall is the removal of specific files from the specific directory.

Design Considerations of an Assembly

An assembly can be a single file that contains all the elements of the assembly including manifest, type meta data, IL code and resources. When we use tools such as Visual Studio.NET to build our application, each project will most likely correspond to a single assembly. As an alternative, we can spread the contents of an assembly into multiple files so that the assembly resides in more than one file in the same directory. In that case, the manifest of the assembly will reside in one of the EXEs or DLLs of the assembly. It is also important to remember that in a multi-file assembly, files are not tied together by the file system. The only thing that makes these files part of the assembly is that they are mentioned in the manifest. Using a command line utility like al.exe (Assembly Generation utility), we can add or remove files from a multi-file assembly.

In the following figure, we have split the contents of the Main assembly into three different files: utility code is separated into a separate DLL and the large resource file is kept in its original location. One of the advantages of this approach is that it optimizes code download to a greater extent. The .NET framework will download a file only when it is referenced, so if the assembly contains code or resources that are not accessed frequently, breaking them out into individual files will increase download efficiency.

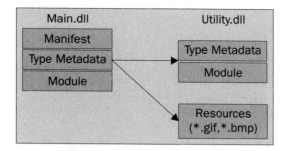

Different Types of Assemblies

Before we categorize assemblies, we need to consider the following two factors.

❑ How assemblies are used – whether they are private to one application or shared among many applications.

❑ How assemblies are constructed – whether the assembly is constructed at design-time or run-time.

Based on the pattern of their usage, we can classify assemblies into Private assemblies and Shared assemblies. Based on the way assemblies are constructed (design time or at run-time), we can classify them into Static assemblies and Dynamic assemblies. Let us look at each of these assemblies in detail.

Private Assemblies

A Private assembly is an assembly that is only visible to one application. Most of the .NET applications will be deployed as private assemblies, as one of the selling points of the .NET framework is its ability to isolate an application from changes made to the system by other applications. When we create private assemblies, we deploy them within the `bin` directory of the application in which it is used. Since the scope of the private assembly is only within the current application, the naming requirements for private assemblies are simple – the names must be unique only within the application.

Since each deployed private assembly is specific only to that particular application that uses it, we need not maintain version information for private assemblies. When the CLR receives a request for the loading of an assembly, the CLR maps the assembly name to the name of the file that contains the manifest. This process is called Probing.

A private assembly is visible to only one application and since it is deployed within the `bin` directory of the application in which it is going to be used, it is one of the building blocks used to create isolated applications in the .NET framework. A private assembly can be installed on a computer just by copying the assembly, whereas installation of a shared assembly (which we look at next) involves copying the assembly file into the global assembly cache, then installing it into the global assembly cache using `gacutil`. So if we want to provide support for `XCOPY` deployment of our applications, we need to use private assemblies.

Shared Assemblies

Another kind of assembly is a Shared assembly and it is shared by multiple applications on the machine. Shared assemblies are stored in the global assembly cache, which is a centralized repository for storing all the shared assemblies in the machine. Since a shared assembly is shared by all the applications in the machine, it allows administrators to deploy bug fixes and all the client applications that use that assembly will start picking up the bug fixes immediately. It is important to note that in .NET, the decision to share code between applications that is made by the developer is completely different from the COM scenario, where developers were *forced* to share their components and hence ran into the risk of some other installation overwriting their components. If you use Visual Studio.NET to add a reference to an external assembly (shared assembly) that is already deployed in the global assembly cache, Visual Studio.NET does not make a local copy of the assembly; instead it directly refers to the one that is deployed in the global cache. This behavior is determined by the CopyLocal property, which is automatically set to False when you add a reference to a shared assembly. We can access this property by right-clicking the referenced assembly and selecting Properties from the context menu. Shared assemblies are designed to avoid the sharing problems we face today. However, shared assemblies should meet the following requirements:

❑ Must have cryptographically strong names that are globally unique.

❑ Must have the built-in infrastructure to prevent someone else from releasing a subsequent version of your assembly and falsely claim that it came from you. This is made possible through the public key cryptography.

❑ Must provide identity on reference. When resolving a reference to an assembly, shared assemblies are used to guarantee the assembly that is loaded came from the expected publisher.

How Public Key Cryptography works in .NET

At the time of building the application, the developer of an assembly generates a key pair that consists of two parts – private key and public key. Once the key pair is created, the developer then signs the file containing the manifest with the private key and publishes the public key to all the client applications that want to use the assembly. When the client application references the assembly, the client application records the public key corresponding to the private key that was used to generate the strong name. At runtime, this recorded information is used to ensure that the assembly loaded is the same as the one that the client application is developed against.

Static Assemblies and Dynamic Assemblies

As we already mentioned, an assembly consists of a collection of physical files and this kind of assembly, which is built at compile time, is called a static assembly. Most of the assemblies we will be creating in this chapter fall into this category. In addition, the .NET framework exposes a set of classes through the Reflection API that we can use to create code on the fly and execute it directly. These assemblies are called Dynamic assemblies and we can also store these assemblies on disk, if we want to. In the later part of this chapter, when we look at Reflection API, we will see an example for creating dynamic assemblies.

Common Type System

The Common Type System is a rich type system built into the Common Language Runtime (CLR) that supports the types and operations found in most programming languages.

System.Object – Root of Everything

All the types in the common type system are ultimately derived from the System.Object type, ensuring that every type in the system has a minimum set of expected behaviors.

Public Methods of the System.Object

MethodName	Description
bool Equals()	Used to see if two objects are equal. For reference types, if the two variables refer to the same object then the return value is true. In the case of value types, this method returns true if the two types are identical and have the same value.
int GetHashCode()	Generates a number that is mathematically derived from the value of an object. The handling of collections in the .NET framework is based on the return value of this method.
Type GetType()	Used to get the Type object that contains useful information about the object. Mainly used with Reflection methods to retrieve the type information of an object.
'string ToString()	For primitive types such as int, bool and string, it returns the string representation of the type's value. For other types, the default implementation of this method returns the fully qualified name of the class of the object. However, it is usually overridden to return a more user-friendly string representation of the object.

Types and Aliases

While the CTS is responsible for defining the types that are required to have cross-language interoperability across languages, most language compilers have chosen to implement aliases to those types. For example, a two-byte integer is represented by the CTS type System.Int16. VB.NET defines an alias for this called Short. Even though there is no advantage to using one technique over the other, it provides the developers with more options to choose from.

CTS Types and Aliases

Type	C# alias	VB.NET alias	Description
System.Object	object	Object	Base class for all CTS Types
System.String	string	String	String
System.Sbyte	sbyte	SByte	Signed 8-bit value
System.Byte	byte	Byte	Unsigned 8-bit value
System.Int16	short	Short	Signed 16-bit value
System.Int32	int	Integer	Signed 32-bit value
System.Char	char	Char	Unicode character value
System.Single	float	Single	Single precision floating point number (32 bits)

Table continued on following page

Type	C# alias	VB.NET alias	Description
System.Double	double	Double	Double precision floating point number (64 bits)
System.Boolean	bool	Boolean	Boolean value of either true or false
System.Decimal	decimal	Decimal	128 bit data type exact to 28 or 29 digits

Value Types and Reference Types

While creating a language where everything is an object allows developers to consume the language in a truly Object Oriented fashion, it has its own disadvantages. The biggest disadvantage is poor performance that is due to the allocation of the objects in the heap even for trivial operations, say for example like adding two numbers. Needless to say, the allocation of an object is extremely inefficient when all we wanted to do was sum two numbers.

The .NET framework design team was faced with the task of creating a rich type system where everything is an object but still works in an efficient way, when required. Their solution to this problem was to separate the CTS into two families: value types and reference types. This classification is based on the following considerations.

1. How they are allocated in memory

2. How they are initialized

3. How they behave in cases of testing for equality.

4. How they are treated in assignment statements

5. How they are dependent on the Garbage Collection (GC) mechanism of CLR

Let us look at the details of the value types and reference types.

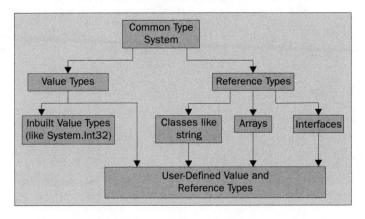

Value Types

The first thing to be noted is that value type variables are allocated memory on the stack and they are initialized to an appropriate value at the time of declaration itself. So when you have a variable that is of value type, it means that you have a variable that contains actual data, which ensures that they cannot be null.

Let us consider the following statement where we create a variable of the CTS type System.Int16 in C#.

```
short s = 10;
```

In the above declaration, a 16-bit space is allocated on the stack for the variable s. In addition, the assignment of a value to s results in that 16-bit value being moved into this allocated space.
The list of value types in the .NET framework includes enumerators, structures and primitives. Anytime we declare a variable of one of these types, we allocate the number of bytes for that type on the stack. We will be working directly with the allocated array of bits instead of with the reference to that allocated memory. In addition, when we assign a variable that is a value type, the copy of the value of the variable is assigned and not a reference to its underlying object. Finally, value types do not expect the GC to reclaim the memory used by them.

Reference Types

Reference type variables are allocated memory on the heap and they are always initialized to null. They also do not contain a reference to a valid object until assigned such a reference either by creating a new instance of the class, or by assigning a reference from an existing valid object.

In the following example, a reference type of string is allocated to the variable s.

```
string s = " This is a reference type";
```

When the above statement is executed, the value is allocated on the heap and a reference to that value is assigned to the variable.

Like value types, there are several types such as classes, arrays, delegates and interfaces defined as reference types in the .NET framework. Anytime you declare a variable of one of these types, you allocate the number of bytes associated with that type on the heap, and you are working with the reference to that object instead of directly with the bits, which is the case with value types.

Even after the reference type variables go out of scope, they will still sit around in memory waiting for the garbage collector to run through its elimination process.

Boxing and Unboxing

Boxing a value means implicitly converting a value type to the type object. When a value type is boxed, an object instance is allocated and the value present in the value type is copied into the new object. Let us consider the following C# code.

```
int iNumber = 10;
Object oNumber = iNumber;
oNumber = 20;
Console.WriteLine ("{0}{1}", iNumber, oNumber);
```

The assignment in the second line implicitly involves a boxing operation and the value of the iNumber variable is copied to the object oNumber. After the value is copied, the two variables are independent of each other and there is no link between them. Because of that, when we change the value of the oNumber variable, it does not affect the value of the iNumber variable.

If we execute the above code, we should get the following output.

10 20

Unboxing refers to the converting of an object type to any value type. In contrast to boxing, unboxing is an explicit operation and we have to explicitly tell the compiler what value type we want to extract from the object type. To understand unboxing, let us consider the following C# code:

```
int iNumber = 10;
Object oNumber = iNumber;
int iNumber1 = (int)oNumber;
```

In the above line, we unbox the oNumber object and assign the extracted integer variable to a variable of type integer. Before we move on with the next topic, let us consider a common scenario where we can implement boxing.

The type system in the .NET framework is called a unified type system because everything is considered as an object regardless of whether it is a value type or reference type. This kind of treatment of types allows boxing and unboxing to be performed automatically on the types depending on the situation that we are dealing with.

For example, let us consider an arraylist called ArrayList that is created using the following line of code.

```
ArrayList oArrayList = new ArrayList();
```

Firstly, we assign an object of type date to the arraylist and then we assign a variable of type integer to the arraylist. When this integer variable is added to the arraylist, it is automatically boxed before being added.

```
//Add a reference type Date object to the arraylist
Date oDate = new Date();
oArrayList.Add(oDate);

//Add an integer to demonstrate the boxing operation
int iTemp  = 123;
//This statement automatically performs the boxing operation and the value is
//converted into an object before it is added to the arraylist
oArrayList.Add(iTemp);
```

From the above, we can see that the boxing is a powerful feature that allows us to treat the types in a consistent fashion across our code. Boxing and Unboxing also enable the common type system to expose a unified and consistent programming model to the .NET developers.

Meta Data

Meta data is information that enables components to be self-describing. Meta data is used to describe many aspects of components including classes, methods, fields and the assembly. Meta data is used by the CLR to facilitate all sorts of things like validating an assembly before it is executed and performing garbage collection while the code is being executed.

Is Meta Data an Evolution of IDL?

If you have done real COM programming, you are probably somewhat familiar with IDL and type libraries. They are used to store all the information that is necessary for COM automation. You can think of meta data as being similar to IDL in the COM world. However, unlike IDL, meta data is much more accurate and complete and it is not optional.

We can simply define meta data as the information used by the CLR to identify everything about the classes, functions, properties, resources, and other items in an executable file. The important point to be noted is meta data is always associated with the file that contains the code; that is, the meta data is always embedded in the same EXE or DLL, making it impossible for the code and meta data to go out of synch. All .NET-compliant compilers are required to give out full meta data information about each and every type class that is present in the compiled source code module.

In COM, meta data is stored separately from the executable. The COM developer has an option to store the component's type library as a separate file. In addition, important COM meta data used at runtime, such as the component's GUID, supported threading model, etc. is stored in the Registry. As meta data is stored separately from the COM or COM+ component, installing and upgrading components can be a nightmare. The component must be registered before it can be used, and if the type library is stored in a separate file, it must also be installed in the proper directory. Once the component is installed, upgrading to a new version can be problematic. Sometimes, you may end up installing a new binary for the component without updating its corresponding meta data (that is spread everywhere in the machine) only to find out that the application has suddenly stopped working. The process of installing and upgrading a .NET component is greatly simplified. Since all meta data associated with a .NET component resides within the file that contains the component itself, no registration is required. Once a new component is copied onto the system, it can be immediately used without having to do any of the configurations that we are used to doing in the COM world. This is called XCOPY deployment, as we touched upon briefly at the beginning of the chapter. Upgrading a component is also less problematic since the component and its associated meta data are always packaged together, they cannot go out of synch.

Attributes

Most programming languages express information either through declaration or code. For example, let us consider the following declaration:

```
public int i;
```

The runtime allocates space for an integer variable and sets its visibility so that it is accessible to other applications. This is an example of declarative information. Generally, the language designers predefine the types of declarative information and we can't extend the language. For example, if we want to associate a predefined value for a class that identifies the characteristics of the class, we must invent a new way of expressing that information. Macros in C++ can solve this problem by storing this information in a field that is part of the object. Such approaches do work; however, they are error-prone and not recommended because of the complexities involved.

The .NET framework comes to our rescue by supporting Attributes, which are merely pieces of information that can be associated with specific elements of source code, such as classes, members, parameters, etc.

We can use attributes to change the behavior of our application at runtime, provide transaction information about an object, or convey organizational information to a designer. The attribute information is stored with the meta data of the element and can be easily retrieved at runtime through a process known as Reflection.

Custom Attributes

Unlike COM+, in .NET we have the ability to extend the meta data exposed by our components with custom attributes. Custom attributes are used extensively throughout the .NET framework. Design-time controls also use custom attributes to store their configuration information.

In the .NET framework, attributes are implemented as classes that derive from the System.Attribute class.

The developer may want to create their own custom attribute for informational purposes like expressing the behavior of the object to the user. For example, we can decorate a class with the custom attribute called Author that records the name of the developer who has created the class.

Now that we have learned what attributes are, let us look at an example of how to use attributes. Consider the following example in which we create a PublisherInfoAttribute that stores the name of the publisher who has published the book. It also has a comment field that contains a brief description of the publisher.

```
[AttributeUsage(AttributeTargets.Class, AllowMultiple=false)]
   public sealed class PublisherInfoAttribute:System.Attribute
   {
     string name;
     string comment;

     public PublisherInfoAttribute(string name)
     {
        this.name = name;

     }
     public string Comment
     {
        get
        {
           return (comment);
        }
        set
        {
           comment = value;
        }
     }

     public string Name
     {
        get
        {
           return(name);
        }

     }
   }
```

We first use the predefined AttributesUsage attribute to indicate how our custom attribute can be used in code. By specifying the AttributeTargets.Class for the AttributesUsage attribute, we indicate that this attribute can be applied only to classes. Other possible values of the AttributeTargets enum include Assembly, Module, Class, Struct, Enum, Constructor, Method, Property, Field, Event, Interface, Parameter, Delegate and All.

As part of the `AttributeUsage` attribute, we can specify one of these or we can OR them together to apply it for combination of entities. `AttributeUsage` can also be used to specify whether an attribute is single-use or multi-use. This is done with the named parameter `AllowMultiple`. We will see what a named parameter is in a moment.

Such an attribute would look like this.

```
[AttributeUsage(AttributeTargets.Method | AttributeTargets.Event,
                AllowMultiple = true)]
```

We then define the attribute class called `PublisherInfoAttribute`, which derives from `System.Attribute`. We also use the optional keyword `sealed` to prevent our attribute class from being extended. Since there can be only one publisher for a book, we set `AllowMultiple` to `False`. The recommended naming convention for attributes class is to append `Attribute` to the end of the class name.

Positional and Named Parameters

The information we store in the attribute can be classified into two groups: Positional parameters and Named parameters. The positional parameters are mandatory and they should be obtained via the constructor of the attribute class. This forces the consumers of this attribute class to specify the values for these parameters. Named parameters are those that can be optionally passed values. Positional parameters should always precede named parameters while passing parameters to an attribute class.

The `PublisherInfo` class defines a single constructor that takes the name as an argument and it is important to note that it is a positional parameter. It also has a comment property that is exposed to the caller through the Property Set and Property Get. Since `Comment` is a named parameter, we can optionally pass values to it.

```
[PublisherInfo("Wrox Press Ltd.",Comment="This is a Wrox Press Release")]
public class Book
{
    public Book()
    {

    }
}
```

In the above example, we create a `Book` class that uses the `PublisherInfo` attribute class to describe the publisher of the book. It is worth noting that we use only `PublisherInfo` as the name of the attribute class. When the compiler comes across this line, it appends the keyword `Attribute` to the name `PublisherInfo` and searches for a class named `PublisherInfoAttribute`, which it will promptly find. If it does not find one, it then searches for a class named `PublisherInfo`.

Putting it all Together

Let us look at how we can use Reflection to enumerate the attributes defined in the `Book` class. We will look at Reflection in detail in the later part of this chapter. For the purpose of this conversation, we will understand that the reflection is the mechanism that allows us to examine the type information at run-time. The C# code for enumerating the attributes defined in our book class looks like this.

```
using System;
using System.Drawing;
using System.Collections;
using System.ComponentModel;
```

```
using System.Windows.Forms;
using System.Data;
using System.Reflection;
```

We use this function to add items to the listbox.

```
private void AddItem(string sMessage)
{
    lstAttributes.Items.Add(sMessage);
}

protected void cmdShowAttribute_Click (object sender, System.EventArgs e)
{
    MemberInfo oMemInfo;
```

Here we get the type object associated with the class type Book.

We then load all the custom attributes that are of PublisherInfoAttribute type into an object array.

```
oMemInfo = typeof(Book);
object[] oAttrs;
oAttrs = oMemInfo.GetCustomAttributes(typeof_
                (PublisherInfoAttribute),true);
if (oAttrs.GetLength(0) !=0)
{
```

As we have only one custom attribute class, the first element in the array will be of type PublisherInfoAttribute. So we cast that object into PublisherInfoAttribute type and then retrieve its values by invoking individual properties.

```
PublisherInfoAttribute oPubInfoAttr = (PublisherInfoAttribute)oAttrs[0];
    AddItem("Publisher Name is " + oPubInfoAttr.Name);
    AddItem("Publisher Comment is " + oPubInfoAttr.Comment);
}

}
```

Common Language System (CLS)

The Common Language system defines a specific set of constructs and constraints that serves as a guide for people who write libraries and compilers. Languages that fit into the .NET framework must satisfy the guidelines set by the CLS. It allows the libraries written using those languages to be fully accessible from any language that supports CLS. We can consider CLS to be a subset of the Common Type System.

From the developer's perspective, when developers design publicly accessible classes following the specifics of CLS, their classes can be easily used from other programming languages. To create an application that is CLS compliant, we need to make sure that we use only CLS-specific features in the following places of the application.

❑   Definitions of the public classes

❑   Definitions of the public members and protected members

❑   Parameters to public methods of public classes and protected methods

From the above constraints, we can understand that CLS enforces constraints only in certain parts of the application, which means that the other parts of the application are free to implement any language-specific features and still create a CLS-compliant component.

Integration of Languages into the .NET Platform

There are actually three levels of CLS compliance that a .NET language can subscribe to.

❑   Compliant producer – the components developed in the language can be used by any other language.

❑   Consumer – the language can consume the classes produced in any other language.

❑   Extender – languages in this category can extend the classes produced in any other language using the inheritance features of .NET.

All the predefined languages in Visual Studio.NET (VB, VC++ and C#) are expected to satisfy all three levels of CLS. If you are writing a language that targets CLR, you can select a level of compliance that fits your requirements. Fully supporting a third-party language in the .NET framework requires a lot of work from the language vendors. The vendor needs to create a compiler for the language that has the ability to create intermediate language code instead of native code. The features of the language must be in compliance with the specifications specified in the CLS. If you go through the process of re-architecting your language to comply with the CLS, your language can enjoy the following benefits in return.

❑   Complete access to the fullset of optimized, scalable .NET framework class libraries

❑   Advanced IDE for development

❑   Sophisticated debugging tools

❑   Complete cross-language integration

An example for this would be creating an interface in COBOL and implementing it in C#.

The third-party languages that are likely to be integrated into the .NET platform are:

❑   APL

❑   Python

❑   COBOL

❑   Eifel

❑   Mercury

❑   PERL

❑   SmallTalk

❑   Scheme

It is difficult at this time to get information about the actual status of these, so keep your eyes on http://msdn.microsoft.com/net/thirdparty/default.asp for more information.

Reflection API

One of the invaluable features of .NET is its ability to access an application's meta data through a process known as Reflection. We can simply define reflection as the ability to discover type information at runtime. In this section, we will first see how we can use reflection to loop through the various elements of an assembly to retrieve their characteristics. Then we will also see several advanced usages of reflection, such as dynamically invoking methods and executing MSIL code, which is created at run-time.

All the reflection-related classes are described in the `System.Reflection` namespace. We can use these classes to logically traverse through assembly and type information. Since the `Reflection` namespace encompasses a great deal of functionality through the use of a huge number of classes, it deserves a separate book on its own. So, we will not be able to cover all these classes in detail. However, we will look at all the key classes that we will be frequently using in our applications.

The System.Type Class

The most important and fundamental class of the Reflection API is the `System.Type` class. It is an abstract class that represents a type in the Common Type System (CTS) and allows us to query an assembly for type name, the module details and namespace, and whether the type is a value type or a reference type.

How to Retrieve the Type

There are two ways by which we can retrieve the type object.

- ❑ By using the instance of an object
- ❑ By using the class name

We will create a VB.NET windows application to demonstrate how to retrieve the type object using both ways. First, we will select a VB.NET windows application from the **New Project** dialog box and name the project Chapter05Example02. We then add two command buttons to the form and name them cmdTypeFromInstance and cmdTypeFromClassName respectively, and also add a listbox called lstMessages. We then double-click on the command button to go to the code editor and associate the following code with the click event of the command button. We follow this for both the command buttons.

```
Private Sub cmdTypeFromInstance_Click(ByVal sender As System.Object, ByVal e
            As System.EventArgs) Handles cmdTypeFromInstance.Click
   Dim oForm1 As Form1 = New Form1()
   Dim oType As Type = oForm1.GetType()
   AddItem("The type name from the instance : " + oType.Name)
   AddItem("....")
End Sub

Private Sub AddItem(ByVal sMessage As String)
   lstMessages.Items.Add(sMessage)
End Sub

Private Sub cmdTypeFromClassName_Click(ByVal sender As System.Object, ByVal
            e As System.EventArgs) Handles cmdTypeFromClassName.Click
Dim oType As Type = Type.GetType("Chapter05Example02.Form1")
AddItem("The type name from the class name : " + oType.Name)
AddItem("....")
End Sub
```

When we execute the above code and click both the command buttons, we get the following output in the listbox.

The type name from the instance: Form1

The Type name from the class name: Form1

We first create an instance of the `Form1` class and then call the `GetType` method of the instance to get its type. Finally, we display the type name in a listbox.

```
Dim oForm1 As Form1 = New Form1()
Dim oType As Type = oForm1.GetType()
AddItem("The type name from the instance : " + oType.Name)
AddItem("....")
```

In the `AddItem` function, we add the passed string to the listbox.

```
Private Sub AddItem(ByVal sMessage As String)
        lstMessages.Items.Add(sMessage)
End Sub
```

Now we will look at how to retrieve a `Type` object from the class name. In this line, we get reference to the type object of `Form1` by calling `GetType` method of the `Type` class, passing in the combination of the project and the name of the class, which is Chapter04Example02.Form1.

```
Dim oType As Type = Type.GetType("Chapter04Example02.Form1")
AddItem("The type name from the class name : " + oType.Name)
AddItem("....")
End Sub
```

In the above example, we can see that we need not create an instance of an object to be able to retrieve its type information. The ability to determine information about a class without even instantiating it allows us to create dynamic and flexible applications using late binding. We will see an example of this when we discuss late binding in the later part of this chapter.

Enumerating through the Types of an Assembly

In this section, we will see an example of how to enumerate all the types in an assembly using the Reflection API. To iterate through all of the types for a given assembly, all we have to do is instantiate an assembly object and get a reference to the `Types` array for that assembly object. We will need a listbox called lstMessages and a button called cmdShowAllTypes. The VB code required for iterating through the assembly is as follows; we'll call this example IterateAssembly (this is because the Reflection API specifies that assembly names are no longer than 15 characters):

```
Public Class DerivedException
    Inherits System.Exception
End Class

Public Enum DaysEnum
    Sunday
    Monday
    Tuesday
```

```
        Wednesday
        Thursday
        Friday
        Saturday
    End Enum

    Public Structure EmployeeStruct
        Dim iEmpNo As Integer
    End Structure

    Private Sub AddItem(ByVal sMessage As String)
          lstMessages.Items.Add(sMessage)
    End Sub

    Private Sub cmdShowAllTypes_Click(ByVal sender As System.Object, _
                ByVal e As System.EventArgs) Handles cmdShowAllTypes.Click
        Dim sAssemblyName As String
        Dim oType As Type
        Dim oProcess As Process
        Dim oAssembly As System.Reflection.Assembly
        Dim oTypes() As Type
        'Get the current process
        oProcess = Process.GetCurrentProcess()
        sAssemblyName = oProcess.ProcessName + ".exe"
        'Load the assembly
        oAssembly = System.Reflection.Assembly.LoadFrom(sAssemblyName)
        oTypes = oAssembly.GetTypes()
        For Each oType In oTypes
            AddItem("The full name is " + oType.FullName)
            AddItem("The full name of the base type is " + _
            oType.BaseType.FullName)
            AddItem("Is Enum Type = " + (oType.IsEnum).ToString)
            AddItem("Is Class = " + (oType.IsClass).ToString)
            AddItem("...")
        Next

    End Sub
```

In the first part of the code, we have declared a class that is derived from System.Exception, an Enumeration and a Structure.

Here, we use the static method GetCurrentProcess of the Process class to get a reference to the currently executing process.

```
    oProcess = Process.GetCurrentProcess()
```

Then we retrieve the name of the current process by invoking the ProcessName property of the Process object, which we obtained in the previous step.

```
    sAssemblyName = oProcess.ProcessName + ".exe"
    'Load the assembly
```

Once we have the name of the assembly, we can easily instantiate the assembly using the LoadFrom method of the Assembly class. To this method, we pass a string that represents the name of the physical file as an argument. From there, a call to the Assembly.GetTypes method returns us an array of Type objects. After that, we show the properties of each type object in the listbox.

```
oAssembly = System.Reflection.Assembly.LoadFrom(sAssemblyName)
oTypes = oAssembly.GetTypes()
For Each oType In oTypes
   AddItem("The full name is " + oType.FullName)
   AddItem("The full name of the base type is " +
   oType.BaseType.FullName)
      AddItem("Is Enum Type = " + (oType.IsEnum).ToString)
      AddItem("Is Class = " + (oType.IsClass).ToString)
      AddItem("...")
Next
```

The output from the above example looks like this.

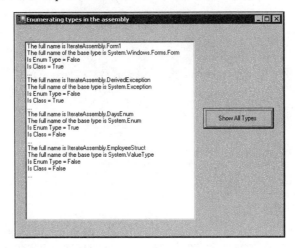

Late Binding with Reflection

We can define late binding as the situation in which the compiler, at the build time, has no clue about the method calls that are going to be made at runtime. Anyone who has done COM programming using late binding by invoking IDispatch methods will know the complexities involved in implementing late binding in COM. We can easily carry out the same task in .NET using the classes present in the System.Reflection namespace.

We will consider the Book class, which we used in our previous code samples, as an example to demonstrate late binding.

As we already know, the Book class we created in the previous examples looks like this.

```
[PublisherInfo("Wrox Press Ltd.",Comment="This is a Wrox Press Release")]
public class Book
{
    public Book()
    {

    }
    public string BuyBook()
    {
        return ("You are buying a Wrox Press Ltd book");
    }
}
```

We are going to add a couple of classes to the form `Form1.cs` that are similar to the `Book` class except for the change in the attributes and will call them `Book1` and `Book2` respectively.

```
[PublisherInfo("ABC Ltd.",Comment="This is a ABC  Release")]
public class Book1
{
   public Book1()
   {

   }

   public string BuyBook()
   {
      return ("You are buying a ABC Ltd book");
   }
}


[PublisherInfo("XYZ Ltd.",Comment="This is a XYZ Release")]
public class Book2
{
   public Book2()
   {

   }
   public string BuyBook()
   {
      return ("You are buying a XYZ Ltd book");
   }
}
```

Now that we have added different types of book-related classes, let us consider the scenario where someone wants to buy a book by Wrox Press using the classes we defined above. The solution for this would be to dynamically enumerate all the book-related classes in the assembly and for each class check the `PublisherInfo` attribute; if the attribute is equal to `Wrox Press Ltd`, instantiate that particular class and finally invoke the `BuyBook` method of that book class.

In the following example, we will see how to implement this (again, remember that the assembly name must be no longer than 15 characters).

```
   protected void cmdBuyBooks_Click (object sender, System.EventArgs e)
{
   string sAssemblyName;
   object[] oAttrs;
   //Get the current process
   Process oProcess = Process.GetCurrentProcess();
   sAssemblyName = oProcess.ProcessName + ".exe";
   //Load the assembly
   Assembly oAssembly = Assembly.LoadFrom(sAssemblyName);
   Type[] oTypes = oAssembly.GetTypes();
   foreach(Type oType in oTypes)
   {
   oAttrs = oType.GetCustomAttributes(typeof_
               (PublisherInfoAttribute),true);
      if (oAttrs.GetLength(0) !=0)
      {
          PublisherInfoAttribute oPubInfoAttr =
                        (PublisherInfoAttribute)oAttrs[0];
```

```
            if (oPubInfoAttr.Name =="Wrox Press Ltd.")
            {
                object obj  = Activator.CreateInstance(oType);
                MethodInfo oMethodInfo = oType.GetMethod("BuyBook");
                AddItem((oMethodInfo.Invoke(obj,null)).ToString());
                AddItem(".....");

            }
        }

    }
}
```

In the following line, we use the `Process` class's `GetCurrentProcess` method to determine the name of the currently-executing application. We then append `.exe` to get the physical exe file of the assembly.

```
Process oProcess = Process.GetCurrentProcess();
sAssemblyName = oProcess.ProcessName + ".exe";
```

Here we instantiate the assembly by invoking the `Assembly.LoadFrom` method and passing in the name of the physical file that contains the assembly. We then call the `GetTypes` method to get an array of `Type` objects.

```
Assembly oAssembly = Assembly.LoadFrom(sAssemblyName);
Type[] oTypes = oAssembly.GetTypes();
```

Now that we have an array of `Type` objects that describes every single type in the entire assembly, we will loop through the array and get a reference to the `PublisherInfoAttribute` object for each of the book classes. We then check the name of the attribute and if it is equivalent to `Wrox Press Ltd.`, we understand that this is the book we need to buy. Then to buy the book, we need to instantiate that identified `Book` class by using the `CreateInstance` method of the `Activator` class, passing to its constructor the `Type` object. We then invoke the `GetMethod` method of the type object to create a `MethodInfo` object, specifying the method name as `BuyBook`. Once we do that, we can then use the `MethodInfo` object's `Invoke` method, passing to it the activated type as an argument. The `BuyBook` method of our `Book` class returns a string, which we show in the `Listbox`.

```
        foreach (Type oType in oTypes)
        {
            oAttrs = oType.GetCustomAttributes(typeof
                        (PublisherInfoAttribute),true);
```

By verifying the `GetLength` method, we can identify the number of attributes present in the class in question.

```
        if (oAttrs.GetLength(0) !=0)
        {
        PublisherInfoAttribute oPubInfoAttr = (PublisherInfoAttribute)oAttrs[0];
            if (oPubInfoAttr.Name =="Wrox Press Ltd.")
            {
                object obj  = Activator.CreateInstance(oType);
                MethodInfo oMethodInfo = oType.GetMethod("BuyBook");
                AddItem((oMethodInfo.Invoke(obj,null)).ToString());
                AddItem(".....");
            }
        }


        }
```

If we execute the above code, we should get an output that is similar to the following.

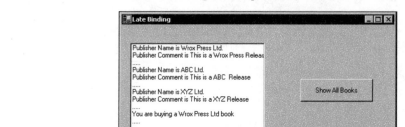

Creating Dynamic Assemblies

Now that we have seen how to use Reflection to retrieve types at runtime, and dynamically execute code using late binding, let us take a step forward and understand how to create code on the fly. Before we see how to create dynamic assemblies, let us first discuss why we need to go for dynamic assemblies.

Let us say, for example, we want to execute a script expression from our ASP.NET page; the first time the user comes to the page, we execute the script by compiling the script expression and save it in the form of a persistable dynamic module that is part of a dynamic assembly. During the subsequent requests, the already persisted assembly can be used instead of recreating it every time from the beginning, which accounts for a tremendous amount of increase in performance.

Creating code on the fly involves using the `System.Reflection.Emit` namespace. The `System.Reflection.Emit` namespace exposes a wealth of functionality, using which we can define an assembly in memory, create a module in an assembly, and emit MSIL code at run-time and of course invoke the created code also.

In the following example, we will create an assembly dynamically, add a module to it, create a class called `Book` (that has a constructor and a `BuyBook` method) and then save the assembly. We will then invoke this saved assembly's methods and see the results. Finally we will see what the saved assembly looks like by dissecting it with `ILDASM` utility.

Let us get started by creating a new C# Windows application, and let us name the project `DynamicAssemblyTest`.

Here we import all the namespaces required for our application. The `System.Reflection` and `System.Reflection.Emit` namespaces are required for importing the classes that implement the functionality to create dynamic assemblies.

```
using System;
using System.Drawing;
using System.Collections;
using System.ComponentModel;
```

```
using System.Windows.Forms;
using System.Threading;
using System.Reflection;
using System.Reflection.Emit;

private void AddItem(string sMessage)
{
    lstMessages.Items.Add(sMessage);
}

protected void cmdCreateAssembly_Click (object sender, System.EventArgs e)
{

    AppDomain curAppDomain = Thread.GetDomain();
    AddItem("Found current application domain");
    // Create a simple name for the Assembly.
    AssemblyName oAssemblyName = new AssemblyName();
    oAssemblyName.Name = "Chapter05Example05";
    // Create the dynamic oAssembly.
    AssemblyBuilder oAssembly = curAppDomain.
    DefineDynamicAssembly(oAssemblyName, AssemblyBuilderAccess.Save);

        AddItem("Assembly creation succeeded");
        //Create a dynamic module named DynamicModule in the oAssembly.
        ModuleBuilder oModule = oAssembly.
        DefineDynamicModule("DynamicModule", "DynamicModule.dll");
        """" AddItem("Module creation succeeded");
        // Define a public class named "Book" in the oAssembly.
        TypeBuilder bookClass = oModule.DefineType("Book",
                            TypeAttributes.Public);

        // Define a private String field named "Message" in the type.
        FieldBuilder sbookVerMessage = bookClass.DefineField("Message",
                Type.GetType("System.String"), FieldAttributes.Private);

        // Create the oConstructor.
        Type[] oConstructorArgs = new Type[1];
        oConstructorArgs[0] = Type.GetType("System.String");
        ConstructorBuilder oConstructor = bookClass.
        DefineConstructor(MethodAttributes.Public,
                        CallingConventions.Standard, oConstructorArgs);

        //Generate IL for the method. The oConstructor calls its superclass
        // oConstructor. The oConstructor stores its argument in the private
        // field.
        ILGenerator oConstructorIL = oConstructor.GetILGenerator();
        oConstructorIL.Emit(OpCodes.Ldarg_0);
        Type oObjectClass = Type.GetType("System.Object");
        ConstructorInfo oConstructorInfo = oObjectClass.GetConstructor
                                    (new Type[0]);
        oConstructorIL.Emit(OpCodes.Call, oConstructorInfo);
        oConstructorIL.Emit(OpCodes.Ldarg_0);
        oConstructorIL.Emit(OpCodes.Ldarg_1);
        oConstructorIL.Emit(OpCodes.Stfld, sbookVerMessage);
        oConstructorIL.Emit(OpCodes.Ret);

        MethodBuilder oBuyBookMethod = bookClass.DefineMethod("BuyBook",
                MethodAttributes.Public, Type.GetType("System.String"), null);

        // Generate IL for BuyBook.
        ILGenerator methodIL = oBuyBookMethod.GetILGenerator();
```

```
            methodIL.Emit(OpCodes.Ldarg_0);
            methodIL.Emit(OpCodes.Ldfld, sbookVerMessage);
            methodIL.Emit(OpCodes.Ret);

            // Make the class Book.
            bookClass.CreateType();

            // Save the oAssembly.
            oAssembly.Save("Chapter05Example05.dll");
            AddItem("Assembly Saved");
            AddItem("....");

    }
```

We start by instantiating the `AppDomain` object from the current domain. Then we instantiate an `AssemblyName` object by using the new keyword. The assembly cache manager uses the `AssemblyName` class to retrieve information about the assembly.

```
AppDomain curAppDomain = Thread.GetDomain();
AddItem("Found current application domain");
// Create a simple name for the Assembly.
AssemblyName oAssemblyName = new AssemblyName();
```

Here, we set the properties of the `AssemblyName` object.

```
oAssemblyName.Name = "Chapter05Example05";
oAssemblyName.DefaultAlias = "Chapter05Example05.dll";
```

Once we create the `AssemblyName` object, the next step is to create the new assembly by calling the `AppDomain.DefineDynamicAssembly`. To this method, we pass the assembly name and the mode in which the assembly will be accessed, as arguments.

```
// Create the dynamic Assembly.
AssemblyBuilder oAssembly = curAppDomain.
DefineDynamicAssembly(oAssemblyName, AssemblyBuilderAccess.Save);
```

The `AssemblyBuilderAccess.Save` parameter in the mode parameter allows us to save the assembly to a `.dll` file. If we set the mode parameter to `AssemblyBuilderAccess.Run`, then we can execute the assembly in memory, but we cannot save it. The `DefineDynamicAssembly` method returns an `AssemblyBuilder` object, which we use for constructing the different elements of the assembly.

Now that we have defined the assembly, let us create a temporary module and add it to the assembly. We begin by calling the `Assembly.DefineDynamicModule` method to retrieve the `ModuleBuilder` object. We then call the `DefineType` method of the `ModuleBuilder` object to create a `TypeBuilder` object, passing to it the name of the type and the attributes used to define it. Since we want to create a type called Book, we pass Book as the first argument. And we want the scope of the Book class to be Public, so we pass `TypeAttributes.Public` as the second argument.

```
ModuleBuilder oModule = oAssembly.
DefineDynamicModule("DynamicModule", "DynamicModule.dll");
AddItem ("Module creation succeeded");
// Define a public class named "Book" in the oAssembly.
TypeBuilder bookClass = oModule.DefineType("Book", TypeAttributes.Public);
```

Now we will add a private field of type string called Message in the book type by invoking the DefineField method of the book type, which we created in the previous step.

```
// Define a private String field named "Message" in the type.
FieldBuilder sbookVerMessage = bookClass.DefineField("Message",
Type.GetType("System.String"), FieldAttributes.Private);
```

In this step, we will add a constructor that takes a string as an argument for our Book class and set the visibility of the constructor to public.

```
// Create the oConstructor.
Type[] oConstructorArgs = new Type[1];
oConstructorArgs[0] = Type.GetType("System.String");
ConstructorBuilder oConstructor = bookClass.
DefineConstructor(MethodAttributes.Public, CallingConventions.Standard,
oConstructorArgs);
```

Now that we have defined the constructor, let us add code to it.

We first get a reference to the ILGenerator by invoking the GetILGenerator method of the ConstructorBuilder object. Once we get a reference to the ILGenerator object, we can directly emit MSIL code into the constructor method using the Emit method of the ILGenerator.
In the following lines written using MSIL, we indicate that the value passed to the constructor should be assigned to the private string field that we defined in the previous step.

```
ILGenerator oConstructorIL = oConstructor.GetILGenerator();
oConstructorIL.Emit(OpCodes.Ldarg_0);
Type oObjectClass = Type.GetType("System.Object");
ConstructorInfo oConstructorInfo = oObjectClass.GetConstructor
                                    (new Type[0]);
oConstructorIL.Emit(OpCodes.Call, oConstructorInfo);
```

By using Ldarg_x (where x specifies the number of the argument to be loaded), we can load the arguments onto the stack. For example, the following line of code is used to load the argument number 0 into the stack that is required for invoking the constructor of the base class System.Object.

```
oConstructorIL.Emit(OpCodes.Ldarg_0);
```

Here, we load the argument 1 onto the stack to enable it to be used in the assignment operation in the next statement.

```
oConstructorIL.Emit(OpCodes.Ldarg_1);
```

The following statement allows us to store the value that is passed to the constructor in the sBookVerMessage variable.

```
oConstructorIL.Emit(OpCodes.Stfld, sbookVerMessage);
```

Using the OpCodes.Ret, we can specify the end of the constructor and signal the return to the caller.

```
oConstructorIL.Emit(OpCodes.Ret);
```

In this step, we create the BuyBook method by invoking the DefineMethod of the bookClass object. We also indicate that the scope of this method is public and the return value of the method is string. The null in the fourth parameter indicates that BuyBook method does not take any parameters.

```
MethodBuilder oBuyBookMethod = bookClass.DefineMethod("BuyBook",
MethodAttributes.Public, Type.GetType("System.String"), null);
```

In the following line written using MSIL, we specify that the BuyBook method will return the value stored in the private string field.

```
// Generate IL for BuyBook.
ILGenerator methodIL = oBuyBookMethod.GetILGenerator();
methodIL.Emit(OpCodes.Ldarg_0);
methodIL.Emit(OpCodes.Ldfld, sbookVerMessage);
methodIL.Emit(OpCodes.Ret);
```

Here, we create the type by invoking the CreateType method of the TypeBuilder object.

```
// Bake the class Book.
bookClass.CreateType();
```

After creating the Type object, then we save the created assembly by calling the Save method of the AssemblyBuilder object.

```
oAssembly.Save("Chapter05Example05.dll");
```

Finally, we have a dynamically created class named Book, which consists of a private string field, a constructor, and a public method named BuyBook.

Now, let us test the dynamically constructed book class by creating an instance of it and then invoking the BuyBook method. To do this, all we have to do is to retrieve the book type member, create an instance using the Activator class, and call the InvokeMember method of this instance.

```
protected void cmdInvokeAssembly_Click (object sender, System.EventArgs e)
{
    // Find the "Book" class
    Assembly oAssembly = Assembly.LoadFrom("Chapter05Example05.dll");
    Type[] oTypes;
    oTypes = oAssembly.GetTypes();
    foreach(Type oType in oTypes)
        {
        if (oType.Name == "Book")
        {
            AddItem("Found Book class");
            Object[] constructorArgs = new Object[1];
            String sMessage = " You are buying 1.0.0.0 version of the book ";
            constructorArgs[0] = sMessage;
    Object oBookObject = Activator.CreateInstance(oType,
        constructorArgs);
```

```
                AddItem("Instantiated Book class");
                //Invoke the "BuyBook" method of the "Book" class.
                AddItem("Invoking BuyBook class");
                Object obj = oType.InvokeMember("BuyBook",
                BindingFlags.InvokeMethod, null, oBookObject, new Object[0]);
                String sReturnMessage = obj.ToString();
                AddItem("BuyBook returned: " + sReturnMessage);
            }
        }
    }
```

In the first step, we instantiate the assembly object by invoking the static method LoadFrom of the Assembly class, passing to it the name of the DLL that we created dynamically.

```
Assembly oAssembly = Assembly.LoadFrom("Chapter05Example05.dll");
Type[] oTypes;
```

Now we get a reference to all the types in the assembly in an array by calling the GetTypes method of the Assembly object. We then loop through elements in the array and check the name of each type object in the array and if the name is equal to Book, we identify that this is the class we created dynamically in the previous step.

```
oTypes = oAssembly.GetTypes();
foreach(Type oType in oTypes)
{
    if (oType.Name == "Book")
    {

    AddItem("Found Book class");
    // Create an instance of the "Book" class.
    Object[] constructorArgs = new Object[1];
    String sMessage = " You are buying 1.0.0.0 version of the book ";
    constructorArgs[0] = sMessage;
```

In this step, we create the instance of the book class passing to its constructor the string value contained in the variable sMessage.

```
            Object oBookObject = Activator.
            CreateInstance(bookClass, constructorArgs);
            AddItem("Instantiated Book class");
            //Invoke the "BuyBook" method of the "Book" class.
            AddItem("Invoking BuyBook class");
```

Now we invoke the BuyBook method by calling the InvokeMember method passing to it all the required parameters. The value returned by the BuyBook method is stored in the variable obj and then it is shown in the listbox.

```
            Object obj = bookClass.InvokeMember("BuyBook",
                    BindingFlags.InvokeMethod, null, oBookObject, new Object[0]);
            String sReturnMessage = obj.ToString();
            AddItem("BuyBook returned: " + sReturnMessage);
        }
    }
```

When we finally execute the code, we should get the following output.

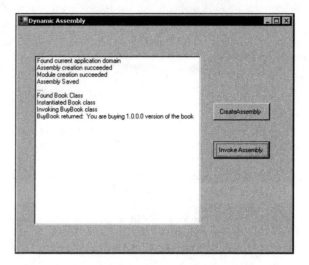

If we examine the module that we created dynamically using ILDASM (the IL Disassembler utility), it looks like this. If we double click on the BuyBook : string() in the following, we can match the MSIL code that appears to the code that we created dynamically.

Versions

One of the primary causes of DLL hell is the sharing model used by current component-based systems. For example, when you install a new version of your DLL, the installation program copies the new version of your DLL to the system directory and makes all the necessary registry entries that overwrite the existing registry entries that were made by the previous versions of the DLL. This installation might potentially have an impact on other applications running on the machine, especially if an existing application was using the shared version of the installed component. If the installed component is backward compatible with the previous versions, then it is fine, but in many cases it may not be possible to maintain backward compatibility with the older versions. If you cannot maintain backward compatibility, you will often end up breaking the existing applications as a result of new installations.

This problem is so widespread that MSDN has a dedicated online service to support customers who are facing this infamous problem. Now that we have understood the problem, let us analyze the infrastructure .NET provides for solving this problem.

Infrastructure provided by the .NET Framework

One of the compelling benefits of .NET is its ability to allow us to create isolated components or assemblies. By isolating an assembly, we are essentially trying to make sure that the assembly is accessed by only one application and not used by the other applications. Since the assembly is isolated and not shared, it cannot be affected by changes made to the other applications in the system. This type of assembly is called a private assembly and it gives a developer the ability to have absolute control over the code used by his application.

However there are times when you might want to share an assembly between applications in your machine. For example, we might write a utility DLL and want that to be used by all the applications on the machine. These assemblies are called Shared assemblies and it is the responsibility of the developer to make the explicit decision whether he wants to share the assembly. When you want to implement shared assemblies, your assembly should meet the following requirements.

- ❑ It should have the ability to have multiple versions of the same assembly installed and run on the same machine.

- ❑ It should follow stricter naming requirements and its name must be globally unique. This name is known as shared name or strong name. Strong names provide security and versioning of components.

- ❑ It should be deployed to the global assembly store, which provides the infrastructure for hosting multiple versions of the same assembly. Administrators can use the store to deploy bug fixes or security patches that they want every application on the machine to use.

- ❑ It should have the version information clearly defined in its manifest. This should include versioning information for the assembly as well as a list of all referenced assemblies and their versioning information.

Let us have a look at the tools provided by the .NET framework for creating and deploying shared assemblies.

Shared Assembly Name Creation Tool

To create a shared assembly, we use the Strong name tool that creates a strong name or shared name for our assembly. Let us look at the benefits of using strong names for the assemblies.

- ❑ It allows us to generate names that are globally unique.

- ❑ Since it uses Cryptography's public and private key combination to differentiate requests, we can clearly identify whether the assembly has been tampered with after its original deployment.

- ❑ It also prevents a third party from releasing a next version of the assembly we built. This is feasible because of the public-private key pair infrastructure; and the third party won't have our private key.

- ❑ When .NET loads the assembly, the runtime can verify that the assembly came from the expected publisher.

To create a key file called `TestKey.key` for our assembly, we need to enter the following at the command prompt.

```
sn -k TestKey.snk
```

As we can see from the above, we can use the Strong Name generation tool (`sn.exe`) for generating a public-private key pair. It can also be used to perform operations such as taking out a public key from a key pair in a file and exporting it to a file and verifying an assembly to check whether it is signed using a particular key file. The switch k indicates the name of the output file that will contain the key. Once we create the key, we can add it to the source file and start using this strong name.

Assembly Cache Utility tools

When you install .NET, you will automatically have a code cache called the Global assembly cache, installed along with it. It is used for the following reasons:

- ❑ Used to store the code downloaded from the Internet or other servers. It is important to note that the code downloaded for a particular application is stored in the private portion of the cache and other applications cannot access it.

- ❑ Used as a centralized repository to store all the components that are installed as shared assemblies. These assemblies are stored in the global portion of the global assembly cache and it is accessible to all the applications on the machine.

- ❑ Sometimes, you can precompile IL source code into native code and you can store it for future use. This is called prejitting and this prejitted code is also stored in the cache. Prejitting allows us to increase throughput of the system because of the saved native code that obviates the need to convert the IL code into native code during the subsequent executions.

Let us look at the tools that can be used to view the contents of the global assembly cache.

Assembly Cache Viewer

.NET features a shell extension (`shfusion.dll`) that allows us to view assembly information, such as the version information, culture, and public key token, and whether the assembly has been prejitted. This assembly cache viewer shell extension not only allows us to determine the list of shared assemblies installed in the machine but also to manipulate its contents. To view the currently installed and shared assemblies using this tool, we open the folder c:\winnt\assembly through Windows Explorer and we should be able to see the list of currently installed shared assemblies. The following figure shows the list of shared assemblies in the machine.

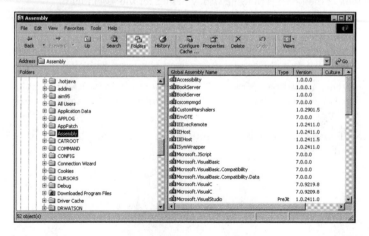

Global Assembly Cache Tool (gacutil.exe)

Using this tool, we can perform several basic tasks by specifying any of the following command line switches. To list the contents of the global assembly cache, including the assembly name, its version number, its location, and its shared name we use the following command.

```
gacutil -l
```

We can uninstall the assembly from the global assembly cache using the –u switch. For example, to uninstall all the versions of the BookServer assembly, we specify the following option.

```
gacutil -u BookServer
```

To uninstall the specified version of the BookServer assembly, we use the following command.

```
gacutil -u BookServer, version=1,0,0,1
```

To install an assembly to the global assembly cache, we use the following command.

```
gacutil -i BookServer.dll
```

From the above command, we can see that installing a shared assembly requires a completely different approach when compared to installing the private assembly. It is important to realize that unlike the private assemblies, shared assemblies cannot be installed using XCOPY deployment. And they need to be moved to the global assembly cache using the above command.

```
C:\WINDOWS\System32\cmd.exe                                     _ □ X

C:\>gacutil -l

Microsoft (R) .NET Global Assembly Cache Utility.  Version 1.0.2901.5
Copyright (C) Microsoft Corp. 1998-2001. All rights reserved.

The Global Assembly Cache contains the following assemblies:
        Accessibility, Version=1.0.0.0, Culture=neutral, PublicKeyToken=b03f5f7f
11d50a3a, Custom=null
        cscompmgd, Version=7.0.0.0, Culture=neutral, PublicKeyToken=b03f5f7f11d5
0a3a, Custom=null
        CustomMarshalers, Version=1.0.2901.5, Culture=neutral, PublicKeyToken=b0
3f5f7f11d50a3a, Custom=null
        IEExecRemote, Version=1.0.2411.0, Culture=neutral, PublicKeyToken=b03f5f
7f11d50a3a, Custom=null
        IEHost, Version=1.0.2411.0, Culture=neutral, PublicKeyToken=b03f5f7f11d5
0a3a, Custom=null
        IIEHost, Version=1.0.2411.5, Culture=neutral, PublicKeyToken=b03f5f7f11d
50a3a, Custom=null
        ISymWrapper, Version=1.0.2411.0, Culture=neutral, PublicKeyToken=b03f5f7
f11d50a3a, Custom=null
        Microsoft.VisualC, Version=7.0.9209.8, Culture=neutral, PublicKeyToken=b
03f5f7f11d50a3a, Custom=null
        Microsoft.VisualC, Version=7.0.9219.8, Culture=neutral, PublicKeyToken=b
03f5f7f11d50a3a, Custom=null
        mscorcfg, Version=1.0.2411.0, Culture=neutral, PublicKeyToken=b03f5f7f11
d50a3a, Custom=null
        Regcode, Version=1.0.2411.0, Culture=neutral, PublicKeyToken=b03f5f7f11d
50a3a, Custom=null
        System.Configuration.Install, Version=1.0.2411.0, Culture=neutral, Publi
cKeyToken=b03f5f7f11d50a3a, Custom=null
```

How Assemblies are Versioned

An assembly's manifest contains a version number as well as a list of all referenced assemblies with their associated version information. We can divide the version information of an assembly into four parts: major, minor, build and revision.

Let us take a look at some VB.NET sample code to understand how to work with assembly versioning and how to implement side-by-side execution. Side-by-side execution can be defined as the ability to run multiple versions of the same assembly simultaneously. The .NET framework provides us with the infrastructure that allows us to run multiple versions of the same assembly on the same machine, or even in the same process. For this example, we will again consider the Book class and we will make it part of the BookServer assembly. We will also create multiple versions of the BookServer assembly to illustrate side-by-side execution. We will also see how we can use XML-based configuration files to create an association between an application and a specific version of an assembly.

We will get started by creating a key pair using the shared assembly name creation tool and we will use this key for signing all versions of our BookServer assembly.

```
sn /k KeyFile.snk
```

To create the BookServer assembly, we need to follow these steps:

❑   First, we create a new VB.NET class library project and name it **BookServer**. While creating the new project, we make sure that we select the path C:\Chapter 4 Examples\Chapter04Example06\BookServer\Ver1000 in the Location textbox.

❑   Secondly, we rename the default class that was created from class1 to Book.

❑   Finally, we add the **BuyBook** method to the **Book** class. The **BuyBook** method is very simple and it just returns a string back to the caller informing the caller about the version of the book he is buying.

The Book class we created looks like the following.

```
Public Class Book
    Public Sub New()

    End Sub

    Public Function BuyBook() As String
        Return ("You are buying version 1.0.0.0 of the book")
    End Function
End Class
```

Now we will add the created key pair to the BookServer assembly. To do this, we right-click on the BookServer assembly in the solution explorer, select **Properties**, navigate to the **Strong name** property page and check the **Generate strong name using** checkbox. Once this option is enabled, we can perform any one of the following operations.

❑   Generate a new key using the **Generate key** option

❑   Add an existing key to this project by navigating to the path of the key file using the **Browse** option

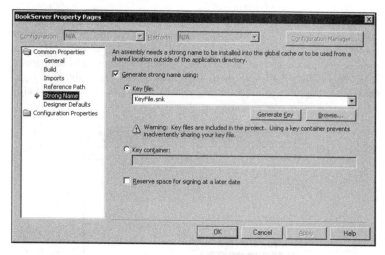

Since we have already created the key using the strong name creation tool, we will just add the KeyFile.snk (which we created in the previous step) to our application by navigating to the path of the file.

We then modify the following lines in the AssemblyInfo.vb file to associate the created key pair with our BookServer application.

```
<Assembly: AssemblyKeyFile("KeyFile.snk")>
<Assembly: AssemblyVersion("1.0.0.0")>
```

We also set the AssemblyVersion attribute to a proper value that is representative of the current version of the assembly. In this example, we set it to 1.0.0.0 to indicate that this is the first version of the assembly. Let us go ahead and compile the BookServer application. Once we compile the BookServer application, the next step is to add the assembly to the global assembly cache. To do this, we type the following command at the command prompt.

```
gacutil -i BookServer.dll
```

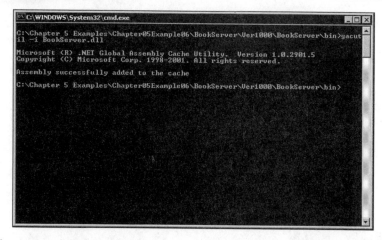

Now that we have created the first version of the BookServer assembly, let us test it by writing a client application that consumes this BookServer assembly.

Client Application for BookServer

We start by creating a new VB.NET windows application in the C:\Chapter 4 Examples\ Chapter04Example06\ folder and we will name it BookClient. We then add a reference to the BookServer assembly, which we created in the earlier step, by navigating to the path of BookServer.dll. After adding the reference to the BookServer assembly, if we right-click on the BookServer assembly in the solution explorer and select Properties, we should be able to see a property window that is similar to the following.

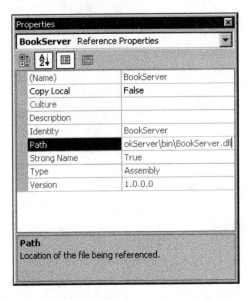

In the above property window, we can see that the CopyLocal property is set to False, which indicates that the BookServer assembly is a shared assembly, and it is stored in the global assembly cache. We can also see that the Path, Strong name and Version properties are set to appropriate values according to the information we specified in our assembly.

```
Imports BookServer

Public Class Form1
    Inherits System.Windows.Forms.Form

    Private Sub AddItem(ByVal sMessage As String)
        lstMessages.Items.Add(sMessage)
    End Sub

    Private Sub cmdBuyBook_Click(ByVal sender As System.Object, ByVal e As_
                        System.EventArgs) Handles cmdBuyBook.Click

        Dim oBook As New Book()
        AddItem(oBook.BuyBook())
    End Sub

End Class
```

Here, we import the `BookServer` namespace into our application.

```
Imports BookServer
```

In the `Click` event of the `BuyBook` command button, we write code to create an instance of the `Book` class and invoke its `BuyBook` method.

```
Private Sub cmdBuyBook_Click(ByVal sender As System.Object, ByVal e As_
                            System.EventArgs) Handles cmdBuyBook.Click
    Dim oBook As New Book()
    AddItem(oBook.BuyBook())
End Sub
```

In the `AddItem` method, as similar to the previous examples, we add the passed string to the listbox.

```
Private Sub AddItem(ByVal sMessage As String)
    lstMessages.Items.Add(sMessage)
End Sub
```

Finally, when we run the application, as expected, we get the following output.

You are buying version 1.0.0.0 of the book.

However, let us see what happens when we install a newer version of the `BookServer` assembly to the global assembly cache.

Second Version of BookServer Assembly

In this step, we will create a new VB.NET class library application in the C:\Chapter 4 Examples\Chapter04Example06\BookServer\Ver1001 folder and name it BookServer. As before, we change the default class to Book and add the `BuyBook` method to the `Book` class. However, this time we will return a different string that represents the current version of the assembly from the `BuyBook` method.

```
Public Class Book
    Public Sub New()

    End Sub
    Public Function BuyBook() As String
        Return ("You are buying version 1.0.0.1 of the book")
    End Function
End Class
```

We also modify the following lines in the `AssemblyInfo.vb` file. We increment the revision part of the version number by one to represent that it is a newer version of the Assembly. We then add the same key file `KeyFile.snk`, which we used for the first version of the `BookServer` assembly to this assembly.

```
<Assembly: AssemblyVersion("1.0.0.1")>
<Assembly: AssemblyKeyFile("KeyFile.snk")>
```

As before, we add the `BookServer` assembly to the global assembly cache by using the following command after navigating to the path of the second version of the `BookServer` assembly.

```
gacutil -i BookServer.dll
```

At this point, we have two versions of the BookServer assembly in the global assembly cache. Now we will go back to our BookClient application and execute the application. When we run the application, we get the following message.

You are buying version 1.0.0.0 of the book.

The above output clearly indicates that the Book client application is not affected by the installation of the second version of the BookServer assembly into the global assembly cache. The version of the assembly loaded is determined by the default versioning policy, which is enforced by the CLR.

Default Version Policy

When we compile our application, the compiler records information about all the static references of the assembly such as name, version, culture, and public token in the assembly manifest. By default, whenever the CLR receives the request for loading of the assembly, it uses the information in the manifest and attempts to bind the application with the exact version of the assembly that the application was built against. This is called Default versioning policy and we can override this default behavior by using XML-based configuration file settings.

Custom Version Policy

As we already mentioned, we can override the default versioning policy with the configuration settings that are specified in XML-based files. There are three different types of configuration files that can be used to enforce custom versioning policy.

- ❑ Application Configuration file
- ❑ Machine configuration file
- ❑ Publisher policy configuration file

All these files use similar XML schema to represent configuration settings. To illustrate custom versioning policy, we will consider our BookServer assembly example and load different versions of the assembly by specifying configuration settings in the above configuration files.

Versioning using the Application Configuration File

Let us say, for example, we want all the requests for the BookServer assembly to be redirected to the second version of the BookServer assembly as the first version of the book has run out of stock. This can be accomplished in two ways.

- ❑ By creating an application configuration file in every client application, which automatically redirects all the requests for the first version of the assembly to the second version of the assembly
- ❑ By making an entry in the global machine configuration file

For this example, we will create an application configuration file and use it for routing the requests to the appropriate version of the assembly.

Let us open the BookClient application, which we used in the previous examples, and add the following entries to a configuration file named BookClient.exe.config and save this file in the bin directory of the application. The name of the configuration file is arrived at by appending .config to the name of the executable. Since this configuration file is a simple text file that is made up of XML entries, it can be created using a text editor like Notepad. Once the file is created, we need to copy this file over to the bin directory of the client application, which we want to redirect to the new version of the assembly.

```
<configuration>
   <runtime>
      <assemblyBinding xmlns="urn:schemas-microsoft-com:asm.v1">
         <dependentAssembly>
            <assemblyIdentity name="BookServer"
               publicKeyToken="29dc6bc05e1c124d" culture=""/>
            <bindingRedirect oldVersion="1.0.0.0" newVersion="1.0.0.1"/>
         </dependentAssembly>
      </assemblyBinding>
   </runtime>
</configuration>
```

Please note that the publicKeyToken value in your machine will be different from the above. As we can see, the above configuration file contains the tags that redirect the binding process at runtime. By specifing the namespace urn:schemas-microsoft-com:asm.v1 with the xmlns attribute in the assemblyBinding element, we indicate that we want to bind our application to an assembly. We then use the dependentAssembly tag to denote that we want to redirect requests for the assembly that identified by the assemblyIdentity tag. The assemblyIdentify tag contains information such as name, publicKeyToken, and culture about the assembly in question. Finally, in the bindingRedirect tag, we state that we want all the requests for the version 1.0.0.0 to be redirected to the version 1.0.0.1 of the BookServer assembly. Now, if we execute the application, we should see the following output.

You are buying version 1.0.0.1 of the book.

This is because of the application configuration file which routes all the requests for version 1.0.0.0 to version 1.0.0.1.

Versioning using the Machine Configuration File

There are times when we may want all applications on our machine to use a specific version of an assembly. This can be accomplished by specifying configuration settings in the machine.config file that affect all the applications in the machine. The settings in the machine.config file take precedence over all the other configuration settings. Let us consider our last scenario and see how we can achieve the same effect using the machine-wide configuration file.

The machine.config file resides in the Config subdirectory of the root directory (<Drive>\Windows\Microsoft.NET\Framework\V1.0.2901\) where the runtime is installed. We open up this file and add the following entry under the configuration tag.

```
<assemblyBinding xmlns="urn:schemas-microsoft-com:asm.v1">
   <dependentAssembly>
      <assemblyIdentity name="BookServer"
         publicKeyToken="29dc6bc05e1c124d" culture=""/>
      <bindingRedirect oldVersion="1.0.0.0" newVersion="1.0.0.1"/>
   </dependentAssembly>
</assemblyBinding>
</runtime>
```

Now, if we go back to our `BookClient` application and run it, we should see the following output.

You are buying version 1.0.0.1 of the book.

This is because of the configuration settings that we made in the `machine.config` file.

Versioning Using the Publisher Policy Configuration File

The publisher policy configuration file, which resides in the global assembly cache, can also be used to redirect requests for one version of assembly to another version of the same assembly. Whenever the CLR receives the request for loading of the assembly, the runtime consults the publisher policy configuration file after checking the assembly's manifest and application configuration file. Let us say, for example, we install the third version of the `BookServer` assembly and we want all the applications in the machine to use this latest version of the assembly. We can accomplish this by specifying the redirection policy in the publisher configuration file that is installed with the third version of the `BookServer` assembly.

It is important to note that we should use publisher policies only when the new version of the assembly is compatible with the assembly being redirected. Sometimes, Shared assemblies, even though they claim to be backwards compatible, can still break the application. To overcome this problem, we can specify the following settings in the application configuration file to bypass the publisher policy.

```
<publisherPolicy apply="no">
```

This setting is placed in the `<dependentAssembly>` tag of the application configuration file. The default setting for the `apply` attribute is `yes`. When we set the apply attribute to `no` at the application level, any publisher policy configuration setting is ignored.

Namespaces

A namespace can be defined as a container, which is used to logically group related classes together. This grouping of classes makes the task of searching and referencing them in our application a whole lot easier. It also avoids the risk of name collision. Let us say, for example we define a class called `Book`; if some other name company also defines a class called `Book`, then there will be name collision. If we have created our `Book` class under the namespace `Wrox` and the other company has created their own namespace, then there would be no conflict. This can be compared to the scenario where files with the same name can be contained in different folders in the Windows file system. It is also possible for namespaces to be nested – one namespace containing another namespace, and so on.

Using and Namespace

When you use Visual Studio.NET to generate your project, it automatically puts your classes in a namespace. Let us say, for example, we create a C# class library called `TestProject`; Visual Studio.NET automatically generates the following code for us.

```
namespace TestProject
{
    using System;
```

There are two keywords which we need to understand – `using` and `namespace`. We will first look at the purpose of the `namespace` keyword.

The `namespace` keyword indicates that everything following the initial opening curly brace is part of the `TestProject` namespace. Later on in the file, we also have a class like this.

```
public class class1
{
```

Since this class is declared inside the namespace `TestProject`, any other code outside this namespace must refer to it as `TestProject.class1` instead of simply `class1`. This naming is known as Fully-Qualified-Name. Code inside the `TestProject` namespace can use `class1`, without the namespace prefix.

Now, let us create a client application that is going to make use of the functionality exposed by the methods of `class1`. We first open up Visual Studio.NET and create a VB.NET client called `TestProjectClient`. Then we add a reference to the `TestProject` class library, which we created in the earlier step. Once the reference to the `TestProject` class library is added, we can have a line like this to instantiate `class1`.

```
Dim oClass1 as new TestProject.class1
```

Let us consider that we are going to create instances of `class1` frequently in our application, then every time we need to qualify the name of the class with the name of the namespace. This might involve a lot of typing if your fully qualified names are lengthy and it makes your code hard to read. However, we can avoid this by typing the following line of code at the top of the file.

```
Imports TestProject
```

The C# equivalent keyword for this would be `using`.

The above line indicates that we can use `class1` without mentioning the fully qualified name. Because of the `Imports` statement, the code that we used for instantiating `class1` can be changed to something like this.

```
Dim oClass1 as New Class1
```

In this case, the compiler will locate the class by searching all the namespaces that have been mentioned in the `Imports` command. However, if it finds a class named `class1` in more than one namespace, then it will generate a compilation error. In that case you have to use the fully qualified name in your source code.

Using Aliases

If you have a very long namespace and you want to use it frequently in your code, then you can substitute a short name for the long namespace. In the code we can refer to the namespace using the short name. The advantages of `using` are more easily readable code and saving the typing out of very long strings.

In C#, we can declare an alias like this.

```
using TestProjectAlias = Wrox.Samples.TestProject
```

The same line can be written like the following in VB.NET.

```
Imports TestProjectAlias = Wrox.Samples.TestProject
```

Once we declare the above, then we can start using the classes contained in the `TestProject` namespace by qualifying them with `TestProjectAlias`.

For example, to refer to the class called class1 in the Wrox.Samples.TestProject, we can use the following line of code in C#.

```
TestProjectAlias.class1 oClass1 = new TestProjectAlias.class1
```

In VB.NET,

```
Dim oClass1 as New TestProjectAlias.Class1
```

Summary

In this chapter, we have covered quite a bit of ground. We started with an introduction to the CLR and then discussed the set of services that CLR provides to applications that are targeted towards the .NET platform. We also discussed the three important entities of a .NET application: Assemblies, Modules and Types.

We then reviewed the CTS and discussed the two kinds of types supported by the CLR: reference types and value types. We then talked about the difference between these types and how the CLR handles these two types.

Next we talked about meta data and understood how meta data is used to make types self-describing. We then looked at examples that showed us how to extend meta data by creating our own attributes. We then went on to discuss what reflection API is and its importance in the .NET framework. We also looked at code examples to understand the usage of reflection API. Specifically we covered:

❑ How to use the reflection API to create applications that use late binding

❑ How to use the reflection API to create dynamic assemblies

We also looked at how versioning is implemented in the .NET framework and learned how to implement side-by-side execution of multiple versions of the assembly. Finally we discussed what namespaces are and how they are used.

In the next chapter, we will further enhance our knowledge of namespaces by taking a tour of all the root namespaces available in the .NET framework.

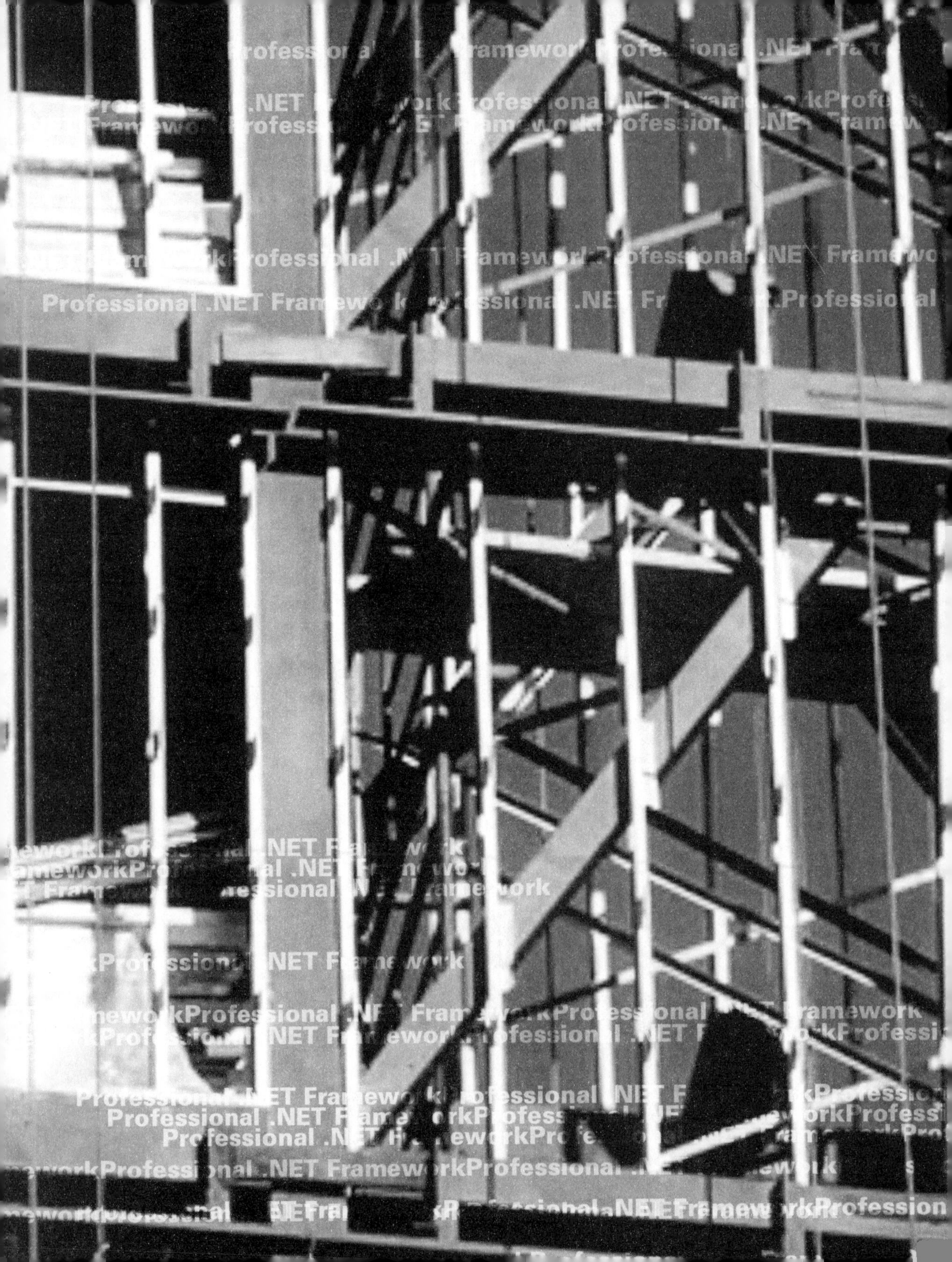
Professional .NET Framework

5

Execution Under .NET

This chapter introduces the infrastructure used to execute code developed within the .NET Framework. A VB.NET or C# developer could go their entire career and ignore the glue that holds together the .NET environment. Such developers "get by", but do not fully understand how their actions in high level code aid or hinder their application's performance, scalability, and reliability. For example, a former C++ developer working in C# may be tempted to often use pointers and unsafe code. A thorough understanding of the .NET Framework's support for type safety and the reliability this represents might curb a bit of this unsafe coding behavior. A VB.NET developer can similarly understand why at times it makes sense to work in .NET style assembly code or how the compilation model used (cached native code versus pseudo machine code) can affect their application's performance.

The code that is deployed and run under .NET is not originally compiled for the CPU architecture on which it will ultimately execute. In fact, what is known as managed code begins life as unmanaged code that is ultimately attached to the Common Language Runtime (CLR). The CLR is the engine provided with .NET that handles object management, security, profiling, debugging, and cross-language support. Once an application is running within the CLR, its code is managed, type safety is assured, and a variety of security issues are resolved with respect to the code. Actually, it is possible to explicitly run code that is unsafe, thus circumventing the reliability provided by the CLR. The rationale behind unsafe coding will be discussed later in this chapter.

.NET ships complete with the infrastructure that facilitates this. This infrastructure is found under each version (where a version number is of the form, vx.x.xxxx) of the .NET Framework installed on a host under the directory [windows folder]\Microsoft.NET\Framework\vx.x.xxxx. This directory (v1.0.2914 at the time this chapter was written) contains compilers for such high-level languages as VB.NET (vbc.exe), C# (csc.exe), and JScript (jsc.exe). This directory also contains the infrastructure responsible for taking applications compiled from these high-level languages and running these applications within the CLR.

This chapter presents the mechanisms that facilitate an application running within the CLR. Once compiled, applications deployed on .NET exist as DLL's and/or EXE's that contain a form of pseudo-machine code generated from Microsoft Intermediate Language (IL). The IL language is reviewed in this chapter, as are the features of .NET used to translate from IL's binary representation to native (CPU-specific) code. The feature that performs this translation is the Just-In-Time compiler (JIT). The various aspects of the JIT will be presented along with the mechanism used to launch managed code within the CLR.

The Code Manager (the portion of the CLR responsible for running the application) and issues such as Type Safety (ensuring objects do not corrupt the memory associated with otherobjects) will also be addressed. Finally, the tool that maps from EXE and DLL back into the IL assembly language will be introduced, the IL disassembler.

A portion of the Help with respect to these topics is found under MSDN. Long before there was a Visual Studio.NET, Microsoft documented these infrastructure features of the .NET Framework. This non-MSDN document is now publicly available when the .NET Framework's SDK or Visual Studio .NET is installed. The purpose of this pre-Visual Studio.NET documentation was to allow compiler writers working on the likes of Pascal, Perl, Cobol, and Python to begin developing compilers that generated IL and also produce applications that could run under the .NET Framework's CLR. The directory where a significant portion of this document is found is: \Program Files\Microsoft.NET\FrameworkSDK\Tool Developers Guide. The specific subdirectories of interest are docs and Samples. What is documented here is raw .NET programming and what is required to work at the level of IL, Runtime Hosts, the JIT compiler, and the Code Manager.

Developing .NET from the Console Environment

A variety of the utilities introduced in this chapter are not included in the PATH environmental variable setup when Visual Studio.NET or the .NET Framework SDK is installed. The VSVars32.bat batch file (directory, \Program Files\Microsoft Visual Studio.NET\Common7\Tools) that ships with Visual Studio.NET can be run from a console window in order to set up the environmental variables and paths required to run these utilities from the command line. This batch file also sets up the paths and environmental variables required to run the C#, VB, JScript, and C++ compilers from the command line. Developers familiar with previous versions of Visual Studio may recall a similar batch file, VCVars32.bat. The VCVars32.bat batch file does still exist under Visual Studio .NET. The batch file, VCVars32.bat, contains a single line of text that simply calls VSVars32.bat.

A .NET ready console window can be launched from the Start menu, by following the route Microsoft Visual Studio .NET 7.0 | Microsoft Visual Studio .NET Tools | Microsoft Visual Studio .NET Command Prompt. This feature became available as of the Enterprise Edition of Visual Studio .NET, Beta 2.

Intermediate Language (IL)

When code (VB, JScript, C#, and managed C++) is compiled for .NET it generates executables (EXEs) and DLLs. So what has changed since back in the mid-to-late 1990's when Win32 code was compiled as executables (EXEs) and DLLs into native (x86) code? The difference is that the .NET EXEs and DLLs are actually in a form of pseudo machine code known as Microsoft Intermediate Language (IL). The documentation refers to IL and MSIL synonymously, with IL being the more contemporary acronym. IL is not hardware specific so using this format facilitates hardware abstraction. For example, IL code can be run on a .NET Framework deployed on Win32 or Win64. IL code could be deployed on the .NET Framework that is running any flavor of Windows CE (Pocket PC) regardless of the underlying CPU. IL could even be deployed on the .NET Framework of a Windows ME/98/95 or Windows XP/2K/NT/CE without worrying about Unicode versus ANSI issues with respect to the operating system's underlying API's.

Legacy Win32 development generated Portable Execution (PE) files that were ultimately composed of native x86 instructions. Other CPUs were supported, but x86 was by far the dominant player. The DLLs and EXEs under .NET are also PE files, but since they contain IL code they are not platform specific. IL is not a high-level language such as C# or VB and at the same time it is not a low-level language such as native x86 or PowerPC instructions. What makes IL a higher-level version of machine code is that it can actually work with constructs such as objects, arrays, namespaces, assemblies, virtual methods, and exception handling.

Before we go any further it is important to note that IL is not an interpreted language. Every few, years interpreted languages make a comeback and each time they do they are viewed as too darn slow. This is why the .NET Framework ships with at least one flavor of the just-in-time compiler (JIT). The JIT is used in order to compile IL into native machine code and does not run the code in its IL format. The next section of this chapter covers the JIT in more detail.

When compiled under .NET, the high-level languages generate IL, but at the same time generate meta data. The purpose of this meta data is to provide a complete definition for every type along with definitions for the other forms of data used by the CLR when an application is executed. The meta data included with the code makes the code self-describing. To put in legacy perspective, much of what meta data accomplishes was previously achieved using type libraries generated using the Interface Definition Language (IDL). C#, VB.NET, and managed C++ do not require a special-purpose language such as IDL in order to generate meta data. Since such languages use data types common to the CLR, it is possible to generate meta data using only the code written in a high-level language.

Programming in IL

The vast majority of developers will use a high-level language (VB, C#, JScript, or managed C++) in conjunction with a compiler to generate IL. Actually, IL can be coded directly using IL assembly language and the IL assembler, `ilasm.exe` (found under directory, [windows folder]\Microsoft.NET \Framework\vx.x.xxxx).

The MSIL Instruction Set specification is shipped as part of the .NET Framework SDK and can be found under the **Tool Developers Guide** directory mentioned at the beginning of this chapter. The Microsoft Word files `Partition II Meta data.doc` and `Partition III CIL.doc` cover the vast majority of the IL specific documentation. Before jumping into the meat of these documents, it is important to remember one thing: IL is case-sensitive so C++/C#/Java developers rejoice and VB developers beware.

Remember that IL works with constructs such as assemblies, classes, methods, and namespaces. In this section we are going to build up a "hello world" application by specifying an assembly for our application, declaring a namespace, declaring a class, specifying an entry point function, and then calling `Console.Out.WriteLine` in order to display "Hello World". This is precisely what is done in a simple console application written in a high-level language such as C# or VB.NET.

In its entirety, our sample ("Hello World") IL example (filename `WXHello01.il`) is as follows:

```
.assembly WXHiWorld01 {}
.assembly extern mscorlib {}

.namespace WXHiWorld01
{
    .class private auto unicode sealed WXLetsIL
        extends [mscorlib]System.Object
    {
```

```
            .method public static void WXTrickyEntryPoint() cil managed
        {
            .entrypoint
            call class [mscorlib]System.IO.TextWriter
                [mscorlib]System.Console::get_Out()
            ldstr "Hello World!"
            callvirt instance void
                [mscorlib]System.IO.TextWriter::WriteLine(string)
            ret
        }
    }
}
```

It is important to remember that when writing in IL an assembly of some kind is being developed. For this reason each assembly written in IL assembly language must specify the `.assembly` directive followed by the name of the assembly. An example of this from the IL source file `WXHello01.il` is as follows:

```
.assembly WXHiWorld01 {}
```

In the previous line of code we are declaring the assembly to be named, `WXHiWorld01`. Following the assembly name is a set of empty brackets `{}`. Inside these brackets other declarations could have been specified such as `.locale` (cultural information for the assembly), `.os` (operating system version used to build the assembly), `.processor` (CPU used to build the assembly) and `.ver` (specifies the assembly's version as four numbers corresponding to major version, minor version, revision number and build number).

The `.assembly` directive can also refer to external assemblies such as the following which refers to assembly `mscorlib`:

```
.assembly extern mscorlib {}
```

The example assembly being developed in IL contains a namespace which is specified using the IL `.namespace` directive followed by the name of the namespace:

```
.namespace WXHiWorld01
{

}
```

Within the brackets associated with the namespace a class will be declared using the `.class` directive followed by the class's name:

```
.namespace WXHiWorld01
{
    .class private auto unicode sealed WXLetsIL
        extends [mscorlib]System.Object
    {

    }
}
```

The class's name is WXLetsIL and this is a private class that is sealed. The term private is a term used in VB.NET, C#, and C++. In IL, private has the same meaning. An instance of this class cannot be created outside of a method found within the class. This is not that restrictive since the class will expose the assembly's entry point and the entry point method would legally be able to create instances of the WXHiWorld01 class. The sealed attribute corresponds to C#'s sealed keyword or VB.NET's NotInheritable keyword. IL's sealed means our class cannot serve as a base class. Our class is derived from [mscorlib]System.Object since it extends this class. The WXLetsIL class could be derived from any base class, provided we set up the external reference to the base class's assembly as we did with mscorlib. In the previous code snippet, auto refers to automatically laying out the data and unicode specifies what type of strings will be marshaled to the underlying OS. It would also have been possible to specify ansi instead of unicode. Another alternative is autochar. This directive causes strings to be marshalled based on the representation of the underlying platform.

Within the class we declare a method, WXTrickyEntryPoint:

```
.method public static void WXTrickyEntryPoint() cil managed
{
    // Fill in what is contained in the method here
}
```

We know this is a method due to the .method directive. It is a public, static method to be precise. The return value of this method is void. This method contains managed code (cil managed) rather than unmanaged code. By this time, the jaw of old-school assembly programmers should be hanging wide open. We have declared a class, and a public, static method that returns a value of type, void. Clearly IL is a higher-level language than standard x86 assembly. Given the concepts understood by IL (classes, methods, namespaces, etc.) it should be simpler for compiler developers to develop native .NET compilers.

However, how does the CLR know that WXTrickyEntryPoint is the first method to be called for our assembly (the entry point for the assembly)? There just so happens to be a .entrypoint directive that can be placed inside the bracket of the WXTrickyEntryPoint method. It is completely legal to have an entry named WXTrickyEntryPoint instead of being named Main.

The body of the WXTrickyEntryPoint method is as follows:

```
.method public static void WXTrickyEntryPoint() cil managed
{
    .entrypoint
    call class [mscorlib]System.IO.TextWriter
                [mscorlib]System.Console::get_Out()
    ldstr "Hello World!"
    callvirt instance void
                [mscorlib]System.IO.TextWriter::WriteLine(string)
    ret
}
```

The first line of IL after .entrypoint is as follows:

```
call class [mscorlib]System.IO.TextWriter
                [mscorlib]System.Console::get_Out()
```

The last line of that snippet called the get_Out (the Out property) method of what is actually Console.Out. But where was the data stored? Those familiar with the internals of Java should recognize how IL works. The value returned by get_Out was placed on the evaluation stack.

Now the evaluation stack contains the value returned by get_Out, a string needs to be declared so it can be displayed. Specifying ldstr "Hello world!" allocates a string of type System.String. This string is allocated behind the scenes by the managed heap and ldstr places a pointer to this object on the stack. Yes, IL understands dynamic memory and the intrinsic types of the CLR.

When callvirt was specified, a method was called using the object placed on the evaluation stack by get_Out and data placed on the evaluation stack by ldstr. The paradigm used here is stack-based evaluation rather than the register-based evaluation associated with x86 assembly. IL is platform generic so it can't just assume R0, R1, and R2 exist as they did in the days of PDP 11 programming. More realistically, it can't assume that EAX, EBX, ECX, and EDX exist as in the days of x86 programming.

This section has barely scratched the surface of programming with IL. There are hundreds more features that could be explored. For instance, our example could have been extended by adding .line directives as follows:

```
call class [mscorlib]System.IO.TextWriter
.line 84
[mscorlib]System.Console::get_Out()
ldstr "Hello World!"
callvirt instance void
    [mscorlib]System.IO.TextWriter::WriteLine(string)
.line 85
ret
```

Using the .line directive, a reference was added to the Portable Debug file (PDB) associated with this module. The .line directive in conjunction with the .module directive is part of a mechanism that allows a debugger to step through the code and how the debugger can run in disassembly mode.

Compiling the previous code is simply a matter of executing the following from a console window: ilasm WXHellow01.il (Don't forget to call vsvars32.bat before attempting to execute ilasm.exe.)

The output generated when our example is executed is none other than: Hello World!

Visual Studio .NET Disassembly Window

In Visual Studio .NET's Debug | Windows submenu there are two assembly-related menu items, Disassembly and Registers. The menu items are only visible when the application is being debugged. If the application is not running in Visual Studio .NET then these menu items are nowhere to be seen. Unfortunately, these menu items are not related to IL assembly. The Registers menu item shows the x86-specific registers being used by the process being debugged.

The Disassembly option shows the code being debugged as disassembled native code (post-JIT code) such as:

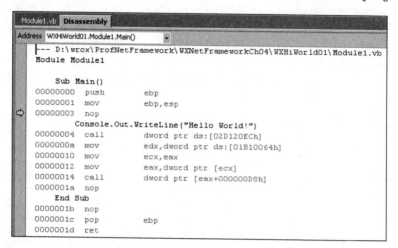

The assembly code in the previous screenshot implements a Hello World application in basically the same manner as WXHello01.il.

The constructs supported by IL make it a bit more legible to programmers more comfortable with high-level languages.

JIT Compilation

IL must be compiled to native code before it can be run on the .NET Framework. When executing IL code under .NET, there is no file with a *.il extension involved in this process. From a C:\ prompt, HelloWorld.exe could be run and behind the scenes this EXE containing IL would be Just-In-Time compiled (JIT'd). For every processor architecture, the .NET Framework will ship with its own flavor of JIT. The 32-bit x86 JIT will differ from the 64-bit x86 JIT and so on.

Rather than compiling the code all at once, the JIT compiler will compile code on an 'as needed' basis. Imagine running an e-mail application. Every time this application is run, the methods related to reading and sending mail are likely to be needed.

It is unlikely that the e-mail packages methods for specifying a different SMTP or POP server will be compiled, because these e-mail settings are rarely altered. This per-method compilation is achieved by creating a stub for each method associated with a given type. Once a method is called, the stub will let the JIT compiler take over and the method will hence get compiled from IL to native code.

It would not make sense to recompile the method each time it is called during execution. Instead, after being compiled, the method is cached and subsequent calls to the method will directly execute the native code.

Yes, it makes sense to reuse code once it has been natively compiled. It is also possible to revert a method that is compiled to native code back to a method that is simply a stub and has yet to be compiled. This reverting is referred to as **code pitching**. Reverting will reduce the memory footprint of an application. When a reverted method is subsequently called, it will be re-JIT'd.

This per-method compilation affords .NET the ability to verify from a security standpoint whether or not a given method should be compiled. The verification process is optional but it does afford a level of additional safety. This topic is reviewed in detail later in the chapter in the section on memory type safety.

The minute JIT compilation is mentioned, any good developer should immediately become concerned with performance. Clearly, Microsoft has gone to great pains in order to ensure that JIT will not degrade performance. Yes, there are overheads attributed to performing JIT when compared to just running native code, but it is minimized as much as possible.

JIT could actually improve performance. To understand this, consider the processor-specific optimizations that are available under Visual C++ 6.0: 80386, 80486, Pentium, and Pentium PRO. What these settings mean is that to optimize for each of these CPU-architectures, different flavors of native code would have to be installed. Clearly it would be simpler to ship IL and let the JIT (which is run per-machine) handle the processor, specific optimizations. JIT will be privy to which flavor of processor is running on the current machine. Notice also the age of the list of processor technologies available for optimization under Visual C++ 6.0. These processors are not particularly current and do not reflect additional processor functionality such as MMX, SSE, SSE II, and AMD-specific processor extensions. The JIT installed on a given machine should be a contemporary of the machine's hardware. Keeping the native code current with respect to a processor's architecture could lead to significant performance improvements. It remains to be seen if Microsoft will take JIT compilation to the MMX, SSE, and SSE II level of optimization.

Depending on the platform on which .NET is deployed, JIT's with different characteristics will be provided. For example, on a small device (hand-held device, set-top box, web appliance) using an operating system such as Windows CE, it might make the most sense to compile each method "quickly but inefficiently". Such devices typically have slower CPU's and smaller memory footprints. Such devices cannot afford the overhead of compiling highly-optimized code. This JIT is referred to as the **economy JIT**. The basic model used by the economy JIT is to translate one IL instruction into a corresponding native instruction or instructions.

The average PC does not suffer the same constraints as a PDA or set-top box. On a normal computer, the JIT will compile each method and generate optimized native code. This flavor of JIT is referred to as the **normal JIT**.

The economy JIT was described as simply mapping an IL instruction to one or more native instructions. This is a simple mapping that does not require a great deal of expertise with respect to optimizing the compiled code. The economy JIT represents the minimum JIT required in order for a platform to support the .NET Framework.

Neither the economy nor the normal flavor of JIT address an application that runs all the time. It makes sense to compile applications that are used frequently (for example your browser, e-mail application, word processor, instant messaging application) directly to native code and to leave such applications compiled natively. On the server-side, ASP.NET DLLs, stored procedure call DLLs and MTS assemblies could also be cached in their natively compiled form. You could refer to such applications as installed because a pre-JIT will be run over the entire application. MSDN provides an article that addresses how to implement such an installer in an article entitled, "Walkthrough: Using a Custom Action to Pre-compile an Assembly During Installation" (mshelp://MS.VSCC/MS.MSDNVS/vsintro7/html/vxwlkWalkthroughUsingCustomActionToPrecompile AssermblyDuringInstallation.htm).

A Pre-JIT Example

The aforementioned article makes use of a .NET Framework utility, NGen.exe. In order to understand this utility, it is important to recognize that the .NET Framework utilizes, as part of its supporting infrastructure, a cache of assemblies (general assembly cache) and a cache of native images (native image cache). The GacUtil.exe utility installs assemblies within the general assembly cache. The NGen utility compiles a managed assembly into native code and installs it in the native image cache. This utility can also remove a native image from the native image cache. The format of the NGen utility's command-line is as follows:

```
ngen [options] [assemblyPath [...]] [assemblyName [...]]
```

The assemblyPath is the path to where the assembly referred to by assemblyName is located. Some of the command-line options supported by NGen are as follows:

- ❑ /debug – the native image generated and placed in the native image cache will contain debugging information.

- ❑ /delete – removes the native image specified by assemblyName from the native image cache.

- ❑ /prof – creates a native image that contains additional information used to determine the execution time of the code and the specific areas of code actually executed. This additional code is referred to as "instrumented code." The profiler uses such a native image.

- ❑ /show – if no assemblyName or assemblyPath is specified then the entire contents of the native image cache are displayed. If an assemblyName or assemblyPath is specified then the contents of the native image cache matching this assembly and/or path are displayed.

The following batch file, TestJIT.bat, found in the directory, WXLotsOfMethods, uses NGen in order to demonstrate the benefit (execution performance improvement) of pre-JIT:

```
@echo off
REM move to where the code is
cd bin\debug
ngen /delete WXLotsOfMethods.exe
echo "Start normal JIT"
WXLotsOfMethods.exe
echo "End normal JIT"
ngen /delete WXLotsOfMethods.exe
ngen WXLotsOfMethods.exe
echo "Start pre-JIT"
WXLotsOfMethods.exe
echo "End time pre-JIT"
```

The previous batch file starts out by removing the WXLotsOfMethods.exe executable from the native image cache using ngen /delete. We remove this executable from the native image cache in order to ensure that, the next time it runs, it will use the normal JIT. The application is written in C#; WXLotsOfMethods.exe contains over thirteen hundred methods. Remember that JIT occurs on a per-method basis, so to demonstrate pre-JIT a large number of methods are required.

Before the first method is called, this application displays the time. It displays the time again after the last method is called. The first time the WXLotsOfMethods.exe executable is run, the normal JIT is used. Right before WXLotsOfMethods.exe is run a second time, this executable is pre-JIT'd by specifying ngen WXLotsOfMethods.exe. When WXLotsOfMethods is run a second time it will not incur JIT overhead.

157

Running the `TestJIT.bat` batch file reveals (on a PIII 650 with 512 MB of RAM) that running `WXLotsOfMethods` in conjunction with normal JIT takes five seconds, while pre-JIT ran almost instantaneously. – these figures will vary depending on the machine. The output displayed by running `TestJIT.bat` is as follows:

```
D:\wrox\ProfNetFramework\WXNetFrameworkCh04\WXLotsOfMethods>testjit
NGen - CLR Native Image Generator - Version 1.0.2914.16
Copyright (C) Microsoft Corp. 2001. All rights reserved.
WXLotsOfMethods, Version=1.0.572.2977, Culture=neutral, PublicKeyToken
=null <debug>
"Start normal JIT"
7/26/2001 2:47:27 AM
7/26/2001 2:47:32 AM
"End normal JIT"
NGen - CLR Native Image Generator - Version 1.0.2914.16
Copyright (C) Microsoft Corp. 2001. All rights reserved.
No matched entries in the cache.
NGen - CLR Native Image Generator - Version 1.0.2914.16
Copyright (C) Microsoft Corp. 2001. All rights reserved.
WXLotsOfMethods, Version=1.0.572.2977, Culture=neutral, PublicKeyToken
=null <debug>
"Start pre-JIT"
7/26/2001 2:47:36 AM
7/26/2001 2:47:36 AM
"End time pre-JIT"

D:\wrox\ProfNetFramework\WXNetFrameworkCh04\WXLotsOfMethods\bin\Debug>
```

The statistics are skewed a bit in favor of pre-JIT. Clearly, pre-JIT benefits from the fact that `WXLotsOfMethods` has "lots of methods" (1302 to be exact). The normal JIT actually took only three milliseconds to compile each method. This number is a bit skewed in favor of normal JIT. The methods of `WXLotsOfMethods` actually contain very little code, so it is no surprise that they compiled quickly. The lesson to be learned is yes, pre-JIT is useful, but clearly it is only necessary when an application is used frequently and/or it contains a large number of methods that must be compiled before the application can even be displayed to the user.

JIT Compilation Performance Counters

During the chapter on managed memory, the concept of performance counters was introduced as a means to gain more intimate knowledge of the inner workings of the .NET Framework. The ".NET CLR Jit" performance counter category provides an insight into the behavior of the JIT compiler with respect to all applications running under the CLR (performance counter instance, `_Global_`) and individual applications running under the CLR. The performance counters associated with the category ".NET CLR Jit" are:

❑   # of Methods Jitted – number of methods compiled.

❑   # of IL Bytes Jitted – number of bytes of intermediate language (IL) compiled by JIT with respect to the methods currently compiled to native code. Methods that have been pitched (reverted from native code back to a stub) are not part of this byte total.

❑   Total # of IL Bytes Jitted – number of bytes of intermediate language (IL) compiled by JIT since the application began execution.

❑   IL Bytes Jitted / sec – bytes-per-second at which Intermediate Language (IL) bytes are JIT compiled.

❑   Standard Jit Failures – the number of methods that failed to compile using the standard JIT.

❑   % Time in Jit – percentage of time spent performing JIT compilation since the last sample was taken.

The Performance Counter associated with JIT Compilation might have a variety of uses. One example might be a web-hosting site hosting numerous web sites implemented in .NET. The cost of JIT compilation would vary tremendously depending on the content of the sites and how web surfers accessed each site. By determining the cost of JIT over time a decision can be made if pre-JIT should be used in order to enhance the performance of certain web sites. For example, the JIT-related performance counters might show some interesting spikes at a precise time for a certain web site. This web site could turn out to be handling stock transactions. The code for this web site might be pre-JIT'd before the market opens (NGen) and then the native versions removed after the market closed (NGen /delete).

An argument could be made to just pre-Jit everything. Remember that the NGen manages the natively compiled cache. This cache is akin to a processes working set. Basically, the natively compiled cache contains the code that is most frequently run on a particular instance of the .NET Framework. Compiling every piece of code natively would fill the cache and, eventually, entries that were deliberately precompiled would be forced from the cache.

The following code creates a PerformanceCounterCategory object associated with our JIT compiler category ".NET CLR Jit" The JIT-specific counters, for instance _Global_, are retrieved. A foreach loop then traverses each counter associated with the global instance (foreach (PerformanceCounter perfCount in perfCounters)) and displays the name (property, CounterName) and data (method, NextValue) associated with the specific counter. The code performing this is as follows:

```
PerformanceCounterCategory perfCat = new
    PerformanceCounterCategory(".NET CLR Jit");
PerformanceCounter [] perfCounters;
int count = 0;

perfCounters = perfCat.GetCounters("_Global_");
Console.WriteLine("Performance Counters *******************");
while (true)
{
    // Log JIT stats every n milliseconds
    foreach (PerformanceCounter perfCount in perfCounters)
    {
        Console.WriteLine("{0}: {1}",
                            perfCount.CounterName,
                            perfCount.NextValue());
    }

    Thread.Sleep(1000);
}
```

The method, Thread.Sleep, is used to have the foreach loop wake up and query every second (1000 milliseconds).

Memory Type Safety

Developers are all too familiar with the Four Horsemen of the Apocalypse: buffer underflow, buffer overflow, invalid memory access, and corrupted pointer. Within the CLR these pesky troublemakers need not be found. This is because code run under the CLR is memory type-safe. The .NET documentation simply refers to this as "type safety", but this terminology should not be confused with ensuring that a floating point value is not misrepresented as a Boolean. For example, type safety within the CLR means that there is no way for one object to access the private data member of another object. The only way to access the data member of an object is by using the methods, properties, and fields exposed by the object. There is no way for code to write too many bytes to a memory location or to refer to an address that is invalid.

The ability of the CLR to enforce type safety enables security enforcement and facilitates assembly isolation. By isolation we mean that one assembly cannot access another assembly (whether adversely or benignly). Windows developers know all too well of scenarios where one DLL (usually written by an uncooperative third party) corrupted the data and/or code of another DLL. The repercussions of this were anything from the process crashing to invalid results being generated.

Type safety of a method is validated as part of JIT compilation to native code. The following diagram demonstrates `MethodB`'s type safety being validated during JIT. The meta data of the assembly that contains `MethodB` is required in order to ensure type safety.

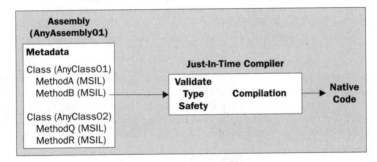

Managed code can bypass JITs type safe verification, since it is not required to be type safe. Just because code is managed does not mean it is type safe. A classic example of this is C# code (a completely managed language) contained in a section marked by the `unsafe` keyword. In order to develop unsafe code, managed code must be configured to explicitly bypass this validation.

The CLR cannot prevent unmanaged code from corrupting managed code. This is why unsafe code is disabled by default in a Visual Studio .NET C# project. The security manager of the CLR requires that permission must be granted in order for unsafe code to be called from type safe code.

Under the covers, the CLR permits unmanaged code to run by creating an instance of `SecurityPermission` from the namespace `System.Security.Permissions`. This class is a collection of flags that specify security permissions. A specific security permission is set, `SkipVerification` from the enumeration `SecurityPermissionFlag`, in order to skip the verification of the code by the assembly. This allows unmanaged code to run within an environment that is otherwise type safe.

PEVerify and Ensuring Type Safety

Compiler writers and the developers of script engines ultimately generate MSIL that should hopefully be type safe. Hope alone is not enough in the real world, so Microsoft has shipped the PEVerify Tool, `PEVerify.exe`. This tool (found under the directory \Program Files\Microsoft.NET\FrameworkSDK\Bin) ensures that IL is type safe. The command-line for `PEVerify.exe` is as follows:

```
peverify filename [/md] [/il] [other options]
```

The filename specified is for the MSIL file whose type safety is to be verified. The option /md enables the algorithm that determines if the file's meta data is valid and /il enables the algorithm that determines that the intermediate language of the file is type safe. If neither of these options is specified then both the /md and the /il check are performed by PEVerify. A variety of other options are available that specify the tool's behavior with respect to such things as: duplicate errors should be ignored (/unique), the maximum number of errors displayed (/break=maxerror), and errors should be displayed in hexadecimal form (/hresult).

To demonstrate PEVerify.exe at its finest, consider the following code snippet from the application WXThisIsUnsafe:

```
static void Main(string[] args)
{
    byte [] byteArray = new  byte [12];

    unsafe
    {
        fixed (byte* pTemp = byteArray)
        {
            // pTemp is read-only so assign it to pTrav to so
            // we can do evil (by type unsafe)
            byte *pTrav = pTemp;

            for (int i = 0; i < 15; i++, pTrav++)
            {
            }
        }
    }
}
```

The previous code takes the value of the pointer of the byteArray and assigns it to pTemp. Since pTemp is read-only (it is fixed), the value of address pTemp is assigned to pTrav. What pTrav is doing is clearly unsafe. The variable traverses through fifteen addresses, when in fact the array contains twelve elements. A partial list of ,running the PEVerify utility against WXThisIsUnsafe.exe is as follows:

D:\wrox\WXThisIsUnsafe\bin\Debug>peverify wxthisisunsafe.exe

Microsoft (R) .NET Framework PE Verifier Version 1.0.2914.16
Copyright (C) Microsoft Corp. 1998-2001. All rights reserved.

[IL]: Error: [d:\wrox\wxthisisunsafe\bin\debug\wxthisisunsafe.exe:
WXThisIsUnsafe.WXShowItIsUnsafe::Main] [local variable #0x00000002] ELEMENT_TYPE_PTR
cannot be verified.
[IL]: Error: [d:\wrox\wxthisisunsafe\bin\debug\wxthisisunsafe.exe :
WXThisIsUnsafe.WXShowItIsUnsafe::Main] [offset 0x00000011] [opcode conv.i] [found address of
SByte] Expected numeric type on the stack.

The output generated by PEVerify was abbreviated: it was significantly longer because WXThisIsUnsafe.exe was extremely unsafe. The code we used to demonstrate PEVerify was C#, but the errors flagged by PEVerify were related to IL. At the end of this chapter, the IL disassembler utility, ildasm.exe, will be presented. Using the disassembler it is possible to determine what PEVerify views as being unsafe. A portion of the IL for the application, WXThisIsUnsafe, is as follows:

```
.method private hidebysig static void Main(string[] args) cil managed
{
    .entrypoint // Code size       40 (0x28)
    .maxstack  2
    .locals ([0] unsigned int8[] byteArray, [1] unsigned int8& pinned pTemp,
             [2] unsigned int8* pTrav, [3] int32 i)
    IL_0000:  ldc.i4.s   10
```

```
IL_0002:   newarr      [mscorlib]System.Byte
IL_0007:   stloc.0
IL_0008:   ldloc.0
IL_0009:   ldc.i4.0
IL_000a:   ldelema     [mscorlib]System.Byte
IL_000f:   stloc.1
IL_0010:   ldloc.1
IL_0011:   conv.i
IL_0012:   stloc.2
IL_0013:   ldc.i4.0
IL_0014:   stloc.3
IL_0015:   br.s        IL_001f
```

PEVerify warns that the variable [local variable #0x00000002] cannot be verified. Look at the local variable [2]; this makes sense since it is defined to be a pointer type, [2] unsigned int8* pTrav. PEVerify warns also of the instruction at offset 11 being unsafe, [offset 0x00000011] [opcode conv.i]. The instruction at this offset, IL_0011:, is conv.i. A quick reference to the Tools Developers Guide document, Partition III CIL.doc, reveals that conv.i takes the following action: "Convert to natural int, pushing natural int on stack"Basically, PEVerify is warning us that it is dangerous to treat that address as an integer.

The vast majority of developers are not compiler developers, so why is PEVerify so important? The answer can be found in a buggy third-party DLL, one that ships with no source code. It causes problems and we never know why. In the time of the .NET Framework, this third-party DLL is a third-party assembly. We can use PEVerify to look inside this assembly to possibly determine if and why it is misbehaving in such a grotesque manner. The idea here is not to fix the third-party assembly but to be able to inform the third party "It's your fault things don't work."

Runtime Hosts

Before an application can be run within the CLR, code must be executed that binds the application to the CLR. The mechanism that performs this task is a piece of unmanaged code referred to as a CLR host (a runtime host). The purpose of a runtime host is to provide a bridge between the operating system that executes the code and the code that runs under .NET. According to MSDN, there will come a time when this bridge is not required and applications run directly within the CLR.

The runtime host configures how the application will run under the CLR. To put this in perspective, consider the fact that both Internet Explorer (IE) and ASP.NET have their own runtime hosts. For IE the runtime host executes .NET components found on web pages, while ASP.NET's runtime executes ASP.NET applications contained in DLLs. These two runtime hosts run under radically different environments. Internet Explorer is fine tuned to keep a human happy. Little things like ensuring the prompt redrawing of windows are important to a human. The runtime host associated with Internet Explorer is aware of this and correspondingly sets CLR to run garbage collection in a less efficient, but screen-refresh-friendly way. Lurking deep in the dark recesses of a server room is a computer that is running Internet Information Server (IIS) and running a web site's ASP.NET code. This computer is most likely headless (no monitor) and contains multiple CPUs. The runtime host for ASP.NET runs garbage collection in the most efficient manner and is optimized to run on a multi-processor computer.

The runtime hosts that are available with the .NET Framework include:

❏ Shell Applications – executables launched from the shell use a runtime host in order to run under the CLR.

❏ Web Server-side Scripts – ASP.NET code is launched from a runtime host. This runtime host is an Internet Server Application Programming Interface (ISAPI) DLL, `aspnet_isapi.dll`, found under the directory where the .NET Framework is installed, [windows folder]\Microsoft .NET\Framework\vx.x.xxxx. This DLL sets up the infrastructure that routes the Web requests to ASP.NET processes.

❏ Web client-side controls – when Internet Explorer (IE) references managed controls it uses a runtime host in order to execute these controls. This runtime host is available as of IE 5.01 or later and is actually a MIME filter.

Reverse Engineering Runtime Hosts with DumpBin

There are times in a project when it is important to know certain intimate details about the code that is being used. For example, developers who truly want to squeeze every last bit of performance from an ASP.NET application should know how such an application is loaded into the CLR and run. The runtime host implemented for ASP.NET is `aspnet_isapi.dll`. This DLL is actually compiled as native, x86 code. In our exploration of runtime hosts it is desirable to dissect this, as well as other modules shipped as part of the .NET Framework. Visual Studio.NET ships with a utility, `dumpbin.exe`, found under \Program Files\Microsoft Visual Studio.NET\Vc7\bin. The `dumpbin` tool is referred to as a Portable Execution file (PE file) `dumpbin` utility and provides tremendous insight into the files of type EXE, DLL, and OBJ. For example, specifying `dumpbin` with its /`IMPORTS` command-line option displays all of the methods imported by a particular PE file. So, to see what the `aspnet_isapi.dll` DLL imports we can execute `dumpbin` as follows:

```
dumpbin /IMPORTS aspnet_isapi.dll
```

It should come as no surprise that the output generated by `dumpbin` shows that `aspnet_isapi.dll` imports functions from the `mscoree.dll`. The information with regard to what `aspnet_isapi.dll` imports from the `mscoree.dll` is as follows (a partiall list of the `dumpbin` generated output):

```
mscoree.dll
        00000001 Characteristics
        5CED866C Address of HMODULE
        5CED4800 Import Address Table
        5CECF9B8 Import Name Table
        5CED023C Bound Import Name Table
        00000000 Unload Import Name Table
             0 time date stamp

     5CECECA6           0 CorBindToRuntimeHost
     5CECEC94           0 CorBindToRuntimeEx
     5CECEC74           0 ClrCreateManagedInstance
```

As we will see, the `CorBindToRuntimeEx` function is used by a runtime host to load the CLR into a process. The `mscoree.dll` (found on a Win32 machine under `%windir%\System32`) is a prime candidate for exploration with `dumpbin`'s /`EXPORTS` command-line option. This command-line option displays all of the functions exported by a DLL. These functions can subsequently be imported by modules such as `aspnet_isapi.dll`. A subset of the output generated by executing `dumpbin` /`EXPORTS` `mscoree.dll` is as follows:

ordinal hint RVA   name

33	0	0000F8E9	CallFunctionShim
34	1	0000F342	ClrCreateManagedInstance
35	2	0000F3EF	CoEEShutDownCOM
36	3	0000390B	CoInitializeCor
37	4	0000EF35	CoInitializeEE
21	5	0000F5FE	CoLogCurrentStack
38	6	0000EFD5	CoUninitializeCor
39	7	0000EF87	CoUninitializeEE
40	8	0000EA76	CorBindToCurrentRuntime
41	9	0000FC30	CorBindToRuntime
42	A	0000FB31	CorBindToRuntimeByCfg
43	B	0000DD47	CorBindToRuntimeByPath
44	C	0000FB0F	CorBindToRuntimeEx
45	D	0000E9C4	CorBindToRuntimeHost
46	E	0000F8AA	CorExitProcess
47	F	0000F5AC	CorMarkThreadInThreadPool
48	10	000084E4	CreateConfigStream
49	11	0000E5E4	DllCanUnloadNow
50	12	0000F943	DllGetClassObject
51	13	0000F996	DllRegisterServer
52	14	0000EE7D	DllUnregisterServer

Not all of the functions exported by `mscoree.dll` are documented. It is interesting to note that this DLL is actually a COM server since it exports functions such as `DllCanUnloadNow` and `DllGetClassObject`. Since `mscoree.dll` is a COM server, it is logical to view the type library associated with this DLL using the **OLE/COM Object Viewer** utility found in Visual Studio .NET **Tools** menu. The type library for this DLL, `mscoree.tlb`, is not contained in the DLL, but can be found under the directory for a specific installed version of the .NET Framework.

Using the **OLE/COM Object Viewer** utility to view the type library, `mscoree.tlb`, we can see documented interfaces such as `ICorRuntimeHost` and `IcorConfiguration`, which are reviewed in detail later in this chapter. Of more interest are the undocumented interfaces revealed by the **OLE/COM Object Viewer** utility, `IGCThreadControl`, `IGCHostControl`, `IGCHost` and `IDebuggerThreadControl`. An example screenshot of **OLE/COM Object Viewer** displaying the contents of `mscoree.tlb` is as follows:

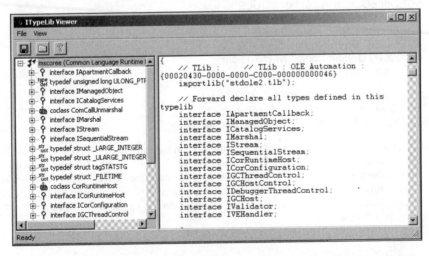

It is not mandated that OLE/COM Object Viewer be used to solely explore runtime hosts. In fact, one of the most insightful offshoots of using this utility was that interfaces supporting the low-level manipulation of garbage collection were discovered (IGCThreadControl and IGCHostControl). The standard disclaimer applies to all these undocumented functions and interfaces. Microsoft does not document them and hence they are not officially supported. This means that such functions and interfaces can be removed. The prototypes of the functions could be altered from version-to-version of mscoreee.dll.

Runtime Host Specifics

A runtime host begins its life as unmanaged code. While executing as unmanaged code, a runtime host calls the function CorBindToRuntimeEx in order to bind the CLR into the currently executing application. One runtime host (such as the runtime host for ASP.NET) could be used to bind a variety of different applications to the CLR. The CorBindToRuntimeEx function is contained in the header mscoree.h and is found in the library mscoree.lib. We are talking about a C++ header file, but the concepts here are equally applicable to VB, JScript, and C# developers. The prototype for CorBindToRuntimeEx is as follows:

```
HRESULT CorBindToRuntimeEx(/*in*/ LPWSTR pwszVersion,
        /*in*/ LPWSTR pwszBuildFlavor, /*in*/ DWORD flags,
        /*in*/REFCLSID rclsid, /*in*/ REFIID riid, /*out*/ LPVOID *ppv);
```

Previously, the dumpbin utility was used to display the functions exported by mscoree.dll. The header file, mscoree.h, provides prototypes for a subset of these functions.

CLR Version and Side-by-Side Execution

The first parameter to CorBindToRuntimeEx (parameter, pwszVersion) specifies the version of the .NET Framework to which the application is to be bound. To understand the implications, consider an application that was built, tested, and validated with CLR version v1.0.2901. Even if the present version of the CLR is v1.0.2914, your application can run on the older version of the CLR. The term for this is referred to as side-by-side execution. This is roughly analogous to being able to run Windows 2000 SP1 and SP2 on the same machine.

Legacy Windows developers recall that even if a version of Windows 98 was installed, the system DLLs could differ depending on which version of Internet Explorer was installed or which version of the C-runtime or VB-Runtime was installed. Conflicts and incompatibilities were common. Testing, validation, and installation were a nightmare. The version parameter removes these problems.

The latest version of the CLR can be specified by an application by passing in a NULL value for this parameter. The "v" character is required to be part of the version name. The previous examples of this parameter referred to specifying a fully qualified version, such as v1.0.2914. Actually, a partially qualified version could have been specified, such as v1.0. In this case, the most recent version, prefixed by v1.0, will be selected. The choice of using NULL or specifying a version is a classic conundrum. Specifying NULL reaps the benefits of any bug fixes or performance enhancements. Specifying a version ensures that a tested configuration is always used.

Developers curious as to what CLRs are installed on their machine can simply look at the contents of their [windows folder]\Microsoft.NET\Framework directory. For a typically set up Windows NT or Windows 2000 machine, this would be the directory of C:\WINNT\Microsoft.NET\Framework, which could contain multiple versions of the CLR such as:

```
05/25/2001  05:11p    <DIR>      v1.0.2204
06/10/2001  12:30a    <DIR>      v1.0.2901
06/22/2001  07:55a    <DIR>      v1.0.2914
```

From a system administrative standpoint this is an incredible boon. As a system administrator, your instant messaging infrastructure can be running on one version of the CLR (a version supported by the instant messaging vendor). The database infrastructure deployed could be running on a newer version that has some critical fixes required by the database server.

A bit of infrastructure is required to support side-by-side execution. The `mscoree.dll` DLL provides this infrastructure by acting as a start up shim. A shim in the classic sense is a small wedge of material that ensures that two larger objects are properly aligned. The `mscoree.dll` DLL acts as shim in that it ensures that the correct version of the CLR is loaded when moving from unmanaged code to using the CLR.

The `mscoree.dll` DLL exposes `CorBindToRuntimeEx` and this function allows a specific version of the CLR to be specified (passed as a parameter). Recall from previous discussions that this DLL is found in the same directory as the operating system (found on a Win32 machine under [windows folder]\System32) and not in a specific version of the .NET Framework. This is because the `mscoree.dll` DLL is responsible for choosing which version of the CLR runs.

An example of `mscoree.dll` acting as a shim and binding managed applications to a different version of the CLR is as follows:

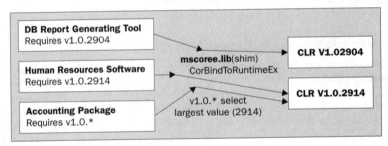

The DLLs that act as the building blocks of the CLRs functionality, `mscorsvr.dll` or `mscorwks.dll`, are contained in a .NET Framework version-specific directory.

Client versus Server Optimized CLR

The second parameter to `CorBindToRuntimeEx` (parameter, `pwszBuildFlavor`) specifies which flavor (client or server) of the CLR should be used. The flavors of the CLR are referred to as builds. Specifying "wks" for this parameter binds an application to the Workstation build. Specifying "svr" for this parameter binds an application to the Server build. Passing `NULL` for this parameter will also bind the application to the Workstation build (the default build). The terms workstation and server should not be confused with an operating system version such as NT Workstation or Windows 2000 Server. The build flavor applies only to the version of the CLR run and is not related to the operating system on which the CLR is installed.

The Server build of the CLR is optimized to take advantage of computers containing multiple CPUs. For example, Garbage Collections on a multi-processor machine can be run in parallel. If "svr" is specified for the `pwszBuildFlavor` parameter, and the machine the application is running on contains only a single processor, then the Workstation build is loaded.

Intuitively, the ASP.NET .NET Runtime should specify "svr" for this parameter while the Internet Explorer .NET Runtime should specify "wks".

Garbage Collection Optimization

The third parameter to `CorBindToRuntimeEx` (parameter, `flags`) specifies the flags that dictate how the application bound to the CLR will handle Garbage Collection and whether or not the assemblies of an application will be shared between application domains. The topic of application domains will be addressed in the next section. Remember that this parameter specifies flags; this means that these unrelated settings (controlling Garbage Collection and how assemblies are loaded) can be combined when passed to the `flags` parameter.

With respect to garbage collection, the following flag value is defined in the header file, `mscoree.h`:

```
STARTUP_CONCURRENT_GC = 0x1
```

When this flag value is specified, the Garbage Collection algorithm is run concurrently. To run concurrently means that the background threads of an application perform Garbage Collection. When this flag value is not specified, Garbage Collection is run non-concurrently. When Garbage Collection is run non-concurrently, it is being executed and run by the threads that are also running the application's code. Do not interpret this to mean that the application must explicitly initiate garbage collection. When Garbage Collection is handled in a non-concurrent manner, the CLR periodically commandeers the threads running the application's code.

On the positive side, non-concurrent garbage collection is more efficient, because it means that there is no context switch required to perform this task. A context switch is when the CPU switches from processing one thread to another. CPUs do this all time, but limiting context switches serves to improve performance.

On the negative side, non-concurrent garbage collection could adversely affect an interactive application such as Internet Explorer. Remember that Internet Explorer is an application designed to keep a human happy by performing tasks such as the redrawing of windows in a timely manner. Humans do not appreciate having their video conference or shoot-em-up game interrupted by garbage collection. For interactive applications, the Garbage Collection flag should be specified as `STARTUP_CONCURRENT_GC` in order to have GC run concurrently.

For non-interactive applications such as ASP.NET, non-concurrent Garage Collection (setting no Garbage Collection flag value for the `flags` parameter) is preferable, because it is more efficient. Web servers in general, databases, e-mail routers, and fax gateways are all candidates for non-concurrent Garage Collection. The `STARTUP_CONCURRENT_GC` flag is mostly independent of which build of the CLR is specified Workstation ("wks") or Server ("srv"). We say mostly, because on a uni-processor machine, the type of garbage collection specified by the runtime host may be ignored. On a uni-processor machine, if concurrent garbage collection is specified (the least efficient form of garbage collection) for build flavor "svr", then non-concurrent garbage collection will be used (the most efficient version).

Application Domains: Sharing and Isolating Assemblies

In addition to configuring Garbage Collection concurrently, the third parameter to `CorBindToRuntimeEx` (parameter, `flags`) specifies whether or not the assemblies of an application will be shared between domains. To understand the concept of a domain we go back in time to the days of Windows 3.1 and DOS. During these primitive times, an application could crash the computer because the operating system was running in the same address space as the application. There was no isolation between the operating system and application. Under Win32, each process maintained its own address space separate from the operating system. Everything worked smoothly so long as one process contained one application. But what happened if a web server loaded a DLL written by an application developer? Similarly, what happened if a database server loaded a DLL written by an application developer? Most of the time things went smoothly, but occasionally the DLL implementing the application would write to memory that didn't belong to it, memory that belonged to the server in which the DLL was loaded. Such random memory corruptions had a tendency to cause web servers, databases, and other such servers to crash. To prevent this from happening, Windows 2000 provided an executable, `dllhost.exe`, which ran a DLL inside a separate process. This provided a level of isolation for applications developed in technologies such as ASP, MTS,, and ISAPI. Although isolation improved reliability, it did degrade performance, because what used to be intra-process were now inter-process.

Fast forward in time to the .NET Framework, CLR, and managed applications. When managed code is run, the .NET Framework has verified that such code is type safe. This means that a .NET application cannot stray into another application's address space, even if they are running in the same process. The .NET construct that allows multiple applications to run within the same process is the application domain. Under .NET, applications are isolated on a per-domain level. Application code in one domain cannot directly access code or data in another domain. Imagine the case of one process containing three application domains. If each of these domains called the same assembly, the CLR would (by default) load three instances of this assembly. This means three separate copies of an assembly's code and data.

Loading three separate copies of an assembly is costly from a memory standpoint, because each application cannot share the code contained in the same assembly. In recognition of this, it is possible to specify that assemblies can be shared between domains. Such an assembly is said to be domain neutral. For an assembly that is domain neutral, code would be shared between all domains in the same process. For such an assembly, static data would not be shared, but would instead be instantiated on a per-domain basis. This isolation of the static data requires additional logic to be executed each time such a data member is accessed. Frequently accessing static data would thus incur a performance hit.

Keeping this in mind, we revisit the application domain-specific flags associated with the `CorBindToRuntimeEx` function (as specified in the header file, `mscoree.h`):

```
STARTUP_LOADER_OPTIMIZATION_SINGLE_DOMAIN      = 0x1 << 1
STARTUP_LOADER_OPTIMIZATION_MULTI_DOMAIN       = 0x2 << 1
STARTUP_LOADER_OPTIMIZATION_MULTI_DOMAIN_HOST  = 0x3 << 1
```

When the `STARTUP_LOADER_OPTIMIZATION_SINGLE_DOMAIN` flag is specified, none of the assemblies are loaded domain neutral (fast performance, but worst memory impact). The one exception to this is the `mscorlib` assembly, which is always loaded domain neutral. This DLL must be domain neutral, because it is what starts things off and it must be accessible to each application domain. Specifying the flag, `STARTUP_LOADER_OPTIMIZATION_MULTI_DOMAIN_HOST`, causes all assemblies to be loaded as domain neutral.

The `STARTUP_LOADER_OPTIMIZATION_MULTI_DOMAIN` flag also causes all strongly-named assemblies to be loaded domain neutral. In order for an assembly to be strongly named, its name must be globally unique and precautions have to be taken to ensure that the assembly is as it was when originally built. This means that a strongly-named assembly cannot be altered, either accidentally or with malicious intent. A strong-named assembly is globally unique due to a combination of its name, version, optional culture information, a public key, and a digital signature. This digital signature is generated using the file in the assembly that contains the assembly manifest. This manifest contains all file names for the assembly and their hashes.

Which of these flags is specified by any of the .NET runtime hosts (shell, ASP.NET, or IE) is not immediately intuitive. When Internet Explorer launches a managed control, an ideal scenario would be for the IE runtime to look at the memory footprint of the machine on which it is running. If the machine has a lot of memory available then `STARTUP_LOADER_OPTIMIZATION_SINGLE_DOMAIN` could be specified as a flag to `CorBindToRuntimeEx`. Given enough memory, we choose speed over memory utilization. If memory is a constraint on the host, the IE runtime could specify `STARTUP_LOADER_OPTIMIZATION_MULTI_DOMAIN` (memory conservation over speed).

Using Application Domains

We have looked at application domains as a way for runtime hosts to specify what level of isolation is used by each application deployed by the runtime host. An application can also create and configure its own application domain using the `AppDomain` class from the `System` namespace.

One use of an application-created Application Domain is to specify how assemblies should be loaded. For example, the Application Domain in which a program is run might declare assemblies are loaded domain neutral (fastest but least safe approach), but by creating an Application Domain, the program can force assemblies to be loaded as single domain (slowest and safest approach).

In order for an application to create an Application Domain, the application must first create a class of type `AppDomainSetup`:

```
AppDomainSetup appDomainSetup = new AppDomainSetup();
```

The `AppDomainSetup` class contains a property, `LoaderOptimization`, that can take a value of `MultiDomain`, `MultiDomainHost`, and `SingleDomain`.

So, in order to specify that that internal resource should not be shared (highest safety level but lowest performance) the following could be specified when setting up the Application Domain:

```
appDomainSetup.LoaderOptimization = LoaderOptimization.SingleDomain;
```

Once the Application Domain setup information has been specified, a new Application Domain can be created using `AppDomainSetup`'s `CreateDomain` method. When this domain is not required anymore it can be unloaded using `AppDomainSetup`'s `Unload` method. The basic shell for an application to use when creating its own Application Domain is as follows:

```
AppDomainSetup appDomainSetup = new AppDomainSetup();
Evidence evidence = new Evidence();
AppDomain ad;

// setup Evidence object (security) here
appDomainSetup.LoaderOptimization = LoaderOptimization.SingleDomain;
ad = AppDomain.CreateDomain(domainName,
                            evidence,
                            appDomainSetup);

//**********************************************************
//Run within AppDomain here
//**********************************************************

AppDomain.Unload(ad);
```

The previous code snippet created an application domain in which an application could run. The specific region in which the application should be run is documented: `//Run within AppDomain here`. All code between the `CreateDomain` method of `AppDomain` and the `Unload` method of `AppDomain` will run within the created application domain.

IL Disassembler (ildasm.exe)

Just as the Intermediate Language (IL) assembly code can be compiled using the IL assembler, `ilasm.exe`, this language can be disassembled using the .NET SDK's IL disassembler, `ildasm.exe`. This utility is found under the directory \Program Files\Microsoft.NET\FrameworkSDK\Bin. By default, this directory is not part of your command-line path and requires that `VSVars32.bat` be run.

Before introducing what the disassembler can do, a reason for using this utility needs to be established. Over the years, the classic use of a disassembler has been to reverse engineer code. This task was always quite difficult because native assembly code was not known for its readability. IL is a different beast. It is higher level and, frankly, readable even to a layperson. This section will introduce the various features of the disassembler. At the end of this sectio,n the `File` class from the `System.IO` namespace will be explored in more detail. Specifically, `File`'s `AppendText` method will be reverse engineered. What is truly terrifying is that reverse engineering the functionality of `AppendText` is truly trivial.

The IL Disassember can display its output to a file, to the console window, or to a GUI provided by `ildasm.exe`. By default the GUI variant is used, but using the command-line option `/TEXT`, the ouput can be directed to the console; using `/OUT=filename`, the output can be directed to a file named "filename".

The assembler (`ilasm.exe`) and disassembler (`ildasm.exe`) can be used together. What the dissembler generates can be re-assembled. Clearly, if command-line options are specified for `ildasm.exe` that limit the output generated, these options might also limit whether or not the IL assembly generated can be assembled. To put the disassembler in perspective, consider the following VB application, `WXHiWorld01.exe`:

```
Module Module1
    Sub Main()
        Console.Out.WriteLine("Hello World!")
    End Sub
End Module
```

From a batch file it would be possible to execute the following, which disassembles `WXHiWorld01.exe` into an IL assembly file, `HiWorld.il`. This assembly language file is then assembled using `ilasm.exe`. At this stage, the new version of the "Hello World" application, `HiWorld.exe`, can be run. The contents of a batch file that performs these task is as follows:

```
ildasm /OUT=HiWorld.il WXHiWorld01.exe
del HiWorld.exe
ilasm HiWorld.il /OUT=HiWorld.exe
HiWorld.exe
```

The `del HiWorld.exe` line is akin to a magician saying, "Nothing up my sleeve". Before `ilasm.exe` is run to create `HiWorld.exe`, the `del` command ensures that no previous version of `HiWorld.exe` exists.

IL Disassember Console Output

The `ildasm` executable contains a variety of command-line options that limit what is disassembled. When using `ildasm` and directing output to a console window it makes sense to limit the output generated. For example, the following is a perfectly legal way to disassemble the entire `mscorlib` DLL and direct the disassembled output to the console:

```
C:\WINNT\Microsoft.NET\Framework\v1.0.2914>ildasm /TEXT mscorlib.dll
```

The output from this operation is 916,881 lines of text (yes, nearly a million). Clearly, it benefits us to limit this output, unless we have taken a course in ultra-speed-reading. Before altering the output generated by `ildasm.exe` we will look at a disassembled example significantly less than a million lines of code. For example, the disassembly of our VB.NET "Hello World" application, `WXHiWorld01.exe`, generates the following:

```
.custom instance void
[Microsoft.VisualBasic]Microsoft.VisualBasic.Globals/StandardModuleAttribute::.cto
r() = ( 01 00 00 00 )
.method public static void  Main() cil managed
{
    .entrypoint
    .custom instance void [mscorlib]System.STAThreadAttribute::.ctor() =
            ( 01 00 00 00 )
    // Code size       19 (0x13)
    .maxstack  8
    IL_0000:  nop
    IL_0001:  call        class [mscorlib]System.IO.TextWriter
                            [mscorlib]System.Console::get_Out()
    IL_0006:  ldstr       "Hello World!"
    IL_000b:  callvirt    instance void
                            [mscorlib]System.IO.TextWriter::WriteLine(string)
    IL_0010:  nop
    IL_0011:  nop
    IL_0012:  ret
} // end of method Module1::Main
```

The disassembled code includes a standard constructor for the class (`.ctor()` in IL). The threading model for the application is specified when the constructor is executed, `System.STAThreadAttribute`. Clearly, the threading model of this application is a single-threaded apartment. This constructor, `.ctor()`, was not implemented in the previous handwritten IL example. Also, in the previous code snippet the size of the evaluation stack is set to eight items using the directive `.maxstack 8`. Each line of IL disassembled code includes a label such as `IL_0000`, `IL_0001`, etc.

Some notable command-line options to `ildasm` that will limit or change the output generated include:

- ❏ `/BYTES` – disassembly generated includes the bytes in hexadecimal of the assembly dissembled. This hexadecimal representation is included as IL assembly comments.

- ❏ `/RAWEH` – disassembly generates the exception-handling portion of code in raw form.

- ❏ `/TOKENS` – disassembly shows meta data tokens of the classes and their members.

- ❏ `/VISIBILITY=<vis>[+<vis>...]` – limits what is disassembled (visible). The permissible values to limit include `PUB` for public item, `ASM` for assembly items and `PRI` for private items.

- ❏ `/PUBONLY` – only public items are included in the disassembly. This is equivalent to the command-line option `/VIS=PUB`.

- ❏ `/SOURCE` – disassembly includes the original source lines as comments in the IL assembly code.

- ❏ `/LINENUM` – disassembly includes the line numbers corresponding to the line numbers in the original source code.

Specifying /SOURCE and /LINENUM for our previous disassembly of WXHiWorld01.exe generates the following:

```
//000003:       Sub Main()
IL_0000:  nop
.line 4:9
//000004:           Console.Out.WriteLine("Hello World!")
IL_0001:  call       class' [mscorlib]System.IO.TextWriter
[mscorlib]System.Console::get_Out()
IL_0006:  ldstr      "Hello World!"
IL_000b:  callvirt   instance void
[mscorlib]System.IO.TextWriter::WriteLine(string)
IL_0010:  nop
.line 5:5
//000005:       End Sub
IL_0011:  nop
IL_0012:  ret
} // end of method Module1::Main
```

In the previous code snippet, line three of the original source code was Sub Main(), while line four of the original source code was Console.Out.WriteLine("Hello World!"). The line number and source code was only available because the build was a debug build. A release build would not produce this information.

The previous command-line options apply to ildasm.exe in console mode, when output is generated to a file, and in GUI mode. The following command-line options only apply and are valid when ildasm.exe generates output to a file or to a console window:

❑   /NOIL – disassembly does not generate IL assembler code. This option lives up to its name and produces nothing except for a line identifying the version of the ildasm.exe executed.

❑   /ITEM=<class>[::<method>[(<sig>)]] – limits disassembly to only a particular item.

❑   /ALL – this options acts as if /HEADER, /BYTES, and /TOKENS had been specified on the command-line.

❑   /HEADER – disassembly output includes information with respect to PE files header information. This header information is similar to information retrievable with DumpBin. A portion of IL generated when this option is specified for WXHiWorld01.exe is as follows:

```
// PE Header:
// Subsystem:                     00000003
// Native entry point address:    000025fe
// Image base:                    11000000
// Section alignment:             00002000
// File alignment:                00000200
// Stack reserve size:            00100000
// Stack commit size:             00001000
// Directories:                   00000010
// 0        [0       ] address [size] of Export Directory:
// 25a4     [57      ] address [size] of Import Directory:
// 6000     [858     ] address [size] of Resource Directory:
// 0        [0       ] address [size] of Exception Directory:
// 0        [0       ] address [size] of Security Directory:
// 8000     [c       ] address [size] of Base Relocation Table:
// 4000     [1c      ] address [size] of Debug Directory:
```

```
// 0         [0        ] address [size] of Architecture Specific:
// 0         [0        ] address [size] of Global Pointer:
// 0         [0        ] address [size] of TLS Directory:
// 0         [0        ] address [size] of Load Config Directory:
// 0         [0        ] address [size] of Bound Import Directory:
// 2000      [8        ] address [size] of Import Address Table:
// 0         [0        ] address [size] of Delay Load IAT:
// 2008      [48       ] address [size] of CLR Header:
```

The /HEADER information displayed includes information on the address where DLLs are loaded, what delay load DLLs are included, what regions handle static thread local storage, the offset of the CLR header, and a variety of other useful information.

IL Disassembler GUI

The ildasm utility can be executed as follows in order to disassemble mscorlib.dll and at the same time to display the disassembled output to a GUI:

```
C:\WINNT\Microsoft.NET\Framework\v1.0.2914>ildasm mscorlib.dll
```

When ildasm.exe is run for this DLL, the following window is displayed:

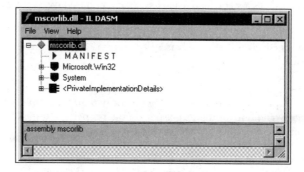

The main window displayed contains a tree of entries each prefixed by a symbol. These symbols are defined as follows:

 – Selecting this icon will reveal more info.

 – The item is a namespace such as System or Microsoft.Win32. Selecting this icon will reveal the contents of the namespace (classes, structures, enumerations, etc.).

 – The item is a class, such as AppDomain and AppDomainSetup, found in the System namespace. Selecting this icon will reveal the contents of the class (methods, properties, fields, etc.).

– The item specifies a type passed by value. For example, with the System namespace Byte is passed by value, as is the DateTime structure.

 – The item specifies an interface. Under the System namespace, interfaces such as IAppDomainSetup and _AppDomain are available.

 – The item specifies a method, such as the get_Second method, exposed by the System's DateTime structure. This method corresponds to the property Second. In method form, this specifies only the get portion of the property. DateTime also exposes methods that are not used to implement a property. ToLocalTime is also a method of DateTime.

 – The item specifies a static method such as the GetSystemFileTime exposed by System's DateTime.

 – The item specifies an enumeration, such as AttributeTargets, found in the System namespace. Remember that an enumeration is actually a class derived from System.Enum, so double-clicking on the enumerator icon will reveal fields and static fields.

 – The item specifies a field, such as MillisPerDay, exposed by the System's DateTime structure.

 – The item specifies a static field, such as ticks, exposed by the System's DateTime structure.

 – The item specifies an event, such as FileSystemWatcher, from the System namespace.

 – The item specifies a property, such as Second, exposed by the System's DateTime structure. A property is represented by one or two methods (one for the get aspect of the property and one for the put aspect of the property). Remember that not all properties support both get and put.

Armed with knowledge of what each symbol in ILDasm's main window means, we can ascertain that for the System assembly's manifest there is "more information" .Double-clicking on this displays a window that basically contains the manifest-related output generated by the console window version of ILDasm.

Using the tree view provided by the ILDasm GUI, it is possible to navigate to namespace, method, class, property, enumeration, etc. within the assembly (mscorlib.dll) or an assembly it references (for example Microsoft.Win32 or System referenced by mscorlib.dll). For example, System.IO's File class could be explored as follows:

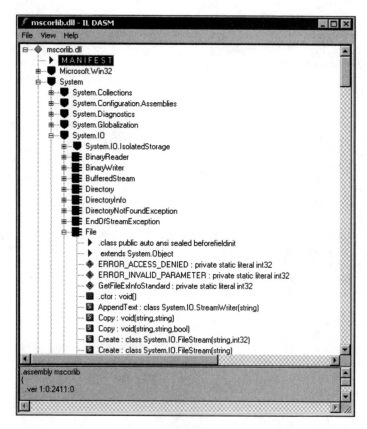

From the previous window, double-clicking on any leaf in the tree will display the IL assembly code for the clicked-up method, enumeration, property, etc. It is vastly simpler to navigate an assembly in this manner than it would be to read the million or so lines generated when the IL assembly code was placed in a file. Double-clicking on `AppendText` reveals:

```
.method public hidebysig static class System.IO.StreamWriter
        AppendText(string path) cil managed
{
  // Code size       28 (0x1c)
  .maxstack  8
  IL_0000:  ldarg.0
  IL_0001:  ldnull
  IL_0002:  call bool System.String::op_Equality(string, string)
  IL_0007:  brfalse.s  IL_0014
  IL_0009:  ldstr      "path"
  IL_000e:  newobj     instance void
            System.ArgumentNullException::.ctor(string)
  IL_0013:  throw
  IL_0014:  ldarg.0
  IL_0015:  ldc.i4.1
  IL_0016:  newobj instance void System.IO.StreamWriter::.ctor(string, bool)
  IL_001b:  ret
} // end of method File::AppendText
```

The implementation is quite informative – for example, it shows AppendText, making sure that the string passed in contains a legitimate value. This check is performed by placing the path argument on the evaluation stack (ldarg.0) followed by placing NULL on the top of the evaluation stack (ldnull). These two values are then compared as follows:

```
IL_0002:  call bool System.String::op_Equality(string, string)
```

If the strings are equal an exception is thrown of type ArgumentNullException, where the parameter that generated this exception is specified to be "path":

```
IL_0007:  brfalse.s  IL_0014
IL_0009:  ldstr      "path"
IL_000e:  newobj     instance void
               System.ArgumentNullException::.ctor(string)
```

If the path parameter is not NULL then the code jumps to line IL_0014 (branch on False, brfalse.s IL_0014, where ".s" is the return value off op_Equality placed on the stack). At this line in the IL assembly code, parameters are pushed on the evaluation stack. Specifically, the path parameter is pushed (ldarg.0) and a value of TRUE is pushed (ldc.i4.1). With two parameters on the stack we can now create a StreamWriter object that will handle the AppendText operation:

```
IL_0016:  newobj instance void System.IO.StreamWriter::.ctor(string, bool)
```

This example clearly showed just how simple it is to use the disassembler to reverse engineer an assembly's functionality. You should be aware that your own assemblies can be disassembled just as easily.

Summary

This chapter looked at how code deployed for .NET is actually executed. Developing directly in IL assembly was introduced using ilasm.exe, along with the pros and cons of the various JIT compilers that translate IL into native code. It is possible to take the JIT for granted, or a developer can be proactive and choose to Pre-JIT. Developers who thoroughly understand the .NET infrastructure and take these extra steps will ship the most efficient .NET applications. This understanding should include a working knowledge of utilities such as ngen.exe and gacutil.exe.

Benefits of the CLR, such as managed code and type safety, were reviewed. Runtime hosts and Application Domains were also introduced. Runtime hosts demonstrated a way for a developer to ensure that their applications were fully optimized. Developing a custom runtime host was demonstrated and once again developers were afforded the opportunity to further optimize the applications deployed under .NET.

Finally, the IL Disassembler was introduced. This is a great tool for gaining insight into how assemblies are implemented and how to examine any piece of code within the .NET Framework. Other utilities, such as tblexe.exe and dumpbin.exe, were also introduced that gave more insight into .NET assemblies.

Probably the biggest lesson learned is that EXEs and DLLs are composed of IL. This might sound obvious in retrospect, but a novice can easily just "assume" that all EXE's and DLL's are native code, because, after all, both IL and native code produce Portable Execution (PE) files. .NET EXEs will not run on a machine unless .NET is installed. Without .NET there is no JIT and without JIT there is no native code. Without .NET there is no runtime host to launch the native code and no CLR in which to run the code, even if the native code was launched.

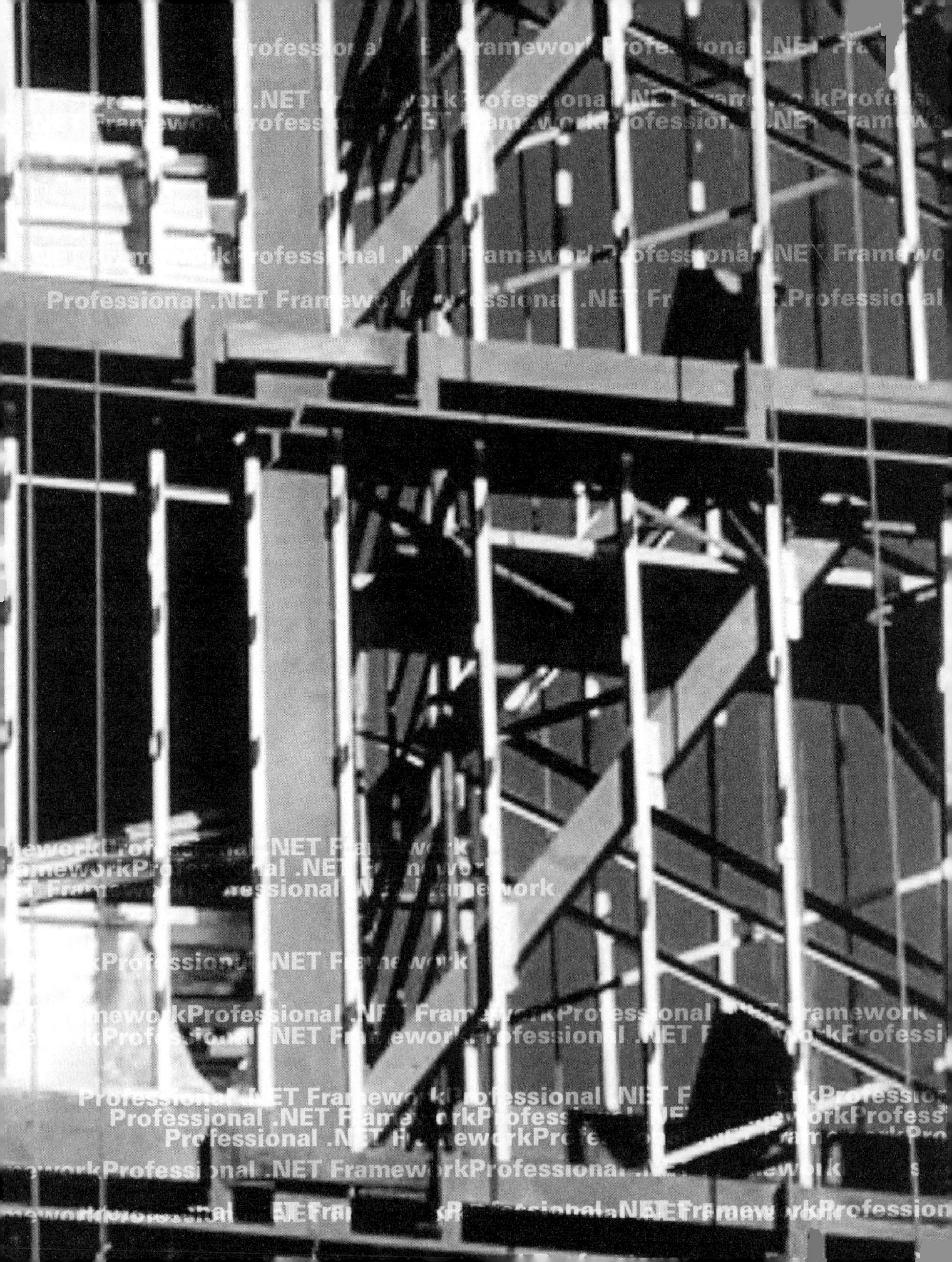
Professional .NET Framework

6
System Classes

In this chapter, we will have a look at the huge number of base classes exposed by the .NET framework that provide a wealth of functionality to applications written in a managed environment. The .NET framework classes can be considered as a replacement for Win32 API functions and the custom COM components like MFC, ATL and the MSXML parser that Microsoft provides. The nice thing about the .NET framework is that once you learn the base classes available, you can use them from any one of the .NET-aware languages like VB.NET, C#, Jscript.NET, MC++ or any other language that compiles to MSIL.

In this chapter, we will see how to carry out some of the frequently performed operations such as reading files, writing to files, accessing the registry and many more, using the base classes supplied by the .NET framework. The number of classes present in the framework is so vast that we cannot hope to give a comprehensive coverage of all the classes; instead we will pick some of the common programming tasks and see how to accomplish them using these set of classes. We will also see how to use the WinCV tool that is bundled with the framework to explore the available base classes. Specifically we will:

- ❑ Understand the importance of the `System` namespace in the .NET framework
- ❑ See how to use the `String` class for the handling of strings
- ❑ Discuss the methods and properties of the `StringBuilder` class and its advantages over the `String` class
- ❑ Use the classes present in the `System.Collections` namespace to create applications that demonstrate the usage of collection classes
- ❑ Learn to debug, trace the execution of code and record events in the Windows 2000 event log
- ❑ Understand how to implement file handling and file monitoring capabilities in applications
- ❑ See how to access the registry programmatically to retrieve registry settings

❑ Connect to the Internet and retrieve resources using the classes present in the `System.NET` namespace

❑ Manipulate date and time by making use of the classes in the `System` namespace

❑ Use the `Array` class to create, search, and sort arrays

❑ Make intelligent use of the `Exception` class for handling and processing errors

❑ Implement the functionalities exposed by the `RegEx` class to create regular expressions

❑ Learn to use the `Math` class to perform common mathematical operations

Applications of the System Namespace

The .NET framework class library is not just one more class library from Microsoft, similar to the ones that are present in the Win32 environment. Instead the .NET framework provides completely new, well-organized, object-oriented and hierarchical classes that expose a unified programming model for the developers to consume functionalities in a manner that is consistent across languages and platforms.

Before we delve into the classes available, we will first look at how to figure out what classes are available in the class library using the WinCV tool.

The WinCV Tool

The Windows Class Viewer (WinCV) tool is used to examine the classes available in the .NET framework. It allows us to quickly look up information about a class based on a search pattern. The class viewer internally uses reflection capabilities provided by the common language runtime to reflect on a type. This tool comes in handy, for example, when we want to find out which namespace to import, or what assembly to reference for using a particular class.

When you type `wincv` at the command prompt, you will get a window that consists of two panes with the left pane showing information about the classes, the namespace and the assembly. When you select a particular class in the left pane, the right pane shows more information about the selected class by showing the properties and methods it contains.

❑ Let us say, for example, we want to search for the class SqlConnection, which is required for establishing a connection with the SQL Server database. If we type in SqlConnection in the Searching For textbox, we see a list of classes that closely match the name SqlConnection. We can see from the search result that the SqlConnection class is contained in the System.Data.SqlClient namespace. We can also see that the System.Data.SqlClient namespace is contained in the System.Data.dll assembly. From this, we can understand that we need to import the System.Data.SqlClient namespace and reference the System.Data.Dll assembly to be able to start using the SqlConnection class in our application.

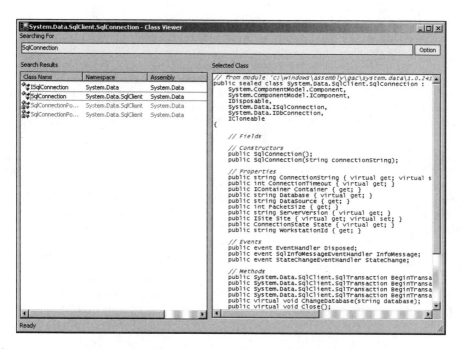

It is also important to point out that when we create a new project using Visual Studio.NET, by default, some of the assemblies are automatically referenced and a few important namespaces that are part of the referenced assemblies are also imported. We can see the list of assemblies referenced in a project by opening up the **References** folder in the Solution Explorer. To see the list of namespaces imported in the project, we need to follow either of the following steps, depending on the language we use to create the project.

❑   If you are creating a C# project, you can see the list of namespaces imported in the current project at the top of the C# class file that was created by default. For example, if you create a Windows application, the following namespaces are imported by default: System, System.Drawing, System.Collections, System.Windows.Forms and System.Data.

❑   If you are creating a VB.NET project, you can see the list namespaces imported by right-clicking on the project name in the **Solution Explorer**, selecting **Properties** from the context menu and then navigating to the **Imports** property page. Through this, we can also import namespaces into our project, which is an alternative approach to writing Imports <namespace> in the code.

Word of Caution

If you choose VB.NET to develop .NET applications, you will often have the option to choose between the functionality available in the VB language and the classes provided by the .NET framework. For example, manipulating arrays and using dates, times, and strings are some of the frequently performed operations that can be performed using any one of the above-mentioned ways. If you are an experienced VB programmer, you will have the tendency to stick with the well-tried and proven ways of implementing things using the core VB language. However, I would encourage you to unlearn these aspects and use the classes supplied by the .NET framework, as it can be guaranteed that Microsoft have optimized these classes to the hilt to allow developers to build high performance, scalable .NET applications.

For example, to find out the length of the string, you would use the `Len` method in VB6. You can use the same `Len` method in VB.NET to determine the length of the string due to the presence of the `Microsoft.VisualBasic` namespace that is imported into any VB.NET project by default. However, the .NET way of doing it is to use the `Length` property of the string object whose length we want to calculate. This approach not only facilitates the use of the consistent programming model supplied by the .NET framework, but also insulates us from the worries of backward compatibility issues that might arise in the future. Also, using the classes supplied by the .NET framework allows us to port our applications to other languages much more easily because of the single programming interface that the CLR exposes.

String Handling

The .NET framework provides the `System.String` class to perform string manipulations such as determining the length of the string, searching for substrings, changing the case of a string, comparing two strings, and many more. In the next section, we will see how to carry out string-related operations using the `System.String` class.

System.String

The `System.String` class provides rich functionality for manipulating strings. We determine the length of the string using the `Length` property. To identify the first instance of a substring within a string, we use the `IndexOf` method. `IndexOf` returns the starting position of the substring if it is found (with the first character located at position 0) or -1 if the substring is not found and it performs a case-sensitive search.

While invoking `IndexOf`, we can also specify optional parameters that let us limit the search by specifying the starting and ending position within the string to search. The `LastIndexOf` method is identical to `IndexOf`, except that it searches for the last instance of a substring. To change the case of a string to uppercase or lowercase, we can use the `ToUpper` and `ToLower` methods of the `System.String` class.

The `Compare` method is used to compare two strings for equality. Compare returns 0 if the strings are equal, a negative number if the first string is less than the second, or a positive number if the first string is greater than the second string. `Compare` is a static method and you can also pass the `Compare` method an optional third parameter with a value of `True`, to ignore case while doing the comparison. The `Split` method can be used to convert a string to an array of substrings. We need to pass the `Split` method a separator character of type `Char` that it uses to split the strings.

We will look at some sample code to understand the usage of the `String` class. The application we create for the demonstration looks like this.

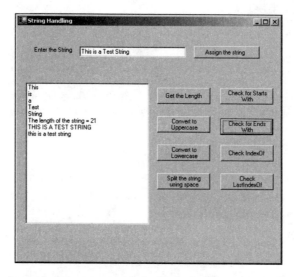

Let us start our explanation with the AddItem method, which takes a string as an argument and adds the passed string to the listbox that is used to display the informational messages.

```
    Private Sub AddItem(ByVal sDisplayMessage As String)
    lstMessages.Items.Add(sDisplayMessage)
End Sub
```

Let us consider the following variable declaration. The variable sMessage is assigned the value entered in the textbox, when we type the string in the textbox and click the command button **Assign the string**.

```
    Private sMessage As String
```

To get the length of the string, we invoke the length property by using the following line of code:

```
    AddItem("The length of the string = " & sMessage.Length().ToString())
```

We convert the contents of the string to uppercase by invoking the ToUpper method. This method returns the converted uppercase string, which we add to the listbox.

```
    AddItem(sMessage.ToUpper())
```

Similarly, to convert the string to lowercase, we call the ToLower method.

```
    AddItem(sMessage.ToLower())
```

The Split method allows us to separate the substrings in a string based on a delimiter, and place the substrings in a string array. The delimiter is made up of one or more characters. In the following line, when we pass the delimiter character to the Split method as an argument, it returns an array of strings.

```
    Dim arrStr() As String
    Dim str As String
    'Split the string using " " as the delimiter
```

```
arrStr = sMessage.Split(" ")
For Each str In arrStr
   AddItem(str)
Next
```

We can also check whether the string starts with a substring by calling the `StartsWith` method. This method returns `True` or `False` depending on whether the string starts with the substring.

```
Dim sCheckStarts As String
sCheckStarts = InputBox("Enter the string to be checked for starting with")
If sMessage.StartsWith(sCheckStarts) Then
   MessageBox.Show("The String starts with " & sCheckStarts)
Else
   MessageBox.Show("The String does not start with " & sCheckStarts)
End If
```

Similar to `StartsWith`, we also have an `EndsWith` method, which checks whether the string ends with the substring.

```
Dim sCheckEnds As String
sCheckEnds = InputBox("Enter the string to be checked for ending with")
If sMessage.EndsWith(sCheckEnds) Then
   MessageBox.Show("The String ends with " & sCheckEnds)
Else
   MessageBox.Show("The String does not end with " & sCheckEnds)
End If
```

As we already discussed, `IndexOf` is used to identify the first occurrence of a substring within the string.

```
Dim sInput As String
Dim iPos As Integer
sInput = InputBox("Enter the string to be used for IndexOf")
iPos = sMessage.IndexOf(sInput)
If iPos < 0 Then
   MessageBox.Show("The String '" & sInput & "' is not found within '" &
                                           sMessage & "'")
Else
   MessageBox.Show("The String '" & sInput & "' is located at the " & iPos
                   + 1 & " position in the string '" & sMessage & "'")
End If
```

`LastIndexOf` is similar to `IndexOf` except that it starts the search for the substring from the end of the string.

```
Dim sInput As String
Dim iPos As Integer
sInput = InputBox("Enter the string to be used for LastIndexOf")
iPos = sMessage.LastIndexOf(sInput)
If iPos < 0 Then
   MessageBox.Show("The String '" & sInput & "' is not found within '" &
                                           sMessage & "'")
Else
   MessageBox.Show("The String '" & sInput & "' is located at the " & iPos
                   + 1 & " position in the string '" & sMessage & "'")
End If
```

StringBuilder

String objects are immutable, which means that once they are created they cannot be changed. We have seen that many of the methods in `String` create and return new strings, which means that every time we use one of the methods in the `String` class, we create a new string object. For example, in the following line of code in C#, we create a string object called `strSentence` and assign a literal to it.

```
String strSentence = "Hello";
```

When we concatenate the literal "world" to the variable `strSentence`, it does not actually modify the `strSentence` variable; instead it creates a whole new string.

```
StrSentence = strSentence + " World";
```

This can be an expensive operation when we allocate multiple strings and perform repeated modifications to strings. If we are going to do only one string operation, then it makes sense to use `String`. However, if we are going to do multiple operations, then it is advantageous to use the `StringBuilder` object, as it allows us to modify a string in place without creating a new object. For example, if we are creating a web page on the fly by concatenating blocks of HTML code based on certain conditions to a certain string type object, then we should use the `StringBuilder` object, as it provides the best possible performance by avoiding the memory consuming string destruction and creation processes.

The `StringBuilder` class is contained in the `System.Text` namespace. The `StringBuilder` object contains a buffer that is typically initialized with a string, but the size of the buffer is usually larger than the string. This buffer can be manipulated in place without creating a new string – we can insert, append, remove, and replace characters. After we are done manipulating the characters, we can use the `ToString` method of the `StringBuilder` class to extract the finished string from it.

To use `StringBuilder`, we need to import the `System.Text` namespace into our application by having this line of code at the beginning of the program.

```
Imports System.Text (In VB.NET)
using System.Text;  (In C#)
```

Let us take a look at some of the important properties and methods that are exposed by `StringBuilder` to perform string manipulations.

The `Replace` method of `StringBuilder` allows us to replace the particular instance of a character or string with an instance of a different character or string. The following is the list of overloaded methods that `Replace` provides.

- ❑ `public StringBuilder Replace(char, char);`
  Replaces a specific occurrence of a character with a new character.

- ❑ `public StringBuilder Replace(string, string);`
  Replaces a specific occurrence of a substring with a new substring.

- ❑ `public StringBuilder Replace(char, char, int, int);`
  This method allows us to specifiy the range of characters to be considered for replacement by allowing us to indicate the index to start and the index to end in the third and fourth parameters respectively.

- ❑ `public StringBuilder Replace(string, string, int, int);`
  Similar to the above method, except that it operates on strings instead of a character.

As we can see from the above, one of the important benefits of the StringBuilder class over the String class is the number of overloads that it provides. For example, using the StringBuilder class, we can replace a specified occurrence of a character with another character in a specified range. For advanced string manipulations that require more flexibility and performance, it is recommended that we use the StringBuilder class instead of the String class due to the previously listed reasons.

Using the Append method, we can append any one of the typed objects like bool, byte, char, decimal, and so on, to the StringBuilder object. Using one of the many overloaded append methods, we can also append a specified number of characters in a string to the end of the StringBuilder. The Append method can be generalized in the following manner.

```
public StringBuilder Append(datatype);
```

The above declaration shows that the Append method takes a typed object, which is to be appended to the StringBuilder, as an argument. The data type can be any one of the following types: bool, byte, char, Decimal, double, short, int, long, object, sbyte, float, string, ushort, uint and ulong.

Let us consider the following declarations.

❑   public StringBuilder Append(bool);
     Used to append variable of type bool to the StringBuilder object

❑   public StringBuilder Append(string);
     Allows us to append a variable of type string to the StringBuilder object

❑   public StringBuilder Append(long);
     Permits us to append a variable of type long to the StringBuilder object

The Capacity property returns the maximum number of characters that the current StringBuilder object is capable of holding. The MaxCapacity property indicates the maximum number of characters that can be contained in the StringBuilder object. It defaults to 2,147,483,647, which is the maximum value that an Int32 variable can hold. We can increase the capacity of the StringBuilder object any time using the EnsureCapacity method.

The Append method allows us to append a string or any type to the end of the StringBuilder. If we pass another type, its ToString method will be called and the result appended to the StringBuilder. The Remove method permits us to remove any number of characters from any position. As we already discussed, the Replace method allows the replacement of individual characters or substrings.

Now that we have understood the different properties and methods supported by the StringBuilder class, let us analyze the overloaded constructors of the StringBuilder class to identify the different ways of constructing the StringBuilder object.

Method	Purpose
public StringBuilder()	Allows us to create a new and empty instance of the StringBuilder class
public StringBuilder(int)	Similar to the above method except that it provides us with the ability to specify the capacity of the StringBuilder

Method	Purpose
`public StringBuilder(string)`	Creates a new instance of the `StringBuilder` object from the supplied string
`public StringBuilder(int, int)`	Allows us to create a string object by indicating the capacity as well as the maximum capacity up to which it can grow
`public StringBuilder(string, int)`	Creates a new instance of the `StringBuilder` object from the passed string using the specified capacity that is supplied in the second parameter
`public StringBuilder(string, int, int, int)`	Constructs a new instance of the `StringBuilder` object using the specified substring and the given capacity. The substring to be used for creating the `StringBuilder` object is determined by using the `startindex` and `length` parameters that are passed in the second and third parameters respectively. The fourth parameter identifies the capacity of the `StringBuilder` that is going to be created

Let us look at an example to comprehend the usage of the `StringBuilder` class. The example application we are going to consider for the illustration of `StringBuilder` functionalities looks like this.

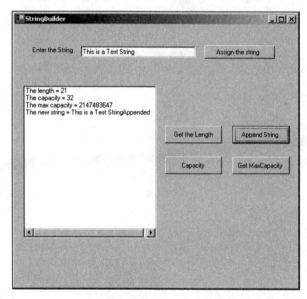

We first declare a variable of type `StringBuilder`.

```
Private mStringBuilder As New StringBuilder()
```

To append a string to the `StringBuilder` object, we execute the following set of statements.

```
Dim sNewString As String
    sNewString = InputBox("Enter the string you want to append ")
    If sNewString <> "" Then
```

```
        mStringBuilder.Append(sNewString)
        AddItem("The new string = " & mStringBuilder.ToString())
    End If
```

We can get the capacity of the `StringBuilder` object by invoking the `Capacity` property.

```
    AddItem("The capacity = " & mStringBuilder.Capacity().ToString())
```

To get the maximum capacity of the `StringBuilder` object, we need to call the `MaxCapacity` method.

Collection Classes

Collection represents a set of objects that are grouped together in a way that allows us to access each of the elements in the collection using a `For...Each` construct. Using collections, we can standardize the way in which groups of objects are handled by our programs. If we use collections, we need not worry about supplying an index to access elements, since the collection itself determines the order in which the elements are returned. Collections can be used in situations where we want to have a group of objects that are read only and we do not require the ability to modify the group of objects, because collections do not allow us to add or modify items from the group.

The `System.Collections` namespace contains a wide assortment of classes, interfaces, and structures used to manage collections. These classes provide a broad range of functionality by exposing a simple unified programming model that is easy to use. The `System.Collections.Specialized` namespace contains classes that are specifically suited for working with strongly-typed collections. An example of this would be the `StringCollection` class that is meant only for dealing with strings. `System.Array` is another collection class that derives from collection interfaces such as `ICollection`, `IList`, and `IEnumerable`.

When Microsoft designed the collections framework, they had some common design goals in mind.

❑ To provide an implementation that is highly efficient and easy to use and that acts as a replacement for the objects used to design collection-based applications in a COM environment.

❑ To allow different types of collections, such as `arraylist`, `hashtable`, `sortedlist` and so on, to work in a similar manner and with a high degree of interoperability.

❑ Since the entire collections framework is designed around a set of standard interfaces, we can easily extend the collections.

All the collection classes in the .NET framework are contained in the `System.Collection` namespace. It contains classes and interfaces that define various collections of objects, such as lists, queues, arrays, hashtables, and stacks. An important item in the collections framework is the `IEnumerator` interface, which provides us with a general purpose, standardized way of accessing the elements within a collection, one at a time. Since each collection implements the `IEnumerable` interface, we can get a reference to the enumerator class by invoking the `GetEnumerator` method of the `IEnumerable` interface.

Once we get a reference to the enumerator, we can access the individual elements in the collection class using the methods of the `IEnumerator` interface. So, with a small change, the code that is used to loop through an `ArrayList` can also be used to cycle through a `SortedList`. Collections often provide off-the-shelf solutions to a variety of problems that we face in our daily life and we should use them whenever the situation presents itself.

For example, let us consider that we are creating a custom third-party component that is designed to provide certain functionality to the consumers. As with any custom component, we might want to access data in a relational database using the classes present in the ADO.NET library. After we obtain the data, we may want to provide this data to the client. There are two ways of exposing the data to the client: we can either expose the data directly in the form of the ADO.NET objects (like `DataSet` or `SqlDataReader`), which means that consumers of our component need to learn a whole set of classes and interfaces to be able to consume the data. The other approach would be to expose all the data in the form of a collection, meaning that the consumers can use a simplified and unified approach to getting information from our component. This also allows us to publish the fact that our component always gives the results back in the form of standard collections that can be enumerated in the simplest possible way, like using a `For...Each` construct.

We will start our discussion of the collection classes by taking an overview of each interface implemented by the collection classes. These interfaces define the fundamental nature of the collection classes.

Overview of the Interfaces Present in the Collection Framework

This section provides an overview of the collection interfaces, as familiarity with the interfaces present in the Collections framework is necessary for the clear understanding of the Collection framework. The `Collection` namespace consists of the following interfaces:

- ❏ `ICollection`
  The `ICollection` interface is the core of the `System.Collections` namespace, as all the collection classes in that namespace derive from `ICollection`.

- ❏ `IList`
  This is implemented by the collection classes that need to have the ability to hold a collection of objects that can be sorted, and also to provide access to the individual elements in the collection using indices. For example, the `ArrayList` class implements the `IList` interface.

- ❏ `IDictionary`
  This is implemented by the classes that have the requirement to hold a collection of similar objects with each individual element in the collection taking the form of key-and-value pair. The `Hashtable` class implements this interface.

- ❏ `IEnumerable`
  Since `ICollection` derives from the `IEnumerable` interface, all the collection classes derive from the `IEnumerable` interface indirectly.

- ❏ `IEnumerator`
  This is implemented by all the collection classes that want to have the ability to loop through all the elements in the collection using a `For...Each` construct.

- ❏ `IDictionaryEnumerator`
  This is implemented by classes such as `Hashtable`, which stores the elements in a dictionary in the form of a key-and-value pair and it is used to enumerate the contents of the dictionary.

The following UML diagram explains the relationship between different interfaces in the `System.Collections` namespace.

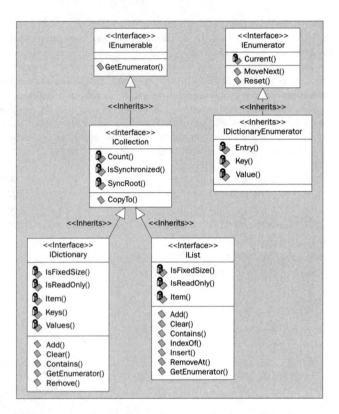

From the above diagram, we can understand that the IDictionary and IList interfaces inherit from ICollection, which in turn inherits from the IEnumerable interface. IDictionaryEnumerator derives from the IEnumerator interface and it is used to enumerate the contents of a dictionary that consists of key and value pair elements. Now that we have understood the relationship between different interfaces, let us discuss the properties and methods exposed by these interfaces.

IEnumerable and IEnumerator

Often, we will want to cycle through the elements in a collection and display each element in the collection. We can accomplish this by using the methods exposed by the IEnumerator interface. To get a reference to the enumerator interface from a collection class, we need to call the GetEnumerator() method of the IEnumerable interface. If we want to use the ForEach semantics to loop through the collection, then we need to implement the interface IEnumerable. The ForEach construct can be used in the following conditions:

- When we want to loop through a collection without modifying the contents of it, as ForEach is read-only. Instead, if we want to have the ability to modify the content, then we need to choose regular looping constructs.

- If we do not need indices while looping through a collection, then we can use ForEach, which is much simpler to use and optimized to provide better performance.

Enumerators are crucial to successful programming in the Collections framework, since they allow us to loop through the elements in the collection in a unified and consistent manner, regardless of the collection we are trying to access. In other words, eumerators provide a forward-only, read-only cursor for a group of similar objects contained in a collection. The IEnumerator interface consists of the following three methods:

❑ MoveNext – used to move to the next item in the collection and it returns true until it reaches the end of the collection, when it returns false.

❑ Current – Current is used to retrieve the value of the current item that the enumerator points to.

❑ Reset – sets the enumerator back to its initial state, which is before the first element in the collection.

Since the initial position of the enumerator is before the first element in the collection, we need to call MoveNext before we call Current, else an exception will be thrown.

ICollection and IDictionary

The ICollection interface is the foundation upon which the entire collection framework is built. The ICollection interface exposes methods and properties that are required to describe the size, enumerator, and synchronization characteristics for all the collection classes.

❑ Count – retrieves the number of elements contained in the collection

❑ IsSynchronized – returns True or False, which indicates whether access to the collection is synchronized

❑ SyncRoot – allows us to synchronize access to the collection by providing us with a synchronized wrapper object around the underlying collection

The IDictionary interface is used to manage groups of unordered objects as key-value pairs. The classes that implement IDictionary include SortedList and Hashtable. The IsFixedSize property of the IDictionary interface returns True or False depending on whether the class that implements the IDictionary interface is of fixed size. As the name suggests, the ReadOnly property allows us to determine whether the collection is read only. The Item property is used to set or get the value of the element in the collection based on the supplied key. The Keys and Values properties are used to get a reference to all the keys or all the values in the collection respectively. Finally, let us consider the properties and methods supported by the IList interface.

IList

The IList interface defines the following properties and methods:

Property or Method	Purpose
IsFixedSize	Determines if a list is of a fixed size
IsReadOnly	Allows us to determine if a list is a read-only
Item	Allows us to retrieve an item in the list using the index
Add	Allows us to add an item to the end of the list
Clear	Removes all the items in the list

Table continued on following page

Property or Method	Purpose
Contains	Allows us to determine if an item is contained within a list
IndexOf	Used to determine the index of an item within a list
Insert	Inserts an item at a specified offset in the list
Remove	Removes an item by reference in the list
RemoveAt	Removes an item by an index in the list

Since the IList interface derives from the ICollection interface, it inherits all of its members, as well as the members of IEnumerable (since ICollection derives from IEnumerable).

List of Collection Classes

Now that we have seen the base interfaces required to successfully implement the collections framework, let us look at some of the important collection classes that we will be frequently using in our applications. We will start our discussion by looking at the ArrayList class.

ArrayList

In the .NET framework, standard arrays are of a fixed length. After arrays are created, they cannot grow or shrink, which means that we must know in advance how many elements an array will hold. Sometimes, though, we may not know until runtime precisely how large an array we need. To handle this situation, the collections framework defines the ArrayList class, which can dynamically increase or decrease the number of elements it can hold. Arraylists are created with an initial size; when this size is exceeded, they are automatically enlarged. When elements are removed, it can be shrunk to a smaller size using the TrimToSize method.

The Capacity property returns the number of elements that the ArrayList is capable of storing, and Count returns the number of elements that are actually in the ArrayList. The value of the capacity is always greater than or equal to Count. While adding elements, if the value of Count exceeds capacity, then the capacity of the list is automatically doubled by resizing the arraylist. The default value for capacity is 16.

Although the capacity of an array can increase dynamically as we add objects, we can also increase the capacity of an ArrayList object manually by setting the Capacity property to an appropriate value. You might want to do this, if you know beforehand that you will be storing many more items in the collection than it can currently hold. By increasing the capacity at the start, you can prevent several costly reallocations later, thereby increasing the performance of the application. It is also possible to reduce the size of the array by invoking the TrimToSize method of the arraylist.

When working with ArrayList, we may sometimes want to obtain an actual array that contains the elements of the list. We can accomplish by invoking the ToArray method of the ArrayList. There are several instances where we will want to convert an arraylist to an array:

❑ Using an array might provide faster processing times for certain kinds of operations. Let us say, for example, we want to process all the elements in a huge arraylist in a random manner – then it is appropriate to convert that arraylist into an array, as using arrays means that we can directly navigate to the particular element in the array using indices and process it.

❑ To pass an array to a method that is not overloaded to accept a collection.

❑ To integrate collections-based code with legacy code that does not understand collections.Arraylists are particularly useful in situations where you would normally use an array, but you do not want to be concerned about things such as allocation and deallocation of memory, searching, and sorting. Since `ArrayList` implements the `IList` interface, it not only has the simplicity of a list, but it can also be considered a sophisticated array because of its ability to dynamically increase or decrease in size.

We will now look at an example application that uses `ArrayList` to demonstrate its usage.

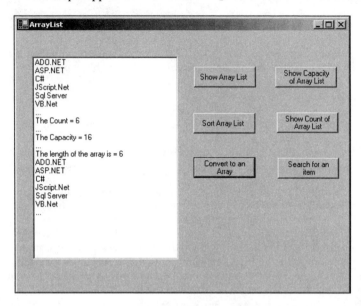

As before, the `AddItem` method is used to add elements to the listbox. For this example, we will consider an arraylist that contains information about the languages. The declaration of the arraylist is as follows.

```
Private marrLangList As New ArrayList()
```

We add elements to the arraylist using the following set of statements:

```
marrLangList.Add("VB.NET")
marrLangList.Add("C#")
marrLangList.Add("ASP.NET")
marrLangList.Add("JScript.NET")
marrLangList.Add("ADO.NET")
marrLangList.Add("Sql Server")
```

When the **Show array list** command button is clicked, we loop through all the elements in the arraylist and show them in the listbox. We use the methods of the `IEnumerator` interface to loop through the arraylist. The `GetEnumerator` method of the arraylist returns a reference to an object that is of a class that implements the `IEnumerator` interface, which is then used to enumerate all the items in the arraylist.

```
Dim oEnumerator As IEnumerator
oEnumerator = marrLangList.GetEnumerator()
While (oEnumerator.MoveNext)
    AddItem (oEnumerator.Current.ToString())
End While
```

To convert the arraylist to an array, we invoke the `ToArray` method of the arraylist that returns an array of languages in this case.

```
oArray = marrLangList.ToArray()
AddItem("The length of the array is = " & oArray.Length.ToString())
For iCtr = 0 To oArray.Length - 1
    AddItem(oArray.GetValue(iCtr).ToString())
Next
```

We can sort the contents of the arraylist using the `Sort` method. The `Sort` method is overloaded to produce different sorting behaviours depending on the requirements of the applications.

```
marrLangList.Sort()
```

The above `Sort` method does not take any arguments and it uses the default implementation of the `CompareTo` method (of the `IComparer` interface), provided by the objects contained in the collection, to sort the collection. We can customize this sorting behaviour by providing a comparer object that implements `IComparer`. We will see an example of this when we talk about the `Comparer` class in the later stages of this chapter.

The `BinarySearch` method provides an efficient and easy way of searching for items in an arraylist. When we search an arraylist using methods like `IndexOf`, the implementation of the arraylist collection class performs the search by comparing every item in the list with the value we are searching for. This sequential search may not be a concern if the arraylist being searched is smaller, but for larger arraylists, it can cause performance overheads. To avoid this overhead, we can use binary search for searching an item in the arraylist. Using binary search, we can locate the items in the collection by doing significantly fewer comparisons, thereby resulting in search times that are significantly smaller than for a linear search.

```
sSearchString = InputBox("Enter the string")
iPos = marrLangList.BinarySearch(sSearchString)
If (iPos < 0) Then
    MessageBox.Show("Item not found in the array list")
Else
    MessageBox.Show("Item is found in the " & (iPos + 1) & " position of
                                                the array list")
End If
```

It is also important to realize that the prerequisite for a binary search of an arraylist to work is that the arraylist needs to be presorted. It does not mean that you will get an error if you try to binary search an arraylist without having it sorted; instead, you will simply get unpredictable results.

Hashtable

`Hashtable` can be considered as a collection of associated keys and values that are arranged based on the hash code of the key. It creates a collection that uses a hashtable internally for storage. It stores information by using a mechanism called hashing. In hashing, the informational content of the key is used to determine a unique value, called its hash code. The hash code is then used as the index at which the data associated with the key is stored. Any object type that overrides the methods `GetHashCode` and `Equals` of the `System.Object` class can be used as keys for a hashtable. Since all the primitive datatypes, like integer and string, override these methods, they can be used as keys. The transformation of the key into hashcode is performed automatically.

The `Hashtable` class implements a hash table data structure. A hash table indexes and stores objects in a dictionary-like structure using hash codes as the object's keys. As we already discussed, hash codes are integer values that determine the identity of the objects. They are computed in such a manner that different objects are very likely to have different hash values and therefore different dictionary keys.

A Hashtable is useful if you want to be able to look up an object using another object as a key – like a dictionary for example. Since Hashtable provides efficient and fast lookups using hash codes, it can be really useful in places where we want to arbitrarily identify an element in the collection without having to go through the overhead of searching for elements in the collection in a linear fashion. For example, a shopping cart implementation of an e-commerce web site can be done efficiently by using hashtables. In the shopping cart, we can maintain a Hashtable object, which holds all the items placed by the customer in the shopping cart, in the memory, and add or remove the individual elements of the hashtable based on the consumer's actions. Since Hashtable also implements the ISerializable interface, we can also serialize and deserialize the elements (items in the shopping cart) of the Hashtable object into a file, or any other medium that is very useful in persisting the elements across multiple requests the user is likely to make to our web site.

It is important to note that Hashtable does not guarantee the order of elements in the collection and the elements in Hashtable are not sorted. If you require the elements to be ordered in your application, then SortedList will be the ideal choice.

Now that we have seen the concepts behind hashtables, let us take a look at some sample code to understand the functionalities of Hashtable.

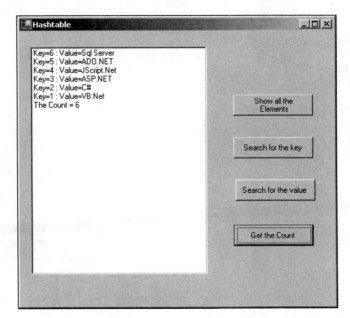

We first declare a variable of type Hashtable.

```
Private mHashtable As New Hashtable()
```

We then add elements to it by executing the following set of statements:

```
mHashtable.Add(1, "VB.NET")
mHashtable.Add(2, "C#")
mHashtable.Add(3, "ASP.NET")
mHashtable.Add(4, "JScript.NET")
mHashtable.Add(5, "ADO.NET")
mHashtable.Add(6, "Sql Server")
```

Since each element in the collection is a key-and-value pair that is of type `DictionaryEntry`, looping through all the elements in the hashtable requires the use of `IDictionaryEnumerator`, which is generally used to enumerate the collection of key-and-value pairs.

In the following line, the enumerator returned by the `GetEnumerator` method is assigned to an object variable of type `IDictionaryEnumerator`.

```
Dim oEnumerator As IDictionaryEnumerator = mHashtable.GetEnumerator()
'Clear the listbox
lstMessages.Items.Clear()
```

Once we get a reference to the enumerator, we can loop through the hashtable and display its contents using the `Key` and `Value` properties of the enumerator.

```
While (oEnumerator.MoveNext)
    AddItem ("Key=" & oEnumerator.Key & " : Value=" & oEnumerator.Value)
End While
```

We can also check to see whether the hashtable contains a particular key or value by calling the `ContainsKey` and `ContainsValue` methods respectively. These methods return `True` or `False` depending on whether the key or value is present in the hashtable. For example, in the following statements, we check to determine whether a particular value is present in the hashtable by invoking the `ContainsValue` method.

```
sValue = InputBox("Enter the value to be located")
If (mHashtable.ContainsValue(sValue)) Then
    MessageBox.Show("Value is found")
Else
    MessageBox.Show("Value is not found")
End If
```

Comparer

Objects of classes that implement `IComparable` can be ordered. In other words, classes that implement `IComparable` contain objects that can be ordered. We can use this class to compare objects and check whether they are equal. It can also be used to perform case-sensitive comparisons of strings. The `Comparer` class provides default implementation for the `Compare` method of the `IComparer` interface. The `Compare` method is used to perform a case-sensitive comparison of two objects of the same type. This method returns less than zero if the first object is less than the second object, zero if both of them are equal, and greater than zero if the first object is greater than the second.

The .NET framework classes provide excellent support for sorting the contents of a collection or an array through the use of built-in functions. However, there are times where we might want to customize the sorting behaviour according to the requirements of our application. To accomplish this, we can override the `CompareTo` method of the `IComparer` interface to produce a sorting behaviour that is in line with the requirements of our application.

Let us consider the following example in which there is a `Student` object that holds the details of a student, such as the name of the student and the marks obtained by the student. Let us say, for example, that we are loading the details of all the students present in the class into a `Student` object array and we want to show the list of students in the descending order of marks they have scored. This requirement necessitates a custom implementation of the `IComparer` interface and the following example will show us how to accomplish this.

We are ultimately aiming to produce the following:

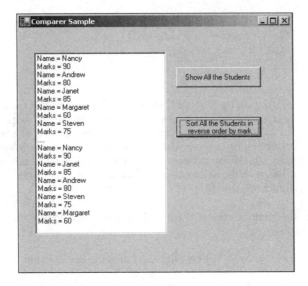

The Student class is defined as follows:

```
public class Student : IComparable
    {
        string sName;
        int iMark;

        public Student(string sName, int iMark)
        {
            this.sName= sName;
            this.iMark = iMark;
        }

        public string Name
        {
            get
            {
                return sName;
            }
        }

        public int Mark
        {
            get
            {
                return iMark;
            }
        }

        int IComparable.CompareTo(object obj)
        {
            Student oStudent = (Student)obj;
            if (this.iMark > oStudent.iMark )
                return -1;
```

```
            if (this.iMark < oStudent.iMark)
                return 1;
            else
                return 0;
        }

    }
```

As we can see from the above code, the Student class has a constructor that takes the name of the student and the marks scored by the student as its arguments. It also contains the public properties Name and Mark, which are used to expose the values present in the private member variables sName and iMark respectively. Now, let us consider the CompareTo method, which allows us to change the default sorting behavior. As we already discussed, the return value of the CompareTo method is the one that determines the sort order. Since we want our sorting to be based on the descending order of the students's marks, we compare the marks of the two student objects and return −1 in place of 1 and 1 in place of -1.

Now that we have seen the implemention of the Student class, let us look at the client code and see how the custom sorting order works.

First, we declare an array of Student objects using the following line of code:

```
private Student[] arrStudent = new Student[5];
```

In the form load event, we load all the details of all the students into the array.

```
private void Form1_Load(object sender, System.EventArgs e)
{
    //Load the details of the Students from the database
    arrStudent[0] = new Student("Nancy",90);
    arrStudent[1] = new Student("Andrew",80);
    arrStudent[2] = new Student("Janet",85);
    arrStudent[3] = new Student("Margaret",60);
    arrStudent[4] = new Student("Steven",75);
}
```

In the click event of the command button, we sort the contents of the array, enumerate them, and show them in the listbox.

```
private void cmdSortReverse_Click(object sender, System.EventArgs e)
{

    Array.Sort(arrStudent);
    foreach(Student oStudent in arrStudent)
    {
        AddItem("Name = " + oStudent.Name);
        AddItem("Marks = " + oStudent.Mark);
    }
}
```

When the static Sort method of the Array class is invoked, the custom implementation that we provided for the CompareTo method in the Student class is internally invoked, as a result of which we have all the Student objects sorted by the descending order of the marks.

NameValueCollection

The `System.Collections.Specialized` namespace contains a class named `NameObjectCollectionBase`, which is used to represent a sorted collection of associated string and string values. The string values contained in this class can be accessed either with the hash code of the key or with the index. The `NameValueCollection` class can be considered a sophisticated version of the `NameObjectCollectionBase` and it is derived from the `NameObjectCollectionBase` class. However, unlike the `NameObjectCollectionBase`, the `NameValueCollection` class can be used to store multiple string values under a single key. Because of its ability to store multiple values under one key, we can use this collection for storing query strings and form data in web pages. The capacity property returns the number of key-value pairs that the `NameValueCollection` can contain. The default initial capacity is zero. The capacity can be increased as required. We will write a simple application to understand the properties and methods of the `NameValueCollection`.

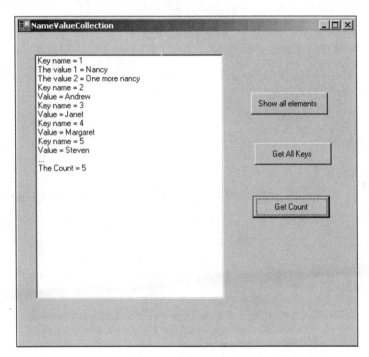

We first declare a variable of type `NameValueCollection` using the following line of code.

```
Private mNameValueCol As New NameValueCollection()
```

We then add elements to the collection using the following set of statements.

```
mNameValueCol.Add("1", "Nancy")
mNameValueCol.Add("1", "One more nancy")
mNameValueCol.Add("2", "Andrew")
mNameValueCol.Add("3", "Janet")
mNameValueCol.Add("4", "Margaret")
mNameValueCol.Add("5", "Steven")
```

Once we add elements to the collection, we can then enumerate the collection using the following code.

```
Dim oEnumerator As IEnumerator = mNameValueCol.GetEnumerator()
'Clear all the elements in the listbox
lstMessages.Items.Clear()
While (oEnumerator.MoveNext)
```

Using the `Current` property, we get the key name of the current item.

```
    sKeyName = oEnumerator.Current
    AddItem("Key name = " & sKeyName)
```

After we get the key name of a particular item, we can get all the values stored under that key by invoking the `GetValues` method of the `NameValueCollection` object.

```
    arrValues = mNameValueCol.GetValues(sKeyName)
    iLength = arrValues.Length
```

We then check the length of the returned array and if it is greater than 1, then we loop through the array and show all the values in the array in the listbox.

```
    If (iLength > 1) Then
        For iCtr = 0 To iLength - 1
            AddItem("The value " & iCtr + 1 & " = " & arrValues(iCtr))
        Next
        Else
```

If the above conditon is not met, we then call the `Get` method passing in the key name as an argument.

```
        AddItem("Value = " & mNameValueCol.Get(sKeyName))
        End If
    End While
```

To get all the keys in the collection, we use the `AllKeys` method, which returns the array of key strings present in the collection.

As we already said, `NameValueCollection` classes are very useful in situations where we want to store the form data and retrieve them at a later stage in a web page. Let us consider a simple web forms application to illustrate this. The web form consists of an `<asp:listbox>` element that provides the users with the ability to select multiple elements, and an `<asp:button>` element. When the user clicks on the button, we show all the list elements the user has selected in the listbox by using the following set of statements.

```
Private Sub Button1_Click(ByVal sender As System.Object, ByVal e As
            System.EventArgs) Handles Button1.Click
    Dim oNameValueCollection As New NameValueCollection()
    Dim arrListItems() As String
    Dim sListItem As String
    oNameValueCollection = Request.Form
    Response.Write("<br>")
    Response.Write("<br>These are the selected elements<br>")
    arrListItems = oNameValueCollection.GetValues("lstItems")
    For Each sListItem In arrListItems
        Response.Write(sListItem)
        Response.Write("<br>")
    Next
End Sub
```

We start by declaring an object of type NameValueCollection that can hold all the form data. Then we assign the Form object to the NameValueCollection object using the following statement:

```
oNameValueCollection = Request.Form
```

To get all the elements the user has selected in the listbox named lstItems, we invoke the GetValues method, passing to it the name of the control whose values we want to get.

```
arrListItems = oNameValueCollection.GetValues("lstItems")
```

Once we get the list of items in the form of an array, we then loop through the array and show it in the web form.

```
For Each sListItem In arrListItems
    Response.Write(sListItem)
    Response.Write("<br>")
Next
```

Queue

A queue represents a First-In-First-Out (FIFO) collection of objects. Queues are useful in places where we might want to do sequential processing of the messages in the same order they were stored in the queue. For example, let us say that we are monitoring a directory or a file for some predefined changes and we want to process the changes that occur in that directory or file in the same order as they occur. In that case, we can use the Queue collection object to store the details of all the changes, and from there we can process them one by one. Queues will also be very useful in creating distributed and asynchronous applications in which there is no guarantee that both sides of the communication point will always be up and running. So, queues can be used to store the intermediate data and then process them in the same order as they were stored.

Whenever we insert an object into the queue, they will be inserted at the front of the queue. Removing an object from the queue results in the object at the end of the queue being removed. When the number of elements added to the queue reaches the current capacity, the capacity is automatically increased to make room for new elements.

To add an object to the queue, we use the Enqueue method, which adds the object to the end of the queue. We can use the Dequeue method to remove and return the object that is present at the beginning of the queue. The Peek method is similar to Dequeue, except that it simply returns the object at the beginning of the queue without removing it. To empty the queue, we can use the Clear method.

Now that we have laid the groundwork, let us look at some code to understand the usage of the Queue class.

We first declare a variable of type Queue by using the following line of code.

```
Private mQueue As New Queue()
```

After the declaration, we add a couple of elements to the queue.

```
mQueue.Enqueue("First Element")
mQueue.Enqueue("Second Element")
```

To remove elements from the queue, we use the `Dequeue` method.

```
Private Sub cmdRemoveItem_Click(ByVal sender As System.Object, ByVal e
            As System.EventArgs) Handles cmdRemoveItem.Click
    Try
        mQueue.Dequeue()
        RefreshListBox()
    Catch ex As Exception
        MessageBox.Show(ex.Message())
    End Try
End Sub
```

The `RefreshListBox` method is used to show all the elements in the queue.

```
Private Sub RefreshListBox()
    Dim oEnumerator As IEnumerator
    'Clear the listbox
    lstMessages.Items.Clear()
    oEnumerator = mQueue.GetEnumerator()
    While oEnumerator.MoveNext()
        AddItem(oEnumerator.Current().ToString())
    End While
End Sub
```

SortedList

`SortedList` consists of a sorted collection of associated keys and its values that can be accessed by key and by index. It internally uses a hashtable to store this information in the list: one contains all the keys and another one contains the associated values. `SortedList` does not allow duplicate values.

Since `SortedList` stores all the entries in a sorted manner, it tends to perform slower compared to a `Hashtable`. However, the `SortedList` offers more flexibility by allowing access to the values either through the associated keys or through the indexes.

Since `SortedList` implements the `IList` interface, it supports methods that are similar to `ArrayList`, which are useful in determining the size and reallocating the size of the list. Like the `ArrayList`, the `Capacity` property indicates the number of elements that the `ArrayList` can hold. We can also modify the size of the `SortedList`, either by calling `TrimToSize` or setting the `Capacity` property to an appropriate value. There are two ways in which we can remove a specified element from the `SortedList`:

❑ To remove an element based on the key, the `Remove` method can be used

❑ To remove an element based on the index, the `RemoveAt` method can be used

In this example we will consider a Banking account situation, where we need to display the name of all the account holders with their account balance, sorted by their name. `SortedList` can provide an ideal solution for this problem as it internally stores all the elements in a specified sort order. We can store the name of all the account holders as the key and their balance can be stored as the value.

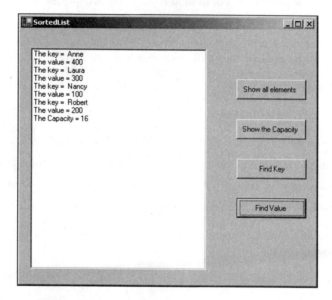

We start by declaring a variable of type `SortedList`.

```
Private mSortedList As New SortedList()
```

We then add elements to the collecction using the following set of statements:

```
mSortedList.Add("Nancy", 100)
mSortedList.Add("Robert", 200)
mSortedList.Add("Laura", 300)
mSortedList.Add("Anne", 400)
```

We show all the elements in the `SortedList` by looping through the collection in the following manner. As we can see, the `GetKey` and `GetByIndex` methods are used to retrieve the key and its corresponding value from the collection respectively.

```
        Dim iCtr As Integer
        For iCtr = 0 To mSortedList.Count - 1
            AddItem("The key = " & mSortedList.GetKey(iCtr))
            AddItem("The value = " & mSortedList.GetByIndex(iCtr))
        Next
```

`SortedList` also exposes the `ContainsKey` and `ContainsValue` methods, which can be used to check whether the collection contains a particular item as its key or its value respectively.

Stack

Stack represents a simple Last-In-First-Out (LIFO) collection of objects. An everyday example of a stack is a pile of papers on a desk in which the item on the top is the one that is most easily accessed. The easiest way to add a new item to stack is to place it above all the current items in the stack. In this manner, an item removed from a stack is the item that has been most recently inserted into the stack, for example, the top piece of paper in the pile.

A classical application of a stack is the implementation of a calculator. Input to the calculator consists of a text string that represents an expression written in Reverse Polish Notation (RPN). Operands, or integer constants, are pushed on a stack of values. As operators are encountered, the appropriate number of operands is popped off the stack, the operation is performed, and the result is pushed back on the stack.

The important methods supported by the `Stack` class are:

❑   `Push` – we can use this method to insert an object at the top of the stack

❑   `Pop` – this method is used to remove and return the object at the top of the stack

❑   `Peek` – whis method is similar to `Pop` except that it does not remove the object from the stack

❑   `Clear` – used to remove all the elements from the stack and count is set to zero

In the following example, we will see how to create a `Stack` object and how to make use of its properties and methods to implement an LIFO type of `Collection` object.

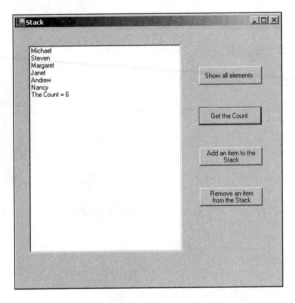

We start with the declaration of a variable that is of type `Stack` class.

```
Private mStack As New Stack()
```

To add elements to the stack, we need to call the `Push` method.

```
mStack.Push("Nancy")
mStack.Push("Andrew")
mStack.Push("Janet")
mStack.Push("Margaret")
mStack.Push("Steven")
mStack.Push("Michael")
```

To enumerate all the elements available in the stack, we get a reference to the `IEnumerator` interface and use its properties and methods to loop through the `Stack` object.

```
Dim oEnumerator As IEnumerator
lstMessages.Items.Clear()
oEnumerator = mStack.GetEnumerator()
While oEnumerator.MoveNext()
    AddItem(oEnumerator.Current().ToString())
End While
```

To remove an item from the stack, all we have to do is call the `Pop` method of the `Stack` object.

```
mStack.Pop()
```

Now that we have understood the usage of `Stack` and `Queue`, let us consider the following example to understand the difference between `Stack` and `Queue` and when to use each of these collections. For example, to determine if a string of characters is a palindrome, we can use one `Stack` and one `Queue` and apply the following strategy: we start by putting the input string on the stack and queue simultaneously; removing the stack elements is the same as reading the string backwards, while removing the queue elements is the same as reading the string forward. With this in mind, we can then match up the characters removed from the stack to the characters removed from the queue one by one. If all the matches return True, we can arrive at the conclusion that the string is a palindrome.

Debugging and Logging

The `System.Diagnostics` namespace provides classes that allow us to perform operations related to troubleshooting, such as debugging your applications, tracing the execution of your application, diagnosing the errors in released code, reading and writing to event logs, and many more. In this section, we will consider the above functionalities and illustrate how to carry out these tasks using the classes available in the `System.Diagnostics` namespace. Towards this end, we will concentrate on the Debug, Trace, and EventLog classes.

Debug and Trace

The `Debug` and `Trace` classes are very similar to each other in terms of the functionalities they provide, except that `Debug` is disabled in release builds by default, whereas `Trace` is enabled in release, as well as debug builds. They furnish extensive diagnostic support for applications through their properties and methods. They provide the following variations of the `Write` method, which can be considered a replacement for the `Debug.Print` statements in VB6.

- ❑ Write – allows us to write debugging or trace information to the listeners that are already registered with the listeners collection.

- ❑ WriteIf – similar to the Write method, except that it writes information only when the expression that is passed as an argument returns True.

- ❑ WriteLine – allows us to write a line of debugging or trace information to the listeners that are already registered with the listeners collection.

- ❑ WriteLineIf – similar to the WriteLine method, except that it writes information only when the expression that is passed as an argument returns True.

They also contain the Assert method, through which we can ensure that the statement of a conditional expression is always True. Asserts are very useful in complex projects to ensure that expected conditions are always met.

In Visual Studio.NET projects, Trace is enabled by default. Therefore, code is generated for all Trace methods in both release and debug builds. This allows us to turn on tracing to help identify the problems without having to recompile the program. The Trace class outputs the messages emitted by the above discussed methods (Writer, WriteLine, etc.) in its Listeners collection. These listener classes are used to monitor debug and trace output. The following table summarises the different types of listeners present in the framework.

Listener	Purpose
EventLogTraceListener	Writes to an event log
TextWriterTraceListener	Used to write to a text file
DefaultTraceListener	Writes the information to the attached debugger

Tracing helps us isolate problems and fix them, even after the system is implemented. However, it is important to understand that the overuse of Trace statements could affect the performance of the application.

We can control the tracing in our application using any one of the following ways:

- ❑ By defining the compilation constant TRACE and setting it to True, we can inform the compiler to keep the tracing code in the compiled binary.

- ❑ Another way of controlling tracing during execution of an application without having to recompile is by using the BooleanSwitch class. We do this by specifying whether the tracing is on or off through a registry value or an environmental variable.

In this example, we will create a VB.NET windows application to demonstrate the usage of the Debug class. For this example, we will consider the scenario where we will try to access the database and see how we can implement the methods of the Debug class to diagnose any exceptional conditions that may occur during the execution of that operation.

```
Imports System.IO
Imports System.Data.SqlClient

Private Sub LoadEmployeesData(ByVal iEmployeeID As Integer)
    Dim oSQLDataReader As SqlDataReader
    Dim oSQLConnection As SqlConnection
    Dim oSQLCommand As SqlCommand
```

```
    Dim sConn As String
    Dim sCommand As String
    Dim oFile As Stream = File.Create("Debuglog.log")
    Dim oTextListener As New TextWriterTraceListener(oFile)
    'Clear all the listeners
    Debug.Listeners.Clear()
    'Register the listener
    Debug.Listeners.Add(oTextListener)
    'This has to be changed to your machine's settings
    sConn = "server=localhost;uid=sa;pwd=;database=Northwind"
    sCommand = "Select * from Employees Where EmployeeID =" & iEmployeeID
    Debug.WriteLine("The connection string used is " & sConn)
    Debug.WriteLine("The SQL Command to be executed is " & sCommand)
    oSQLConnection = New SqlConnection(sConn)
    oSQLCommand = New SqlCommand(sCommand, oSQLConnection)
    oSQLCommand.Connection.Open()
    Debug.Assert(oSQLConnection.State = ConnectionState.Open, "Connection
                              is not established")
    oSQLDataReader = oSQLCommand.ExecuteReader()
    While (oSQLDataReader.Read())
       MessageBox.Show(" The value returned is " &
                       oSQLDataReader("EmployeeID"))
    End While

    oTextListener.Flush()
    oTextListener.Close()
    oSQLConnection.Close()

End Sub

Private Sub Form1_Load(ByVal sender As System.Object, ByVal e As
                       System.EventArgs) Handles MyBase.Load
    LoadEmployeesData(1)
End Sub
```

We will start by importing a couple of namespaces required for our application.

```
Imports System.IO
Imports System.Data.SqlClient
```

The System.Data.SqlClient namespace contains optimized, high-performance classes that can be used to access a SQL Server database from a managed code environment.

In this case, we use the Employees table of the Northwind database that comes bundled with SQL Server for the retrieval of information. The SqlDataReader object provides a means of reading forward-only cursor from a SQL Server database. The SqlConnection object represents an open connection to the SQL Server database.

In the following line, we create an instance of the file object and assign it to a stream.

```
Dim oFile As Stream = File.Create("Debuglog.log")
```

Here, we declare an object of type TextWriterTraceListener that is used to direct the debugging output to the stream object that we created in the previous step.

```
Dim oTextListener As New TextWriterTraceListener(oFile)
```

By default, the `Assert` method shows the debugging output in the form of a prompt with the options like `Abort`, `Continue` and `Ignore`. Since we want to avoid getting this prompt, we clear all the default listeners by calling the `Clear` method of the `Listeners` collection.

```
Debug.Listeners.Clear()
```

Now, we add the `TextWriterTraceListener` object that we created to the collection of listeners that are going to be monitoring the debug output.

```
Debug.Listeners.Add(oTextListener)
sConn = "server=localhost;uid=sa;pwd=;database=Northwind"
sCommand = "SELECT * from Employees WHERE EmployeeID =" & iEmployeeID
```

In the following lines, we log the connection string that is used for connecting to the database and the SQL command to our log file by invoking the `WriteLine` method of the `Debug` class.

```
Debug.WriteLine("The connection string used is " & sConn)
Debug.WriteLine("The SQL Command to be executed is " & sCommand)
```

Here, we create an instance of the `SqlConnection` object, passing in the connection string as an argument.

```
oSQLConnection = New SqlConnection(sConn)
```

We then instantiate the `SqlCommand` object and we pass the command and the connection object as arguments to its constructor.

```
oSQLCommand = New SqlCommand(sCommand, oSQLConnection)
```

This line of code opens the connection to the database by calling the `Open` method of the connection object.

```
oSQLCommand.Connection.Open()
```

Once the connection is opened, we then verify the state of the connection by checking the `State` property of the `Connection` object. If the evaluation of the condition returns `False`, we log the message to the log file.

```
Debug.Assert(oSQLConnection.State = ConnectionState.Open, "Connection is not
established")
```

Here, we execute the command by calling the `ExecuteReader` method of the SQL command object and then we loop through the SQL data reader object and display its contents.

```
oSQLDataReader = oSQLCommand.ExecuteReader()
While (oSQLDataReader.Read())
MessageBox.Show(" The value returned is " & oSQLDataReader("EmployeeID"))
End While
```

In this line, we flush the output of the buffer for the writer.

```
oTextListener.Flush()
```

Finally, we close the `TextWriterTraceListener` object by invoking its `Close` method.

```
oTextListener.Close()
```

If you execute this program and open the `Debuglog.log` file, it looks like this.

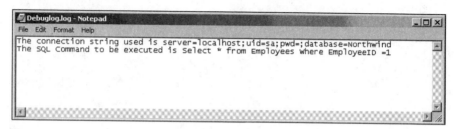

EventLog Class

`EventLog` exposes properties and methods that allow us to interact with the event log. They are mainly used to record information about important software and hardware events that may fall into any one of the following categories: Warning, Information and Error. Windows 2000, by default, has three event logs, namely Application, System and Security. We can use the `EventLog` class to perform the following operations.

- ❑ Enumerate log entries from existing logs
- ❑ Write entries to application and system logs
- ❑ Delete logs
- ❑ Read the event log information of a remote computer

Let us look at some of the important properties and methods exposed by the `EventLog` class. The `Source` property specifies the name of the event source that logs the events. For example, if you are writing an application and you want to log all the errors that may occur in your application to the event log, then you can set the `Source` property to the name of your application. The name of the source must be unique and duplicate names are not allowed. We can use the `SourceExists` property to check whether an event source is registered on the computer.

The `Log` property allows us to indicate the name of the log that we want to operate on. It can be Application, System, Security, or a custom log name. If we are dealing with event logs in a remote machine, then we need to set the `MachineName` property to appropriate value. If we do not specify a value for this, the `MachineName` property defaults to the local computer, which is indicated by ("."). The `WriteEntry` method allows us to write an entry to the event log, and at the time of writing an entry, we can also specify the value for the `EventLogEntryType`, which allows us to indicate the type of the event. The event type can be Error, FailureAudit, Information, SuccessAudit, or Warning. `EventViewer`, which is shipped with Windows 2000 and Windows XP, uses this `EventLogEntryType` value to display the appropriate icon in the event viewer. The `EventLogEntry` class represents a single entry in the event log.

Now that we have covered a bit of ground, let us create a C# windows application to illustrate how to enumerate all the log entries in a specified computer of the local machine. There are times when administrators might want to see the event log entries in a remote machine. In this example, we will create a utility application that has the ability to connect to any computer and show all the event log entries in that particular machine, assuming that we have proper credentials to access that computer.

The way the application works is like this: when the user enters the name of the computer and clicks the command button GetEventLogs, we show the list of all the logs available in that particular machine in a listbox. When a particular log is selected in the listbox, we then show the list of log entries present in that log in a listview.

```csharp
using System;
using System.Drawing;
using System.Collections;
using System.ComponentModel;
using System.Windows.Forms;
using System.Data;
using System.Diagnostics;

private void cmdGetEventLog_Click(object sender, System.EventArgs e)
{
    EventLog[] oEventLogs;
    //Get all the Event Logs in the computer
    oEventLogs = EventLog.GetEventLogs(txtComputerName.Text);
    lstEventLogs.Items.Clear();
    foreach (EventLog oEventLog in oEventLogs)
    {
        lstEventLogs.Items.Add(oEventLog.Log);
    }
}


private void lstEventLogs_SelectedIndexChanged(object sender,
                                        System.EventArgs e)
{
    EventLog oEventLog = new EventLog();
    ListViewItem oListViewItem;
    oEventLog.Log = lstEventLogs.Text;
    oEventLog.MachineName = txtComputerName.Text;
    //Clear all the Entries in the Listview
    lvwEventEntries.Items.Clear();
    foreach(EventLogEntry oEventLogEntry  in oEventLog.Entries)
    {
        oListViewItem = new ListViewItem();
        oListViewItem.Text = oEventLogEntry.TimeGenerated.ToString();
        ListViewItem.ListViewSubItem  oListViewSubItem = new
                    ListViewItem.ListViewSubItem();
        oListViewSubItem.Text = oEventLogEntry.EventID.ToString();
        oListViewItem.SubItems.Add(oListViewSubItem);
        ListViewItem.ListViewSubItem oListViewSubItem1  = new
                    ListViewItem.ListViewSubItem();
        oListViewSubItem1.Text = oEventLogEntry.Source;
        oListViewItem.SubItems.Add(oListViewSubItem1);
        //Add the ListViewItem to the ListView
        lvwEventEntries.Items.Add(oListViewItem);
    }
}
```

We start by importing all the namespaces required in our application. It is important to note the presence of the System.Diagnostics namespace, which contains the EventLog class and the related classes.

```
using System;
using System.Drawing;
using System.Collections;
using System.ComponentModel;
using System.Windows.Forms;
using System.Data;
using System.Diagnostics;
```

To get all the logs, including custom logs, we execute the following set of code. We first declare an array of EventLog and then get a reference to the array of logs by invoking the static method GetEventLogs of the EventLog class. To this method we pass the name of the computer whose event log entries we want to enumerate as an argument.

```
EventLog[] oEventLogs;
//Get all the Event Logs in the computer
oEventLogs = EventLog.GetEventLogs(txtComputerName.Text);
```

Here, we clear the listbox of any entries.

```
lstEventLogs.Items.Clear();
```

Finally, we loop through the array of Eventlogs and display it in the listbox.

```
foreach (EventLog oEventLog in oEventLogs)
{
    lstEventLogs.Items.Add(oEventLog.Log);
}
```

When a particular log is selected in the listbox, we then need to show all the eventlog entries in that selected log in the EventLog entries listview. Towards this end, we execute the following statements.

```
EventLog oEventLog = new EventLog();
ListViewItem oListViewItem;
```

We set the Log property of the EventLog object to the name of the selected item in the listbox.

```
oEventLog.Log = lstEventLogs.Text;
```

Here, we assign the name of the computer to which we want to connect, to the MachineName property of the EventLog.

```
oEventLog.MachineName = txtComputerName.Text;
```

In this line of code, we clear the contents of the listview.

```
lvwEventEntries.Items.Clear();
```

As we already discussed, the `EventLogEntry` object represents an entry in the event log.

Finally, we loop through the `Entries` collection of the referenced event log and show all its EventLog entries in the listview.

```
foreach(EventLogEntry oEventLogEntry  in oEventLog.Entries)
{
    oListViewItem = new ListViewItem();
    oListViewItem.Text = oEventLogEntry.TimeGenerated.ToString();
    ListViewItem.ListViewSubItem  oListViewSubItem  = new
              ListViewItem.ListViewSubItem();
    oListViewSubItem.Text = oEventLogEntry.EventID.ToString();
    oListViewItem.SubItems.Add(oListViewSubItem);
    ListViewItem.ListViewSubItem oListViewSubItem1  = new
              ListViewItem.ListViewSubItem();
    oListViewSubItem1.Text = oEventLogEntry.Source;
    oListViewItem.SubItems.Add(oListViewSubItem1);
    //Add the ListViewItem to the ListView
    lvwEventEntries.Items.Add(oListViewItem);
}
```

Finally, when we execute the application, the output we get is similar to the following:

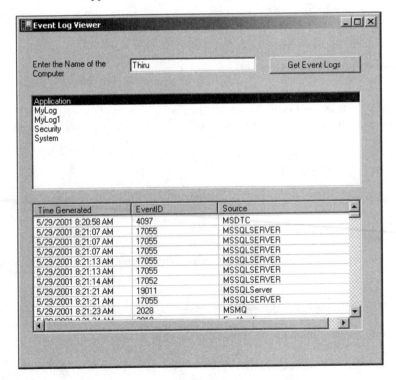

File Handling and File System Monitoring

The .NET framework provides a number of classes to perform operations such as accessing the file system, reading from and writing into files, copying files, moving files, and so on. All these classes are contained in the System.IO namespace.

Overview of the Classes

Using the classes present in the System.IO namespace, we can perform synchronous and asynchronous reading and writing of data streams and files. The File class provides static methods for carrying out tasks such as creating files, copying files, deleting files, opening of files, and so on.

The following diagram gives an overview of the important classes contained in the System.IO namespace. It also provides an idea of the capabilities of the different classes by showing the inter dependencies between them. For example, since StreamWriter derives from TextWriter, we can understand that it is used to deal with a sequential series of characters (since the TextWriter class declares methods for handling a sequential series of characters).

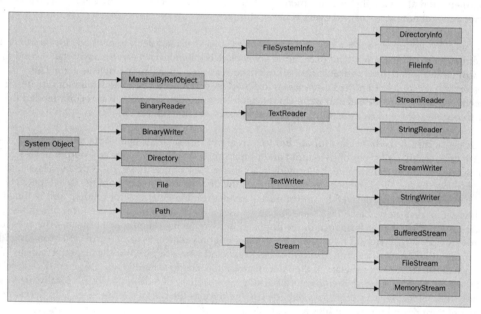

From the above diagram, we can see that the classes MarshalByRefObject, BinaryReader, BinaryWriter, Directory, File and Path derive from the System.Object class. MarshalByRefObject is the base class that contains all the methods for applications to implement remoting of objects using marshal by reference. FileSystemInfo, TextReader, TextWriter and Stream are some of the many classes that derive from MarshalByRefObject. The BinaryReader and BinaryWriter classes are used to read and write primitive types such as bool, int, or string to a stream in binary format. The File class is a utility class that exposes static methods for creating, copying, deleting, moving, and opening files. Similar to the File class, the Directory class also exposes static methods for creating, moving, and looping through contents of the directory.

The static methods exposed by the Path class can be used to accomplish the following important functionalities:

❏ Allows us to change the extension of a file using the ChangeExtension method.

❏ Using the Combine method, we can combine two different file paths to produce a single file path.

❏ To return the directory path of a file, we can use the GetDirectoryName method.

❏ Using the GetExtension and HasExtension methods, we can determine the extension and whether the path includes a filename extension respectively.

As we can see from the diagram, the FileSystemInfo class is an abstract class that acts as the base class for both the FileInfo and DirectoryInfo classes. The FileInfo and DirectoryInfo classes are similar to the File and Directory classes in terms of the functionalities they provide, except for the difference that they expose instance methods, meaning that we need to create an instance of them before we start using them. It is also important to understand that, since the File and Directory classes provide only static methods, everytime we use them security checks are internally performed and this might have impact on the performance of the application. If we are going to use a File or Directory object several times, it is recommended that we use the instance methods of the FileInfo and DirectoryInfo classes, as security permissions will not be performed every time.

As we already discussed, the TextWriter and TextReader classes declare methods for handling a sequential series of characters. The StringReader class implements a TextReader that is used to read data from a string and the SteamReader allows us to read characters from a byte stream. The StreamWriter and StringWriter classes are used to write data into a byte stream or a string respectively. If we want to read and write characters from a standard text file, it is recommended that we use the StreamReader and StreamWriter classes to carry out that operation.

The Stream class is the base class for all the streams and is designed for byte input and output. It exposes a generic view of different types of byte input and output, such as a file, an input and output device, and an inter-process communication pipe. By providing a generic view of the above, the Stream class abstracts away the specific details of the operating system and the underlying devices from the developer. The BufferedStream class, derived from Stream, provides implementations for reading and writing bytes to the destination data store. Since BufferedStream uses a block of memory in the form of a buffer to cache data, it can improve the performance of the application by reducing the number of read-write calls to the underlying operating system. The FileStream class not only allows us to perform synchronous and asynchronous I/O operations, but also buffers and read and writes to give out better performance. We will see more of the FileStream class in the later stages of this chapter. Finally, the MemoryStream class is used to create streams that use memory as a backing store instead of a disk, which is typically used as a backing store. Since MemoryStreams directly use memory as the backing store, they help decrease the number of temporary buffers and files in an application.

File and Directory

In the first example, which is written using C#, we will demonstrate how to list the attributes of a file and a directory. In this example, we first create an instance of the object of type File class by passing in the full path of the location of the file to the constructor of the File class. The snapshot of the application we are going to create for this example looks like the following:

Let us walk through the code that is required to implement the application.

```
using System;
using System.Drawing;
using System.Collections;
using System.ComponentModel;
using System.Windows.Forms;
using System.Data;
using System.IO;

private void cmdFileOpen_Click(object sender, System.EventArgs e)
{
    dlgFileOpen.ShowDialog();
    //Assign the selected file to the textbox
    txtFileName.Text = dlgFileOpen.FileName;
}

private void AddItem(String sMessage)
    {
        lstAttributes.Items.Add(sMessage);
    }

    private void cmdGetAttributes_Click(object sender, System.EventArgs e)
    {
    Try
        //Get the reference to the file
        FileInfo  oFileInfo = new FileInfo(txtFileName.Text);
        String sDirectoryName;
        lstAttributes.Items.Clear();
        AddItem("The File Attributes are ...");
        AddItem("Creation time = " + oFileInfo.CreationTime.ToString());
        AddItem("Size = " + oFileInfo.Length.ToString());
        AddItem("Directory name = " + oFileInfo.DirectoryName);
```

```
        AddItem("Full Path = " + oFileInfo.FullName);
        AddItem("Last Access Time = " + oFileInfo.LastAccessTime.ToString());
        AddItem("Last Write Time = " + oFileInfo.LastWriteTime.ToString());
        AddItem("File Extension = " + oFileInfo.Extension);
        //Get the name of the directory in the local variable
        sDirectoryName = oFileInfo.DirectoryName;
        DirectoryInfo oDirInfo =new DirectoryInfo(sDirectoryName);
        AddItem("...");
        AddItem("The Directory Attributes are ...");
        AddItem("Creation time = " + oDirInfo.CreationTime.ToString());
        AddItem("Size = " + oDirInfo.GetDirectories().Length.ToString());
        AddItem("Directory name = " + oDirInfo.Parent.Name);
        AddItem("Full Path = " + oDirInfo.FullName);
        AddItem("Last Access Time = " +oDirInfo.LastAccessTime.ToString());
        AddItem("Last Write Time = " + oDirInfo.LastWriteTime.ToString());
    Catch ex As Exception
        MessageBox.Show(ex.Message())
    End Try
    }
```

At the start of the program, all the namespaces required by our application are imported using the following statements. Please note that we also have the System.IO namespace imported, which contains the classes required for implementing file system related operations.

```
using System;
using System.Drawing;
using System.Collections;
using System.ComponentModel;
using System.Windows.Forms;
using System.Data;
using System.IO;
```

When we click the command button, we get a **File Open** dialog box in which we select the file whose attributes we want to display. After we select the file and click **OK**, the selected file name is assigned to the textbox. For the file opening, we use the class OpenFileDialog that is present in the System.Windows.Forms namespace.

```
private void cmdFileOpen_Click(object sender, System.EventArgs e)
{
    dlgFileOpen.ShowDialog();
    //Assign the selected file to the textbox
    txtFileName.Text = dlgFileOpen.FileName;
}
```

When the **Get Attributes** command button is clicked, we create a FileInfo object, passing to its constructor the selected file name as an argument. Once we get a reference to the FileInfo object for the selected file, then we can easily display, as well as modify, the attributes of the file like CreationTime, Length, DirectoryName, FullName, LastAccessTime, LastWriteTime and Extension using the get and set properties of the FileInfo class.

```
        //Get the reference to the file
        FileInfo  oFileInfo = new FileInfo(txtFileName.Text);
        String sDirectoryName;
        lstAttributes.Items.Clear();
        AddItem("The File Attributes are ...");
```

```
AddItem("Creation time = " + oFileInfo.CreationTime.ToString());
AddItem("Size = " + oFileInfo.Length.ToString());
AddItem("Directory name = " + oFileInfo.DirectoryName);
AddItem("Full Path = " + oFileInfo.FullName);
AddItem("Last Access Time = " + oFileInfo.LastAccessTime.ToString());
AddItem("Last Write Time = " + oFileInfo.LastWriteTime.ToString());
AddItem("File Extension = " + oFileInfo.Extension);
//Get the name of the directory in the local variable
sDirectoryName = oFileInfo.DirectoryName;
```

In this line, we create a `DirectoryInfo` object and we pass the directory name of the previously selected file as an argument. Then we display the properties for that directory in the listbox.

```
DirectoryInfo oDirInfo =new DirectoryInfo(sDirectoryName);
AddItem("...");
AddItem("The Directory Attributes are ...");
AddItem("Creation time = " + oDirInfo.CreationTime.ToString());
AddItem("Size = " + oDirInfo.GetDirectories().Length.ToString());
AddItem("Directory name = " + oDirInfo.Parent.Name);
AddItem("Full Path = " + oDirInfo.FullName);
AddItem("Last Access Time = " +oDirInfo.LastAccessTime.ToString());
AddItem("Last Write Time = " + oDirInfo.LastWriteTime.ToString());
```

Copying, Moving and Deleting Files

The `File` class provides static methods such as `Move`, `Copy`, and `Delete`, which can be used to carry out operations like moving files from one directory to the other, copying files, and removing files. For example, to copy a file from one folder to another, the following command can be used:

```
File.Copy(txtFileName.Text, sTargetPath & "\" & sTargetFileName, True)
```

In the above line, `txtFileName.text` returns the name of the source file to be copied, and the combination of `sTargetPath` and `sTargetFileName` returns the target directory as well as the target file name. The `True` value in the third parameter is used to indicate that the file can be overwritten, if a file with the same name exists.

To delete a file, we need to invoke the `Delete` method, passing in the name of the file to be deleted as the argument.

```
File.Delete(txtFileName.Text)
```

The `Move` method of the `File` class is similar to `Copy`, except that there is no third parameter to indicate the overwriting of the file.

```
File.Move(txtFileName.Text, sTargetPath & "\" & sTargetFileName)
```

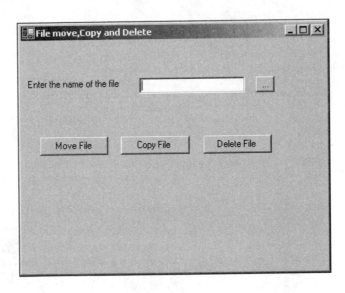

StreamReader and StreamWriter

The StreamReader and StreamWriter classes are designed to handle character input and output. The StreamReader class is used for reading information from a text file and the StreamWriter class is used for writing information into a text file.

StreamReader provides the following variations of reading that can be useful in many situations. The Read method is used to read the next available character from the input stream into a local variable. To read one full line of characters from the stream, the ReadLine method can be used. We can use the ReadToEnd method to read all the characters from the current position to the end of the stream. The Peek method will be useful in situations when we want to read a character without moving the current pointer to the next character.

Similar to StreamReader, StreamWriter exposes a set of methods that facilitate the writing of data into a file. The Flush method of the StreamWriter class can be used to clear all the buffers of the current writer and write the underlying data to the stream. Like StreamReader, it also exposes methods Write and WriteLine – the Write method is used to write a specified of set of characters to the stream whereas the WriteLine method writes a single line of characters to the underlying stream.

These classes differ from FileStream in the way that they are designed for handling character input and output of files, whereas FileStream classes provide a means of handling byte input and output.

Let us consider the following application, which we will use for understanding these classes:

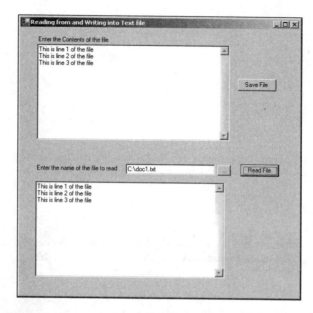

Once we enter the values in the first textbox and click Save File, we then show a file save dialog box asking the user to select the path and name of the file for the entered contents. After that, the file is saved to the location we selected. To read the same file, we can either enter the path of the file directly in the textbox or click on the command button that brings up the file opening dialog box. Through that we can select the file, and after selecting it, when we click Read File, the contents of the file are read and shown in the bottom text box. Now let us look at the code required to create this application in C#.

```csharp
using System;
using System.Drawing;
using System.Collections;
using System.ComponentModel;
using System.Windows.Forms;
using System.Data;
using System.IO;
using System.Text;
private void cmdSaveFile_Click(object sender, System.EventArgs e)
{
    String sFileName;
    dlgSaveDialog.ShowDialog();
    //Assign the name of the file to the variable
    sFileName = dlgSaveDialog.FileName;
    StreamWriter oStreamWriter = new StreamWriter(sFileName);
    oStreamWriter.Write(txtWriteFile.Text);
    oStreamWriter.Close();
    MessageBox.Show("File is successfully saved");
}

private void cmdFileRead_Click(object sender, System.EventArgs e)
{
    String sLine;
    StreamReader oStreamReader = File.OpenText(txtFileName.Text);
    StringBuilder sBuilder = new StringBuilder();
//Read the contents of the file and show it in the textbox
    while (oStreamReader.Peek() != -1)
    {
```

```
            sLine = oStreamReader.ReadLine();
            sBuilder.Append(sLine);     }
            txtReadFile.Text = sBuilder.ToString();
    }

    private void cmdFileOpen_Click(object sender, System.EventArgs e)
    {
        dlgOpenDialog.ShowDialog();
        txtFileName.Text = dlgOpenDialog.FileName;
    }
```

The following namespaces are not imported by default. We import the System.IO namespace to have access to the file-related classes and the System.Text namespace is for making use of the StringBuilder object.

```
using System.IO;
using System.Text;
```

When the **Save File** button is clicked, we execute the following lines of code. We start by opening the open file dialog box and assign the name the user has given for the file to a variable.

```
String sFileName;
dlgSaveDialog.ShowDialog();
//Assign the name of the file to the variable
sFileName = dlgSaveDialog.FileName;
```

Here, we create an instance of the StreamWriter object, passing to its constructor the name of the file to be created as an argument. We write the contents of the textbox into the file using the Write method and then we close the file by calling the Close method of the StreamWriter object.

```
StreamWriter oStreamWriter = new StreamWriter(sFileName);
oStreamWriter.Write(txtWriteFile.Text);
oStreamWriter.Close();
MessageBox.Show("File is successfully saved");
```

To read a file from the file system using the StreamReader, we need to instantiate the StreamReader object. Here, we get a reference to the StreamReader object by calling the static OpenText method of the File class.

```
String sLine;
StreamReader oStreamReader = File.OpenText(txtFileName.Text);
StringBuilder sBuilder = new StringBuilder();
```

We then invoke the Peek method to check for the end of the file. The Peek method returns the next available character in the stream without changing the pointer location. It returns −1 if no more characters are available to be read in the file. Inside the loop, we read every line in the file by calling the ReadLine method and we append the read contents to a StringBuilder object. Finally we show the contents by calling the ToString method of the StringBuilder object.

```
while (oStreamReader.Peek() != -1)
{
    sLine = oStreamReader.ReadLine();
    sBuilder.Append(sLine);
}
txtReadFile.Text = sBuilder.ToString();
}
```

FileStream

FileStream classes are useful for reading and writing files on a system using a byte array of stream. It is also useful in situations when we want to perform asynchronous reading and writing operations. By default, when we open a file using FileStream, it will be used in synchronous mode. One more reason why FileStream classes are preferred over all other classes is because of its ability to allow applications to perform random access of files. The Seek method of the FileStream class can be used to move the file position pointer anywhere within the file. When we create a FileStream object, we can specify the mode in which we want to open the file by supplying an appropriate value to the FileMode parameter. The FileMode parameter in the constructor of the FileStream class can take any one of the following values: Append, Create, CreateNew, Open, OpenOrCreate, and Truncate. At the time of creating the file, we can also indicate the kind of access we want to have on the file using the FileAccess parameter. The FileAccess enum can have any one of the following values: Read, Write and ReadWrite.

Let us see the code we need to execute to be able to write contents into a file. To write information into a text file, we need the following lines of code.

We first create an instance of the FileStream object, passing to its constructor the following arguments: the name of the file to be created, the mode in which we want to open the file, and the kind of operation we want to perform on the file.

```
Dim oFileStream As FileStream = New FileStream("FileStreamLog.txt",
                 FileMode.OpenOrCreate, FileAccess.Write)
Dim oStreamWriter As StreamWriter = New StreamWriter(oFileStream)
```

In this line, we set the file pointer to the end of the file by calling the Invoke method.

```
oStreamWriter.BaseStream.Seek(0, SeekOrigin.End)
```

In the following lines, we write contents to the file using the WriteLine method of the StreamWriter.

```
oStreamWriter.WriteLine("This is the first line in the file")
oStreamWriter.WriteLine("This is the second line in the file")
```

Finally, we close the Writer object by invoking its Close method.

```
oStreamWriter.Close()
```

Now that we have seen how to write contents to the file, let us see what it takes to read from a file.

As before, we create an instance of the FileStream object, passing appropriate values to its constructor. Since we want to read the file this time, we pass FileAccess.Read in the third parameter.

```
Dim oFileStream As FileStream = New FileStream("FileStreamLog.txt",
FileMode.OpenOrCreate, FileAccess.Read)
Dim oStreamReader As StreamReader = New StreamReader(oFileStream)
    'Set the file pointer to the beginning.
    oStreamReader.BaseStream.Seek(0, SeekOrigin.Begin)
    MessageBox.Show(oStreamReader.ReadLine())
    MessageBox.Show(oStreamReader.ReadLine())
```

After we set the file pointer to the beginning of the file, we can read the information in the file by using the `ReadLine` method.

```
MessageBox.Show(oStreamReader.ReadLine())
MessageBox.Show(oStreamReader.ReadLine())
```

FileSystemWatcher

One of the new exciting features of the .NET framework is the ability to create applications that can interact with the File System and raise events at scheduled intervals based on the activities in the File System. The `FileSystemWatcher` component provides a good alternative approach to mechanisms like MSMQ for creating asynchronous solutions. If you have ever done any work in MSMQ, you might have created an application that receives the events from the message queue whenever a new message arrives in the queue. This is implemented using the object `MSMQEvent`. Creating and maintaining an application of this kind is not the easiest thing in the world, because of the complexities involved. However, in .NET we can use `FileSystemWatcher` in conjunction with the Windows service applications to accomplish the same set of functionalities in a flexible and easier manner.

The `FileSystemWatcher` component that is contained in the `System.IO` namespace exposes methods and properties through which we can watch for changes to directories and files and take specific actions when these changes occur. Using the `FileSystemWatcher` component, we can watch for files on a local machine, a network drive, or a remote machine.

The `FileSystemWatcher` component can be created in two different ways:

❑ We can drag an instance of the `FileSystemWatcher` component from the **Components** tab of the **Toolbox** and drop it in designer.

❑ We can create an instance of the `FileSystemWatcher` component programmatically after importing the `System.IO` assembly.

The following table discusses the important properties exposed by the `FileSystemWatcher` class.

Properties	Purpose
EnableRaisingEvents	Allows us to determine whether the component is enabled for monitoring.
Filter	Allows us to get or set the filter string that determines the files to be monitored.
Path	Allows us to specify the path of the directory that is to be watched for changes.
IncludeSubDirectories	Allows us to indicate whether the subdirectories within the specified path should be monitored.
NotifyFilter	Accepts an enum constant as an argument that indicates the different types of changes to watch for.
InternalBufferSize	Allows us to retrieve or set the value of the size of the internal buffer that is used to store the file system changes momentarily before they are passed to the applications that are interested in receiving notifications. The default size of the buffer is 8K.

As we already discussed, the NotifyFilter enumeration allows us to specify the changes that we want to monitor in a file or folder. It can have any one of the following values, which determine the changes to watch for.

- ❑ Attributes
- ❑ CreationTime
- ❑ DirectoryTime
- ❑ FileName
- ❑ LastAccess
- ❑ LastWrite
- ❑ Security
- ❑ Size

Now that we have understood the important properties whose values need to be set for us to be able to start receiving notifications, let us go forward and understand the different notifications (or events) the FileSystemWatcher can raise in response to the above properties.

Events	Purpose
Changed	Raised when changes occur in the file or directory that is being monitored. These changes include changes in the size, system attributes, last write time, last access time, or security permission changes of the file or directory.
Created	Raised when a file or directory is created in the path set by the Path property.
Deleted	Raised when a file or directory is deleted in the path set by the Path property.
Renamed	Provides us with a the notification when a file or directory is renamed in the path indicated by the Path property.
Error	Allows us to determine the exception condition that is caused by the internal buffer overflow.

In the following example, written in C#, we will see how to create an application that is set up to monitor a directory for the creation of new files and also to respond to the action of the creation of new files.

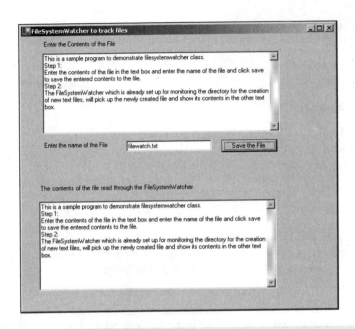

```
using System;
using System.Drawing;
using System.Collections;
using System.ComponentModel;
using System.Windows.Forms;
using System.Data;
using System.IO;
using System.Text;

FileSystemWatcher oWatcher = new FileSystemWatcher();

public Form1()
{
    InitializeComponent();
    oWatcher.Path = Application.StartupPath.ToString();
    oWatcher.Filter = "*.txt";
    oWatcher.EnableRaisingEvents = true;
    oWatcher.Created += new FileSystemEventHandler(OnCreated);

}
    private void OnCreated(object source, FileSystemEventArgs e)
    {

        String sLine;
        StreamReader  oStreamReader  = File.OpenText(e.FullPath);
        StringBuilder sBuilder =new StringBuilder();
        //Read the contents of the file and show it in the textbox
        while(oStreamReader.Peek() != -1)
        {
            sLine = oStreamReader.ReadLine();
            sBuilder.Append(sLine);
        }
            txtReadFileContents.Text = sBuilder.ToString();
```

```
    }

    private void cmdSaveFile_Click(object sender, System.EventArgs e)
    {
        StreamWriter oStreamWriter = new StreamWriter(txtFileName.Text);
        oStreamWriter.Write(txtWriteFileContents.Text);
        oStreamWriter.Close();
    }
```

We start by importing all the required namespaces.

```
using System;
using System.Drawing;
using System.Collections;
using System.ComponentModel;
using System.Windows.Forms;
using System.Data;
using System.IO;
using System.Text;
```

In this line, we create an instance of the FileSystemWatcher class and assign it to a module level variable.

```
FileSystemWatcher oWatcher = new FileSystemWatcher();
```

In the constructor of the Form1 class, we set the properties of the FileSystemWatcher object to appropriate values. We set the Path property to the application startup path, which indicates that we want to monitor the application path for the creation of files. We also specify that we want to watch only for text files by setting the Filter property to *.txt.

```
oWatcher.Path = Application.StartupPath.ToString();
oWatcher.Filter = "*.txt";
```

We then indicate that we want events to be raised by the FileSystemWatcher object to our application to enable our application to process the newly created files. We do this by setting the EnableRaisingEvents property to true.

```
oWatcher.EnableRaisingEvents = true;
```

Finally, we specify that FileSystemWatcher call back our application by notifying the OnCreated method whenever a new file is created.

```
oWatcher.Created += new FileSystemEventHandler(OnCreated);
```

In the OnCreated method, we get the name of the file that was created and we then read the contents of the file using the StreamReader object. The FullPath property of the FileSystemEventArgs object returns the name of the file along with the directory location of the file. Similarly to the previous examples, we read the contents of the file using the combination of Peek and ReadLine methods.

```
private void OnCreated(object source, FileSystemEventArgs e)
{
    String sLine;
    StreamReader  oStreamReader  = File.OpenText(e.FullPath);
    StringBuilder sBuilder =new StringBuilder();
    //Read the contents of the file and show it in the textbox
    while(oStreamReader.Peek() != -1)
    {
        sLine = oStreamReader.ReadLine();
        sBuilder.Append(sLine);
    }
    txtReadFileContents.Text = sBuilder.ToString();
}
```

In the `Click` event of the **Save File** command button, we write the contents of the textbox into a file by invoking the `Write` method of the `StreamWriter` object.

```
private void cmdSaveFile_Click(object sender, System.EventArgs e)
{
    StreamWriter oStreamWriter = new StreamWriter(txtFileName.Text);
    oStreamWriter.Write(txtWriteFileContents.Text);
    oStreamWriter.Close ();
}
```

Now that we have seen what a `FileSystemWatcher` is and how to use it, let us consider the following problem and see how we can solve it by incorporating the features of the `FileSystemWatcher` component. If you have ever created an application that has a lot of dependency on data files for its input, then you might have coded your application in such a way that it waits and processes the files that show up in a particular directory. Your application might even import data from a file, which is downloaded from a mainframe or from any other external resources, into a database. In that situation, instead of constantly polling the directory for new files, you can wait for notifications indicating that a new file has been created. `FileSystemWatcher` can be a perfect fit for this kind of requirement as it provides an elegant and consistent approach to coding up this application.

Registry Access

The registry can be considered a centralized storage facility for storing information about applications, users, and default system settings. For example, we can use the registry to store information that needs to be persisted across different running sessions of our application. For instance, we can store connection strings to the database and some important settings in the registry and allow our application to pick up these values from the registry at runtime. The entire registry-related classes are contained in the `Microsoft.Win32` namespace.

In this section, we will take a look at a code sample to understand how to read values from the registry programmatically. Since the registry is structured in a hierarchical fashion, to reach a particular key, we need to navigate down the path to get to the key. The `Registry` class contains the following static fields that are used to identify the registry hives present in the registry.

- ClassesRoot
- CurrentConfig
- CurrentUser
- DynData
- LocalMachine
- PerformanceData
- Users

All the above static fields are of type `RegistryKey`. Once we get a reference to the field of type `RegistryKey`, we can easily perform operations like accessing the keys, enumerating the subkeys, and reading and modifying values.

To read the string value `"Path"` that is present under the HKEY_LOCAL_MACHINE \SOFTWARE \Microsoft\ASP.NET\1.0.2914.16\ hive of the registry, we need to execute the following set of statements:

```
Imports Microsoft.Win32

Dim oHKLM As RegistryKey = Registry.LocalMachine
Dim oSoftware As RegistryKey = oHKLM.OpenSubKey("SOFTWARE")
Dim oMicrosoft As RegistryKey = oSoftware.OpenSubKey("Microsoft")
Dim oASP As RegistryKey = oMicrosoft.OpenSubKey("ASP.NET")
Dim oVer As RegistryKey = oASP.OpenSubKey("1.0.2914.16")
        AddItem("{HKEY_LOCAL_MACHINE\SOFTWARE\Microsoft\ASP.NET\1.0.2914.16\}")
AddItem("Path = " & oVer.GetValue("Path").ToString())
```

By importing the namespace, we ensure that we can use the registry classes without having to type the fully-qualified name every time we mention the registry classes.

```
Imports Microsoft.Win32
```

In the following lines of code, we navigate through the registry hierarchy to get the value contained in the string value `Path`.

```
Dim oHKLM As RegistryKey = Registry.LocalMachine
Dim oSoftware As RegistryKey = oHKLM.OpenSubKey("SOFTWARE")
Dim oMicrosoft As RegistryKey = oSoftware.OpenSubKey("Microsoft")
Dim oASP As RegistryKey = oMicrosoft.OpenSubKey("ASP.NET")
Dim oVer As RegistryKey = oASP. OpenSubKey("1.0.2914.16")
```

After we reach the **Books** hive, we then directly call the `GetValue` method passing in the name of the string value to be retrieved.

```
AddItem("{HKEY_LOCAL_MACHINE\SOFTWARE\Microsoft\ASP.NET\1.0.2914.16\}")
AddItem("Path = " & oVer.GetValue("Path").ToString())
```

The above example clearly shows that we can access the registry easily using the classes provided by the .NET framework. However, it is also important that we carefully consider the other options for storing the global configuration settings, such as an XML-based file (like `web.config`) instead of the registry, because storing the values in the registry introduces dependency on the registry, which defeats the whole purpose of XCopy deployment, one of the core features of the .NET platform.

Connecting to the Internet

There are times when we might want to download a resource from the Internet from our application programmatically. It is basically a two-step process that involves making a request to the resource, receiving the response, and processing the response by reading it through the `StreamReader` class.
The `System.NET` assembly contains a number of classes that allow us to perform the above operations.

The classes present in the `System.NET` namespace provide a simple and unified programming model for writing networked applications in managed code. The .NET classes expose a robust implementation of the HTTP protocol and allow us to write scalable, high-performance, middle-tier applications. We can compare these classes with the WinInet API in terms of the functionalities like allowing applications to send and get data using Internet protocols. However, the .NET classes differ from the API in that they are designed with an emphasis on standing up to a high stress server environment. The .NET classes contain the following three layers.

❑   The request/response layer

❑   Application protocols layer

❑   Transport layer – sockets exist in the Transport layer and it is contained in the `System.NET.Sockets` namespace

The `Sockets` class implements the Berkeley Sockets interface, which provides a general-purpose interface to both connection-less and connection-oriented network transport communication. The .NET framework uses the `Sockets` class to provide Internet connections to .NET classes such as `UdpClient`, `TcpClient`, `WebRequest` and so on. For example, a client application that uses the `WebRequest` class to programmatically obtain resources from the Internet uses sockets internally and it performs the following steps:

❑   Create a socket

❑   Connects to server port (endpoint)
    Connection to the endpoint or port is established using the `Connect` method. After the connection is established, we can bind the socket to the specific endpoint by invoking the `Bind` method.

❑   Read from connection
    `Receive` and `ReceiveFrom` methods are used to read data from the socket.

❑   Write to connection
    This is carried out using the `Send` and `SendTo` methods.

❑   Close connection
    After we are done using the socket, we need to disable it using the `ShutDown` method and then finally close it using the `Close` method.

The important classes in the `System.NET` namespace, which provide the applications with the capability of connecting to the Internet and downloading a resource, can be represented using the following diagram:

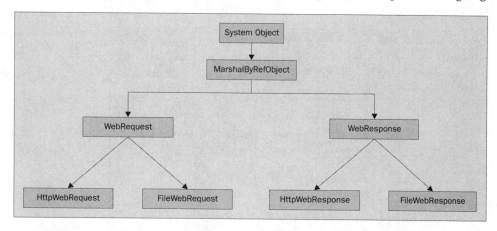

From the above diagram, we can see that the `MarshalByRefObject` class derives from `System.Object`. The `MarshalByRefObject` class exposes the functionality to perform remoting of objects using marshal by reference. `WebRequest` is an abstract class and it is derived from `MarshalByRefObject`. Because of the abstract nature of the `WebRequest` class, classes such as `HttpWebRequest`, `HttpWebResponse`, `FileWebRequest` and `FileWebResponse`, which inherit from the `WebRequest` class, are required to provide the actual implementation for the `WebRequest` class.

The `FileWebRequest` and `FileWebResponse` classes implement the `WebRequest` abstract class and they are used to formulate requests for local files using the request scheme file://. We can create an instance of the `FileWebRequest` class using the `Create` method of the `WebRequest` class.

When we want to make an HTTP request, we do it through the instance of the class `HttpWebRequest`. However, we cannot create an instance of `HttpWebRequest` directly – instead it needs to be constructed by invoking the `Create` method of the `WebRequest` class. This method returns a reference to the `WebRequest` object and it needs to be cast to the `HttpWebRequest` object.

Once we get a reference to the `HttpWebRequest` object, we can actually make the request by calling its `GetResponse` method. This method returns the `WebResponse` object that contains the information returned by the web server as a result of the request that we made through the `WebRequest` object.

After we get a reference to the `WebResponse` object, we can use a `StreamReader` to retrieve the contents of the response. To do this, we use the `StreamReader` constructor, which takes two parameters: a `Stream` object and an enumeration that indicates the encoding type. For the encoding type, we specify `Encoding.ASCII` to indicate that this stream contains ASCII text data.

The HTTP classes implement the generic request/response model, along with some additional properties that provide a greater level of control over such HTTP-specific features as access to the HTTP protocol in an object model for property-level control over headers, chunking, or setting the User Agent string. In most cases, using `WebRequest` and `WebResponse` will be sufficient for sending and receiving data. We need to use the `HttpWebRequest` and `HttpWebResponse` classes only when the level of details exposed by `WebRequest` and `WebResponse` is not sufficient.

Let us look at the following example to understand the usage of .NET classes. In this example, we will retrieve the resource from the Internet based on the URL (using the HTTP protocol) that the user enters. The running application looks like this:

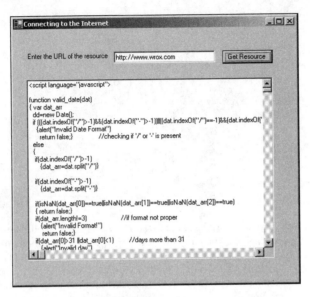

We will create this application using the VB.NET windows application template.

```vbnet
Imports System.IO
Imports System.NET
Imports System.Text

Public Class Form1
    Inherits System.Windows.Forms.Form

Private Sub cmdGetResource_Click(ByVal sender As System.Object, ByVal e As
            System.EventArgs) Handles cmdGetResource.Click
    Dim oWebRequest As HttpWebRequest
    Dim oWebResponse As HttpWebResponse
    Dim oStmReader As StreamReader
    Dim sURL As String
    Dim sLine As String
    'Clear the Listbox
    lstResource.Items.Clear()
    sURL = txtURL.Text
    oWebRequest = CType(WebRequest.Create(sURL), HttpWebRequest)
    oWebResponse = CType(oWebRequest.GetResponse(), HttpWebResponse)
    oStmReader = New StreamReader(oWebResponse.GetResponseStream(),
                        Encoding.ASCII)
    While (oStmReader.Peek <> -1)
        sLine = oStmReader.ReadLine()
        AddItem(sLine)
    End While
    oStmReader.Close()
End Sub

Private Sub AddItem(ByVal sMessage As String)
    lstResource.Items.Add(sMessage)
End Sub
```

First, we import the namespaces that we will be specifically using, apart from the default namespaces that VB.NET automatically imports. The `System.IO` namespace is for the `StreamReader` that we need to use, `System.NET` is for the web classes, and `System.Text` is for the helper enumeration that we require while creating the `StreamReader` object.

```
Imports System.IO
Imports System.NET
Imports System.Text
```

When we enter the URL of the resource and click the **Get Resource** command button, we execute the following set of statements to retrieve the resource:

```
Dim oWebRequest As HttpWebRequest
Dim oWebResponse As HttpWebResponse
Dim oStmReader As StreamReader
Dim sURL As String
Dim sLine As String
```

Now, we clear the contents of the listbox and then capture the entered URL into a variable called `sURL`.

```
'Clear the Listbox
lstResource.Items.Clear()
sURL = txtURL.Text
```

In this line, we cast the `WebRequest` object returned by the `Create` method of the `WebRequest` class into an `HttpWebRequest` and assign it to a variable.

```
oWebRequest = CType(WebRequest.Create(sURL), HttpWebRequest)
```

Now, we invoke the `GetResponse` method of the `HttpWebRequest` object and get the response returned by the web server into a variable that is of type `HttpWebResponse`.

```
oWebResponse = CType(oWebRequest.GetResponse(), HttpWebResponse)
```

We then get the response into a `StreamReader` object by invoking the `GetResponseStream` method of the `HttpWebResponse` object.

```
oStmReader = New StreamReader(oWebResponse.GetResponseStream(),
                 Encoding.ASCII)
```

Finally, we loop through the contents of the `Stream` object and show it in the listbox.

```
While (oStmReader.Peek <> -1)
    sLine = oStmReader.ReadLine()
    AddItem(sLine)
End While
oStmReader.Close()
```

We use the `AddItem` method to add the passed string arguments into the listbox called `lstResource`.

```
Private Sub AddItem(ByVal sMessage As String)
    lstResource.Items.Add(sMessage)
End Sub
```

Exception Handling

Exception can be defined as an event that occurs during the execution of a program that disrupts the normal flow of execution. `System.Exception` defines several properties and methods that are used to store and manage information about the exceptions that may occur in an application. It is the base exception class for all the exception-related classes in the .NET framework. If you are writing your own custom-defined exception class, you then need to derive from the `Exception` base class.

The cause of exceptions can be anything, ranging from serious hardware problems to simple programming errors, such as trying to access an out-of-bounds array element. When such an error condition occurs, the method creates an `Exception` object and hands it the runtime. The `Exception` object contains information about the error condition, including its type and the state of the program when the error occurred.

After a method throws an exception, the runtime searches backwards through the call stack, beginning with the method in which the error occurred, until it finds the method that contains the matching error handler that can handle the raised exception. This process is called **exception bubbling** and while searching for the appropriate exception handler, if the runtime does not find an appropriate one, the program terminates abnormally raising an error message. For example, the following `DivideByZeroException` exception message is displayed when there is no exception handler to handle the divide-by-zero exceptional condition.

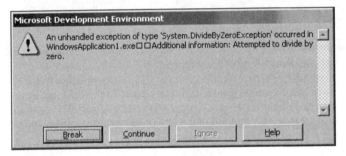

The `Message` property of an `Exception` class contains the human-readable description of the cause that has created this exceptional condition. When an exception is created, and before it is raised (or thrown), the CLR captures the info about the call stack and stores it with the `Exception` object. We can retrieve the stored info by calling the `StackTrace` method of the `Exception` class. This is especially useful for debugging purposes when the application consists of nested method calls.

When we invoke the unmanaged code, and if an exception occurs during the execution of that code, then the CLR automatically converts the COM `HRESULT` failure values into `Exception` objects, so that the managed code can handle the exceptional condition in a consistent way. Similarly, when calling into managed code from unmanaged code, and if an exception occurs, the CLR automatically converts the `Exception` object's information into an `HRESULT` value, which the unmanaged code can understand.

One of the major drawbacks of writing applications in unmanaged code (COM environment) is the lack of an elegant and standard approach to handling errors. Traditionally exceptions are handled by using the return codes returned by the function, which does not lend itself to the construction of robust exception handling systems. There are a lot of disadvantages to handling errors in that way.

Advantages of the Exception Handling Approach in .NET

- ❏ Allows us to separate error-handling code from regular code, thereby improving the readability of code.

- ❏ Allows us to propagate errors up the call stack so that it can be handled in the appropriate context.

- ❏ Allows us to group different kinds of error conditions into logical groups.

- ❏ Allows us to throw exceptions from constructors
  Object construction is one of the major areas where we could not return error codes to the caller to indicate exceptional condition. However, in .NET, we can raise or throw errors even from the constructor. All we have to do is wrap the statements in the `Try` block and the runtime will take care of raising the error to the caller.

- ❏ Allows us to catch exceptions and handle them from any language, regardless of the language from where the exception is thrown.

- ❏ By implementing custom exception classes, we can specify more exception-related information that allows us to provide a clear picture of the exceptional condition.

Steps to be Followed when Writing an Exception Handler

- ❏ The `Try` block
  The first step in writing an exception handler is to enclose the statements that might throw an exception within a `Try` block.

- ❏ The `Catch` block
  Next, you associate exception handlers with the `Try` block by providing one or more `Catch` blocks directly after the `Try` block.

- ❏ The `Finally` block
  The `Finally` block provides a way for the method to perform cleanup regardless of whether statements in the `Try` block are executed successfully or not.

Now that we have defined the various elements that form an exception handler, let's go ahead and build a sample application that exercises these concepts. Accessing the database is something that we will be performing frequently in our daily life. So in this example, written using C#, we will access the database to retrieve employee information and see how to handle errors that may occur during the execution of those statements. The execution flow of the application can be easily understood by considering the following diagram.

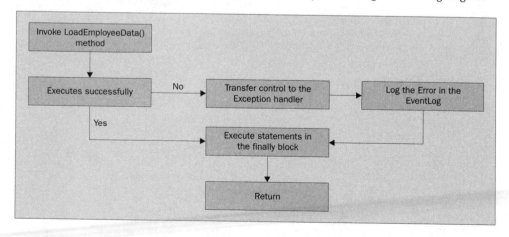

The method LoadEmployeesData is the meat of the example, as it not only contains all the code to retrieve the employee information from the database, but also shows how to handle errors (in this case logging the error into the event log) when an exception condition occurs.

```csharp
using System;
using System.Drawing;
using System.Collections;
using System.ComponentModel;
using System.Windows.Forms;
using System.Data;
using System.Data.SqlClient;
using System.Diagnostics;


private void LoadEmployeesData()
{
    SqlDataReader oSQLDataReader;
    SqlConnection oSQLConnection = new SqlConnection();
    ListViewItem oListViewItem;
    try
    {
        String sConn = "server=localhost;uid=sa;pwd=;database=Northwind";
        String sCommand = "SELECT * FROM Employees";"
        oSQLConnection.ConnectionString = sConn;
        SqlCommand oSQLCommand  = new SqlCommand(sCommand, oSQLConnection);
        oSQLCommand.Connection.Open();
        oSQLDataReader = oSQLCommand.ExecuteReader();
        //Clear all the items in the listview
        lvwEmployees.Items.Clear();
        while (oSQLDataReader.Read())
        {
            oListViewItem = new ListViewItem();
            oListViewItem.Text = oSQLDataReader["EmployeeID"].ToString();
            ListViewItem.ListViewSubItem oListViewSubItem = new
                        ListViewItem.ListViewSubItem();
            oListViewSubItem.Text = oSQLDataReader["LastName"] + "," +
                        oSQLDataReader["FirstName"];
            oListViewItem.SubItems.Add(oListViewSubItem);
            ListViewItem.ListViewSubItem oListViewSubItem1 = new
                        ListViewItem.ListViewSubItem();
            oListViewSubItem1.Text = oSQLDataReader["Title"].ToString();
            oListViewItem.SubItems.Add(oListViewSubItem1);
            lvwEmployees.Items.Add(oListViewItem);
        }
    }
    catch(SqlException ex)
    {
        EventLog oEventLog;
        String sLogName;
        String sSource;
        //Write the errors into the Windows 2000 event log
        oEventLog = new EventLog();
        sLogName = "MyLog";
        sSource = "Chapter15Example23";
        oEventLog.Source = sSource;
        if (!EventLog.SourceExists(sSource))
```

```
            {
                EventLog.CreateEventSource(sSource, sLogName);
            }
            oEventLog.WriteEntry(ex.ToString(), EventLogEntryType.Error);
            throw new Exception("SQL Exception occured,Please try     again");
        }
        catch (Exception ex)
        {
            throw new Exception("Exception occurred,Please try again");
        }

        finally
        {
            if (oSQLConnection.State == ConnectionState.Open)
            {
                oSQLConnection.Close();
            }
        }
    }

    private void cmdLoadEmployee_Click(object sender, System.EventArgs e)
    {
        try
        {
            LoadEmployeesData();
        }
        catch(Exception ex)
        {
            MessageBox.Show(ex.Message);
        }
    }
```

We start by importing all the required namespaces.

```
using System;
using System.Drawing;
using System.Collections;
using System.ComponentModel;
using System.Windows.Forms;
using System.Data;
using System.Data.SqlClient;
using System.Diagnostics;
```

In the following line, we create a SqlConnection object:

```
SqlDataReader oSQLDataReader;
SqlConnection oSQLConnection = new SqlConnection();
ListViewItem oListViewItem;
```

We enclose all the executable statements in a try block to catch any errors that may occur during the execution of those statements.

```
try
{
```

In the following lines, we assign the connection string to the database to a string variable and then assign the SQL statement to be executed, to another string variable.

```
String sConn = server=localhost;uid=sa;pwd=;database=Northwind";
String sCommand = "Select * from Employees";
```

Here, we set the connection string property of the `SqlConnection` to the value of the string variable.

```
oSQLConnection.ConnectionString = sConn;
```

Now, we create an instance of the `SqlCommand` object, passing its constructor the SQL command to be executed and the `SqlConnection` object that was created in the previous step as arguments.

```
SqlCommand oSQLCommand  = new SqlCommand(sCommand, oSQLConnection);
```

By invoking the `Open` method, we establish the connection to the database.

```
oSQLCommand.Connection.Open();
```

In this line, we invoke the `ExecuteReader` method of the command object, create an instance of the `SQLDataReader` object and assign it to the variable of type `SQLDataReader`.

```
oSQLDataReader = oSQLCommand.ExecuteReader();
```

Before displaying the employee information in the listview, we clear the contents of the employees listview.

```
lvwEmployees.Items.Clear();
```

Now, we set up a `while` loop to loop through the `SQLDataReader` object and display all the records in the listview. The `Read` method of the `SQLDataReader` returns `True` if there are more records, otherwise it returns `False`.

```
while (oSQLDataReader.Read())
{
    oListViewItem = new ListViewItem();
    oListViewItem.Text = oSQLDataReader["EmployeeID"].ToString();
    ListViewItem.ListViewSubItem oListViewSubItem = new
            ListViewItem.ListViewSubItem();
    oListViewSubItem.Text = oSQLDataReader["LastName"] + "," +
            oSQLDataReader["FirstName"];
    oListViewItem.SubItems.Add(oListViewSubItem);
    ListViewItem.ListViewSubItem oListViewSubItem1 = new
            ListViewItem.ListViewSubItem();
    oListViewSubItem1.Text = oSQLDataReader["Title"].ToString();
    oListViewItem.SubItems.Add(oListViewSubItem1);
    lvwEmployees.Items.Add(oListViewItem);
}
}
```

Whenever an exception occurs during the execution of the above statements, control will be transferred to the `catch` blocks and each `catch` block will be matched against the kind of exception that was generated. In this case, we want to handle all the error conditions of type `SQLException` by logging them into the Windows 2000 event log. We handle the remaining exceptional conditions by raising them back to the client.

```
catch(SqlException ex)
{
    EventLog oEventLog;
    String sLogName;
    String sSource;
    //Write the errors into the Windows 2000 event log
```

In this group of statements, we create an instance of the EventLog and set its Source property to an appropriate value.

```
    oEventLog = new EventLog();
    sLogName = "MyLog";
    sSource = "Chapter15Example23";
    oEventLog.Source = sSource;
```

We also check whether the specified source exists by invoking the SourceExists method of the EventLog class. If it does not exist, we create the source by using the CreateEventSource method of the EventLog class, passing in the property source and log name as arguments.

```
    if   (!EventLog.SourceExists(sSource))
    {
        EventLog.CreateEventSource(sSource, sLogName);
    }
```

Here, we write an entry into the event log using the message that is present in the Exception object.

```
    oEventLog.WriteEntry(ex.ToString(), EventLogEntryType.Error);
```

After writing the message into the event log, we also raise the error back to the caller using the throw statement.

```
    throw new Exception("SQL Exception occurred,Please try again");
}
```

In this catch block, we handle all the errors other than the SQLException errors.

```
catch (Exception ex)
{
    throw new Exception("Exception occurred,Please try again");
}
```

As we already said, the finally block allows us to provide a set of statements that are always executed, regardless of whether statements in the try block are executed successfully or not.

```
finally
{
    if (oSQLConnection.State == ConnectionState.Open)
    {
        oSQLConnection.Close();
    }
}
}
```

Now that we have gone through the code of the LoadEmployeesData method, let us look at the code that is required for invoking this method and for handling the exceptions raised by this method in a graceful manner.

```
private void cmdLoadEmployee_Click(object sender, System.EventArgs e)
{
    try
    {
        LoadEmployeesData();
    }
    catch(Exception ex)
    {
        MessageBox.Show(ex.Message);
    }
}
```

When the Load Employee Data command button is clicked, we call the LoadEmployeesData method and display the results in the listview. We enclose the code that is required for calling the LoadEmployeesData method in the try block so as to handle the errors raised by the called method in a graceful manner.

If we run the application, we should get the following output:

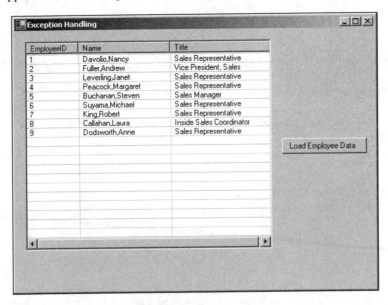

Now let us test the effectiveness of the exception handler by setting the connection string to an incorrect value and then execute the application. We should get a message box saying "SQL Exception occurred, Please try again". If we open up the event viewer, we can also see that the exception handler has also recorded the exception information in the event log.

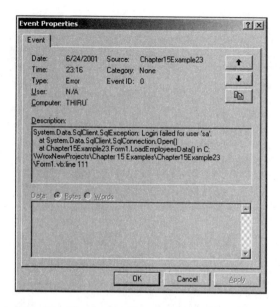

Everything seems to be working fine. However, when we want to have this logging facility of the exceptional conditions to be implemented across our application, we need to duplicate the logging code in all the other parts of the application. An elegant solution for this problem would be to have the logging code moved over to a user-defined exception class that can encapsulate this operation for us.

Deriving User-Defined Exception Classes

As we have already discussed, there are times when we might want to provide additional information or formatting to an exception before we raise it back to the client code. Also, by having our own exception class, we can publish the fact that our class will throw only one type of exception to the clients. One more reason to derive a user-defined exception class would be to log the error information or take a follow-up action if an exception has occurred in the application, which is precisely the reason why we are going to write our own exception class that is derived from the Exception base class.

The example is similar to the previous one except that we are going to derive our own exception class and have the logging code moved over to the constructor of that class.

```
public class InValidConnectionException : Exception
{
public InValidConnectionException(String sMessage,Exception ex) :base(sMessage,ex)
    {

        EventLog oEventLog;
        String sLogName;
        String sSource;
        //write the errors into the Windows 2000 event log
        oEventLog = new EventLog();
        sLogName = "MyLog";
        sSource = "Chapter15Example24";
        oEventLog.Source = sSource;
        if (!EventLog.SourceExists(sSource))

        {
            EventLog.CreateEventSource(sSource, sLogName);
```

```
        }
        oEventLog.WriteEntry(ex.ToString(), EventLogEntryType.Error);
    }
}

private void LoadEmployeesData()
{
    SqlDataReader oSQLDataReader;
    SqlConnection oSQLConnection = new SqlConnection();
    ListViewItem oListViewItem;
    try
    {
        String sConn = "server=localhost;uid=sa;pwd=;database=Northwind";
        String sCommand = "Select * from Employees";
        oSQLConnection.ConnectionString = sConn;
        SqlCommand oSQLCommand  = new SqlCommand(sCommand, oSQLConnection);
        oSQLCommand.Connection.Open();
        oSQLDataReader = oSQLCommand.ExecuteReader();
        //Clear all the items in the listview
        lvwEmployees.Items.Clear();
        while (oSQLDataReader.Read())
        {
            oListViewItem = new ListViewItem();
            oListViewItem.Text = oSQLDataReader["EmployeeID"].ToString();
            ListViewItem.ListViewSubItem oListViewSubItem = new
                        ListViewItem.ListViewSubItem();
            oListViewSubItem.Text = oSQLDataReader["LastName"] + "," +
                        oSQLDataReader["FirstName"];
            oListViewItem.SubItems.Add(oListViewSubItem);
            ListViewItem.ListViewSubItem oListViewSubItem1 = new
                        ListViewItem.ListViewSubItem();
            oListViewSubItem1.Text = oSQLDataReader["Title"].ToString();
            oListViewItem.SubItems.Add(oListViewSubItem1);
            lvwEmployees.Items.Add(oListViewItem);
        }
    }
    catch(SqlException ex)
    {
        throw new InValidConnectionException("SQL Exception
                    occurred,Please try again", ex);
    }
    catch (Exception ex)
    {
        throw new Exception("Exception occurred,Please try again");
    }

    finally
    {
        if (oSQLConnection.State == ConnectionState.Open)
        {
            oSQLConnection.Close();
        }
    }
}
```

Let us examine the code of the constructor of the InValidConnectionException class that encapsulates the logging of the exceptions as part of its object construction process.

As we can see, the constructor passes the arguments supplied to it also to the base exception class by using the following line of code.

```
public InValidConnectionException(String sMessage,Exception ex) :base(sMessage,ex)
{
```

The rest of the constructor code is used for logging the exceptions to the Windows 2000 event log.

```
EventLog oEventLog;
String sLogName;
String sSource;
//write the errors into the Windows 2000 event log
oEventLog = new EventLog();
sLogName = "MyLog";
sSource = "Chapter15Example24";
oEventLog.Source = sSource;
if (!EventLog.SourceExists(sSource))
{
    EventLog.CreateEventSource(sSource, sLogName);
}
oEventLog.WriteEntry(ex.ToString(), EventLogEntryType.Error);
}
```

Now let us look at the code used for invoking the constructor of the InValidConnectionException class to log the errors. In the following line, we use the throw statement and create an exception object of type InValidConnectionException, passing in the message and the exception object as arguments to its constructor. So whenever SQLException occurs, control will be transferred to the catch block where it is logged by the constructor of the InValidConnectionException class, and then the exception is raised back to the client.

```
catch(SqlException ex)
{
    throw new InValidConnectionException("SQL Exception
            occurred, Please try again", ex);
}
```

Date and Time Related Operations

In this section, we will look at two important date and time related classes: DateTime and TimeSpan. These classes are used to represent date and time. The DateTime data type can be used to represent dates and times ranging from 12:00:00 AM, 1/1/0001 to 11:59:59 PM, 12/13/9999. In contrast to DateTime, the TimeSpan class is used to represent the time interval. Using Timespan, we can find out the difference in dates between two instances of DateTime variables.

The DateTime class provides a number of methods for working with date and time values. To create a DateTime value, we simply declare a variable of type DateTime and invoke one of the many overloaded constructors.

In the following example, we will take a look at the important properties and methods of the `DateTime` class, most of which are self-explanatory.

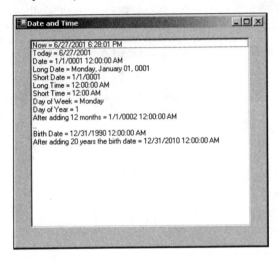

```
Date and Time                                          _ □ x
Now = 6/27/2001 6:28:01 PM
Today = 6/27/2001
Date = 1/1/0001 12:00:00 AM
Long Date = Monday, January 01, 0001
Short Date = 1/1/0001
Long Time = 12:00:00 AM
Short Time = 12:00 AM
Day of Week = Monday
Day of Year = 1
After adding 12 months = 1/1/0002 12:00:00 AM
..
Birth Date = 12/31/1990 12:00:00 AM
After adding 20 years the birth date = 12/31/2010 12:00:00 AM
```

We start by declaring two variables of type `DateTime`: one holds the current date and another one holds the date 12/31/1990.

```
Dim dtCurrentDate As New DateTime()
Dim dtBirthDate As New DateTime(1990, 12, 31)
```

In the following lines, we invoke the different properties and methods of the `dtCurrentDate` variable and display the results in the listbox.

```
With dtCurrentDate
    AddItem("Now = " & .Now())
    AddItem("Today = " & .Today())
    AddItem("Date = " & .ToString())
    AddItem("Long Date = " & .ToLongDateString())
    AddItem("Short Date = " & .ToShortDateString())
    AddItem("Long Time = " & .ToLongTimeString())
    AddItem("Short Time = " & .ToShortTimeString())
    AddItem("Day of Week = " & .DayOfWeek().ToString())
    AddItem("Day of Year = " & .DayOfYear().ToString())
    AddItem("After adding 12 months = " &
            dtCurrentDate.AddMonths(12).ToString())
    AddItem("..")
```

Now we manipulate the `dtBirthDate` variable by adding 20 years to it and then display its results.

```
    AddItem("Birth Date = " & dtBirthDate.ToString())
    AddItem("After adding 20 years the birth date = " &
            dtBirthDate.AddYears(20).ToString())
End With
```

Array Manipulation

In the .NET framework, the `System.Array` class serves as the base class for all arrays in the common language runtime. `System.Array` implements several collection interfaces, such as `ICloneable`, `IList`, `ICollection`, and `IEnumerable`. This means that we can cast an array to any of the above-mentioned interfaces, which gives us the ability to pass an array to a method that takes any one of the above interfaces as an argument.

Due to the collection interfaces it is derived from, `System.Array` is similar in functionality to many of the collection classes contained in the `System.Collections` namespace and `System.Collections.Specialized` namespace.

If we want to create a collection that provides standard functionalities, such as storing, manipulating, and searching a group of elements, then `System.Array` would be the ideal choice. Instead, if we want to create a sophisticated array that can be dynamically increased or decreased, then we should opt for the `ArrayList` class that is part of the `System.Collections` namespace.

The most basic way that information is stored in a computer program is by putting it into a variable. However, this method is limited to relatively simple usage. Sometimes, you may want to store the groups of related variables that are of the same type. In that case, arrays can be used to store that information. We can create arrays for any type of information that can be stored as a variable. Like variables, we create arrays by stating the type of the variable being organized into the array and the name of the array. For example, the following statements create an array of variables:

```
String[] arrEmployeeNames;
int[] arrEmpIDs;
```

The previous examples create arrays, but they do not store any values in them initially. To do this, we must either use the new statement, along with the variable type, or store values in the array within { } marks. We must also specify how many different items will be stored in the array. Each item in the array is called an element. The following creates an array and sets aside space for the values that it will hold.

```
int[] arrNumber = new int[50];
```

The above example creates an array of integers called `arrNumber`. The array has 50 elements in it that can be used to store the numbers from 1 to 50. For arrays that are not extremely large, you can set up their individual values at the same time as you create them. The following example creates an array of strings and gives them initial values:

```
String [] arrEmployeeNames = {"Nancy", "Andrew", "Janet", "Margaret",
                              "Steven", "Michael"}
```

In the above example, the number of elements in the array is not specified in the statement, because it is set to the number of elements in the comma-separated list. Each element of the array in the list must be of the same type. It is important to point out that the first element in the array is numbered 0 instead of 1. This means that the highest index of an array is one less than the total number of items in the array. For example, let us consider the following statement:

```
String[] arrEmployeeNames = new String[3];
```

This statement creates an array of string variables that are numbered from 0 to 2. If we refer to `arrEmployeeNames[3]` somewhere else in our program, we would get the `System.IndexOutOfRangeException`. To check the upper limit of an array, we can use the `Length` method. By using this method we can avoid getting beyond the maximum limit of the size of the array. The `Length` method returns an integer that contains the number of elements an array can hold.

Once we group a bunch of similar items together into an array, one of the things we might want to do is sort them into a specific order. Sorting an array is easy in .NET, because the `Array` class does all the work for us. This is accomplished by invoking the `Sort` method of the `Array` class. The methods `GetLowerBound` and `GetUpperBound` return the lower bound and the upper bound of the specified dimension in the array respectively. Using the `Rank` of an array, we can find out the number of dimensions in the array. Using the `Reverse` method, we can reverse the order of the elements in a one-dimensional array.

Like the `String` class, `Array` also contains the `IndexOf` and `LastIndexOf` methods that allow us to find out the index of the occurrence of a value, either from the start or from the end.

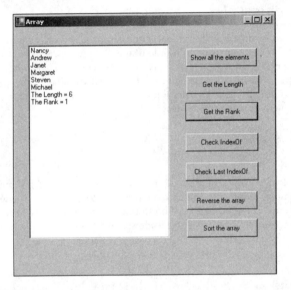

Regular Expressions

If you have ever typed *.doc in the Windows Find dialog box to search for files that end with a specific extension, you have already used a simple regular expression. If you are a PERL programmer, you will agree that regular expressions are arguably one of the most powerful and useful tools provided by PERL.

Regular expressions figure in all kinds of text-manipulation tasks. For example, searching and search-and-replace are some of the very common uses of regular expressions. They can also be used to test for certain conditions in a text file or data stream. For example, we can use regular expressions as the basis for a short program that separates incoming mail from incoming spam. In this case, the program might use a regular expression to determine whether the name of a known spammer appeared in the From: line of the e-mail. E-mail filtering programs, in fact, very often use regular expressions for exactly this type of operation.

The power of regular expressions lies in the pattern string that is used to perform matching operations such as searching, extracting a specified substring from a string, or replacing sub strings and so on. The patterns available in regular expressions are so comprehensive that we will not be able to cover all of them in this section. Instead, we will consider the frequently used special characters that are used in pattern matching in the following table.

Element	Description	Example Pattern	Matching Example
*	Zero or more matches	`wor*d`	world and word
+	One or more matches	`wor+d`	word and worrd
?	Zero or one match	`wor?d`	word and world
\s	Any whitespace character	`Hello\sWorld`	Hello World
\S	Any non-whitespace character	`Hello\Sworld`	Helloworld
\d	Any digit character	`VB\d`	VB6
\D	Any non-digit character	`SQ\D`	SQL
\b	Position that is a word boundary	`*NET\b`	Visual Basic.NET
\B	Position that is not a word boundary	`*basic\B`	Visual basic.NET

Realizing the usefulness and the power of the regular expressions, the .NET team created a separate namespace called `System.Text.RegularExpressions`, which contains a number of classes that provide us with access to the .NET framework regular expression engine, which provides a very effective and easier way to do certain things, such as advanced searches/replaces and many more. In .NET, these regular expression classes form an integral part of highly optimized cross-language libraries that make up the backbone of the .NET platform.

The base class for all regular expressions is `Regex`, whose constructor takes a regular expression as a string parameter, and creates and compiles a regular expression object. The `Regex` object is immutable once it is created, but it can be used as many times as we wish without the need to recompile, which in turn helps performance to a great extent.

It is important to understand the way .NET compiles regular expressions. When a regular expression is evalutated, a sequence of byte codes representing the regular expression is generated and interpreted at runtime. If performance is critical, it is possible to compile the regular expression directly to explicit IL. This is achieved by constructing a `Regex` object with the `RegexOptions.Compiled` option. Because the IL is at a lower level than byte codes, the performance increases many times. However, the increase in performance comes at a cost. We cannot unload the generated IL till we unload all of our application's code. That may not be an issue if we only compile very few regular expressions that are used repeatedly, but if a great number of regular expressions are used, it is better to stick with the proven interpreted expressions rather than compiled expressions.

We create a `Regex` object by using the following syntax:

```
Dim oRegex As New Regex("Expression")
```

The `Match` method can be used to search an input string for an occurrence of a regular expression. This method returns a `Match` object as the return value, which represents the results of that single matching operation. Once we get the `Match` object, we call the `Success` property to check whether the regular expression matches the input string.

```
Dim sMatch As String
Dim oMatch As Match
Dim oRegEx As New Regex("World")
sMatch = InputBox("Enter the string to be matched")
oMatch = oRegex.Match(sMatch)
AddItem("Is the string matched = " & oMatch.Success.ToString())
```

The `Matches` method is similar to `Match`, except that it is used to perform multiple matches and it returns a `MatchCollection` as the return value. Once we get the collection object, we can then loop through it to display the matched elements.

```
Dim oMatchCollection As MatchCollection
Dim sMatch As String
Dim iCtr As Integer
```

In the following line of code, we indicate that we want to compile the regular expressions directly to MSIL by passing the value `RegexOptions.Compiled` to the second argument of the `RegEx` class constructor:

```
Dim oRegEx As New Regex("World", RegexOptions.Compiled)
sMatch = InputBox("Enter the string to be matched")
oMatchCollection = oRegex.Matches(sMatch)
For iCtr = 0 To oMatchCollection.Count - 1
    AddItem(oMatchCollection.Item(iCtr).ToString)
Next
```

The `Replace` method exposes quite a few overloads and in this example we use one of them to replace the occurrence of one string with another string.

```
Dim sReplace As String
sReplace = InputBox("Enter the new string you want to place")
AddItem(Regex.Replace("This is a string used for the entire example",
                      "This", sReplace))
```

Finally, the `Split` method can be used to split a string expression to an array of strings based on the character delimiter that is passed in.

```
Dim arrString() As String
Dim str As String
arrString = Regex.Split("This is a string used for the entire
                        example", " ")
For Each str In arrString
    AddItem(str)
Next
```

The `Regex` class also exposes two static methods, namely `Escape` and `Unescape`, that are used to perform escaping and unescaping respectively while handling a set of meta characters that are used in the pattern matching.

Now that we have seen the regular expression related classes present in the
System.Text.RegularExpressions namespace, let us look at some of the frequently used regular
expressions that are supplied in the .NET SDK documentation.

Expression	Example
[\w-]+@([\w-]+\.)+[\w-]+	Internet E-mail address (for example peter@dotnet.com)
\d{3}-\d{2}-\d{4}	Matches US social security number pattern (for example 123-45-6789)
\d{5}(-\d{4})?	US postal code (for example 85283-3841)
\d{4}-?\d{4}-?\d{4}-?\d{4}	Major credit card (for example 1111-1111-1111-1111)

Before we finish the discussion of the regular expressions, we also need to keep in mind that regular
expressions tend to be easier to write than they are to read. This will be less of a concern if you are the only
one who ever needs to maintain the program, but if several people need to watch over it, the syntax can turn
into more of a hindrance than an aid. So we need to exercise caution before flooding the application with the
regular expressions.

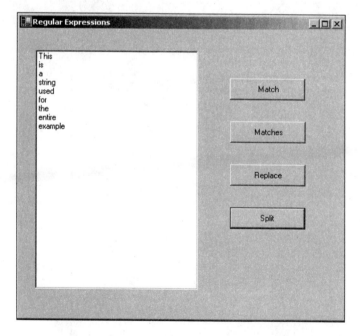

Mathematical Operations

The .NET framework makes available a wealth of functionality to perform mathematical calculations in an easy and flexible manner. It includes the ability to perform trigonometric, logarithmic and other common mathematical operations. The Math class is contained directly under the System namespace.

The Math class provides the following two public shared fields:

❑   E – returns the natural logarithmic base

❑   PI – gives the ratio of the circumference of a circle to its diameter

In the following examples, we invoke the properties and methods of the Math class to perform commonly performed mathematical operations. As you can see from the names of the methods, all of them are self-explanatory.

```
AddItem("E = " & Math.E.ToString())
AddItem("PI = " & Math.PI.ToString())
AddItem("Log of 10 = " & Math.Log(10).ToString())
AddItem("Max of 10, 20 = " & Math.Max(10, 20).ToString())
AddItem("Min of 10, 20 = " & Math.Min(10, 20).ToString())
AddItem("Sin 30 = " & Math.Sin(30).ToString())
AddItem("Cos 30 = " & Math.Cos(30).ToString())
AddItem("Floor of 12.8 = " & Math.Floor(12.8).ToString())
AddItem("Exp of 2 = " & Math.Exp(2).ToString())
AddItem("Square Root of 25 = " & Math.Sqrt(25).ToString())
```

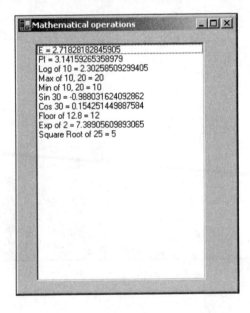

Summary

In this chapter, we have taken a tour of the important classes provided by the .NET framework. We started with an introduction to the `System` namespace and then went on to discuss how to use the WinCV tool to explore the classes available in the class library. We also discussed the importance of using the .NET framework classes in our applications, as opposed to using the same set of functionalities supplied by a language such as VB. We then talked about the important classes in the .NET framework and discussed their role in creating effective, maintainable, scalable and flexible applications. Specifically we covered:

❑　How to handle strings effectively using the `String` and `StringBuilder` classes

❑　How to use collection classes to engineer a powerful set of well-defined solutions to some of the most common programming tasks

❑　How to implement the classes in the `System.NET` namespace to connect to the Internet and retrieve resources

❑　Debugging and tracing the execution of code as well as logging events in the Windows 2000 event log

❑　How to carry out file handling and file monitoring operations

❑　Accessing the registry programmatically by making use of the classes available in the `Microsoft.Win32` namespace

❑　Creation of easy-to-maintain applications by employing the robust exception handling system provided by .NET

❑　How to perform common mathematical operations

We also covered classes, such as `Array`, `Regex`, `Math` and `DateTime` classes, to carry out frequently performed operations in the .NET framework.

In the next chapter, we will discuss the migration issues that we need to consider while trying to port existing applications to run under the .NET framework.

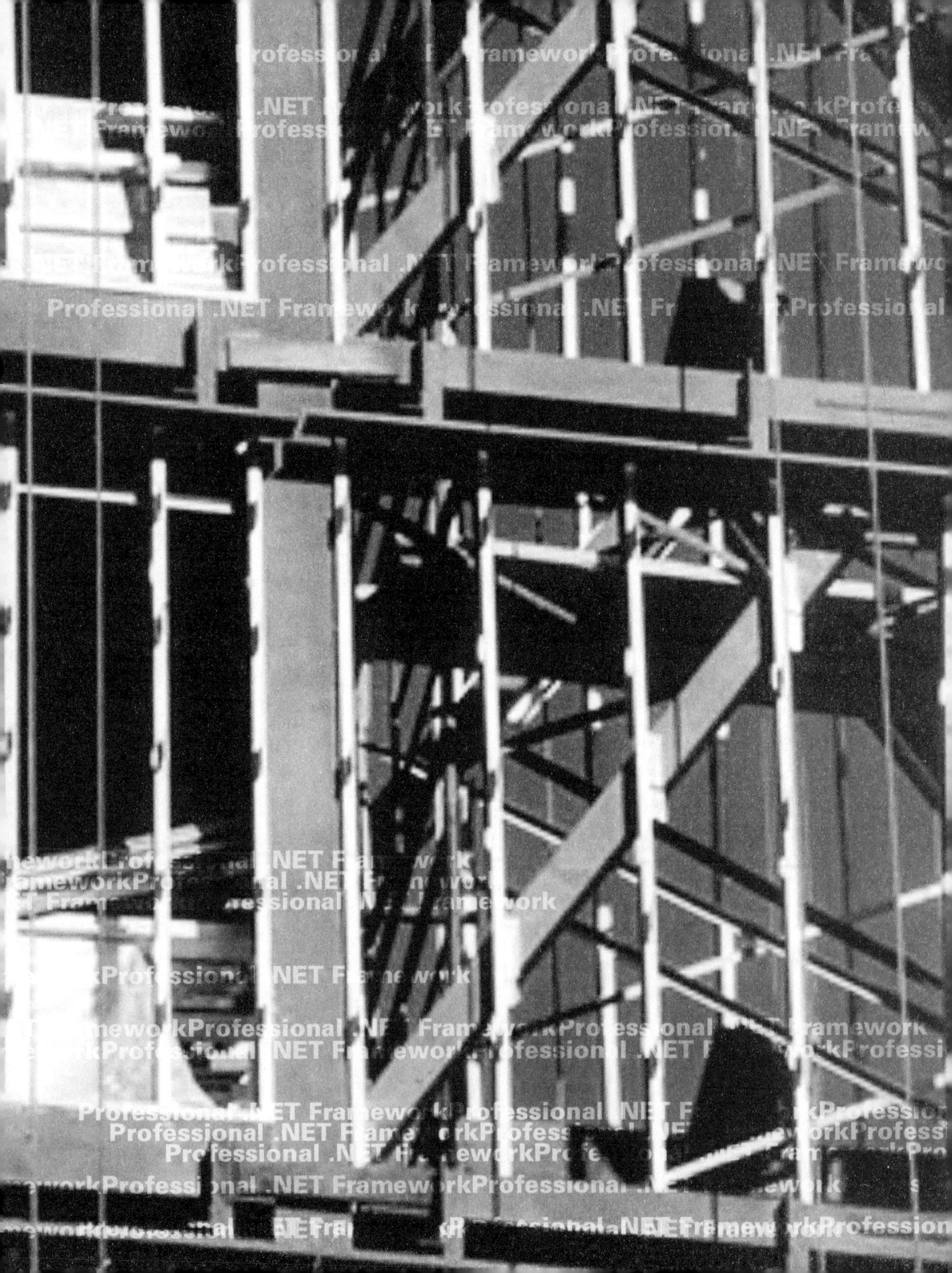
Professional .NET Framework

7

Engineering Applications

One of the first things that most experienced programmers learn is that there is an enormous difference between simply writing code and *engineering* an application. Writing code involves looking at samples, finding a minute task (such as utilizing an array), and accomplishing it. On its own the small section of code may be very impressive, but apart from a solid engineering and design process, it won't sell any software.

This chapter will give a thorough overview of good engineering practices with respect to Object-Oriented Programming (OOP) and *Component-Oriented Design*. While these topics may have already been discussed many times over in different publications and on various web sites, this chapter will attempt to apply these good design paradigms and best practices specifically to engineering n-tier applications within the scope of the .NET framework.

Throughout this chapter we will progressively develop components and classes that illustrate our concepts of good engineering, design, and OOP practices. This code will be able to be used by either a Web front-end or a Windows front-end, illustrating the main point that an application's presentation layer should be thin and versatile and the underlying tiers (business and data services) should not depend on the presentation layer for anything.

This chapter should give you a good understanding of the following concepts:

❑ Component Design

❑ Layer and Tier Separation in an n-Tier model

❑ Creating a robust, reusable set of back-end components

❑ Separating the presentation tier from a reusable back end infrastructure

By the time we complete the chapter, we will have fully developed a sample Video Store application that contains a core collection of business and data services that can be utilized by either a Windows presentation layer or Web Forms.

OOP in Practice

In Chapter 7, you learned all about how the .NET framework supports and embraces Object-Oriented Programming. When engineering your application, good Object-Oriented Design (OOD) and Object-Oriented Programming (OOP) are absolutely crucial to the success of your application.

The Framework itself is so much more than a hodgepodge collection of randomly gathered utilities, classes, types, enumerations, and assemblies. Instead, it should be considered a template. The framework's class library is built entirely upon good OOD practices. Once you start using the framework more often, you will begin to realize just how beneficial its good OOD practices are to the programmer.

Anyone who remembers spending hours sifting through Win32 API and MFC manuals, on-line references, and even newsgroup postings to find out where a specific piece of data resides, can truly appreciate the need for good OOD in an application. The .NET framework is arranged in an object hierarchy: therefore, when looking at an object, you immediately know its lineage, and know whether or not a specific piece of data or method is supported by that lineage. I'm thoroughly convinced that the time it takes to find what you're looking for in the .NET framework class library is less than a tenth of that required to find a useful function or type in the Win32 API. Other vendors have provided OOP frameworks as well. Java sports the WFC, Microsoft produced MFC, and Delphi has its Visual Component Library (VCL), all of which are built on strong inheritance models. The difference between these and the .NET framework is that these other OOP frameworks are built on top of flat, non-OOP cores, so the object model could only go so far before requiring functional interface. With the .NET framework, the entire thing, all the way up to the CLR, is built on a hierarchical object model, and is designed for extensibility.

Utilizing good Object-Oriented paradigms in your application will allow you to create applications that are scalable, flexible (or *agile*, depending on who you're talking to), easily maintainable, robust, and that support easy troubleshooting and diagnosis.

Component Design versus Application Design

One symptom of bad engineering practice very evident in the software industry today is lack of attention to *Component Design*. An application should be considered a collection of individual components. The Application provides the glue between those components and ties them together in related activities. As such, each individual component should be given as much design consideration as an entire application.

Obviously, the application must have an extremely strong, well thought-out design before design work on the components should begin. The application architects and designers (and usually some programmers) provide a high-level design of the application as a whole, while the programmers are typically responsible for iterating through the component life cycle.

This may seem like a radical idea, but in truth it will save you time and effort in the end. If each component has received as much attention to detail as applications do, then you can be reasonably sure that the component will function properly, be reasonably scalable, reusable, and save the programmers a considerable amount of time. Also, components developed in this fashion are considerably more reliable than components built with little or no design or attention to the component life cycle. If all of the components in your "collection" of components are functioning properly, then you have a very good chance of having your entire application function properly.

Component Life Cycle versus Software Life Cycle

In an object framework like the .NET framework, it is a crucial mistake to not treat each of your application's components with their own life cycle. In general, a software development life cycle consists of the following phases (obviously this varies depending on application, industry, software type, etc.):

- ❑ **Concept** – this phase should be an initial, very high-level concept development of the application.

- ❑ **Specifications / Requirements** – at this point, a concept has been solidified, and designers begin working out detailed requirements and specifications. These specifications and requirements are often based on user requests or user-supplied requirements when the project is being sponsored by a customer or a user.

- ❑ **Specifications Testing** – the specifications and requirements are typically tested by having walk-throughs of intended functionality and applying specific Use Cases to the design. At this point, "holes" in the design are often found, in which case the process returns to the specification stage.

- ❑ **Internal Documentation** (design, specs, use cases, UI, flow, requirements, etc.) – there are very few things in the software development life cycle more important than documentation. During this phase, the requirements, specifications, designs, use cases, and more are all documented and laid out clearly to give the developers as much information and background as possible.

- ❑ **Code and Testing** – this is a repetitive stage where the actual development of the application takes place. Testing of the application should be taking place concurrently with the development of the application, as well as afterwards by external testers.

- ❑ **Customer Documentation** (often outsourced) – this phase includes manuals, guides, on-line help, tutorials, training materials and outlines, etc. Your application may perform a million and one amazing feats, but if the customer has no idea how to use it, they won't use it.

In general, what happens to many application engineers is that they will thoroughly follow a development cycle that looks like the one above, or more than likely they will follow a much larger and rigorous development cycle. However, the problem arises when all "component work" shows up in the *Code* step and no additional work is done for them. For example, if the application design calls for the ability for a user to plot data in a graph form, it is likely that the programmers will develop some kind of graphing or plotting component. Rather than iterating the component through its own life cycle, including its own design, use case testing and more, many times the life cycle for the component will consist solely of the "code it" stage. This leads to very narrow-purpose components that are hard to reuse, maintain, and scale.

If you think of components as smaller, specialized applications then you should come to the conclusion that they need their own development cycle. If a component fails in a production application, the results can be disastrous, yet programmers habitually ignore all phases of development with regard to components except for programming. Another benefit of developing components with their own individual life cycles is that their usefulness isn't tied to the usefulness of a given application, and the component can remain useful long after its original host application becomes obsolete or unsupported.

The following example of a component life cycle should look very similar to that of an entire application. Again, keep in mind that all development projects are different and life cycles vary based on team structure, timelines, finances, and all kinds of other factors:

❑ **Concept** – this phase should be an initial, very high-level concept of the component. Designers will attempt to focus in on what the nature and purpose of the component are. Note that the component should rarely be designed specifically for one application, as that limits its ability to be reused for multiple applications.

❑ **Specifications / Requirements** – at this point, a concept should have been decided upon. Now the development and design team should focus on what functionality the component provides and to whom it should provide this functionality.

❑ **Specifications Testing** – once a solid set of specifications and requirements have been defined, it is time to run the component "through the ropes", so to speak. Use cases and hypothetical integrations with various applications should be examined to determine if the component's design holds up. If it fails to satisfy the conditions, development returns to the specifications and requirements stage.

❑ **Internal Documentation** – internal documentation for the component should consist of a detailed list of all methods, properties, constructors and anything else relevant to any programmer utilizing the component. Documentation for each function should indicate any appropriate pre- and post-conditions, as well as any data validation that must occur prior to invocation.

❑ **Code and Unit Testing** – this is a repetitive stage where the actual development of the component takes place. Each component should have its own test harness that verifies that all functionality, as defined by the requirements specification, works properly, even under the harshest conditions. No bugs should be tolerated here.

❑ **Integration Testing** – once the component has been coded and completely tested and verified standalone via its test harness, it should then be integrated into the main application and tested for individual functionality and that it does not adversely affect any functioning portion of the existing application. No component should ever be considered "done" until it has passed both unit and integration testing without a single detectable bug.

Applications are structures built of many small, specialized bricks that all fit together a certain way. If no attention to detail is paid to the construction of the bricks, the entire structure will eventually crumble.

A good practice to get into is to follow an entire software development life cycle for each component. Each component you build in your application should have its own requirements, its own specifications, and design. In addition, it should have its own internal documentation. The internal documentation for a component can be anything from a web page, a word document, or a full web report generated by VS.NET. Regardless of the form the internal documentation takes, it should be enough to allow any programmer on the development team to program against that component without requiring lengthy conversations with the component's programmer. Each component you produce should not only have its own dedicated time for testing, but each component builder (or some other dedicated programmer) should produce a harness for testing that component.

By following these practices, you can ensure that when each component is considered "finished" the first time around, it works without any bugs on its own within the context of its test harness. Then, you can place all the components together into the application and perform integration testing. This allows you to focus all of your testing and debugging efforts on the integration and communication of the components as a collection, rather than worrying about the individual functionality of the component in a standalone environment.

It may seem like a lot of effort to begin with, but it will pay for itself over and over again when you deploy a commercial application that you can not only feel proud of, but also feel secure in its stability, reliability, and scalability.

The last thing to remember about component and application life cycles is that they are interconnected. As each component's life cycle progresses, it then impacts the stage of its Application's life cycle. Conversely, when the application's life cycle progresses, it affects the integration portion of the component's life cycle. The following diagram illustrates this principle using the analogy of interconnected gears representing the life cycles of the components and an application.

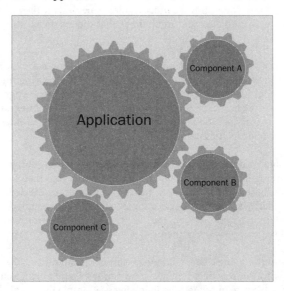

Everyone should agree by now that for every extra hour of effort you spend in design, you earn yourself many times that amount in saved debugging and repairing time. This, of course, should be taken with a grain of salt. It is very, very easy to be caught in the trap that some programmers refer to as "the design abyss". Other, more colorful terms are available to describe the situation where so much time is being spent designing that no development is being done and nothing is being completed. Documentation is an absolutely necessary piece of the development cycle of your application and each of your components. Document as much as you can. If you aren't sure if something should be documented, document it.. Every method and property (especially publicly exposed ones) of every class should be well documented. With the ability for VS.NET to automatically generate web reports based on code structure, as well as the ability for C# to supply XML comments, internal documentation of components should be a snap for any programmer.

Simply by selecting the **Build Web Reports** option from the **Project** menu in VS.NET, you can choose to build a report for a single project or your entire solution. The result is a drill-down, structured set of web pages that describes the structure of each project, including the classes, their properties, method definitions, private data, and more. C# allows additional notations to be made about these constructs, which are placed directly in the HTML output of these reports. There is no word as to whether or not other VS.NET languages will eventually support the XML comment syntax.

In short, the embracing of good Object-Oriented designs and techniques will go far to improve the stability, scalability, and reliability of your application. One inevitable result of using good OOP is building your application on a series of interrelated, but separated components. Each of those components should have its own design, its own testing phase, and its own documentation in order to be considered complete and ready for integration into the main application. This gives you a rock-solid foundation on which to build the presentation tier for your application.

Modeling

There are many different opinions on when (or if) modeling should be used in a software development project. Some Unified Modeling Language (UML) purists believe that the day will come when the models themselves will actually be able to be executed by some kind of UML run-time engine, and programmers won't actually have to write any code; they'll simply model the behavior they need and the programs will run that way. Those on the other end of the spectrum believe that there's no substitute for just sitting down and churning out code.

No matter where you rest in your opinion of modeling and its usefulness on a software development project, it can't be denied that pictures and diagrams are extremely useful for viewing the "big picture". While it may be useful for each of the programmers to have written specifications when programming their own individual components, they need to know how that component is to be used when integrated into the main application. Modeling application and component behavior also provides a common, non-technical way to communicate application design and behavior with customers.

Modeling can be an invaluable design tool. It is extremely helpful to diagram out how you think things should work. With everything in front of you, you can change your mind, add or remove classes, add relationships, child classes, base classes, and more with very little effort. Modeling can be used in many different places including hardware design, application or component design, database design and more. Once you've finally decided on a good model, you can then go ahead and start implementing your specifications for each of the components in the model.

For our particular sample, we're going to be building a solution that automates the day-to-day functioning of a Video Store. This store allows customers to rent and return movies, and enables employees to keep track of inventory as well as movies that are overdue. The following is a sample of the rough-draft model that we came up with when building our fictitious Video Store application. It shows individual classes and their parent-child relationships. The model is actually of the business services layer. Typically, other models would include use case flow charts, User Interface samples, and a class relationship model for the Data Services components.

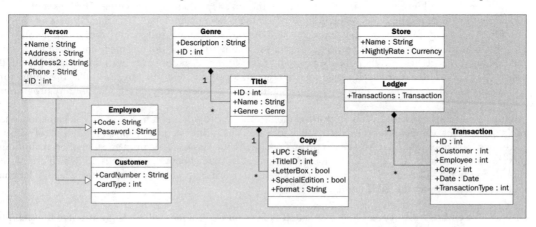

In the UML model above, you can see that the **Employee** and **Customer** classes are specific types of the **Person** generalization. This indicates that these classes will be inheriting or deriving from the **Person** class. Also obvious in the model above is the fact that a **Genre** can contain 0 or more **Titles**, and each **Title** can contain 0 or more **Copies**. The numbers on the ends of the generalization arrows in the above UML diagram indicate the cardinality of the classes. The 1 beneath **Genre** means that in the relationship between **Genre** and **Title**, for any 1 **Genre**, there are 0 or more (indicated by the asterisk) **Titles**. Further down the line, the 1 below **Title** indicates that for every 1 title, there are 0 or more **Copies**.

Providing all of the programmers on a given project with access to this model will give them a frame of reference when thinking about how their component fits into the "big picture" and will generally provide for a more cohesive focused development effort from start to finish.

Separation of Tasks

One of the most important points to remember about OOP and component-oriented programming is to maintain a clear separation of tasks and responsibilities, as well as appropriate encapsulation of functionality (or "black box" theory). Consider that each component is a specialist. It is given a certain area of specialization and is then considered the expert in that area. All other components should defer to the expert when dealing with its particular area of expertise.

What this means is that each component should maintain its own area of functionality and not duplicate functionality contained in other components or provide functionality that it isn't considered an expert on.

For example, if you have a component called `TriangleMath` and a component called `SquareMath`, you might expect what functionality each component provides. In the case of the `TriangleMath` component, you might expect to find methods allowing access to the Pythagorean Theorem, whereas the `SquareMath` component might provide Area-type calculations. If, however, the `SquareMath` component is asked to perform a complex operation that involves computing the length of a diagonal, good separationist philosophy indicates that it should then use `TriangleMath` to perform the sub-calculation, because it is, after all, considered to be the expert on Triangles. If, through some cataclysmic tragedy, the Pythagorean Theorem were to be changed, all we would have to do to keep up with the change is inform the expert (`TriangleMath`) of the new formula. If functionality hasn't been duplicated across many different classes or tiers, it is a simple matter of "replacing the expert" to bring our code up to date with new changes.

However, if we've all been bad programmers and have duplicated functionality across multiple components, we've mixed tiers so that some components have built-in data access and some defer to a Data Services component, and we've allowed UI code to bleed into the business tier, then updating our application (as well as developing it initially) becomes an absolute nightmare.

n-tier Applications

The classic division of tasks generally involves an initial grouping of components into three distinct logical groupings referred to as levels or *tiers*:

- ❑ Presentation Tier (User Interface)

- ❑ Business Tier (Business Rules, abstraction, encapsulation, etc.). This tier is frequently divided up into smaller sub-tiers or units containing other components, agents, etc.

- ❑ Data Services Tier (direct data access, invocation of stored procedures, transactions, etc.)

The following diagram illustrates an n-tier architecture, but with specific regard for our purpose during this chapter. It shows an architecture that includes multiple presentation tiers for the same set of back-end tiers.

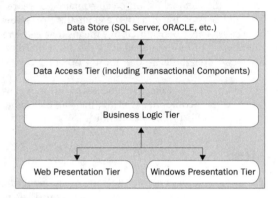

Presentation Tier (User Interface)

The functionality that you provide in your presentation tier should *only* concern itself with conveying information to the user and conveying the user's requests across to the Business Tier. This tier should *never* have direct access to the database; in fact it would be entirely for the best if this tier had no idea where its source data came from.

In a Windows application, the presentation tier consists mainly of Windows Forms. It commonly contains controls that are bound to data passed to it from Business Tier components and passes on to the Business Tier requests to Create, Retrieve, Update, or Delete specific pieces of data. Even though the Business Tier is reserved for housing the particular business rules of your application, you may find that a bit of "cheating" occurs here. It is often too costly to submit invalid data to the business tier and await a response indicating whether or not the data is valid according to the business rules. In such a case, it is quite acceptable to include simple validators (such as date range, numeric-only, numeric range, etc.) to avoid the unnecessary round-trip to validate simple data. More detailed business rules (such as rules that prevent violation of unique constraints, foreign keys, or unstable data conditions) should be enforced in the business tier. Round trips should always be considered when validating on the client. Edit checks that are dependent on data that changes infrequently are better served by being performed on the client side. The client should generally validate to the best of its ability before handing data to the business tier.

Business Tier

The business tier is often referred to as a *middle tier*. The business tier fits into the logical n-tier hierarchy model between the user interface (or another tier of UI-supporting tool components) and the data services tier. Components within this tier are responsible for providing an encapsulated, logical view of the application's underlying data. This view of application information typically provides a view of information that closely resembles how the information will be viewed and manipulated by users of the application.

Components in this tier are stateful (although they may not necessarily persist for a long time), in that they maintain an internal state that can be queried using properties and methods. The components in this tier are the ones that most closely resemble the design models that may have been produced at the initial startup of the development project.

In addition to providing a stateful, object-oriented representation of the data within the system, they also apply all appropriate business rules to the data. For example, if phone numbers are to be stored within the database stripped of their parentheses and dashes, then it is the job of a business tier component to perform that stripping before passing data along to the Data Services tier.

Typically, these are also the fanciest components, often creating collections and indexed properties to represent caches of list data retrieved in batches from the Data Services tier. Extreme care should be taken when designing the components within this tier as to the method by which the components convey to the User Interface that a business rule has been violated, and in particular, which rule was violated and why.

Data Services Tier

The Data Services tier is the workhorse of the entire application. It is responsible for pulling data from a data source. Typically, this will be an RDBMS like SQL Server or ORACLE, or an OLAP provider, though there is nothing preventing that data source from being a directory of XML files, a single text file, or even an older flat-file database like Paradox or BTrieve, or some other form of data such as an LDAP server, directory services, Web Services, e-mail, etc. By abstracting the data access into components that provide stateless, single-call data load, update, delete and insert operations, the underlying database (or any generic data store) can be changed or upgraded without significant impact on the application.

Components in the Data Services tier are responsible for creating, completing, and canceling component and database transactions where appropriate and providing methods by which the business tier can communicate changes, new records, deletions, etc. to the data store. The Data Services components are supposed to be *stateless*.

Anyone who has done any large-volume programming in the Data Services tier knows that *stateless components* are a myth. There is absolutely no such thing as a component that can remain completely stateless. Instead, a more accurate way to describe the state management of these components is that they have *transitory state*. When a Data Services component is activated (by instantiating it from disk, or pulling it from the COM+ object pool, or by having it JIT-activated) its state should be loaded as quickly as possible. The operation requested should then be performed relative to that state and completed as quickly as possible. When the component is de-activated, its state should then be either disposed of completely or serialized for later restoration.

As an example, the *state* of a component might actually only consist of its connection to the database. When it is activated, a new connection is instantiated and configured with a connection string (also part of the component's state) and opened. Then requests for operations come in and are serviced. Once the component is through performing its task and de-activated, the connection can be closed and disposed of, and if memory was being used to store the connection string (that is, it may have been stored in some external resource accessible via a handle or an unsafe pointer, etc.) then it can also be reclaimed.

It may sound trivial, but the point actually has a large impact on component design and encapsulation of functionality. The dogma may have been previously that all Data Services components should be *stateless*, but the truth is that with JIT, object pooling and COM+ services, and the increase in size and complexity of the tasks being performed by Data Services components, *statelessness* is nearly impossible. Instead, strive to maintain *transitory state*, a state that is loaded when the component is activated and disposed of and/or serialized when the component is disposed of or returned to the object pool.

Another good example of why you might need a Data Services component to temporarily load some state is the case of updating something like a sales log. If the ID of the employee performing the sale is passed to the Data Services component, then the component may need to load into its state information such as the employee's commission rate, the employee's unique employee code, possible discounts based on the time of day, etc. in order to properly create new sales log entries in the database. Once the operation is complete, the state is no longer needed and can be reclaimed.

The difference between pure *statelessness* and *transitory state* is that pure statelessness requires that an object maintain *no state between any two method calls*, whereas *transitory state* requires only that an object maintain *no state between any two object activations*. An object activation is when COM+ activates the component. Keep in mind that COM+ may not necessarily activate a component when it instantiates it. If an object pool is designed to pre-instantiate several copies of the component, it will instantiate them ahead of time, but only activate them when needed. If you know ahead of time that the state per activation won't change, then you can save the overhead of loading state with each method call and cache it ahead of time, drastically increasing performance on repeated function calls to the same component. On the other hand, if each function call contains information that makes its required state (such as employee ID) unique from the previous function call, you must use a *stateless* model and load state with each function call.

Class Design

You could read volume after volume in book after book on how to properly design your classes. Eventually, a few common ideas will emerge that vary only slightly throughout all the different publications you may find on class design, especially those written with respect to the .NET framework. The following is a short list of guidelines that might help you avoid unnecessary debugging or redesigning late in your project's lifetime. They are listed in no particular order of importance.

❑ **Consistent Multiplicity**
When building your classes, you should be completely consistent with your class' multiplicity. By multiplicity, we mean the plurality of the entity (or entities) that your class represents. For example, if you have a class that represents a Point (x and y co-ordinate), it should not also be used to represent a list, collection, or array of points. If you have need to represent the plurality of a Point, you should consider creating a Points enumerator or providing a host class that returns a collection of Point instances as the result of a method call or an indexed property.

❑ **Narrow Scope**
The scope of your class should stay as focused as possible on the model the class represents or the task it is supposed to accomplish. It is far too easy to come up with an initial design for a class, start coding, and then find more functionality that needs implementing. Rather than re-factoring at that point and coming up with one or more new classes, many programmers simply stuff the new functionality into the class, extending its functionality beyond its original design, purpose, and model. You can save yourself and all other programmers on your team a lot of trouble in the long run by taking the time to analyze the class structure each time you need new functionality.

❑ **Serialization Support**

When building your classes, you should consider serialization. When classes are transmitted across AppDomain boundaries, which include COM InterOp Marshaling, they are serialized at one end and deserialized at the other. If you don't provide your own serialization implementation, the CLR will provide one for you by converting to XML all public members of the class. The downside to having the CLR decide on a serialization scheme for you is that your data may not deserialize to the same representation, or it may not appear exactly as you expect. If your class requires the use of private or protected members to accurately represent its own state, you will have to provide the serialization code yourself. You may not intend for your class to be used in a way that requires being serialized to a stream, but if you aren't sure about how other consumers (other team members or external parties) are going to be utilizing your class, you should probably provide serialization support to be safe.

❑ **Properties versus Methods**

When designing your classes, it is often a tough decision as to whether to use properties in favor of methods, or vice versa. The first and foremost thing to keep in mind is to use a property whenever the member is logically an attribute of the model that the class represents. For example, the Name of an instance of a class is logically a property of that class; however an operation like FindFirst should not be a property, because it is an operation on a member data, rather than a member itself.

You should use methods in favor of properties when you are performing conversions (such as `ToString()`) or the operation is computationally much more expensive than a single field set/get. In addition, you should never use a property when sequential accesses to the same member do not return the same results or when the order of accesses to the member is important.

❑ **Method and Operator Overloading**

Method and Operator overloading are extremely valuable programming tools and allow the programmer to perform some extremely useful tricks with classes and structs. However, you must keep in mind that not all .NET languages support Overloading, neither does the COM InterOp system (it renames method overloads sequentially rather than providing the overloaded name multiple times). For example, if a .NET component exposes two overloaded methods called `DoTask()`, each with varying arguments, the COM InterOp system will actually display those methods to a COM client as `DoTask()` and `DoTask1()`, a result that can cause unpredicted results. At this point, VB.NET does not support operator or method overloading. Any time you overload an operator, you should also provide an override for the operators verbose method, such as the `Equals` method when overloading the "=" operator. This way, you ensure that your class can be used by multiple languages and/or the COM InterOp system.

❑ **Constructor Guidelines**

Following these few guidelines for constructs should help you efficiently manage instantiation of your classes. First, if your class contains only static members, then you should provide a private default constructor that prevents the class from being instantiated. You would do this simply by changing the default constructor (parameterless constructor) from public to private. This prevents your class from being instantiated, but allows its static members to be accessed.

Secondly, your constructor should execute as quickly as possible, performing as little work as possible. Constructors should not do much other than capture the construction parameters. The real work should be delayed until the client invokes a particular feature within the instance. You should also provide a `protected` (or `Friend` in VB.NET) constructor that derivative classes can utilize. You should also use parameters in constructors as shortcuts for setting properties. If you know at instantiation-time a subset (or all) of the property values, you should provide a constructor that allows you to set them all at once.

Classes versus Structures

The difference between a class and a structure (`structs` in C#, user-defined `Types` in VB.NET) has never been more blurred than it is now. For those of you who aren't familiar with the C term "struct", a struct is an in-memory representation of structured and related data. In classic C programming, structs were used to represent related groups of data for easy maintenance, easy access, and easy serialization (structs and VB User-Defined Types were quite easy to serialize to random access binary files).

Occasionally you may be able to use a "light-weight" class alternative to give you some performance gains. That would be a struct. The following is a list of the features that classes and structs support and where they differ.

Struct	Class
Value type	Reference type
Stack Allocated	Heap Allocated
Passed by value (copied) to functions	Passed by Reference to functions
Constructors require parameters	Supports overriding default constructor
Members cannot have initializers	Members support initialization
Can instantiate without new keyword	Must use new keyword to instantiate
No inheritance supported	Single inheritance supported
Supports Interface implementation	Supports Interface implementation

We won't go into too much detail on implementing structs as opposed to class implementations. However, you should at least be aware of the fact that structs provide faster, stack-based access to their data than classes. However, because they are on the stack, they consume more "precious" resources. If what you are looking for is a way to represent a simple grouping of related data (such as the co-ordinates of a point, vertices of a triangle, etc.) then a struct will be far more useful and efficient. Structs (User-Defined value types) are used in various places throughout the framework, extensively in the GDI+ libraries, structs are used in threading code, when working with fonts, and in places you might not expect, such as the Int64 type and others.

In general, it is recommended that you use a struct if the type you are trying to create is to act like a primitive or intrinsic type, has an instance size of under 16 bytes, is immutable, or where value semantics are desirable over reference.

Exception Handling

Exception handling is an important part of any application. Your application's ability to properly handle exceptions generally results in the difference between the user seeing a message explaining a failure and the user seeing your application crash in an extremely unfriendly manner (which is usually followed up shortly thereafter by a call to tech support).

The general rule of thumb for exception handling is that, wherever possible, no unexpected condition should ever cause your application to terminate without at first informing the user in a friendly, polite fashion that something unexpected has happened.

The .NET framework allows you to derive subclasses from the base Exception class, giving you unlimited flexibility with which to design your own exception handling system. Defining your own exception class is as simple as the following code:

```
public class ReallyBadException: ApplicationException
{
    // there are three constructors that exceptions define.
    public ReallyBadException() { }

    public ReallyBadException( string Message ) : base( Message ) { }

    public ReallyBadException( string Message, Exception inner ) { }
}
```

Once you've created your custom exception, you can throw and catch it just like any other exception, so long as both callee (server) and caller (client) know where the assembly that defines your exception is located. Microsoft's .NET Framework Developer's Guide contains a good section on Exception handling best practices for more information.

To Throw or Not to Throw

Whether or not to throw an exception is actually a far more difficult decision than it might first appear. Throwing exceptions, which might include instantiating your own custom exception handler, is an expensive and slow operation.

Your application should *never* rely on exceptions to detect predictable conditions. What this means is that exceptions should *only* be used when an *unexpected* result has occurred. Therefore, if while executing a stored procedure ADO.NET throws an exception complaining that the connection has been lost (or someone pulled the plug out on the server, etc.), that is a valid use for an exception. However, throwing an exception when the record you are about to insert into the database is a duplicate of an already existing record is an inefficient use of exceptions. Those kinds of results should be handled with return values (possibly returning values in an enumeration of trappable error conditions) rather than actually interrupting the flow of execution.

Samples

After spending a few pages covering some basics of Object-Oriented Design, Component-Oriented Design, and a few pointers on good class design and exception handling, we're ready to take a look at a few examples. These examples are taken from our sample Video Store application, and illustrate principles of good class design along with the concepts of narrow functionality scope, proper use of properties and methods, constructor guidelines, and *transitory state* for the Data Services classes.

The samples will show a few of the classes that provide our back-end, or core functionality of our application. This will show that the components provide a specific set of functionality, and nothing more. They are designed to be used by calling clients, whether they are Business Tier objects, or Windows Forms, or Web Forms. Keep in mind that in an n-tier architecture, components from one tier shouldn't be invoking components from within that same tier. For example, an object in the business tier should not be using another business tier object. The direction of flow is always up or down, and never laterally.

Business Classes

All of the classes we're going to look at in the business tier are in the UML diagram shown previously in this chapter. As we said earlier, the business tier objects should be responsible for providing an easy-to-use, near-model representation of the data within the data store.

Our first sample class, the `Ledger` class, is a business tier class solely responsible for providing a read-only view of the Transactions within the system. This class is a small portion of the classes that make up our sample video store application that we described and modeled briefly earlier in the chapter. It has a couple of constructors, and uses a public property to provide access to a strongly-typed `DataTable` containing rows of Transactions.

```
/*
 * Ledger.cs
 * Contains the definition and implementation of the Ledger class.
 */

using System;

using ReelGoodVideo;
using ReelGoodVideo.Common;

namespace ReelGoodVideo.BLL
{
    /// <summary>
    /// The Ledger class is an abstraction surrounding the Transactions
    ///within the Database.
    /// A Ledger is a list of transactions beginning on a certain date.
    /// </summary>
    public class Ledger
    {
        private TransactionDataSet _TrxDS;

        /// <summary>
        /// Default constructor. If the Ledger is instantiated without an
        /// explicit start date, it is assumed to be today at midnight (ideal
        /// for looking at "today's activity" screens).
        /// </summary>
        public Ledger()
        {
            LoadFromDate( System.DateTime.Today );
        }

        /// <summary>
        /// Parameterized constructor used when an explicit starting date for
        /// the Ledger is used.
        /// </summary>
        /// <param name="StartDate">Sytem.DateTime representing the starting
        /// date of the ledger</param>
        public Ledger( System.DateTime StartDate )
        {
            LoadFromDate( StartDate );
        }

        /// <summary>
        /// Private function that populates the private DataSet based
        /// on the initial startup date.
        /// </summary>
        /// <param name="StartDate"></param>
        private void LoadFromDate( System.DateTime StartDate )
```

```
        {
            DAL.Store dStore = new DAL.Store();
            _TrxDS = dStore.GetTransactions( StartDate );

            dStore.Dispose();
        }

        /// <summary>
        /// Property allowing public read-only access to the Transactions
        /// table contained within the private DataSet.
        /// </summary>
        public TransactionDataSet.TransactionsDataTable Transactions
        {
            get
            {
                return _TrxDS.Transactions;
            }
        }
    }
}
```

Even though it appears like a fairly simple class, because it is actually providing some encapsulation for a strongly-typed `DataSet` class, it makes several common programming tasks extremely easy. For example, once we have an instantiated `Ledger` object we can write code against it that looks like the following:

```
Console.WriteLine( oLedger.Transactions[index].CustomerName );
```

As the property `Transactions` actually represents a strong `DataTable` nested class, we can reference our rows by array index, and then reference the columns within each row directly as members rather than dealing with `Object` types (`variants` in VB6 terminology).

With the `Ledger` class, you may notice that both constructors refer to a single, private method. This is handy, but it can lead to problems later on if at some point one of the constructors is upgraded and the other is not. We can solve that situation by placing the code from `LoadFromDate()` into the date-specific constructor, and modifying the default constructor so that its declaration looks like this:

```
public Ledger() : this( System.DateTime.Today ) { ... }
```

This allows the default constructor to always call the parameterized constructor, creating a single point of update for later maintenance. In VB.NET, the above line of code might look like this:

```
Public Sub New()
  MyBase.New( System.DateTime.Today )
End Sub
```

Our next sample class is the `Employee`. This class is good to examine because it shows an example of a business tier class inheriting from an abstract base class (`Person`).

```
/*
 * Employee.cs
 * Contains the implementation and definition for the Employee class
 */
using System;
```

```
using ReelGoodVideo;
using ReelGoodVideo.Common;

namespace ReelGoodVideo.BLL
{
    /// <summary>
    /// The employee class extends the basic "person" support provided by the
    /// Person class by adding a Code and Password to those standard fields
    /// offered by the base class.
    /// </summary>
    public class Employee : Person
    {
        private int _EmployeeID;
        private string _Code;
        private string _Password;

        /// <summary>
        /// Default constructor
        /// </summary>
        public Employee()
        {
            //
            // TODO: Add constructor logic here
            //
        }

        /// <summary>
        /// Parameterized constructor for specifically instantiating this
        /// class based on a given EmployeeID.
        /// </summary>
        /// <param name="EmployeeID">ID on which to base the new instance of
        /// the class</param>
        public Employee( int EmployeeID )
        {
```

The first thing we're going to do in our employee business class constructor is to obtain an instance of the Employee Data Services class which resides in our DAL (Data Access Layer) namespace. EmployeeDataSet is a Typed DataSet created in the Common namespace for this application and is the data type returned by the Load() operation of the DAL.Employee class. We know that we're only returning a single employee, so we grab a reference to the first row of the result set and use that row to populate this class' private member data.

```
        DAL.Employee dEmployee = new DAL.Employee();
        EmployeeDataSet empDS = dEmployee.Load( EmployeeID );
        EmployeeDataSet.EmployeesRow empRow = empDS.Employees[0];

        _EmployeeID = EmployeeID;
        _Code = empRow.Code;
        _Password = empRow.Password;
```

The following four member variables aren't actually defined by the Employee class. This class inherits from the "Person" class, which defines the following four as "protected" members. This means that only classes deriving from the Person class have access to the following four member variables.

```
                // -- "person" data
                _Name = empRow.Name;
                _Address = empRow.Address;
                _Address2 = empRow.Address2;
                _Phone = empRow.Phone;
```

Even though we're in a garbage collected environment, we want to indicate to the GC that we're done using this stuff as soon as possible, so the memory can be reclaimed as soon as possible.

```
                empDS.Dispose();
                dEmployee.Dispose();
        }


        /// <summary>
        /// Creates a new Employee in the database based on the employee
        /// represented by internal state
        /// </summary>
        /// <returns>ID of newly created employee</returns>
        public int Create()
        {
            DAL.Employee dEmployee = new DAL.Employee();

            _EmployeeID = dEmployee.Create( _Name, _Address, _Address2, _Phone,
                                    _Code, _Password );
            dEmployee.Dispose();
            return _EmployeeID;
        }


        /// <summary>
        /// Updates the employee in the database based on internal state
        /// </summary>
        /// <returns>1 upon success</returns>
        public int Update()
        {
```

Here the code is creating an instance of the Employee class in the DAL namespace (it is a Data Access Layer component). It stores the return value of the Update function in the result variable so it can dispose of the reference to the DAL object before returning the result code.

```
            int result;
            DAL.Employee dEmployee = new DAL.Employee();

            result = dEmployee.Update( _EmployeeID, _Name, _Address, _Address2,
                                    _Phone, _Code, _Password );
            dEmployee.Dispose();
            return result;
        }


        /// <summary>
        /// Deletes the employee indicated by internal state
        /// </summary>
        /// <returns>1 upon success</returns>
        public int Delete()
        {
```

As with the `Update()` code above, an instance of the Data Access Layer component `Employee` is being created here. From there, the `Delete()` method is invoked and the return value passed along to the calling client after disposing of the reference to the DAL object.

```
        int result;
        DAL.Employee dEmployee = new DAL.Employee();

        result = dEmployee.Delete( _EmployeeID );
        dEmployee.Dispose();
        return result;
    }

    /// <summary>
    /// ID of the Employee
    /// </summary>
    public int EmployeeID
    {
        get
        {
            return _EmployeeID;
        }
        set
        {
            _EmployeeID = value;
        }
    }

    /// <summary>
    /// Employee's 4-character unique login code.
    /// </summary>
    public string Code
    {
        get
        {
            return _Code;
        }
        set
        {
            _Code = value;
        }
    }

    /// <summary>
    /// Password of the employee
    /// </summary>
    public string Password
    {
        get
        {
            return _Password;
        }
        set
        {
            _Password = value;
        }
    }
    }
}
```

Even though the employee has a name, an address, and a phone number, the `Employee` class doesn't need to provide any implementation for private members to hold that data, nor does it have to provide any public properties to access that data. All of that functionality is inherited from the `Person` base class. You can see that the `Employee` class provides full CRUD (Create, Retrieve, Update, Delete) functionality by relying on functions in the Data Services tier.

To finish off our business tier examples, we'll show you the code for the abstract base class `Person`. All of the source code for the entire video store application is available for download from **www.wrox.com**.

```
/*
 * Person.cs
 * (C) 2001 Wrox Press Ltd
 * Person class implementation
 */

using System;

using ReelGoodVideo.Common;
using ReelGoodVideo;

namespace ReelGoodVideo.BLL
{
    /// <summary>
    /// Summary description for Person.
    /// </summary>
    abstract public class Person
    {
```

The following member variables are all given the `protected` access modifier. This means that only classes that inherit from this class can have access to these members. If we had added the "`internal`" modifier to these as well, access would be restricted to only those inheriting classes within this particular Assembly.

```
        protected string _Name;
        protected string _Address;
        protected string _Address2;
        protected string _Phone;

        /// <summary>
        /// Default person constructor
        /// </summary>
        public Person()
        {
            //
            // TODO: Add constructor logic here
            //
        }

        /// <summary>
        /// Name property shared by all classes deriving from Person
        /// </summary>
        public string Name
        {
            get
```

```
        {
            return _Name;
        }
        set
        {
            _Name = value;
        }
    }

    /// <summary>
    /// Address (Line 1) Property shared by all classes
    /// deriving from Person
    /// </summary>
    public string Address
    {
        get
        {
            return _Address;
        }
        set
        {
            _Address = value;
        }
    }

    /// <summary>
    /// Address (Line 2) property shared by all classes
    /// deriving from Person
    /// </summary>
    public string Address2
    {
        get
        {
            return _Address2;
        }
        set
        {
            _Address2 = value;
        }
    }

    /// <summary>
    /// Phone # property shared by all child classes. Note that the set
    /// accessor strips all chars in (, ), and -.
    /// </summary>
    public string Phone
    {
        get
        {
            return _Phone;
        }
        set
        {
```

Any time the Phone property is set on any class inheriting from this one, the protected member _Phone will become that phone number, minus all commas, dashes, and parentheses.

```
            _Phone = value.Replace("(", "");
            _Phone = _Phone.Replace(")", "");
            _Phone = _Phone.Replace("-", "");
        }
    }
  }
}
```

Data Services Class

Because we firmly believe that stored procedures are just about the fastest way possible to retrieve and modify data, our Data Services classes are very centralized around the concept of stored procedures. Each Data Services class inherits from a single abstract class called DALObject). This class provides overrides for COM+ activation, as well as several routines that facilitate executing stored procedures quickly and in very readable and efficient code.

We won't go into too much detail about COM+, transactions, activation, and the like in this chapter as it is outside our scope. However, the beauty of the new attributes in the .NET framework allows us to simply declare how we'd like our class to behave under COM+ hosting and not have to worry about the underlying structure and low-level code being activated on our behalf.

The DALObject class:

```
/*
 * DALObject.cs
 * This file houses the DAO class, the base class from which all data-tier
 * classes inherit.
 */

using System;
using System.EnterpriseServices;
using System.Data;
using System.Data.SqlClient;
using System.Diagnostics;
using System.Runtime.InteropServices;

namespace ReelGoodVideo.DAL
{
    /// <summary>
    /// DALObject is a ServicedComponent class, meaning that it runs natively
    /// within the context of a COM+ Application. It provides standard, low-
    /// level data access functionality that the data classes will use.
    /// This class is abstract, as such it can only be inherited, not
    /// instantiated.
    /// </summary>
    abstract public class DALObject: ServicedComponent
    {
        protected SqlConnection Connection;
        private string m_DSN;

        /// <summary>
        /// This method creates a SqlCommand object designed to execute a
        /// stored procedure.
        /// </summary>
        /// <param name="sprocName">String representing the name of the stored
```

```
/// procedure to execute</param>
/// <param name="parameters">SqlParameter[] array of arguments (not
/// including argument for return value)</param>
/// <returns>Newly instantiated SqlCommand object</returns>
private SqlCommand CreateCommand(string sprocName, IDataParameter[]
                                 parameters)
{
   SqlCommand command = new SqlCommand( sprocName, Connection );
   command.CommandType = CommandType.StoredProcedure;

   // Populate the Sql Command's parameter array.
   foreach (SqlParameter parameter in parameters)
   {
      command.Parameters.Add( parameter );
   }

   /// Add a SqlParameter representing the return value from the
   /// stored procedure.
   command.Parameters.Add( new SqlParameter ( "ReturnValue",
      SqlDbType.Int,
      4, /* Size */
      ParameterDirection.ReturnValue,
      false, /* is nullable */
      0, /* byte precision */
      0, /* byte scale */
      string.Empty,
      DataRowVersion.Default,
      null ));

   return command;
}

protected string DSN
{
   get
   {
      return m_DSN;
   }
}

/// <summary>
/// Executes a stored procedure within the database
/// </summary>
/// <param name="sprocName">String representing the name of the stored
/// procedure to execute</param>
/// <param name="parameters">SqlParameter[] array of arguments to the
/// stored procedure</param>
/// <returns>Integer representing the integer value returned from the
/// stored procedure</returns>
protected int RunSP( string sprocName, IDataParameter[] parameters )
{
   int result;
   Connection.Open();
   SqlCommand command = CreateCommand( sprocName, parameters );
   command.ExecuteNonQuery();
   result = (int)command.Parameters[ "ReturnValue" ].Value;
   Connection.Close();
```

```
         return result;
    }


    /// <summary>
    /// Executes a stored procedure, placing results in a DataSet.
    /// </summary>
    /// <param name="sprocName">String representing the name of the stored
    /// procedure to execute.</param>
    /// <param name="parameters">SqlParameter[] array of arguments to the
    /// stored procedure.</param>
    /// <param name="dataSet">DataSet into which to place return results
    /// from stored procedure</param>
    /// <returns></returns>
    protected int RunSP( string sprocName, IDataParameter[] parameters,
                         DataSet dataSet )
    {
        int result;
        SqlDataAdapter sqlDA = new SqlDataAdapter();
        Connection.Open();

        sqlDA.SelectCommand = CreateCommand( sprocName, parameters );
        sqlDA.Fill( dataSet, "SourceTable" );
        result = (int)sqlDA.SelectCommand.Parameters[ "ReturnValue"
                                                    ].Value;
        Connection.Close();
        return result;
    }


    /// <summary>
    /// This function will more than likely be used to populate strongly-
    /// typed DataSets. The TableName is required to properly conform to
    /// the schema. Note that this function doesn't actually treat the
    /// dataset as a strongly-typed DataSet, one of the great things
    /// about inheritance.
    /// </summary>
    /// <param name="sprocName">String representing the name of the stored
    /// procedure to execute.</param>
    /// <param name="parameters">SqlParameter[] array of arguments to the
    /// stored procedure</param>
    /// <param name="dataSet">DataSet to be populated with results from
    /// stored procedure.</param>
    /// <param name="TableName">TableName within the dataSet to populate
    /// w/results.</param>
    /// <returns>Int representing return value of the stored
    /// procedure</returns>
    protected int RunSP( string sprocName, IDataParameter[] parameters,
                         DataSet dataSet, string TableName )
    {
        int result;
        SqlDataAdapter sqlDA = new SqlDataAdapter();
        Connection.Open();

        sqlDA.SelectCommand = CreateCommand( sprocName, parameters );
        sqlDA.Fill( dataSet, TableName );
        result = (int)sqlDA.SelectCommand.Parameters[ "ReturnValue"
                                                    ].Value;
```

```
        Connection.Close();
        return result;
    }

    /// <summary>
    /// Overridden ServicedComponent method. Takes the ConstructionString
    /// (found by right-clicking the component
    /// in COM+ console, getting properties) and stores it privately as
    /// the DB connection string (DSN)
    /// </summary>
    /// <param name="ConstructString">String sent to the object as a
    /// construction string from COM+</param>
    public override void Construct(string ConstructString)
    {
        m_DSN = ConstructString;
    }

    /// <summary>
    /// Overridden ServicedComponent method. Called when COM+ JIT-activates
    /// this component. Used to instantiate the database connection.
    /// </summary>
    public override void Activate()
    {
        Connection = new SqlConnection(m_DSN);
    }

    /// <summary>
    /// Overridden ServicedComponent method. Called when COM+ JIT-
    /// deactivates this component. Used
    /// to dispose of the Sql Connection object.
    /// </summary>
    public override void Deactivate()
    {
        Connection = null;
    }

    }
}
```

There is actually quite a lot going on here. The first thing to notice is that the DAO class is maintaining its own *transitory state* by instantiating and releasing (it's more like indicating to the GC that it isn't using it any longer) the Connection object during object activation and deactivation.

The next thing to notice is the Construct method. It is called almost like an activation constructor. If you right-click any component in the COM+ explorer (you can find it in your Component Services control panel on Windows 2000) you'll see that you can set a **Construction String**. This construction string can be anything you like, and mean anything you want. For our purposes, we decided to use it as a good place to store the DSN, relieving the responsibility of passing the DSN along from the business tier (since the business tier should realistically not have any knowledge of the type or even location of the data store). One of the biggest benefits of using the DSN in the component Construction String is that the data source/connection string can be changed at a moment's notice without having to recompile anything.

To keep things brief, we'll show only one of the Data Services classes:

```
/*
 * Employee.cs
 * DAL component providing read/write data access to
 * employee data.
 */
using System;
using System.EnterpriseServices;
using System.Data;
using System.Data.SqlClient;
using System.Data.SqlTypes;

using ReelGoodVideo.Common;

namespace ReelGoodVideo.DAL
{
    /// <summary>
    /// Employee Dclass.
    /// Transactions are "supported" to retain Activate/DeActivate
    /// functionality, but are not required as all of the data access
    /// takes place through stored procedures that can create much
    /// faster transactions than COM+
    /// </summary>
    [Transaction( TransactionOption.Supported )]
    [ConstructionEnabled( Default = "Data Source=localhost; Initial
                        Catalog=ReelGoodVideo; User id=sa; Password=;" )]
    public class Employee : DALObject
    {
        /// <summary>
        /// Will verify the employee code and password of an employee.
        /// </summary>
        /// <param name="Code">Employee's ID code</param>
        /// <param name="Password">Employee's Password</param>
        /// <returns>The EmployeeID of the employee. If the code/password
        /// combination fails, then  a -1 is returned.</returns>
        public int VerifyLogin( string Code, string Password )
        {
            int result;
            SqlParameter[] parameters =
            {
                new SqlParameter( "@Code", SqlDbType.VarChar, 4),
                new SqlParameter( "@Password", SqlDbType.VarChar, 8)
            };

            parameters[0].Value = Code;
            parameters[1].Value = Password;

            return RunSP( "sp_VerifyEmployee", parameters );
        }
        /// <summary>
        /// Will load a particular employee
        /// </summary>
        /// <param name="EmployeeID">ID of the employee to load</param>
        /// <returns>EmployeeDataSet containing the employee's
        /// information</returns>
```

```
        public EmployeeDataSet Load( int EmployeeID )
        {
            SqlDataAdapter empDA = new SqlDataAdapter( "SELECT EmployeeID,
                Code, Password, Name, Address, Address2, Phone FROM Employees "
                + "WHERE EmployeeID = " + EmployeeID, Connection );
            EmployeeDataSet empDS = new EmployeeDataSet();

            empDA.Fill( empDS, "Employees" );

            empDA.Dispose();
            return empDS;
        }


        /// <summary>
        /// Creates a new Employee.
        /// </summary>
        /// <param name="Name">Name of the new employee</param>
        /// <param name="Address">Address Line 1</param>
        /// <param name="Address2">Address Line 2</param>
        /// <param name="Phone">Character-stripped phone #. Takes only 10
        /// digits</param>
        /// <param name="Code">Employee's 4-character employee code.</param>
        /// <param name="Password">Employee's password</param>
        /// <returns>ID of the newly created employee.</returns>
        public int Create( string Name, string Address, string Address2,
                           string Phone, string Code, string Password )
        {
            int result;
            SqlParameter[] parameters =
            {
                new SqlParameter( "@Name", SqlDbType.VarChar, 30),
                new SqlParameter( "@Address", SqlDbType.VarChar, 255),
                new SqlParameter( "@Address2", SqlDbType.VarChar, 255),
                new SqlParameter( "@Phone", SqlDbType.VarChar, 10),
                new SqlParameter( "@Code", SqlDbType.VarChar, 4),
                new SqlParameter( "@Password", SqlDbType.VarChar, 8)
            };

            parameters[0].Value = Name;
            parameters[1].Value = Address;
            parameters[2].Value = Address2;
            parameters[3].Value = Phone;
            parameters[4].Value = Code;
            parameters[5].Value = Password;

            result = RunSP( "sp_CreateEmployee", parameters );
            return result;
        }


        /// <summary>
        /// Updates a specific employee's information
        /// </summary>
        /// <param name="EmployeeID">ID of the employee to update</param>
        /// <param name="Name">New employee's name</param>
        /// <param name="Address">New Address Line 1</param>
        /// <param name="Address2">New Address Line 2</param>
```

```
        /// <param name="Phone">New stripped Phone #</param>
        /// <param name="Code">New Employee Code</param>
        /// <param name="Password">New Password</param>
        /// <returns>1 upon successful update</returns>
        public int Update( int EmployeeID, string Name, string Address,
            string Address2, string Phone, string Code, string Password )
        {
            int result;
            SqlParameter[] parameters =
            {
                new SqlParameter( "@EmployeeID", SqlDbType.Int, 4),
                new SqlParameter( "@Name", SqlDbType.VarChar, 30),
                new SqlParameter( "@Address", SqlDbType.VarChar, 255),
                new SqlParameter( "@Address2", SqlDbType.VarChar, 255),
                new SqlParameter( "@Phone", SqlDbType.VarChar, 10),
                new SqlParameter( "@Code", SqlDbType.VarChar, 4),
                new SqlParameter( "@Password", SqlDbType.VarChar, 8)
            };

            parameters[0].Value = EmployeeID;
            parameters[1].Value = Name;
            parameters[2].Value = Address;
            parameters[3].Value = Address2;
            parameters[4].Value = Phone;
            parameters[5].Value = Code;
            parameters[6].Value = Password;

            result = RunSP( "sp_UpdateEmployee", parameters );
            return result;
        }


        /// <summary>
        /// Will delete a specific employee.
        /// </summary>
        /// <param name="EmployeeID">ID of the employee to delete</param>
        /// <returns>1 if successful, -1 if employee has made at least one
        /// transaction</returns>
        public int Delete( int EmployeeID )
        {
            int result;
            SqlParameter[] parameters =
            {
                new SqlParameter( "@EmployeeID", SqlDbType.Int, 4)
            };

            parameters[0].Value = EmployeeID;

            result = RunSP( "sp_DeleteEmployee", parameters );
            return result;
        }

    }
}
```

Windows Forms and the .NET Framework

Windows Forms is a library of classes for providing a Windows-based User Interface for applications running on the .NET framework. It contains a standard set of components such as Forms, Panels, Buttons, Images, DataGrids, ListBoxes, ComboBoxes and more.

Even though the .NET framework provides many tools that speed development and make programming easier, the framework itself cannot force you to design your applications properly. It does, however, make sure that poorly designed applications are far more visible as such than in previous environments (Win32 API, for example).

Effective Form Design and Usage

Even the smallest of Windows applications is still usually composed of at least one form. There are exceptions to this when applications do not have a main form. The form is the container or surface for other interface controls that will interact with the user; when an application displays a dialog box that interacts with the user in some way, it is displaying a custom type of form; whenever you open an MDI child window to edit another document in an application, this is also another type of form. Pretty soon, even medium-sized applications begin to require some serious form-juggling effort.

Back when Visual Basic first appeared, and people could double-click a button and write code that would execute in response to that event or message, it was so easy that not too many people thought about effective form usage.

There are a couple of things that I've discovered to be invaluable in designing Windows Forms applications that can help avoid a tangled mass of "spaghetti-form" code where some buttons have functional code in their event handlers and others don't, some forms have public fields and some don't, while other forms are entirely self-contained.

❑ **A Form is a Class**
Far too many people get lost in the WYSIWYG editor and point-and-shoot coding interface and lose sight of the fact that the form is really just a specialized class. As such, you must also remember that when the user is navigating through your application, they are navigating through *instances of your forms*, and not the actual forms themselves.

Because of this, your forms should follow all the guidelines of good design that were discussed earlier in this chapter. The form should have a narrow purpose, it should maintain its scope and multiplicity, and should be considered the expert on its given task.

Therefore, if you have a form that asks the user for input of a name, address, and phone number, then that form should be considered the expert on that task, and no other form should provide the same functionality.

❑ **Forms can have Constructors**
As classes, forms can have constructors. If you have a form that provides an interface to edit a user, or a book, or a video title, you should consider providing a constructor for that form that will pre-populate any appropriate data on that form with data belonging to the ID passed into the constructor.

So, for example, your code might look like this:

```
frmUserEditor UserEditor = new frmUserEditor( UserID );
UserEditor.ShowDialog();
```

❑ **Forms can inherit from other forms**

Because forms are classes, you can actually have forms that inherit from other forms. This provides for some very advanced functionality, but it should be done with caution, as visibility issues can get messy with inherited forms.

Emulate "CodeBehind"

VS.NET ASP.NET projects provide a functionality known as "CodeBehind". This functionality splits the events and functions in a programming language from the markup tags and user interface. This allows for incredible flexibility and encourages code reuse and true separation of UI and underlying code.

Windows Forms don't have anything called "CodeBehind", but your design can strive to emulate its goal and essential concept. What you are trying for is a pure separation of UI code and elements from logic and data code elements.

The biggest debate concerning Windows Forms development is whether to include all of the code logic in the form class itself, or in the calling form. Personally, I think a combination is most appropriate. Remember that your form is a class; it is the expert at providing a user interface for a specific task. It should provide that interface however possible, including pre-loading ComboBoxes with lookup data, binding data from a database read done during a Load method, etc. However, it should only provide the interface and the validation for user input. The change in data should come as a result of the calling form testing its DialogResult. This is an example of a typical dialog-type editor load, showing where the line is drawn between the calling form and the new form:

```
frmUserEditor UserEditor = new frmUserEditor( UserID );
UserEditor.ShowDialog();
if ( UserEditor.DialogResult == DialogResult.OK )
{
    // .. perform processing in response to successful edit.
}
. .
```

If you treat forms as you would any other well-designed class, and keep in mind the guidelines for good class design, the concept of separating UI code from the underlying business rules, and data access, you will find that designs and implementations of your forms will be very straightforward and easy.

Working with Windows Forms Classes

The Windows Forms classes should look very familiar to most programmers who have worked with Windows in Visual Basic, MFC, or even Delphi. Most of them are actually just .NET framework wrappers for controls residing in the COMCTLxx.DLL family. WindowsXP actually supplies its own completely new set of common controls that support extra features. If your control sets its FlatStyle property to "System", it will automatically take advantage of WindowsXP styles when run in a WindowsXP environment.

Basic Windows Forms Controls Overview

This chapter is about engineering applications, and as such Windows and Web Forms are merely tools to that end. We'll briefly go over the use of some common controls in Windows Forms, but will leave the detailed reference to the book, *Professional Windows Forms*, also published by Wrox Press. The following is a screenshot of the VS.NET designer with a couple of commonly used Windows controls, with descriptions of those controls below.

Label

The Label is a simple control for displaying regular text on a surface. You can do the normal things to it such as set its location, size, height, font, and its Text property. The Text property is probably the most often used. Labels are commonly used in conjunction with other controls to provide descriptive text to guide the user through the interface.

Link Label

The Link Label works much the same way as the Label control. However, this label acts like a URL link. The link can change color based on its Link Visited property and programmers can write navigation code in response to user clicks. The new control is just one more UI feature that VS.NET supports that allows you to give your Windows applications a much more "web-like" feel.

Button

The Button is the basic unit of interactivity between the user and the application. The application will typically present to the user a list of controls on a form, and when the user is done, wants to cancel, or wants further details on something, they will typically activate a button. A Button has the standard set of properties, plus a DialogResult property to indicate to the form what the form's DialogResult should be after the button is pressed.

TextBox

The TextBox is the basic control for allowing the user to type information into a form. TextBoxes can be single or multiple lines, can hide entered characters based on a PasswordChar, and can be bound to virtually any bindable Data Source.

CheckBox

The CheckBox is the most basic way of representing a Boolean (Yes/No) condition on a form. If the box is checked, its Checked property is true, otherwise it is false. CheckBoxes are usually used to represent options in an application that can be toggled on or off.

ListBox

The ListBox is used to represent a simple list of items. It is often used to display a list to the user that as to be used for drilling down to further detail, either through the Click or DoubleClick event. If there is need to display more than a single column of information, then a ListView control might be more appropriate than the light-weight ListBox control.

ComboBox

The ComboBox is a composite control that contains a listbox. By clicking the attached down arrow button, it will pop up a listbox control. When you select from that listbox control, that item becomes the currently selected item. ComboBoxes (often abbreviated simply as "dropdowns") are ideal for prompting the user to select a single item from a list.

MonthCalendar

The MonthCalendar control is a very nice-looking control that allows a user to navigate to a specific date. The format of the text displayed next to the word "Today:" is actually localized, so you will see you own local date format there. For example, the previous screenshot above shows 7/31/2001, but in the UK it would show 31/7/2001.

Forms Inheritance

At some point in your application's development (probably fairly soon if you're working on a large application) you may find that you are constantly configuring forms in the same way, with only slight variations. Your company may have a certain visual style that sets up a tiled background, a certain set of base fonts and colors, etc.

To save yourself (and other programmers on your team) time and effort, you may find it easier to create a base form and then create multiple other forms that inherit from the base. This forms inheritance is called **Visual Inheritance**. It is called this because the child form visually inherits the style of the parent as well as other properties and members (according to access modifiers). VS.NET allows you to easily create a new form inherited from a parent by providing the **Add Inherited Form** option from the **Project** menu. You can also inherit from another form manually by editing the class definition of your form to inherit the parent form, just like you would inherit any other class.

One common use for Forms Inheritance is for your application to build a single base class that acts as a template for all application forms to inherit from, providing a common set of matching functionality (or even look and feel as well) for all forms in that application.

DataBinding

DataBinding is a concept that has been around in visual languages for quite some time. In a nutshell, it is the ability for you to programmatically or visually bind the contents of a control or component to an external data source represented by an instance of a class, an intrinsic type like an array, or an ADO.NET object like a DataSet.

Some programmers in the past opted to skip past DataBinding because it was slow and rigid, and did not allow customization of the binding behavior and other attributes. Also, DataBinding to a connected source would tightly integrate data access into the GUI, which violates many of the principles of n-tier architecture. With the .NET framework, DataBinding can be an extremely fast operation, especially when binding to intrinsic types like arrays. Binding to a `DataSet` actually binds to a completely disconnected entity, allowing databinding to take place without violating n-tier architecture principals. Databinding in the .NET framework is also incredibly flexible and customizable, allowing you to do many things previously impossible through databound operations.

ADO.NET

DataBinding in ADO.NET is a relatively simple process. You simply take the control that you want bound and bind it (or a single property on it) to an ADO.NET object like a `DataSet`. Most ADO.NET binding is done against a `DataSet`. This is because the `DataSet` maintains its data in an offline, disconnected fashion, making things like sorting, seeking, and iterating extremely fast and seemingly tailor-made for Databound operations.

The following code creates a `DataSet` from scratch (it could easily have been one loaded from SQL Server or an XML file, or even a strongly-typed `DataSet` with its own internal schema). The great thing about binding to a `DataSet` is that it doesn't matter where the data came from, what it used to look like, or even what kind of data store it was; all binding to the DataSet functions the same.

Once the `DataSet` has been created from scratch, a few sample rows are added to it and then it is bound to a `ListBox` control. As an added bonus, the "Name" column of the `DataSet` is then manually bound to the `Text` property of a `Label` control. If you run the DataBinding sample included in the code for this chapter, you'll notice that this label control *automatically* updates itself and changes its text to the value of the "Name" column of whatever row is being selected by the ADO-bound `ListBox`.

```
dsCities.Tables.Add( "Cities" );
dsCities.Tables["Cities"].Columns.Add( new DataColumn( "Name",
System.Type.GetType("System.String") ) );

myRow = dsCities.Tables["Cities"].NewRow();
myRow["Name"] = "Atlanta";
dsCities.Tables["Cities"].Rows.Add( myRow );

myRow = dsCities.Tables["Cities"].NewRow();
myRow["Name"] = "Portland";
dsCities.Tables["Cities"].Rows.Add( myRow );

lbCities2.DataSource = dsCities.Tables["Cities"];
lbCities2.DisplayMember = "Name";
```

To add a column to the new `DataTable` we created, we use a little bit of Reflection to obtain a static reference to the "String" type by using the `System.Type.GetType()` function. This function returns an actual data type, and not just an enumerator indicating a data type (like ADO's `adInteger` etc.). From there we create a couple of rows and set the `DataSource` of the `ListBox` to our new `DataTable`. Then we choose which member (column) within the bound datasource that we're going to display. Finally, we manually bind the `Text` property of our label to the "Name" column of the current row in our `DataSet`:

```
lblBoundLabel.DataBindings.Add( new Binding("Text", dsCities.Tables["Cities"],
"Name") );
```

When you consider that the `DataSet` in our example could be data from an Oracle server, SQL Server, an XML file, a text file, or manually created by user interface, the ability to bind tables within that set to controls becomes an incredibly powerful tool. Because the `DataSet` is an implementation-indifferent data store, you can actually have one table in it that came from SQL Server, and another table alongside it (complete with relations, keys, and constraints with respect to the first table) that was populated by data from Oracle. In addition to being able to have tables from multiple sources, you also get an added benefit in that the schema of that data is loaded into the `DataSet` at the time it is filled. Therefore, you can find out which columns are integers and strings, etc. by asking the `DataSet`; you don't need to know any server-specific commands for querying schemas.

Intrinsic

One of the best new things I've seen in the .NET framework is the ability to bind controls (Web or Windows) to intrinsic data types like arrays or instances of classes, etc. The following example is also code from the DataBinding sample. It shows the instantiation of an array and the single line of code required to bind a `ListBox` to the array, creating an entry in the `ListBox` for each item in the array.

```
private string[] Cities = {
        "Washington D.C.",
        "Dallas",
        "Portland",
        "Seattle",
        "Atlanta",
        "New York",
        "Bellevue",
        "Kansas City",
        "Topeka",
        "Cincinnati",
        "Chicago",
        "Cheyenne",
        "Denver" };

lbCities.DataSource = Cities;
```

That's all it takes. All we have to do is set the `DataSource` of the `ListBox` to the array and everything else is handled for us. This example can also be used on the `Array` type, which we can dynamically add more items to, sort, manipulate, etc.

Using Components from Windows Forms

We've covered the concepts of good OOP within the .NET framework, good class design, effective form design, the basic WinForms controls, and a basic overview of DataBinding. Now that we've covered all that, we'll put that all together and actually use our core business tier components from within the Windows Forms UI.

Our video store application, Reel Good Video, is fairly simple. The main form displays a `DataGrid` containing the current day's transaction activity (`Ledger`). From there we gain access to other functions like browsing the store's titles and logging customer rentals and video returns.

The first thing we're going to look at is the binding of the main form's `DataGrid`. The following code initializes a `Ledger` object and then binds the `DataGrid` to the appropriate data.

```
private void frmMain_Load(object sender, System.EventArgs e)
{
    // the default constructor for the Ledger configures it to pull
    // "today's activity"
```

```
    oLedger = new Ledger();
    dgLedger.DataSource = oLedger.Transactions;
    dgLedger.Refresh();
}
```

That's it. That's all we have to do in order to bind our `DataGrid` to our `DataSet`. Of course, we have to go into the `DataGrid`'s `TableStyles` property, and from there into the `ColumnStyles` property to configure which columns we're going to display and how. The really nice thing about this is that the `MappingName` property of each of our `ColumnStyles` is going to be the name to which we're mapping. This allows us to set different `DataGrid` styles for different tables (and columns) within the `DataSet`, providing a great deal of flexibility and control. The `DataSet` is a strongly typed `DataSet`, allowing us to reference the table and columns by name.

Let's look at a sample of the code that our VS.NET Form's designer (for our `frmMain` form) builds for us to configure one of our `ColumnStyles`:

```
//
// TitleColumn
//
this.TitleColumn.Format = "";
this.TitleColumn.FormatInfo = null;
this.TitleColumn.HeaderText = "Title";
this.TitleColumn.MappingName = "TitleName";
this.TitleColumn.NullText = "";
this.TitleColumn.ReadOnly = true;
this.TitleColumn.Width = 75;
```

Our `TableStyle` has a `MappingName` of `"Transactions"`, which is the name of the table in our strongly-typed `DataSet`. Within that, the above column simply needs a `MappingName` of `"TitleName"` and everything works just great.

This really illustrates one feature of the .NET framework: there is always more than one way to accomplish something, but certain methods end up being remarkably quick, simple, efficient, and easy to implement. DataBinding with a strongly typed `DataSet` is one of those methods.

The `TreeView` in our Title Directory form (shown on the next page) is a bit more complicated. `TreeViews` aren't nearly as easy to provide custom mappings for due to the hierarchical nature of their data, but they are easy to populate manually. The code we're about to look at shows us using the `Store` business tier object to populate a `TreeView` three levels deep.

```
//
// TODO: Add any constructor code after InitializeComponent call
//
TreeNode RootNode;
TreeNode ChildNode;
TreeNode ChildNode2;

Store oStore = new BLL.Store();
TitlesByGenreDataSet titleDS = oStore.GetTitles();
RootNode = new TreeNode( "Reel Good Video", 0, 0 );
trvStoreTitle.Nodes.Add( RootNode );
```

```
foreach (TitlesByGenreDataSet.GenresRow gRow in titleDS.Genres )
{
   ChildNode = new TreeNode( gRow.Description, 1, 1 );
   trvStoreTitle.Nodes[0].Nodes.Add( ChildNode );
   foreach (TitlesByGenreDataSet.TitlesRow tRow in
            gRow.GetTitlesRowsByGenresTitles() )
   {
      ChildNode2 = new TreeNode( tRow.Name, 2, 2 );
      ChildNode.Nodes.Add( ChildNode2 );
   }
}
```

First we grab an instance of the business tier object `Store`. Then we use the `GetTitles()` method, which fills a `TitlesByGenreDataSet` (defined by an XML Schema (XSD) file in our Common Assembly). Because our `DataSet`'s nested row classes implement the enumeration interface, they can be traversed easily through the `foreach` operator. For each genre, we obtain the list of related titles by invoking the XSD relation called "GenresTitles". Our `DataSet` class created its own method for invoking that relation by prefixing the relation name with "GetTitlesRowsBy" where `TitlesRows` is the collection of `TitlesRow` objects to be returned.

The method naming conventions may seem a bit lengthy, and you can override them by a process called *annotation* that you can do to your XSD schema file, but that's a topic for an entirely different book.

You can see from the following screenshot what the final output of the `TreeView` looks like.

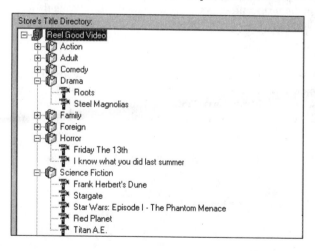

WebForms, ASP.NET, and the .NET Framework

WebForms is a library of server-user interface controls that provides never-before-seen flexibility, cross-browser interoperability, and functionality for the ASP.NET platform. ASP.NET is the successor to Active Server Pages (ASP). However, the capabilities of ASP.NET simply blow away those of its predecessor.

While Windows Forms may seem impressive, nobody is all that shocked to see a library of Windows-based interface classes: after all, MFC has been around a while, and people have been using various versions of VB, OCX, and ActiveX controls for a long time as well.

Aside from third-party component packages, no one has yet produced a suite of server-side, programmable component classes for use on web pages. The new paradigm of ASP.NET allows web application programmers to utilize more traditional programming methods, styles, design patterns, and development techniques. It encourages and rewards good design, good class design, and carefully considered code.

Effective Form Design and Usage

ASP.NET tries to do away with the concept of considering a web page as nothing more than a temporary stream of data from a web server, or others now, for example SSL, etc.). Instead, ASP.NET wants the programmer to treat their web pages in a similar fashion to the way in which Windows programmers treat forms.

As such, instead of trying to deal with stuffing information into the `Session` object as a kludge for going between pages, or spending days writing code to worry about whether the strings you're passing into your URLs contain &s or 's or even +s, the programmer should instead now be concerned with making their buttons respond to events via the `PostBack` mechanism that is already built into the system, databinding robust DataSets to their controls, and providing a top-notch user experience. They should be thinking about where they want to place validation controls and how the interface should facilitate their business rules and core design.

Microsoft has spent a considerable amount of effort in trying to take the pain and suffering out of actually writing the code so that the programmers, architects and designers devote their time to designing and engineering their application instead of debugging "spaghetti-code".

CodeBehind

With the introduction of ASP.NET comes the introduction of the code-behind concept. ASP.NET provides a rich, object-oriented model to all facets of its functionality, including pages. Using VS.NET with CodeBehind, programmers can now create separate classes that perform the code work behind the ASP.NET page, rather than mixing code and interface elements in a messy jumble like the following, which is so prevalent in current ASP pages.

A classic ASP example for populating the items in an HTML drop-down box:

```
<%
    Set oRS = component.GetRecordSet
%>
<select name="MySelect">
<%
    Do while not oRS.EOF
        Response.Write "<option value=" & chr(34) & oRS("ID") & chr(34)
    Response.Write oRS("Description") & "</option>"
        oRS.MoveNext
    Loop
    Set oRS = nothing
%>
</select>
```

As you can see, it's far from pretty, and if you can imagine an entire page filled with code like this, it gets really ugly really fast. The following is an example of populating a select box from within a CodeBehind class in ASP.NET:

```
foreach (MyDataSet.MyRow myRow in MyDataSet.MyTable.Rows)
{
    DropDownList1.Items.Add( myRow.Description, myRow.ID );
}
```

More examples of code-behind behavior will be shown later in *the "Using Components from WebForms"* section. Obviously, the ASP.NET approach looks the most familiar to Windows programmers, is the easiest to read, and is far easier to debug and interpret than sifting through all of the muddled text-printing in the classic ASP example previously.

In short, the concept of CodeBehind allows ASP.NET programmers to truly create web *applications* rather than hodgepodge collections of ASP and HTML pages.

Working with the ASP.NET WebForms Classes

The ASP.NET WebForms classes are a library of extremely useful server controls that provide cross-browser display with uniform property naming conventions and uniform usage conventions. If you use the WebForms controls, you don't have to worry about whether Netscape calls an argument value "middle" and IE calls it "center" and yet another browser calls it "theMiddle". The controls themselves have built-in advanced browser detection and know how to render themselves appropriately based on the capabilities of the viewing browser. *All* of the work of browser detection for common UI elements is now done completely on the programmer's behalf by ASP.NET, with the HTML for the server-side components being generated entirely on the server.

The WebForms UI classes provide not only a way to be placed on ASP pages by means of <asp:xxx> tags, but can also be programmatically instantiated and added to a page's (or another control's) child control list. This functionality allows for incredible flexibility, especially when programmers find out how easy it is to extend these controls by deriving their own server-side control classes.

The Page Class

The Page class is an incredible feature of ASP.NET. Anytime you add a Web Form to your project in Visual Studio.NET, it will create a .aspx page for your user interface tags, and then create a CodeBehind class that derives from the System.Web.UI.Page base class. The Page class provides access to properties like Application (the newest version of the classic ASP global dictionary), IsValid, which is used to indicate whether the user's input was valid on that form, the Request and Response objects, and a User object that obtains information about the viewing user and his/her security context.

The Page class is the basic class that you're going to work with all of the time when engineering applications for the web. One of its biggest uses, however, is actually to be used as a base class for your own custom Page classes. For example, if you have a large set of pages that all need to display a certain header, and all need to retrieve a specific DataSet to provide information for that header, you can create a Page sub-class that provides all that information and functionality automatically. In general, if you have two or more pages that have a lot of data and/or UI in common, then you might want to consider making them inherit from a sub-classed Page.

The following is an example of a code-behind `Page` class that inherits from a common `Page` base class. The `Page` base class is also included here:

```
public class HomePage : Company.Web.BasePage
{
    // code for implementing the code-behind page, including the
    // Page_Load() event.
}
```

The `Company.Web.BasePage` class can be defined in an entirely separate Assembly that can be anywhere on the system:

```
namespace Company.Web
{
  public class BasePage : System.Web.UI.Page
  {
      // implementation of behavior and properties to be shared
      // among all inheriting pages.
  }
}
```

User Interface Classes

The following is a brief overview of some of the server-side User Interface classes available within ASP.NET. It isn't within the scope of this book to cover any of these in detail, but we'll give you a quick run-down of the classes you'll find yourself using most often so that you can get more information on them from other references or books. Also keep in mind that there are a host of server controls that aren't mentioned here.

Label

This is the simplest form of output to a web page. Depending on the browser and the configuration of your `PageLayout` (VS.NET designer property), this may or may not end up as a client-side <SPAN> tag.

TextBox

The `TextBox` is a programmable server-side <INPUT> tag. It allows you to provide all kinds of styling information, colors and configurations. Because `TextBox` (and all other default ASP.NET default server-side input controls) implements `INamingContainer`, it can reload its own values after the page is posted back. This behavior is common to quite a few of the controls listed here.

Button

The `Button` control is an ASP.NET implementation of the standard <SUBMIT> tag, though with quite a few configurable options. You can programmatically, or through tags, configure the size, text, and location of the `Button`.

DropDownList

The `DropDownList` control is the ASP.NET implementation of the <SELECT> tag. We showed a really quick example of how easy it is to populate this list programmatically, allowing for easy debugging and very legible, robust code. In addition to manually setting the items, the `DropDownList` (as well as many other of the controls listed here) can be bound to a `DataSource`.

RadioButtonList & RadioButton

These controls are exceedingly useful. A set of radiobuttons on their own provide a way of displaying a list of choices to users and allowing them to select only one of them. A `RadioButtonList` is a control that is ripe for databinding. You can bind the text display of each button to a column in a `DataSet` to automatically populate the list.

ImageButton

The `ImageButton` is an ASP.NET implementation of the specific type of `<INPUT>` tag that allows for a single, clickable image to represent a button. Because you don't have to worry about cross-browser functionality, you can set all kinds of great configuration options on this control, and it will take care of which browser gets to see which options.

DataGrid

If you're an ASP programmer now, then the `DataGrid` ASP.NET control is your new best friend. You can AutoFormat this grid just like you can Tables in MS Word just by right-clicking it and picking a visual style. Also, you can create your own visual style so that other programmers can have quick access to commonly used color schemes and styles. You can bind the Grid to Arrays and other intrinsic types as well as ADO.NET `DataSets` based on XML files, SQL results, Oracle results, or results from any other supported OLE DB database.

CheckBox & CheckBoxList

The `CheckBox` is an ASP.NET implementation of the standard `Boolean` User Interface control. Even a control this simple can be configured, colored, styled, edited and more. The `CheckBoxList`, much like the `RadioButtonList`, is a control designed with DataBinding in mind. It allows you to bind the text of the `CheckBoxes` to a column, as well as bind the `Boolean` value of each checkbox to another column in a `DataSet`.

Calendar

The `Calendar` control is a composite control that places a calendar onto the web page. This control can then be queried by a code-behind class (or inline code if you feel like it) for its current date or have its date set programmatically.

Low-Level Page Utilities

In addition to all of the user-interface power that ASP.NET places in your hands, the ASP.NET core actually provides quite a bit more power in the form of some low-level utilities. ASP.NET allows you to control a page data cache, gives you access to both Session and Application level state, and even gives you fine-grained control over how data is posted back to your pages in response to user activities. Wrox provides a full coverage of these topics and many more in their *Professional ASP.NET* book, so we'll just skim the surface in this chapter, describing a couple of things you should keep in mind when engineering your web applications.

Cache Object

Each page class exposes a `Cache` object that allows the programmer fine-grained control over storing frequently accessed data to dramatically increase performance and avoid unnecessary round-trips. The `Cache` object implements the `IEnumerable` interface, so each cached item can be accessed individually and the cache can be traversed with the `foreach` command.

One of the beauties of caching individual objects is that you can avoid unnecessary round-trips to data stores or repeated calculations. For example, one excellent use for caching is to cache a frequently requested set of data, only requesting data from the database when the associated tables in the database change. You can use caching to pre-emptively store the results of long or processor-intensive calculations or requests, dramatically increasing the performance of the application.

Trace Object

You can use the `Trace` object (`TraceContext` class) to add detailed tracing information to your page so that you can more effectively debug its flow and execution path. This kind of debugging was only possible in classic ASP by placing dozens of `Response.Write` calls mingled throughout the ASP code and HTML tags. Now you can literally run a debug up to breakpoints in ASP pages just like you could with Console or Windows applications using VS.NET's integrated debugger.

Web Services

You've probably heard more than you care to about Web Services lately. People are writing articles on web sites and in magazines that range from touting Web Services as the newest revolution in Internet content, to claiming that they're yet another half-baked idea from Microsoft that isn't ready for prime-time yet.

The truth is that Web Services are more than ready for prime-time, they're out there, and they're already running and growing. A common misconception is that Web Services are unique to Microsoft and the .NET framework. **WSDL** (Web Services Description Language) is a W3C standard, and many companies, including IBM and Sun, have their own infrastructures for publishing and consuming Web Services.

To keep things short and in the scope of this chapter, Web Services are a way of exposing the functionality of an application as an industry-standard XML service hosted by a web server. Visual Studio.NET contains wizards and built-in functionality for creating and consuming these services, but you don't need the .NET framework for Web Services. Microsoft recently released version 2.0 SP2 of the SOAP Toolkit that allows you to host traditional COM objects as Web Services (that is, VB6 ActiveX DLLs). You can download plenty of sample code for using the SOAP toolkit from Microsoft's MSDN Downloads web site.

Using Components from WebForms

Throughout this chapter we've gone over OOP concepts, class design, good form design and usage for Windows applications, and using .NET components from a Windows Forms application. The main point of this chapter is to demonstrate that the back-end components can be shared, only being differentiated by a thin presentation layer.

So, without further delay we'll get into showing off some of the features of our Reel Good Video application with a WebForms front-end. This next sample shows the default home page of the video store application. The home page is essentially the same as the main form in the Windows application. It displays "Today's Activity" in a bound `DataGrid` control and provides methods by which the employee can perform other functions from there.

The C# code for the `CodeBehind` class for the `default.aspx` page:

```
/*
 * Default.aspx.cs
 * Reel Good Video "Home" Page
 * (c) 2001 Wrox Press Ltd
 * Shows "Today's Activity" all Transactions since "Today" at midnight.
 */
using System;
using System.Collections;
using System.ComponentModel;
using System.Data;
using System.Drawing;
```

Use the relevant namespaces that contain the various web-related classes that we might need. These are all automatically added to the page if you use VS.NET to create the `.aspx` page.

```
using System.Web;
using System.Web.SessionState;
using System.Web.UI;
using System.Web.UI.WebControls;
using System.Web.UI.HtmlControls;
```

Now use the application and company-specific namespaces for ease of use.

```
using ReelGoodVideo;
using ReelGoodVideo.Common;
using ReelGoodVideo.BLL;

namespace ReelGoodVideo.Web
{
    /// <summary>
    /// Class that drives the default.aspx page.
    /// </summary>
    public class CDefault : System.Web.UI.Page
    {
        public string CvtType(int TrxType)
        {
            if (TrxType == 0)
                return "Rent";
            else
                return "Return";
        }
        protected System.Web.UI.WebControls.DataGrid dgTransactions;

        public CDefault()
        {
            Page.Init += new System.EventHandler(Page_Init);
        }

        private void Page_Load(object sender, System.EventArgs e)
        {
            // Put user code to initialize the page here
            if (!Page.IsPostBack)
            {
                Ledger oLedger = new Ledger();
                dgTransactions.DataSource = oLedger.Transactions;
                dgTransactions.DataBind();
            }
        }

        private void Page_Init(object sender, EventArgs e)
        {
            //
            // CODEGEN: This call is required by the ASP.NET Web Form Designer.
            //
            InitializeComponent();
        }

    // VS.NET designer code snipped out...
    }
}
```

There's quite a bit of interesting stuff going on in this page. The first thing you'll notice is that there isn't a single piece of user interface HTML tag mingled into the code. The second might be the Page_Load() event. This event is called every single time your page is loaded. The interesting thing to point out here is that if you bind a DataGrid and post back to the page, you don't need to re-bind it again: the ASP.NET system will have saved that grid's internal state for you, because it implements the INamingContainer interface.

The other really good thing here is that it only takes three simple lines to completely populate our DataGrid (complete with paging and sorting support!) with the data that bubbled up from our data access tier:

```
Ledger oLedger = new Ledger();
dgTransactions.DataSource = oLedger.Transactions;
dgTransactions.DataBind();
```

You may remember from the Windows application that the Transaction Type field is displayed as a 0 or a 1, depending on whether the transaction was a rental or a return. With ASP.NET, we could convert the TransactionType databound column to a TemplateColumn, which allowed us to supply a function return value for the grid's display rather than the column itself. Windows Forms DataGrids don't work in quite the same way, and providing this functionality is a bit more difficult in Windows than it is here in ASP.NET.

Here is the grid's TemplateColumn definition:

```
<asp:TemplateColumn HeaderText="Type">
  <ItemTemplate>
    <asp:Label id="Label1" runat="server" Text='<%#
                    CvtType((int)DataBinder.Eval(Container,
                    "DataItem.TransactionType")) %>'>
  </asp:Label>
  <ItemTemplate>
</asp:TemplateColumn>
```

This code tells the ASP.NET rendering engine that the "Type" column should be displayed by sending the integer form of the "TransactionType" column to the CvtType function and displaying the return value. You may have noticed that the CvtType function, in keeping with UI separation, is actually sitting in the CodeBehind class that we listed above:

```
public string CvtType(int TrxType)
{
    if (TrxType == 0)
        return "Rent";
    else
        return "Return";
}
```

These few straightforward lines of code and completely visually designed `.aspx` page all combine to display a page that looks like this in a web browser:

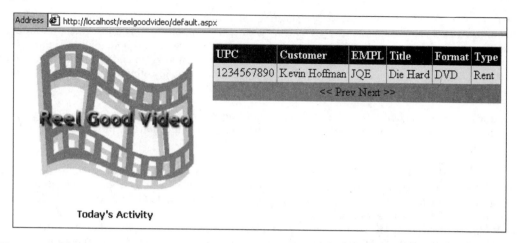

You can see that the Type column is actually displaying the word Rent and not the rather un-friendly 0 or 1 that the `DataSet` contains and that is stored internally in SQL Server. Being able to customize the display behavior of any bound column so that it can perform calculations and modifications on the bound column is an incredible feature. Also, you can create columns in your `DataGrid` that don't exist in your `DataSet`, which might be combinations of columns. For example, you could have a Customer Name column that really just combines the `"First"` and `"Last"` fields within a `DataSet`.

Deployment

We won't go into too much detail on deploying your applications here. The thing to take away from this chapter is that you can deploy your core set of back-end components (business and data tiers, our BLL and DAL projects in the ReelGoodVideo solution), and then deploy the presentation tiers separately on top of the core components. So long as the Assemblies housing the core components are either in the same directory as the web's `bin` directory or the Windows executable, or in the Global Assembly Cache (**GAC**), you won't need to register anything or do any more work than simply launching the application. The sample video store uses Assembly Attributes to automatically create a COM+ package for the data access tier, so deployment won't even have to create a COM+ package.

Xcopy deployment isn't a myth, and so long as your Assemblies are strongly named, properly versioned, and visible to your client applications, you should have no trouble deploying your application.

Summary

This chapter has shown you the basics of engineering applications for the .NET framework. The .NET framework makes many common programming tasks easier by supporting, encouraging, and rewarding good design practices and good implementation of OOP concepts. If you maintain good, solid code throughout your back-end tiers, then your presentation layer (either Web or Windows) should be much easier to create than it has been in the past, and should provide the same features that any other presentation tier for the same back-end components could provide.

Following practices of good class design, tier separation, encapsulation and Object-Oriented Design, your applications should be able to take full advantage of the rich pool of functionality provided for them by the .NET framework.

As an exercise to put to practical use the things you've learned throughout this book up to this point, you can extend the sample video store application. The sample that is included with the code downloads for this book doesn't actually include any login ability – everything is done by an employee with an ID of 1. You can start expanding by adding Forms Validation to the ASP.NET project and by creating a login dialog box for the Windows application. The code to verify an employee's login is already included in the core business and data tier objects. As well as adding authentication, you can experiment with providing reports and informational displays showing late rentals and expected returns. The real test is to use your imagination and figure out how you can add to the basic shell that has been provided for you. It's always been my experience in the past that I learn far more and far quicker by being given a quick nudge in the right direction and then be allowed to "tinker" with my new toy until I've completely figured it all out. Hopefully the "Reel Good Video" application will be a good toy for you to play and experiment with, implementing the various technologies you learn about in this book and others.

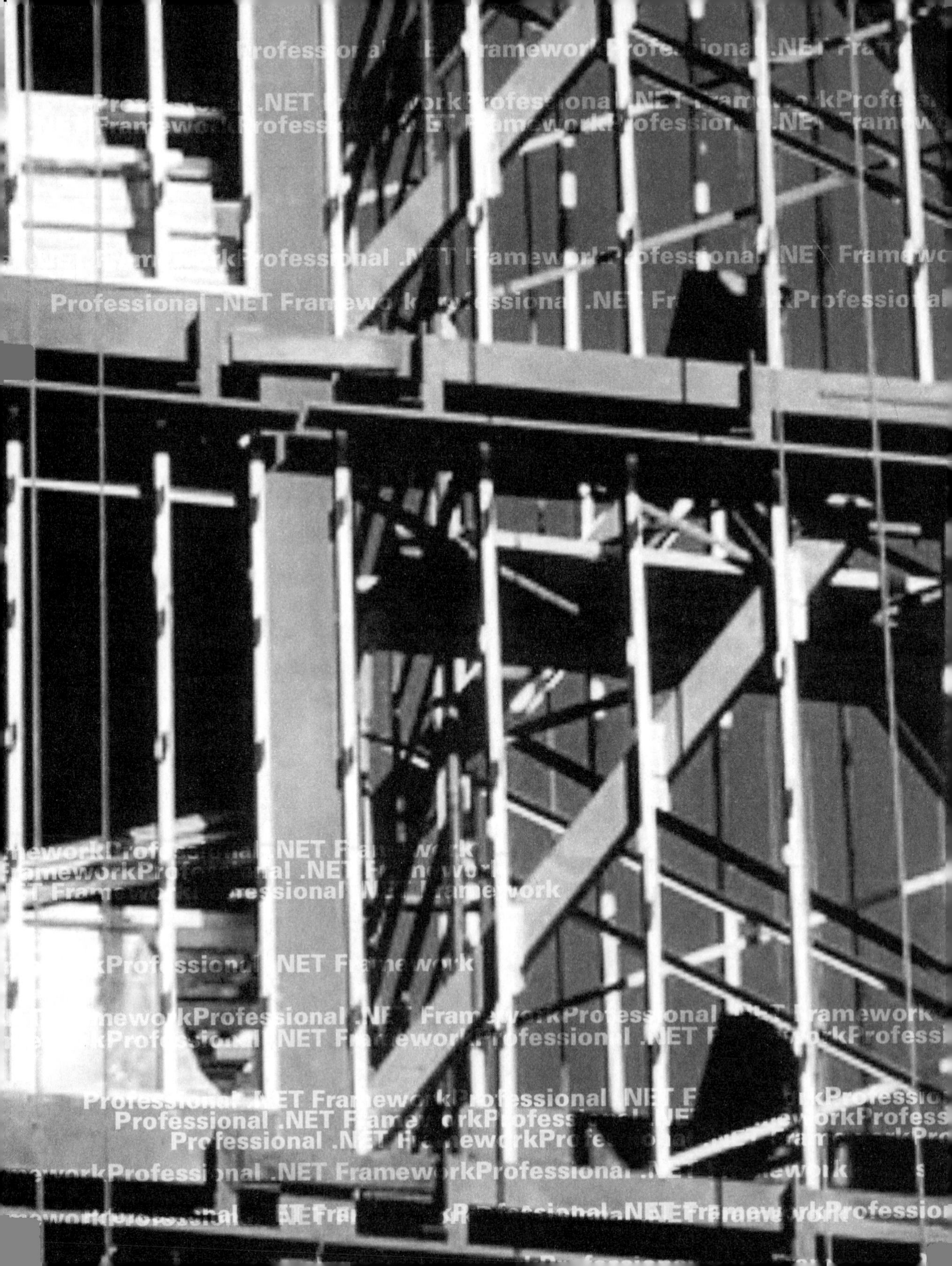
Professional .NET Framework

8

.NET Components and Controls

Component writing for the .NET framework is an entirely new and different experience to component writing in the classic COM environment. In the past, and in many cases today, the world of components has belonged to C++ programmers writing COM at the lowest levels and VB (or Delphi, etc.) programmers creating tools and utilities for all kinds of applications.

These components are used in everything from stand-alone desktop applications to n-Tier enterprise distributed applications. The days of isolated, bloated, and monolithic applications are long gone. It is extremely hard these days to create a modern application that doesn't use or implement components.

The goal of this chapter is to introduce you to building components for the .NET framework. In addition, it will give you some good examples of Interoperability with classic COM components and some information on building and using your own .NET custom controls.

By the time you have finished reading this chapter, you should have learned:

- ❑ The difference between a component and a control
- ❑ How to build native .NET framework components
- ❑ How to use .NET components in your COM-based applications
- ❑ How to use classic COM components in your .NET applications
- ❑ How to create Windows Forms and WebForms controls

Components versus Controls

Before we can discuss the difference between a component and a control, we need to actually cover what a component is. Without even considering a computer-related definition, the word *component* implies that it is a portion, or piece of a larger entity. One problem with trying to define components is that there are literally hundreds of different definitions for them. Some languages consider an ActiveX DLL a component, while others consider the classes contained within that DLL a component. Even UML has its own definition for a component, which translates pretty close to the first definition (a DLL). I personally prefer a slightly more abstract definition.

A **Component** is an abstract, self-contained logical subset of software functionality. It is an incomplete, useless tool until invoked by an *Application* or another component. What this means is that a component relates to a class nearly one-to-one. The reason I say *nearly* is that classes can contain nested classes in the .NET framework, and they can be derivative classes of parent classes. The instantiable form (including all code inherited from parents and contained by nested classes) is the actual component.

Therefore, if you have a class called Fork that inherits from a class called Utensil, which in turn inherits from a class called Dinnerware or some such, there are several different possibilities for components. If the Fork is the only instantiatable (non-abstract) class, then the Fork is the component in this example, and the other classes are simply contributing parent classes. However, you could just as easily have instantiatable forms of the Utsensil and Dinnerware classes. The key point to take from this example is that the component is the *instantiatable unit* of code (such as a class).

If you're used to programming in COM, then you are probably used to thinking of components as classes that implement an IUnknown and IDispatch interface. The flexibility of building components on the .NET framework allows you to build components that more closely resemble the design models for your abstracts. In other words, .NET components don't have to adhere to rigid interface guidelines.

Now that you know what a .NET component is, we can contrast it with a .NET Control. A .NET Control is a .NET component that contains code and logic for rendering its own User Interface (or the interfaces of child controls contained within it). This is the essential, and only, difference between controls and components.

For example, a component that exposes methods that in turn call Console.WriteLine() is not a control. The reason for this may seem a bit fuzzy. Granted, the component can affect the display of the console, but it does not render its *own* User Interface. What this means is that when added to a container within a Windows Form or a Web Form, it does not know how to display itself, either in design mode or at run-time.

Therefore, in short, components are logical subsets of program functionality. Controls are components that contain additional code and logic for rendering themselves onto a given display surface (for example, a Windows Form or a Web Form).

Building Components in .NET

Building components for the .NET framework may seem similar in some respects to building classic components, but there are actually quite a few differences. The first and foremost thing that all programmers need to keep in mind when building their components is that .NET components are **managed**.

Programming a **managed component** involves working with some features and language constructs that programmers may not be familiar with. Some of the other things that you need to deal with when working with .NET components are constructors, namespaces, class access levels, versioning and side-by-side execution, data visibility, and a concept introduced with the .NET framework, *Attributes*. *Attributes* are a feature of the .NET Runtime that allows a programming language to define *meta data* about a given class, method, property, etc. that can be then read and interpreted at run-time for various purposes. More information on Attributes will be given later in this chapter.

Create and Destroy

When the Runtime creates an instance of a class, it invokes a constructor on that class that is used to set any private data within that class to an appropriate initial state.

Constructors can have parameters, allowing programmers to create instances of classes under varying conditions. For example, you might use a parameterized constructor to create an instance of a class, passing to it a unique database key so that it can appropriately load its own data from the database. You can also have multiple different constructors, depending on what information is available at the time.

The following is an example of a class that has two constructors:

```
class MyUser
{
    private string _Name;
    private string _Login;

    MyUser()
    {
        // This is the default constructor, called when
        // the class is instantiated without arguments.
        _Name = "New User";
        _Login = "new";
    }

    MyUser( string Name, string Login )
    {
        // This is called when two strings are passed to the
        // class when instantiated.
        _Name = Name;
        _Login = Login;
    }
}
```

The above is actually poor component design. In a commercial environment, all constructors, regardless of arguments, should eventually boil down to some private function that creates the data, providing one and only one internal method for instantiating private data, and using the constructors as simple front-ends to that function.

Here's an example of how we might make the above example a bit more scalable and easier to maintain:

```
public class MyUser
{
    private string _Name;
    private string _Login;

    private void InitializeUser( string Name, string Login )
```

```
    {
        _Name = Name;
        _Login = Login;
    }

    MyUser()
    {
        // This is the default constructor, called when
        // the class is instantiated without arguments.
        IntializeUser( "New User", "New" );
    }

    MyUser( string Name, string Login )
    {
        // This is called when two strings are passed to the
        // class when instantiated.
        InitializeUser( Name, Login );
    }
}
```

With the above example, even though we have two constructors, they both end up calling the same function to initialize the class. Therefore, any time we need to make changes to how the class's private members are initialized, we can do it from one function, rather than duplicating the changes throughout each constructor.

Namespaces

Namespaces are already covered in several other places throughout this book. However, it is important to mention them when discussing component building for the .NET framework. Namespaces provide a logical hierarchy and grouping of related classes, enumerations and types.

In the days of COM, many companies that made components that served common purposes, such as Address Books, Phone Dialers, etc., had to resort to strange and confusing naming conventions to prevent duplication of component names on a given customer's system. For example, without the benefit of namespaces in the COM world, if you had a class called `AddressBook` that provided business rules functionality, plus another `AddressBook` class that provided read-access from within MTS, and another class that provided transactional data update functionality within MTS, you would quickly find out that the traditional COM PROGID naming convention of `Company.ClassName` comes up short. In a case like this, a programmer might resort to the following naming conventions for the classes:

`Company.AddressBook` (Business Layer)
`Company.rAddressBook` (Data Layer, Read-Access)
`Company.wAddressbook` (Data Layer, Write/Transactional Access)

Now that namespaces are available for .NET programming, the namespace is actually part of a class's identity, allowing a class named `AddressBook` to exist in your company's namespace while another address book vendor may have an `AddressBook` class in their own namespace. In addition, namespaces allow you to retain the same classname regardless of the tier in which the class resides. For the example above, where the programmers had to prefix class names with intended functionality, we could use namespaces to identify the above classes as follows:

`Company.Application.Business.AddressBook`
`Company.Application.Data.AddressBook`
`Company.Application.Data.Transactional.AddressBook`

If those get a bit too long to write, VB.NET and C# both allow you to alias a particularly long namespace name, so that, assuming the proper using or import statement, you could refer to the last class above as:

```
Trans.AddressBook
```

In short, the general rule of thumb is to use a namespace hierarchy that begins with your company's name, and then beneath that contains a namespace for an application or suite of applications.

Object Hierarchies and Access Level

In many object-oriented programming languages available today, there are ways of controlling the access (sometimes referred to as protection or visibility level) and hierarchy of classes. The .NET framework is no exception, and contains a rich and full featured set of modifiers that you can use to not only indicate inheritance, but various levels of access and visibility.

Allowing for inheritance, especially across language and vendor barriers, allows for potential abuse or accidental misuse of your code by other programmers on your team or third parties consuming your component or framework.

There are several class modifiers available that allow you to fine-tune and restrict the visibility and access level of your classes, as well as define how class hierarchies can and cannot be formed. The following is a list of the various class modifiers and how they affect the classes you create:

- ❑ Abstract
- ❑ Public
- ❑ Protected
- ❑ Internal
- ❑ Private
- ❑ Sealed

We won't go into too much detail here since there is a good deal of coverage on Object-Oriented concepts in this book already. However, we'll recap some of the access modifiers with special attention paid to how they affect your .NET components.

Abstract

An Abstract class is just that; a class definition that remains an abstraction. As such, it cannot be instantiated. It is only used to provide a model from which child classes may inherit. Those child classes can then be instantiated. An abstract class is indicated by the keyword MustInherit in VB.NET and the keyword abstract in C#.

```
'Visual Basic.NET
Public MustInherit Class Fan
    Sub New()
        ' Constructor for the Fan class.
    End Sub

    Public MustOverride Sub On()
    Public MustOverride Sub Off()
```

```
End Class

// C#
abstract class Fan
{
    public Fan()
    {
        // constructor
    }

    abstract public void On();
    abstract public void Off();
}
```

Public

The public keyword is the same for both Visual Basic.NET and C#. It defines the visibility of the class. If a class is defined as public, then any other class or application has access to that class definition, even if the consumer was written in a different language, or resides in a DLL on another disk. Public access does not restrict access to the class in any way.

You should be wary about using this keyword, and only use it whenever it is absolutely necessary. The default accessibility for classes is Internal (discussed below). You should try accomplishing your tasks with internal accessibility first before trying public.

Protected

The protected keyword is a member-access keyword that indicates that access to the member is restricted to the containing class, or types that are derived from the containing class. The following is a small console application that won't compile because the protected member is being accessed from an illegal scope.

```
using System;

namespace Wrox.ProDotNet.Chapter9.ProtectedSample
{
public class Fan
{
    // protected member, allow only deriving classes to access
    protected int Speed;
}

public class OscillatingFan: Fan
{
    public OscillatingFan()
    {
        Speed = 12;
    }
}

class Class1
{
    static void Main(string[] args)
    {
        // this will work
        OscillatingFan MyFan = new OscillatingFan();
        Fan MyOtherFan = new Fan();
```

```
        // this will not work.
        MyOtherFan.Speed = 12;
    }
  }
}
```

Internal

The internal keyword indicates that the class is only accessible within the context of the current project (DLL or EXE, that is, a compiled target). Internal is the default access level for all classes unless you specify otherwise. What this means is that if you create a component and do not set the access to anything other than internal (internal is the default), that component is only usable from within your project.

A very common use for the internal keyword is for helper and utility classes that only serve a purpose when being accessed by other classes and functions within that project or assembly. Visual Basic.NET uses the keyword Friend, while C# uses internal.

```
using System;

namespace ConsoleApplication1
{
    /// <summary>
    /// Summary description for OscillatingFan.
    /// </summary>
    internal class OscillatingFan
    {
        public OscillatingFan()
        {
            //
            // TODO: Add constructor logic here
            //
            Console.WriteLine("Oscillating...");
        }
    }
}
```

In all but one case, there is only one access modifier allowed for a member or type. The exception is the protected internal modifier. This modifier indicates that access to the class on which it is applied is limited only to the current project or to types derived from the containing class. This allows you to secure a class while allowing other classes deriving from it, but contained in other assemblies, to retain access. A class marked as just internal cannot be accessed, instantiated, or inherited from anything outside the current Assembly. Protected Internal gives classes deriving from that class in other assemblies access to that class.

Private

The private class is the most prohibitive access modifier. It restricts access to the containing type only. This modifier is seen most often when declaring private member variables contained within a class. Only that class (not even deriving child classes) has the ability to read or modify those values. Access is typically granted to these internal values by wrapping properties that may contain business rules around the private data.

Sealed

The language-neutral nature of the .NET framework allows components contained in one assembly to inherit components contained in another assembly. While this may immediately seem like a good thing, there is a downside – if you aren't careful, you could have customers inheriting and extending your commercial components without your knowledge. If you remember from above, deriving classes have more privileges on class data than simple instantiation. This could allow third parties access to data you don't intend them to have access to.

If you know that a class is at the "bottom" of a particular class hierarchy, you should mark it as such with the `sealed` modifier. This modifier doesn't follow the one-modifier rule, and can be added to `private`, `public`, or `internal` types.

By *sealing* a class, you are indicating that it cannot be inherited from, no matter what the access or privilege level of the inheriting class is. If all of the classes that your `sealed` class derives from are `protected internal`, then no class but yours can inherit from the bases, and no one can inherit from your `sealed` class.

The following trivia question should be obvious at this point:

Can you have a `sealed abstract` class? Explain why. If you're stumped, try compiling a project with a `sealed abstract` class and see what happens.

Exposing Component Data

Now that you know how to prevent unauthorized use of your classes and hide data from the outside world, you should learn how to expose the data from your component. The only components that don't actually expose data are *stateless* components, typically found in host services like COM+, but that's a topic for another book. And, even in their case, data is still exposed, but through different means.

So we can pretty reliably assume that if we are going to be building .NET components, we need a way to allow the consumers of our components to work with the data that they represent. There are a couple of different ways to expose component data and information about our component: we can use things like properties, indexers, public fields, methods, and attributes. Attributes are a topic all on their own.

Properties

Anyone familiar with object-oriented programming concepts should be familiar with the concept of properties. No matter what language we're programming for, a property consists of up to three different sets of code:

- ❑ Property Name
- ❑ Read Accessor
- ❑ Write Accessor

The first piece of code required to create a property is the name or description of the property. Once the name of the property is defined, then two optional methods can be defined that provide read and write access to the internal data that represents the value exposed by the property.

The following is a really brief example of what an implementation of properties might look like to expose some simple data about an `AirConditioner` class.

```vbnet
'Visual Basic.NET
Class AirConditioner
    'private member variable to be represented by a property
    Private BTU as Integer
    Private CostPerBTU as Integer

    Public Property TotalCost() As Long
        Get
            Return BTU * CostPerBTU
        End Get
    End Property

    Public Property BTU() As Integer
        Get
            Return BTU
    End Get
    ' We use "Value" here for consistency, but you can name this
    ' anything you want.
    Set(ByVal Value as Integer)
        BTU = Value
    End Set
    End Property
End Class
```

```csharp
// C#
public class AirConditioner
{
    private int _BTU;
    private int _CostPerBTU;

    public int BTU
    {
        get
        {
            return _BTU;
        }
        set
        {
            // value is a keyword reserved for use in properties
            // by C#.
            _BTU = value;
        }
    }

    public int TotalCost
    {
        get
        {
            return _BTU * _CostPerBTU;
        }
    }
}
```

Indexers

Indexers are a concept that may take some getting used to for some programmers not used to OOP programming with Collections or Templates. Die-hard MFC programmers will probably yawn through this section and skip to the next.

An indexer is a custom property that allows the calling code to supply an index as well as the name of the property. This allows a class to expose a collection, a list, an array, or any other kind of indexed data as a property and publish full access to all elements in that list through a property. To the code making use of an Indexer, the class with an indexer, especially in C#, may look exactly like a Dictionary, an object that many programmers (VB and C++ alike) are familiar with.

The following is a short example that demonstrates how to implement an indexer. Note that the indexer has no actual name, as the class instance itself is what takes the array index indicator [].

```
using System;

namespace ConsoleApplication1
{
    /// <summary>
    /// Summary description for IndexerSample.
    /// </summary>
    public class IndexerSample
    {
        private int[] myArray = {5, 4, 3, 2, 1};
        public IndexerSample()
        {
            //
            // TODO: Add constructor logic here
            //
        }
```

The this keyword here is actually the keyword that indicates the current instance of the class. Therefore we know that this indexer is an indexer against a given instance of the class, and will be used whenever someone indexes this class instance with an integer. Note that you can have multiple indexers of various different types on the same class (to allow you to index the same data from various keys).

```
        public int this[int Index]
        {
            get
            {
                return myArray[Index];
            }
            set
            {
                myArray[Index] = value;
            }
        }
    }
}
```

Now take a look at the code that makes use of this class's indexer property, allowing the class instance itself to be treated as if it were an array. The ability to treat a class as if it were an array, or a dictionary, and to be able to enumerate through all of its indexed items is an incredible asset. It allows you to iterate through all of the Orders belonging to a Customer with a single class, or all of the line items on a given Order with a single class. The possibilities for using indexers are limited only by the imagination of the programmer.

```
using System;

namespace ConsoleApplication1
{
    /// <summary>
    /// Summary description for Class1.
    /// </summary>
    class Class1
    {
        static void Main(string[] args)
        {
            //
            // TODO: Add code to start application here
            //
            IndexerSample test = new IndexerSample();

            Console.WriteLine("3rd Element: {0}", test[2]);
            test[2] = 45;
            Console.WriteLine("New 3rd Element: {0}", test[2]);
        }
    }
}
```

Public Fields

The simplest way of exposing component data is to simply make the component data public, allowing any calling code to read and write the information in that variable. Typically, if you're using nothing but public fields, you might want to consider using a `struct` type instead of a class. The following is a very simple example of a class that exposes data via public fields:

```
public class FieldExposer
{
    public FieldExposer()
    {
        // Constructor
    }

    public int IntData;
    public string StringData;
}
```

As they are public properties that don't define `get` or `set` accessors, you can access and modify the above members directly. Again, this isn't exactly the best design model, so make sure that you really need public fields before you use them. There are very few times when public fields are a practical choice. If you can avoid them at all, you would be far better served by defining your own accessors to privately maintained data. If all you need is simple data storage for a very small amount of data, and don't need some extra features of classes, you might want to rewrite the above as a `struct` (shown in C#):

```
public struct FieldExposer
{
    public int IntData;
    public string StringData;
}
```

The only visible difference here is that we didn't need to define a default constructor, and we used the `struct` keyword instead of `class`.

Modules, Assemblies, and Namespaces

Unlike traditional COM programming, where there really wasn't any kind of hierarchy to speak of, there is a hierarchy of "containers" in the .NET framework. This hierarchy is not the same as the class hierarchy generated by classes inheriting from other classes. Instead, it is more of a logical container tree, as shown in the following diagram.

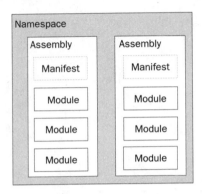

One point that the above diagram illustrates is that multiple assemblies can be part of the same namespace and reference components in other assemblies within that namespace as if they were built into the same assembly.

The following example shows how you can access functionality from a different assembly within the same namespace, with the code still looking as though you were accessing a class from within your own assembly:

```
using System;

namespace Wrox.ProDotNet.Chapter9.AssemblyExample
{
class ClassMain
{
static void Main(string[] args)
{
      AssemblyTester MyObject = new AssemblyTester();
      Console.WriteLine( "Same-namespace Assembly, value: {0}", MyObject.Number );
}
}
}
```

Note the namespace on the code for the `Console` application above. In order for it to work, all we had to do was add a project reference to our example assembly, which contains the following class:

```
using System;

namespace Wrox.ProDotNet.Chapter9.AssemblyExample
{
public class AssemblyTester
{
private int _Number;

public AssemblyTester()
```

```
    {
        _Number = 12;
    }


    public int Number
    {
        get
        {
            return _Number;
        }
        set
        {
            _Number = value;
        }
    }
    }
    }
```

Again, you can see that the namespace is the same. We can have an unlimited number of classes, in an unlimited number of assemblies scattered across our hard disk and still are able to reference them all as if they were internal (provided the access modifiers and references are set properly).

For reference, the official definition of an Assembly is a unit of reuse, versioning, security, and deployment.

In addition to assemblies, there is a smaller unit of compiled code: the module. In most cases, if you're using Visual Studio.NET, you won't need to concern yourself too much with modules. A module is a precompiled component that can then be linked into an assembly. At some point, you might feel that you need to compile some of your classes ahead of time and link them into an assembly later.

One practical use for this that I have found is linking the same class into multiple assemblies. This isn't something you'll probably be doing often, but to accomplish it, you can simply compile the single class into a .NET module (using the `/t:module` parameter to the compiler, for example).

The following shows an example of how you can module-build your own assembly from precompiled .NET modules (module targets using the compiler).

The AlarmClock Class, to be compiled into a module (AlarmClock.cs):

```csharp
using System;

namespace ModuleSample
{
    public class AlarmClock
    {
        public AlarmClock()
        {
            Console.WriteLine("Wake Up!!!");
        }
    }
}
```

The **AlarmClockClient** class, also to be compiled into a module (ClockClient.cs in the downloadable samples):

```
using System;
using ModuleSample; // Namespace created by the other module.

class AlarmClockClient
{
    public static void Main()
    {
        AlarmClock clock = new AlarmClock();
        Console.WriteLine("Created a Clock.");
    }
}
```

The two classes are then built into standalone, precompiled binary modules with the extension .netmodule (the default if you don't specify one) using the following two command-line compiles:

```
csc /t:module AlarmClock.cs
csc /addmodule:AlarmClock.netmodule /t:module ClockClient.cs
```

The /addmodule directive tells the C# compiler that the module it is about to compile references a namespace in the module indicated. Then, to build the actual executable from the two module files created using the command lines above, we issue a command to the Assembly Linker:

```
al ClockClient.netmodule AlarmClock.netmodule /main:AlarmClockClient.Main↵
/out:ModuleSample.exe /target:exe
```

The above command tells the linker to create an assembly from the two listed .netmodule files, specifying the fully-qualified method name of the Main() entry point as well as the output filename of the executable file.

Again, Visual Studio.NET will almost always be doing this kind of work for you behind the scenes, but it is always helpful to know how things can be done manually if need be, and how things are built internally, even if you never have to do it yourself. By default, Visual Studio.NET will compile all of your code into a single module, which is then linked into your assembly. If you want to change this behavior you'll have to modify your project settings.

Side-by-Side Execution (The End of DLL Hell)

One of the major problems that have plagued programmers over the past few years is a condition known as "*DLL Hell*". If the words "GUID", "DLL Versioning", and "Binary Compatibility" don't make you want to reach for the nearest antacid, then you probably have not experienced this particular phenomenon.

Before we can discuss how the .NET framework solves this problem, it might help to briefly discuss the nature of the problem. In the world of COM, a COM library is defined solely by its filename. Within that library, the components and their methods are identified by GUIDs (Globally Unique IDentifiers). When a project references a COM component in VB6, it is actually referencing the GUID representing that component within that component's Type Library. One problem that arose from this is that any time the interfaces changed for a given component (which would cause VB to generate a new GUID), anything using that component would then be broken and unable to use that component. Other languages didn't have automated methods for generating GUIDs, and so encountered entirely different problems when working with COM components.

There are a host of other problems that arise from using the COM binary standard that contribute to *DLL Hell*. The availability of a COM component depended entirely on valid entries in the Registry. Much of *DLL Hell* arises from issues with the Registry, and mismatches between Registry entries and file locations (in other words moving a registered DLL to a new directory, etc.). The important problems to remember about COM components are that you can't have multiple versions of the same DLL on the same machine co-existing happily: you must globally register your component on the machine for all to see, even if your component is only used in your application. The worst of the problems is that if your application depends on a particular version of a DLL, there is nothing stopping the owner of the machine from registering a new version and completely breaking all of the functionality in your application. Obviously, the COM application programmer would want to check for COM dependencies before starting the application, but changes in the registration information and/or file location of dependent COM objects still worry even the most veteran COM programmers.

The .NET framework solves all of the above problems and many more. It allows you to distribute private assemblies that reside in your application's directory. If the owner of the machine happens to install an application that brings with it a newer version of that component, it won't matter. Both copies of the component can reside on the machine at the same time, each servicing their own application without interfering with the operation of the other. The framework also supports multiple versions of the same component to being *shared* globally across the entire machine if you choose. In addition, you don't even need to register anything to use a .NET component in your application's private directory, and you don't have to use the Registry to store globally accessible .NET Assemblies.

Assembly Versioning

The version stamp in the compiled VB projects was a useful piece of information, and helpful for tracking build numbers, but didn't really help much more than that. In fact, the version stamp could actually cause more problems than it solved if not updated properly. If you referenced a COM component from a VB project, you referenced its GUID and invoked all kinds of nightmarish registry issues.

The .NET framework has an entirely different scheme for versioning assemblies. Each assembly within the framework has a version number that consists of four numbers. These typically represent the *Major*, *Minor*, *Revision*, and *Build* segments of a full version. Instead of being useful for decoration and information, the assembly versions are used when referencing .NET components.

If an assembly has a strong name (discussed shortly), then its version number is automatically used to distinguish it from other components like it. In fact, ten different components with all of the same information, differing only by version number, can co-exist on the same machine and still service their respective applications. As well as being able to co-exist, each different version can execute at the same time, with their own private, in-memory copies of the components without interfering with the operation of the other versions.

A strongly-named assembly is identified as unique by the following four characteristics:

- ❏ Filename/Assembly Name (.DLL, .EXE, etc.)
- ❏ Version Number (that is 1.0.0.5)
- ❏ Public Key (Part of encrypting a valid publisher)
- ❏ Culture (for example, "en-us")

What this means is that two assemblies, both produced by the same vendor, both with the same filename, both with the same version number, can co-exist on the same machine differing only by the language culture. Each client invoking that component knows the four identifying characteristics of the assembly it bound to at compile time, so it can easily distinguish which assembly to use to obtain the type definitions it needs in order to execute properly.

Strong Names

All of the documentation you'll find tells you that you don't need to provide a strong name for your assemblies. I tend to disagree. About the only time you shouldn't supply a strong name for your assemblies is when you're testing locally and you're the only one who is going to use your code.

A strong name is essentially a hash of the above uniquely identifying characteristics. When you reference a component, rather than storing in your assembly a reference to a GUID, or a type library, or anything else, the compiler will store the strong name of the referenced assembly.

You might be wondering just what else the strong name is good for. Aside from providing a way to distinguish two apparently identical components from each other, it is also a very useful authentication and security tool. The strong name guarantees that your code will always run against an absolutely specific version of a given assembly. If someone upgrades the globally shared version of an assembly that you have in your application directory to a new version, your application will, in most cases, continue to use the version against which it was compiled. Because the version number is part of the strong name, if your application referenced a strongly-named assembly, your application will continue to use the *exact* version against which it was compiled, regardless of how many newer versions of that assembly are placed in the Global Assembly Cache.

The exceptions are when a special assembly is installed called a *Publisher Policy*. This is a special entry in the global assembly cache that indicates that the publisher of a given component wants all applications compiled against a specific strong name (version, public key, etc.) to now run against the new version of the component. You can also configure your application through a `.config` file to ignore publisher policy and always run against your specific version of the component.

The possibilities are endless, and the amount of configuration you can supply is great. At first, the entire concept of strong names and public keys and versions may seem confusing. It is a little complicated, but in the end it allows you, as the developer of a given application, absolute and final say in exactly which versions of which components your application can and will run against. You no longer have to worry about a new DLL being installed that breaks your code, or an old one being removed from an uninstall, nor do you have to worry about the GUID for a shared component changing and breaking your code, even though the DLL is still there and functional.

To build a strong name into your component, all you need to do is provide a version number and a *key file*. This key file contains an RSA signature that uniquely identifies you as the vendor any time you strong name a component with that key. We'll cover what an RSA signature is (and what RSA stands for) in a minute. To generate the key file, you can either have Visual Studio.NET generate it for you in the Project Properties dialog, or you can manually build the file at the command prompt with the following command:

```
sn -k (filename.snk)
```

The `sn.exe` program generates RSA signature files that can then later be used to strongly name assemblies. As I stated earlier, you're going to want to do this to *all* of your components that go anywhere beyond simple demonstration and testing phases. Once you've built your assembly key file, you can indicate to the VS.NET compiler the name of that file with the `AssemblyKeyFile` attribute, like the one below:

```
[assembly:AssemblyKeyFile("MyKey.snk")]
```

To illustrate the generation of strong names, we created a class library called `StrongAssembly`. In Visual Studio.NET, any time you create a new project you get an "`AssemblyInfo`" file (in both VB.NET and C#) in which you can place your meta data attributes that contain versioning information, descriptions, copyrights, and more. The following is a snippet from this file (the pre-generated comments have been removed):

```
using System.Reflection;
using System.Runtime.CompilerServices;

[assembly: AssemblyTitle("Strong Assembly")]
[assembly: AssemblyDescription("Strong Assembly")]
[assembly: AssemblyConfiguration("")]
[assembly: AssemblyCompany("Wrox Press Ltd")]
[assembly: AssemblyProduct("Strong Assembly")]
[assembly: AssemblyCopyright("(c) 2001 Wrox Press Ltd")]
[assembly: AssemblyTrademark("")]
[assembly: AssemblyCulture("")]

[assembly: AssemblyVersion("1.0.0.1")]

[assembly: AssemblyDelaySign(false)]
[assembly: AssemblyKeyFile( @"..\..\MyCompany.snk" )]
[assembly: AssemblyKeyName("")]
```

You can see from the above code that we used the `SN.EXE` tool to generate our own `MyCompany.snk` file in the project directory (the builds default to the obj\debug directory, or obj\release, so we use the `..\..\` convention to look for the key file in the project root directory.

If we take a look at the Global Assembly Cache after adding our assembly to it, we can see how the framework identifies the assembly by its strong name, which includes the assembly name, version, the culture, and the public key portion of the `.snk` file we generated.

Global Assembly Name	Type	Version	Culture	Public Key Token
Office		2.2.0.0		b03f5f7f11d50a3a
Regcode		1.0.2411.0		b03f5f7f11d50a3a
SoapSudsCode		1.0.2411.0		b03f5f7f11d50a3a
StdFormat		1.0.0.0		b03f5f7f11d50a3a
stdole		2.0.0.0		b03f5f7f11d50a3a
StrongAssembly		1.0.0.1		27f0cb23a72ae22a
System	PreJit	1.0.2411.0		b77a5c561934e089
System		1.0.2411.0		b77a5c561934e089
System.Configuration.Install		1.0.2411.0		b03f5f7f11d50a3a

All of the code for the above assembly can be found in the `StrongAssembly` directory in the downloads for this chapter.

Encryption and Keys

Some of you may not be entirely familiar with the concept of public and private keys. You can think of public and private keys as if they were two halves of a secret decoder ring: separately, they are useless; together, they form a cipher key that is used to encrypt and decrypt information.

The particular form of encryption used by the .NET framework is called RSA. RSA is a method for obtaining digital signatures and public-key cryptosystems. (Incidentally, it stands for the initials of the last names of the three people who invented it, R. L. **R**ivest, A. **S**hamir, and L. M. **A**delman. The RSA encryption algorithm was originally formed in 1977, and the RSA company held a private patent on the algorithm until September of 2000).

The algorithm itself is represented by an equation that works by creating two exponents and a modulus. If you want more detail on how exactly the algorithm works, websites describing it in detail are plentiful. The W3C site that contains all the information you will need for learning about the RSA/SHA1 encryption and Digital Signatures is at www.w3.org/PICS/DSig/RSA_SHA1_1_0.html. So now that you know who invented the RSA encryption algorithm, you may just be able to avoid being the weakest link the next time tech trivia comes up at your next tech conference!

What happens when you create a strong-name key file is that an RSA signature is built into the file, containing both the public and private keys. When you build your assembly against that key file, the public portion of the key is built into the assembly. That is where the security comes in. No one else in the world can generate assemblies with the same public key as you can, unless they get access to the .snk file you created.

Needless to say, if you're planning on releasing strongly named components to the public, you need to make sure that your key files are tucked away somewhere safe. Also, to ensure consistency and avoid returning to *DLL Hell*, once you create a key for an assembly, **ALL** versions of that assembly should be built with that key, giving them all the same public key. That public key is essentially your vendor identification. You must have the same public key in order to release *Publisher Policy* assemblies into the Global Assembly Cache.

Obviously there are some topics that were discussed here that are worth doing more research on. You should, however, now have enough information to be aware of how the .NET framework avoids *DLL Hell* conditions and allows you to provide a reliable, consistent versioning story for .NET components.

Self-Describing Components (Meta Data)

Earlier, we discussed a few ways in which you can expose static and instance data contained within a class to calling clients. In addition to that kind of data, the framework provides a mechanism that allows you to expose additional information to the compiler, to the runtime itself, and even to your own application.

Attributes

Attributes are keyword-like tags that allow you to provide additional data and information about entities defined in .NET framework programs. Attributes can be used to define all kinds of custom options, configurations, and behaviors.

For example, there is an entire set of attributes that allow you to define versioning, copyright, culture, and company information for your assembly. Also, there is another set of attributes that allows you to define how your class and/or assembly will behave when being managed by COM+ Services, such as defining the object pool size and transactional affinity.

Attributes are attached to entities by being placed directly in the code above the entity to which they belong. The following is a list of attribute examples in VB.NET:

```
<Assembly:AssemblyTitle("Sample Assembly Application")>
<WebMethod>
<Assembly:ComVisible(true)>
```

These are those attributes applied in a C# program:

```
[assembly:AssemblyTitle("Sample Assembly Application")]
[WebMethod(false)]
[assembly:ComVisible(true)]
```

There are countless attributes within the framework's class library. Thankfully, they are all organized into the namespaces where their application has meaning. This means that you'll find `InteropServices`-related attributes in the `System.InteropServices` namespace, making it easy to find their associated documentation.

The following is a list of some of the more important assembly attributes that you can use in your `AssemblyInfo` file that VS.NET should generate for you when you create a new project:

❑ `AssemblyTitle` – specifies the title of the Assembly.

❑ `AssemblyDescription` – specifies an extended description for the Assembly.

❑ `AssemblyCompany` – specifies the company that produced the Assembly.

❑ `AssemblyProduct` – specifies the product to which the Assembly belongs.

❑ `AssemblyVersion` – specifies the version of the Assembly. This is very significant for supplying strong names and proper versioning. If you leave trailing portions of the version with asterisks (such as 1.0.*) the compiler will build a version for you.

❑ `AssemblyCulture` – specifies the culture for the Assembly. The default is the neutral culture. If your Assembly is specific to the US or the UK you can specify cultures such as "en-us" and "en-uk". Note that the culture of an Assembly is part of its strong name, and that projects referencing two different cultures of the same version numbered assembly will actually work against two different Assemblies.

❑ `AssemblyKeyFile` – specifies the RSA signature file used to obtain the public/private key pair for aiding in strong-naming an Assembly.

❑ `ApplicationName` – COM+ application name into which to install all components within the Assembly. This is done automatically the first time the Assembly is referenced without the programmer having to do any work.

❑ `ComVisible` – indicates whether or not the Assembly is visible to COM InterOp services.

Custom Attributes

In addition to being able to give fine-grained instructions to the compiler, to the Runtime, and to other hosting services like Remoting, ASP.NET, and COM+ Services, you can define your own custom attributes. These attributes can store any information that you want to store on any kind of entity that you want. Using `Reflection`, you can actually query at run-time the values of attributes assigned to an entity at compile-time.

The following is a custom `Attribute` class. Creating a custom attribute is actually pretty simple. You specify (using an attribute!) to what type of entities the attribute can apply. Then, you simply create a class that has a constructor and properties that derive from `System.Attribute`.

The `ProgrammerAttribute` custom attribute class (`ProgrammerAttribute.cs`):

```
using System;

namespace AttributeSample
{
    /// <summary>
    /// Summary description for ProgrammerAttribute.
    /// </summary>

    [AttributeUsage(AttributeTargets.Class)]
    public class ProgrammerAttribute : System.Attribute
    {
        private string _Name;
        private string _Email;
        private string _Team;

        public ProgrammerAttribute( string Name, string Email, string Team)
        {
            _Name = Name;
            _Email = Email;
            _Team = Team;
        }

        public virtual string Name
        {
            get
            {
                return _Name;
            }
        }

        public virtual string Email
        {
            get
            {
                return _Email;
            }
        }

        public virtual string Team
        {
            get
            {
                return _Team;
            }
        }
    }
}
```

The `SampleClass`, which has a `ProgrammerAttribute` defined (`SampleClass.cs`):

```
using System;

namespace AttributeSample
{
    /// <summary>
```

```
    /// Summary description for SampleClass.
/// </summary>

    // the following attribute is a custom attribute that indicates to the
//compiler, the runtime, and anyone else who'll listen which programmer
//is responsible for maintaining the following class
    [Programmer("A. Programmer", "aprogrammer@someplace.com", "Framework Team")]
    public class SampleClass
    {
        public SampleClass()
        {
            Console.WriteLine("Sample class instantiated.");
        }
    }
}
```

It is as simple as that. Simply start defining an attribute as if you were using an attribute provided by the class library. If you're using VS.NET, it will even pop up a Help window displaying the potential arguments to the attribute.

Finally, the main portion of the Console application uses Reflection to obtain at run-time a custom attribute on a given class. Note that it isn't obtaining information on an instance, but on the class itself as it was compiled in VS.NET. To compile and run this sample, simply load the AttributeSample.sln file into Visual Studio.NET and build the solution. You can then run the AttributeSample.exe from the obj\debug directory or directly from the Debug menu in VS.NET.

Class1.cs, containing the Main function to query the custom Attributes at run-time:

```
using System;

namespace AttributeSample
{
    /// <summary>
    /// Summary description for Class1.
    /// </summary>
    class Class1
    {
        static void Main(string[] args)
        {
            //
            // TODO: Add code to start application here
            //
            Type t = typeof(SampleClass);
            ProgrammerAttribute tempAttribute = (ProgrammerAttribute)
                    Attribute.GetCustomAttribute(t, typeof(ProgrammerAttribute));
            Console.WriteLine("Programmer Information for the SampleClass class:");
            Console.WriteLine("-----------------------------------------------");
            Console.WriteLine("Programmer: {0}", tempAttribute.Name);
            Console.WriteLine("E-Mail: {0}", tempAttribute.Email);
            Console.WriteLine("Team: {0}", tempAttribute.Team);
        }
    }
}
```

When I first saw the attributes and how they were used to act like compiler and runtime properties and tags, I was impressed. Attributes allow you to define within the meta data of your own assembly how the classes and other entities within it behave and interact with the rest of the framework and host machine.

I was a bit skeptical about custom attributes, not having found a good use for them. Then I came up with the example above and it was as if a light went on. At first, the above sample may not appear all that important – big deal, you can describe the name and e-mail of the programmer that worked on a given class. However, picture this: your application uses a custom exception class that it throws whenever something drastic happens. This exception class knows about a system-wide flag that indicates whether or not your application is in debug mode. If it is, it can use Reflection to find out which programmer is responsible for maintaining the class that threw the exception. From there, it can actually *e-mail* to the programmer the entire contents of the error, including the entire call stack and any other tracing information available, and other application-specific information like what user was logged in, and so on.

Here's another scenario that might get your creative juices flowing: someone on your team has made a custom attribute that looks like this:

```
[Revision("A.Programmer", 15055, "Woops, fixed a typo.")]
```

At first glance, it may not seem all that useful. However, if you consider that 15055 is actually the number of a defect within your company's internal defect tracking system, it begins to appear far more powerful. With the use of Reflection and custom attributes, you can actually push a button in your defect tracking system and *pull* live revision history directly from the class definition in a compiled DLL. In addition, you could use the same defect tracking system to log bugs directly into the code, so that the next time a developer looks at the code, they'll see the bug, fix it, and add a [Revision()] attribute to the class.

The number of possible uses for custom attributes is virtually unlimited. The key is finding out what types of meta data you could place in your assemblies to describe your code that might make your development process, and that of your team, faster, easier, and more productive.

COM and .NET

COM Interoperability may seem like a single, generic topic, but it actually has two distinct sides. It affects the programmer differently depending on which direction they're going. For example, as we discussed above, when consuming .NET components from COM, you don't have access to a wide variety of the features that are commonplace and frequently used within managed code.

The same is true when operating in the opposite direction. When you're working with a COM object from within managed code, you don't have access to overloaded operators, static members, parameterized constructors, implementation inheritance, and many other managed concepts. The reason is simple: COM doesn't support any of that.

The really important thing to keep in mind when working with Interoperability in either direction is that despite the seemingly magical workings of the CCW and the RCW, all they do is hide the transformation process; they don't actually compensate for lack of functionality in either environment. Knowing exactly what you can do in COM and exactly what you can do in managed code, and exactly what things can be communicated, will go a long way toward making your next InterOp project a success.

Data Marshaling

Marshaling is the process that transmits information across process boundaries. As COM cannot communicate directly with managed code, and managed code cannot communicate directly with COM, *wrappers* need to be created as arbiters to massage and forward information heading in either direction. Managed code is considered to be any code that is running underneath the Common Language Runtime.

Traditional COM data marshaling consisted of reducing program data from intrinsic types to the limited type system supported by COM. In many cases, many languages had an extremely tough time attempting to map their type systems to the COM type system.

Data Marshalling now consists of communicating with *wrappers*. Each wrapper is designed to appear as if it were native to the model from which it is being called. Therefore, the COM-Callable Wrapper (**CCW**) works to hide the complexity of communicating with a .NET component by presenting a COM-like interface to clients. Likewise, the Runtime-Callable Wrapper (**RCW**) works to present a native, managed interface to clients, encapsulating the inner workings of the destination COM object in managed code. There is a bit of a performance hit in invoking these wrappers (or proxies, if that term makes them a bit easier to understand). Each function call to a wrapper incurs a hit of an average (just an estimate, it varies with the function calls) of 70 additional instructions. Therefore, if you are using an InterOp wrapper to continually call many short functions on the "other side" of the proxy, it is a fairly inefficient proposition. However, if you are making a few calls to long and complex operations on the other side of the proxy, then the initial hit of 70 instructions should be barely noticeable.

The wrappers are not only responsible for encapsulating and abstracting interfaces and functionality. There is actually an enormous amount of code involved in these wrappers. Each of the wrappers is responsible for things like maintaining thread affinity, providing proxies to STA (Single-Threaded Apartment, the only option for VB6 components) model components, and allowing free-threaded access to MTA (Multi-Threaded Apartment) components, and so on. In addition to maintaining thread affinity, the wrappers are responsible for marshaling data across from one native environment to the other.

Using .NET Components in COM Applications

To consume .NET components from the .NET framework, it's a simple matter of just instantiating the component and going from there. All of the plumbing is handled for you. To consume .NET components from within a COM application, the COM-Callable Wrapper also provides the plumbing for you.

When most of the truly hard work has already been done for you, it is easy to forget about the underlying architecture of the system you're using. Unfortunately, if you do that with Interoperability, you may end up with some unpredictable results. The main thing to remember is that the wrapper you are using may also be in use by other components or applications, so you should avoid manually disposing of the wrapper. The following diagram shows the basic architecture involved in consuming .NET components from a COM application.

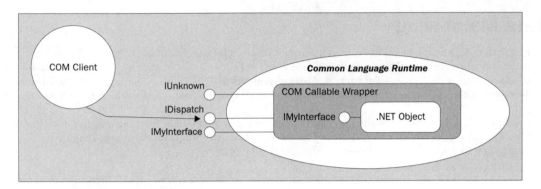

COM InterOp

As I said, it can become very easy to simply forget about the existence of the wrappers or about marshaling or anything else and simply assume that everything is handled for you. There are some restrictions and design best practices that you should be aware of in order to get the most out of COM Interoperability by exposing your .NET components to the COM environment.

Some of the restrictions on .NET components being exposed to COM are:

❑ **Only public types are visible**
A limitation of the COM binary standard is that there is no way for it to distinguish between public, private, or internally exposed types. Therefore, the only types that can be exposed visibly to the COM environment through wrappers are public types.

❑ **Classes require the default constructor**
COM doesn't actually support the concept of a constructor. Therefore, when the CCW instantiates a .NET component on behalf of the COM client, the only constructor that it can invoke is the default, parameter-less constructor.

❑ **No static members**
COM can only deal in exposed interfaces. Therefore, there is no way for the CCW to distinguish to its clients the difference between a class and an instance of a class, so it cannot then support the notion of static members.

❑ **Method overloads are renamed**
The COM binary standard doesn't support the notion of method overloading, even though it is a concept frequently used in the .NET framework. So, in order to provide the COM client with access to overloaded methods, the CCW will append an underscore and a number to generate unique method signatures.

The COM-Callable Wrapper (CCW)

The CCW is a managed object that is dynamically created whenever a COM client calls a .NET object. This object is effectively a proxy that provides access to the .NET component. This proxy exposes itself to COM as a COM object, allowing for the model to be transparent. This way, the code used by the COM application to invoke a .NET object looks just like any other code it would use to invoke any standard COM object, hiding the programmer from the details of the wrapper's implementation. The two should have the same functional accessibility within the COM application.

One and only one CCW is created for each .NET component being accessed. This means that if ten different COM components from multiple applications are accessing the same .NET object, only one CCW will have been created. The wrapper itself allows multi-threaded access to the component on the other side of the wrapper. In other words, the wrapper will not affect the threading support of the .NET object on the other side. The .NET object that the CCW was asked to instantiate is allocated on the garbage-collected heap, allowing the framework to move it around while compacting as it would a normally invoked .NET object. However, the CCW itself is allocated on a non-collected heap, allowing the COM components direct (and location-stable) access to the CCW.

Once the CCW's reference count has reached zero (no more COM applications/components are holding active references to it), it releases its own reference to the .NET component and is de allocated. The now free .NET object will then be garbage collected during the next collection cycle.

Exposing .NET Assemblies to COM

There are several ways to physically expose your assemblies to COM. When you have created your class and you are satisfied that what you have will be usable from within COM via the CCW, you can either have Visual Studio.NET expose your assembly or you can do it yourself.

Once you've written your .NET component and are satisfied that it's working properly, you need to export that component and make it available to COM-calling clients.

Exporting Type Libraries via Visual Studio.NET

Making sure that your class has the [ComVisible(true)] attribute, open up the Project | Properties configuration page. Check the Register for COM Interop box. By doing this, each time your project is built, a Type Library is generated and the appropriate registry entries are generated.

I know, you were told that you'd never have to use the registry ever again. Well, unfortunately, to allow for some InterOp with components from COM some registration is needed. However, it is pretty minimal and quite painless.

Exporting Type Libraries Manually

There are a few things that I prefer doing manually. In certain cases, I like having the final control over how and when something is done. Building type libraries for my .NET components is one such case. You can use the TlbExp and RegAsm tools to register your strong-named DLL in the registry as if it was a COM component.

You should know exactly what information the registry has on your .NET component when it is registered for COM Interop. In the screenshot of RegEdit that follows, you can see that the actual DLL that the registry knows about is mscoree.dll. A few additional keys are stored that allow the mscoree.dll to locate the .NET Assembly, such as its strong name and CodeBase.

Deep down, underneath all of the smoke and mirrors of the call wrappers, you still end up needing to expose your code to COM, and the only way to do that is to go back into the registry. You can infer from this that instead of referencing your code directly, the COM client must first go through mscoree.dll, a proxy that is basically an interface between the COM world and the managed world.

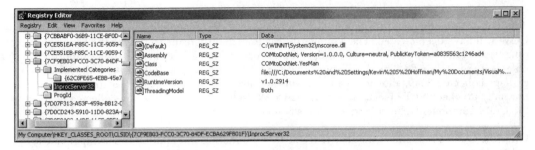

Sample "COM to .NET" InterOp Application

The following is a sample class written in C# that was exposed to COM by giving it a strong name and using VS.NET's Register for COM InterOp property. The class was built by creating a new Class Library project in VS.NET. If you open up the `COMtoDotNet.sln` file, you'll see the `YesMan.cs` file below.

```csharp
using System;
using System.Runtime.InteropServices;

namespace COMtoDotNet
{
    /// <summary>
    /// Summary description for Class1.
    /// </summary>
    public interface IYesMan
    {
        string GetAgreement();
    }

    [ComVisible(true)]
    public class YesMan: IYesMan
    {
        public YesMan()
        {
            //
            // TODO: Add constructor logic here
            //
        }

        public string GetAgreement()
        {
            // no argument to the constructor gives us
            // a time-dependent random # table.
            System.Random r = new System.Random();
            string Phrase;
            int x = r.Next(5);

            Phrase = "I simply don't know what to say.";
            switch (x)
            {
                case 0:
                    Phrase = "You're the man!";
                    break;
```

```
        case 1:
            Phrase = "I couldn't have done it better myself, sir!";
            break;
        case 2:
            Phrase = "I don't know how you do it. Being perfect is such a
            burden.";
            break;
        case 3:
            Phrase = "Your genius is blinding...And me without my sunglasses.";
            break;
        case 4:
            Phrase = "Masterful. Absolutely Masterful. You're so right.";
            break;
        case 5:
            Phrase = "I couldn't agree more. A supremely wise and enlightened
            idea!";
            break;
    }

    return Phrase;

    }
  }
}
```

A very highly recommended design practice when exposing .NET classes to COM is to explicitly define the interfaces to which the class conforms. This way, the tools don't have to guess about class definition when the class is exported into a type library. The following section of code is the Visual Basic 6 application that is consuming the above .NET class. The VB6 project is actually referencing the .NET component as if it were a standard COM component in the registry via the Project | References option. As you can see, through the magic of the CCW, the VB6 code looks no different to any other COM client code. The Visual Basic 6 project is showing the .NET component in the References dialog. This component appears in the registry after the .NET component is compiled in Visual Studio.NET with COM InterOp turned on.

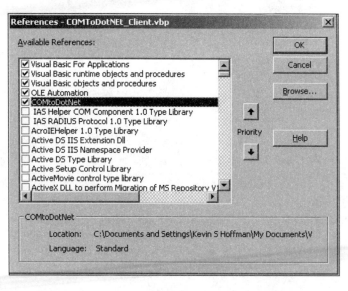

Form button click event handler in the `ComToDotNet_Client` VB6 application:

```
Private Sub Command1_Click()
    Dim objYesMan As COMtoDotNet.YesMan
    Dim strPhrase As String


    Set objYesMan = New COMtoDotNet.YesMan

    strPhrase = objYesMan.GetAgreement

    MsgBox strPhrase, vbOKOnly, "Opinion"

    Set objYesMan = Nothing
End Sub
```

In response to clicking the button on the form, a variable of type `ComToDotNet.YesMan` is created. As far as VB6 is concerned, this is just another COM object.

Consuming Managed Types from COM

As we've already discussed, when your COM application creates a reference to a managed type (such as a `ComVisible`, registered component like the one on the previous pages), a CCW object proxy is created on your behalf to maintain model transparency. As far as the client is concerned, all calls to the CCW proxy look just like calls to a COM component.

However, if you are writing InterOp components, you should know exactly how your .NET managed types are going to be converted into COM types. One thing to watch out for is that some COM-compatible languages support data types that are very close to .NET managed types, but since COM doesn't support them, and you're using COM as your gateway to the managed code, your CCW will not supply those types to you.

COM native Data Type	.NETManaged Type
DATE	System.DateTime
CURRENCY	System.Decimal
VARIANT	System.Object
Interface IMyInterface	interface IMyInterface
CoClass MyClass	class MyClass
BSTR	System.String
Safearray of Int	int[]
2 or 4-byte value, True is 1 or –1	Boolean

Custom Marshaling

For the most part, you should be fine using whatever marshaling scheme the CCW has determined is best for the managed types to which it is providing access. However, there may be a few cases where you may be writing both the consumer and the managed component. In this case, you may actually want to maintain fine-grained control over exactly how your managed types are marshaled.

You can obtain this fine-grained control over the marshaling by either using the `MarshalAs` attribute, or actually writing your own custom marshaler that implements the `ICustomMarshaler` interface. We're not going to cover writing your own marshaler here, but using the attribute is pretty straightforward.

The following code instructs the runtime to marshal the result of the `GetGreeting()` as an `LPWStr`.

```
[MarshalAs(UnmanagedType.LPWStr)]
public string GetGreeting();
```

Managed Type Interoperability

One thing that we didn't mention above is that there are two different types that can be marshaled: **blittable** and **non-blittable** types. A *blittable* type is a type that has the same in-memory representation in managed code as it does in COM code. Don't confuse the term *blittable* here with the old Win32API definition of Blit. For example, a 4-byte integer in managed code is a 4-byte integer in COM code. Marshaling blittable types is always the fastest because no conversion needs to take place.

The following is a table of blittable types that shows both the VB.NET and the C# language type. Keep these in mind when thinking about what information needs to be marshaled during InterOp calls.

VB.NET	C#
N/A	SByte
Byte	byte
Short	short
N/A	ushort
Integer	int
N/A	UInt
Long	long
N/A	ulong
Single	float
Double	double

Non-blittable types include `Arrays`, `Booleans`, `Class Interfaces`, `Variants/Objects`, etc. For more details on how these various data types are converted to native types, see the documentation for the language participating in the InterOp and the MSDN documentation for InterOp marshaling conversions.

For *non-blittable* types, there is no common representation of the data type across managed and unmanaged code. By default, if you don't exert some control over the marshaling process, the marshaler will infer a COM representation of the data from the managed representation. Obviously this process can be much slower than marshaling blittable types. Additionally, the inference that the marshaler makes may not be the one you expect and your code may perform unexpectedly.

You can use the `MarshalAs` attribute as described above to manually map the data types between managed and unmanaged code. In addition, you can use the `MarshalAs` attribute to define a custom marshalling class responsible for providing the runtime with the appropriate wrapper objects. Code to indicate such a class looks like this:

```
[MarshalAs(UnmanagedType.CustomMarshaler,
MarshalType="Company.Utilities.MyMarshaler")]
```

Not only does this give you the ability to specify your own marshaler, but also, in doing so, it allows you to add company or application-specific logic and calculations to the data conversion. For example, if your `CustomerIDs` in your COM application are all single-byte numbers (why you would do this, no one knows), and in the managed code, they are all 4-byte numbers, you could use a custom marshaler to allow your COM object to supply native "old" customer IDs to your custom CCW, which then modifies the old `CustomerID` into a 4-byte number, possibly doing some calculations on it to indicate that it was an "old" customer.

The possibilities are, as usual, virtually limitless. If you're willing to take a little extra time to sit back and really evaluate the goals you have for your Interoperability applications and components, you may find that you can do some amazing things with your classic COM applications without having to rewrite very much code at all.

In many cases, people have rewritten some old COM components in managed code, created a custom marshaler and then simply dropped the new component in place without have to re-write a single line of their old code. They simply had to change the reference to the component from the old COM object to the new registry entry created either by VS.NET's automatic registration or the `RegAsm` utility.

Using COM Components in .NET Applications

Consuming COM components from within managed components maintains just as much model transparency as when consuming .NET components from within COM code. One of the major differences is that the limitations of the COM components will be far more visible from within managed code.

As with anything you do as far as Interoperability is concerned, if you jump into it blindly without knowing the underlying structure of what is happening with your components, you may end up experiencing some unexpected results in your application.

The following diagram shows you the basic structure of an environment where managed code is consuming a COM component or automation server. Of all the many things that consuming COM objects from .NET code allows us to do, probably my favorite and most welcome feature is that you don't have to interpret a single `HRESULT` value. All `HRESULTS` are interpreted into exceptions (if the `HRESULT` indicated an error) while `[out,retval]` parameters to COM components become return values from .NET functions.

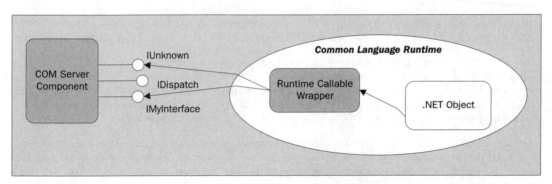

The Runtime-Callable Wrapper (RCW)

As you can see in the diagram on the previous page, all traffic to and from the COM component is routed through a managed object called the **Runtime-Callable Wrapper**. One and only one RCW is created for each COM component being consumed. The RCW appears to all calling code as if it were a native .NET object, though its primary purpose is to marshal calls between managed and unmanaged code.

The truly important thing to note, as with both of the wrappers, is that both ends of the conversion are completely unaware that they are communicating with anything other than a native object. All of the function calls and return values from the .NET object are done using native .NET types. The COM component on the other end receives nothing but native COM types and returns nothing but native COM types.

Exposing COM Libraries to .NET

When an application or component makes a request for a COM object from within the COM environment, the GUIDs stored in that object's type library are used to find the appropriate IUnknown interface. Once that is found, a series of queries can be done to obtain more information about how to interact with that component.

Because of the way COM InterOp and the RCW works, you can actually call any COM component from .NET in the same way that you would have called it from any other platform. In fact, through the wrapper, you can utilize ActiveX controls on your Windows Forms, or call COM components to populate ASP.NET WebForms controls.

The same is true when consuming that same COM component from within .NET code. In order for managed code to make use of a COM component, it must have access to an assembly that contains meta data that provides the same description of functionality as the COM component's type library. In order to provide this assembly, you must obtain it in one of two ways.

The first way is to manually import the assembly from an existing COM type library. This is done through the use of the TlbImp.exe tool that ships with the Framework SDK. This creates an assembly that managed code can then reference and use to provide access to the COM component as if it were a native .NET component.

The second way is from within Visual Studio.NET: simply add a reference and click the COM tab. This will give you a list of all registered COM components that you can reference. VS.NET may complain about the lack of a Primary InterOp Assembly (discussed below).

Primary InterOp Assembly (PIA)

When you use TlbImp to create an export assembly from a Type Library, you create an InterOp Assembly that can be referenced by .NET components that will provide a transparent interface into the COM component, hiding the details of the implementation of the RCW from the client.

A disadvantage to that is that you might end up with hundreds of InterOp Assemblies floating around, many of them probably without version stamps and weakly named. The TlbImp.exe tool creates the InterOp Assemblies and allows you to sign them with a key file, effectively stamping that InterOp Assembly as having been authorized.

In addition to signing the InterOp Assembly, you can also specify the /primary command-line argument to the TlbImp tool, creating a *Primary InterOp Assembly*. A Primary InterOp Assembly is an InterOp Assembly that has been signed and marked as the official, Authorized Version of that assembly.

The Primary InterOp Assembly should always be your first choice when trying to obtain references to COM types. MSDN (Microsoft Developer's Network) will eventually be publishing dozens of PIAs providing managed type interfaces for things like Word, Excel, and other currently COM-exposed servers.

Sample ".NET to COM" InterOp Application

The following is a VB6 COM component class that basically provides the same type of functionality as our previous sample. It provides a COM visible method called `GetOpinion` that returns a string phrase to the calling client.

```
Public Function GetOpinion() As String
    Dim X As Integer
    Dim result As String
    Randomize
    X = Int((5 * Rnd) + 1) 'random number between 1 and 5

    Select Case X
        Case 1:
            result = "You're so remedial."
        Case 2:
            result = "That would be a good idea, if it wasn't old and tired."
        Case 3:
            result = "If ignorance is bliss, then you must be a truly happy person."
        Case 4:
            result = "What is that smell? Oh, it is just you."
        Case 5:
            result = "Too bad your IQ isn't graded on the curve."
    End Select

    GetOpinion = "Your phrase: " & result

End Function
```

In Visual Studio.NET, we create a new Windows Forms application. Then we drag a button from the Toolbox onto the main form. Then, right-click the References link in your Solution Explorer and choose Add Reference. Then we clicked the COM tab and found our newly built VB6 COM DLL. VS.NET (Beta 2) will give you a warning that there is no Primary InterOp Assembly found for that component. It then asks if you want it to build a manually exported assembly for you. We then choose Yes and place the following code in the event handler for the button's click event.

```
//(C#)
private void button1_Click(object sender, System.EventArgs e)
{
```

You can see here that the code is creating an instance of the class "NegativityMan" which is in the COM component "DotNetToCOM_VB6". All of this is visible through Intellissense from within VS.NET.

```
    DotNetToCOM_VB6.NegativityMan oNeg = new DotNetToCOM_VB6.NegativityMan();
    string Phrase;

    Phrase = oNeg.GetOpinion();
    MessageBox.Show(this, Phrase, "Opinion");
}
```

As you can see from the following screenshot, there's no visibility to the fact that the .NET code is calling COM code, or that the Message Box displayed is anything other than a classic Message Box, instead of the managed class.

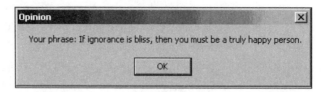

Creating .NET Controls

For a long time, control building was considered a "Black Art". Not too many people knew how to do it, and even fewer knew how to do it well. Companies began appearing that did nothing but create reusable visual controls for people to use. They were successful because they were providing a service that was either too hard or too time-consuming for developers to implement on their own.

Unfortunately for those companies, control programming has just got much easier, and much faster. As I said earlier, controls are really just specialized components that have code and logic for interacting with a design environment as well as rendering themselves at runtime.

In the past, if you wanted to create a textbox that had rounded edges to give it a bit of flare, even in Visual Basic it was an annoying, time-consuming, difficult process. Now, you simply create a new control that inherits from the standard `TextBox` control, override the paint method to round the edges, and you're done.

Creating WebForms controls is just as easy. The only essential difference between a WebForms control and a Window Forms control is that the Window Forms controls render themselves graphically using the Win32 API and GDI+, while WebForms controls render themselves by generating HTML. Window Forms controls use the `Paint` method, while WebForms controls use the `Render` method (and other associated methods).

The coverage here of controls may seem entirely too brief, but that is intentional. For a far more detailed look at WebForms controls, check out Wrox's *Professional ASP.NET* book. For all the information you'll need to create your own custom Window Forms controls, check out *Professional Windows Forms*.

Writing your own Window Forms Controls

Creating a Windows Forms control is easier than you might think. To get started, the first thing you need to do is know what you're trying to build. You'll end up with a horrible, tangled mess if you start coding before you're sure of exactly what behavior and display you want your control to contain.

Once you've got your design ready, go into Visual Studio.NET and create a new Windows Control Library. The really great thing about this is that you can house multiple controls within the same assembly. So, if your company has designed its own unique look-and-feel for all of its Windows Forms applications, all the front-end developers need to do is reference this Windows Control Library and their Toolbox can then have access to all of the custom controls.

Visual Studio.NET will automatically create the first control for you, deriving it from `System.Windows.Forms.UserControl`. For our example we're going to change that to `System.Windows.Forms.Label`, so that our control can inherit the border ability without having to recode it manually ourselves.

For our sample, we're going to create a control that derives from `Label`. It displays label text on top of a configurable gradient background. Let's take a look at what our control class looks like and then we'll analyze each section in detail. Before we look at the code, let's look at the end result of the control in action.

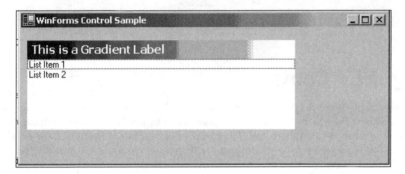

GradientLabel.cs

```csharp
using System;
using System.Collections;
using System.ComponentModel;
using System.Drawing;
using System.Data;
using System.Windows.Forms;
using System.Drawing.Drawing2D;
using System.Drawing.Design;

namespace Wrox.Samples.WinFormsControls.GradientLabel
{
    /// <summary>
    /// Custom Gradient Label Control
    /// It will display label text just as normal labels do, but this
    /// text will appear on a gradient background.
    /// </summary>
    public class GradientLabel : System.Windows.Forms.Label
    {
        /// <summary>
        /// Required designer variable.
        /// </summary>
        private System.ComponentModel.Container components = null;

        // Private information for our own custom properties.
        private Color _GradientStartColor = Color.Blue;
        private Color _GradientEndColor = Color.White;
        private float _Angle = 0;
        private string _Text = "Gradient Label";

        public GradientLabel()
        {
            // This call is required by the Windows.Forms Form Designer.
            InitializeComponent();
// TODO: Add any initialization after the InitForm call
```

```
    }

    /// <summary>
    /// Clean up any resources being used.
    /// </summary>
    protected override void Dispose( bool disposing )
    {
        if( disposing )
        {
            if( components != null )
                components.Dispose();
        }
        base.Dispose( disposing );
    }
```

The following is the code of the overridden paint event. We've modified the code so that any time the control is to be painted, our code is called rather than the default code for the label. We obtain a solid brush, measure the size of the text, and then center our text paint vertically within the bounds of the label. We then create a gradient, going from our starting color to our ending color, and paint the gradient onto the label surface, finishing up the operation by actually placing the text onto the label.

```
    private void GradientLabel_Paint(object sender,
System.Windows.Forms.PaintEventArgs e)
        {
        SolidBrush b = new SolidBrush(this.ForeColor);
        SizeF fontSize = e.Graphics.MeasureString( _Text, Font );
        int newX = 3;
        int newY;
        if (this.Height == fontSize.Height)
            newY = 0;
        else
            newY = (int)(this.Height - fontSize.Height) / 2;
        LinearGradientBrush bgrnd = new LinearGradientBrush( new Rectangle(0,0,
        this.Width,
                        this.Height), _GradientStartColor,
                        _GradientEndColor,_Angle, true);
        e.Graphics.FillRectangle( bgrnd, 0, 0, this.Width, this.Height);
        e.Graphics.DrawString( _Text, this.Font, b, newX, newY);
    }
```

Any time that data is vital to how your control is displayed is changed, you need to make sure that you Invalidate the surface of the control. This forces Windows to repaint your control. You can invalidate only a portion of your control to optimize the repainting to only those areas affected by the data change, but that is a bit out of the scope of this chapter.

```
    private void GradientLabel_ForeColorChanged(object sender,
    System.EventArgs e)
    {
        Invalidate();
    }

    private void GradientLabel_FontChanged(object sender, System.EventArgs e)
```

```
    {
        Invalidate();
    }

    private void GradientLabel_Resize(object sender, System.EventArgs e)
    {
        Invalidate();
    }

    /// <summary>
    /// GradientStartColor Property. Graphics color representing the
    /// color the gradient begins with.
    /// </summary>
    [
    Category("Gradient"),
    Description("Starting Color of the Gradient Fill"),
    ]
    public Color GradientStartColor
    {
        get
        {
            return _GradientStartColor;
        }
        set
        {
            _GradientStartColor = value;
            Invalidate();
        }
    }
/// <summary>
/// GradientEndColor property allows the user to define the
/// ending color of the gradient background.
/// </summary>
    [
    Category("Gradient"),
    Description("Ending Color of the Gradient Fill"),
    ]
    public Color GradientEndColor
    {
        get
        {
            return _GradientEndColor;
        }
        set
        {
            _GradientEndColor = value;
            Invalidate();
        }
    }

    /// <summary>
    /// GradientAngle property allows the user to define the angle at which
    /// the colors flow from start to finish, in degrees from the X axis.
    /// </summary>
    [
    Category("Gradient"),
```

```
        Description("Angle at which the Gradient flows (degrees clockwise from the X
Axis)")
        ]
        public float GradientAngle
        {
            get
            {
                return _Angle;
            }
            set
            {
                _Angle = value;
                Invalidate();
            }
        }
        /// <summary>
        /// Text property. There is no real reason to do this except
        /// to demonstrate how easy it is to override and hide properties
        /// defined by the base class (Label)
        /// </summary>
        [
        Category("Appearance"),
        Description("The text to be displayed on the label")
        ]
        public override string Text
        {
            get
            {
                return _Text;
            }
            set
            {
                _Text = value;
                Invalidate();
            }
        }

    }
}
```

The definition of the private variables, the constructor, and property definitions should all look pretty familiar, as they use the same code as you would use to create a regular component. The first thing that might look odd is that in the property set definitions, they all make a call to an Invalidate() method.

Those of you familiar with graphics programming in general or "classic" Windows control creation might already be familiar with the term. Invalidate() indicates to the drawing sub system that the surface being invalidated (you can invalidate smaller rectangles instead of the entire control rectangle) is "dirty", or in need of being repainted. It is always a *really* good idea to Invalidate your control (or some smaller rectangle within the control) any time that the data used in rendering changes.

The next things that might not look familiar to you are the custom attributes being used to affect the properties of the control.

```
    [
    Category("Gradient"),
    Description("Angle at which the Gradient flows (degrees clockwise from the X
Axis)")
    ]
```

The previous attributes indicate to the VS.NET designer (or any other designer) that the property being described should appear in the property category called Gradient. It also provides a small Help text that is displayed in the **Properties** window when the property is selected. The following is a screenshot that shows the effect the previous attributes have on your VS.NET experience:

You can see that the Gradient property category contains the three custom properties that our control defined above.

Finally, let's look at the Paint event. All controls have a Paint event that is called whenever a rectangle within that control is Invalidated. This allows us to provide our own drawing code so that we can place a gradient behind the label text.

```
private void GradientLabel_Paint(object sender,
System.Windows.Forms.PaintEventArgs e)
{
    SolidBrush b = new SolidBrush(this.ForeColor);
    SizeF fontSize = e.Graphics.MeasureString( _Text, Font );
    int newX = 3;
    int newY;
    if (this.Height == fontSize.Height)
        newY = 0;
    else
        newY = (int)(this.Height - fontSize.Height) / 2; LinearGradientBrush bgrnd =
        new LinearGradientBrush( new Rectangle(0,0, this.Width,_
```

```
                                _this.Height), _GradientStartColor, _GradientEndColor, _Angle,
                            true);
        e.Graphics.FillRectangle( bgrnd, 0, 0, this.Width, this.Height);
        e.Graphics.DrawString( _Text, this.Font, b, newX, newY);
    }
```

There is some GDI+ code at work here that we don't need to spend too much detail on. Basically, the code will vertically center the string stored in the control's overridden `Text` property. Also, a `LinearGradientBrush` is used to build a gradient and then use that gradient as a fill on a rectangle.

When the control is all set, and we've modified our toolbox in our Windows Forms application, we can generate output in our application that looks like this (although 256 color grayscale doesn't do gradients much justice):

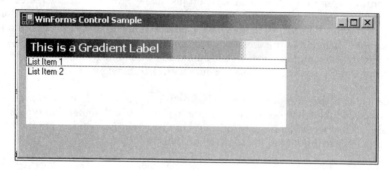

Make sure that when you're working with this sample, you're using the Visual Studio.NET solution (`GradientLabel.sln`) provided. The Windows Form sample references the control by project, so trying to compile the code outside of VS.NET means that you may fail to find the reference properly.

Composite Window Forms Controls

A *Composite Control* in Windows Forms is a custom control that is made up of one or more other controls. Suppose, for example, that you're writing a custom control that is a rounded textbox, but, because of your rounding code, you need to make sure that the label for that textbox is always above the box and right justified. Instead of forcing the forms designer to create a new label control each time, and force it to be right justified, you can actually include a custom-formatted label control within your custom control.

There are countless other reasons for composing controls, the most significant being that you never want to re-invent the wheel. If your custom control needs to display some kind of behavior that already exists in a previously coded control (including another custom control), then, by all means, drag that existing control onto your control's surface in the designer and you're ready to go.

Another use for composing controls is to link related functionality. For example, VS.NET includes a `DateTimePicker`, which is a `ComboBox` with customized drop-down behavior, displaying a calendar that allows you to select a date. In our example, we'd like to provide a `FilePicker`. It is an edit box that is linked to a **Browse** button that operates an `OpenFile` dialog. All of the functionality will be linked together, and we can then simply access the `FileName` property of the control, not worrying about any nested controls or their properties.

When our sample composite control is finished, we can drop it onto a form and manipulate it as a single control, even though it consists of a `TextBox`, a `Button`, and an invisible `OpenFile` dialog.

Our custom `FilePicker` control on a new form in the VS.NET designer.

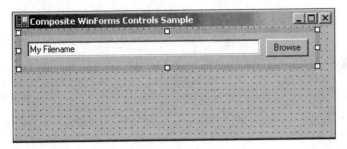

To build our custom, composite control we start off just like we did last time. Create a new Windows Control Library project in VS.NET. Expand the surface of the control a bit and then drag a `TextBox` and a `Button` from your Toolbox onto the control surface. Then drag an `OpenFile` dialog onto the form. In our sample (included in the downloads in the `CompositeControl` directory), we've named the textbox `txtFileName` and the browse button `btnBrowse`. Being remarkably creative, we have used the default `openFileDialog1` name for our `OpenFile` dialog box.

This next code listing is the extremely simple class definition for our `FilePicker` class. All we did to generate this was to double-click our browse button in the control designer and type in some code for the event handler. Then we created a new property to allow read/write access to the file name directly without having to expose the private `txtFileName` control.

FilePicker.cs

```
using System;
using System.Collections;
using System.ComponentModel;
using System.Drawing;
using System.Data;
using System.Windows.Forms;

namespace Wrox.Samples.CompositeControls.CompositeControl
{
    /// <summary>
    /// Summary description for UserControl1.
    /// </summary>
    public class UserControl1 : System.Windows.Forms.UserControl
    {
        private System.Windows.Forms.TextBox txtFileName;
        private System.Windows.Forms.OpenFileDialog openFileDialog1;
        private System.Windows.Forms.Button btnBrowse;
        /// <summary>
        /// Required designer variable.
        /// </summary>
        private System.ComponentModel.Container components = null;

        public UserControl1()
        {
            // This call is required by the Windows.Forms Form Designer.
            InitializeComponent();

            // TODO: Add any initialization after the InitForm call

        }
```

```
/// <summary>
/// Clean up any resources being used.
/// </summary>
protected override void Dispose( bool disposing )
{
   if( disposing )
   {
      if( components != null )
         components.Dispose();
   }
   base.Dispose( disposing );
}


#region Component Designer generated code
/// <summary>
/// Required method for Designer support - do not modify
/// the contents of this method with the code editor.
/// </summary>
private void InitializeComponent()
{
   this.openFileDialog1 = new System.Windows.Forms.OpenFileDialog();
   this.btnBrowse = new System.Windows.Forms.Button();
   this.txtFileName = new System.Windows.Forms.TextBox();
   this.SuspendLayout();
   //
   // btnBrowse
   //
   this.btnBrowse.Location = new System.Drawing.Point(264, 8);
   this.btnBrowse.Name = "btnBrowse";
   this.btnBrowse.Size = new System.Drawing.Size(56, 23);
   this.btnBrowse.TabIndex = 1;
   this.btnBrowse.Text = "Browse";
   this.btnBrowse.Click += new System.EventHandler(this.button1_Click);
   //
   // txtFileName
   //
   this.txtFileName.Location = new System.Drawing.Point(8, 8);
   this.txtFileName.Name = "txtFileName";
   this.txtFileName.Size = new System.Drawing.Size(248, 20);
   this.txtFileName.TabIndex = 0;
   this.txtFileName.Text = "";
   //
   // UserControl1
   //
   this.Controls.AddRange(new System.Windows.Forms.Control[] {
                                         this.btnBrowse,
                                         this.txtFileName});
   this.Name = "UserControl1";
   this.Size = new System.Drawing.Size(328, 40);
   this.Resize += new System.EventHandler(this.UserControl1_Resize);
   this.ResumeLayout(false);

}
#endregion
```

Here is the core of most of the functionality of this control. Any time the browse button is clicked, the code will open a file dialog and place the resulting filename from that dialog in the textbox. Note that both the textbox and the browse button are private controls within this particular user control.

```
private void button1_Click(object sender, System.EventArgs e)
{
    openFileDialog1.ShowDialog();
    txtFileName.Text = openFileDialog1.FileName;
}
```

Just as an added bonus, when the entire control is resized, it is a simple matter to just resize the textbox and reposition the browse button so that they both expand appropriately when the control is resized. This event applies not only to when it is resized in the design environment, but when modifying the control's properties causes the control to resize at run-time.

```
private void UserControl1_Resize(object sender, System.EventArgs e)
{
    txtFileName.Width = this.Width - 80;
    btnBrowse.Left = txtFileName.Width + 16;
}

[
Category("File Dialog"),
Description("Title description of the Open File Dialog box.")
]
public string DialogTitle
{
    get
    {
        return openFileDialog1.Title;
    }
    set
    {
        openFileDialog1.Title = value;
    }
}
```

Here the properties of our control are actually just forwarding on requests for properties of the child controls.

```
[
Category("File"),
Description("Full Filename")
]
public string FileName
{
    get
    {
        return txtFileName.Text;
    }
    set
    {
        txtFileName.Text = value;
    }
}
}
}
```

The first really nice thing you should notice about this control is that I didn't override any `Paint` event. As all I did was link together two already created controls with some common functionality, I didn't need to override any event. I could have, and actually have created a gradient for the background surface of the `FilePicker` control, but you can probably figure that out by combining the two samples.

Writing your own WebForms Controls

Those of you used to working with classic ASP and HTML will know just how hard it is to provide reusable user interface experiences. In ASP, the typical trick would be to provide some kind of rendering code that you would then embed into an ASP page through the use of a server-side include. Many felt that this method was nothing more than a hack and was unacceptable.

Other, far more enterprising programmers went so far as to create COM objects that would take parameters, properties and other information and provide some method that would return a string or Stream of HTML. This approach is very similar to the ASP.NET/WebForms control paradigm, but the programmers still had to create all of the rendering logic and the entire infrastructure of re-usable HTML generators. Not too many developers had the time or the resources to bring this approach up to the level where it was truly effective.

A WebForms control, however, is a very simple thing to create. As we showed above, to create a Windows Forms control, you simply create a component that inherits from a particular *control* class, and modify the rendering behavior and you are done. With WebForms, the process is actually the same. You create a standard .NET component that inherits from the `WebControl` class, provide properties and private data, and specify how the control is to be rendered (this time in HTML rather than GDI+) and you have a functioning WebForms control.

I'm sure you've read enough about code reuse and good Object-Oriented principles in this book and others to know why custom controls should be used. I won't go into too much detail, as a large amount of WebForms control creation detail can be found in *Professional ASP.NET*.

We've written a fairly straightforward sample control to illustrate the basics of getting up and running with a custom WebForms Control. To get started, we opened up VS.NET and created a new project, selecting **Web Control Library** as the type. This gets us set up with a project that will build an assembly containing one or more WebForms controls. You'll need to be running at least Windows 2000 in order for this example to work, as ASP.NET does not work on NT 4.0. If you are compiling the samples manually, you'll need to copy the control's compiled assembly to the web site's /bin directory. If you're using the VS.NET solution provided (`WebControlSamples.sln`) then VS.NET will take care of publishing the compilations to the /bin directory.

The control we created actually duplicates the functionality found in the *COM to .NET* sample earlier in this chapter. We've re-implemented the `YesMan` component as a WebForms control. Every time a page is refreshed with this control on it, the control will automatically render itself as one of the six choice catch-phrases.

YesManLabel.cs

```
using System;
using System.Web.UI;
using System.Web.UI.WebControls;
using System.ComponentModel;

namespace Wrox.WebControls.SampleControls
{
```

```
/// <summary>
/// Summary description for YesManLabel.
/// </summary>
[DefaultProperty("Text"),
    ToolboxData("<{0}:YesManLabel runat=server></{0}:YesManLabel>")]
public class YesManLabel : System.Web.UI.WebControls.WebControl
{
    protected override void Render(HtmlTextWriter output)
    {
        Random x = new Random();
        string Phrase;
        int Number = x.Next(5);


        Phrase = "I simply don't know what to say.";
        switch (Number)
        {
            case 0:
                Phrase = "You're the man!";
                break;
            case 1:
                Phrase = "I couldn't have done it better myself, sir!";
                break;
            case 2:
                Phrase = "I don't know how you do it. Being perfect is such a
                burden.";
                break;
            case 3:
                Phrase = "Your genius is blinding...And me without my sunglasses.";
                break;
            case 4:
                Phrase = "Masterful. Absolutely Masterful. You're so right.";
                break;
            case 5:
                Phrase = "I couldn't agree more. A supremely wise and enlightened
                idea!";
                break;
        }

        output.Write(Phrase);
    }
}
}
```

The first new thing we see in this code (since we're already familiar with component building in general) is the new set of custom attributes.

```
[DefaultProperty("Text"),
    ToolboxData("<{0}:YesManLabel runat=server></{0}:YesManLabel>")]
```

The ToolboxData attribute is actually a macro. It defines the exact ASP.NET code that will go in the .aspx page when the control is dragged from the ToolBox onto the page. The {0} parameter is the TagPrefix of the control as it is defined on the destination .aspx page.

You should recognize the random number and phrase-building code from the COM InterOp sample earlier in this chapter. The method `Render` is a method that is given to all custom WebControls. We are overriding the default implementation of the `Render` method so that we can provide our own code. The `HtmlTextWriter` object is a `Stream` interface to the actual output of the ASP page. By calling `output.Write()` we can issue text to the ASP page as if it had been in the source code of the `.aspx` file.

When we get to the `YesManDemo.aspx` page, we see that we can reference our new custom control as if it were natively part of the ASP.NET framework, wrapped in semantics strikingly similar to standard HTML code.

```
<%@ Register TagPrefix="WROX" Namespace="Wrox.WebControls.SampleControls"
Assembly="SampleControls" %>
<%@ Page language="c#" Codebehind="YesManDemo.aspx.cs" AutoEventWireup="false"
Inherits="WebControlSamples.YesManDemo" %>
<!DOCTYPE HTML PUBLIC "-//W3C//DTD HTML 4.0 Transitional//EN" >
<HTML>
    <HEAD>
      <meta name="GENERATOR" Content="Microsoft Visual Studio 7.0">
      <meta name="CODE_LANGUAGE" Content="C#">
      <meta name="vs_defaultClientScript" content="JavaScript (ECMAScript)">
      <meta name="vs_targetSchema"
    content="http://schemas.microsoft.com/intellisense/ie5">
    </HEAD>
    <body>
    <form id="YesManDemo" method="post" runat="server">
     <asp:Label id="Label1" style="Z-INDEX: 102; LEFT: 25px; POSITION: absolute;
     TOP: 23px" runat="server">Here's your YesMan Quote for the Day:</asp:Label>
      <br>
      <br>
      <WROX:YesManLabel runat="server">
      </WROX:YesManLabel>
    </form>
    </body>
</HTML>
```

The `WROX TagPrefix` is created at the top of the page by the following code:

```
<%@ Register TagPrefix="WROX" Namespace="Wrox.WebControls.SampleControls"
Assembly="SampleControls" %>
```

This provides ASP.NET with enough information to locate the custom control. It then knows that anytime a control is referenced with `WROX:YesManLabel`, it should look for the class `Wrox.WebControls.SampleControls.YesManLabel` in the assembly `SampleControls.dll`.

Composite WebForms Controls

Composite WebForms controls extend standard WebForms controls in the same way that Composite Window Forms controls extend standard Window Forms controls. A composite WebForms control is a control that contains one or more *child* controls.

The default implementation of the `Render` method actually starts a recursive process that continually calls the `Render` method in all of the control's child forms. What this means is that in the same way that I didn't have to override the `Paint` method for my composite Windows Forms control, you don't necessarily have to override the `Render` method for a composite WebForms control. It is very possible that each of the child controls is perfectly capable of rendering itself, and all you need to supply is the manipulation of the properties of the control and its children.

Our sample composite WebForms control is very simple. It is a TextBox WebForms control that has a piece of text associated with it as a label. Quite often when displaying forms on a web page, TextBoxes have caption or label text associated with them. Our sample control links the two together, allowing us to drop one control onto a form and have both the TextBox and the label appear on the final web page.

Code for the `LabeledTextBox` WebForms control:

```
using System;
using System.Web.UI;
using System.Web.UI.WebControls;
using System.ComponentModel;

namespace SampleControls
{
    /// <summary>
    /// Summary description for LabeledTextBox.
    /// </summary>
    [DefaultProperty("Text"),
        ToolboxData("<{0}:LabeledTextBox runat=server></{0}:LabeledTextBox>")]
    public class LabeledTextBox : System.Web.UI.WebControls.WebControl
    {
        private string _Label;
        private TextBox _childText;

        [Bindable(true),
            Category("Appearance"),
            DefaultValue("")]
        public string Text
        {
            get
            {
                // Use EnsureChildControls to force a CreateChildControls call if
                // it hasn't been done already. This way we know the TextBox is
                // always there.
                this.EnsureChildControls();
                return _childText.Text;
            }

            set
            {
                this.EnsureChildControls();
                _childText.Text = value;
            }
        }

        public string Label
        {
            get
            {
                return _Label;
            }
            set
            {
                _Label = value;
            }
        }

        protected override void CreateChildControls()
        {
            _childText = new TextBox();
```

```
        _childText.Text = "";

        this.Controls.Add( new LiteralControl( _Label + ":" ) );
        this.Controls.Add( _childText );
    }
  }
}
```

You can see that instead of overriding the `Render` method, we delete override the `CreateChildControls` method, which allocates and instantiates any child controls that belong to this custom control. In our case, we create two child controls, a `LiteralControl`, which is basically raw HTML text that represents the label of our textbox, and a `TextBox`.

The `Bindable` attribute allows ASP.NET and ADO.NET to actually bind some form of data source to the `Text` field. This means that in, order for us to allow our new custom control to be databound, we simply add one custom attribute and it works.

The only other new thing in the above class is the `EnsureChildControls` method. This method checks to make sure that the child controls for the control have been created. If they have not, then the `CreateChildControls` method is invoked automatically. This allows us to feel pretty comfortable about accessing member data on the child controls without having to obfuscate the code logic with a bunch of redundant error checking.

One of the most useful things that comes with WebForms controls out of the box is the ability to reference properties of a control class instance with HTML-style attributes. The following is the code in the `.aspx` page that contains the tag for our new, composite custom control:

```
<%@ Page language="c#" Codebehind="CompositeControlTest.aspx.cs"
AutoEventWireup="false" Inherits="WebControlSamples.CompositeControlTest" %>
<%@ Register TagPrefix="WROX" Namespace="SampleControls" Assembly="SampleControls"
%>
<!DOCTYPE HTML PUBLIC "-//W3C//DTD HTML 4.0 Transitional//EN" >
<HTML>
<HEAD>
    <meta name="GENERATOR" Content="Microsoft Visual Studio 7.0">
    <meta name="CODE_LANGUAGE" Content="C#">
    <meta name="vs_defaultClientScript" content="JavaScript (ECMAScript)">
    <meta name="vs_targetSchema"
    content="http://schemas.microsoft.com/intellisense/ie5">
</HEAD>
<body MS_POSITIONING="GridLayout">
    <form id="CompositeControlTest" method="post" runat="server">
    <WROX:LabeledTextBox id="LabeledTextBox1" Label="My Label" Text="My Text"
    runat="Server">
    </WROX:LabeledTextBox>
    </form>
</body>
</HTML>
```

Note that the `Label` and `Text` attributes of the `<WROX:LabeledTextBox>` control tag are actually nothing more than public properties in our class control. This mapping between tag attributes and class properties is done for you automatically. If you instantiate the control in code, rather than on the designer, you can still reference those properties as if they were normal properties.

Summary

This chapter covered a wide variety of information and code applications. We showed you a brief overview of building native .NET components, including such topics as versioning, strong-naming and side-by-side deployment. We compared and contrasted the models for consuming COM components from managed code and consuming managed code from COM applications and components. Lastly, we spent some time showing you how to build custom Windows Forms and WebForms controls.

The most important thing that you can take away from this chapter is that everything you do in the .NET framework relating to components has a consistent model. If you know how to create components, then you can leverage that knowledge and ability to create custom controls, whether you're creating Web or Windows controls.

In addition to that, in everything we did throughout this chapter we reinforced the idea that a good object model and design will always provide for an easier implementation. There is much more to working with the .NET framework than you might initially think, and if you spend enough time and thought designing your components, custom controls, and COM InterOp applications, you'll find that the actual implementation of your design is the easiest part of the software development life cycle.

9

Working with Data in .NET

Data comes in a myriad of forms. Today, virtually anything can be described by data of some kind. In short, data is information and, as we all know, information is power. Any statistic, number, fact, figure, or seemingly unimportant little detail can also be considered data. Data isn't just the bits and bytes that you store in your mammoth data store high in your Ivory Tower, locked away behind an army of IT professionals.

Traditionally, many of us grew up thinking that data consisted of the DATA statements at the end of a BASIC (I dropped off the trailing "A" so as not to date myself *too* much), or the holes in a set of punched cards or the sequential storage of bits and bytes in a binary file on disk. In our modern world of RDBMSs, XML, and remote data stores, we've come to think that we have a more advanced view of data now.

As more and more people needed quick, easily-programmed, reliable access to popular data stores, Microsoft provided DAO, or Data Access Objects, based on their JET Database Engine. From this evolved ADO, a faster, more efficient system of accessing data that allowed a wider community of programmers to easily access SQL servers, Oracle databases, and many more data sources, all with a uniform API. The world was good.

Unfortunately, the reliance on ADO for all things data gave many people tunnel vision. If you ask your average programmer the question, "What is data?", they are very likely to respond with a lengthy discourse on SQL, Oracle, mySQL, or any other host of database servers or database file formats like Btrieve or Paradox. ADO actually provided a high level abstraction from a concrete data source, advancing Microsoft's concept of Universal Data Access. Unfortunately, many of the features of ADO that dealt with non-relational data went unnoticed.

With the release of the .NET framework, Microsoft is trying to widen people's perception and remove some of the tunnel vision and "data crutch" created by reliance on ADO. While ADO was (and still is) a remarkably good tool, it is not the solution to all problems. With the .NET framework, Microsoft is trying to reinforce the statement that *data is data*, and nothing more. They believe that programmers should be able to program data without the hang-ups of relying on the nuances of a given data provider to allow them to do so. Whether you obtain the circumference of your thumb from an Oracle server, a SQL Server, a Btrieve file, an XML file, or an XML stream pumped to your application over a network socket, the fact remains that you are still simply dealing with the circumference of your thumb. The source of that information should not be allowed to impact how you handle it.

Throughout this chapter you will see how the System.Data namespace is structured and how to utilize many of the classes within it. As well, we'll go over the pros and cons of using ADO.NET, and then compare and contrast current ADO functionality with that of ADO.NET. After that we'll go into using the System.Xml namespace. While reading this chapter, keep in mind that this is a high-level overview of working with data in .NET.

> *For truly in-depth coverage of all the material in this chapter and then some, consult* Professional ADO.NET Programming from Wrox Press, ISBN 186100527x *due to be published shortly after this book.*

What this chapter hopes to accomplish is to present the idea that we have yet again returned to the days where people think of data as data without regard for the physical means by which that data is obtained. By the time you complete this chapter, you should:

❑   Be familiar with the basic architecture of ADO.NET

❑   Know the benefits and drawbacks for using ADO.NET

❑   Know when to use ADO versus ADO.NET and why

❑   Be familiar with the core XML classes provided by the framework

❑   Be aware of how the System.XML and System.Data namespaces are intertwined

System.Data

There is a specific reason why this section of the chapter is not referred to as ADO.NET: the reason being is that ADO is actually a bit of a misnomer. It has been kept in marketing campaigns, documentation and other references to keep programmers within a familiar frame of reference. However, there is no longer any reference to the acronym ADO within the System.Data namespace.

This fact is not an oversight. If there is one important thing you take away from this chapter before moving on to the next, it should be the memory that System.Data is *not* ADO's direct successor. The System.Data namespace is so much more than that. It is a highly object-oriented, extensible library of classes for manipulating structured *data*. That data can be from SQL, Oracle, text files on your disk, XML streams, or virtually anywhere else.

System.Data Architecture

Illustrated in the following diagram are a couple of things that you may not be familiar with. On the right are what are called Managed Providers (or Data Providers, depending on which documentation you're reading during Beta 2). These managed providers provide a managed, object-oriented set of functionality for accessing a data store. The two that currently ship with the .NET framework's System.Data namespace are the OleDb managed provider and the SqlClient managed provider. In addition, Microsoft is offering the Odbc Data Provider as a separate download. All of its functionality can be found in the System.Data.Odbc namespace. On the left is the keystone of ADO.NET, the DataSet object. The diagram illustrates a clear separation (yet easy communication) of the DataSet and the actual store from which the data originates.

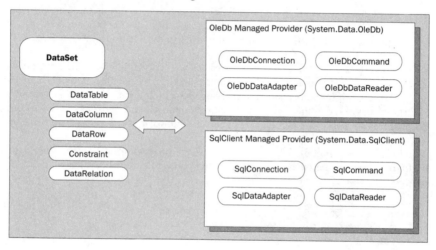

Data Providers

Data Providers within the context of the .NET framework are managed, object-oriented wrappers around database functionality. They essentially provide a layer of abstraction above their specific data source. A data provider provides methods for connecting to a database, retrieving data from the database, committing changes to a database, and executing database commands.

Shipping with the .NET framework are two data providers, the OleDb provider and the SqlClient provider.

❑ **OleDb Provider**

The OleDb provider uses the native OLE DB functionality through the COM Interoperability services of the .NET framework. Just as with previous uses of OLE DB providers, you still need to specify which OLE DB provider (not to be confused with the OLE DB managed provider. Clear as mud?) to use. You can use the SQLOLEDB provider or one for Oracle or one for the Microsoft JET Database engine. There is a limitation on the use of the OLE DB provider in the Beta 2 release of the framework SDK. The OleDb Managed Data Provider cannot be used to access OLE DB providers that require a version 2.5 interface, such as the OLE DB provider for Microsoft Exchange.

The OleDb managed provider is an excellent choice when using SQL Server 6.5 or earlier, Oracle, or Microsoft Access. This is the recommended provider for single-tier, Access-based solutions or for other data sources that have OLE DB providers such as Active Directory, LDAP, etc.

❑ **SqlClient Provider**
The SqlClient managed provider is a lightweight, highly optimized Data Provider. It uses its own protocol (Tabular Data Stream) to directly access SQL Server 7.0 (or later) without requiring an OLEDB provider or the use of the ODBC layer. The bottom line is that if you're using SQL Server 7.0 and above, you should *absolutely* be using the SQL Server .NET Data Provider because of its improved efficiency, smaller memory footprint, and improved speed over the SQL OLE DB provider.

❑ **Odbc Provider**
Available as a separate download from Microsoft, this provider exposes traditional ODBC data sources to managed code.

You might be thinking that once more and more data providers start to appear, we'll be back in the same mess we used to be before the advent of ODBC for standardizing data access across multiple vendors. This might be true, had Microsoft not enforced some rules on the .NET Data Providers.

At the core of each Data Provider are four classes (discussed shortly): The Connection, the Command, the DataAdapter, and the DataReader. Even though each provider implements their own version of these classes, each class implements a specific interface to which it must conform. Remembering your knowledge of Interfaces, we can then say that a Connection class, regardless of which provider it came from, can be programmed with the same code because it conforms to the IDbConnection interface.

Therefore, the following snippet of code illustrates that the programmer doesn't really care which provider originally supplied the class. We can treat the classes as their basic interfaces and program to the common denominators.

```
IDbCommand GenericCommand = Connection.CreateCommand();
GenericCommand.CommandText = "SELECT Flavor FROM Coffees";
// . . . continue on with source-agnostic data access code
```

The connection in our sample could have been an OleDbConnection, a SqlConnection, or if we're thinking ahead, it could have been some third party extension like BDEConnection (for the Borland Database Engine).

We won't cover the how or the why in this book, but you should be aware of the fact that you can create your own custom .NET Data Provider if you choose. All you really need to do is fill a namespace with your own derivatives of the core classes such as Connection, Command, DataReader, and DataAdapter and you can then easily begin writing data access code against your own proprietary, optimized provider.

The Connection

A Connection is a class that implements the IDbConnection interface. This should be one of the most familiar concepts in ADO.NET to classic ADO programmers. The Connection provides the essential link between your code and the data store housing your data. In traditional implementations, the Connection typically connects to an RDBMS across a network wire. However, it is best if you don't make that assumption about connections. With the ability for vendors to be producing their own managed .NET Data Providers, it is possible that this Connection could be a link to something else entirely (an Active Directory, Exchange Server, a proprietary security system, or anything else you can think of that might be considered a viable source of data).

The `IDbConnection` interface dictates that a `Connection` provides implementations for properties like the database connection string, the connection timeout, the name of the database, and methods for opening and closing the connection. Second only in importance to providing the link to the data store, is the `Connection`'s ability to create a `Command` object based on that `Connection`. This way, the consumer of the `Connection` object is guaranteed to get a `Command` object that belongs to the same managed provider.

We'll put the `Connection` object and the other components of the managed providers together in some samples once we've had a chance to go over each component individually. The following is a quick example of how a SQL connection can be instantiated and used, and a couple of its useful properties:

```
using System;
using System.Data;
using System.Data.SqlClient;

namespace ConnectionExample
{
class ConnectionSample
{
static void Main(string[] args)
{
    // declare and instantiate a new SQL Connection.
    SqlConnection Connection = new SqlConnection();

    Connection.ConnectionString =
        "Data Source=localhost; Initial Catalog=Northwind; User id=sa;
                                            Password=;";

    Connection.Open();

    // Use a couple of SQL specific connection properties.
    Console.WriteLine("SqlClient Connected from {0} to SQL Server v{1}",
                    Connection.WorkstationId, Connection.ServerVersion );

    Connection.Close();
}
}
}
}
```

The output generated by this program on my test machine produces the following line of text:

```
SqlClient Connected from MEPHISTOPHOLES to SQL Server v08.00.0100
```

The Command

The `Command` object represents a SQL statement or stored procedure that is executed through its `Connection`. The `IDbCommand` interface requires that any deriving class must implement properties to set and retrieve the command string and command type, as well as the ability to execute the command, storing the results in a `Reader` object, or executing the command without any return results.

Programmers of ADO should find this concept familiar as well, as they had to create an instance of the ADO `Command` object to utilize a stored procedure, etc. The provider-specific versions of the `Command` class are `SqlCommand` and `OleDbCommand`. Of all the ADO.NET classes, this has the most resemblance to an ADO counterpart, the ADO `Command` object. Aside from syntactic differences, the two classes perform generally the same roles.

The following example is a quick glimpse at the operation of a Command object, enabling us to execute one of the stored procedures against the Northwind database:

```
using System;
using System.Data;
using System.Data.SqlClient;

namespace Wrox.ProDotNet.Chapter10.CommandExample
{
class CommandSample
{
static void Main(string[] args)
{
   // Create a connection to Northwind on SQL 2000
   SqlConnection Connection = new SqlConnection();
   Connection.ConnectionString =
      "Data Source=localhost; Initial Catalog=Northwind; User id=sa;
                        Password=;";
   Connection.Open();

   SqlCommand MyCommand = new SqlCommand( "CustOrderHist", Connection );
   // Need to set the command type, otherwise it defaults to text.
   MyCommand.CommandType = CommandType.StoredProcedure;

   // The stored procedure we're calling asks for the CustomerID parameter.
   SqlParameter CustID = new SqlParameter( "@CustomerID",
             SqlDbType.NChar, 5);
   // Pick one of the customers in Northwind to grab history for.
   CustID.Value = "DRACD";
   MyCommand.Parameters.Add( CustID );

   SqlDataReader MyReader = MyCommand.ExecuteReader();

   // Do something with the data returned from the command.

}
}
}
```

The DataAdapter

The DataAdapter can be considered to be like the electrical "plug" of the ADO.NET architecture. The Adapter's sole purpose in life is to fill DataSets and propagate DataSet changes to the data source. As we'll find out shortly, the DataSet is a completely source-agnostic data store. This means that it can never know the nature of the source of the data it contains. The job of the DataAdapter is to *adapt* the data from any of its Command objects (which as we now know, have an associated Connection object) and pour that data into the DataSet by using the DataSet's native methods for creating data, as well as take data from the DataSet and place it into the data source using Command objects.

The Adapter actually is a container for four separate Command objects. It contains a SelectCommand, an InsertCommand, an UpdateCommand, and a DeleteCommand. Any class implementing the IDbDataAdapter interface must provide these four properties. By housing these commands, it can successfully adapt any changes made in an associated DataSet by transferring those changes through the appropriate command (and hence to the final destination on the other side of the appropriate Connection object).

Therefore, by looking at the following diagram, we can see how the flow of data travels up a food chain of sorts, housed by a managed provider:

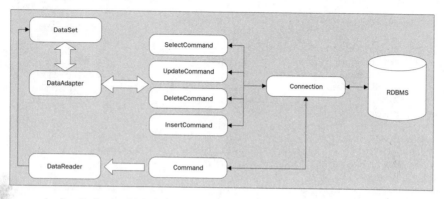

The figure may look a little confusing initially, but once you get the hang of working with data in .NET, it will seem like second nature to you. Firstly, we can follow the food chain from the RDBMS (note that this could easily be an Access database or some other custom database from a third party vendor) all the way back to the DataSet.

Another interesting thing to point out about our diagram is that we only have a single Connection object in use. One of the really incredible things that we can do with the DataAdapter and its command objects is actually have the Command objects referencing different connections. The implications of this are enormous, but you can see how it might facilitate possibly having a highly optimized read-only store on one connection, and the modifiable store on the other connection.

Without knowing anything about the performance implications of ADO.NET, we can immediately form the guess that if we only need single-direction, read-only loading of DataSets or controls, we can bypass the Adapter entirely and utilize a DataReader.

The DataReader

The DataReader is an implementation of a way of navigating a forward-only stream of data. There are many cases in which you would opt to use the DataReader over the DataSet. The DataReader is an extremely fast, low-overhead way of retrieving information from a data stream. You might be traversing a result set to display it on a web page or you could be pulling information to dump into a text file, etc. Chances are that, if your application doesn't need anything beyond forward-only, read-only data access for a given purpose, it can achieve significant performance benefits by using a DataReader.

It can accomplish this performance boost because it doesn't need to maintain the overhead of caching previously traversed records. The DataReader only maintains a single row of data in memory at any given time.

The previous example we used for the Command object lends itself very well to being used with a DataReader. If we add a few lines of code to the previous sample, we can actually display the results of the stored procedure. The new code for our CommandExample project looks like this:

```
using System;
using System.Data;
using System.Data.SqlClient;

namespace Wrox.ProDotNet.Chapter10.CommandExample
```

```
{
class CommandSample
{
static void Main(string[] args)
{
    // Create a connection to Northwind on SQL 2000
    SqlConnection Connection = new SqlConnection();
    Connection.ConnectionString =
        "Data Source=localhost; Initial Catalog=Northwind; User id=sa;
                            Password=;";
  Connection.Open();

    SqlCommand MyCommand = new SqlCommand( "CustOrderHist", Connection );
    // Need to set the command type, otherwise it defaults to text.
    MyCommand.CommandType = CommandType.StoredProcedure;

    // The stored procedure we're calling asks for the CustomerID parameter.
    SqlParameter CustID = new SqlParameter( "@CustomerID",_
                SqlDbType.NChar, 5);
    // Pick one of the customers in Northwind to grab history for.
    CustID.Value = "DRACD";
    MyCommand.Parameters.Add( CustID );

    SqlDataReader MyReader = MyCommand.ExecuteReader();

    // Do something with the data returned from the command.

    Console.WriteLine("Order History for Customer ID: DRACD");
    Console.WriteLine("Product:Quantity");
    Console.WriteLine("----------------");
    while (MyReader.Read())
    {
        Console.WriteLine("{0}:{1}", MyReader.GetString(0),
                MyReader.GetInt32(1) );
    }
    Connection.Close();
}
}
}
```

The output of the above code returns the following results:

```
Order History for Customer ID: DRACD
Product:Quantity
----------------
Gorgonzola Telino:20
Gumbär Gummibärchen:12
Jack's New England Clam Chowder:9
Konbu:25
Lakkalikööri:12
Perth Pasties:20
Queso Cabrales:20
Raclette Courdavault:30
Rhönbräu Klosterbier:12
```

Using the SQL Server .NET Data Provider

Now that we've had a quick sample of some of the facilities available to use for accessing data in the .NET framework, let's put it to the test. Our sample is fairly simple. We've written a simple console application that opens up a connection to the SQL Server 2000 Northwind sample database using the SQL Server .NET Data Provider. Once we have the connection, we create a command based on that connection. Continuing to follow the food chain as we described above, we create a DataReader based on that new command and simply iterate through our newly obtained results.

Let's look at the output of our sample application and then we'll get into the code that produced it.

From this we can see that there are three fields (Customer ID, Contact Name, and Company Name) that are being displayed.

To build our sample application, all we did was create a new Console Application using the VS.NET New Project wizard. After that, we added a reference to the System.Data Assembly (Project | Add Reference ...). From there, we entered the following code into our new class:

```
/*
 * SqlProviderTest
 * Console application to demonstrate simple DataReader access
 * of the Sql managed provider
 */

using System;

// lets us reference System.Data and Sql managed provider class names
// without long prefixes.
using System.Data;
using System.Data.SqlClient;

namespace Wrox.ProDotNet.Chapter10.SqlProviderTest
{
    /// <summary>
    /// Summary description for Class1.
    /// </summary>
    class MainApp
    {
```

```
static void Main(string[] args)
{
string SqlQuery = "SELECT CustomerID, ContactName, CompanyName FROM
                   Customers";
```

This will create a new instance of the `Connection` object implemented by the SQL data provider and then use that connection object to create a new `Command` object.

```
SqlConnection Connection = new SqlConnection("Data Source=localhost;
            Initial Catalog=Northwind; User id=sa; Password=;");
SqlCommand Command = Connection.CreateCommand();
Command.CommandText = SqlQuery;

Connection.Open();
SqlDataReader Reader = Command.ExecuteReader();
```

Working with the forward-only model of the `DataReader`, we loop until `Reader.Read()` returns a `false` value. While in the loop, we use the Getxxx methods to access the various columns of our result set from the reader. In our case, we're using `GetString` with the 0 indicating the first column.

```
while (Reader.Read())
{
    Console.WriteLine( "{0}\t{1}\t\t{2}", Reader.GetString(0),
            Reader.GetString(1), Reader.GetString(2) );
}

Reader.Close();
Connection.Close();
    }
  }
}
```

The code is pretty straightforward. The first thing we do is create a new `Connection`, providing a connection string indicating that we want to use the `Northwind` database (note that the server must be configured for SQL Server and Windows security). After that, we create a new command object by asking the `Connection` to create one for us and set its command text to our SQL query. Opening the connection is a simple matter of just calling `Connection.Open ()`.

Once we have an open connection, we create a new `DataReader` by calling the `ExecuteReader()` function. This function will execute the SQL statement in our `Command` object and store the result set in a new `DataReader` object.

From there, we call the `Read()` method in a `while` loop to fetch new rows continuously. The `Read()` function returns a `boolean` indicating a successful (or not) read operation. After it returns `true`, we can then use the GetXXX() functions to retrieve a given column, casting the value to a given data type. In our case all of our columns are strings, so we can just fetch them all using `GetString(x)`, where x is the ordinal position of the column we want to retrieve.

Coding Provider-Agnostic

Earlier on in this chapter, we made the bold statement that you could, in theory, write code to the level of the common interfaces, which would allow your code to function the same whether or not you were using an `OleDb` Data Provider pointing at an OLEDB Provider or the SQL Data Provider working against a SQL Server 2000 database.

Some of you are probably thinking that it's all well and good to say these things, but you'll believe it when you see it. Just to set you at ease, we've prepared an example that demonstrates exactly this point. Our example is an enhancement of the code above. We prompt the user for a provider type, and then create a connection, and from there all of the code is the same, regardless of the provider. Our example demonstrates running code and queries against the Northwind MS Access database (converted to Access 2000 format) and the SQL 2000 `Northwind` example.

Let's take a look at the output and then we'll go into the code. You'll notice that the output is identical to the previous sample, even though we're programming generically without prior knowledge of the Data Provider.

You can see that the application prompts the user for which type of provider they want to use. This in turn affects the connection string provided to the connection. However, once the connection has been established, all of the code from that point on is generic and is coded against the interfaces and not the provider-specific features.

```
using System;
using System.Data;
```

Here we can see that we're using both the `OleDb` and the `SqlClient` namespaces. This is only to make our code for creating a connection a little easier; we're still only referencing the `System.Data` Assembly.

```
using System.Data.OleDb;
using System.Data.SqlClient;

namespace Wrox.ProDotNet.Chapter10.DataProviders
{
    class MainExample
    {
```

```
        static void Main(string[] args)
        {
            string Input;
            string OleConnectionString  = @"PROVIDER=Microsoft.Jet.OLEDB.4.0;
                    DATA SOURCE=C:\NorthWind2k.Mdb;";
            string SqlConnectionString = "Data Source=localhost; Initial
                    Catalog=Northwind; User id=sa; Password=;";
            string SqlQuery = "SELECT CustomerID, ContactName, CompanyName FROM
                    Customers";
```

Rather than instantiate an `OleDbCommand` or a `SqlCommand`, or an `OleDbConnection` or a `SqlConnection`, we instead declare our variables at the interface level. Thinking back to our basic component and class designs, we know that we can treat a class as an interface that it implements without changing its internal structure or implementation. Being able to treat a class as one of its ancestors, or an interface that it implements, is a feature of object-oriented programming called **polymorphism**.

```
            IDbCommand GenericCommand;
            IDataReader GenericReader;
            IDbConnection GenericConnection;

            Console.Write("How do you take your data? (1 - Slap some OleDb on
                            it!, 2 - Slathered in SqlClient):");
            Input = Console.ReadLine();

            // our only conditional code will be in building our connection,
            // we'll use common interface-based code for the rest of the sample
            if (Input == "1")
                GenericConnection = new OleDbConnection( OleConnectionString );
            else
                GenericConnection = new SqlConnection( SqlConnectionString );

            GenericCommand = GenericConnection.CreateCommand();
            GenericConnection.Open();

            GenericCommand.CommandText = SqlQuery;
            GenericReader = GenericCommand.ExecuteReader();

            while (GenericReader.Read())
            {
                Console.WriteLine( "{0}\t{1}\t\t{2}",
                        GenericReader.GetString(0), GenericReader.GetString(1),
                        GenericReader.GetString(2) );
            }

            GenericReader.Close();
            GenericConnection. Close ();

        }
    }
}
```

Taking a close look at the code, you can see that the only thing that is different between the two providers is the connection string supplied to the connection, and the original connection type. The true beauty of this architecture is that even though we can refer to a SqlConnection as an IDbConnection, when we invoke the CreateCommand() function on it, we actually get back a class that internally deals with SqlConnections while conforming to the standard basic set of functions defined by the IDbCommand Interface.

The DataSet

The DataSet is a class devoted to providing a fully functional in-memory data store. It maintains a completely disconnected cache of data. The basic structure of a DataSet actually looks quite a bit like a miniature relational database on its own. It contains a set of tables, relationships between those tables, constraints and keys on those tables, and each of those tables contains a set of rows and columns very much like that of SQL Server or Access or any other relational database. It is important that you keep in mind that the DataSet is absolutely nothing like the ADO RecordSet and you should avoid trying to draw comparisons.

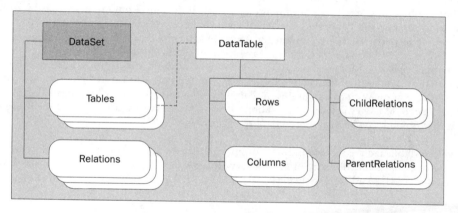

You can see from the illustration above that the DataSet is the parent to both tables and relations. The tables contained within the DataSet belong to the DataTable class. In turn, this class is home to collections of Rows, Columns, and Parent and Child Relations.

The internal data within a DataSet is maintained entirely in XML. In addition, the structure of the DataSet is actually defined by an XSD (XML Schema Definition language) schema. We'll talk more about how XML plays into the role of the DataSet later. For now, it's sufficient to say that a DataSet is built entirely upon XML and you cannot separate one from the other.

The truly important things to remember about the DataSet are that it is source-agnostic and that it operates in a completely disconnected model. By source-agnostic, we mean that the DataSet is designed so that it has no information as to where the data contained within it came from. It operates on its own set of data without concern for whom or what supplied the data to begin with, or where the data is eventually going to reside. The ability for the DataSet to operate without specific knowledge of the source or destination of its data makes it an incredibly versatile tool that can not only be marshaled easily through XML serialization, but it can in theory be decomposed and reconstructed on any platform that supports the DataSet without losing any of its functionality.

In addition to providing a completely disconnected, source-neutral data store with an internal XML format, the DataSet provides a facility for establishing complex hierarchies of data. Using *Relations* (discussed shortly), a programmer can establish master/detail relationships and parent or child relationships simply by adding new items to collections in the appropriate tables.

You might be asking yourself at this point, "What's so good about a source-neutral data store?" After all, the more a program knows about the nuances of the environment in which it is operating, the better it can perform, right? Well, yes, but no. Creating code that is *too* dependent on a specific condition causes maintenance problems. In addition to the benefits of the source-neutral data store, you also gain all the benefits of a completely disconnected operating model. This allows your data to potentially come from multiple disconnected and disparate sources on multiple platforms. If you hard-code the directory where your data files are, you can't change that directory without crashing your app. Having source-neutral data actually insulates the DataSet programmers from many headaches that other programmers might have to deal with.

Consider the following: millions of people own handheld devices or PDAs. One popular brand is the PalmPilot. Having done extensive programming for this little gem, I found out the hard way that when integers are stored on the Palm, they are actually stored in reverse byte order from those of their Windows counterparts. Therefore, an integer that comes from a PalmPilot is *not* the same as an integer that originated on Windows. Programmers have to know about this quirk and program extensively for it and make sure they don't forget about it. If they wrote all of their code to work against a source-neutral, in-memory representation of their data, they simply wouldn't have to care whether the native integer storage is different on Windows than it is on PalmOS – the DataAdapter responsible for populating the DataSet would have made that translation ahead of time. This is just the tip of the iceberg of the long list of problems that source-neutral data storage solves.

Once we've established a good groundwork of information on the individual pieces of a DataSet and how to use their basic functionality in the code, we'll cover in more detail the relationship between the DataSet class, XML, and XML Schemas.

DataTable

The DataTable is one of the core objects within the System.Data namespace. The table, in standard database design terms, is an organized collection of columns that can have any number of associated rows. We're all quite familiar with what a table constitutes in SQL or Access terms, so it should be fairly easy to understand the function of a table. The DataTable exposes the following properties that you should pay close attention to when learning the ADO.NET architecture:

❑ **Columns**
The Columns collection contains the list of all of the columns contained within a table. For example, in a Customers table, the Columns collection might contain column definitions for the Customer's ID, name and address. This property contains a collection of DataColumn objects.

❑ **Constraints**
Constraints are data rules that are applied to the table. A constraint enforces a certain condition on a table that cannot be broken. If changes to a DataTable will violate a constraint, then an exception will be thrown. This is also a collection object.

❑ **ChildRelations**
The DataSet provides the unique ability to establish a hierarchy of tables within its schema or structure. The ChildRelations collection is a collection of relations that define the relationships that establish the child tables of this DataTable.

❑ **ParentRelations**

This is the opposite of the ChildRelations collection. This collection contains a list of all of the relations necessary for establishing the parent tables of this DataTable.

❑ **PrimaryKey**

If you've done a lot of work with databases before, you know that most tables have primary keys. Tables within a DataSet are no different. In fact, there is complete support for composite keys, or primary keys that are composed of more than one column. For example, if you require not only an e-mail address, but also a credit card number to establish a unique user identity, you would create a composite key of the user's e-mail address and their credit card number.

The PrimaryKey property is an array of DataColumn objects that represents all of the columns that comprise the primary key of a particular DataTable, allowing for incredibly robust and complex representations of data to be stored in the DataSet.

❑ **Rows**

Where the Columns collection provides the schema structure of the DataTable, the Rows collection provides the actual data contained within that table. It contains a collection of DataRow objects.

❑ **TableName**

The TableName is fairly self-explanatory. It represents the name of the DataTable. Even though it appears simple, it is actually a crucial property. The TableName of a given table can be used as the index in the parent DataSet's DataTableCollection (DataSet's Tables property).

When this property is used to locate a table within a DataSet's Tables property, it is conditionally case-sensitive. That means that if two tables exist in the collection that differ in name only by case, then the search for *just those two tables* is case-sensitive. In all other cases, locating tables by name is case-insensitive.

This list of properties is by no means complete, and is here to give you somewhere to start when researching the DataTable in more detail and a quick reference as to some of the most often used properties.

DataColumn

The DataColumn is the core of building the schema (structure) for the DataTable and, indirectly, the DataSet in which the parent table belongs. When you define DataColumns, you provide data type, size, and name information that will be used to control how data is accessed within the table. The DataColumn exposes quite a few properties and methods, and we've listed a few of the most often used ones here for reference:

❑ **AllowDBNull**

A Boolean flag indicating whether nulls are allowed in the column for rows in the column's parent table.

❑ **AutoIncrement**

Another Boolean flag, indicating whether or not the column will automatically increment the column's value for new rows inserted into the column's parent table.

❑ **Caption**
The caption of a column is its human-readable description. This is the description of the column that will be displayed in databinding controls such as a `DataGrid`, etc. Due to limitations of the architecture in the past, many programmers would select columns from SQL using a syntax like `SELECT ColumnName as 'Column Name' FROM Table` in order to obtain a "pretty-printable" name for the column. With the use of the caption property, you can appropriately separate the data-store relevant column name from the UI-relevant column caption.

❑ **ColumnName**
This is the actual name of the column, rather than its displayable caption. This name is used to locate the column in the parent table's `Columns` property (of type `DataColumnCollection`). This property is also used by `DataAdapters` for transferring data to and from `Connections`.

❑ **DataType**
Rather than using an enumeration or some error-prone data type encoding system, the `DataType` property is actually able to store an actual .NET framework data type. This is possible through the use of Reflection and the `System.Type` class. Not only does this allow the programmers to specify actual data types rather than trying to remember strange enumeration names and mappings, but because `System.Type` represents language-neutral CTS types, the columns of a `DataSet` thereby can take on language-neutral data types as well, making the `DataSet` fully portable across any .NET framework language.

The following .NET framework data types are supported as valid column data types:

❑ `Boolean`

❑ `Byte`

❑ `Char`

❑ `DateTime`

❑ `Decimal`

❑ `Double`

❑ `Int16`

❑ `Int32`

❑ `Int64`

❑ `SByte`

❑ `Single`

❑ `String`

❑ `TimeSpanUInt16`

❑ `UInt32`

❑ `UInt64`

❑ **ReadOnly**
A Boolean flag indicating whether or not the value in the column of a row in the table can be modified. An exception will be thrown if code attempts to modify the value of a column that is marked as `ReadOnly`.

❑ **Unique**
A Boolean flag indicating that all values in the column for all rows in the table must remain unique. If a change to the table causes duplicate values in this column for the rows of the table then an exception will be thrown.

DataRow

The DataRow is the essential component of a DataTable object. The DataRow is a formatted, structured data container for rows of data within a table. The DataRow object is what houses the Create, Retrieve, Update, and Delete functionality (affectionately abbreviated as CRUD by many programmers) for rows of data within a table.

Before you start to think that you've seen it all before, and you know what rows are, you should stop right there. This isn't your grandmother's old-fashioned DataRow! One of the most impressive things about ADO.NET DataRows is that they are *versioned*. No, you are not seeing things, and no you don't have to write any additional code to take advantage of row versioning support. It's all there for you, like a big cake on your birthday. Versioning allows for various different states of a given DataRow to be retained in memory and retrieved. This provides the programmer with the ability to at any given time, view or cancel the changes pending to a row, or when rows are selected, only a specific version of that row can be retrieved, etc. Versioning is indicated by the DataRowVersion enumeration, which contains the following values: Current, Original, Default, and Proposed.

We've selected a few of the most frequently used and important methods and properties of the DataRow class to give you a feel for how it is used and where it sits in the ADO.NET scheme of things.

❑ RowState – the RowState property is of the enumerated type DataRowState. It indicates to the programmer (and to the GetChanges() and HasChanges() methods) the current state of the DataRow. That state can be indicated by any one of the following enumerated values:

    ❑ **Added** – the row has been added to the table and the AcceptChanges() method has not yet been called.

    ❑ **Deleted** – the row was deleted from the table using the Delete() method of the DataRow.

    ❑ **Detached** – the row is not actually part of a table. It has either just been created without being part of a collection or has just been removed from a collection.

    ❑ **Modified** – the data within the row has been modified and AcceptChanges() has not yet been called.

    ❑ **Unchanged** – the data within the row has not changed since the last call to AcceptChanges().

❑ Item – the Item property is heavily overloaded to allow for many different ways of obtaining the data stored in a specific column in the row. You can supply a column's name, allowing you to both set and retrieve the value. You can supply a DataColumn object, which also allows you to both set and retrieve the value. In addition, you can supply the ordinal position of the column and it will allow you to set and retrieve the value. If you also supply a DataRowVersion enumerated value as well as one of the previous three indexing methods, you will be allowed to retrieve a specific version (Current, Original, Default, or Proposed) of the data stored in the specified column. In C# you can choose to either use the Item property or use the indexer property, which affords you a syntax that resembles array indexing.

❑ BeginEdit() – this function places the DataRow into edit mode, which temporarily suspends event triggering, allowing the code to modify data for more than one row at a time. A programmer might want to do this to suspend validation rules by placing several rows in edit mode, loading the data, and then committing the changes.

❑ CancelEdit() – this function will take the DataRow out of edit mode and discard any changes made to the row since the BeginEdit() method was called.

❏   `Delete()` – this function will delete the current row.

❏   `EndEdit()` – this function will complete edit mode for the current row, saving changes made to the `DataSet` since the `BeginEdit()` method was called.

❏   `AcceptChanges()` – this function will implicitly invoke the `EndEdit()` method. If the `RowState` of the row before this function was called was `Added` or `Modified`, the `RowState` then becomes `Unchanged`. If the `RowState` was `Deleted` before the function call, it will then be physically removed.

DataRelation

The `DataRelation` class is an incredibly powerful tool, yet it is equally simple to use. The `DataRelation` class is designed to contain the data required to describe a relationship between two `DataTable` objects through `DataColumn` objects. The `DataRelation` functions within a `DataSet` in much the same way as relationships between tables function in SQL Server.

When creating a `DataRelation`, you are creating a parent/child relationship between two tables where the matching columns used to establish the relationship must be of the same data type. Therefore, you cannot have a primary key in the parent table as an integer and the related column in the child table as a string. Using `DataRelations` in combination with constraints, you can actually allow for changes to cascade downward from parent to child or upward from child to parent.

The following example snippet of code demonstrates how to create a new `DataRelation` and place it into the `Relations` collection of the associated `DataSet`. As usual, we'll be using tables from the Northwind database.

```
DataColumn Parent;
DataColumn Child;

Parent = CustomerDataSet.Tables["Customers"].Columns["CustID"];
Child = CustomerDataSet.Tables["Orders"].Columns["CustID"];

DataRelation CustomerOrders =
    new DataRelation( "CustomersOrders", Parent, Child );
CustomerDataSet.Relations.Add( CustomerOrders );
```

Once the relation is in place, you can navigate to a given row in the `Customers` table and obtain all of that customer's orders by using the `GetChildRows()` function. Simply specify the name of the relationship that you're using to obtain the child rows as follows and everything else is handled for you.

```
DataRow[] Orders;
Orders = CustomerDataSet.Tables["Customers"].Rows[0].GetChildRows(
"CustomersOrders" );
foreach (DataRow OrderRow in Orders)
{
    // display or process an order
}
```

Another one of the great features of using a `DataRelation` is that when using the `GetChildRows()` function, you can actually pass a value from the `DataRowVersion` enumeration. This allows you to effectively obtain all child rows with the `Current` values, or `Default` values, or `Original` values, or even `Proposed` values (changes have not been accepted yet). So, you could change the line above that retrieves child rows to only retrieve the `Original` values of the rows:

```
Orders = CustomerDataSet.Tables["Customers"].Rows[0].GetChildRows(
    "CustomerOrders", DataRowVersion.Original );
```

Updating Data with the DataSet

As we've said before, the DataSet is a completely disconnected, source-neutral data store. So, if it is completely disconnected, how can we use it to update data? The answer is through the use of the utility class, DataAdapter. The DataAdapter can be compared to a communication wire in that its sole responsibility in life is to relay information across a wire between two normally disconnected entities.

Using the UpdateCommand, DeleteCommand, InsertCommand, and SelectCommand properties of the IDbDataAdapter implementation, you can then use that adapter to populate your DataSet as well as transfer all of the changes made to it back to the original data source. It is important to note that a connection to the database (or some other data store) will only be maintained for the duration of the specific command being executed. The DataSet will remain completely disconnected the entire time.

We'll show a small snippet of code for updating information in a database from a DataSet, and then later we'll show a fully functional sample of updating data in both a connected and disconnected fashion using the DataSet. This particular example uses a fictitious table so don't fret if you can't find it in the Northwind database.

```
// The default constructor for the adapter populates the SelectCommand
// property.
SqlDataAdapter FileDA = new SqlDataAdapter( "SELECT FileName, Description FROM
Files", Connection );
FileDA.UpdateCommand = new SqlCommand("UPDATE Files SET Description = @Description
WHERE FileName = @FileName", Connection );
FileDA.UpdateCommand.Parameters.Add( "@Description", SqlDbType.VarChar, 30 );

SqlParameter KeyParam = FileDA.UpdateCommand.Parameters.Add( "@FileName",
SqlDbType.VarChar, 8 );
KeyParam.SourceColumn = "FileName";
KeyParam.SourceVersion = DataRowVersion.Original;

Connection.Open();
FileDA.Fill( MyDS, "Files" );

// just because we can, modify the 12th row.
```

The following line of code obtains a reference to a specific row within the "Files" table.

```
DataRow MyFile = MyDS.Tables["Files"].Rows[11];
```

Use the MyFile reference to modify the value of a single column within that row.

```
MyFile["Description"] = "Semi-Useful File.";
// Don't be fooled by the name, the Update method calls
// ALL of the appropriate UPDATE, DELETE, or INSERT commands
// for those records with the appropriate state.
FileDA.Update(MyDS);
```

One thing that might not be immediately obvious is that the `UpdateCommand` (and all other command properties respectively) can take any form of database command. This includes stored procedures. What this means is that not only can you rig up your own SQL statements to carry your data changes across to the database, but you can also supply the prototypes for stored procedures, allowing for some incredibly advanced (and efficient) processing in response to changes made to your `DataSet`.

XML Schemas

We gave a brief indication earlier that the core structure and data within an ADO.NET `DataSet` is entirely built on XML. It is very useful that any programmer working with a `DataSet` knows that its internal structure is represented by an XML Schema. Knowing how the `DataSet`s form their internal structure gives you more control over what you can do with `DataSet`s, including creating strongly-typed `DataSet`s (another topic entirely).

For those not familiar with XSD (XML Schema Definition), it is an XML dialect for describing relational data structures. Not only is it the internal format in which the structure of a `DataSet` is maintained, but XSD is used extensively throughout the entire .NET framework, including Web Services, Remoting, and in many other places.

For a detailed reference and excellent examples of how to write your own XSD and learn all of the ins and outs of this technology, you should pick up a copy of *Professional XML Schemas* from Wrox Press.

There are two different types of XML Schemas utilized by the `DataSet` object:

❑ **Inferred Schema** – when a `DataSet` loads data from a source from which it cannot also determine the schema (such as an XML file that does not include an in-line schema), the `DataSet` must infer this schema. It does this by examining the data that it has found and extrapolating relations and constraints. However, you should know that when a `DataSet` reads from an XML file without a schema, all of the column data types will be strings as there isn't enough information to reliably infer data type. The following is a quick example that loads some data from a standard XML document and outputs a .XSD file that represents the schema that the `DataSet` inferred from the data. Note that we didn't have to do anything to generate the schema. As we've said before, the schema is an integral part of the `DataSet`, and you cannot ever have a `DataSet` without a schema.

```
using System;
using System.Data;

namespace Wrox.ProDotNet.Chapter10.Schemas2
{
    class ClassMain
    {
        static void Main(string[] args)
        {
            DataSet WidgetDS = new DataSet();

            WidgetDS.ReadXml( "WidgetSource.XML", XmlReadMode.InferSchema );
            WidgetDS.WriteXmlSchema( "Schema2.XSD" );
        }
    }
}
```

The above code is only a few lines, but there's a lot of stuff going on in the background. When the `DataSet` is loaded, a schema representing the structure and relations of the data is inferred and stored as the `DataSet`'s internal structure. In order to compile and run the above code, place the `WidgetSource.XML` file in the **obj\debug** directory beneath the project directory and compile with a reference to `System.Data.dll`. The output of the `Schema2.XSD` file looks like this:

```xml
<?xml version="1.0" standalone="yes"?>
<xsd:schema id="WIDGETS" targetNamespace="" xmlns=""
xmlns:xsd="http://www.w3.org/2001/XMLSchema" xmlns:msdata="urn:schemas-microsoft-
com:xml-msdata">
  <xsd:element name="WIDGETS" msdata:IsDataSet="true">
    <xsd:complexType>
      <xsd:choice maxOccurs="unbounded">
        <xsd:element name="WIDGET">
          <xsd:complexType>
            <xsd:sequence>
              <xsd:element name="WIDGETID" type="xsd:string"
                           minOccurs="0" />
              <xsd:element name="DESCRIPTION" type="xsd:string"
                           minOccurs="0" />
            </xsd:sequence>
          </xsd:complexType>
        </xsd:element>
      </xsd:choice>
    </xsd:complexType>
  </xsd:element>
</xsd:schema>
```

The raw XML File, `WidgetSource.XML`, that generated the above schema looks like this:

```xml
<WIDGETS>
  <WIDGET>
    <WIDGETID>1</WIDGETID>
    <DESCRIPTION>Nice Widget</DESCRIPTION>
  </WIDGET>
  <WIDGET>
    <WIDGETID>2</WIDGETID>
    <DESCRIPTION>Angry Widget</DESCRIPTION>
  </WIDGET>
</ WIDGETS>
```

❑ **Supplied Schema** – instead of letting the `DataSet` infer a (possibly inaccurate) schema, you can supply your own. You can invoke the `ReadXmlSchema()` method on the `DataSet` itself or load a schema from a stream or from a `TextReader`. If a `DataAdapter` fills the `DataSet`, it is the responsibility of the `DataAdapter` to supply the schema. The `SqlDataAdapter` will supply the `DataSet` with a completely accurate schema, including data types. The other way to supply your own schema is to build the `DataTable` and `DataColumn` objects on your own. Using these objects, you will implicitly build the schema in your `DataSet`. The following is a quick sample that shows manually building a `DataSet` and then outputting its schema to a text file. You can build the following example by simply compiling with a reference to `System.Data.dll`.

```
using System;

using System.Data;

namespace Wrox.ProDotNet.Chapter10.Schemas1
{
    /// <summary>
    /// Summary description for ClassMain.
    /// </summary>
    class ClassMain
    {
        static void Main(string[] args)
        {
            DataSet SampleDS = new DataSet();
            DataTable Widgets = new DataTable( "Widgets" );
            Widgets.Columns.Add( "WidgetID", typeof(int) );
            Widgets.Columns.Add( "Description", typeof(string) );


            SampleDS.Tables.Add( Widgets );
            SampleDS.DataSetName = "WidgetDataSet";

            SampleDS.WriteXmlSchema( "schema1.xsd" );
        }
    }
}
```

The above code creates a `DataSet` and then calls the `WriteXmlSchema()` method, which creates the following schema:

```
<?xml version="1.0" standalone="yes"?>
<xsd:schema id="WidgetDataSet" targetNamespace="" xmlns=""
xmlns:xsd="http://www.w3.org/2001/XMLSchema" xmlns:msdata="urn:schemas-microsoft-
com:xml-msdata">
  <xsd:element name="WidgetDataSet" msdata:IsDataSet="true">
    <xsd:complexType>
      <xsd:choice maxOccurs="unbounded">
        <xsd:element name="Widgets">
          <xsd:complexType>
            <xsd:sequence>
              <xsd:element name="WidgetID" type="xsd:int" minOccurs="0" />
              <xsd:element name="Description" type="xsd:string"
                            minOccurs="0" />
            </xsd:sequence>
          </xsd:complexType>
        </xsd:element>
      </xsd:choice>
    </xsd:complexType>
  </xsd:element>
</xsd:schema>
```

You've already seen code that reads from a SQL Server, so we won't bore you with that (it is readily available in the download section for this chapter, anyway). What we *would* like to demonstrate is the result of a supplied schema through the use of a `SqlDataAdapter`. Remember that we said that the `DataSet` cannot infer data type, it can only infer columns and table relations. So, based on the following XSD file generated by our third schema sample, we know that the `SqlDataAdapter` is actually retrieving schema information from SQL Server and placing it directly into the `DataSet`. Quite a lot of work is being done on your behalf without you even needing to worry about it.

```xml
<?xml version="1.0" standalone="yes"?>
<xsd:schema id="NewDataSet" targetNamespace="" xmlns=""
xmlns:xsd="http://www.w3.org/2001/XMLSchema" xmlns:msdata="urn:schemas-microsoft-
com:xml-msdata">
  <xsd:element name="NewDataSet" msdata:IsDataSet="true">
    <xsd:complexType>
      <xsd:choice maxOccurs="unbounded">
        <xsd:element name="Customers">
          <xsd:complexType>
            <xsd:sequence>
              <xsd:element name="EmployeeID" type="xsd:int" minOccurs="0" />
              <xsd:element name="LastName" type="xsd:string"
                      minOccurs="0" />
              <xsd:element name="FirstName" type="xsd:string"
                      minOccurs="0" />
              <xsd:element name="Title" type="xsd:string" minOccurs="0" />
              <xsd:element name="TitleOfCourtesy" type="xsd:string"
                      minOccurs="0" />
              <xsd:element name="BirthDate" type="xsd:dateTime"
                      minOccurs="0" />
              <xsd:element name="HireDate" type="xsd:dateTime"
                      minOccurs="0" />
              <xsd:element name="Address" type="xsd:string" minOccurs="0" />
              <xsd:element name="City" type="xsd:string" minOccurs="0" />
              <xsd:element name="Region" type="xsd:string" minOccurs="0" />
              <xsd:element name="PostalCode" type="xsd:string"
                      minOccurs="0" />
              <xsd:element name="Country" type="xsd:string" minOccurs="0" />
              <xsd:element name="HomePhone" type="xsd:string"
                      minOccurs="0" />
              <xsd:element name="Extension" type="xsd:string"
                      minOccurs="0" />
              <xsd:element name="Photo" minOccurs="0">
                <xsd:simpleType>
                  <xsd:restriction base="xsd:base64Binary" />
                </xsd:simpleType>
              </xsd:element>
              <xsd:element name="Notes" type="xsd:string" minOccurs="0" />
              <xsd:element name="ReportsTo" type="xsd:int" minOccurs="0" />
              <xsd:element name="PhotoPath" type="xsd:string"
                      minOccurs="0" />
            </xsd:sequence>
          </xsd:complexType>
        </xsd:element>
      </xsd:choice>
    </xsd:complexType>
  </xsd:element>
</xsd:schema>
```

If you've got good eyes, you'll notice that the parent element in this schema is actually called "Customers", and not "Employees", even though the code actually selects all columns from the Employees table. This was done deliberately to show you that we can control the name of the table into which the results from SQL are placed, but the rest of the schema is supplied entirely by the data structure of the SQL table itself.

One other tip on XML Schemas and DataSets before we move along: if you aren't all that comfortable with generating your own schemas by hand, or you don't like using Visual Studio.NET's Schema editor, then you have one other option. You saw how easy it was for us to use the DataSet to infer and store to disk a schema based on existing data. If you want to build a schema based on a pre-existing XML file or set of data that you have, you can simply load the data into the DataSet, save the schema, and then make minor tweaks and changes such as configuring the data types properly.

ADO.NET Pros and Cons

So far throughout this chapter, you've been given a fairly straightforward, objective overview of the many features and uses for ADO.NET. Believe it or not, there may actually be a few occasions where you might not actually want to use ADO.NET. I know how you feel; I was shocked nearly to the point of fainting when I first found out myself!

No programmer should ever jump ship on tried and true methods without first exploring both the positive and the negative side of any new technology. This next section of the chapter should give you a good idea of not only the good things that come with ADO.NET, but also some of its drawbacks.

Pros

ADO.NET is rich with plenty of features that are bound to impress even the most skeptical of programmers. If this weren't the case, Microsoft wouldn't even be able to get anyone to use the Beta. What we've done here is come up with a shortlist of some of the more outstanding benefits to using the ADO.NET architecture and the System.Data namespace.

- ❑ **Performance** – there is no doubt that ADO.NET is extremely fast. The actual figures vary depending on who performed the test and which benchmark was being used, but ADO.NET performs much, much faster at the same tasks than its predecessor, ADO. Some of the reasons why ADO.NET is faster than ADO are discussed in the ADO versus ADO.NET section later in this chapter.

- ❑ **Optimized SQL Provider** – in addition to performing well under general circumstances, ADO.NET includes a SQL Server Data Provider that is highly optimized for interaction with SQL Server. It uses SQL Server's own TDS (Tabular Data Stream) format for exchanging information. Without question, your SQL Server 7 and above data access operations will run blazingly fast utilizing this optimized Data Provider.

- ❑ **XML Support (and Reliance)** – everything you do in ADO.NET at some point will boil down to the use of XML. In fact, many of the classes in ADO.NET, such as the DataSet, are so intertwined with XML that they simply cannot exist or function without utilizing the technology. You'll see later when we compare and contrast the "old" and the "new" why the reliance on XML for internal storage provides many, many advantages, both to the framework and to the programmer utilizing the class library.

- ❑ **Disconnected Operation Model** – the core ADO.NET class, the DataSet, operates in an entirely disconnected fashion. This may be new to some programmers, but it is a remarkably efficient and scalable architecture. Because the disconnected model allows for the DataSet class to be unaware of the origin of its data, an unlimited number of supported data sources can be plugged into code without any hassle in the future.

- ❑ **Rich Object Model** – the entire ADO.NET architecture is built on a hierarchy of class inheritance and interface implementation. Once you start looking for things you need within this namespace, you'll find that the logical inheritance of features and base-class support makes the entire system extremely easy to use, and very customizable to suit your own needs. It is just another example of how everything in the .NET framework is pushing toward a trend of strong application design and strong OOP implementations.

Cons

Hard as it may be to believe, there are a couple of drawbacks or disadvantages to using the ADO.NET architecture. I'm sure others can find many more faults than we list here, but we decided to stick with a shortlist of some of the more obvious and important shortcomings of the technology.

❑ **Managed-Only Access** – for a few obvious reasons, and some far more technical, you cannot utilize the ADO.NET architecture from anything but managed code. This means that there is no COM interoperability allowed for ADO.NET. Therefore, in order to take advantage of the advanced SQL Server Data Provider and any other feature like DataSets, XML internal data storage, etc, your code must be running under the CLR.

❑ **Only Three Managed Data Providers (so far)** – unfortunately, if you need to access any data that requires a driver that cannot be used through either an OLEDB provider or the SQL Server Data Provider, then you may be out of luck. However, the good news is that the OLEDB provider for ODBC is available for download from Microsoft. At that point the down-side becomes one of performance, in which you are invoking multiple layers of abstraction as well as crossing the COM InterOp gap, incurring some initial overhead as well.

❑ **Learning Curve** – despite the misleading name, ADO.NET is not simply a new version of ADO, nor should it even be considered a direct successor. ADO.NET should be thought of more as the data access class library for use with the .NET framework. The difficulty in learning to use ADO.NET to its fullest is that a lot of it does seem familiar. It is this that causes some common pitfalls. Programmers need to learn that even though some syntax may appear the same, there is actually a considerable amount of difference in the internal workings of many classes. For example (this will be discussed in far more detail later), an ADO.NET DataSet is nothing at all like a disconnected ADO RecordSet. Some may consider a learning curve a drawback, but I consider learning curves more like scheduling issues. There's a learning curve in learning anything new; it's just up to you to schedule that curve into your time so that you can learn the new technology at a pace that fits your schedule.

ADO.NET Samples

So far, we've covered the basic architecture of the System.Data namespace, and we've gone into a bit of detail on some of the major players in ADO.NET's data access scheme, like the Connection class, the Command class, the DataAdapter and more. Now it's time to put all of this overview together into some coherent samples. Our first sample shows the creation, updating, deleting, and retrieval of data using a DataSet and an adapter that communicates with SQL Server 2000. The next example illustrates the same CRUD principle utilizing an offline data store (an XML file on disk).

A Server Connection Data Example

The first of our ADO.NET review examples will demonstrate using a DataSet and a DataAdapter to retrieve data from SQL Server, and post changes such as inserts, updates, and deletes through the adapter and their appropriate IDbCommand objects.

This is the listing for the ClassMain.cs file, the main file of our little sample Console Application. A few of the tabs have been removed to try to fit all the code into the space of the pages here.

```
using System;
using System.Data;
using System.Data.SqlClient;
```

```
namespace Wrox.ProDotNet.Chapter10.ADONET_Connected
{
class ClassMain
{
static void Main(string[] args)
{
   DataSet SampleDS = new DataSet( "SampleDS" );
   string ConnectionString = "Data Source=localhost; Initial
         Catalog=Northwind; User id=sa; Password=;";
   SqlConnection Connection = new SqlConnection( ConnectionString );
   SqlDataAdapter SampleDA = new SqlDataAdapter( "SELECT RegionID,
         RegionDescription FROM Region", Connection );
   DataRow TempRow;
   // now lets provide SQL statements that support the rest of the
   // UPDATE, DELETE, and INSERT functionality.
```

There is a way to get VS to build all these commands for us, but it will only work if VS is connected directly to the source to interrogate it. If we were working on an n-tier solution where VS only sees derived classes, we'd have to do this manually anyway.

It's worth noting here than when creating commands to commit changes for the `DataAdapter`, it is important to indicate the source column. You can do that by setting the `SourceColumn` property on the `Parameter` object, or by passing it as the argument immediately following the parameter's data type size.

For example, the parameter, `@RegionDescription`, when the `DataAdapter` attempted to invoke the `Update` command, couldn't decipher on its own that the value to be supplied for `@RegionDescription` was the `RegionDescription` column. By supplying the `SourceColumn` to the `Parameters.Add()` method on our own, we guarantee that the adapter will supply the right column values for the right arguments.

```
// -- UPDATE --
SqlCommand UpdateCommand = new SqlCommand( "UPDATE Region SET
         RegionDescription = @RegionDescription WHERE RegionID =
         @RegionID", Connection );
SqlParameter UpdateKeyParam = new SqlParameter( "@RegionID",
         SqlDbType.Int );
UpdateKeyParam.SourceColumn = "RegionID";
UpdateKeyParam.SourceVersion = DataRowVersion.Original;
UpdateCommand.Parameters.Add( "@RegionDescription", SqlDbType.NChar, 50,
         "RegionDescription" );
UpdateCommand.Parameters.Add( UpdateKeyParam );
SampleDA.UpdateCommand = UpdateCommand;
```

The other thing to keep in mind in the code, both above and below, is that instead of supplying raw SQL statements, we could easily be supplying stored procedures. For example, if we wanted to use a stored procedure for the above `UpdateCommand`, we would change the first line of code to the following two lines:

```
SqlCommand UpdateCommand = new SqlCommand( "sp_UpdateRegion", Connection );
UpdateCommand.CommandType = CommandType.StoredProcedure;
```

Using this particular construct, we can create incredible amounts of functionality with very little work on our part and very few lines of code.

```
// -- DELETE --
SqlCommand DeleteCommand = new SqlCommand( "DELETE Region WHERE RegionID
        = @RegionID", Connection );
SqlParameter DeleteKeyParam = new SqlParameter( "@RegionID",
        SqlDbType.Int );
DeleteKeyParam.SourceColumn = "RegionID";
DeleteKeyParam.SourceVersion = DataRowVersion.Original;
DeleteCommand.Parameters.Add( DeleteKeyParam );
SampleDA.DeleteCommand = DeleteCommand;

// -- INSERT --
SqlCommand InsertCommand = new SqlCommand( "INSERT INTO
        Region(RegionDescription, RegionID) VALUES(@RegionDescription,
        @RegionID)", Connection );
InsertCommand.Parameters.Add( "@RegionDescription", SqlDbType.NChar, 50,
        "RegionDescription" );
InsertCommand.Parameters.Add( "@RegionID", SqlDbType.Int, 4,
        "RegionID" );
SampleDA.InsertCommand = InsertCommand;

// now load the dataset with the results of our SQL Query.
// notice that we're not explicitly opening our connection. Our
// DataAdapter is doing all that work for us, closing it as soon as it
// completes its task.
SampleDA.Fill( SampleDS, "Region" );

// create a new row
// the Region table doesn't have an autonumbering identity,
// so we have to supply our own region ID.
DataRow NewRow;
NewRow = SampleDS.Tables["Region"].NewRow();
NewRow["RegionDescription"] = "Central";
NewRow["RegionID"] = 5;
Console.WriteLine("New Row Created using NewRow(), RowState is: {0}",
        NewRow.RowState );

SampleDS.Tables["Region"].Rows.Add( NewRow );
Console.WriteLine("New Row Added to Table RowState is: {0}",
        NewRow.RowState );

// modify the first row
TempRow = SampleDS.Tables["Region"].Rows[0];
Console.WriteLine("Modifying First Row, Pre-Change State is: {0}",
        TempRow.RowState );
TempRow["RegionDescription"] = "Reeeeeaalllly Far East";
Console.WriteLine("Modifying First Row, Post-Change State is: {0}",
        TempRow.RowState );
// call the update method to save the new row and update the first
Console.WriteLine("Calling Update() to Commit New Row and First Row
        Change.");
SampleDA.Update( SampleDS, "Region" );

// delete the second row
Console.WriteLine("Deleting Our New Row, Post-Delete State is: {0}",
        NewRow.RowState );
NewRow.Delete();
Console.WriteLine("Deleting Our New Row, Post-Delete State is: {0}",
```

```
                   NewRow.RowState );
       // now call the update method.
       Console.WriteLine("Calling Update() - this will post ALL of our changes,
               not just the update.");
       SampleDA.Update( SampleDS, "Region" );
       Console.WriteLine("Region Table after Update()\n------------------------
               -----");

       foreach (DataRow tRow in SampleDS.Tables["Region"].Rows )
       {
           Console.WriteLine( tRow["RegionDescription"] );
       }

       SampleDS.Dispose();
       SampleDA. Dispose ();
       }
   }
 }
```

After going through the source code above, you can take a look at what the output of the example produces. It is especially interesting to see how the RowState property changes with each line of code, and that it changes implicitly without the programmer having to keep track of changes on his/her own.

The code creates a new region called "Southern". Then it modifies the first region to change its name to "Reeeeaalllly Far East". Then the Update() method is called to commit both the new row, and the change to the name of the first region. After that, the code deletes the "Southern" region simply by calling the Delete() method on the DataRow object, and then Update() is called again to commit that change. If you don't believe what's going on, you can always add a breakpoint to this code immediately before the second Update() that deletes the new row and go and verify that it actually has been inserted into the database.

```
New Row Created using NewRow(), RowState is: Detached
New Row Added to Table RowState is: Added
Modifying First Row, Pre-Change State is: Unchanged
Modifying First Row, Post-Change State is: Modified
Calling Update() to Commit New Row and First Row Change.
Deleting Our New Row, Pre-Delete State is: Unchanged
Deleting Our New Row, Post-Delete State is: Deleted
Calling Update() - this will post ALL of our changes, not just the update.
Region Table after Update()
-------------------------------
Reeeeeaalllly Far East
Western
Northern
Southern
```

An Offline Data Example

What we've done for our offline example is take the regions and place them into an XML file. Also, we've created an XSD schema representing the Regions table (we did this by adding a line of code to the above connected example calling the WriteXmlSchema() method to create the .XSD file).

For practical purposes, you will want to use the DataSet's ability to save its own data as an XML file (or stream) when you are exporting data, possibly for some kind of business-to-business document exchange or for later import into another application. Also, some small desktop applications that don't connect to high-end RDBMSs for their data use XML as their sole data store in files on disk.

This example is going to perform the same exact operations on an offline data store (XML file) as the previous example. The only differences will be in that we don't need to use an adapter, we'll use the `AcceptChanges()` method instead of `Update()`, and we'll use the `WriteXml()` method to save our `DataSet` to disk rather than stream it to a database.

Let's look at the code we wrote for the offline, XML-based ADO.NET sample. To make sure that this code works properly, make sure that the `Region.XSD` file is in the **obj\debug** directory of the project so that the executable can find the file, and make sure that it is compiled with a reference to the `System.Data` DLL.

```
using System;
using System.Data;

namespace Wrox.ProDotNet.Chapter10.ADONET_Offline
{
class ClassMain
{
static void Main(string[] args)
{
    DataRow TempRow;
    DataSet SampleDS = new DataSet( "SampleDS" );
```

`ReadXmlSchema()` supplies the `DataSet` with the XSD indicated by either the stream or text file that we supply as an argument. An interesting thing to do is put a watch on your `DataSet` variable and breakpoint before and after this call. Immediately following this call, you'll see that all of the column definitions have been created, data types have been modified, and any `DataRelations` or `Constraints` that are applicable have also been placed into the `DataSet`.

```
SampleDS.ReadXmlSchema( "Region.XSD" );
// loading the data from the XML file after importing a supplied schema
// accomplishes the same thing for the DataSet as having an Adapter
// plug in data from a connected store like SQL.
SampleDS.ReadXml( "Region.XML" );
```

Note that all of the code from this point on, with the exception of calling `AcceptChanges()`, is accomplished in the same fashion as our previous example. It is another illustration of one of the benefits of having a source-neutral data store.

```
DataRow NewRow;
NewRow = SampleDS.Tables[ "Region" ].NewRow();
NewRow["RegionDescription"] = "A little to the Left";
NewRow["RegionID"] = 5;
Console.WriteLine("New Region Created using NewRow(), RowState is: {0}",
        NewRow.RowState);
SampleDS.Tables[ "Region" ].Rows.Add( NewRow );
Console.WriteLine("New Region RowState After adding to Table: {0}",
        NewRow.RowState);

// modify the first row
TempRow = SampleDS.Tables[ "Region" ].Rows[0];
Console.WriteLine( "First row Pre-Modify State is : {0}",
        TempRow.RowState );
TempRow["RegionDescription"] = "Reeeeeaalllly Far East";

// commit changes to dataset.
Console.WriteLine( "Calling AcceptChanges() in DataSet to commit
```

```
                    values." );

        SampleDS.AcceptChanges();

        // now delete the row we created.
        Console.WriteLine( "New Region, Pre-Delete RowState is: {0}",
                NewRow.RowState );
        NewRow.Delete();
        Console.WriteLine( "New Region, Post-Delete RowState is: {0}",
                NewRow.RowState);

        Console.WriteLine(" Calling AcceptChanges() in DataSet to commit deletion
                of new region" );

        SampleDS.AcceptChanges();

        Console.WriteLine( "Writing new DataSet to XML." );
```

WriteXml() serializes the internal data storage format of the DataSet to either a stream or a text file. In our case, we're writing to a different file to the one we opened to allow the reader to compare and contrast the XML files. We could just as easily have written our modified XML to the source document, truly committing the changes to disk.

```
        SampleDS.WriteXml( "Region_Changed.XML" );

        Console.WriteLine( "SampleDS Regions after changes:" );
        Console.WriteLine( "-----------------------------" );

        foreach (DataRow tRow in SampleDS.Tables[ "Region" ].Rows )
        {
        Console.WriteLine( tRow["RegionDescription"] );
        }

        SampleDS.Dispose();

    }
  }
}
```

Now let's take a look at the output we generated by running our offline ADO.NET sample:

```
New Region Created using NewRow(), RowState is: Detached
New Region RowState After adding to Table: Added
First row Pre-Modify State is : Added
Calling AcceptChanges() in DataSet to commit values.
New Region, Pre-Delete RowState is: Unchanged
New Region, Post-Delete RowState is: Deleted
Calling AcceptChanges() in DataSet to commit deletion of new region
Writing new DataSet to XML.
SampleDS Regions after changes:
-------------------------------
Reeeeeaalllly Far East
Western
Northern
Southern
```

In our sample output, you can see that the modification of the first region was successful, changing its description to "Reeeeeaalllly Far East". You can also see that the "A little to the Left" region is not in the DataSet. As with our previous sample, if you really aren't convinced of what's going on, you can breakpoint the sample immediately before the second `AcceptChanges()` method is called and examine the contents. You will see the fifth region in there, waiting to be removed.

As for the final XML, the resulting XML document looks like this:

```xml
<?xml version="1.0" standalone="yes"?>
<SampleDS>
  <Region>
    <RegionID>1</RegionID>
    <RegionDescription>Reeeeeaalllly Far East</RegionDescription>
  </Region>
  <Region>
    <RegionID>2</RegionID>
    <RegionDescription>Western
    </RegionDescription>
  </Region>
  <Region>
    <RegionID>3</RegionID>
    <RegionDescription>Northern
    </RegionDescription>
  </Region>
  <Region>
    <RegionID>4</RegionID>
    <RegionDescription>Southern
    </RegionDescription>
  </Region>
</ SampleDS>
```

You should notice that after the Western, Northern, and Southern regions, there is a large amount of whitespace in the XML file, the reason being that in SQL, those were originally defined as Nchar(50), which will actually pad remaining room in the string with whitespace. Region 1, which we edited without such a restriction, does not have padded whitespace. Situations similar to this where the DataSet loads an XML file and saves one in a slightly different format is what is known as a *loss of* **fidelity** in the underlying XML document. We'll discuss fidelity loss and preventing occurrences like this (and other far more damaging issues) later when we discuss using the `XmlDataDocument`.

ADO versus ADO.NET

You might be thinking that we took our sweet time getting to this particular section of the chapter. The reason it's so late in the chapter is so that you really appreciate all of the differences between ADO and ADO.NET, and when might be the appropriate time to use either of them: you need to be familiar with the basic features and functionality of ADO.NET. We're assuming that you're familiar with ADO already. If you aren't familiar with ADO and are just learning ADO.NET, you may want to skim this section and read those things that apply to ADO.NET and ignore the ADO descriptions.

Choose your Weapon

When we were looking at the Pros and Cons of ADO.NET previously, we mentioned that there might actually be times when you don't want to use ADO.NET. Despite the startling nature of this statement, it is true.

❑ **When to use ADO.NET** – if the code that you are writing that needs underlying data access is managed (that is, it runs managed by the CLR) then you really don't want to be using anything but ADO.NET. ADO.NET is a set of managed classes, and they are optimized to be run in a managed environment. The only time this doesn't apply is if your data source simply cannot be reached by anything that the two ADO.NET Data Providers can offer. Note that it is physically impossible to use any ADO.NET feature through COM InterOp or in any other way from an unmanaged application.

❑ **When NOT to use ADO.NET** – there may be times where you are writing your native .NET code, but the data source to which you need access cannot be reached by any of the three ADO.NET Data Providers (though Odbc's Data Provider must be downloaded separately). In this case, you could use ADO through COM InterOp (though this is not recommended), or you could simply write classic VB or C++ code to utilize ADO.

The general rule is that if you are writing code in a managed language like C# or VB.NET, then you should try to use ADO.NET for as much as you possibly can. Only use ADO from .NET when there is no other alternative. If you are writing your code in unmanaged languages like VB6 or C++, then you should continue using classic ADO.

ADO.NET DataSet versus ADODB.RecordSet

You can't discuss ADO without discussing the RecordSet, nor can you discuss ADO.NET without discussing the DataSet. They are both core components of their respective technologies. What we're going to provide here is a feature-by-feature comparison of how each of these objects implements those features. The ultimate goal of this exercise is to prove that the ADO.NET DataSet is NOT the same thing as an ADO RecordSet, and that they are in fact two different solutions to two different paradigms.

❑ **Table Multiplicity** – the traditional ADO Recordset provides the ability to navigate through a single table of information. Sure, that single table may be the result of multiple joins done at the server level, but it is still a single-table access. The DataSet, on the other hand, has support for many, many tables within the same DataSet that can be iterated separately or by navigating parent/child relationships in a robust hierarchy of tables, rows, constraints and relations. With its ability to support multiple tables with keys, constraints and interconnected relationships, the DataSet can be considered a small, in-memory relational database cache.

❑ **Navigation** – Navigation in the ADO Recordset is based on the cursor model. Even though you can specify a client-side cursor, you must still move a navigation pointer from one location to the next. Primitive seeking and filtering routines allow you to navigate in bursts, but the model is still based on the cursor. The DataSet, on the other hand, is an entirely offline, in-memory, cache of data. As such, all of its data is available all the time. At any point, the programmer can retrieve any row or column, constraint or relation simply by accessing it either ordinally or by retrieving it from a name-based collection.

Incidentally, it is worth pointing out that the ADO RecordSet was not originally designed to operate in a disconnected fashion. All of that functionality was added later as demand for more features rose. This caused a bloat in the featureset of the ADO RecordSet that made it try to accomplish too many tasks. Early users of ADO will remember that the `Recordset` was originally designed to be a simple, server-side iterator tool and not much more than that. As demand for offline functionality and extra features rose, features were slapped onto the original design, bloating the functionality and internal code of the `Recordset`.

❑ **Connectivity Model** – we mentioned briefly in the navigation section that the `DataSet` is a completely offline, in-memory cache of data. As well, the `DataSet` is designed specifically to have information about the source of the data contained within it. It has one purpose and one purpose only. The ADO `RecordSet` was originally designed without the ability to operate in a disconnected fashion. This functionality was added later, and many programmers complain that the offline functionality seems kludgy and stamped on like an afterthought. Even the ability to create a recordset manually column-by-column without a database connection was something that was added on afterward. As we demonstrated earlier, the `DataSet` can accept and post information to/from connected servers through the help of a `DataAdapter`, and it can maintain a completely disconnected, offline XML representation of data being defined by an XSD schema and an XML document. The pure disconnected connectivity model of the `DataSet` gives the `DataSet` much more scalability and versatility in the amount of things it can do and how easily it can do them.

❑ **Marshaling and Serialization** – in the world of COM programming, any time you pass data from one COM component to another that data needs to undergo a process called *marshaling*. Marshaling involves copying and processing data so that a complex type can appear to the receiving component the same as it appeared to the sending component. In fact, many dictionaries list "assembly" as a synonym for marshaling. A marshaler is, in a sense, decomposing and re-assembling your data in a new location. Any COM programmer can tell you that marshaling is an expensive operation. The `DataSet` and the `DataTable` components support Remoting (discussed in the next item) in the form of XML serialization. Rather than spending all the time and effort using COM marshaling to transfer the `DataSet` across a wire, it is simply converted into XML (an easy task, since we know it is internally stored as XML already) and sent across process boundaries.

❑ **Firewalls and DCOM and Remoting (Oh My!)** – those who've worked with DCOM enough will know that it is nearly impossible to marshal a DCOM component across a router. Obviously people have come up with their own tricks and workarounds to get around this limitation, but the inherent limitation is still there. As such, it is very, very difficult to utilize DCOM components or transfer DCOM components in and out of a firewall, across the Internet itself, etc. Through the use of Remoting (.NET's answer to DCOM), a `DataSet` or `DataTable` component can be serialized into XML, sent across the wire to a new AppDomain, and then deserialized back into a fully functional `DataSet`. Because the `DataSet` is completely disconnected, and has no external dependencies, you lose absolutely nothing by serializing it and transferring it through Remoting.

❑ **Rich Object Model (or lack thereof)** – COM is based on a binary standard that has no support for inheritance. As such, any COM object can't actually externally inherit from any other COM object. This essentially forces a very flat object model and one that can be cumbersome at times for people to use. As you saw earlier in this chapter, ADO.NET is based on a very logical, well-designed hierarchy of classes and interface implementation. This type of robust object model fosters code reuse and actually makes it far easier for programmers to use the classes and learn their functions. As such, ADO can be said to have a fairly flat object model while ADO.NET has a large, robust object hierarchy.

System.Xml

This chapter is all about working with data in the .NET framework. It might not be immediately obvious, but the `System.Xml` namespace is an integral player in the data access scheme for the .NET framework. We've covered pretty well that the `DataSet` relies entirely on XML for its own internal schema and data representation.

We'll learn in this section what the difference is between `System.Xml` and `System.Data`, as well as their similarities and how their functionality is intertwined with somewhat parallel hierarchies. We will also learn that XML is worth just as much consideration in a chapter about data access as is SQL Server or Oracle or OLE DB.

Before we get into more detail on the `System.Xml` namespace and its components, we should make sure that you are reminded that `System.Xml` is NOT simply the managed version of MSXML. Its functionality may overlap that of the MSXML COM library, but it contains much more and sports a rich object model and hierarchy. The `System.Xml` namespace provides standards-based support for many kinds of XML processing, including:

- ❑ XML 1.0
- ❑ XML Namespaces
- ❑ XML Schemas (XSD)
- ❑ XPath
- ❑ XSL/T Transformations
- ❑ DOM Level 2 Core (XmlDocument)
- ❑ SOAP 1. 1

If our coverage of the `System.Xml` namespace seems a bit cursory, that's intentional. This isn't the right forum for an in-depth chapter on XML (an entire book could be written on .NET XML, in fact look out for *Professional .NET XML* from Wrox Press), so we're just going to skim the surface as it relates to data and ADO.NET `DataSets`.

System.Xml and System.Data

The two different namespaces both provide different answers to various data issues. The key to getting a handle on where they diverge and where they meet is in determining the needs of your application. Some applications may use nothing but the `System.Data` namespace, working purely in a `DataSet` with its internal XML format and `DataAdapters`, `Commands` and `Connections`.

In the not-so-distant past, many people thought that XML was just another buzzword; a fad that was going to quickly fade from sight and never be used again. Now, XML is a part of millions of people's lives, whether they know it or not. Knowing the abilities of an `XmlDocument`, what can be done using XML, SOAP, XSL/T and related technologies, will go far toward helping you make the right decision as to which technology you need to use and when.

There isn't nearly enough room in this chapter to provide a full coverage of all of the various classes and technologies residing in the `System.Xml` namespace. We're going to cover two things that are very closely related to the `System.Data` namespace – the `XmlDocument` and the `XmlDataDocument`. One of the samples earlier in this chapter loaded a `DataSet` with a standard XML document. In the .NET framework, we have the `System.Data` namespace, which provides us with the ability to manage structured data with a relational model or view by working with DataSets. As well, there is the System.Xml namespace, which provides us with the ability to manage hierarchical XML documents and streams. In addition, we also have classes that provide a bridge between relational data in DataSets and hierarchical data in XML documents. The XmlDocument class provides the ability to work with DOM documents, while the XmlDataDocument provides a synchronization bridge between relational and XML data.

The XmlDocument

The XmlDocument provides us with an in-memory representation of an XML document according to the W3C Core DOM Level 1 and Core DOM Level 2 standards. It is essentially a container for a list of XmlNodes. Of course, each of those nodes can then have its own list of XmlNodes, and so on and so on. This section of the chapter is going to assume that you have some familiarity with XML and have used the MSXML.DOMDocument object before, as it provides a good frame of reference when dealing with the .NET XmlDocument. For more information on the XML DOM, you can consult the W3C (http://www.w3.org) or the Wrox Press book *Professional XML*.

Let's get right into a sample and then we'll analyze it and pick it apart afterward. Our sample is actually going to take the Region.XML source file from the last DataSet example and load it into an XmlDocument. From there, it is going to use the document model to make some changes to the document. The end result of this experiment should look very much like the result of our last DataSet example. This, of course, is not a coincidence.

Here's our sample code in C#.

```
using System;
using System.Xml;

namespace Wrox.ProDotNet.Chapter10. XmlDocument1
{

class XmlSample
{
static void Main(string[] args)
{
   XmlDocument SampleDoc = new XmlDocument();
   XmlNode RootNode;
   XmlNode RegionNode;
   XmlNode RegionDescription;
   SampleDoc.Load( "Region.XML" );

   // This is going to be our "SampleDS" root node
   RootNode = SampleDoc.DocumentElement;

   // modify the first region, like we did in the previous sample.
   RegionNode = RootNode.ChildNodes[0];
   // select the RegionDescription child of the Region node.

   RegionDescription = RegionNode.SelectSingleNode("RegionDescription");
   RegionDescription.InnerText = "Reeeeeaaalllly Far East";
   SampleDoc.Save( "Region_Changed.XML" );
}
}
}
```

The code is pretty straightforward. We first load the `XmlDocument` with the XML in the `Region.XML` file. Then, grabbing a reference (careful not to say pointer!) to the `DocumentElement` object, we then find the first Region by grabbing the first child of the `RootNode`. We use just about the simplest XPath statement possible (we'll go into a pinch of `XPath` later) to select the `"RegionDescription"` node. Once we have a reference to that node, we change its `InnerText` property and save the document to disk.

The code generates a `Region_Changed.XML` file. Note that it is identical to the one we created with our `DataSet` example earlier.

```
<?xml version="1.0" standalone="yes"?>
<SampleDS>
  <Region>
    <RegionID>1</RegionID>
    <RegionDescription>Reeeeeaaalllly Far East</RegionDescription>
  </Region>
  <Region>
    <RegionID>2</RegionID>
    <RegionDescription>Western
    </RegionDescription>
  </Region>
  <Region>
    <RegionID>3</RegionID>
    <RegionDescription>Northern
    </RegionDescription>
  </Region>
  <Region>
    <RegionID>4</RegionID>
    <RegionDescription>Southern
    </RegionDescription>
  </Region>
</SampleDS>
```

The XmlDataDocument

The `XmlDataDocument` class is designed specifically to work in tandem with a `DataSet`. It allows a structured XML document to be viewed and manipulated through a `DataSet` object, retaining the original **fidelity** (we talked about that earlier) of the underlying XML document. It can be considered a relational view of a subset of an XML document.

The `XmlDataDocument` allows for a two-way link between the `DataSet` and an XML document. In terms of data access, the relationship between the `DataSet` and the `XmlDataDocument` is similar in nature to the relationship between the `DataSet` and the `DataAdapter`. The following diagram illustrates a sample use of the `XmlDataDocument` where, through the use of a `DataSet` and an XML document, the `DataSet` is limited in its scope to only the main `<Customers>` node of the document. All other data in the document, including the `<Orders>` node, is completely inaccessible to the `DataSet`. By providing full fidelity on the XML document, we can be guaranteed that any change made to the `<Customers>` node via the `DataSet` will have absolutely no impact on the `<Orders>` nodes. Assuming that we configure our mapping types properly, we can also be assured that attributes in the document will remain attributes and elements will remain elements, even though they may all appear as columns in the `DataSet`.

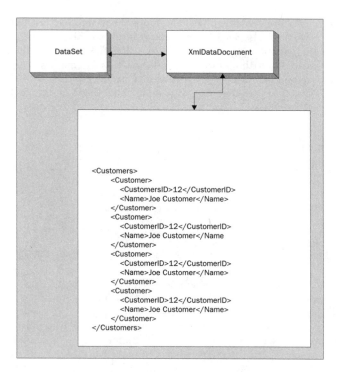

```
<Customers>
    <Customer>
        <CustomersID>12</CustomerID>
        <Name>Joe Customer</Name>
    </Customer>
    <Customer>
        <CustomerID>12</CustomerID>
        <Name>Joe Customer</Name
    </Customer>
    <Customer>
        <CustomerID>12</CustomerID>
        <Name>Joe Customer</Name>
    </Customer>
    <Customer>
        <CustomerID>12</CustomerID>
        <Name>Joe Customer</Name>
    </Customer>
</Customers>
```

There are many reasons for implementing a solution using an XmlDataDocument rather than simply using the XmlDocument DataSet component. If you link an XML document to the DataSet through this class, then your XML document can become *versioned* in the same way as the DataSet. This allows you to track changes to a custom XML document. In addition, with the XmlDataDocument, you are able to run XPath queries (covered shortly) against your data. You can also choose which method you use to traverse your data, and at any point you can load a DataRow for a given node, and the reverse.

The quick sample we're going to walk through shows you in detail the effects of using an XmlDataDocument against a schema-loaded DataSet. The issue here is that if your DataSet represents, and has access to, everything in your XmlDocument, you may not need to use the XmlDataDocument. Also, keep in mind that the XmlDataDocument is a complex thing and we could spend dozens of pages using it. It works bi-directionally, so you can modify the DataSet and see the changes in the XmlDocument, and if you modify the XmlDocument *outside* the scope defined by the DataSet's schema, the DataSet doesn't care.

Let's walk through the code and then take a look at the output.

```csharp
using System;
using System.Data;
using System.Xml;

namespace Wrox.ProDotNet.Chapter10XmlDataDocument
{
class ClassMain
{
static void Main(string[] args)
{
```

Here we create a new `DataSet`, which we've seen before. Then we have the `DataSet` load a pre-defined schema (which we have also seen in previous examples). This schema, included further below, describes only information about a region table that exists one level beneath the root document. It contains no information about anything else. Once we load the schema, we create an `XmlDataDocument` based on the `RegionDS` `DataSet`. This links the `DataSet` and the `XmlDataDocument`. What is happening under the hood is that the data document is subscribing to the `DataSet`'s events in order to link the two.

```
DataSet RegionDS = new DataSet();
DataRow RegionRow;
RegionDS.ReadXmlSchema( " Region_More.XSD" );
XmlDataDocument DataDoc = new XmlDataDocument( RegionDS );
DataDoc.Load("Region_More.XML" );

Console.WriteLine("DataSet has data now, even though we never loaded the
        DataSet.");
Console.WriteLine("Because of the Schema in our XSD file, RegionDS has no
        access to the MoreData table.");
Console.WriteLine("DataSet Tables Found: {0}", RegionDS.Tables.Count );
```

This is where some people's alarm bells start going off. We're iterating through the list of tables in the `DataSet`, and we're iterating through the list of rows in those tables. All of this is fine and good, but we never actually loaded any XML explicitly from the `DataSet`, nor did we use a `DataAdapter` to load it. Remember what was said a little earlier in this section about the similarity between the `XmlDataDocument` and the `DataAdapter`. The `XmlDataDocument` populated the `DataSet` with the data that was appropriate and performed a good deal of other work behind the scenes.

```
foreach (DataTable tTable in RegionDS.Tables)
{
   Console.WriteLine("Table: {0}", tTable.TableName );
   Console.WriteLine("-----------------------------------");
   foreach (DataRow tRow in tTable.Rows)
   {
      Console.WriteLine( tRow["RegionDescription"] );
   }
}

RegionRow = RegionDS.Tables[0].Rows[0];

Console.WriteLine();
Console.WriteLine("Without doing anything, first row pre-mod state: {0}",
        RegionRow.RowState);
RegionDS.AcceptChanges();
Console.WriteLine("About to Modify the first region, pre-mod state: {0}",
        RegionRow.RowState);
RegionRow["RegionDescription"] = "Reeeeeaalllly Far East!";
Console.WriteLine("Just modified the row, post-mod state: {0}",
        RegionRow.RowState );
RegionDS.AcceptChanges();
Console.WriteLine("Commit changes to disk, using the XmlDataDocument,
        NOT the DS!");
DataDoc.Save( "Region_More_Modified.XML" );
}
}
}
```

This is another area that may confuse some programmers. We're actually calling the Save method on the XmlDataDocument, which should look pretty familiar to anyone who has used the XmlDocument class. The reason we're calling Save() on the XmlDataDocument is that we need to preserve fidelity. If we had saved the DataSet itself, we would have only saved the subset of information to which the DataSet's schema allows us access. As an exercise for yourself, modify this sample code so that the DataSet saves its own copy of the data in a file called Region_More_DSModified.XML and compare the two. If you can answer the question *Why are the two files different?* then you have really understood the content of this section.

Now that we've looked at the code, let's take a look at the output:

The first thing that should strike you immediately is that the RowState of the row is set to Added. This differs from our previous DataSet examples where the RowState was Unchanged. The reason for this is that, because the DataSet was loaded and linked by virtue of the XmlDataDocument, it has no original state, therefore all of the data in the DataSet at that time is considered to be Added data. We call AcceptChanges() once and then the rows look normal with the Unchanged state.

To illustrate the full impact of what this application does, let's take a look at the source XML document that this console application loads.

```xml
<?xml version="1.0" standalone="yes"?>
<Root>
  <Region>
    <RegionID>1</RegionID>
    <RegionDescription>Eastern
    </RegionDescription>
  </Region>
  <Region>
    <RegionID>2</RegionID>
    <RegionDescription>Western
    </RegionDescription>
  </Region>
  <Region>
    <RegionID>3</RegionID>
    <RegionDescription>Northern
    </RegionDescription>
  </Region>
  <Region>
    <RegionID>4</RegionID>
    <RegionDescription>Southern
    </RegionDescription>
  </Region>
```

Again, keep in mind here that because the schema we provided didn't contain a definition for MoreData, the dataset cannot see it when linked to the XmlDataDocument for this XML. Not only can it not see it, but changes made to the DataSet cannot modify this section of the XML.

```
<MoreData>
  <Column1>12</Column1>
  <Column2>Hi There</Column2>
</MoreData>
```

We've trimmed some redundant data here to make the file more readable.

```
<MoreData>
  <Column1>12</Column1>
  <Column2>Hi There</Column2>
</MoreData>
</Root>
```

What it looks like we have here is an XML file that contains the data for two tables. One table, Region, contains two columns and we've seen this before in our previous examples. The second table we made up and stuffed into the XML file for demonstration purposes. It too has two columns.

When we apply the following schema to the DataSet, we are in effect completely hiding the MoreData table from the XmlDataDocument because, as we know, DataSets will not allow visibility to, nor modify access to, any piece of data not described in its internal schema.

The Region_More.XSD schema that we "pre-filter" our DataSet with:

```
<?xml version="1.0" standalone="yes"?>
<xsd:schema id="Root" targetNamespace="" xmlns=""
xmlns:xsd="http://www.w3.org/2001/XMLSchema" xmlns:msdata="urn:schemas-microsoft-
com:xml-msdata">
  <xsd:element name="Root" msdata:IsDataSet="true">
    <xsd:complexType>
      <xsd:choice maxOccurs="unbounded">
        <xsd:element name="Region">
          <xsd:complexType>
            <xsd:sequence>
              <xsd:element name="RegionID" type="xsd:string"
              minOccurs="0" />
              <xsd:element name="RegionDescription" type="xsd:string"
              minOccurs="0" />
            </xsd:sequence>
          </xsd:complexType>
        </xsd:element>
      </xsd:choice>
    </xsd:complexType>
  </xsd:element>
</xsd:schema>
```

Finally we come to the conclusion of our output, the Region_More_Modified.XML file. This file contains the output as saved by the XmlDataDocument, not by the DataSet itself. You'll notice that fidelity has been preserved in that the MoreData information still remains. This is a significant point to remember, because if we had done the same load, modify, save operation on only the DataSet, the MoreData table would have evaporated into thin air and we would have lost all of that data!

Here is the final output of our program in the form of the modified XML Data File.

```xml
<?xml version="1.0" standalone="yes"?>
<Root>
  <Region>
    <RegionID>1</RegionID>
    <RegionDescription>Reeeeeaalllly Far East!</RegionDescription>
  </Region>
  <Region>
    <RegionID>2</RegionID>
    <RegionDescription>Western
    </RegionDescription>
  </Region>
  <Region>
    <RegionID>3</RegionID>
    <RegionDescription>Northern
    </RegionDescription>
  </Region>
  <Region>
    <RegionID>4</RegionID>
    <RegionDescription>Southern
    </RegionDescription>
  </Region>
  <MoreData>
    <Column1>12</Column1>
    <Column2>Hi There</Column2>
  </MoreData>
```

Again, we've skimmed out some data here to make the file more readable on the printed page.

```xml
  <MoreData>
    <Column1>12</Column1>
    <Column2>Hi There</Column2>
  </MoreData>
  <MoreData>
    <Column1>12</Column1>
    <Column2>Hi There</Column2>
  </MoreData>
</Root>
```

A Brief Introduction to XPath

Obviously we don't have the room in this chapter to give any form of detailed discussion on XPath. Wrox has other books that cover Xpath in much greater detail that we can here. XPath is a simple query language used for selecting lists of nodes from an XmlDocument. Many people have dubbed it "SQL for XML" or "Internet SQL".

We're not going to go into detail at all on the semantics or tokens involved in the XPath language. Instead, we'll show a brief example of how you can use an XPath query on an XmlDataDocument to retrieve a list of matching nodes. For syntax information on the XPath language itself, you can consult any number of Wrox books or the W3C (www.w3.org) home page for more information.

Our XPath sample takes the previous sample and modifies the Region_More.XSD schema such that the RegionID column is no longer a child element but an attribute of the <Region> tag. This also demonstrates an incredibly powerful use for schemas in that we can have a mix of attribute columns and element columns defined by the schema. We then load the Region_More.XML file and select those region's whose RegionID attribute is greater than 2.

```
using System;
using System.Data;
using System.Xml;

namespace Wrox.ProDotNet.Chapter10.XPath_XmlDataDocument
{
class ClassMain
{
static void Main(string[] args)
{
    DataSet RegionDS = new DataSet();
    DataRow RegionRow;
    RegionDS.ReadXmlSchema( " Region_More.XSD" );
    XmlDataDocument DataDoc = new XmlDataDocument( RegionDS );
    DataDoc.Load( " Region_More.XML" );
```

The XPath statement in the below code translates roughly into English as "Select all Region nodes that are children of a Root node that have a RegionID attribute value greater than 2". The NodeMatches variable will then contain an array of XmlNode objects. Because the DataSet is linked with this XmlDataDocument, we can obtain any DataSet row for any given node so long as the node represents the uppermost level of that row (for example, you cannot select a child-element column node and obtain a row for it, that will result in a null).

```
    // Now we'll select all of the regions that have
    // a RegionID > 2.
    XmlNodeList NodeMatches =
            DataDoc.SelectNodes("//Root//Region[@RegionID>2]");

    Console.WriteLine( "------------------------" );

    foreach ( XmlNode tmpNode in NodeMatches )
    {
        // pull up corresponding row in the DS.
        RegionRow = DataDoc.GetRowFromElement( (XmlElement)tmpNode );
        Console.WriteLine(RegionRow["RegionDescription"]);
    }

}
}
}
```

The code above results in the following output:

```
------------------------
Northern
Southern
```

Obviously the XPath queries can become quite complex and provide the programmer with an incredibly valuable resource for locating specific data and selecting batches of data that match a certain criteria. The ability to utilize XPath on an XmlDataDocument is not only useful when working against on-disk offline stores, but can be extremely valuable to query offline XML that was populated from a server to avoid making multiple round-trips to re-query and re-sort various pieces of data.

We won't go into it in this chapter, but you should at least be aware of the fact that just as easily as you can perform XPath queries against a given XmlDataDocument, you can also perform XSLT (eXtensible Stylesheet Language Transformations) transformations against that data.

The possibilities for uses for all of these XML technologies are limited only by your ability to think of them. There are thousands of different things that you can utilize the XmlDataDocument / DataSet combination for, and when you consider that you can then add XPath and XSLT support to it, the number of possibilities grows exponentially.

Summary

In the first section of this chapter, you were given an overview of the System.Data namespace (ADO.NET), which included overviews of the Connection, the Command, the DataAdapter, and the DataReader. That section then gave you an overview of the DataSet and its capabilities. Then you were given some information to help you compare and contrast ADO and ADO.NET, as well as the benefits and drawbacks of ADO.NET.

Once we completed our brief tour of ADO.NET, we then went through a very quick introduction to the System.Xml namespace, introducing you to the XmlDocument and XmlDataDocument classes. Once we got into the XmlDataDocument class and discovered how it can be used to link directly with a DataSet, and provide XPath and XSLT services against an XmlDataDocument (thereby indirectly an ADO.NET DataSet), we realized and discovered the true depth of the link between the System.Xml and System.Data namespaces.

Data is simply a representation of information. ADO.NET (System.Data) allows you to represent facts in DataSets, tables, rows, columns and relational data. System.Xml allows you to represent facts in the form of XML documents. Linking the two namespaces, you can perform XML-based operations on relational data, and relational operations on XML data.

Hopefully you now have a good idea of what is involved in working with data in the .NET framework, and how you cannot simply exclude XML when considering the concept of "data" as a whole. At this point you should be ready to start working with and learning more about ADO.NET and the .NET framework XML support.

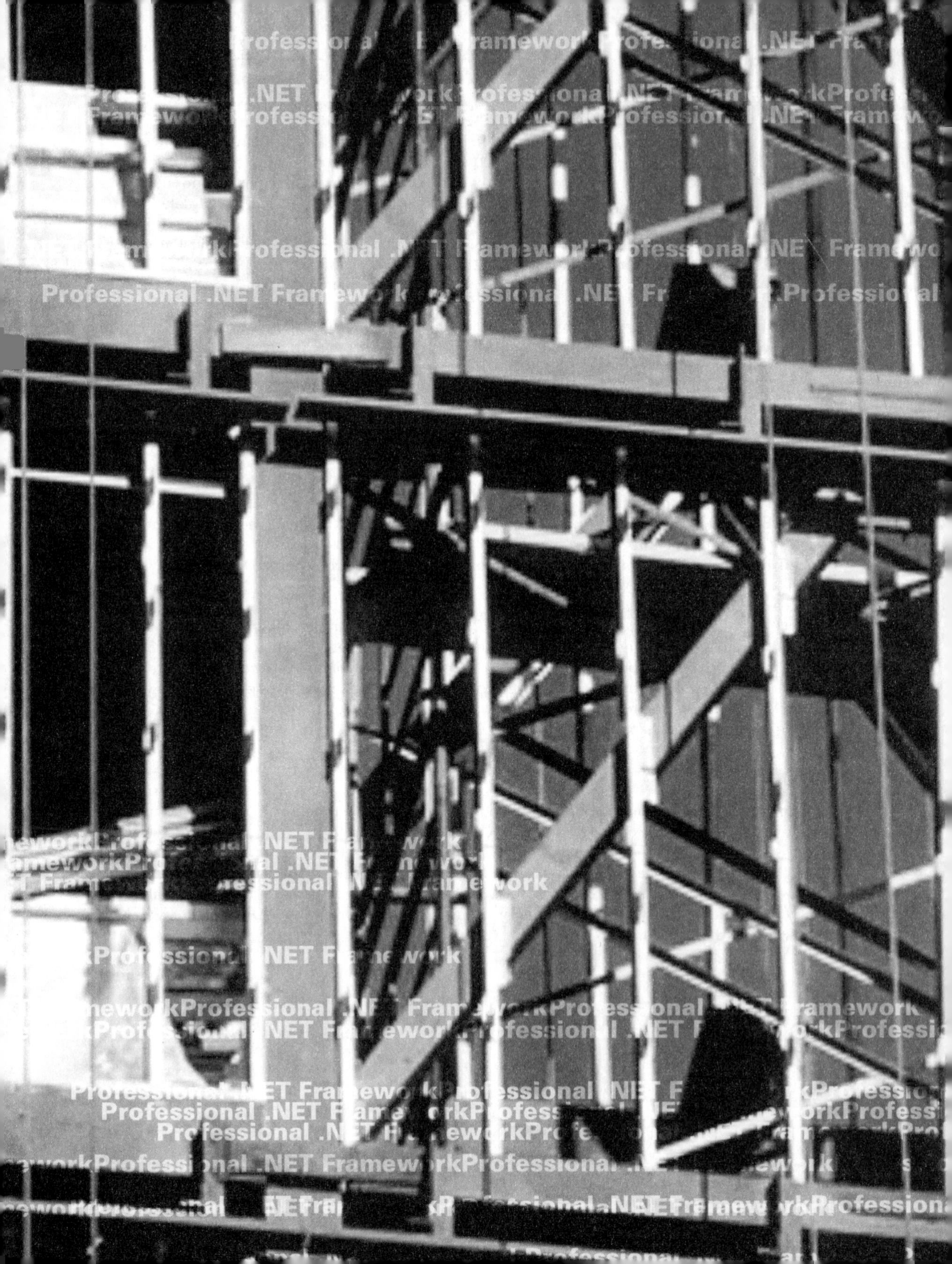
Professional .NET Framework

10

Engineering Web Services

In the last chapter, we saw how to work with data in .NET using ADO.NET and its base classes. In this chapter, we will learn about a very exciting topic – how to engineer web services. Web services are reusable web components that can be invoked from any platform capable of communicating over the Internet. Web Services solve a lot of the problems of the past communicating with remote computers and they will allow systems to talk to each other that previously were never able to. This chapter will specifically cover the following:

❑   Why we need web services and what they replace

❑   The Web Service Wire Formats (HTTP-GET, HTTP-POST, and SOAP)

❑   Describing a web service with Web Service Description Language (WSDL)

❑   Discovering web services with DISCO and UDDI

❑   Designing, creating, testing, and consuming web services

❑   Creating transactional and asynchronous web services

❑   Extending web services using SOAP extensions

❑   A brief introduction to Microsoft Hailstorm, a set of off-the-shelf web services

Finally, we will review some key points to remember about web services.

What are Web Services?

Web Services are reusable components that are based on standard Internet protocols for platform and language independence. In simplest terms, web services are nothing more than procedures or functions that perform some task that an application can easily invoke using Internet technologies such as TCP/IP. Web services can be invoked either in intranet or Internet environments, and in the case of intranet environments don't necessarily require an Internet connection. Web services can share data across platforms and languages. In addition, the application that invokes the capability of the web service doesn't have to know any details about how the underlying web service is functioning. All the invoking application needs to know is where the service is located, the type of parameters it requires, and the type of information it will return.

You are probably thinking to yourself that being able to call functions and procedures on remote computers is not a new concept. If so, you are absolutely correct. With the Distributed Component Object Model (DCOM) and other similar technologies, we have been able to call functions and procedures on different computers for some time now. However, in such cases, it was difficult to communicate across platforms and with computers across firewalls. Even when communication across firewalls was possible, it was often very slow or limited in functionality. Web services solve the communication problems of the past and make it easier than ever for diverse applications to talk to one another. A single web service can easily be called by web-and non-web-based applications on a variety of platforms from all around the world – as long as the application can communicate using standard Internet protocols.

The biggest advantage to web services is that they open up new ways to allow businesses and individuals to easily share information and to capitalize on offering new and existing services worldwide. We will most likely see an emergence of web services available for use for a small fee and probably just as many, if not more, available for free. For example, a real-time stock ticker web service might prove extremely useful to investment companies who want to display real-time stock information on their web sites for their customers. An individual or company who creates a full featured stock ticker might sell the rights to use the web service to many different investment companies. As another example, a company that sells merchandise might want to convert some of its existing business logic into web services to allow their customers and suppliers to have access to information that previously was only available inside the company.

Another important advantage of web services is that when updates and new features are made to them, all applications that use it will immediately see the changes without having to perform installation steps on the client. This feature is true of all web applications that are server-based and is not unique to web services.

It really is overwhelming to think about the possibilities that web services can provide for businesses and individuals, in light of how much easier they make cross-platform communication. Developers may even want to consider creating and selling some web services of their own! With this as the backdrop, let's move on to learning all the important details about what web services consist of and how you can create them.

The Building Blocks of a Web Service

There is much more to a web service than just the web service itself. A web service that sits on a computer somewhere doesn't serve any purpose if there isn't a way to get to it, to know that it exists, and to know what information it expects and provides in return. That's exactly where the web service building blocks come in. They address all these issues to make discovery and communication with a web service possible.

Web Service Wire Formats

A very important aspect of communicating with a web service is the physical aspect of being able to reach it. Web services are based on standard Internet protocols and the web service wire formats that allow you to communicate with them include: HTTP-GET, HTTP-POST, and SOAP. **HTTP-GET** and **HTTP-POST** are standard Internet protocols based on the Hypertext Transfer Protocol (HTTP) language. Using HTTP-GET, data is sent as part of the URL to the web service. Using HTTP-POST, data is sent in the HTTP message body. HTTP-GET and HTTP-POST return data from web services as simple XML documents. They are limited in the respect that they only support simple types, such as int, string, arrays, etc; they cannot support complex types such as structures, datasets, and classes. Thus, depending on the type of information being exchanged with a web service, HTTP-GET and HTTP-POST may or may not successfully communicate with that particular web service.

The **Simple Object Access Protocol (SOAP)** is a lightweight XML-based protocol for exchanging structured and type information over the Internet. The SOAP specification defines several items, such as:

❑ An extensible message format (called an envelope) required for encapsulating data. The envelope is the only required part of a SOAP message.

❑ Rules for how to use XML to represent data, such as for application-defined data types. Usage is Optional.

❑ The syntax for representing remote procedure calls (RPCs). Usage is Optional.

❑ Binding between SOAP and HTTP. Usage is Optional.

SOAP, unlike HTTP-GET and HTTP-POST, supports both simple and complex types. Thus, complex types such as structs, datasets, and classes can be used in SOAP communications. SOAP is the primary message format used by the .NET Framework for communicating with XML Web Services. The good news for developers is that Visual Studio.NET handles the SOAP communication for us. But let's take a look at what a SOAP message looks like so we can better understand what it is and what it does:

```
POST /test/simple.asmx HTTP/1.1
Host: 155.555.55.55
Content-Type: text/xml; charset=utf-8
Content-Length: length
SOAPAction: "http://www.xyzcorp.com/GetNameById"

<?xml version="1.0" encoding="utf-8"?>
<soap:Envelope xmlns:xsi="http://www.w3.org/2001/XMLSchema-instance"
xmlns:xsd="http://www.w3.org/2001/XMLSchema"
xmlns:soapenc="http://schemas.xmlsoap.org/soap/encoding/"
xmlns:tns="http://soapinterop.org/"
xmlns:soap="http://schemas.xmlsoap.org/soap/envelope/">
  <soap:Body soap:encodingStyle="http://schemas.xmlsoap.org/soap/encoding/">
    <tns:GetNameById>
      <CustId>A1234</CustId>
    </tns:GetNameById>
  </soap:Body>
</soap:Envelope>
```

The example SOAP message above will call the `GetNameById` method available at www.xyzcorp.com and passing the A1234 value (John Doe's id in this hypothetical example) for the `CustId` string field. The response you get in return from the server might look something like this:

```
HTTP/1.1 200 OK
Content-Type: text/xml; charset=utf-8
Content-Length: length

<?xml version="1.0" encoding="utf-8"?>
<soap:Envelope xmlns:xsi="http://www.w3.org/2001/XMLSchema-instance"
xmlns:xsd="http://www.w3.org/2001/XMLSchema"
xmlns:soapenc="http://schemas.xmlsoap.org/soap/encoding/"
xmlns:tns="http://soapinterop.org/"
xmlns:soap="http://schemas.xmlsoap.org/soap/envelope/">
  <soap:Body soap:encodingStyle="http://schemas.xmlsoap.org/soap/encoding/">
    <tns:GetNameByIdResponse>
      <Return>John Doe</Return>
    </tns:GetNameByIdResponse>
  </soap:Body>
</soap:Envelope>
```

Notice that the data is again included within the XML, and this time, the result is shown in the `Return` part of the XML. We can see from this that John Doe was the customer with that particular customer id. Hopefully, this gives you a better idea of what SOAP is, but don't worry if this isn't totally clear, since Visual Studio.NET hides these details from you.

We will see examples of communicating with web services using SOAP (although it is done behind the scenes) later in this chapter when we learn how to consume a web service.

Web Service Description Language (WSDL)

Web Service Description Language (WSDL) is an XML-based language that is being jointly developed by Microsoft and IBM. WSDL is a standard way to document what messages the web service accepts and generates – that is, to document the **web service contract**. A web service contract document describes how to communicate with web services in a means they will understand and to know what to expect in return. The good news is that Visual Studio.NET and the .NET Framework, along with other tools, can generate WSDL documents for you, so you do not have to know all the details of the WSDL specification.

The document below is a small portion of a WSDL file that describes a simple web service we are going to be creating later in this chapter. This web service contains two methods: `CalculateShippingCost` and `RetrieveShippingMethods`. You can see in the XML document below that a variety of details about the web service are described, such as the fact that these two methods are available. Since the WSDL language specification is very detailed, and since you don't have to create the WSDL document for a web service yourself, don't worry about understanding every detail about the example below. It is provided here for illustration purposes only to give you some idea about what information a WSDL document contains.

```
<?xml version="1.0" encoding="utf-8?>
<definitions xmlns:s="http://www.w3.org/2001/XMLSchema"
xmlns:http="http://schemas.xmlsoap.org/wsdl/http/"
xmlns:mime="http://schemas.xmlsoap.org/wsdl/mime/"
xmlns:urt="http://microsoft.com/urt/wsdl/text/"
xmlns:soap="http://schemas.xmlsoap.org/wsdl/soap/"
xmlns:soapenc="http://schemas.xmlsoap.org/soap/encoding/"
xmlns:s0="http://tempuri.org/" targetNamespace="http://tempuri.org/"
xmlns="http://schemas.xmlsoap.org/wsdl/">
  <types>

<s:schema attributeFormDefault="qualified" elementFormDefault="qualified"
targetNamespace="http://tempuri.org/">
```

```
       <s:element name="CalculateShippingCost">
         <s:complexType>
           <s:sequence>
             <s:element minOccurs="1" maxOccurs="1" name="dblWeight"
                        type="s:double" />
             <s:element minOccurs="1" maxOccurs="1" name="strShippingMethod"
                        nullable="true" type="s:string" />
           </s:sequence>
         </s:complexType>
       </s:element>
   (...portions omitted...)
    <service name="ShippingService">
     <port name="ShippingServiceSoap" binding="s0:ShippingServiceSoap">
       <soap:address location="http://goz/Shipping/CalculateShipping.asmx" />
     </port>
     <port name="ShippingServiceHttpGet" binding="s0:ShippingServiceHttpGet">
       <http:address location="http://goz/Shipping/CalculateShipping.asmx" />
     </port>
     <port name="ShippingServiceHttpPost" binding="s0:ShippingServiceHttpPost">
       <http:address location="http://goz/Shipping/CalculateShipping.asmx" />
     </port>
   </service>
 </definitions>
```

Later in this chapter, when creating and testing our web services, we will learn a simple way to view the WSDL document associated with a given web service. So for now, just know that WSDL is the specification for describing a web service contract and that a WSDL document describes the web service contract for a particular web service (that is, how to communicate with that web service). Let's move on to learning about the ways you can discover which web services have been made available by others.

Discovery of Web Services (DISCO)

A web service isn't going to be very useful if no one knows about it. **The Discovery of Web Services (DISCO)** specification defines an XML-based discovery document format as well as a protocol for retrieving the discovery document. The DISCO document, which typically resides at the root of a web server, contains references to the location of available web services. This allows discovery of services at a known URL. However, creating discovery documents for your web services is certainly not required. There may be times when you purposely don't want to advertise the availability of a particular web service, such as one you created for private use. Just because you don't advertise the web service, however, doesn't mean that you shouldn't take steps to implement proper security and other such mechanisms to ensure its private use. When your web services are not private-only use, however, creating a DISCO file to allow the services to easily be discovered is a good idea. Now let's take a look at what a DISCO file looks like and how they can be discovered.

Suppose, for example, that you know that XYZ Corporation has web services available, but you only know their corporate web site address. If they have a DISCO file that is located on their web server, then the web services they have available and the location of the WSDL documents describing how to communicate with those web services can be determined. Their DISCO file (named `default.disco` or anything ending with `.disco`) may look something like the following:

```
<?xml version="1.0" ?>
<disco:discovery    xmlns:disco="http://schemas.xmlsoap.org/disco"
xmlns:wsdl="http://schemas.xmlsoap.org/disco/wsdl">
   <wsdl:contractRef ref="http://www.xyzcorp.com/WebService1.asmx?WSDL"/>
   <wsdl:contractRef ref="http://www.xyzcorp2.com/WebService2.asmx?WSDL"/>
</disco:discovery>
```

As in the example DISCO file on the previous page, there can be multiple references to web services listed. In this example, XYZ Corporation has `WebService1` and `WebService2` listed in the discovery document. It is important to point out that the first web service is in their main xyzcorp.com domain while the second one is in their xyzcorp2.com domain. What this means is that the web services you are listing as available do not have to be located on the same web server as the one where the discovery document resides. Also, you should know that if the URL paths specified in the discovery document are relative paths, they are assumed to be relative to the location of the discovery document.

Now, how would you go about discovering what web services XYZ Corporation has made available? One way is to use a command line tool provided with the .NET Framework and the other way is to use the graphical tool in Visual Studio.NET. The command line tool, `disco.exe,` comes with the .NET Framework. Suppose you want to use it to search the www.xyzcorp.com URL looking for DISCO files. You could select Start | Run, and issue a command similar to the following:

```
disco.exe /out:TempResults http://www.xyzcorp.com
```

You may need to specify the complete path to the `disco.exe` file, which by default is `c:\Program Files\Microsoft.NET\FrameworkSDK\Bin\`. The `/out` parameter shown above specifies the directory where you want the results of the search placed. If this parameter is not specified, then the results will be placed in the current directory. The parameter immediately following the out parameter is the URL you want to discover web services for. There are several other parameters that can be specified with the disco utility, such as `username`, `password`, `proxy`, and so on. Here is the syntax for those examples:

❑ /password:*password* (for servers that require a password for authentication)

❑ /proxydomain:*domain* (the domain to use when connecting to a proxy server requiring authentication)

❑ /proxyusername:*username* (the user name for connecting to the proxy server)

❑ /proxypassword:*password* (the password for connecting to the proxy server)

More information about these and other available parameters can be found in the .NET Framework documentation under the disco.exe topic.

The effect of running the disco program against a URL that has discovery documents is that copies of those documents will be placed in the local directory you specified. You can then open these discovery documents and see for yourself the details about what web services are available by that company and where you can get more information (for example, the location to the WSDL document describing how to communicate with a particular web service).

If you're like most people, however, you probably prefer an easier way. Visual Studio can perform these steps for you and display the results graphically. When you add a web reference to a project, Visual Studio searches a URL for you automatically to let you know what web services that URL has made available. You can then click on any result in the list and view the contract details, and if you desire, add a reference to that web service in your project. This will be demonstrated later.

In the next section, we will learn about another way to discover web services that are out there – using a national web service directory.

Universal Description, Discovery, and Integration (UDDI)

DISCO, as we just learned, is very useful for allowing discovery of services at a known URL. However, there will be instances when you don't know the URL of where web services can be found, but instead need to look up which web services are available. The **Universal Description, Discovery, and Integration (UDDI) specification** describes a set of standards that XML web service providers should follow to advertise the fact that their web service exists. In addition to the specification is a **UDDI Business Registry** that allows companies to list information about their web services in a central place, similar in concept to the yellow pages in a phone book. Once added to the Business Registry, web services can be looked up by category, company name, etc.

The UDDI Business Registry and details about the UDDI specification can be accessed at http://www.uddi.org. From this site, you can register your company and the web services you offer, or you can search for the web services that other companies have made available. When registering your company or searching for web services, you will be prompted to choose a Business Registry Node to search, such as the Ariba, IBM, or Microsoft Business Registry Nodes. Or you can visit the Microsoft or IBM nodes directly using http://uddi.microsoft.com and https://www-3.ibm.com/services/uddi/protect/home.jsp, respectively. Similar to Internet registration of a domain name, there are multiple vendors authorized to perform the registration. When registering your company and your services with one of the UDDI Business Registry Nodes, the information you enter is shared with the other registries. Thus, you do not have to input the data multiple times with each registry. Unlike Internet domain registration, however, registry with UDDI is presently free.

You only want to register web services that you want others to easily be able to find. If the web service is designed for limited or private use, then registering it in the UDDI directory doesn't make sense – just like you wouldn't want to put an unpublished phone number in the phone book so anyone could find it.

Let's look at a sample search in the UDDI directory to see how it works. Let's go to http://uddi.microsoft.com and search the Microsoft directory. From the main page that comes up, click the Search option under the Tools heading in the left portion of the screen. A screen like the following will appear:

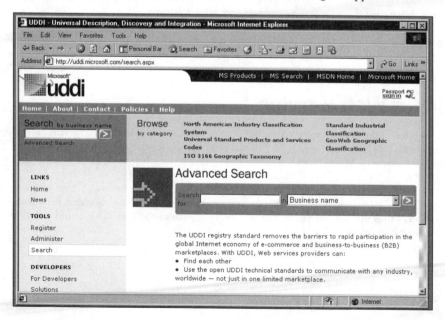

Next, in the Search For field type *stock* and in the drop-down where it defaults to Business Name, change it to *service type by name*. This will allow us to search for any stock web services registered with UDDI. Click the go arrow and you should get results similar to the following:

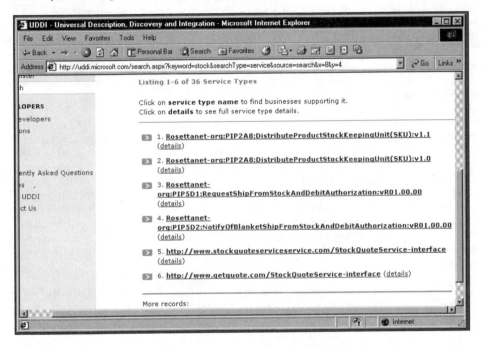

Notice how there are 36 service types related to stocks that are returned. Click on the details hyperlink next to one of the stock services and see what results you get. You will see information such as a link to the web service itself or a hyperlink to the WSDL or other documents containing information that you can view to see more details about what the web service expects and what it returns.

Now that we've covered the building blocks of web services, including how to discover and communicate with them, let's move on to the fun part of actually creating them.

Creating a Web Service

ASP.NET web services can be created with or without using Visual Studio.NET. The language compilers are included free with the .NET Framework, so you can create a web service using any tool you want. There are many advantages to using Visual Studio.NET to create web services, however, as we will see later in this section.

ASP.NET web services are saved with a `.asmx` file extension. This lets the web server know to interpret it as a web service. The `.asmx` file is technically the only required file you have to create for a web service. There are other types of files that should be used as well though, such as the DISCO file, and we will look at what those are and how they are useful.

Creating a Web Service without Visual Studio.NET

The compilers for VB.NET, C#, etc. are free and come with the .NET Framework. Thus, as long as the code you write complies with the .NET Framework standards (that is, will compile with the language compiler of the language in which it is written), it can be created in any application you desire, such as Notepad. There are good reasons for using Visual Studio.NET to create web services instead of simple editors like Notepad, as we will see later. For now, let's create our first web service using Notepad to see how easy it can be. After we create our web service using Notepad or any other text editor, we will then see how to test and run the web service using a tool that is built-in with the .NET Framework.

A New Web Service – the Shipping Cost Example

Suppose you want to create a web service that will calculate shipping costs based on the shipping method and weight of the package. You want to create a method that will return the shipping cost of a given package, based on the following criteria:

❑ There is a minimum handling charge of $2.00, no matter how large the package.

❑ The additional shipping costs will be determined by using a formula that multiples the weight times a multiplier for a given shipping method (Overnight, 2nd Day, or Regular Mail).

❑ Thus, the heavier a package and the sooner you need it delivered, the more expensive it will be.

Further suppose that you want to create another method that just returns a string containing the shipping methods ("Overnight, 2nd Day, or Regular Mail"). In reality, this exact business logic would not be the best method for calculating shipping costs and returning shipping methods, but this example will still give you a good idea of what a web service might be created for and how to actually create it.

Creating a web service is not much different to creating any other method. Below is an example that demonstrates how to create a web service based on the business rules we've specified. Create a folder on your web server called `shipping`, then open Notepad and create a file called `CalculateShipping.asmx` that looks like this:

```
<%@ WebService Language="VB" Class="ShippingService" %>

Imports System.Web.Services
Imports Microsoft.VisualBasic

Public Class ShippingService
    Inherits System.Web.Services.WebService

    <WebMethod()> Public Function CalculateShippingCost(ByVal dblWeight as _
        double, ByVal strShippingMethod as String) As Double

    Dim dblHandlingCost as Double
    Dim dblShippingCost as Double

    dblHandlingCost = 2.00   'handling cost

    Select Case strShippingMethod
       Case "Overnight"
          dblShippingCost = dblWeight * 6
       Case "2nd Day"
```

```
            dblShippingCost = dblWeight * 4
    Case "Regular Mail"
            dblShippingCost = dblWeight * 1.5
        End Select

    CalculateShippingCost = dblHandlingCost + dblShippingCost

    End Function

    <WebMethod()> Public Function RetrieveShippingMethods() As String

    RetrieveShippingMethods = "Overnight, 2nd Day, Regular Mail"

    End Function

End Class
```

Notice that the first line describes details about the fact that this is a web service, the language being used, and the name of the class. In this case, the web service is being created with Visual Basic.NET, although it could have just as easily been created using C#. Next are the `imports` statements that reference the namespaces (libraries) being used later in the code. Following the `imports` statements is the `public class` declaration and then the declaration for our two functions: `CalculateShippingCost` and `RetrieveShippingMethods`.

On first glance, this doesn't look a whole lot different to a typical Visual Basic.NET class, does it? The few differences that actually make this a web service instead of just a traditional class module are shown highlighted below.

The first difference is with the first line of code:

```
<%@ WebService Language="VB" Class="ShippingService" %>
```

A traditional class module would not need this line of code, which identifies this class as a web service.

The second difference is in the namespaces that are imported:

```
Imports System.Web.Services
Imports Microsoft.VisualBasic
```

Only web services need to import the `System.Web.Services` namespace to make use of its functionality.

The third difference is in the class declaration:

```
Public Class ShippingService
```

To be a web service, the class must be declared as public. Traditional class modules are not required to be public.

The fourth difference is that directly following the public class declaration, an `inherits` statement is included to inherit all the functionality of the `System.Web.Services.WebService` namespace:

```
Inherits System.Web.Services.WebService
```

The final difference from a traditional class module is in the function declarations, such as here:

```
<WebMethod()> Public Function CalculateShippingCost(ByVal_
    dblWeight as double, ByVal strShippingMethod as String) As Double

    Dim dblHandlingCost as Double
    Dim dblShippingCost as Double

    dblHandlingCost = 2.00   'handling cost

    Select Case strShippingMethod
      Case "Overnight"
        dblShippingCost = dblWeight * 6
      Case "2nd Day"
        dblShippingCost = dblWeight * 4
      Case "Regular Mail"
        dblShippingCost = dblWeight * 1.5
    End Select

    CalculateShippingCost = dblHandlingCost + dblShippingCost

    End Function
```

and here:

```
<WebMethod()> Public Function RetrieveShippingMethods() As String
    RetrieveShippingMethods = "Overnight, 2nd Day, Regular Mail"

    End Function

End Class
```

Notice how the <WebMethod()> prefix precedes the Public Function declaration. This identifies each function as a web method that will be exposed in the web service. Private methods can also be in the web service, but only the public web methods will be exposed in the web service. To use a private method in a web service, do not include the WebMethod() declaration and declare it as a Private Function.

Those are the only differences between a web service and a regular class module that is not a web service. Now that we have the text for our web service created, let's learn how to run and test it out.

Running and Testing your Web Service

If you open up a web browser and type the URL to the web server where the `CalculateShipping.asmx` file you just created is located, a screen similar to the one below will appear:

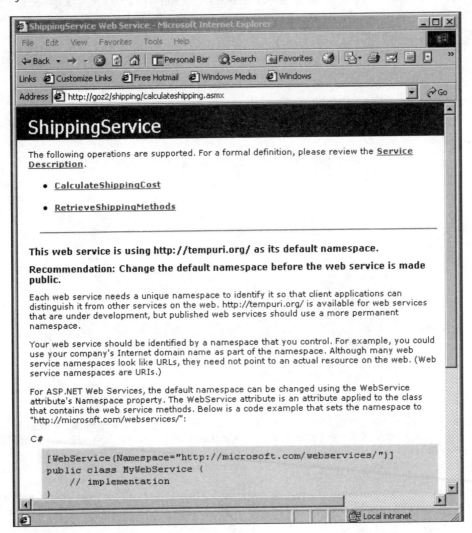

Notice at the top of the browser how the Shipping Service is being described and the two methods it supports (CalculateShippingCost and RetrieveShippingMethods) are listed; at the bottom of the screen is some helpful information reminding us to change the default namespace. All we did was create the `.asmx` file with our web service code and browsed to its location and we can see information about it. Next, click on the CalculateShippingCost hyperlink and you will see a screen similar to this:

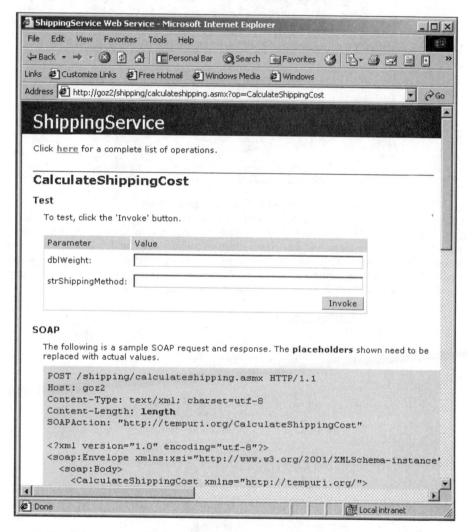

At the top portion of the screen notice how the dblWeight and strShippingMethod parameters are specified followed by an Invoke button. This actually allows you to test your own web service and see if it is working, or to test the web service of someone else to see how it works. Then, in the bottom portion of the screen there is an example of the SOAP, HTTP-GET, and HTTP-POST formats that can be used to invoke the web service.

Fill in a value of 5 for the dblWeight field and Overnight (case-sensitive) for the strShippingMethod field. Then, click the Invoke button and a screen similar to the following will appear:

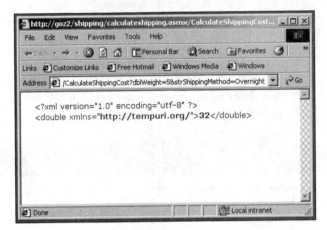

The response from our web service is displayed in XML, as shown above. We see that the ShippingCost being returned is 32, which is correct based on the formula we created for calculating shipping costs. This is a very powerful tool within the .NET Framework for testing your web services and the web services of others, as well as for learning how to invoke them. Another great feature provided by the .NET Framework is allowing you to view the web services contract (the WSDL document) associated with a given web service so that you will know even more details about how to communicate with it. To view the web services contract for our shipping service, all you have to do is append ?WSDL to the end of the original URL, like that shown below:

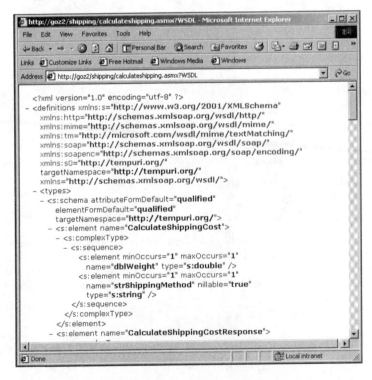

Note that you need a browser capable of viewing XML documents (such as Internet Explorer 6) in order to see this document. Does this document above look familiar? This is the exact same WSDL document we briefly looked at (in a much-abbreviated form) in the WSDL section in the beginning of this chapter. Remember in that section how you were instructed not to worry too much about the details of how to create a WSDL document? Well, in this instance, the .NET Framework automatically created one for us by interpreting the asmx file when we accessed the hyperlink with the ?WSDL parameter at the end.

Creating a Web Service with Visual Studio.NET

In this section, we will create the same ShippingService web service using Visual Studio.NET. In the process, we will see the advantages to using the Visual Studio.NET development environment to create web services, instead of just a simple text editor like Notepad.

Creating the ShippingService Web Service in Visual Basic.NET

In the previous section, we created the ShippingService web service in Notepad, and named the file CalculateShipping.asmx. Now let's walk through the steps of creating that exact same web service using Visual Studio.NET.

Open Visual Studio.NET and select File | New | Project. In the New Project dialog box, do the following:

❑ Select Visual Basic Projects (since our previous one was created with Visual Basic).

❑ Select the ASP.NET Web Service icon in the Templates list.

❑ In the Name field, type ShippingService.

❑ In the Location field, choose the web server where the service should be created. If you want to put the web service on your local development machine, this value might be http://localhost.

An example of what the screen looks like is shown below:

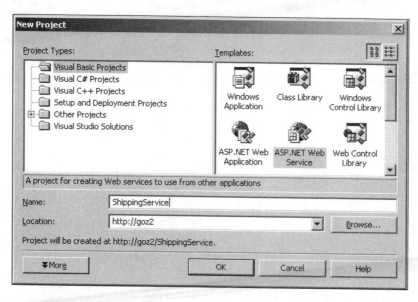

After filling in all the necessary information in the **New Project** dialog box, click the **OK** button. Visual Studio.NET creates a web service project for you and when finished, displays the .asmx file in Design View, as shown below:

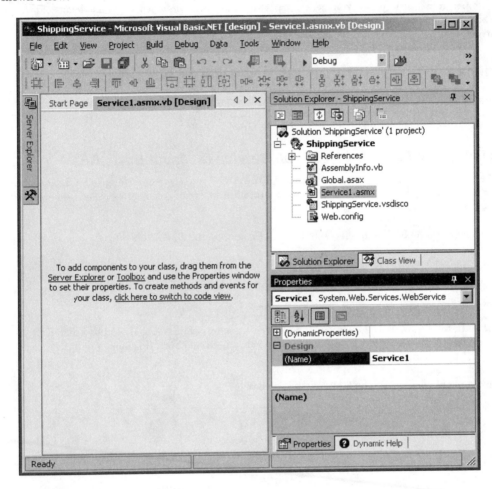

We need to change a few things, so do the following:

- ❑ In the Properties window, where it says Service1 System.Web.Services.WebService, change the name property from Service1 to ShippingService.

- ❑ In the Solution Explorer, select Service1.asmx, right-click, select Rename, and change the name of the file to CalculateShipping.asmx.

- ❑ Again in the Solution Explorer, select CalculateShipping.asmx, right-click, and select View Code on the shortcut menu. A screen with a code template for your new web service will be displayed, like the following:

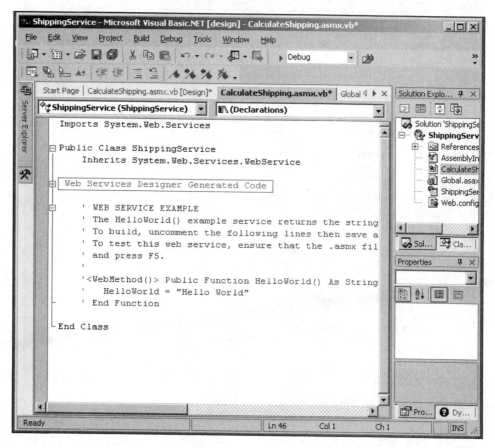

Fill in the missing code sections by adding the `Imports Microsoft.VisualBasic` statement and the `CalculateShippingCosts` and `RetrieveShippingMethods` functions. You can also delete the `Hello World` example that is commented out and being displayed for sample purposes only. Your final version should look as follows:

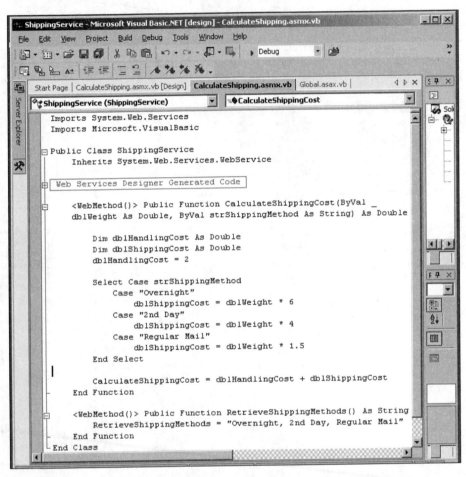

Notice that the `CalculateShippingCost` function declaration above has a line continuation character (_) in it. Further notice on screen how the keywords appear in blue and visually indicate that they are correct. As you type, IntelliSense will assist you by showing, for example, methods and properties that are available for a given object. These are just a few examples of the benefits of using Visual Studio.NET to develop your web service versus Notepad or other text editors. To demonstrate this, type something in the code window that you know isn't programmatically correct (such as your name) and see how it underlines the code and visually indicates a syntax error. Then make sure you remove the offending code.

It is now time to save our work, so select File | Save All. We now need to compile our code, so select File | Build and Browse to build the project and display it in a web browser. Visual Studio.NET will display the integrated web browser within the development environment. Your ShippingService web service will be displayed in the web browser if there were no errors:

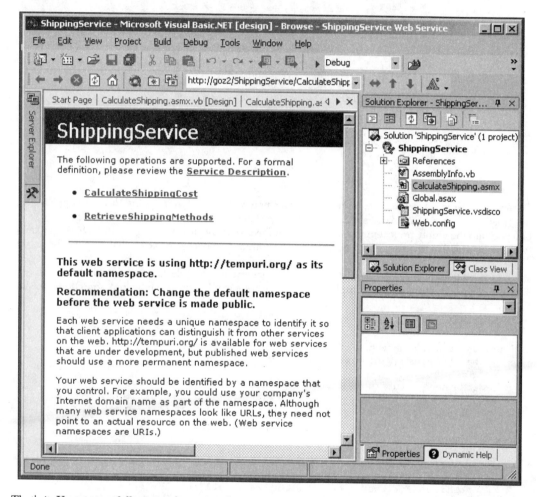

That's it. You successfully created a new web service using Visual Studio.NET. Now let's take a look at how to modify an existing class module into a web service.

Creating a Web Service from an Existing Class Module in Visual Studio.NET

We already learned earlier that there are only a few differences between a typical class module and a web service class module. However, to further demonstrate how easy it is to turn an existing class module into a web service, we'll quickly look at another example to solidify this concept in your mind.

Suppose that you have a class module that contains a function for calculating monthly mortgage payments based on principal, interest rate, and number of payments to be made. Further suppose that the fully-functional code for the class module looks like this in Visual Basic.NET code:

```
Public Class clsMortgageCalc

    Public Function CalculateMonthlyPayment(ByVal intNumPayments As_
                Integer, ByVal dblAnnualInterest As Double,_
                ByVal dblPrincipal As Double) As Double

        Dim dblTemp As Double
        Dim dblMonthlyInterest As Double

        dblAnnualInterest = dblAnnualInterest / 100
        dblMonthlyInterest = dblAnnualInterest / 12
        dblTemp = Math.Exp(intNumPayments * Math.Log(1 + dblMonthlyInterest))
        CalculateMonthlyPayment = (12 * dblMonthlyInterest * dblPrincipal *_
                        dblTemp) / (12 * (dblTemp - 1))

    End Function

End Class
```

To turn this class into a web service, we first create an empty web service project using Visual Studio.NET as described in the prior `ShippingService` web service example, then copy the `CalculateMonthlyPayment` function into the empty project in the Code View of the `.asmx` file (overwriting the `Hello World` template text). Make sure that the `Class` and `Function` are both declared as `Public` so that they will be accessible.

We now need to modify the `CalculateMonthlyPayment` function declaration to include the `<WebMethod()>` attribute. The complete code in the code window should now look something like this:

```
Imports System.Web.Services

Public Class MortgageCalc
    Inherits System.Web.Services.WebService

    <WebMethod()> Public Function CalculateMonthlyPayment(ByVal _
                intNumPayments As Integer, ByVal dblAnnualInterest As _
                Double, ByVal dblPrincipal As Double) As Double

        Dim dblTemp As Double
        Dim dblMonthlyInterest As Double

        dblAnnualInterest = dblAnnualInterest / 100
        dblMonthlyInterest = dblAnnualInterest / 12
        dblTemp = Math.Exp(intNumPayments * Math.Log(1 + dblMonthlyInterest))
        CalculateMonthlyPayment = (12 * dblMonthlyInterest * dblPrincipal * _
                        dblTemp) / (12 * (dblTemp - 1))

    End Function

End Class
```

Now save your work and let's test this web service to see how it works. To test it, from the `Debug` window, select **Start** (or hit *F5* on the keyboard). This will open the web service in the browser and will show the interface that allows you to test it, as shown on the next page:

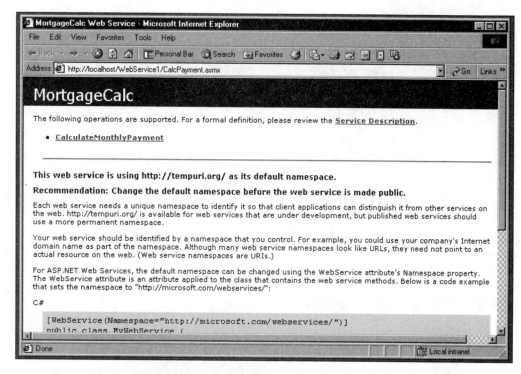

Click on the CalculateMonthlyPayment hyperlink and the screen with the web service parameters appears. Type in the values for the web service as shown below:

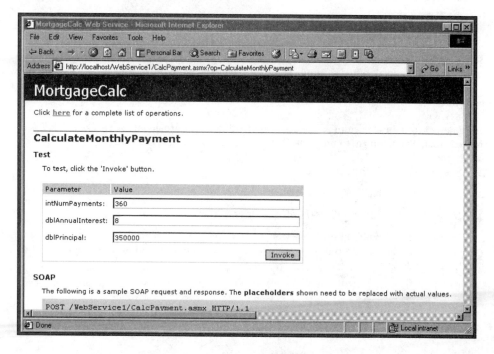

In this example, we want to find out what our monthly payment would be to borrow $350,000 at 8% for 30 years (360 payments). The following results should be displayed:

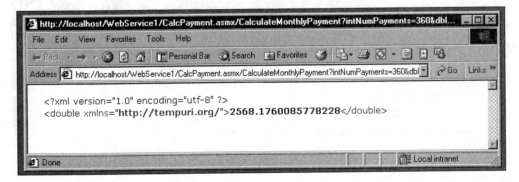

Well, it looks like that new house is going to cost you $2568+ per month. It's pretty amazing that this is all you had to do in order to create a web service out of the existing mortgage class in Visual Studio.NET.

Consuming a Web Service

There are multiple tools you can use to create the code to consume a web service: from Visual Studio, from text editors like Notepad, from a web browser by passing the parameters in the URL, and so on. In this section we will explore some of these in more detail.

Consuming a Web Service from Clients created using Visual Studio.NET

This time, let's create a traditional web application using Visual C#, instead of Visual Basic.NET, to consume our ShippingService. This web application will have textboxes to allow the user to input the weight of the package and the shipping method desired. Then, after clicking a button, a call will be made to our web service and the shipping cost returned from it will be displayed on the screen. Let's get started with making this happen.

Starting a new project in C# is almost the same as creating a new project in Visual Basic.NET – the only difference is that, when you get to the New Project dialog box, do the following:

❑ Select Visual C# Projects.

❑ Select the ASP.NET Web Application icon in the Templates list.

❑ In the Name field, type ShippingConsumer.

❑ In the Location field, choose the web server where the web application consumer should be created. If you want to put it on your local development machine, this value might be http://localhost.

An example of what the screen looks like is shown below:

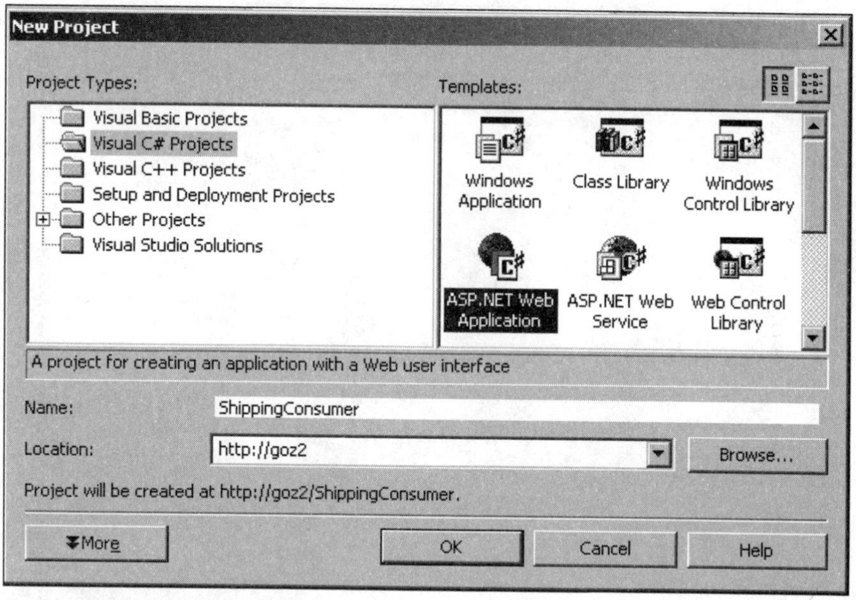

After filling in all the necessary information on the New Project dialog box, click the OK button. Visual Studio.NET creates a web application project for you and when finished, displays the result. In the Solution Explorer, rename WebForm1.aspx to ShippingConsumer.aspx.

The next bit is slightly different, as we need to add items to the form so that the consumer can use them! Here is what to do:

- ❏ Using the toolbox, place two textboxes on the form. \

- ❏ In the Properties Window for each textbox, set the (ID) to txtWeight and txtShipMethod, respectively.

- ❏ Using the toolbox, place four labels on the form and set their text properties to: Calculate Shipping Costs, $0, Weight, and Shipping Method.

- ❏ Add a button to the form, then, in the Property Window for the button, change the text to Calculate.

- ❏ In the Properties Window for the label that says $0, change the (ID) to lblShippingCost. Also, change the ForeColor property of the label to Red to make it stand out better. This label is where we are going to show the shipping cost results that get returned from the web service, so it needs to have a meaningful name.

An example of what the form should look like at this point is shown below:

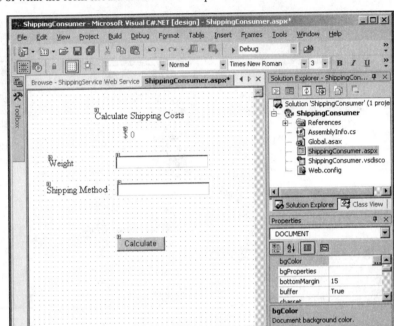

Now that we have the basic user interface for our web application, we are ready to add a reference to the `ShippingService` web service that we created earlier. To do so, select Project | Add Web Reference. The screen below will appear:

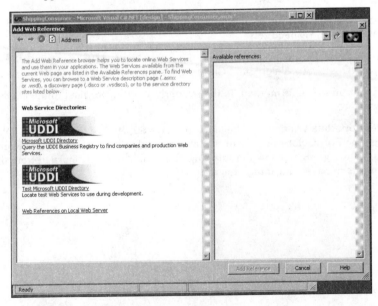

This screen allows you to discover web services that are available. You could search the UDDI Business Registry for web services from here, specify a URL to a web site that you think contains DISCO documents, specify an explicit URL to a `.asmx` or `.disco` file, or simply have it discover the web services on your local web server. In our situation, we are going to click the hyperlink to have it discover web services on our local web server.

After clicking on the hyperlink to have it discover web services locally, the right pane will list all of the available web services on the local machine:

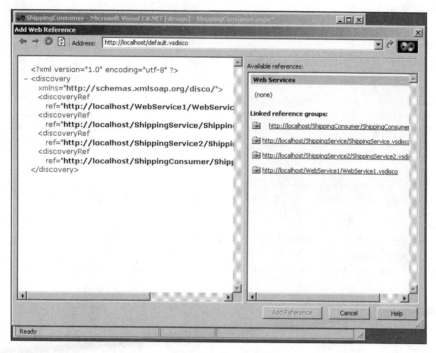

Scroll down the list under Linked Reference Groups until you find the ShippingService that you created earlier (it will probably say something like ShippingService.vsdisco). Click on the hyperlink to it so that you can see the details about it. Then, click the Add Reference button, which should now be enabled, to add a reference to the ShippingService web service to our C# web project.

After Visual Studio.NET does some thinking, a Web References node will be added to the Solution Explorer. If you expand the Web References node, you will probably see LocalHost as the reference, as shown below:

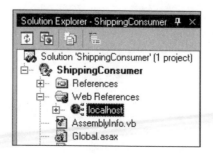

Right-click on localhost and select Rename to rename LocalHost to ShippingService, which is a more meaningful name that we will use later in our code.

Next, we need to double-click on the Calculate button to open the code window. You should be taken to the click event of the Calculate button, and it is there you need to add the following code (noting that it is Case Sensitive):

```
private void Button1_Click(object sender, System.EventArgs e)
{
ShippingService.ShippingService wsShip = new ShippingService.ShippingService();
double dblPkgWeight = Convert.ToDouble(txtWeight.Text);
string strShipMethod = Convert.ToString(txtShipMethod.Text);
double dblShipCost = wsShip.CalculateShippingCost(dblPkgWeight, strShipMethod);
lblShippingCost.Text = "$ " + dblShipCost;
}
```

The first line declares a new instance of our ShippingService. Then, the values in the textboxes for Weight and ShipMethod are converted to double and string variables, respectively. The next line declares a new double to hold the results of the web service call, plus it actually invokes the web service CalculateShippingCost method. The last line of code sets the results of the web service to the Label, so that the user will see the results.

Now we need to save our work by selecting File | Save All. Again, we need to compile our code, so select Build | Build. If the code doesn't compile, resolve any typographical errors and continue building the project until it compiles.

Once the project compiles, select File | Build | Browse. After a short delay, Visual Studio will display your user interface in the integrated web browser. As an alternative, you can also open your complete web browser and specify the path to the .aspx file and run it that way, as shown below:

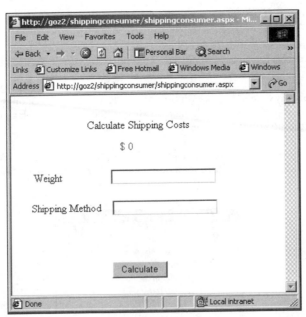

From the user interface, specify a value of 5 for the weight and Overnight (which is case-sensitive) for the Shipping Method, as shown below:

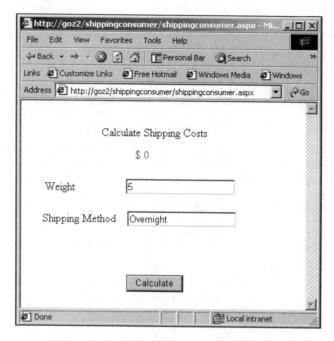

Click the Calculate button. The `ShippingService` gets invoked (consumed) and the results are translated behind the scenes, from the XML that the web service returned, into the format that is actually displayed on the screen:

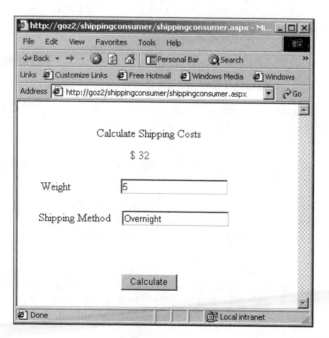

Notice how the screen is updated to reflect a shipping cost of $32, as returned by the web service. Note that if the web service didn't exist or was unavailable at the time, you would see a message in the browser generated by the .NET Framework indicating that an error occurred on the line calling the web service.

Congratulations! You have now built and consumed a web service using Visual Studio! In this example, we created a WebForms application to consume the web service. We could have just as easily created a Windows Forms or Console application using Visual Studio to consume the same web service.

Consuming a Web Service from Clients created with Text Editors such as Notepad

It is important to point out that when you added a reference to the web service, Visual Studio.NET did a lot of work behind the scenes for you and created what is called a **Web Service Proxy DLL Class**. This proxy class contains details about the methods available for a given web service. Each method in the class then contains the appropriate marshaling code and network invocation to invoke and receive a response from the remote Web Service method. You can think of this as the way to early bind to a web service in your code.

If you were simply using Notepad or another text editor to create the `.aspx` web application file to consume the web service, then there are some extra steps that you would have to take to bind to the web service. In brief, those steps include:

❑ Creating the Web Service Proxy Class DLL manually using the `WSDL.exe` command line tool. Here is an example of creating a namespace called nsShippingService for the ShippingService web service:

```
wsdl.exe /language:VB /out:nsShippingService ↵
http://localhost/ShippingService/CalculateShipping.asmx
```

❑ Adding a line of code in your `.aspx` file (which in our case happened to be created with C#) to import the namespace of the Web Service Proxy Class DLL.

❑ Adding the lines of code to declare an instance of the Web Service Proxy Class DLL and to invoke its methods.

Consuming a Web Service using HTTP-GET

There is another way to consume web services without adding a reference (either manually or by using Visual Studio.NET): that method is by explicitly passing parameters in a URL calling a web service, like that shown below:

```
http://localhost/shipping/calculateshipping.asmx/CalculateShippingCost?dblWeight↵
=5&strShippingMethod=Overnight
```

This is using the HTTP-GET method to pass parameters in the URL. If you simply type this information in a web browser or call it from within a program, the results will be displayed as XML. If you are calling this from within a program, you might want to apply a style sheet (XSLT) to the XML document to format it in a meaningful way for the reader.

Note that, using this method, there is no need to create the proxy DLL class since you are invoking the web service explicitly in the URL. From within a program, the compiler has no knowledge at compile time that this URL is actually a web service. You can sort of think of this like late-binding to the web service and the prior two methods as early binding to the web service.

Beyond the Basics

In this section, we will look at some more advanced concepts of web services, such as design considerations, transactions in web services, asynchronously calling web services, and SOAP extensions.

Design Considerations

There are some design considerations you should keep in mind when building web services.

Using Descriptions to Document your Web Service

Recall that earlier we converted the Monthly Payment Mortgage Calculator into a web service. If we were to use the testing tool to view information about that web service, it would look something like this:

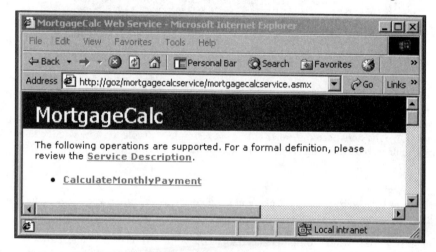

In the example above, the `CalculateMonthlyPayment` method contains no explanation of some sample values it expects and returns or the details about what it does. The `WebMethod` attribute accepts a `Description` parameter that should be used to describe each `WebMethod` that you create. You can use the `WebMethod` attribute to describe in plain English what you want someone to know about your web service method. For example, suppose that we modify the `mortgagecalcservice.asmx` file so that the `WebMethod` attribute declaration contains this description:

```
<WebMethod(Description:="Calculates the Monthly Mortgage Payment --- Example:
Suppose you want to borrow $100,000 at 8% for 30 years.  The parameters will look
like this --- intNumPayment: 360 (12 X 30 years is 360 payments);
dblAnnualInterest:  8 (for 8%); dblPrincipal: 100000 (for $100,000)")>
    Public Function CalculateMonthlyPayment(ByVal intNumPayments As Integer, ByVal
dblAnnualInterest As Double, ByVal dblPrincipal As Double) As Double
```

Then, suppose you saved your changes to the file and re-ran it in the web browser testing tool. What is the effect of adding this description? Let's have a look:

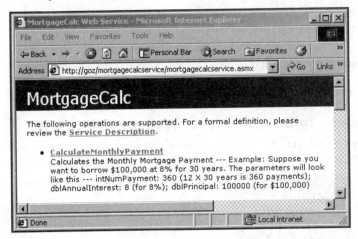

Notice how now the CalculateMonthlyPayment method is described in much more detail with examples of parameters that can be passed in and what exactly they mean. Without this description, would you have realized that the interest rate should be in the format people talk about it versus the mathematical representation of a percent (8 versus .08)? You may not have realized it until you tested the web service and tried to track down the unexpected results. This is just a simple example to show you the importance of documenting your web service using the Description of the WebMethod attribute.

Security

You enforce security in web services just like you would do with any other web application. Let's take a quick look at what some of these options are.

First, if you know exactly which computers need to access your web service, you can always use a firewall to restrict access to known IP addresses. In most scenarios, however, you will not know the IP address of the computers that need to access your web service. Thus, in those situations, you can take advantage of the authentication methods associated with the protocols being used, such as HTTP. Internet Information Services (IIS) supports several authentication methods for HTTP:

- ❏ Anonymous – allows anonymous users access without authentication, thus providing virtually no security.

- ❏ Basic – information sent in plain text, thus no good for applications that need higher levels of security.

- ❏ Basic over SSL – same as Basic, except the username and password are sent encrypted using Secure Sockets Layer (SSL). This authentication method is slower than anonymous and basic methods due to the extra effort involved in encrypting the content.

- ❏ Digest – transmits username and password using hashing. However, not widely supported on platforms other than Microsoft Windows.

- ❏ Integrated Windows Authentication (formerly called Windows NT Challenge/Response) – uses NTLM or Kerberos security methods to determine whether the user has a valid user account on the domain. Works only in Internet Explorer.

- ❏ Client Certificates – each client must obtain a certificate, which is then mapped to their user account.

To take advantage of these authentication methods, you open Internet Information Services, browse to the directory where your web service is located, right-click on **Properties**, and select the **Directory Security** tab. From the **Directory Security** tab, click the **Edit** button to view and modify security levels for that particular directory where the web service is located.

Another option for securing web services might include implementing security on your own such as by having credentials passed in as parameters or as part of the message sent to the web service. In such a case, however, you will have to create your own logic (such as looking up in a database) to translate and validate the credentials.

Additionally, a .NET Web Service Proxy DLL Class (such as the one automatically created behind the scenes by Visual Studio.NET, or one created manually using `WSDL.exe`,) contains properties called `Username`, `Password`, and `Domain`. Thus, a client application can set these properties and pass them in to the web service.

Another possibility is to use the Microsoft Passport service to validate users. This can work great in the instances when individuals use web services, but it may be the case that another system (independent of the user) is calling the web service. Passport is not necessarily the best solution in the latter scenario, because a particular application or server would not have a Passport account. There may be ways around this issue, but it's something to keep in mind when considering Passport.

These are just some examples of the many possible ways to go about securing your web services. Hopefully, there are enough ideas here to help you determine your security approach.

Managing State

Web Services are typically stateless. What this means is that once the web service is invoked, a new instance is created and then destroyed at the end. The result of one invocation of the web service is not available to the next one. This stateless model works fine in scenarios where the service always performs the same action without caring about the result of carrying out that same action for someone else. A perfect example of this might be our Shipping Service and our Mortgage Calculator service. From one call to the next, it doesn't make any difference what shipping method the prior person chose and what the package weight was. Nor does it make any difference with our mortgage calculator what parameters the previous user specified. These are stateless web services in the truest sense.

There can be times, however, when it would be helpful to be able to retain certain bits of information across invocations of the web service. In such cases, ASP.NET provides you with the ability to use Session and Application State variables to store certain bits of information. The web service is still created and destroyed just like before, but the only difference is that now some information is being stored in these State variables that the web service can access. Session State variables live for the entire session of that particular user and only contain information provided by that user. A great example of using Session State variables is for keeping track of a shopping cart in an e-commerce application. The Application State variables, on the other hand, are available to every user in the application and not just to a particular user – that is, they are available to the entire application.

These state variables are implemented in ASP.NET using the `Cache` object. This allows you to keep an object in memory across HTTP requests, with its lifetime tied to that of the application. The `Cache` object is recreated with each instance of the application. Here is one example of a Visual Basic.NET syntax that can be used to add and retrieve information from the cache:

```
cache.insert("KeyName", ValueOfTheObject)
strSomeLocalVariable = cache("KeyName")
```

For example, if you want to insert a value containing the person's first name for personalization, it might look like the following:

```
cache.insert("FirstName", "Denise")
```

Then, if you wanted to retrieve the FirstName from the Cache into a local variable, it would look something like this:

```
strFirstName = cache("FirstName")
```

When designing web services, you should avoid using the state variables unless you need them, because they take up resources and may slightly impact application performance. If you do need them, however, they are definitely available for you to take advantage of.

Transactions in Web Services

A very useful feature of ASP.NET web services is the ability to participate in transactions. The transaction model for ASP.NET web services is based on the same transaction model of MTS and COM+. When a web service participates in a transaction and the method executes without errors, the transaction is automatically committed. On the other hand, when an error occurs in the method, the transaction is automatically rolled back.

Let's walk through an example to see how to take an existing web service and modify it to participate in transactions. Suppose that you have a web service called CustomersService.asmx that updates data in the Northwind sample database that you want to modify to participate in transactions. That web service currently looks like this:

```
<%@ WebService Language="VB" Class="Customers" %>
Imports System
Imports System.Data
Imports System.Data.SqlClient
Imports System.Web.Services

Public Class Customers
    Inherits System.Web.Services.WebService

    <WebMethod()> _
        Public Function UpdateCustAddress(ByVal strCustID As String,_
            ByVal strCustAddr As String, ByVal strCustCity As String,_
            ByVal strCustState As String, ByVal intCustZip As Integer)_
            As Integer

        Dim UpdateCmd As String = "Update Customers SET Address = '"_
            & strCustAddr & "', " & "City = '" & strCustCity &_
            "', Region = '" & strCustState & "', PostalCode = " & _
            intCustZip & " WHERE CustomerId = '" & strCustID & "'"

        Dim sqlconn As New SqlConnection("user _
            id=sa;password=pwd;database=northwind;server=goz")
        Dim sqlcomm As New SqlCommand(UpdateCmd, sqlconn)

        sqlcomm.Connection.Open()
        Return sqlcomm.ExecuteNonQuery()

    End Function

End Class
```

The above `Customers` web service contains one method, `UpdateCustAddress`, that updates the address of the customer based on the parameters passed to it. Now, let's take a look at how you can modify this web service to make it transactional. The process is really pretty easy. There are three simple elements that need to be added to your web service code in order to make it transactional:

❑ Adding an assembly directive to `System.EnterpriseServices`

❑ Adding a reference to the `System.EnterpriseServices` namespace

❑ In the declaration of the web service method, setting the `TransactionOption` property of the `WebMethod` attribute to `TransactionOption.RequiresNew`

So, if we modify our `CustomersService.asmx` file to make it transactional, it now looks like this:

```
<%@ Webservice Language="VB" Class="Customers" %>
<%@ Assembly name="System.EnterpriseServices" %>
Imports System
Imports System.Data
Imports System.Data.SqlClient
Imports System.Web.Services
Imports System.EnterpriseServices


Public Class Customers
    Inherits System.Web.Services.WebService

   <WebMethod(TransactionOption:=TransactionOption.RequiresNew)> _
       Public Function UpdateCustAddress(ByVal strCustID As String,_
           ByVal strCustAddr As String, ByVal strCustCity As String,_
           ByVal strCustState As String, ByVal intCustZip As Integer)_
           As Integer

        Dim UpdateCmd As String = "Update Customers SET Address = '" &_
           strCustAddr & "', " & "City = '" & strCustCity & "',_
           Region = '" & strCustState & "', PostalCode = " & _
           intCustZip & " WHERE CustomerId = '" & strCustID & "'"

        Dim sqlconn As New SqlConnection("user _
           id=sa;password=pwd;database=northwind;server=goz")
        Dim sqlcomm As New SqlCommand(UpdateCmd, sqlconn)

        sqlcomm.Connection.Open()
        Return sqlcomm.ExecuteNonQuery()

    End Function

End Class
```

Notice the three lines of code that were added as shown in the highlights: the assembly for `System.Enterprise` services, the reference importing `System.EnterpriseServices`, and the `TransactionOption` property of the `WebMethod` declaration. If an error occurs in the web service, ASP.NET automatically aborts the transaction, and if it is successful, it automatically commits. It is that simple to set up a web service to automatically be transactional! So let's move on to another great feature: calling web services asynchronously.

Calling Web Services Asynchronously

We learned earlier that when you add a Web Reference in Visual Studio it automatically generates the Web Service Proxy DLL Class for you. We also learned that you can manually generate the proxy class by using the WSDL.exe utility. A proxy class generated by either of these methods is capable of being called asynchronously – which means that you can perform other operations while waiting for the web service to respond. This can provide a huge performance improvement in web applications.

Luckily for us, no additional configuration is required in order to take advantage of calling web services asynchronously. The proxy class is capable of handling both synchronous and asynchronous calls.

Here is a C# example of how to implement an asynchronous callback:

```
private void button1_Click(object sender, System.EventArgs e)
{
    ServiceName.Service1 wsServiceName = new ServiceName.Service1();

    // cb is essentially a pointer to the CallbackService function below
    AsyncCallback cb = new AsyncCallback(CallbackService);

    // Call the Begin method of the proxy class to start the
    // asynchronous call to the Web Service method.
    wsServiceName.BeginLongProcess(txtInput.Text, cb, wsServiceName);
}

public void CallbackService(IAsyncResult ar)
{
    // Retrieve the original state for the proxy
    ServiceName.Service1 wsServiceName = (ServiceName.Service1)ar.AsyncState;

    // Get the web service results by calling the End method of proxy class
    txtOutput.Text = wsServiceName.EndLongProcess(ar);
}
```

Notice that a pointer is created to the CallbackService function so that the function will be called when the web service returns results. Then, when the web service returns, the result is displayed in a textbox called txtOutput and the process ends.

This is a basic introduction to how to create an asynchronous call to a web service. A more detailed explanation is beyond the scope of this chapter. However, you can find more information in the .NET documentation.

SOAP Extensions

The SOAP extension architecture in ASP.NET allows you to gain access to SOAP messages at specific points in time during the message processing. One example of what SOAP extensions might be useful for is implementing an encryption algorithm over the top of the web service call. Another example where SOAP extensions might be useful is for implementing a data conversion routine or a compression routine on the data going in or coming out of the web service.

ASP.NET SOAP extensions derive from the SoapExtension class. More information about implementing SOAP extensions can be found in the Visual Studio.NET online documentation or in a March 22, 2001 MSDN article called Fun with SOAP Extensions, located at the time of this book's writing at:
http://msdn.microsoft.com/library/default.asp?url=/library/en-us/dnaspnet/html/asp03222001.asp

What is Hailstorm?

You may have already heard about **Hailstorm** – the set of core off-the-shelf XML web services that Microsoft is in the process of developing at the time of this book's writing. The main objective behind Hailstorm is to put people in control of their information, to be able to access it from a variety of locations and devices, while protecting their personal information from unauthorized individuals. Hailstorm is based on the Passport authentication system, which authenticates you one time for all applications that utilize Passport. Hailstorm is initially expected to contain the set of web services listed below:

- ❑   myAddress – geographic and electronic address to identify me
- ❑   myApplicationSettings – my application settings
- ❑   myCalendar – my calendar and tasks
- ❑   myContacts – electronic address book
- ❑   myDevices – devices I have, their settings, and their capabilities
- ❑   myDocuments – document storage
- ❑   myFavoriteWebSites – my favorite URLs
- ❑   myInbox – my e-mail inbox
- ❑   myLocation – geographic and electronic location
- ❑   myNotifications – subscriptions, management and routing
- ❑   myProfile – name, nickname, picture, etc.
- ❑   myServices – services provided for an identity
- ❑   myUsage – usage of these other web services
- ❑   myWallet – coupons, payment instructions, receipts, etc.

Beta versions of some Hailstorm web services are available today, with the full release expected some time in 2002. We can expect other web services to be created beyond this initial set of offerings. In addition, many applications developed by others will be able to take advantage of these core services. Hailstorm is one example of off-the-shelf web services being developed by companies (in this case, by Microsoft).

Summary

In this chapter, we've certainly covered a lot of ground. We learned a lot about web services, how to create and consume them, and have really only scratched the surface of what web services can do. At this point, you should have a good understanding of:

❑   Web Services – reusable web components based on standard Internet protocols

❑   Communicating with web services using HTTP-GET, HTTP-POST, and SOAP web service wire formats

❑   Using the Web Service Description Language (WSDL) to describe a web service

❑   Discovering web services from the DISCO file

❑   Discovering web services from the UDDI Business Registry

❑   Creating a new web service from scratch using a text editor and from Visual Studio

❑   Using the built-in testing tool to view documentation and test a web service

❑   Creating the client code to consume a web service from Visual Studio, a text editor, and through a web browser

❑   Running the client code to consume the web service

❑   Web Service design considerations (documentation, security, and state)

❑   Making a web service transactional

❑   Creating asynchronous web services

❑   Using SOAP extensions to extend web services

❑   Microsoft Hailstorm – Microsoft's initial set of web service offerings centered around people allowing them convenient access to their information

The possibilities are truly exciting about where web services are going to take us technologically this is an exciting time to be a developer!

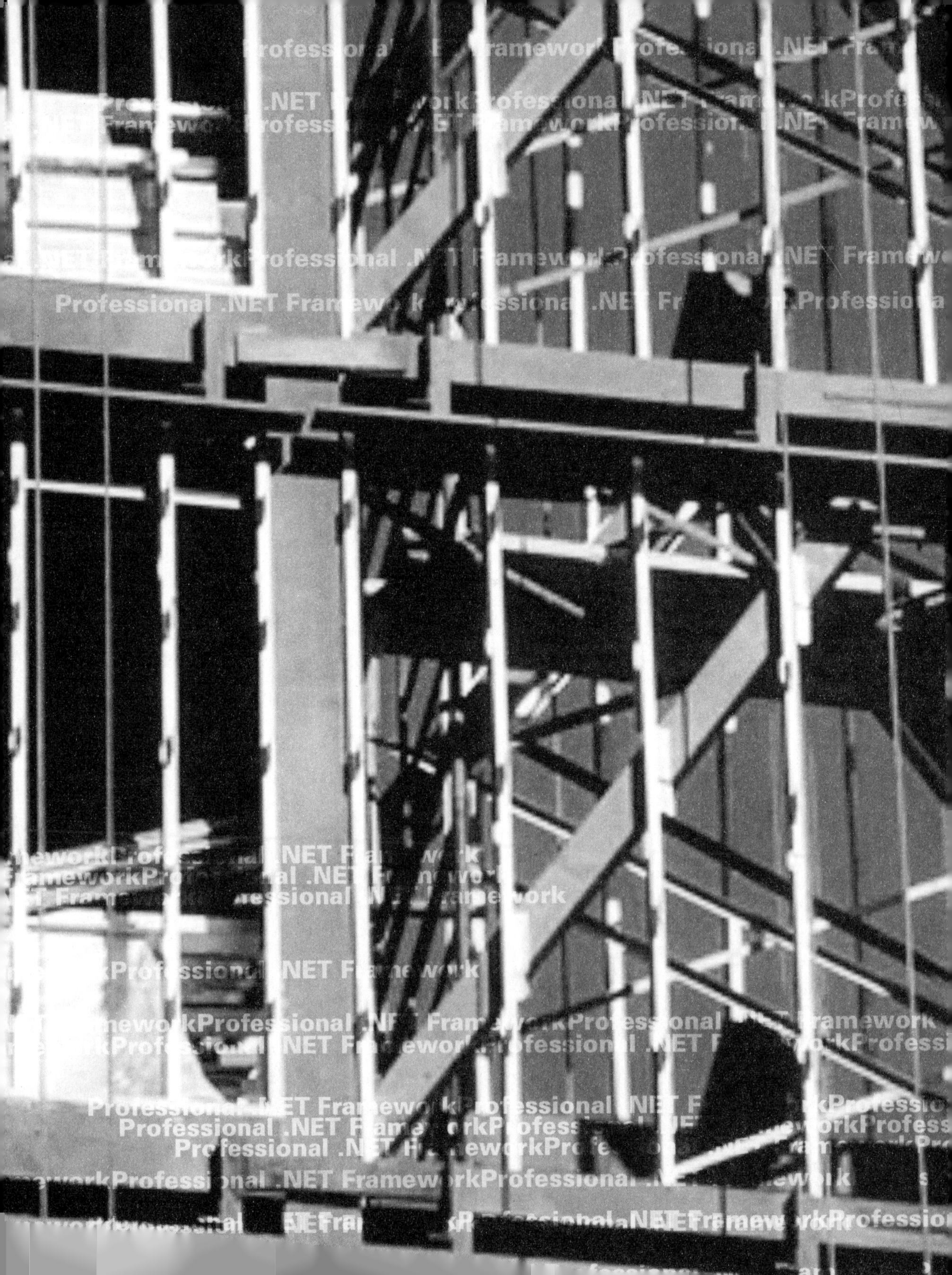
Professional .NET Framework

11

.NET Remoting: the New Infrastructure for Distributed Systems

What is Remoting? This is probably a very good question at this point, as Microsoft has really changed the rules of the game for creating distributed applications. The change is for the better, but there are a lot of new concepts to learn. If you have become accustomed to DCOM, Object Context, Object Control, and learning how to use IUnknown, you can still do everything you did before, but will have to learn a few new methods, and a bit of terminology.

In this chapter, I will be taking you through the basic architecture of .NET Remoting, and how you can use it in your applications. After we have had the opportunity to get introduced, we will begin to build an application that requires remote objects. This will hopefully bring you to the point of being able to use remoting where appropriate, and give you some sense of how you will make decisions about implementing remoting in your own applications. This chapter will not delve into Web Services, as these are covered in-depth in their own chapter of this book. If you are already familiar with Remoting from the .NET beta 1 framework, you will already know the concepts, but the namespace, class, and configuration changes are important. You can get up to speed by checking out the explanation of changes at the end of this chapter.

> Though I will point out the availability of other protocols and serialization methods in this chapter, I will be using the built-in serialization formats and protocols of the .NET Framework in my explanations and examples, namely, TCP/IP with binary SOAP, and HTTP with both binary and text-based SOAP. If you aren't sure this is relevant to you, then you can safely read on.

What is Remoting?

Okay, so what is Remoting? Remoting is the way in which inter-process communication is handled in .NET. When objects need to talk to one another, remoting is at work. You may interact with Remoting in your architecture when you want objects you have created to communicate with objects created on other servers, whether those servers reside within your own network as part of a scaling solution, or somewhere else in the world as hosts for objects that you do not own.

Let's take a step back and consider a few general concepts. Even if your application is running locally and dependent only on local objects, it must still work with the threads of execution of those objects helping it. If you need to call a method on a system service for instance, you cannot simply import the whole service into your application and run a method from it: you must insert a call into the running process and retrieve the result. Additionally, you cannot just insert such a thread from anywhere you want, or at any time. You will have to obey rules that help your object remain safe and effective as a participant with all the other processes currently managed by the operating system.

This sort of inter-process communication is handled with various threading models and marshaling. In a distributed application, the issue of process boundaries grows considerably. While you still have the threading models and marshaling, what if you want to "marshal" a thread to a server over the Internet: what rules will govern how you gain access to that object? How can you package an object so it will be transported properly over common protocols? In .NET, the concept of such boundaries is called **Application Domains**. In short, application domains are units of processing which isolate applications from each other, similar to notions of processes or threads of execution. If you want .NET-managed applications to communicate from one application domain to the next, remoting must be involved. Again, .NET Remoting is a framework that provides the necessary services to allow objects to interact with one another across application domains.

Rest assured, .NET Remoting is working under the covers during more mundane procedures, but we will concern ourselves with those times when we need to interact with Remoting to reap its benefits. The Remoting system will allow us to determine such things as the transportation protocol, the lifetime of objects, how those objects are created, and how messages between objects are packaged.

The Remoting system lets you easily choose between:

❑ TCP/IP, HTTP, or any other common or custom-built transport protocol

❑ XML/SOAP, Binary SOAP, or any other common or custom serialization format

❑ Server-activated or client-activated objects. Activation determines the lifetime of objects, and who will control that lifetime. A server-activated object's lifetime is controlled by the server, while the client controls a client-activated object.

These communication options can be handled at compile time with configuration files, or embedded in the program logic utilizing the `RemotingConfiguration` and `ChannelServices` classes.

If you are familiar with DCOM, you may be putting two and two together at this point, and recognizing the area in the .NET framework that remoting is attempting to fill. We will consider the similarities and difference with DCOM a bit later in the chapter. However, at this point we can say one thing: in the past you may not have had to think an awful lot about DCOM when developing distributed applications. In .NET, Remoting has not been abstracted away from the programmer to the same degree as DCOM. Mainly, this has been done to give you more control over the inter-process communication of your objects. The ability of the application architect to control communication at varying stages of the process is key to understanding the beauty of .NET Remoting.

When do I need Remoting?

I mentioned above that Remoting is at work more often than we need to concern ourselves with. Then it is appropriate to ask, "When should I involve myself with the object communication process?" To answer that question we should look at what is happening under the covers during communication.

When we talk about remote object communication we are talking about a server-hosted object which has some publicly exposed interface, and a client object which desires the functionality available from the hosted object. The client makes calls on the server object, and the message is carried along some transport mechanism. In this situation, the calling object either copies the server object to the client process, or makes calls on a stand-in for the object, which describes the object's public interface, known as a proxy, and receives the results of the call back on the transport mechanism. These types of calls are known as **pass-by-value** and **pass-by-reference** respectively. In this chapter we are concerned with making objects available by reference.

Consider that when you pass by value, the entirety of an object is carried across the wire to the client process, possibly carrying many methods that will not be required by the client. Conversely, if you pass by reference, every method called by the client must be marshaled anew. You can see that this will quickly affect your architectural decision making in a distributed application.

Marshaling by value is always desirable when calling an object within the same application domain. Such an object does not even require marshaling, and therefore will be very fast. Additionally, marshaling by value is excellent for dealing with simple return types that do not represent the state of the called object. It makes sense to return XML by value rather than returning an XMLReader object by reference if the recipient object doesn't need to affect the XML represented by the XMLReader in the original object. On the other hand, we may want to pass by reference if we want to affect the original object, such as passing an array by reference so it may be filled and returned for use. Or, marshaling by reference makes sense if the object we want to call cannot operate outside of its original location, such as an object that makes use of local operating system properties.

> Objects that will be marshaled by value implement the **ISerializable** interface, while those that should by marshaled by reference extend **System.MarshalByRefObject**.

Furthermore, when you make objects available for inter-process communication, you need to decide on whether an object may even be passed around outside a particular server, or even outside the current process. The point of all this is that .NET Remoting lets you configure the behavior of each of the steps in communication. So, in order to understand when you need to work with remoting, you need to think through how the steps in the communication process are going to affect performance, security, and object behavior. No surprise in this, right? Let's take moment then to look at some possible steps in your decision process.

Should this object be accessed remotely? Does this object have a fragile or complex internal state?	In other words, does the object depend on a number of properties that could not be determined outside its local domain? Are properties set upon activation that come from the local operating system, or are set by calls from other local objects? The greater the number of dependencies your object has on local environmental factors, the greater the likelihood it will be difficult or impossible to work with a copy of the object in a remote application domain. Such an object should be marshaled by reference. If the state of the object is such that, on the other hand, your object simply performs some standard operation based on input parameters, it is essentially stateless, and may be better off marshaled by value.
Can your object handle multiple threads of execution?	If your object is single threaded, how will it manage multiple calls on the local object? Certainly it can be done, but you may want to consider forcing such an object to be marshaled by value.
Is the object overly large, such that it will be expensive to copy to the client?	This would be a question best answered by your own knowledge of the size of the data pipe you will be transmitting upon. In general, most objects will be of a reasonable size for marshaling by value.
Is the object dependent on the local machine or process for information that will not be present in the client process?	This sounds similar to the question of state, but deals with a different issue of accessible objects. For instance, does your object call a database that is unreachable from the client process? If so, you will have to marshal your object by reference so that calls will actually occur in a domain where the database server exists.
Is the client making extensive use of the server object, such that multiple round trips will be required to complete the calls?	For instance, if your object is providing a calculation method from which a client will be looping through a data set and calculating numerous values, it would be best to provide a copy of the object to the client. On the other hand, a client that requires your calculation one time, before using that data, may not want to copy everything else that accompanies this method just for the single usage.

Is the server object only returning data, rather than actionable objects?	When an object is returning simple data collections, that are essentially complete "as is", there is no need to maintain a reference to the original object. Conversely, a data set that needs to be changed by the client will have to be passed by reference.
Should the object be created once and live forever?	If, during the creation of your object, you must make several expensive operations, it will be best to let the object live for a long time. For instance, if you retrieve numerous configuration settings from a file, and call a few objects to set the object's internal state, you don't want to repeat this operation again and again if you don't have to. In this case, it will be necessary to control lifetime carefully, such that your object is created once per client.
Should the object be created and destroyed every time it is needed?	If your object is simple to create, perhaps such that it maintains no state, or holds on to scarce resources such as database connections, you may want to kill this object as soon as the client is done with it. This need will have to be balanced with the expense of creating the object, including the expense of creating database connections.
Can several instances of the object be created and called repeatedly?	If an object is stateless, such that no properties are set for use at a later time, it may easily be executed numerous times without changing the outcome. This would be the case with an object that executes a query based on certain input parameters, and returns a recordset object. The query results are independent of any other execution of the object, and will be reliable each and every time they are requested, whether on a new instance of the object or the same object over and over.
Will the server object live behind a firewall, such that I should use HTTP, or will the object be created on an internal network?	If firewalls are preventing your object from executing methods, you may almost always route traffic out using HTTP. In any sane installation you will not be permitted to use RPC over the open internet. The presence of such obstacles will determine what protocols are acceptable.

Table continued on following page

Should the internal state of this object be passed outside a secure network DMZ? Should the calls to this object be encrypted?	If an object contains state data, such as a database connection string, it may be unwise to pass a copy of the object so the connection string property can be read. Instead, pass this object by reference and keep your database connection method private. You should also consider whether or not the parameters, or results, of a request will contain data that should not be read. This will come into play in making calls over networks where you are not sure who may be listening, such as the Internet or within a large corporation. If your calls shouldn't be read, then you will need to choose a protocol that supports encrypted packets.
Is there a range of ports that is acceptable to use in my network? Should I avoid using port 80, even for HTTP calls?	Since you may configure port usage in .NET Remoting, you should take the time to figure out which ports will be allowed on your corporate network, or that will make it through your firewall configuration. In classic DCOM, a range of ports had to be permitted; here you have the opportunity to make your network admin happy, and choose a specific port for each application, or set of applications. You may want to consider using non-standard ports for standard protocols to segregate traffic for a particular purpose, say browsing the Internet, from traffic intended for your object.

Simply put, .NET Remoting is the mechanism for relaying messages between application domains in the .NET Framework. Of course, that sentence is really a mouthful. To get at the *how* of the questions asked above, we should get into the architecture of the remoting system itself.

Overview of the Remoting Architecture

I have been throwing a lot of terms at you, even while explaining the basics of object communication. Now that you have some idea of the issues involved, we can look at how the remoting system intends to provide you with the tools to make the best decisions possible. In this section, we will look at the concepts of **Channels, Application Domains**, and **Application Contexts**, as this forms the basis for configuring your remote applications.

Channels

What is a Channel?

A channel is a transportation mechanism for messages. Just as when you tune into a particular television channel, you are setting your TV to receive information at that particular bandwidth range, you set your remote applications to talk over particular protocols and formats within the .NET Framework. If broadcast engineers will forgive me, I will take the TV analogy a bit further. If you want to receive HDTV, you need a TV that is configured (hardware in this case) to understand the HDTV encoding and decoding algorithms (CODEC), amongst other things. In .NET, a channel is a combination of **Channel Sinks**, called a **Sink Chain**, that provide for messages to be sent and received in a particular format with a particular protocol. A sink is a .NET type that provides information about the messages flowing between objects on the client and server.

The basic Channel Sinks can be understood in the following categories:

Formatter Sink	The sink that generates the necessary headers and serializes the message to the stream. Formatter sinks are generally the first sinks in a sink chain; however, it is possible to place other sinks first that can manipulate the message before serialization occurs. You may use the formatters included with .NET, or make your own.
User Sink	User-defined sinks may be used to write additional information to the headers or stream. However, the serialized message cannot be manipulated at this point.
Transport Sink	Transport sinks read and write messages to the stream. The client transport sink is the last sink on the client-side sink chain, providing information about the protocol used to send messages. This sink communicates directly with the server-side transport sink, the first sink in the server-side sink chain.

Taken together, a sink chain will provide the basic communication objects for your chosen channel. Depending on the format and transport method, a particular channel will include various sinks in the chain. Whether they reside on the client or the server, and whether they send or receive messages may further segment channels.

Two complete channels have been provided for you in the .NET framework: the `TcpChannel` and the `HttpChannel`. These channel types reside in the `System.Runtime.Remoting.Channels.Tcp` and `.Http` namespaces respectively. These channels provide types for both client and server channels that will both send and receive messages. In other words, you may implement channels of these types in your objects without dallying in too many of the details of implementing a channel interface. You may even use some of the individual sinks provided by the framework, such as the binary formatter sink.

> **Channels are an enormous subject, and have been treated here in a manner that helps us understand remoting only. If you want to get into the details of creating your own channel sinks, check into the .NET MSDN library articles entitled: Channel Sink Concepts, Channels, Sinks and Sink Chains, and IChannel Interface. Also, please note that MSDN references throughout are to the .NET-specific MSDN documentation installed with the .NET beta Visual Studio installation. Due to this, article reference numbers, or Internet URLs are not available at this time, but searching by article titles will be sufficient.**

Let me make a few final notes about channels before we move on, firstly regarding client and server channels.

Before your objects are able to communicate using remoting, a channel must be available in the framework's remoting configuration table. Channels are made available through a registration process handled by the `Configuration` class provided by the .NET framework. Both the server and client must have registered channels.

If a client wants to communicate with a server object, the client does not have to register a channel for sending. However, if the client application expects to receive a call back from the server object, that is you are getting an object or value in return, you must register a client-side listening channel that is compatible with the channel in use by the server. Calls to a server object, even from clients expecting a return value, can be made on any registered channel. The need for a compatible listener on the client is still necessary. A compatible channel is one that is using the same formatter sink and protocol, so that messages may be routed, serialized, and de-serialized. Secondly, the port that you choose to use for a particular channel registration may only be registered with one channel. The marriage of channel with port creates a unique transport path. If you have more than one object communicating on the same port, they will have to do so with the same channel. Also, if you do not wish to set a particular port, then simply enter the port as 0, and the remoting framework will provide an available port for the application. Of course, this last option leaves you open to random port assignment, which is often a headache in a distributed application.

Application Domains

Application Domains are the .NET implementation of execution boundaries for an application. Application Domains are not themselves specific to remoting, in that they are the mechanism for isolation within the entire framework. However, remoting is needed whenever such domains will be crossed by communication between objects. Whenever calls on objects occur across domain boundaries, remoting must get involved to make the call succeed. Domain boundaries are either set by the .NET Framework runtime hosts such as ASP.NET, Internet Explorer, or specifically by you when you create a new server host. The framework uses application domains as a way of isolating application processes. You may most easily think of operating system process isolation when referring to application domains, but there may be many processes within a single application domain. You should think of application domains as logical processes, where isolation occurs for managed code. Furthermore, the reasons for isolation, whether for OS processes or app domains, remain the same: safety, performance, and security. Application domains are created for you if you don't create them yourself, and we won't deal with configuring your own domain in this chapter, though you should be aware this is available to you through the `System.AppDomain` class.

The most common places in which you will communicate across application domains are:

❑ When you communicate across different servers. Objects created on different physical servers cannot be in the same application domain.

❑ When for safety or security reasons, you want an application to be isolated during execution. In this way, an application can fail without taking other processes down, or require that some internal state of the object not be copied outside the logical process.

The boundaries set by application domains protect objects from each other. For instance if a rogue object fails to use memory wisely and crashes, it will not bring the other objects outside its domain with it. For this you may want to force out questionable or potentially dangerous objects into some other domain, even when called locally.

A Very Simple Example

To understand something about application domains, let's take a look at two simple C# client objects, one that calls a method on an object being hosted remotely (though on the same machine), and the other that calls a similar method on an instance of an object that it creates. Though we don't want to become bogged down in remoting details at this time, I am going to show you a very simple host object called `SimpleHost` that registers a channel and hosts an object called `SimpleLibrary1`. The host object is a console application that contains references to the `System.Runtime.Remoting` library, and to `SimpleLibrary1`. `SimpleLibrary1` has one class, called `SimpleClass1`, which exposes the `remoteConcat` method. Similarly, another console application called `AppDomainTestClient1` references an object called `AppDomainTestLib1`, which exposes `localConcat()`.

If we look at a very simple diagram of the objects in their domains, you can see logically what our test is trying to prove.

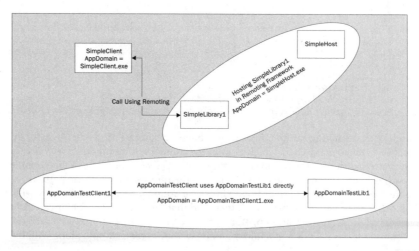

The two libraries, `SimpleLibrary1` and `AppDomainTestLib1`, perform the same function and have been created and compiled in the same way. Each has also been referenced in their respective client in a similar manner. However, the `SimpleClient` app is going to register the `SimpleLibrary1` type with the remoting framework, and look for an instance of the object through remoting. The result is that the application domain of the `SimpleLibrary` is that of its host. The application domain of the `AppDomainTestLib1` library is that of the client. Let's take a look at how this looks in the code.

To set up these examples, you can use the Visual Studio.NET IDE, or the great and powerful Notepad. Either way, we have five class files, as shown in the following table:

Object	Class File Name	Purpose
SimpleClient	Class1.cs	This is the remoting client sample that will call a method on `SimpleLibrary1`
SimpleHost	HostClass1.cs	This is the remoting host for `SimpleClass1`

Table continued on following page

Object	Class File Name	Purpose
SimpleLibrary1	SimpleClass1.cs	This is the library that provides the RemoteConcat function
AppDomainTestClient1	Client1.cs	This is the local client that makes use of AppDomainTestLib1
AppDomainTestLib1	Class1.cs	This is the local library that provides the LocalConcat function

Once you have each of the class files created, and filled with the code to follow, you may compile them with the C# command line compiler using the following directives:

```
csc /out:SimpleLibrary1.dll /t:library SimpleClass1.cs
        /r:System.Runtime.Remoting.dll
csc /out:SimpleClient.exe /t:exe Class1.cs /r:System.Runtime.Remoting.dll
        /r:SimpleLibrary1.dll
csc /out:SimpleHost.exe /t:exe HostClass1.cs /r:System.Runtime.Remoting.dll
        /r:SimpleLibrary1.dll
csc /out:AppDomainTest/AppDomainTestLib1.dll /t:library
        AppDomainTest\Class1.cs
csc /out:AppDomainTest/AppDomainTestClient1.exe /t:exe
        AppDomainTest\Client1.cs /r:AppDomainTest/AppDomainTestLib1.dll
```

Notice that each of the remoting sample objects must have a reference directive (/r:) for the System.Runtime.Remoting DLL, which lives in the framework install directory. This directory must be in your system path in order for the samples to compile correctly (if you can call the compiler command, your system path is fine). Also note that each client, and the remoting host, SimpleHost, has reference directives for the libraries that they use or host. This set of commands assumes that you will compile each client with the referenced library in the same folder, and that you have a sub folder called AppDomainTest for the AppDomainTestClient1 and AppDomainTestLib1 source files. A complete makefile.bat, plus all the required files, is included in a folder named MakeSimpleExample along with the download for this book.

Each class library will report its application domain, as will the client objects. First we will create the remoting host:

```
using System;
using System.Runtime.Remoting;
using System.Runtime.Remoting.Channels;
using System.Runtime.Remoting.Channels.Tcp;

namespace SimpleHost
{
    class HostClass1
    {
        static void Main(string[] args)
        {
            try
            {
                Console.WriteLine("Configuring Host...");
                TcpChannel chan = new TcpChannel(8085);
                ChannelServices.RegisterChannel(chan);
                Type thisType = Type.GetType
                    ("SimpleLibrary1.SimpleClass1,SimpleLibrary1");
```

We need to offer a type reference to the RemotingConfiguration system so that it can create a proper registration. The simplest way to get a type that is of type Type is call GetType with the full name of the class and the name of the assembly. As you may have learned in previous chapters, the assembly provides all necessary type information to the .NET Framework.

Having retrieved the type and placed it in the variable thisType, we can call the registration method for the host service.

```
RemotingConfiguration.RegisterWellKnownServiceType(thisType,
        "SimpleLibraryEndpoint",WellKnownObjectMode.SingleCall);
```

The RemotingConfiguration class contains methods for registering remote types within your code. The method we have used here, RegisterWellKnownServiceType, is specific to an object that will be hosted, and have its activation controlled by, the server. We will see other registration classes used for client registration, and for objects that will have their activation controlled by the client. Moving on, we catch any exceptions that occurred during registration, and write out a simple message to the console, which lets the user know that the host is ready to go.

```
            }
            catch(Exception theExcep)
            {
                Console.WriteLine ("ErrorOccurred: " + theExcep.Message + "
                                    Source: " + theExcep.Source);
            }
            Console.WriteLine ("Hit enter key to end hosting");
            int theEnd = Console.Read ();
        }
    }
}
```

You can see how easy it is to use the built-in framework channels. However, notice in this code that we have not specified an application domain, but have simply registered the SimpleLibary1 object with remoting via the RegisterWellKnownServiceType method of the RemotingConfiguration class.

The hosted object itself is also straightforward:

```
using System;
using System.Runtime.Remoting;
using System.Runtime.Remoting.Channels;
using System.Runtime.Remoting.Channels.Tcp;

namespace SimpleLibrary1
{
    public class SimpleClass1:MarshalByRefObject
    {
        public SimpleClass1()
        {
            Console.WriteLine("SimpleClass1 activated");
            //Get a reference to the current appdomain,
            //so we can display the friendly name.
            AppDomain app = System.Threading.Thread.GetDomain();
            Console.WriteLine("AppDomain: " + app.FriendlyName);
        }
```

```
        public string RemoteConcat(string string1, string string2)
        {
            return string1 + ":" + string2;
        }
    }
}
```

Here you will notice two things. Firstly, this class object extends `MarshalByRefObject`. We'll talk more about this later, but for now recognize this as the mechanism that makes it possible to remote this object. You should understand that is still possible to use this object locally, even if you extend `MarshalByRefObject`. Secondly, note the commented lines, which show how we are getting a reference to the `AppDomain` object, and then writing out one of its properties, `FriendlyName`.

```
AppDomain app = System.Threading.Thread.GetDomain();
Console.WriteLine("AppDomain: " + app.FriendlyName);
```

The `AppDomain` type provides methods and properties for you to interact with an application's `AppDomain`. We are using it here to show the `AppDomain` in which each object is currently executing. The `FriendlyName` property simply shows us a human-readable name for the `AppDomain`.

Finally, let's look at our simple client that calls the remote object and gets a concatenated return value.

```
using System;
using System.Runtime.Remoting;
using System.Runtime.Remoting.Channels;
using System.Runtime.Remoting.Channels.Tcp;

namespace SimpleClient
{
    class Class1
    {
        static void Main(string[] args)
        {
            if(args.Length < 2)
            {
                Console.WriteLine("Please provide 2 words as input parameters");
                return;
            }
            AppDomain app = System.Threading.Thread.GetDomain();
            Console.WriteLine("AppDomain: " + app.FriendlyName);
            TcpChannel chan = new TcpChannel();
            ChannelServices.RegisterChannel(chan);
            Type thisType = typeof(SimpleLibrary1.SimpleClass1);
            SimpleLibrary1.SimpleClass1 myService =
                        (SimpleLibrary1.SimpleClass1)
                        Activator.GetObject(thisType,
                        "tcp://localhost:8085/SimpleLibraryEndpoint");
```

For the client, we are able to obtain an object reference using the `Activator` class's method, `GetObject`. This method returns a proxy reference for a remote object that is already running as a Well Known object. Recall that we set up the host with a `RegisterWellKnownServiceType` method. It is important that the client use a method of obtaining references that is compatible with the registration method of the hosted object. We also need to know the name of the endpoint where the host is making the remote object available. The endpoint name given here, `SimpleLibraryEndpoint`, is exactly what was registered by the host. This name, however, has no other particular significance, and could as easily have been something like "foo".

We finish the remote client by calling the `RemoteConcat` method, and writing it to the console.

```
        // use appropriate interface to access object.
        string retData = myService.RemoteConcat (args[0], args[1]);
        Console.WriteLine("ReturnValue: " + retData);
        return;
    }
  }
}
```

Once you have each of the classes written and compiled, you will need to bring up a different command line to run the host, and each of the clients. You must execute the host first, before trying to run the remote client, `SimpleClient`. If you do not have a host for the referenced object, the host will offer a remoting exception that explains that the server has removed this object, or it cannot be found at the endpoint specified. If you are following along, go ahead and type SimpleHost at the command line opened for the host.

You may then call `SimpleLibrary1` from the client with any two parameters you choose. After execution we will see the following on the client side, where the current application domain is clearly the local executable itself, SimpleClient.exe:

```
C:\WINNT\System32\cmd.exe                                         _ □ ×

D:\my documents\Wrox\Remoting\SimpleClient\bin\Debug>simpleclient Wrox Rocks!
AppDomain: SimpleClient.exe
ReturnValue: Wrox:Rocks!

D:\my documents\Wrox\Remoting\SimpleClient\bin\Debug>
```

Over at the host, we should then see that both the host and the activated object occur in the application domain of the host.

```
D:\my documents\Wrox\Remoting\SimpleHost\bin\Debug\SimpleHost.exe    _ □ ×
Configuring Host...
Hit enter key to end hosting
SimpleClass1 activated
AppDomain: SimpleHost.exe
SimpleClass1 activated
AppDomain: SimpleHost.exe
```

When we execute the `AppDomainTestClient1`, which simply uses the new operator on the library class that it has referenced, we see the following output:

This shows clearly that the .NET Framework has created the instance of the library object within the application domain of the calling client application. This makes sense, as there is no reason the library object cannot be copied into the local domain. The programmer has not configured it this way, and the object is locally available.

Though it takes a bit of work to see application domains at work, I hope this helps you to get a feel for what the framework is doing under the covers. As you consider building your distributed applications in .NET, you will need to understand where different application domains will apply. You may then become involved in the communication process between domains, and properly configure your application to take advantage of the appropriate level of isolation. The last detail we will cover with application processes is the application context.

Application Contexts

An application context is at a finer level of granularity than the application domain. A single application running in one domain may have many contexts, each configured for different aspects of the application's objects. As in the example above, when no particular attention has been paid to context, objects are created in the default context of the application domain.

Suffice it to say for now that contexts are associated with a domain and deal with issues of security and transactional behavior, and may set properties that require an object to be created in a different domain to the caller.

Understanding the Remoting Architecture

Let's finalize this section by trying to put the concepts I have outlined above into a coherent whole that explains how remoting works. When you want to call a method on a remote object, you need to configure the client to talk over an appropriate channel. You can register a channel for the client as we saw above:

```
TcpChannel chan = new TcpChannel(8085);
ChannelServices.RegisterChannel(chan);
```

or in a configuration file, as we will see later. Either way, having registered the channel, you can use it to access the remote object you want by specifying the URI, again as we saw above

```
SimpleLibrary1.SimpleClass1 myService =
        (SimpleLibrary1.SimpleClass1)
        Activator.GetObject(thisType,
        "tcp://localhost:8085/SimpleLibraryEndpoint");
```

or in a configuration file.

Having so registered a channel and requested the object, the remoting runtime will create a proxy for us in the client application domain. The messages to the object are handled by the remoting system, and carried over the registered channel, having been serialized by the client formatter sink. These messages are received on the server and deserialized by the server formatter sink, and the return value is passed back the way it came. Refer to the figure below for a simple illustration of the objects involved in this process.

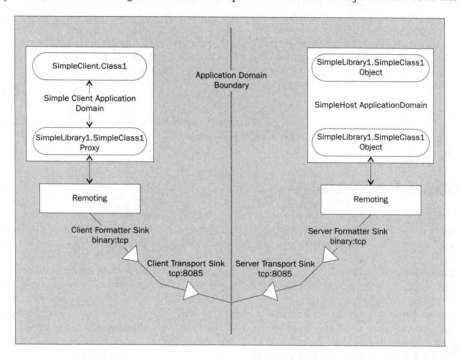

What have we Learned?

Remoting is the system in .NET for transferring object messages between application domains. Application Domains are process boundaries in .NET that extend the concept beyond threads of execution. Application Domains may contain multiple processes, and all processes in an application domain may occur on one thread. You can configure the communication process at every step along the way. You can affect how and where an object is created, how long it will live, and who is allowed to access it. Channels handle a major piece of the communication process. Channels can be custom made, or provided by the framework. Channels are made up of various channel sinks that handle serialization formatting, transportation details, and any client-configured details that affect the messages before sending. Furthermore, you can configure which port a channel communicates over. The combination of a channel and its communication port is unique per machine, and you only need to configure a client channel if you expect a response from the remote object; if you don't need two-way communication, you don't need a client channel configuration. If you understand each of these concepts, we'll dive into a few more specifics before considering a simple distributed application.

The System. Runtime.Remoting Namespace

The `System.Runtime.Remoting` namespace, obviously enough, contains the classes and interfaces we will be using to create our remote objects. While I would enjoy running through everything you can do with remoting, a whole book could be written on this subject alone.

> If you want to study the other important classes in the remoting namespace, check out **ObjRef**, and **RemotingServices**. These classes allow you to work with remote objects at a more basic level, giving you the opportunity to affect the lifetime of objects, create custom proxies, and other exciting remoting tricks.

During our introduction I have thrown several terms at you and promised to get to them soon. Let's turn our attention now to a more in-depth review of remoting activation.

Remoting Activation

How an object is activated generally controls where it lives, how many instances will exist, and how long it is going to live there. In .NET, a remote object may be either **Server-Activated** or **Client-Activated**. The main difference between the two activation types lies in when the object will be created, and how long it will live.

The question of where an object lives is somewhat moot in remoting, as we will assume it lives in the hosting application domain on the server. All remotely activated objects will make use of a proxy on the client, which has its messages marshaled to and from the server with an `ObjRef` object. We talked above about objects being created either by-reference or by-value, and that remoting is concerned with by-reference objects. Obviously you may choose to copy an object to the local application domain in order to benefit from performance gains. However this is not always possible due to issues of state, size, or complexity of the object you wish to use. If you decide that you would like to create an object by reference, then you will still need to consider the state and performance of your object reference. These architectural decisions are made in remoting with Activation.

Server Activation

A server-activated object is one that has its lifetime controlled by the hosting service on the server, and that is not activated until the client makes a method call on the object. A hosting service is simply terminology for an application that acts as host to a particular library, or set of libraries. Whether or not an object is server activated is controlled by the way in which the client configures its creation of the object. When the client configures a well-known object, as we saw in the examples created above, the object will be server-activated. Recall that we have seen two ways of getting an object reference in the client: one with the `Activator.GetObject` call:

```
SimpleLibrary1.SimpleClass1 myService =
        (SimpleLibrary1.SimpleClass1)
         Activator.GetObject(thisType,
        "tcp://localhost:8085/SimpleLibraryEndpoint");
```

and another with the new operator after we had configured the well-known client object:

```
RemotingConfiguration.RegisterWellKnownClientType(thisType,
            "tcp://localhost:8085/  SimpleLibraryEndpoint");
SimpleClass1 myService = new SimpleClass1();
```

In both cases, our client is dependent on the type information it has locally referenced for the `SimpleLibrary` object to be available at the specified endpoint. When either `new` with a well-known configuration, or `GetObject` is used on the client, the local proxy is created from the known type without making a call to the server. This is the reason that the server object will not be created until a method call is made by the client. This also makes it impossible to use parameterized constructors on that particular remote object.

> **If you need to use parameterized constructors on a remote object, you must use client activation.**

Obviously, there is a slight network performance gain in not having to call the server to receive a reference to the object proxy. While on a LAN, this may be inconsequential; it could make a big difference calling a remote object halfway around the world.

Client Activation

Client-activated objects control lifetime on the client side, and make a call to the server to create an instance of the object when they get an object reference. In other words, the server will create the object as soon as the `new` operator, or `Activator.CreateInstance`, is called. The object is then available for all subsequent method calls. By default the object on the server will be destroyed when the client object call completes. Calls to the same object from different instances of the client, or different clients, will receive new instances of the object. You can set a remote object to be client activated with a call to `RemotingConfiguration.RegisterActivatedClientType`. Just like the call we saw previously to register a well-known type, this call requires the type of the object, and its URI:

```
Type thisType = typeof(SimpleClass1);
RemotingConfiguration.RegisterActivatedClientType(thisType,
                            "tcp://localhost:8085");
SimpleClass1 myService = new SimpleClass1();
```

Notice in this call that we have left off the name of the type on the server side. That's because client-activated registration on the server does not call for publishing an endpoint. In order for the server to activate the object on client request, it must use `RemotingConfiguration.RegisterActivatedServiceType` instead of well-known.

```
Type thisType = Type.GetType("SimpleLibrary1.SimpleClass1,SimpleLibrary1");
RemotingConfiguration.RegisterActivatedServiceType(thisType);
```

Again, this method differs in that an endpoint name is not required for registration on the server. Note that it is possible to configure each of these activation settings in the application configuration file also. To configure your client for client activation in the configuration file, you need to change the object reference tag from `<wellknown>` to `<activated>`.

```
<application>
<client url="tcp://localhost:8085/SimpleLibraryEndpoint">
<activated type="SimpleLibrary1.SimpleClass1"/>
</client>
</application>
```

When an object's lifetime is to be managed by the server, the server considers the type to be well-known. That is, the server has a registration of the type matched with the object's endpoint. If an object is client activated, the server must use the object URL to locate the activator for that object. Thus, the url attribute in the client tag is used as the endpoint identifier when used with an activated type object, forming that object's Uniform Resource Identifier (URI). This URI forms the key in the remoting configuration table, and therefore is mandatory when configuring client activation, and optional for a registering well-known objects. This makes sense when we recall that the type information for a client-activated type is retrieved from the server at the moment of instantiation, while a server-activated type will rely on the client's type information until the first method call.

Finally, in our introduction to Activation, let's look at lifetime services. We will then consider configuration more closely before we get on with the real work of building a small, distributed application.

Lifetime Services

Server-activated objects will have their lifetime controlled by whether they are configured to be **Singletons** or **SingleCall** objects. SingleCall objects are created on the first method call from the client, and destroyed after the call has been returned. This can be very useful for objects that have no internal state and are inexpensive to create, such as utility objects on a web server. Singletons are objects that are created by a method call, but then live for a configurable amount of time on the server, whether they have more work to do or not. In other words, if the object is not in use at the present time, it will live on according to its **lease**, not its apparent usefulness to client objects. In remoting, lifetime is handled by something called a lease. A lease is a lease on life for the object. The initial time for an object to live is set either by the object host, or within the object itself. If no other clients request the object before the lease expires, the garbage collector will come to take it away. However, the object may request a new lease time, be used again, or be renewed by a client call.

Server-Activated Lease Configuration

Well-known types may have their leases configured by the host service, or may control their own lifetime. If neither the service, nor the remote object specify lifetime configuration, then the default machine configuration file will be used. The default in my machine configuration file is 30 seconds on first activation, and a 2 second renewal if called again before the lease expires.

> As stated in the .NET documentation in the article titled *Machine Configuration Files*:
> "The machine configuration file includes settings that apply for the entire machine. The file is located at **%runtime install path%\Config\Machine.config**. **Machine.config** contains information such as machine-wide assembly binding, built-in remoting channels, and ASP.NET configuration settings."

Objects that will interact with their lifetime must have a reference to the System.Runtime.Remoting.Lifetime namespace. Several methods exist for initializing the lifetime service for an object, and then changing the properties of the lease established. When a client interacts with the lifetime of a server-activated object, a reference to the lease may be obtained by a call to InitializeLifetimeService() on the server object:

```
ILease lease;
if(bServerActivated)
{
    lease = (ILease)myService.InitializeLifetimeService();
}
```

Client-Activated Lease Configuration

A client holding a reference to a client-activated object may still interact with the object's lifetime services, but obtains a reference to the lease with `RemotingServices.GetLifetimeService`.

```
lease = (ILease)RemotingServices.GetLifetimeService(myService);
```

Once the lease has been obtained, the method calls on the lease are no different to for those for a server-activated object. We will take a closer look at these in the application examples that follow this section. One more subject before we apply the material is to consider the `RemotingConfiguration` class.

Remoting Configuration

The `RemotingConfiguration` class provides for the general configuration of remoting within your object. You will call methods on this class to obtain specific remote class locations, and register remote types. I will introduce you to this class by looking at a couple of the most important methods.

Configure(string filename)

The `Configure` method simply loads and parses the information within a configuration file. This method then makes use of other methods to make the proper configuration settings a reality. On the client side, this may be the only method you ever need for a simple remoting client. In fact, if you configure your client yourself, you will probably not need the `RemotingConfiguration` class at all. We will look at file versus direct configuration in a little bit. However, once we look at configuration files, this may be your favorite method of all time. With a simple configuration file, you can set up your channel, and set the location of your remote type, without calling any extra methods. The call to `RemotingConfiguration.Configure` looks like this:

```
RemotingConfiguration.Configure("YourObject.exe.config");
```

where the string parameter is the location of the configuration file for your type, whether this is for the server or the client. This configuration file should be named under the convention, `resourcename.filetypeextension.config`. You don't have to follow this to make this particular method work, but other .NET Framework options will require this name for a local application configuration file.

Using the Application Configuration File

The application configuration file may contain a section for remoting under the tag `<system.runtime.remoting>`. This configuration file is an XML file, which is parsed by the application at runtime, and by requests from various services. The file may reside anywhere, but I find it is most convenient to keep it with the compiled executable or library. The `RemotingConfiguration.Configure` method will parse the contents of the `config` file under this element. The configuration file contents will differ for client configuration and server. Keep in mind that when the `Configure` method parses this file, it then calls the methods you could call yourself from within the applications. However, this file makes it possible to make configuration changes at runtime, rather than compile time. This could be of great service if your port suddenly needs to change, or even your protocol. A simple client configuration file for our example above would look like this:

```
<configuration>
   <system.runtime.remoting>
      <application>
         <client url="tcp://localhost:8085/SimpleLibraryEndpoint">
         <wellknown type="SimpleLibrary1.SimpleClass1, SimpleLibrary1"
                        url="tcp://localhost:8085/SimpleLibraryEndpoint" />
         </client>
         <channels>
            <channel type="System.Runtime.Remoting.Channels.Tcp.TcpChannel,
                        System.Runtime.Remoting" />
         </channels>
      </application>
   </system.runtime.remoting>
</configuration>
```

With this simple file, we are taking care of channel registration and well-known type registration. The `url` attribute of the `<client>` tag will be used as meta data for a well-known client type, but will be used as the resource URI in a client-activated type.

> Channel registration for a particular application goes inside the **`<application>`** tags. However it is possible to configure whole channels with a **`<channel>`** tag inside a **`<channels>`** tag outside the **`<application>`**. In fact, almost any type of configuration and registration can be done with this file. The documentation on this file is not complete at the time of this writing, but I am sure that you will want to become very familiar with this very flexible method of configuring your applications.

A Server registration file for our simple example would look something like this:

```
<configuration>
   <system.runtime.remoting>
      <application name="SimpleLibraryEndpoint">
         <service>
            <wellknown mode="Singleton" type="SimpleLibrary1.SimpleClass1,
                        SimpleLibrary1" objectUri="SimpleLibraryEndpoint" />
         </service>
         <channels>
            <channel port="8085"
                        type="System.Runtime.Remoting.Channels.Tcp.TcpChannel,
                        System.Runtime.Remoting" />
         </channels>
      </application>
   </system.runtime.remoting>
</configuration>
```

With server configuration files, notice that the `<client>` tag has been replaced by a `<service>` tag. This is a straightforward change. Also notice the `objectUri` attribute, which in this case contains only the name we assigned to the endpoint, not the protocol, server, and port. The `<channel>` tag is nearly identical to the client, save the `port` attribute.

RegisterWellKnownServiceType(Type type, string Object URI, WellKnownObjectMode mode)

This registration method is for use on the server side of remoting. This method will cause **Well-Known** types to be registered in the remoting system's registration table on the server. Recall that Well-Known objects are either singleton or single call objects that have a registered URI with the remoting framework. This URI can be used to activate the object on the server. So then, a server service which desires to make a remotable object available must register the type with the remoting system. This method call will take care of that detail for you. When we saw this method used in the example above, we received a reference to the proper Type using `GetType`, made up a name for the endpoint URI: "`SimpleLibraryEndpoint`", and set the mode to `SingleCall` using the `WellKnownObjectMode` enumeration.

```
Type thisType = Type.GetType("SimpleLibrary1.SimpleClass1,SimpleLibrary1");
RemotingConfiguration.RegisterWellKnownServiceType(thisType,
        "SimpleLibraryEndpoint",WellKnownObjectMode.SingleCall);
```

Having already registered a channel on the service, this configuration call completed the registration information needed for the remoting system to return proxies to clients. The methodology is similar on the client side, which we will look at next.

RegisterWellKnownClientType(Type type, string ObjectURI)

This configuration call sets up a known reference to the remote type. When we activated the remote object in our example above, we obtained a reference using `Activator.GetObject`.

```
SimpleLibrary1.SimpleClass1 myService = (SimpleLibrary1.SimpleClass1)
Activator.GetObject(thisType, "tcp://localhost:8085/SimpleLibraryEndpoint");
```

This required a URI to be provided, so we could obtain an instance of the object of the specified type. If we first register the type as known to the client in this application domain, we then simply call new to obtain an instance of the object:

```
RemotingConfiguration.RegisterWellKnownClientType(thisType,
            "tcp://localhost:8085/  SimpleLibraryEndpoint");
SimpleClass1 myService = new SimpleClass1();
```

Neither one will save you any typing over the other, but in lieu of a configuration file, I think registering the type with the remoting system allows you to write cleaner code that has a more obvious intent. Furthermore, you only need to register a `WellKnownClientType` once in the application, whereas `GetObject` will always require the URI.

By this point in the chapter, I hope you have become familiar with the basic procedure for getting a remote object running. In very simplistic terms, you find some way to point to the object through a channel, and then the framework takes care of marshalling the calls.

Before we move on to the application examples, it may be good to take stock once again of the principles we have learned so far.

Remoting is the framework that handles the interaction of remote objects in the .NET Framework. Remoting creates object references for clients that have requested objects through a particular channel and endpoint URI. Client objects that do not require a call back from the server object do not need to configure a channel before remoting, as a proxy will be created. However, clients receiving data from the server object must configure a channel that can receive the call. When the client creates the object reference it may use client activation or server activation. Client-activated objects are retrieved either by the new operator on a configured activated object, or CreateInstance. When a client-activated object is referenced, the proxy is created by calling the server and retrieving the type information directly. Server-activated objects created either with the new operator on a registered well-known type, or with GetObject, create a proxy based on the locally registered type, and the server object is not created until the first method is called.

Objects may be configured as well-known or activated either by using configuration methods in the RemotingConfiguration class, or by using the application configuration file.

Distributed Application Example

Now that you have seen a lot of the basics, and understand the remoting framework, we will attempt to pull everything together in a simple distributed application. This will help you to see everything I have detailed above in a working environment that you could duplicate, and to discuss a few implementation details.

The Application

This will be a C# Windows Forms application that uses TCP/IP to communicate with various remote objects. As far as Visual Studio is concerned, this application will all be housed in a solution called NewCar, which may be downloaded from the Wrox web site. If you are working with these samples outside of the VS.NET IDE, or do not have the download file, you will need the following files:

Object Name	Class File	Purpose
CarInventory	CarData.cs	This is the remote library object that returns data from a database in order to populate the data grid in the ShowVehicles form. This object is hosted by the InventoryHost console host.
RemoteHost	Service1.cs	This is a Windows service created using the service template. If you do not have VS.NET installed, you will have to read up on how to create a service.
InventoryHost	Inventory.cs	This is the remote host for the CarInventory object. It is a console application much like the host in the simple example at the beginning of the chapter.
LoanCalculator	FigureLoan.cs	This is the remote library object that is used by the LoanCalc class to perform the actual calculations. It is hosted by the RemoteHost service.

Object Name	Class File	Purpose
NewCarBuyer	LoanCalc.cs	This is the main WindowsForms class, and is the start object for the NewCarBuyer application. It is also the client of the first remote object, LoanCalculator.FigureLoan.
NewCarBuyer	Preferences.cs	This is a WindowsForms class that receives information from the LoanCalc form, and is the client of the remote CarInventory.CarData object.
NewCarBuyer	ShowVehicles.cs	This is a simple WindowsForms class that uses a datagrid object to display information returned from the CarData class.

If you do not have the VS.NET IDE installed, these examples will be difficult to run unless you get the code from the download site. If you do have the IDE, you can create a solution that will hold a WindowsForms application, a console application, and a WindowsService application. Use the table provided as a guide for placing each class in the proper application.

Again, I will leave the broad topic of web services to the appropriate chapter in this book. Web services are getting all the press anyway, right? We will be building several parts of one application in each example, so you have one complete solution at the end.

Business Case

As a top developer at a cutting-edge firm, you are charged with developing an application for a car dealership that helps their salesmen to make intelligent recommendations to customers, while helping to prequalify the customer. Your client has charged you with the following requirements:

❑ Build a GUI application that receives input from a customer about their finances and relevant tastes before showing the salesman a list of cars that fit the profile.

❑ The application must conform to their existing n-tier application environment, utilizing presentation, business, and data objects.

❑ Relevant database information is stored only at the central office and cannot be reached directly from satellites.

❑ Database-driven sections of the application will communicate to the satellite via the corporate LAN in a secure manner.

❑ The application must be simple enough to be used in a book example.

While the last requirement really helps us out, all of these requirements may be met by using remoting in the .NET framework.

Design

We have decided to develop the user interface as a three step process, which will start with the amount the customer can afford, then ask about details such as seating capacity, and finally produce a listing of cars from the home office database. We will require two business objects: one to calculate the loan amount, and another to communicate with the database at the home office. The interaction of the objects is shown overleaf.

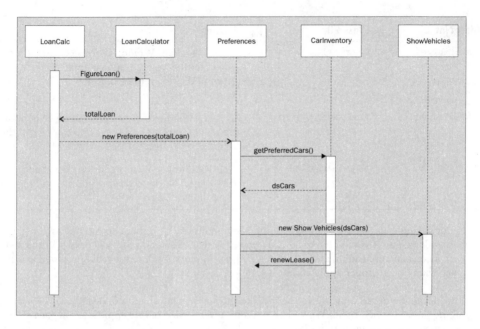

I have not shown the use of the hosting service objects, as they do not interact with the application; however, I will be discussing their development below. The role of each object is detailed in the following table:

Object Name	Role
LoanCalc	This is the central form class and receives the data entry for a customer's financial information. This form is responsible for using the LoanCalculator object to get a total amount the customer can afford for their new vehicle. This object lives throughout the application so that new data can be entered to tweak financial details.
LoanCalculator	This is our calculation utility object that will live on the application server in the satellite offices. This object will be client activated due to its low activation overhead. We would also like to be able to kill the object when we are done with it.
Preferences	LoanCalc activates the preferences form as soon as a calculation is satisfactory to the customer. This form offers a few options to help understand the customer's needs and passes these to the CarInventory object. Once a DataSet of available cars has been retrieved, the data display form, ShowVehicles, is called with the data set as a parameter. Preferences may choose to renew the CarInventory object's lifetime, but otherwise the object will be server controlled. Server activation also makes sense here because we don't want to make a call on the actual object until we are ready to use it.
CarInventory	A database call is made here to retrieve appropriate cars. This data is used to fill a data set object, which is returned to Preferences.
ShowVehicles	This simple form utilizes a data-bound grid to display available cars with all of their features.

The requirements for this project will be met by making the correct decisions about when and where to activate objects, and by developing objects that can easily support the physical separation requirements. We will be working with a simple database that has the following schema:

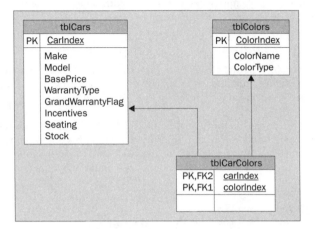

> If you want to get the data for this database, or the Visio document to create the database itself, you can download the scripts along with the rest of the code at the Wrox web site.

With this overview of the architecture firm in our minds, I am sure you are itching to get at the development phase, so let's move on.

Example 1 – Loan Calculation

In this section we will look at the two objects used to retrieve the total loan amount that is passed to the rest of the application. Loan calculation requires a data-entry form, and a calculation object. The form we will use has some standard questions used in the calculations.

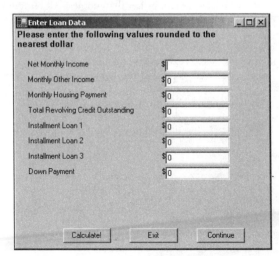

The car dealer will fill in the data from the customer and select the **Calculate!** button, which will access the calculation object and print a loan total to the screen. If the customer decides to move on (or the dealer sees they have enough credit to do so), the dealer selects **Continue**, which will send them on to choosing preferences. To keep focused on remoting, we won't be looking so much at how to create such a form, but on where in the development of the form remoting usage occurs.

LoanCalculator::FigureLoan

The calculation business object, `LoanCalculator`, is a simple class library assembly with a double return type. Let's look at this object first, and then how to wire the form to use it. Recall that in our make-believe world, this business object lives on a different server.

When you first create a class object in the Visual Studio.NET IDE, it will contain references to the `System`, `System.XML`, and `System.Data` assemblies. In order to remote this object, you will also need to get a reference to `System.Runtime.Remoting`. It will also be useful to put the following `using` statements at the top of the class file in order to reference their members without fully qualifying them:

```
using System;
using System.Runtime.Remoting;
using System.Runtime.Remoting.Channels;
using System.Runtime.Remoting.Channels.Tcp;
using System.Runtime.Remoting.Lifetime;
```

Having done this, it's best to go ahead and set a namespace, and declare the `FigureLoan` class to extend `MarshalByRefObject`.

```
namespace LoanCalculator
{
    public class FigureLoan:MarshalByRefObject
    {
        public FigureLoan()
        {
            //Construction logic goes here.
        }
```

The `MarshalByRefObject` class is the base class that makes it possible – or requires, if you like – that our object return references to itself when requested, rather than copies. All remotely-activated objects must extend `MarshalByRefObject`, and all objects that extend your remote objects will be Marshal-By-Reference also.

As with our original remoting samples above, little else occurs in this class specific to remoting. The `getAvailableLoan` method is declared as public, and contains our loan calculation formula.

```
public double getAvailableLoan(double totalIn, double totalOut, int Down)
{
    //write out for illustration only...
    Console.WriteLine("Beginning Calculation...");
    //12 payments per year
    const int PAY_FREQUENCY = 12;
    /*term years, longest term available produces largest number for
    * available loan*/
    const int LOAN_TERM = 5;
    /*current rate, this would be a good opportunity to connect to
    * the bank and get real rates*/
    const double INTEREST_RATE = 0.0749;
```

```
        //simple available cash scenario
        double statedAvailable = totalIn - totalOut;
        //reduce the income figure by 30% for normal living expenses
        double cashPadding = .3 * totalIn;
        double cashAvailable = statedAvailable - cashPadding;
        /*Calculate largest possible loan using P = M(1-[1+(i/q)]-nq)q/i.
        * where M = cashAvailable, i = interestRate, q = frequency,
        * and n = Term*/
        double totalLoan = cashAvailable*(1-
            (Math.Pow((1+(INTEREST_RATE/PAY_FREQUENCY)),
            -(LOAN_TERM*PAY_FREQUENCY))))*PAY_FREQUENCY/INTEREST_RATE;
        /* add the downpayment in to get the total.
         * We want this calculation in this tier
         * so future decisions that may include the downpayment don't require
         * an interface change*/
        return totalLoan + Down;
    }
```

If we consider what the object is doing, it becomes obvious that this object could easily be marshaled by value. In this case, we have stated that the object will live on another server and, therefore, must be accessed outside of its application domain. Our other main consideration for this object is how it will be activated, and how long it should live. As the object has little overhead associated with its construction, and it will have almost no bandwidth impact, it makes sense to have the object activated by the client. This will enable our client form to create and destroy the object on an as needed basis. Furthermore, if it should become desirable to create this object with parameters for the term, or rate to be retrieved prior to calculation, this will only be possible with a client-activated object.

It may also be possible in a real-world solution to use a web service for such a remote service. This would work well enough, but would negatively impact performance in this case as a network connection is available that doesn't require an Internet-based request and response. Furthermore, with our TCP channel, we can return objects and native types, which are often easier to deal with than strings, as you would find in a SOAP message.

This server object will be hosted by a console application for the purposes of our illustration, but could also be hosted by a Windows service, as I will show in the second example. In any case, the host will differ from our previous host examples only in that it is configuring a client-activated object. The host, called `ConsoleHost`, will need references to `System.Runtime.Remoting`, and to the `LoanCalculator` assemblies. All of the logic for configuring the remoting system is contained in the `Main` constructor method.

```
static void Main(string[] args)
{
    try
    {
        //use configuration services...
        Console.WriteLine("Configuring Calculator Host...");
        ChannelServices.RegisterChannel(new TcpChannel(8086));
        Type calcType =
            Type.GetType("LoanCalculator.FigureLoan,LoanCalculator");
        RemotingConfiguration.RegisterActivatedServiceType(calcType);

    }
    catch(RemotingException theExcep)
    {
        Console.WriteLine(theExcep.Message);
    }
    Console.WriteLine("Select Enter to End Hosting");
    Console.Read();
}
```

Recall that a server host for a client-activated type registers the object as an `ActivatedServerType`, using the `RegisterActivatedServiceType` method of the `RemotingConfiguration` class. This registration makes it possible for clients desiring an reference to that type to query the server appropriately. If you define the server host as creating a well-known endpoint, you will receive an error from the client stating:

Object </RemoteActivationService.rem> has been disconnected or does not exist at the server.

Conversely, if the client is misconfigured, you will see:

Value null was found where an instance of an object was required.

The difference between the two errors serves as a good illustration of the differences in the modes of activation. When the client is looking for an activated service type, it does so when the new operator is called to retrieve the type information from the server. As the server does not have a registration entry, the client reports that the server does not have the object. On the other hand, when the client is expecting a well-known type, it keeps type information locally, and does not 'discover' the configuration error until it goes to use the object it has already instantiated. On the first method call to the object, the requested type is not an object, and no instance is available from the server.

Let's now turn our attention to the client.

LoanCalc::loanForm

As stated above, this form gathers information about the customer's current financial situation in an attempt to prequalify them on the types of vehicles they can afford. This form is the start-up form for the `NewCarBuyer` project, which contains all of the other forms. Once this form is loaded, it may be hidden, but will not be unloaded until the application is shut down. A completed use of this form prints the customer's prequalified amount at the bottom of the form.

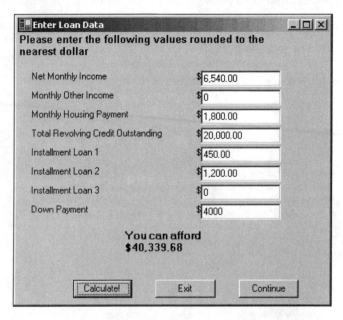

You guessed it, the NewCarBuyer project will need a reference to System.Runtime.Remoting, as well as to the LoanCalculator assembly. To make sense of the NewCarBuyer project, I've provided a shot of the NewCar Solution Explorer:

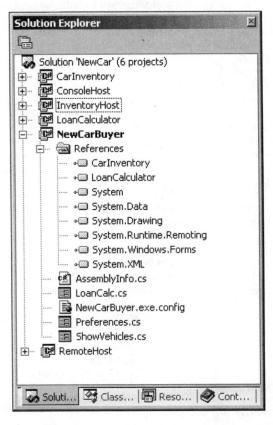

In order to take advantage of only one instance of the calculator object, we declare the variable to hold our remote type in the class declaration section.

```
LoanCalculator.FigureLoan loanCalc = null;
```

The registration of the remote channel and type are taken care of in the constructor logic for this form.

```
public loanForm()
{
    InitializeComponent();
    //use remoting configuration...
    ChannelServices.RegisterChannel(new TcpChannel());
    Type calcType = typeof(FigureLoan);
    RemotingConfiguration.RegisterActivatedClientType
        (calcType,"tcp://localhost:8086");
    loanCalc = new LoanCalculator.FigureLoan();
}
```

All constructor logic must follow the `InitializeComponent()` method, so we begin there, registering a channel over which to receive our callback message. Per the usual practice so far, we then get our Type reference, and configure the client's remoting system with an entry for this activated type. Having registered the type in this way, we will be able to instantiate the object with the `new` operator anywhere else in the form. Here, we have instantiated the object directly. Additionally, because this form will be active throughout the use of the application, we could call this remote object anywhere in the project without additional configuration. Every form created in the project will live in the same Application Domain unless you specify otherwise programmatically.

> **A note about lifetime services would be prudent here. The single instantiated `LoanCalculator` object will live until the client's use of the object is complete (sets its reference to `null` or is closed). The client controls the lifetime. With a server-activated object, the object will live for the default time set by the application's configuration. The object's lease will be renewed for a certain amount of time after each additional method call. If the object is not called within the lease lifetime, a new object instance will be created for any method calls that follow. You can prove this to yourself by placing a console statement in the remote object's constructor logic. The console host will print a "new object" message the first time the object is called, and then again if you wait for the lease to run out, probably about 60 seconds.**

Our use of the calculator object is trivial then, in that it behaves just like any other object. In this case, the **Calculate!** button `On_Click` event will gather up the data from the textboxes on the form and perform a bit of summation before handing the results to the `LoanCalculator` and getting the `totalLoan` result.

```
private void btnCalculate_Click(object sender, System.EventArgs e)
{

    //Validate income as the only mandatory field.
    if(txtMonthlyNet.Text.Length == 0 && txtMonthlyNet.Text != "0")
    {
        MessageBox.Show("You must enter your monthly net income");
        txtMonthlyNet.Focus();
        return;
    }
    /*If income is >0, get all the values, and calculate using remote
     * object turn total outstanding revolving debt(credit cards)
     * into a monthly figure using a 2% mandatory payment per month*/
    double netInstallments = Convert.ToDouble(txtRevolving.Text)*.02;
    double totalIncome = Convert.ToDouble(txtMonthlyNet.Text)
        + Convert.ToInt32(txtOtherIncome.Text);
    double totalPayments = Convert.ToDouble(txtHousing.Text)
        + Convert.ToDouble(txtInstall1.Text)
        + Convert.ToDouble(txtInstall2.Text)
        + Convert.ToDouble(txtInstall3.Text)+ netInstallments;
    int down = Convert.ToInt32(txtDown.Text);
    LoanCalculator.FigureLoan loanCalc = new
        LoanCalculator.FigureLoan();
    totalLoan =
        loanCalc.getAvailableLoan(totalIncome,totalPayments,down);
    lblResults.Text = "You can afford " + totalLoan.ToString("C");
    lblResults.Visible = true;

}
```

The results of the calculation are printed to the form object, formatted to appear as currency. The calculation can be tried again and again. Each time, the same object instance can be used.

> If **LoanCalculator** were a server-activated, **WellKnown SingleCall** object, a new
> instance would be created for each method call. By definition, Single Call objects will only
> respond to one request before being deactivated and made available for garbage collection.

If the customer decides to move on, the auto dealer can select Continue, which will simply create a new `Preferences` form, and hide this one.

```
private void btnContinue_Click(object sender, System.EventArgs e)
{
    NewCarBuyer.Preferences newForm  = new
                NewCarBuyer.Preferences(totalLoan,this);
    newForm.Activate();
    this.Hide();
    newForm.Show();
}
```

At this point, you can congratulate yourself on having used a remote object in a working application. To try something a bit more advanced, you could actually host the remote object on a remote server. In order to get this object you would then simply need to change the configured URI in the `RegisterActivatedClientType` call:

```
RemotingConfiguration.RegisterActivatedClientType
    (calcType,"tcp://remoteserver:8086")
```

After compiling your form, you could then delete your local copy of the `LoanCalculator`, and prove that remoting is really working! If you'll take my word for it for now, let's move on to the `Preferences` form, and its use of a server-activated data object.

Example 2 – Preferences

The `Preferences` form begins by reminding the user how much money is available to the prospective buyer, and then offering preference questions on mileage per year, and how many people will need to ride in the vehicle. These choices will be used to create selection criteria when it is time to query the database. The `Preferences` form is shown below.

Preferences::Preferences

The three command buttons available give us the equivalent of forward, back, and quit options. The Get Cars! action will utilize our second remote object to get a data set from the database and load the final form, `CarInventory`. The creation of the `Preferences` form in the middle of the application gives us some interesting programming issues to consider.

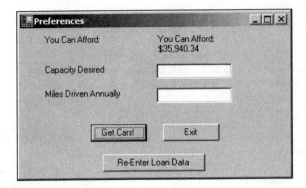

Firstly, when the `Preferences` form is created, the `loanForm` has already been activated, and is still in memory. You'll recall that we registered the TCP channel in that form; because the client channel is not specific, and contains no particular endpoint to call, the single registration works for any other remote object using TCP. So, we drop channel registration from this remote client's activities, as we only need to register the remote type.

We also have a registration issue with the type, if this form is called multiple times during one lifetime. The registration of the type occurs in the application domain, which spans the entire `NewCarBuyer` executable. So, we have to check the existence of the registered type before we try to register it again. Let's look at the code surrounding these issues.

First, we make a couple of declarations in the class:

```
const string configPath = @"My Documents\Visual Studio" +
          Projects\NewCar\AvailableLoan\NewCarBuyer.exe.config";
CarData dInventory = null;
```

You can see that we are preparing to use a configuration file this time, and have also prepared a container for the remote object to be used throughout the class.

```
public Preferences(double Cash, Form LoanForm)
{
    InitializeComponent();
    loanForm = LoanForm;
    WellKnownClientTypeEntry thisEntry = RemotingConfiguration.
            IsWellKnownClientType("CarInventory.CarData","CarInventory");
    if (thisEntry == null)
    RemotingConfiguration.Configure(configPath);
    dblCash = Cash;
    lblLoanResults.Text = "You Can Afford: " + Cash.ToString("c");
    dInventory = new CarData();
}
```

Notice that the signature contains a few input parameters:

```
public Preferences(double Cash, Form LoanForm)
```

The `Cash` parameter just allows us to carry the `totalLoan` amount from `loanForm`. The other parameter is actually a reference to the calling form, so we can easily reference the form. I confess this is a WinForms detail, but you'll see it used next.

Next, we call the `Configure` method during the `Constructor` method. As I said above, this call needs to be embedded in an `if()` statement to protect against duplicate registration. Be careful, as the `IsWellKnownClientType()` method does not return a Boolean as expected, but in fact returns a type registration entry. However, it will return a `null` if nothing is in the remoting catalog for the given type, and this is what we check against. Once we are satisfied that a duplicate registration will not occur, the configuration file is parsed. Again, note that the configuration file does not contain a channel registration.

```xml
<configuration>
   <system.runtime.remoting>
      <application>
         <client url="tcp://localhost:8087/InventoryEndpoint">
            <wellknown type="CarInventory.CarData, CarInventory"
                       url="tcp://localhost:8087/InventoryEndpoint" />-->
         </client>
      </application>
   </system.runtime.remoting>
</configuration>
```

In order to avoid conflict with the port used by our other remote object, this object has been registered at port 8087. Recall that the remoting system will not allow registration of two channels on the same port. If you were running these examples on three different computers, as they are designed to be, this wouldn't be an issue. However, to run them all on your own machine, you will need different ports to differentiate the hosts. In any case, we also note that this object is being registered as a well-known, server-activated object. Before we look at the rest of the `Preferences` form class, we'll set up the hosting service. Once we have the host in place, we'll return to the function that utilizes the remote object.

Instead of using a console this time, let's take a quick look at creating a Windows service to host your application. This is closer to what you would do in the real world, and is worth mentioning here. Using the Windows Service project template actually makes this a simple operation.

> In order to stay within the scope of this chapter, I will not look at everything you need to do to configure a Windows service here. There is an excellent .NET MSDN article entitled **"Walkthrough: Creating a Windows Service Application in the Component Designer"**. This walkthrough will give you the basic service, to which you only need make minor changes as directed below. A complete service is also included in the downloadable examples for this book.

Once you have a service application, you only need to add code to the `OnStart` procedure.

```csharp
protected override void OnStart(string[] args)
  {
    string configPath = @"C:\My Documents\Visual Studio Projects\"+
      @"RemotingHost\Service1.exe.config";
    try
    {
      RemotingConfiguration.Configure(configPath);
    }
    catch(RemotingException theExcep)
    {
      eventLog1.WriteEntry(theExcep.Message, EventLogEntryType.Error);
    }

  }
```

I have instituted an `EventLog` object for this service, but you could just as easily write errors to a custom event log you create. The configuration file for the service is straightforward.

```
<configuration>
    <system.runtime.remoting>
        <application name="CarBuyer">
            <service>
                <wellknown mode="Singleton" type="CarInventory.
                    CarData,CarInventory" objectUri="InventoryEndpoint" />
            </service>
            <channels>
                <channel port="8087"
                    type="System.Runtime.Remoting.Channels.Tcp.TcpChannel,
                        System.Runtime.Remoting" />
            </channels>
        </application>
    </system.runtime.remoting>
</configuration>
```

Our main goal in using this remote object is to make sure that we send as little traffic over the WAN lines as possible. The first way to handle this is with a server-activated object. This means that a call will not be made to the server service until a method is called on the object. We also configure the service to be in `Singleton` mode. This means that the same object will be available to the calling client until either the lifetime runs out, or the client is destroyed. We will look at the lifetime issue when we consider how the remote object itself is set up. Once this service is running, it will behave like any of the console examples you have seen so far. If you are ready to experiment, a good exercise would be to change the `LoanCalculator` host into a service also.

> You may be wondering at this point, what happened to COM+ services? "Isn't there a nice application server to take care of these hosting issues?" Well, not yet. You can be sure that a nice GUI application will be created before long, but in the meantime you have to write the hosts yourself. It's kind of like getting back to the good old days of writing your own proxy/stub code. Until Microsoft does it for you, you can see this as a feature that allows you the greatest level of control over your own application.

Getting back to `Preferences`, we have a registered remote type `CarInventory.CarData`, and we have gathered a couple of pieces of new data from the customer. If the car dealer is ready to look up the available cars, he selects **Get Cars!** and we handle the data in the `cmdGetCars_Click` procedure.

```
private void cmdGetCars_Click(object sender, System.EventArgs e)
{
    string warrantyChoice = "simple";
    int miles = Convert.ToInt32(txtMiles.Text);
    if(miles > 36000)
    {
        warrantyChoice = "extended";
    }

    if(dInventory == null)
        dInventory = new CarData();
    DataSet dsCars = dInventory.getPreferredCars
```

```
                (Convert.ToDouble(dblCash),warrantyChoice,
                Convert.ToInt32(txtCapacity.Text));
        NewCarBuyer.ShowVehicles newForm = new NewCarBuyer.ShowVehicles(dsCars);
        newForm.Activate();
        newForm.Show();
        dsCars = null;
        ILease lease = (ILease)dInventory.InitializeLifetimeService();

        if (lease == null)
            MessageBox.Show("lease is null");
        else
        {
            TimeSpan lifetime = TimeSpan.FromMinutes(2);
            lease.Renew(lifetime);
        }

    }
```

After going through some code to set up the parameters for our query, we check to see if the remote object reference has been instantiated.

```
    if(dInventory == null)
        dInventory = new CarData();
```

This is again related to our need to be able to go back and forth through this form. If we are calling this procedure a second time not instantiating the form, and have lost our original reference, we will need to get a new reference to the object. The getPreferredCars() method is called, and the return fills a dataset we can pass off to the data-bound grid form. The piece of code that may have caught your eye is the use of the Ilease.

```
    ILease lease = (ILease)dInventory.InitializeLifetimeService();

    if (lease == null)
        MessageBox.Show("lease is null");
    else
    {
        TimeSpan lifetime = TimeSpan.FromMinutes(2);
        lease.Renew(lifetime);
    }

}
```

I have talked about lifetime in several places, and here we see a possible use. As the creation of this object is somewhat expensive, we really don't want to do it twice. If we lose our lease on this object, we will have to call the server twice to regain the proxy: once to get the type definition, and again for the method call. In order to avoid losing the lease, we get a reference to the object's lifetime services lease object, and renew the lease. We set the lease for another two minutes.

```
    TimeSpan lifetime = TimeSpan.FromMinutes(2);
        lease.Renew(lifetime);
```

This way we won't lose our lease if the user decides to come back and enter new criteria after reviewing the cars displayed. The getPreferredCars method is really entirely involved with retrieving a data set, so we won't review it; however, we should take a look at the method that makes the lease reference possible.

CarData::InitializeLifetimeService

In this remote data object, we once again need our reference to the remoting assembly. The class is defined as extending `MarshalByRefObject`, and in this case we again have an empty constructor.

```
public class CarData:MarshalByRefObject
{
    public CarData()
    {
        //for illustrative purposes only...
        Console.WriteLine("Inventory Object activated");
    }
```

We then override the `InitializeLifetimeService` method from the `MarshalByRefObject` class.

```
public override Object InitializeLifetimeService()
{
    ILease lease = (ILease)base.InitializeLifetimeService();
    if (lease.CurrentState == LeaseState.Initial)
    {
        lease.InitialLeaseTime = TimeSpan.FromMinutes(1);
        lease.RenewOnCallTime = TimeSpan.FromSeconds(2);
    }
    return lease;
}
```

By overriding this method within the remote class, we make it possible for the object to set its own lifetime settings. Otherwise, these settings are handled either in the host's application configuration, or from the default system configuration. This method first obtains the lease from the base class, and then sets several properties for the lifetime services. Each property is fairly straightforward.

```
        lease.InitialLeaseTime = TimeSpan.FromMinutes(1);
        lease.RenewOnCallTime = TimeSpan.FromSeconds(2);
```

The initial lease is the time this object will live from the first call from a client if no other method calls are made, or the lease is not renewed. The `RenewOnCallTime` property is for resetting the lease time for each subsequent method call the object receives. In our case, we also renew the lease from our client by getting the lease through the execution of this method.

In our application, the lease has been safely renewed, and the object lives on. When we make the call from `Preferences`, `CarData` returns a `DataSet`, and our application is complete. The final form can display the results from the database.

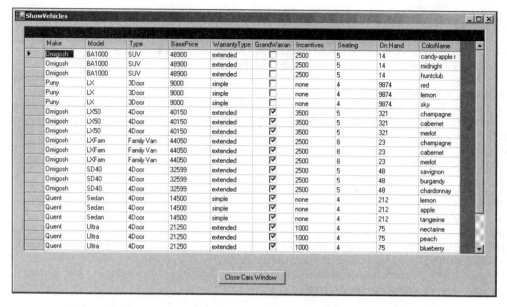

In this case, I have populated a single `System.Windows.Forms.DataGrid` object with the `DataSet` type. You'll recall that the data grid is retrieved in the `Preferences cmdGetCars_Click` event handler.

```
DataSet dsCars = dInventory.getPreferredCars
(Convert.ToDouble(dblCash),warrantyChoice,
Convert.ToInt32(txtCapacity.Text));
NewCarBuyer.ShowVehicles newForm  = new NewCarBuyer.ShowVehicles(dsCars);
```

The `ShowVehicles` form class constructor takes in the data set as a parameter and simply associates the `DataSet` with the `DataGrid` object utilizing the `SetDataBinding` method.

```
public ShowVehicles(DataSet dsCars)
{
    InitializeComponent();
    dgCars.SetDataBinding(dsCars,"Table");

}
```

Mission Accomplished

You've done it. You have lived up to your reputation as a top application developer and delivered a distributed application using the latest technology available. But are you finished? Well, what would developing be without continuous new developments in technology? There is more, much more to be learned about remoting, but hopefully you are now armed with the information you need to dig into the complexities of your own applications.

Summary

We have discussed a lot of concepts and ideas in this chapter, so much so that reviewing what we have learned about remoting in logical groups will be beneficial here.

Objects by Reference, Objects by Value

The first step is to decide whether or not you need a remote object, or if you would be better off using a local instance of the object. Objects that will be created by reference are Marshal-By-Reference objects, and must inherit from `MarshalByRefObject`. A proxy will be created and packed as an `ObjRef` object to be sent over the registered remoting channel. Copied objects are copied into the calling application domain in their entirety. When dealing with distributed applications, we are most often interested in marshaling by reference.

Channels and Ports

Channels are the finished product of several Channel Sinks put together in a Sink Chain that contain information about how to serialize object messages, and which transport mechanism to use to marshal the messages. Channel sinks can also be created for other types of interaction that you want to have with your objects' messages. You may create or use sinks that deal with security issues, or use protocols other than those provided by the framework. The combination of a channel and a port create a particular transport mechanism, which cannot be repeated on a single machine. You configure channels on servers and clients, and must have a compatible channel on a client if your client needs callback messages from the server object.

System.Runtime.Remoting

Several helpful classes are available which help you to configure your remoting application. The `RemotingConfiguration` class provides ways for us to manually register our server and client types, or to parse our application configuration files. If application configuration files are used, the `RemotingConfiguration.Configure()` method simply parses the file to retrieve the parameters with which to make the appropriate configuration calls.

Activation

Activation may either be Server or Client. Server-activated types are known as `WellKnown` types, and may be either `Singleton` or `SingleCall` objects. `Singleton` objects will be created once for each client that calls and will live until the client is destroyed, or the object lease runs out. Client-activated types control their own lifetime, and by default will live as long as the client object. Client-activated types get the type definition from the server when the type is instantiated, and thus may use constructor parameters. Server-activated objects are not referenced by the client until the first method call, the client gets the type definition from the assembly that was present at compile-time.

Leases and Lifetime

Objects in the .NET framework have their time-to-live determined by a lease, rather than polling client objects to see if they are still alive. This is very friendly to network traffic, and allows for a greater level of lifetime control. Leases for server-activated objects may be renewed by the client, or will live according to properties set by the host application, or their own when they override the `InitializeLifetimeService` method. Leases may additionally be refreshed by new method calls on the server object.

So, now you should know enough about remoting to attempt it yourselves!

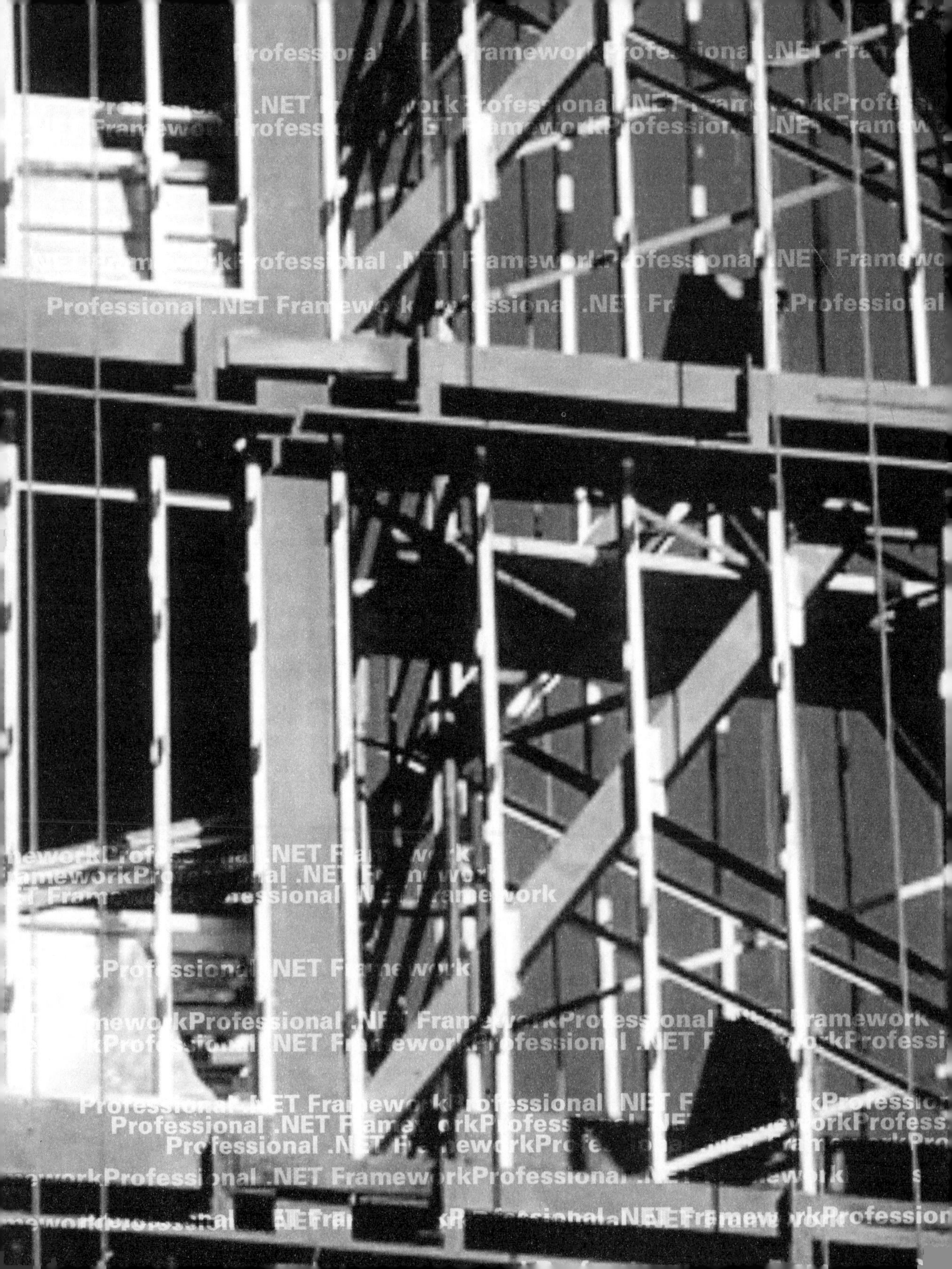
Professional .NET Framework

12

Best Engineering Practices with the .NET Framework

Now that you have spent all this time learning about the .NET Framework, what are some of the best practices in developing applications with it? There are two basic parts to this chapter: techniques to optimize your .NET code and infrastructure, and good engineering practices for any code and framework.

As some of my former colleges will attest, I have been at times downright militant when it comes to writing code with the best and fastest techniques. This comes from the days of single machine applications in Visual Basic 3. If you didn't write the best code possible and use every trick in the book, your code was slow. Compared to today's n-tier Windows DNA applications, there was very little outside interaction with other applications. Some applications used a bit of DDE (Dynamic Data Exchange – a predecessor to Object Linking and Embedding (OLE) for inter-application communication) or use of some VBX's (used in Visual Basic version 1 through 3, 16 bit custom controls) but there wasn't ASP.NET, managed code, Web Services, and Namespaces etc. across multiple domains running on tens to potentially hundreds of servers and using multiple tiers of application architecture.

There are so many different areas of a .NET application and all the parts must work together to produce a manageable, reliable, secure, maintainable, auditable, traceable, and available application from both a production and development aspect. If you don't plan your application development, implementation, and infrastructure from beginning to end, it won't matter how fast your code is, because the other interrelated parts of your application will be potential bottlenecks.

I know myself and many developers out there have worked on applications where it was only important to get the application completed. This, in many cases, sacrificed the ability of the developers to include many of the parts that make up a successful application, as previously listed. It should be stressed that all areas that create a successful application should not be an afterthought, but included up front in the initial design and continually refined throughout the development process. If these areas are addressed after the features of the application are complete, you will most certainly run over schedule, over budget, and will be subject to countless potential problems.

In most large-scale e-commerce applications today, there is more than just the development team involved. You may have any combination (in smaller companies some may be the same person or team) or more of the following teams working with you in its creation and maintenance:

- ❑ A graphics/asset team to provide images and other media for the site
- ❑ A Project Management person or team that keeps the schedule on track and interacts with the customer
- ❑ An ASP/HTML team that works on the layout of the site
- ❑ A development team that creates the front-end presentation components
- ❑ A development team that creates the middle-tier infrastructure components
- ❑ A development build team that prepares the builds for testing
- ❑ A code maintenance team that reviews the code and keeps it safe
- ❑ A database team that creates new schema and stored procedures
- ❑ A release management team that prepares the next release of code or content
- ❑ An engineering team that configures and maintains the web farm
- ❑ A quality assurance team that finds all the bugs in all areas

However, there are many smaller companies today that simply can't employ this large a team, or some of the projects that you may be working on may not require such a large team. Many times it is possible that one person will work in a couple of different roles. For instance, the graphics and ASP/HTML team might be the same person, perhaps someone with a good set of presentation layout skills. If you have a project where you have a very small database, it may be very feasible for the developers to do the back end *and* database development. I have worked in a number of small companies where the build, source control, and release management teams were one person (myself). It is very possible, depending on the size of the project and the skills sets of the people involved, for one person to do a couple of different jobs, as long as all the work gets done.

Each of these teams has a very important role in how your application is created and maintained, but if it is not planned and managed properly, you will end up with an application that may have problems.

This chapter will discuss some of the best engineering practices and how you can apply these to your .NET applications. These practices will help you plan your application infrastructure as well as help you maintain your code for several iterations and revisions of the application. If you plan ahead, you will be able to continue engineering your application for several versions; otherwise, Version One may be the only one your customer ever sees.

The following areas will be discussed, with emphasis on using these with Microsoft's .NET Framework for creating large-scale e-commerce applications; however, they are applicable to all types of development applications. Many of the techniques discussed will work just as well for small teams creating more traditional client-server applications as for the individual developers who are looking at .NET to create a custom application or a great new piece of shareware.

- **Planning your Application**
  This section of the chapter will discuss some best practices and examples of how to plan for your application to have some of the best availability, manageability, reliability, scalability and securability, as well as actual performance. These will include some .NET servers and their best use, general design goals, and ongoing maintenance.

- **The Code**
  This section of the chapter will discuss coding standards in general and some ideas for .NET, techniques for conducting code reviews, and how to manage your code in the long term and protect it from accidental loss with source code control software.

- **Testing the Code**
  This section of the chapter will look at testing strategies and practices so that when your application is complete it will work on time. This will include looking at the new Microsoft stress test tool, MS Application Center Test.

Planning Your Application

The business analyst has given you and your teams the detailed functional specification for your new application and you are dying to write it in the .NET framework. What are some issues that should be addressed to guarantee success (no matter what development framework you are using)? If you do not start planning your application with the following in mind, you will most likely make mistakes in key areas preventing you from delivering a successful release. These areas may seem broad but they are very important in today's large multi-user applications.

We will look at the following areas:

- **Availability**
  No matter what type of application you create it should be designed in a way that it will always be available to the intended target (a real person or software consumer etc.) for the required documented need. This may be as simple as a small database application not running out of hard drive space, to a mission critical web application that must run 24 x 7 without any interruption or loss of data, even during application maintenance and upgrades.

- **Manageability**
  All applications need to be managed once they have been deployed. Is the application working correctly? How do I configure security for all the servers? Do all the servers have the same version of components? There are ways to plan and design your application so that these type of problems are easier to take care of and address on an ongoing basis throughout the lifecycle of the application.

- **Reliability**
  This planning and design consideration is closely related to availability. If your application is not reliable (code that always crashes, operational errors etc.) most likely it won't stay available to its intended target.

❑ **Scalability**
Designing an application that is scalable can be a very large and ongoing task. As your application has to handle a greater load in either the area of users or data, can it still provide the same level of service? You can scale an application vertically, by adding larger more powerful hardware, but if your code is not designed well, you may reach a point of diminishing returns where adding new hardware won't be able to handle the load as it could before. By scaling an application vertically, you provide a means of just adding average hardware that shares the load equally. If designed correctly, scaling vertically can provide a linear increase in scalability without a loss of returns.

❑ **Securability**
Designing for securability requires up front knowledge of the actual security requirements for your application so that you can provide the adequate level of authentication, authorization, data protection and security auditing.

Utilize Clustering Technologies (Availability, Scalability)

Utilize the Clustering features included in Windows 2000 Advanced Server and Application Center 2000: Network Load Balancing (NLB), Cluster Service, and Component Load Balancing (CLB). Each of these are discussed below:

Use Network Load Balancing (Availability, Scalability)

Network Load Balancing (available in Windows 2000 Advanced Server and above) distributes incoming IP traffic across a cluster of up to 32 servers. It is ideal for enabling incremental scalability and outstanding availability for e-commerce web sites. This enhances the availability of your application by detecting server utilization and automatically redistributing traffic to other servers running at a lower capacity. Network Load Balancing provides both availability with minimal operational support, and increased scalability with easily added capacity. Other methods of Network Load Balancing can also be achieved by hardware implementations (for example, Cisco LocalDirector Content Switches).

Another useful technique to help load balance your network traffic is to segregate your web farm. (A web farm is two or more web servers networked together to share request and resource load. A web farm generally supports load balancing and can include the abilities of fault tolerance. To a single user connecting via a single IP address, it looks to them as if they are connecting to a single server.) If you are running an e-commerce site, customer traffic will spend more time viewing pages such as products and services and (much to the dismay of the company's shareholders) there will be less traffic to the purchase of these products and/or services. Browse, product and services type pages tend to be configured for non secure or HTTP port 80 Internet traffic. When a customer buys any one of these products and/or services, you will want to protect this data by securing the information using secured sockets layer (SSL) on HTTP port 443. Depending on the volume of traffic to the individual pages for your site (this can be determined with Commerce Server 2000 and analysing your Internet Information Server traffic logs), you may want to employ a technique of hardware network load balancing and configuration of your web farm so that a greater percentage of the farm is used for port 80 traffic and less for port 443 (by using SSL accelerator cards you will also increase the performance of secured web pages). This will provide greater availability to the area of the site that is visited the most. With continuous monitoring of site traffic, you will be able to reconfigure your farm as traffic changes. An example of this may be that if, over a period of time, you know that a special sales promotion brings in 20% more orders, you can reconfigure your hardware load balancing to handle the increased load to the farm.

Use Clustering Services (Availability, Scalability)

Microsoft Cluster Services provides high availability for applications such as file services, databases and messaging. If a server (node) is part of a cluster, it will automatically take over the workload of a server if it fails without loss of data. Both Windows 2000 Advanced Server (2-node clustering) and Windows 2000 Datacenter Server (4-node clustering) employ Microsoft Cluster Services. Clustering provides the servers in your web farm with a fault tolerance option: if one server in the cluster fails, one or the other will take over (this of course requires fault tolerant hardware support, such as redundant RAID controller cards etc.). With clustering enabled and configured you will have instant fail over to an available server upon the failure of another. The more servers that you have per cluster, the greater degree of load balancing and fault tolerance that can be implemented. Microsoft Cluster Services provides a high level of server availability for the data and storage tier of your application. Application Center 2000 provides availability through load-balanced, shared-nothing clustering for the Internet Information Server and COM+ components tiers of your application. By implementing both types of clustering you will provide a level of end-to-end availability for all your servers and web farms.

Use Component Load Balancing (Availability, Scalability, Manageability)

Component Load Balancing distributes workload across multiple servers for running an application's business logic components. It complements both Network Load Balancing and Microsoft Cluster Services by acting on the middletier of a multi-tiered, clustered network.

Application Center 2000 provides Component Load Balancing but this feature should only be used under the correct circumstances. When using Application Center 2000's Component Load Balancing with COM+ components, depending on the availability of a component, you may be forced to access a component on another server. Accessing any component on any server other than the one that it resides on is a very costly operation as you will be limited to the speed of the network that you are connected to. Currently, Component Load Balancing can only work with COM+ components. Since .NET marshals (marshal means the action of passing function calls etc. of a COM object across process boundaries) COM+ between managed and unmanaged code, you should keep the usage of all COM+ objects to a minimum as there is a performance loss when marshalling between managed and unmanaged code. Depending on how many COM+ components you may have to use with your .NET application, the benefits of Component Load Balancing may not be worth it.

Constant Security Reviews (Securability, Availability)

As you plan and execute your application, and as your infrastructure grows, your security needs will change also. If your security implementation is not constantly reviewed for needed improvements and policy changes, you will be opening yourself up to possible problems. You want to provide an application that is available to the right people all the time and to the wrong people none of the time. You will have to continually check the security options on distributed objects, database access, all types of users (registered and unregistered) and all points of access to the infrastructure, whether they are physical (building) or electronic (Internet and network access).

If the application is mission critical and has the available budget, it is a good idea to hire an independent security expert to review and recommend changes to your security policies and infrastructure. This may be very costly but it will be cheaper in the long run if your application's site is compromised and valuable data is removed.

Create a Production Support Team (Availability)

Once your application has gone to production (depending on your company's development goals) there is usually very little time before most developers will start to work on the next feature set or a separate application. This leaves very few developers, if any, to fix any issues that may arise in production. The creation of a production support team to handle these issues in a controlled and timely manner is key to a continued level of high availability and customer satisfaction. Depending on the size of the team or company, and the experience with an application, a developer from the production team may have to fix an issue if it can't be resolved through the regular support channels.

This team should be informed of any serious issues as quickly as possible. This can be accomplished by providing them with pagers or cell phones for extremely urgent issues. Many of these issues can be communicated through automation. Providing all other teams with an information contact list with names, methods of contact, and area of expertise in the application will provide nearly anyone with the means to get the right person working on the issue as quickly and effectively as possible. The Production Support Team should also keep track of all incident issues for a history of possible reoccurrence; this may be accomplished with an advanced issue tracking system.. This will provide a means to solving reoccurring issues faster.

Restoring your Application (Availability)

What will happen to your application if some form of catastrophe took place and your application goes offline? Do you have the means and plan to restore it completely from scratch if needed? And if you do have this plan completely worked out, have you tried it?

The restoration plan must be tested repeatedly for issues ranging from a simple hard drive failure to the entire web farm being destroyed (mind you if this happens there may be other priorities that come first). The restoration plan must be constantly maintained and updated based on any changes or updates that are made to your application over its life cycle. Whenever possible you should test your restoration plan under simulated conditions to help find and work out any potential problems before a real emergency occurs. If your restoration plan does not work, it is only worth the paper you wrote it on.

A restoration plan should contain: all detailed instructions to rebuild the network, servers, server tools, applications and configuration details on paper. This should not be on a server in the corner because what will you do if that server goes down as well. For the restoration of small issues, you may need replacement parts for anything hardware related. For the loss of application software, copies of the last working production application (it may be prudent to keep several previous versions) as well as easy access to redundant copies of off-site application development code.

Conduct Scheduled Backups (Availability)

As part of your overall maintenance plan, all your vital servers should have a means of backing up their relevant data. With the possibility of data corruption, or loss, or hardware failure, a regularly scheduled backup is crucial to a maintenance plan in keeping your applications running with the highest level of availability.

By performing full backups every night you will be able to provide a level of confidence in a full recovery in a short amount of time.

If your database is SQL Server, you can also use application transaction logs with a full backup to improve the level of confidence when needing to restore a database. With this information available, you will be able to use the Database Consistency Checker (DBCC) to repair possible corruption in your database.

Hardware (Availability)

Consistent standardized hardware is a great way of making sure that your application stays available to its intended audience. By using the same type of hardware for development and production, there will be a less likely chance of possible issues with improperly configured hardware or hardware that does not behave the same. Having standardized hardware also provides you with no need for different replacement parts and the operations team will not have to be familiar with different equipment. This option is not always feasible due to budget and the logistics. Having a small representative test lab for the application with the same hardware will allow you to basically achieve the same result in a more realistic fashion.

Since the hardware will be the same right down to network and video drivers, you will be able to use one of many software duplication programs to provide the ability to recreate a server configuration with a greater degree of success. If all machines require different drivers due to different configuration then this type of software is of little use.

From time to time you may require support directly from the software vendor (in the case of Windows 2000 and .NET this would be Microsoft). You will want to make sure that the software you have chosen is compatible with the hardware. Microsoft provides a very thorough and broad range of support options as long as your chosen hardware is on their Windows Hardware Compatibility List. If your hardware is not supported, you may not be supported.

Most e-commerce applications today are deployed on a web farm or other server arrangement. The following hardware guidelines will also provide an increased degree of application availability.

- ❑ Use error corrective coding memory.
- ❑ All servers should have redundant network interface cards in case of failure.
- ❑ All servers should have redundant disk controllers.
- ❑ All servers should have redundant power supplies.
- ❑ All servers should have some level of RAID support.

Networking (Availability, Securability)

By creating a web or distributed application, you will then have to access or be part of a network. Depending on the nature of the application, you will have to implement network connectivity that may be public and/or private. If this is the case, then every server should have two network interface cards to provide isolated public and private connectivity. For mission critical applications, the prevention of a single point of failure for your network is required. This can be accomplished by implementing several redundant network paths to critical application components.

Internal networks that need access to the Internet should be secured by a form of firewall, either hardware or software. The .NET server, Internet Acceleration and Security Server 2000 is a firewall as well as an Internet content cache tool to increase performance when accessing pages. You can get more information on this product from the web site http://www.microsoft.com/isaserver/.

Constant Surveillance (Securability)

By maintaining constant surveillance over all aspects of the security of your network and applications, you will be able to combat any unforeseen risks. Have a good auditing policy in place to record all events, and make sure that this record is reviewed on a very regular basis for abnormal activity.

In highly visible e-commerce applications it should be reviewed every day, with alerts sent upon activity beyond a certain threshold. By not reviewing your records regularly, it may be too late to stop an intruder, as it only takes a short time before the damage is done and you didn't even know it.

Implement Security Rules (Securability)

Never say never in the world of security: no matter how secure you think you have your application, there are new ways and issues that come up to break security barriers. With this in mind, you must look at the cost and goals of your application and then implement a set of security rules that fit accordingly. By implementing the best set of security rules possible, and maintaining and reviewing these rules, you are giving your application a fighting chance of staying secure.

Secure Data (Securability)

Just securing the outside external access is not adequate in most situations, because what if someone finds a way into your system? Your data will be fully exposed. In many applications today, data does not always stay on the inside of the application: it can either be sent to other applications or be exposed over a wire. You have to implement a set of rules to secure every aspect of your application infrastructure including the data no matter where it is.

By implementing the security options built in to the .NET servers, you will be on your way to providing a secure site with relative ease. Several of these share a common security model (Windows Active Directory) and implement their own as well. Some items below cover dual roles of securing access as well as data.

The following can be implemented with little effort:

❏ Windows 2000 password options

❏ Windows 2000 NTFS File Permissions

❏ Internet Security and Acceleration Server 2000

❏ Certificate Server 2000

❏ Internet Information Server Secure Sockets Layer (SSL)

❏ Internet Information Server secured logins or anonymous

❏ Microsoft Component Services

❏ COM+ security in the code (if .NET interoperability required)

❏ Microsoft SQL Server 2000

❏ Windows 2000 Active Directory (will require personnel with Active Directory experience to setup optimally)

Provide as Little Visibility as Possible (Securability)

An easy way to prevent access is by making your application as invisible as possible to outside interaction. This means limiting access to as few people as possible. Part of the security review process and password implementation is to either remove access as soon as it is not needed, or force expiration of security after a certain period of time. The more network and physical access available, the easier it will be for someone to gain access.

To limit unnecessary access via the Internet, remove all unnecessary Internet access (only port 80 and 443 TCP/IP traffic if required). Stop as many services as possible if your project does not require them (FTP, Index Services, SMTP etc.). Start with making your system completely closed and then open only entry points that are required to start. If a security breach occurs you will have very few areas to review to prevent it from happening again.

Strong Authentication (Securability)

For highly sensitive data based applications you will want to use the most security possible. This, however, comes at a cost of performance. As you add another layer of security, it will decrease overall performance due to an extra security check for every execution.

Windows 2000 has a couple of integrated features that can provide this level of security. Through the use of Kerberos v5 authentication protocol, you can limit the accessibility of passwords through the distribution of security tickets. It also provides extra secure access to resources on your network.

If your application requires another level of strong authentication and is accessible from the Internet, you may want to implement public-key client certificate authentication. This allows users with a public and private key pair to access your application via the Internet without passwords. Every packet of communication is inspected to match the registered public and private key pair; if they do not match, the request is denied. This can be implemented with the help of Certificate Services in Windows 2000 Server (and above). A note to remember about using certificates is that they contain an expiry date. Since the certificates do expire, you must also implement a plan for the scheduled renewal of those certificates. If these certificates expire it will prevent users from accessing certain areas of your site.

System Access (Securability)

When developing your .NET application, you will have to plan how and to what level it needs to be secured. Many applications have the ability to secure their data, either through application level access, or system integration access, through the operating system. The .NET servers integrate to Windows 2000 and Active Directory so you can implement network-wide authentication, providing ease of management of accessibility.

To gain access to application resources (printers, file servers, applications etc.) you can implement discretionary access control lists (DACLs). This takes the application's security token and compares it to DACL for the requested resource. If the user of that application has permission for that resource, then access is granted.

When you do give access to a user, their security is only as good as their password. By enforcing a strict password implementation you will reduce the use of common passwords, forcing passwords to be changed on a frequent basis, or stipulating that they must meet complexity requirements. These options can be set in the Local Security Policy component of Windows 2000 Server (and above).

Give only the level of access that is required for that user for the applications that they have been assigned to; this will prevent unauthorized or accidental access to areas or features of the application, as well as prevent possible damage if that application executes the wrong instruction.

If you are creating a multi-tier application, you should test access on all levels. This will prevent someone bypassing the front level and directly accessing a middle-tier component, or the database. You can also secure the route of application access so that the multiple layers (depending on the feature or functionality) are accessed in the correct sequence.

Validation (Securability)

All data that is entered into the system must be validated, especially if the action that is being attempted is of a destructive nature or of a non-rollback nature. Also, make sure that the request is coming from the correct location and is not been executed through a back door or invalid path.

Frequent Microsoft's Site for Security Documents and Updates (Securability)

As mentioned above, as application bugs are fixed and improvements are made, new security issues are exposed or created. Microsoft has a very extensive website dedicated just to security issues (http://www.microsoft.com/security) in its products, as well as overall issues. Include visiting their site on a regular basis as part of your security review. The site contains the latest documents on improving security, as well as patches for the latest security issue fix. You can even sign up to be e-mailed security bulletins. How to get and apply this information should also be documented for your customer so that they can keep the systems up to date themselves if you don't have a maintenance agreement with them.

Another great place for general security information on the web is the National Security Agency (http://nsa1.www.conxion.com/index.html). This site provides recommended security guides for different software and hardware implementation.

With all these options available, there is no reason to be caught off guard. One of the biggest problems today with security breaches is that nobody is bothered to apply the available fix. Microsoft does its best to provide solutions but they can't make you apply them. This point should also be made for all software that is being used in your application, whether it is Microsoft or not. It only takes one application to be hacked and your application security is compromised.

Software Tuning (Scalability, Performance)

Most enterprise level applications require an extensive level of integration with Microsoft .NET server software. If any of these applications is not configured properly, then it may not matter what type of hardware you have implemented. The design decisions that have been made may still not be able to scale and perform the way the software was intended.

Listed below are particular server software applications, and ways to improve scalability and performance, as well as information on improving performance and scalability for your application.

SQL Server Tuning

SQL Server 2000 is Microsoft's premier enterprise-level database application, but, if not properly configured, it will not provide the level of scalability that it was designed for. Making sure that the following items are implemented as well as possible means that you will improve the scalability of your overall application.

- ❑ Keep transactions as short as possible and as simple as possible
- ❑ Avoid full table scans unless necessary
- ❑ Do not abuse the use of temporary tables
- ❑ Keep indexes to only the required ones and no extras

❑ Use the appropriate data access technology when required (if the application requires pessimistic locking or server-side cursors you must still use regular ADO)

❑ Use the SQL Server .NET-specific data provider instead of an OLEDB .NET provider

❑ Know when to normalize and denormalize your data

❑ Use Data Partitions for large sets of information (customers, orders etc.)

❑ Use Microsoft Knowledge Base article to troubleshoot performance issues (http://support.microsoft.com/support/kb/articles/Q224/5/87.ASP)

Development Application

Listed below are simple principles and design concepts to keep in mind when you are developing your .NET application. These will help in the scalability and performance of your application.

❑ Keep web pages as small as possible.

❑ Release resources as soon as they are not needed where .NET garbage collection isn't involved (an example of this is if you are required to use ADO or are interoperating with COM components).

❑ Choose asynchronous operations (COM+ loosely coupled events, message queues) before synchronous.

❑ Divide managed components in to transactional and non transactional.

❑ Use the Dataset features of ADO.NET instead of regular ADO with disconnected recordsets.

❑ Use as many forms of resource caching as possible (be careful with memory access if the cache becomes too large) browser, proxy, Internet Information Server, ASP.NET, on a page and fragment level.

❑ Test and tune application under load (this is discussed later in the chapter).

❑ Profile your code with Visual Studio Analyzer.

❑ Keep all operations as stateless as possible.

❑ Run ASP or ISAPI in process or process-isolated, but run COM+ package in process (library package) when possible in mixed .NET COM application.

❑ In the .NET managed framework keep COM+ components calls to a minimum.

❑ Use Internet Information Server Session and application objects as little as possible for state management.

Use Application Center 2000 (Manageability)

Application Center 2000's role in .NET is providing server management functionality and content deployment for servers running Windows 2000 (and higher) and Internet Information Server 5.0.

Application Center 2000 provides ease of managing member servers of its cluster by being able to monitor events and performance counters of those servers. This allows fewer people to manage more machines in the web farm as well as making sure that they are all configured and deployed with the same content.

When deploying content through a manual process, it is possible to either miss or deploy the wrong content to servers on your web farm; it can also take a lot of time, especially if you have to manually restart Internet Information Server services. By using the content deployment features of Application Server 2000, these errors will be eliminated, ensuring that you will have the same content across the farm and in a timelier manner. Application Center 2000 provides you with the ability to also install and configure automatically COM + objects and ISAPI filters.

Application Center 2000 also uses the Network Load Balancing in Windows 2000 to distribute requests across the farm.

Self Monitoring Applications (Manageability)

Having a very large application running on a web farm can make it very difficult to manage all machines at the same time. By building into your application the means to monitor and test itself, then informing a member of the team of errors, you will be better able to manage your application in a 'real time' manner. The application will make period diagnostics on itself to make sure everything is under normal parameters. These could be common functions executed in a test mode. The results would be compared to documented normal responses and in the case where they differ, e-mail or contact the system administrator with as much information as possible.

Application and Infrastructure Monitoring (Availability, Securability, Manageability, Reliability)

By providing continuous monitoring of your application's infrastructure, it can help to prevent problems, or solve problems faster, as there is more information available about the issue. Keeping accurate comprehensive information on all issues that have occurred helps build a knowledge database for staff that they can refer to in order to fix issues easily.

When monitoring your application there are three types of information that will be received: one being a failure message, another telling you of a change in a metric, and one informing that the monitoring cycle completed without errors (this provides a level of confidence because you know the monitoring is still working). It can be difficult to tell if a change in a metric piece of information (for example, increase in SQL Server CPU utilization) is actually a cause for concern unless you have a baseline. This baseline should be obtained and maintained over the life of the application. All monitoring information should be compared to this baseline to determine if something is not functioning correctly. The baseline should contain information on dates and times, load, consumed resources, and throughput, as well as all version information about the software installed.

By monitoring continuously with all information possible, if there is a continual increase or reoccurring sequence, you must find the source of the issue to determine if the problem is related to the process or the software. Process-related issues could be something like having a particular scheduled event occur during peak user volume. A software related issue could be that, after the installation of a new component, there is a slow progressive memory leak.

Having different members of the team from different areas (development, quality assurance, operations etc.) evaluate and analyze the gathered information on a regular basis will help track and find the cause of potential problems before they bring down the application. Results from the analysis may include actual infrastructure changes or procedural changes.

The easiest way to monitor and keep track of your application's infrastructure is by installing and using monitoring tools. These tools provide information on everything from server performance to server application security.

Microsoft provides several tools that can be easily installed and configured to help monitor many aspects of your application:

- ❑ Windows Management Instrumentation: using WMI, an application can access information useful for managing resources on your computers. There is an extensive amount of information available through WMI, including hardware, performance, driver, application, component, event log information, and more. An application that has been constructed with WMI can inform monitoring users of issues. Implementing WMI in an application can take time and effort, but the return on investment is worth it when you can increase reliability, manageability, and availability. By using WMI in conjunction with Application Center 2000, you will be able to track and monitor the health of your servers and the web applications in your web farm. For more information on WMI, follow the link to Microsoft's site: http://msdn.microsoft.com/library/default.asp?URL=/library/psdk/wmisdk/wmistart_5kth.htm.

- ❑ HealthMon (Part of Application Center 2000): HealthMon is a tool that provides a means to monitor your servers from a centralized application. It provides a graphical, real-time status view of your server computers.

- ❑ Performance Logs and Alerts: this is the Windows 2000 performance monitor tool that helps to analyze and track information from various workload counters. Many .NET servers provide counters, which can be monitored by Performance Logs and Alerts. This tool can be configured to alert a user when a particular monitor threshold has been met or exceeded.

- ❑ Application Center 2000: Application Center 2000 has a set of utilities and tools to help manage, synchronize, and scale large Web-based applications. Application Center provides load balancing and server synchronization; cluster configuration services, and handles Network Load Balancing (this is described in this and the previous chapter).

Windows 2000 (Availability, Reliability)

As with standardized hardware, you will want to make sure that all third-party software that is included in your application is "Certified for Windows". Microsoft has a set of guidelines that all software must meet if it is to pass the Windows 2000 Certification program. If this software does not meet these guidelines it may be difficult to obtain the best support from Microsoft.

Windows 2000 provides a number of features that provide very high levels of reliability and availability compared to Windows NT 4.0. These include:

- ❑ Memory Protection: web applications can be set to run out of process to prevent memory leaks from crashing the application.

- ❑ Storage Management: dynamic partition growth; recoverable file system with transaction-based disk I/O; smart space monitoring; dynamic volume management.

- ❑ Windows File Protection: this feature protects all system files from corruption and accidental deletion. This is for all the .SYS, .DLL, .EXE, .TTF, .FON and .OCX files shipped on the Windows 2000 CD.

- ❑ Recovery Features: easy to use recovery console for repairing a machine that will not start due to a misbehaving service. One step restarts Web services without rebooting. Task Manager now has the ability to cleanly shut down an entire process tree for errant applications.

❑   Diagnostic Tools: quick restart of Web services without reboot; clean Task Manager shutdown of the entire process tree for errant applications.

❑   Reboot-Free Maintenance: Plug and Play system configuration; fewer system restarts; RAID rebuilds without reboot.

Environment (Availability)

Securing the availability of your application through better software design and hardware infrastructure is required, but what is protecting it? The environment and attributes of the physical location need to be protected to make sure that the application infrastructure stays running. Test and plan the physical security of access to the infrastructure, for the possibility of fire and in the case of mission critical applications, fire suppressant systems. No matter where the systems are located, they must have power to run. A backup generator or battery backup UPS is essential to continued operation of your application or controlled shutdown in case of a power failure.

Synchronize All Clocks (Availability)

Many automated operations require accurate file timestamps to operate. If the servers that are accessing the applications do not have their clocks synchronized, they become confused, shut down or crash, they may create incorrect data or they may start up an automated process at the worst possible time (for instance, archiving orders on your database during the day). By keeping all server clocks synchronized, operations should run smoothly and without any surprises.

If you are running an application that is distributed in different time zones, and a server in one time zone may affect another in a different time zone, you have two possible choices. The first is that all applications and servers will have to be configured to run in the same time zone; this could either be the time zone of the headquarters, or your central office, or Greenwich Mean Time (GMT). The other option is the use of UTC (Universal Time Coordinate), which is the same everywhere; however, this option can only be used if all applications understand and/or have this option. Below you will find a couple of links to the Microsoft Knowledge Base for articles on how to configure and synchronize your server clocks.

❑   How to Set Up And Synchronize with Domain Time Source Servers
http://support.microsoft.com/support/kb/articles/Q131/7/15.asp

❑   Using TIMESERV to Set and Synchronize Time
http://support.microsoft.com/support/kb/articles/Q232/2/55.ASP

Staffing (Availability, Reliability)

The application that is being developed can only be as good as the people that work on it. The more experience and expertise that the staff has, the more reliable and available the application will be. Once the design and planning of the application have been completed, there may be an area of technical implementation where the level of expertise on the staff is not adequate enough for the task. The staff must be trained in the architecture and tools that have been chosen for the task, otherwise they will not be able to create and maintain the application. By developing a regularly reviewed training plan and budget, individually and as a whole team, the team will become stronger and better prepared to complete any application on time and budget.

Since the .NET Framework and Visual Studio .NET are very new, a detailed training plan for all staff is recommended before working on the first major production .NET application. Microsoft has extensive training materials included in the DVD versions of Visual Studio.NET. Microsoft's training and certification web site has a complete listing of courses and materials for .NET. Also, seminars and books (Wrox Press books, of course!) are great training tools as well.

Here are some links to various web sites for training material on .NET and .NET Servers:

- ❑   http://www.wrox.com/Books/books.asp?sub_section=1&subject_id=63&subject=%2ENET
- ❑   http://www.microsoft.com/education/training/cert/default.asp
- ❑   http://www.microsoft.com/trainingandservices/redirect/dotnet.htm
- ❑   http://www.microsoft.com/seminar/

Staying within Budget (Availability, Reliability)

Depending on the type of application that is being created, you may have to re-evaluate your budget if you require your application to be available and reliable all the time. Many features that are designed to increase the uptime of your application can cost a lot of money. This cost benefit may not be worth the expense if the application is not mission critical to yourself or the customer. There are many features and techniques that can be implemented that can increase the availability and reliability of your application; choose the combination that fits the budget and the need of the application.

Software Engineering Methodology (Reliability)

It is difficult to achieve a high level of reliability in your application through code alone. By following a well documented and understood software engineering methodology, you can achieve a very high level of reliability in any large-scale application. By following the chosen methodology from start to finish, you will be able to accurately assess the success of the application. This will help in refining company practices and standards, which in turn should increase reliability in your next application. In most cases, if a design methodology is not implemented, and the coding of an application begins right away, you will have visible returns almost immediately, but will run into issues later in the development cycle that may ultimately prevent you from completion with a high degree of acceptance.

A good software engineering methodology does not rely on a particular development language; it is for the design and managing the construction of the application in its complete lifecycle.

Microsoft has a very well documented software engineering methodology framework called Microsoft Solutions Framework. Microsoft Solution Framework is a guide or set of ideas for planning, building and managing applications. There are six models that make up the Microsoft Solution Framework. They are: Team and Process Models, the Application Model, the Solution Design Model, the Enterprise Architecture Model, Total Cost of Ownership Model and the Risk Management Model. These models also provide information on procedure for documenting each process as well as who should be part of the documentation creation and delivery. The following is a brief description of the use of each model:

- ❑   **Team and Process Model**
  This model provides a guide on how to organize projects and the people that will be working on them. This is the core model for Microsoft Solution Framework.

- ❑   **Application Model**
  This model provides a guide for designing applications and distributed applications.

❑ **Solution Design Model**
This model provides a guide to how applications should be designed from a user and business point of view in regards to the Application Model.

❑ **Enterprise Architecture Model**
This model provides a guide to help you maximize the benefits of new technology in your application designs.

❑ **Total Cost of Ownership Model**
This model provides a guide to increasing the value of technology through assessing, improving and managing its overall cost.

❑ **Risk Management Model**
This model provides a guide to managing risks in designing and development of your application.

There are other design methodologies, which will provide you with other approaches to designing applications in a development cycle; these are Rational Unified Processes (RUP) and Carnegie Mellon Software Engineering Institute Capability Maturity Model (CMM). For more information, follow these links:

❑ http://www.microsoft.com/business/microsoft/mcs/msf.asp

❑ http://www.rational.com/products/rup/index.jsp

❑ http://www.sei.cmu.edu/cmm/cmm.html

Quality Assurance (Reliability)

Your application is only as good as the quality assurance testing that has been conducted on it. All functionality must be working as specified in the design and technical specification. All use cases must be working without error. The quality assurance cycle should continue until the level of reliability is met to the documented metrics and customer satisfaction. Several techniques to improve the quality assurance process are documented later in this chapter.

Change Implementation (Reliability)

Once your application is implemented, to keep it reliable you will have to maintain it. However, if all aspects of maintenance are not implemented in a controlled manner, then there is a possibility that you may introduce new issues, which may result in failure.

Throughout the life cycle of an application you may be required to make changes in a number of different ways: for example, the server it is running on requires a new version of another application, or the installation of another application, the executing machine is having an application removed as it is no longer required, or you have to install a new patch to your application due to fixing a bug. These scenarios may remove a component that your application requires, install a new version of a component that your application can't work with, or your own component might introduce new bugs or expose existing bugs. All of these changes to the system can have adverse reactions to your application if the change is not fully tested.

All changes must be handled with more care than a brand new installation. If possible, all changes should be tested in the lab to make sure there are no errors in the repeatable implementation process. To help in the process of implementing changes, a good approach is using a set of environments that emulate the different stages leading to release in production. All potential changes will start off in the development environment, move to the quality assurance department, go back to the staging environment, and then to production. If at any point a problem is found, cycle back to the beginning and start over.

If the change has any possibility that it can be rolled back in case of error, a comprehensive tested rollback plan should be prepared. If the change can't be rolled back, what preparations can be made in case of error? A controlled, and preferably automated, implementation plan will help make sure that the change is done correctly. By using an automated process of implementation you will remove the human error factor and increase reliability in the change.

Don't make changes for the sake of change. Depending on the lifecycle of the application, the change may not be required, as the application may be retired in a short amount of time. If the application is currently working and the change is not absolutely required, it may be a good idea not to implement it. Also, be very careful in trying to implement too many changes at once. It is very tempting to say that since we are already changing one component, why don't we just make this change too? The more changes you make, the more testing of those changes you will have to do, and the greater the chance of error.

If you must make changes, it is a very good idea to make as few changes to production as possible. You must plan all changes in great detail and pool the required changes together to form a service pack type release, test the release thoroughly, and make as few updates to production as possible.

A reliable application is possible only when all of the components, services, and configurations are synchronized. A quality deployment process requires timely communication, necessary skills, formal procedures, clear authority, and a problem resolution process.

The Code

Now that you have planned to implement your application with the best practices for the overall availability, manageability, securability, scalability and reliability of your application, what about the actual code for that application?

The code is the most important part of any application and there is more to just writing it than making sure that it works without any problems. In the past you may have started a new job and upon reviewing the actual code realized that you would have to spend the next two weeks learning what the code does, because there are no coding standards and almost no documentation on just what each piece of code does. Anyone can read the code and figure it out, but why should you have to? If you have to spend all your time just trying to figure out if a word is a variable, method, or object, and you then afterwards have no idea what it is actually used for, or why is it there, you know there are going to be errors and no best practices for any aspect of development is going to save the code.

If the code is well documented, with technical and functional specifications, well commented, and the code follows very clearly defined coding standards, you should be able to read what the code is doing as it applies to the business rules of the application in almost no time at all. The goal of all coding standards is to be able to read the code and not be able to tell which developer did which piece or when. The only personalization should be the developers name in the comment blocks.

All teams, whether they are a team of one or many, should work together to create a naming and code standard that all members agree with and are willing to adhere to. There currently exists several naming conventions (such as Hungarian notation) and coding standards that go to various degrees of completeness. The more detail that your coding standards document has, the less chance there is for developer discrepancy when reviewing code with the team members.

Code Reviews

Your team has written a new Web Service with .NET following the company's naming conventions and standards but what about the code itself? If you work in a team of ten developers, how do you know that the ten pieces will work together, that some people have not duplicated code, and that the code is free of potential unseen bugs? Your design and technical specifications should address the previous issues, but, due to communication problems (someone didn't read an e-mail) or a developer couldn't wait for another developer to complete their work, this does not always happen.

I have met some senior developers who don't find code review sessions necessary: they feel that their code is fine and with all their experience, they don't create code with bugs anymore. With the vast size of .NET and the fact that it is so new, everyone is a junior developer and can learn at least one or two things in a code review session.

Everyone has their own thoughts of how code review sessions should be conducted (or even if they should be). I have found over the years that the technique that is most productive and beneficial for the developers and the application is conducting code review sessions with the entire development team, all at one time. There are many benefits for this format as compared to one person reviewing everything or a one-on-one type situation. Below you will find a few direct benefits and the methods for this format and some of their advantages.

Accountability

By presenting code in front of the team, each developer is given a level of accountability to make his or her code the best that it can be. They, of course, should be putting their best foot forward anyway, but a bit of competitiveness and peer pressure never hurt anyone. That peer pressure of knowing that code will be reviewed by all team members with a fine-toothed comb tends to push developers to find new ways of doing common tasks, to learn new techniques, and to triple check their code for any possible errors. Throughout the entire code review process it should be made clear that no developer should be made to feel victimized or stupid. It should be stressed that, even though everyone is accountable for their own work during a review, it is not the idea to criticize mistakes, but help improve the overall talent of the whole team.

Apprentice / Mentorship

Presenting code to a group of developers that have mixed skill sets is a great way for all team members to learn, regardless of whether they are senior or junior. I have experienced that at first the junior developers may feel that they are being criticized or being picked on in this type of session. It must be stressed that all comments and feedback are meant to be communicated in a very constructive manner. Everyone is there to learn and help each other. The junior developers have a great opportunity to learn, as well as the senior developers, who can pass along knowledge that in the long run makes the team stronger. Senior developers who have a wealth of experience in different environments will be able to spot potential problems in the code that maybe others didn't even think of. The more senior developers should also take the time to help the more junior staff as much as possible as they will then become more productive and contribute to the application more quickly.

Teamwork

By working on your own piece of code for a few days, you may start to lose touch with the other developers' code (and if not careful the other developers themselves). Bringing the team together helps each developer remember the big picture of the entire application. It gets everyone thinking about each other's code and how it will all work together. The more often the code reviews sessions occur, the more each developer will think of the team and what each can do to help. This may be hard to do at times due to conflicts of schedules and deadlines, so get as many developers together as possible. This will at least provide the code and team with some level of visibility to make sure all is on track. Bascially, take the approach that a small team code review is better than no code review at all.

The following are some techniques in the actual performing of code reviews:

Time

Depending on the development schedule, size and scope of the application, you may want to have one or more code reviews per week. I don't suggest scheduling each session any farther apart than that, or the time in between will be too long to have a memorable impact on all developers. Once the developers get into a routine that they know that their code will be reviewed, they will accept that practice and be better prepared for it.

Keep the actual time during the day that a code review is conducted consistent. The more often you change the time that the actual code review occurs, the greater the possibility that developers will think that they are not as important as they should be.

Keep the length of the code review sessions to a reasonable level, but also make sure that everyone's code is reviewed. If this takes longer, it takes longer. Everyone needs their fair time to make sure that they feel as important and included as the rest. This may be difficult at crunch time, but again, any time saved in finding bugs in the code review sessions are of more benefit than spending the time trying to roll back a change to production.

Preparation

Make it mandatory for each member of the team to prepare his or her code at least a day before the code review. Either provide printed copies to the other members of the team or point them to a very well marked place in the code in your source code control database.

Upon going to the code review session make sure that every member of the team has actually reviewed the other members' code. The best way to do this is just as your teacher marked your homework and tests in school: take a printed copy and mark it with a red pen. It may seem somewhat simple, but it can be very effective.

If for some reason a developer does not have time to prepare, or just doesn't do it, don't let them off. Have that developer do the preparation as soon as possible and do a manual one-on-one code review or convene a special code review session. This will help stress the fact that code reviews are a very necessary part of development and aren't to be taken lightly. This may sound harsh, but if a code review finds a bug that could crash your application it is worth it.

During the Review

To allow all participants of the review to be focused on the code that is being reviewed, it is a good idea to have one person document what code changes have been accepted. This allows that developer to concentrate on code being discussed and not have to write down every little change. This also provides a comprehensive list of the changes that are to be made for all the code being reviewed.

Also, don't let the actual review process get sidetracked by other development issues, such as the current deadline, or whether the hardware is installed yet. Nobody likes a meeting that runs longer than is necessary; by concentrating on the code review at hand you will have a better chance of enforcing standards, find bugs, and learning ways to code.

Consistency

The code must be reviewed against the well-documented and detailed coding standards that have been approved by the entire team. If you review the code against how you, as an individual, feel, it isn't fair to the developer who did the code, as he based his code on the standards that are in place. This makes sure that there is always a level of reinforcement and a solid baseline when it comes to reviewing the code. Don't make exceptions for one developer or one particular type of code. If there is an issue with the standards for that particular item, apply the current standards and bring it up in the next standards review meeting.

After the Review

Once you have finished the actual code review session, you are not done. It is now time for each member of the team to go back and implement the required changes to their code. By going back and making changes, it provides a level of reinforcement of the company standards that are in place, as well as giving time to review the new techniques that were learned.

Once the code is updated, ask each developer for the actual printed code review code back. This can be used as a reference check later, in case any issues come up later in production that you thought were fixed. It can also be used to provide an area of metrics for improvement for the more junior members of the team – how have they improved in areas of adhering to commenting, naming conventions, and class creation etc. over a period of time?

As new techniques, tools, and other languages are brought in to the development process, it is a very good idea to have regular coding standards review meetings. This provides a forum for all developers to discuss anything that they may find difficult or incorrect in the coding standards and to work towards changing it. The items listed previously, or maybe new developers brought on to the team, will help dictate how often this type of meeting should take place. If every person knows that there is a forum to discuss changes in the coding standards, no one will feel like they are being forced to comply with something they don't believe or have a hand in.

Once the code has been distributed, all code must not be changed unless there is a change request and the changed code is then also reviewed. This will prevent non-reviewed code from possibly being distributed to production.

If all these items are done in a consistent manner, each member of the team will learn a great deal and it will help them to work much closer together, as well as build a better application.

Version Control

Visual SourceSafe and .NET

As you continue building your .NET application, you come to the same problem that has always existed – managing the actual code. Code management and version control software has been marginally improved in .NET. Visual Studio .NET Enterprise contains a very slightly modified version of Visual SourceSafe called Visual SourceSafe 6.0c. These modifications to Visual SourceSafe are only a couple of integration issues to the new .NET IDE and some GUI changes to pop-up windows. Visual Studio .NET contains its own source control services, so you don't have to use the Visual SourceSafe client; everything is self-contained in the developer's environment.

Visual Studio.NET has introduced new file types that are only recognized by Visual SourceSafe 6.0c natively, so to ensure that your source control services are properly and fully integrated, this is the version that should be installed.

The major functionality of Visual SourceSafe has not changed. This is a good thing in that all that you have learned in the past with Visual SourceSafe is still completely valid. I guess this is also a bad thing, as we are still stuck with all the things that make Visual SourceSafe a program most developers love to hate (at least in my experience). This was mainly due to the awkward and feature-incomplete Visual SourceSafe add-in that could be used with Visual Basic 6.0

Inside the .NET IDE, you have the ability to have predefined default source code control settings (more than the four previously offered in Visual Studio 6). There are three predefined combinations of option settings: standard Visual SourceSafe, Team Development, Independent Developer. There is also one that is your own custom combination.

This new addition allows for ease of setup for different types of developers. In previous versions of VB, when you have loaded up your latest project, found the method of code that requires modification, and started typing, the IDE will beep at you and say that it can't edit this code. The file has not been checked out of Visual SourceSafe. This was a real problem if you were on the road and needed to make changes to the code and were not able to connect to your Visual SourceSafe database. The new settings in .NET allow you to set different options for when this situation happens. You can either have the IDE prompt the user to check out the file, prompt for exclusive checkouts (which isn't mentioned in any documentation – I am assuming this will check out the file exclusively if you have configured your Visual SourceSafe environment to have share checkouts), check out the file automatically (if it is not checked out already), or act as in previous versions of VB and not do anything.

As part of the new feature, when you try to edit checked-in files as per above, there is another option available, which will allow you to edit the file even though it has been checked in. This new option in the .NET IDE allows a user to edit a particular file in their own environment, even if another developer has that file checked out. This will allow developers to keep working on their code, or try new ideas, without having to force another developer to check in his or her code. The last new option in the .NET IDE is also to do with editing a checked-in file. Now that you have edited a checked-in file you have three options when you try to save the file: you will be prompted to check out the file (if possible) so that you can then check your changes back in to Visual SourceSafe; you can change the setting so that upon trying to save your changes, the file that you are working on will be checked out automatically; or, the last option is to save your changes to the checked-in file to somewhere else on your system as a Save As.

As much as I always hated that when I tried to edit a file that was already checked in, the IDE would beep at me, there is serious potential for problems with certain combinations of settings with the new options provided by the .NET IDE.

If you have the **Allow checked in items to be edited** option checked (see the following figure), the when checked in items are saved set to Check out automatically and the regular .NET IDE option of automatically save changes upon running the application, the following scenario could happen: with the above settings set, you start to edit a checked in file, make several changes, and run your application – your changes will be saved automatically, and upon closing the application the Visual SourceSafe check in dialog will appear. If enter is pressed and the developer is not paying attention, they will have inadvertently checked in code that was never meant to be checked-in. The two ways to revert back to the previous version are to re-check out the file and remove your changes (that is if you remember what changes you made!) or have your Visual SourceSafe admin roll back your changes to a previous Visual SourceSafe version. This scenario could have disastrous effects if you are just about to compile code that is going to production and the build engineer gets the latest version from Visual SourceSafe and does not pay attention to any changes that have been made (this should not happen; it is best to form a quality assurance test label of the code before making a build that will be going to production). This scenario does require several 'ifs' to happen first, but there are other combinations of the new .NET IDE features that can still be effective, although not as harmful.

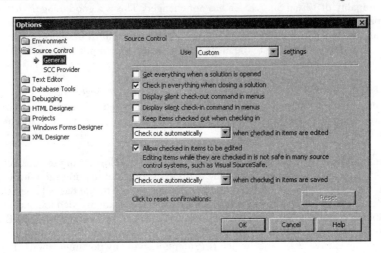

If you are going to be working in a team environment, it is a very good idea to make sure that everyone on the team uses the same settings for source code control.

Another new feature in the .NET IDE is the ability to have menu items for having silent check in and out processes. By choosing these menu items, you can check out or in files without displaying the appropriate dialog box. By using this option you will not be able to add comments to your check out and in process. This in most situations is not ideal. By providing comments when you check out and in files you give other users more details of why you did the action in the first place. This is a perfect place to put comments regarding bug fixes. These comments, of course, should be in the code as well, but it allows a build engineer to find the differences between different checked-in versions of code and print out what were the changes. When comments have been added they can be matched up with your quality assurance information to provide an automatic change log for the next build.

Below you will find information about the different settings in the .NET IDE for configuring the interaction with your source code control tool.

❑ **Visual SourceSafe Settings**
These settings provide very little automation to the source code control process. By default, you will not get the latest version of code when you open a project, nor will you check anything in. When attempting to edit items that are checked in already, you will be prompted to check them out. These settings provide a level of safety for your code, so you don't make any mistakes due to unnecessarily checking in files or overwriting them because of an automatic process.

❑ **Team Development Settings**
These settings are the same as the above Visual SourceSafe settings, except it has the exact settings of the scenario that I described above in regard to editing a checked-in file. I don't recommend this setting at all for the above reason. If you are using Visual SourceSafe as your source code control, use a combination of the Custom settings that avoids the above scenario.

❏ **Individual Developer Settings**

This combination of settings is fine if you are a single developer working in your own environment. It gives you all the benefits of source code control, without the slight inconvenience of checking in and out files manually. The only item that I recommend to be changed is Display silent check in command in the menus.

❏ **Custom Settings**

This setting allows you to custom-choose any combinations of settings you choose.

Now that you have your code being stored and versioned in Visual SourceSafe, you have to be just as careful with those files as you would be with any other file of great importance. This is your code; this is the information that is making you your money. If you don't protect this then you might not be a developer for much longer.

Visual SourceSafe Best Practices

Do Not Use Allow Multiple Checkouts

Shared checkouts are an option that should only be used by experienced developers who are aware of the risks in its use. Shared checkouts provide the ability for more than one developer to check out a particular file. This defeats one of the key purposes of source code control – generally, you don't want two developers working on the same file at the same time. The first person that checks that file in will think that his changes are safe and secure. When the other developer checks in his or her file, it will overwrite the changes of the previous developer.

Synchronize All Developers Systems Clocks

Make sure that all Visual SourceSafe server and client systems clocks are synchronized on a regular basis. This prevents file check ins and outs from appearing as if they were conducted out of sequence. This can become a very large problem if you are working with Visual SourceSafe from different time zones. Visual SourceSafe uses the timestamp from the client machine when performing any operation, it does not have any means for understanding time zones or to use the Universal Time Coordinate (UTC). The only way to prevent any time-related issues is for all clients to be set to the same time zone as the server (again synchronize for exact time). This can be more than just an inconvenience if you are offsite for more than a short time and must conduct other tasks that are time-dependent.

The other option for getting around this issue is to use a product called SourceOffsite. It is designed primarily for remote access to Visual SourceSafe databases. We can find more information about this product at www.sourcegear.com. It processes all transactions based on the server time (but also keeps track of the client's time); this prevents any problems with time-based file operations. The other great feature of this product is that it is much faster over just about any connection (Internet to direct dial up) than using the standard Visual SourceSafe client. This can be a great benefit if you have many developers out of the office and need a quick connection to the Visual SourceSafe server.

One other issue with synchronizing systems clocks is that all files should be checked in before the time is changed. Visual SourceSafe uses the system date and time to determine if a file is within a valid range for a label. Changing the system clock to a date preceding the creation date of the project being searched causes serious damage to the labeling structure of that project, which results in a loss of project history.

Sharing and Branching

If you are a single developer working on a couple of applications, sharing files between Visual SourceSafe projects provides a level of convenience when you have to fix a bug or add a new feature. Once you get the latest version of the code, you will have the new bug fix code as well. However, when you get into a large team with multiple parallel development tracks (for example, maintenance patch project, next minor release, prototype for next major release), sharing files can cause problems if not handled correctly. If your maintenance patch project and next minor release project share the file common.bas, and a developer makes a change for a new feature in the next minor release project, if the file is not branched that change will be compiled with the maintenance patch project. There is a big possibility that this sequence of events will cause problems in the compiled code.

Remove Destroy Permission for All But the Most Trusted Developers

Do not give too many developers on the team Destroy permission in Visual SourceSafe. Once a file is destroyed there is no way to retrieve the file unless you want to retrieve it from a database backup. If a file is destroyed, and it is required for a previous version of the application, and you try to get that version from the history, you will not be able to. Since that file is destroyed, you won't be able to get that version of the application and compile it if you require a previous version of the application. It is fine to allow developers to delete files as long as they don't have destroy rights. These files are not completely removed from the system, but held in a Purge container (similar to Windows Recycling Bin). These files can be retrieved from the Deleted Items tab of that project's Properties dialog.

This permission should only be given to tech leads or senior developers, and is only to be used when they are absolutely positive that destroying the file will not do any harm.

Keep Shared Common Files in One Project

If you are implementing sharing in your Visual SourceSafe database, and you are working on a set of applications that share several objects, it is very common to have each of those objects in each project being shared with the others. If you are relying on Visual SourceSafe sharing to have all applications use the same objects, no matter what operation you perform on the database, then you may be in for a surprise. If you check in a shared object and realize that you have to roll back the checked-in file, Visual SourceSafe will roll back the file, but it will also break the share. If you are unaware of this behavior, the next time you make a change to what you thought was a fully-shared object, one or more of the applications will not get the change.

The best way to share a set of files between a set of applications is to place these files in a Common project just under the root project and have all your .NET projects in the set of applications point to the same directory on your development machine. Your projects will all reference the same file directory and all will receive the latest version (this may require you to do two 'get latest versions' from Visual SourceSafe: one for the Common project and one for your application); they won't know the difference, you will not have problems with sharing, and you will save disk space.

Visual SourceSafe Maintenance Plan

The SourceSafe Data directory is the main directory where the Visual SourceSafe database stores its data. It contains all of your files, code and projects. Microsoft has made every precaution possible to ensure the integrity of all SourceSafe files. There are certain events that can cause the data in this database to become corrupted. These corruptions can be in the shape of an inaccessible file, links to shared files that are duplicated, orphaned files, etc. If the database is maintained properly, you should never come across any of these issues. SourceSafe database corruption can be caused by a variety of factors. Listed below are a few events that can cause database corruption:

- ❏ Power loss

- ❏ Server System crashes

- ❏ User terminating a long process

- ❏ Running out of disk space

- ❏ Network problems

- ❏ Operating system problems

If too many of these events occur and the Visual SourceSafe database becomes substantially corrupt, it may become nearly impossible to retrieve your files. It is very important to have a strict maintenance plan in place to discover and fix these errors before it is too late. As Visual SourceSafe databases grow in size, the potential for problems becomes greater.

According to Microsoft's recommendations, the maximum size your Visual SourceSafe database should get to is between 3GB and 5GB, depending on usage and type of information being stored. The more history, shared files, labels, and files there are, they will force this maximum size to become smaller. A Visual SourceSafe database with many projects (over 200) with thousands of very small files (possibly a typical e-commerce web site), many of them shared with a year's worth of history, can become very corrupt by the time it becomes about 1GB in size.

Microsoft has a very good document on **Best Practices with Visual SourceSafe** on the MSDN network (http://msdn.microsoft.com/library/default.asp?URL=/library/techart/vssbest.htm). Use this document as a base for your maintenance plan; I have included several observations that should be used in addition to the above document. A couple of these items may seem contradictory, but as with all development issues, your environment will be different from everyone else's, so use these as a guideline and keep monitoring it yourself until you feel comfortable.

Run Full Backups

It is best not to run incremental backups with Visual SourceSafe as there can be difficulty in restoring all files. It is best to always conduct a full backup. It is a very good idea to test your full backup on a regular basis. This may seem like a fairly standard thing to do in this day of computers, but not testing backups is a very common problem. I am sure that you, or someone you know, has been left out in the cold over a backup that didn't restore. Restore your backup to a completely different machine and test it by opening it with your usual client machine. Browse around the project structure and check out and in some files, make sure that everything is fine. If it does not work you may be looking at some serious rebuilding.

Shadow Directories

To provide yourself with an extra level of protection against loss of data, you can implement a Shadow Directory of your key development projects. A Shadow Directory is a directory on a server that receives the latest changes to its related project when a file is checked in. It does not contain any history. The Shadow Directory can be set up to be anywhere on any server. In the case where we want to provide an additional form of backup, it would be best to point this to a different server to your main Visual SourceSafe server. It does not receive updates when project-related information (for example, the renaming of a project) is changed; if these are changed you must resync the Shadow Directory manually or through the Reconcile method of the Project Difference dialog. If this Shadow Directory is maintained, you will always have another backup of your latest code. This Shadow Directory is updated upon every file check in, so this will slow the performance down of your overall server. For this reason you will only want to use this option if the benefit outweighs the cost. If you are a single developer with no form of major backup (I don't have to tell you how shameful that is in the first place!) at least you will have a file-based copy of your Visual SourceSafe database somewhere else on your system in case of accidents.

Increase Performance of Visual SourceSafe By Decreasing Size

On a regular basis, depending on your development schedule, archive the oldest projects to some form of permanent storage. This will keep the Visual SourceSafe database from getting too big with files that are rarely accessed. As the size of the Visual SourceSafe database increases, the performance will decrease. It won't be very noticeable when you are doing a 'get the latest version', but it will be noticeable when you, for example, do a recursive view on the project's history.

Another reason to keep branching of files to a minimum is that once a file is branched in SourceSafe, there are four associated files that are not deleted from the disk at this point. The reason this occurs is so that the reference between the branch and original file is maintained. There is no way to undo this behavior after the branching has occurred.

Purging Old Files

If you know that you are never ever going to do a get from an old label you can purge all deleted files from a project. This should be only done if you are very tight on space and there are no other means of obtaining more. If you try to do a get from an old label, and a file that was there at the time the label was created is now purged from the database, you will not be able to get that label.

There are two ways to purge files, either from the client user interface of Visual SourceSafe, or from the command line. Both these options only allow you to purge one project at a time. The only way to purge a set of projects all at one time is to write a tool with the Visual SourceSafe automation objects. A better practice, which is safer, would be to archive old code and projects if you really want to get space back on your Visual SourceSafe server.

Analyzing for Errors

The `Analyze` tool is used to find and fix errors in the Visual SourceSafe database. It also can delete files and compress the database to help conserve space. This tool takes four separate paths through the Visual SourceSafe database for each time it is run, so depending on the size of your Visual SourceSafe database, you should allow for a long execution time. Do not allow your scheduled backup program to run while the `Analyze` tool is executing, as this will cause it to not complete its task.

When you run the Visual SourceSafe `Analyze` tool you must first delete the current `Backup` directory. You should make sure that there are no outstanding issues reported with possible missing information after the last analyze. Next you must make sure that you lock the Visual SourceSafe database so there is no user interaction while `Analyze` is executing. It is generally a good idea to automate the execution of this task during the night due to the above problems.

Run the Visual SourceSafe `Analyze` tool with the `Fix` and `Delete` options on a regular basis, depending on total Visual SourceSafe usage (for a large heavy usage database once every two weeks). The only time `Analyze` will delete files when you use the `-D` switch is when it detects a file that was involved in a branch at one point, and there are no other branched versions of the file that are now active.

```
Analyze.exe c:\Visual SourceSafe\data -F -D
```

Run the Visual SourceSafe `Analyze` tool with the `Compress` option on a regular basis, depending on total Visual SourceSafe usage (for a large heavy usage database once every month). This feature does not do that much on most Visual SourceSafe databases for various reasons (when you branch files and then delete them, the space is not recovered until all copies of the branched file are destroyed in the database).

```
Analyze.exe c:\Visual SourceSafe\data -C
```

Clean Up Temp Directory

As you work with Visual SourceSafe, it will create temporary files on the server in the `TEMP` directory on the root database directory. These files are supposed to be destroyed once they are not required; however, due to circumstances, this does not always happen. These files don't cause any problems other than the fact that they take up space in the file system.

The Visual SourceSafe administrator can remove these files and restore space by executing the `Cleanup Temp Directory` command from the Visual SourceSafe `Admin` tool.

Each client also has a temporary file directory on each machine that, as good practice, should be cleaned up from time to time. The location of this directory is set in the Options of the Visual SourceSafe client. It can be either a local or network drive. It should be set to a local drive to speed performance of Visual SourceSafe operations, but this will require a manual process from each developer to execute the clean up.

Coding Standards

As mentioned a few times in this chapter, coding standards can, and will, make all developers' jobs easier as long as they are strictly adhered to. Microsoft has prepared a very good document about design goals for creating classes in .NET. They have drawn out a set of guidelines for the naming of managed classes to best allow all developers to easily understand their use in a cross language development application. This document is almost a chapter unto itself so I won't be going into this subject myself. The name of the document is .NET Framework Design (`designguidelines.doc`). It should be easy to find on the Visual Studio.NET CD or DVD.

This section will discuss some general ideas of coding standards, a big change in variables in VB.NET, and the use and look of comments, and briefly look at the change in Visual Studio.NET's code indentation rules.

There are a number of general rules to follow when creating a coding standard. It is okay to have your own preferences as long as they are very well documented to all developers and each one agrees to them fully. If it is not well communicated then it can't be much of a standard.

There should be a section for the naming of all objects, methods, handlers, variables etc. The standard should include a physical code layout standard for all elements of your code (variables, construct blocks, and commenting etc.). If you do not have a layout standard already in place, the VS.NET IDE allows you configure an option for Smart Indenting per language. This smart indenting takes care of the enforcement of the correct indentation of all constructs for a language; if all developers configure this option it will provide the consistency needed for a layout standard. There should be a well documented set of rules for the new structured error handling, setting and testing of all return values, object creation, and variable initialization (should you use the new variable declaration initialization functionality or just initialize code when needed). It should contain a detailed description of how, where, and when you should be inserting comments into the code (this is described in greater detail below). There should also be set rules in regard to the actual formatting and layout of the code; this can enhance the readability as well as the presentation of code if the source code is required for delivery.

Use of Regions

A new feature of VS.NET that can help organize large blocks of code for easy viewing is the use of `#Region` directives. A region directive allows you to be able to collapse or expand a section of code when outlining in the VS.NET IDE. An example of this built in to VS.NET is the automatically generated Windows code. They are all enclosed in region directives.

Enterprise Templates

The Enterprise Edition of Visual Studio.NET has a new feature called Enterprise Templates. Its main goal is to provide prebuilt code templates for an application. These templates take the approach of providing a template for a particular type of application, not focusing primarily on what language it should be written in. These templates are completely customizable to the point where you can build your own from scratch. This will allow you to create a set of templates based on proven development approaches, but coded against your own coding standards. This will help enforce your coding standards, but also greatly ease the development process.

VS.NET Code Reuse

The Visual Studio.NET IDE provides a few ways to help reuse code to make it easier to enforce coding standards. If you want to only use a snippet of code while the VS.NET IDE is running, you can use the new Clipboard Ring that saves all the code that you have copied or cut. This will allow you to reuse code that you have already used once. The VS.NET IDE also has a new macro recording functionality so you can record actions and code and assign it to a button. This will allow you to save standardized snippets of code for reuse in other programs. Also, if you don't have the Enterprise Edition of Visual Studio.NET and need similar functionality as the Enterprise Templates, you can always create your own code repository addin. VS.NET IDE has an expanded and upgraded automation object model so you could code your own add-in to store company-wide common standardized coding blocks. It is a great way to learn .NET as well as help ease development and enforce coding standards.

Variables

The handling of variables in the coding standard can have a huge impact on the actual performance of the code itself. A big change in coding in VB.NET is the default variable type. In all previous versions, the Variant was the default if you didn't type cast your variables; in VB.NET it is now an Object class. This change will have the most impact on code that is converted from standard ASP classes to VB.NET, if they are left as objects and each variable is not type cast.

The Object class can hold a reference to any other type of variable. It should be well documented in the coding standard when this type of variable usage is accepted and when it should be reviewed on a case-by-case basis in the code review sessions. The difference is that, as with all objects in previous versions of VB, they will be late bound during run-time. This can have a big impact on performance depending on the number of times of execution. When running a simple test of just assigning a value to an object or a proper type cast variable it was 20 times slower. Granted this test is greatly simplified and the actual execution time was small, but if that variable was a class instead (perhaps a textbox), the measurable difference becomes greater. Over the execution life span of an application it may actually save a very large noticeable amount of time if type casted correctly.

```
    Private Sub btnTest_Click(ByVal sender As System.Object, ByVal e As
            System.EventArgs) Handles btnTest.Click
        'Dim objTotal as Long
        'Change declaration based on test to be run
        Dim objTotal As Object
        Dim intCounter As Integer
        Dim dblStartTime As Double

        dblStartTime = Timer

        For intCounter = 1 To 100000
            objTotal = objTotal + intCounter
        Next

        Debug.WriteLine(Timer - dblStartTime)
    End Sub
```

Another area that will affect the use of variables is the use of the new statement Option Strict (On | Off). This language statement forces that all data type conversion be explicitly coded when it is turned On. The default for this statement is Off. This statement is used to ensure that there is no data loss when implicitly converting to a data type of smaller capacity or precision. If an explicit conversion statement is not used, the developer will be notified upon compiling the code. Other errors will occur as the use of Option Strict On also implies Option Explicit, even if this statement isn't used. Also, the use of late binding of an object will cause a compile error, since there is no way for the compiler to know what the proper conversion of a variable should be.

Comments

The following are suggested best practices for style and type for the commenting of your code. Use this as a guide for your own style and implementation in your coding standards document.

General Commenting in .NET

One of the nice new features of the VS.NET IDE is the TODO comment. Whenever and wherever in your code you want to create a reminder to yourself or your fellow developers, you just have to enter the comment ' TODO (and the actual comment you want to enter) and the VS.NET IDE will place that comment in the Task Window. This Task Window is very similar to the Visual Interdev feature. This will allow you (and your team) to keep track of all unfinished work and any implementation details that need to be done.

If you are using C#, you should include the use-specific XML tags and the /doc switch so the comments in your code can be used to create code comment web reports that can viewed by just about anyone on your team. By inserting /// followed by a specific XML tag in the code window you can document the description of classes, structure, interfaces etc. and have those comments displayed in a structured format on a special web site that can automatically be created by using the **Build Comment Web Pages** feature of the **Tools** in the Visual Studio.NET IDE. This new feature provides a great way to self document your application and aids all developers in using the objects within.

Module Level Comments

All modules and classes should have a comment block preceding any code. This comment should outline the name, purpose, what other objects this object calls, what objects call this object, and any other relevant factors with regard to the method or class. The purpose should contain any comments in regard to special 'how to' instructions on the use of the module. When a developer has any questions about what this particular module or class' functionality is, all they should have to do is read this comment block.

Example:

```
'*****************************************************************
'
' Class: PageService
'
' Purpose: This module provides a centralized place for all code
' that handles generic page creation and behavior.
' This service will instantiate and call a
' custom business object to handle non-generic (page
' specific) logic.
'
' Calls: DataService
' CacheService
```

```
' Custom Business Object
'
' Called From: ASPX Pages
'
' Author:    Scott Wylie - June 21, 2001
'********************************************************************
```

Method Level Comments

All methods, no matter what their declaration (`Public Function`, `Private Property` etc.) should contain header comments containing the method name, purpose, detail description of the use of the parameters that are passed in (and out) and what other objects call this method. If there are any significant assumptions made, those should also be stated, such as this method requires the completed execution of another method before the correct results can be obtained.

Example:

```
'********************************************************************
' Function: GetOrderDetails
' Purpose: This function returns a Dataset of the item details
'          for an order id
' Parameters: OrderID: value of the order to be searched
' Called From: OrderSearch
'              OrderEntry
'              OrderStatus
'    Author:    Scott Wylie - June 21, 2001
'********************************************************************
```

Line or Section Level Comments

Every few lines of code should contain a comment where appropriate (comments such as Turn on Error Handler for a `Try...Catch...Finally` block are not needed). The more complicated a method or block of code, the more frequent the comments should be. Generally, a comment should precede the line of code it is meant to comment, but if it is very short it can be on the same line. When writing comments, make sure that you explain any and all business processes in the code with detailed descriptions. This will help the next developer looking at your code to quickly understand the processes involved in its execution. Once the code has been updated, the comment must also be updated; if this is not done for every change, the comments may be meaningless for the associated code and be of no help to you or the next developer.

Example:

```
'Set work area path if we are reading from file.
mstrReadFromFile = pstrReadFromFile
blnContinue = SetPathForReadFromFile()

'Attempt to Read Requested Page From Cache
If blnContinue Then
    If Not mobjCacheService.CacheReadPage(pstrPageName, vbNullString,
                 mlngPageRow, mobjPageContentArray, mobjPageFields,
                                 mlngPageContentArrayCount) Then
        'Page Does Not Reside in Cache
        'Initialize page content retrieval
```

```
        If ContentInit() Then
            'Build Page Content from database
            blnContinue = ContentBuild()
        Else
            blnContinue = False
        End If
    End If
End If
```

Inline Code Maintenance Comments

Once you have completed your code and it has gone into the quality assurance process or production, you still may need to fix a bug. When you fix this bug you should indicate that a section of code has changed due to the bug with detailed inline code maintenance comments. The comment should indicate the bug fixed, the date, the developer's name and a quality assurance bug tracking number. This will help other developers later when fixing the code to know why a developer made a particular change, or if you have to find a reference to a particular bug number.

Example:

```
' Begin Maintenance Comment: #234546 - Scott Wylie - 11/05/01
' Modification: Boolean Logic Reversed
'
<Code to be changed>
'
' End Maintenance Comment: #234546 - Scott Wylie - 11/05/01
```

Indentation

In all previous Microsoft IDE's there was very little in the way of auto-formatting of code. If your line was indented, the next line you typed would be indented at the same position. This method still exists in Visual Studio .NET, and is called Block Indenting. Visual Studio.NET has a new Smart Indenting feature that you can control per language. It provides much more automated indentation of code to the degree of automatically entering the 'end' code for a construct.

The reason I bring this up is that not everyone wants his or her code formatted and presented in the same way. As long as this is clearly documented in the coding standards, and all developers on the team use the same settings in their .NET IDE options, there will be no problem when it is time to merge code together for the application's continuity.

Testing Your Code

So you have planned your project, coded it, and have secured the code base against unknown disaster, but does it do everything you planned for it to do? Testing your code in as many scenarios as possible is probably one of the most important areas of development and in many situations when there is little time to complete the application, it is one that is cut first. You have three months to complete a project, but you run into some unforeseen problems and you get two weeks behind; this leaves little time to test the application. In most good, well thought-out project plans, the quality assurance testing cycle is left to about the last one third of the project (I have seen a number of projects where there is no quality assurance cycle at all, but you as a professional developer would never do that!).

The quality assurance cycle should start almost the day design starts. As soon as you have started design, your quality assurance team should be looking at every use case and planning out their resources to make sure that the right amount of quality assurance time is given to the project.

Once the final design is complete, the quality assurance team should know exactly what scenarios they would have to test. In projects where quality assurance is more of an afterthought, the code will be completed and then the application will be given to the quality assurance team, who at this point have no idea of the new features or even what the application is supposed to do. The sooner they know the use cases in the application, the sooner they will be able to help find potential problems in design.

Once the quality assurance team knows what use cases they will have to test for, they will need to know what technologies and infrastructure they will need to be testing on. It is at this time that the build team should be preparing at least two environments for development effort: one for the development teams themselves, and one for the quality assurance team, both matching as closely as possible the production hardware. This in itself is a big testing quality assurance issue. It is a good idea if the developers work on an environment that is close to production so they will be able to find performance issues long before they reach production. However, if your quality assurance team is testing the application on a quad server with multiple gigabytes of RAM and the customer only has purchased a dual server with 256MB of RAM you will not be able to adequately test the application, especially when it comes to stress and duration testing.

Once the development team has been provided with screen designs and technical specifications, the quality assurance team will be able to start creating their test scripts. Depending on the size of the application, life span of the application, and the size of team and money available to the company, you may be limited in the type of test scripts you can use. You should have a set of written instructions that mimic the operation flow of the application based on the use cases. Each use case should have a test script to match. These test scripts should be as repeatable as possible. That is the issue to remember with testing: if you can only create the error once and never again, it is nearly impossible to fix. How many times have you heard a quality assurance person say "well I got this error, but I was not able to get it again"? Probably about as many times as a developer says "well it works fine on my machine"!

As the developers start work, they should, after a short period of time, provide early builds for the quality assurance team to test. The testing of these early builds is going to be very different to the final testing. These early builds will be to validate concepts and design. No member of the quality assurance team should be too worried about whether the validation of an e-mail address is working at this point in development; this is not what needs to be tested. If the concepts and design do not pass quality assurance, then the entire application may have a fundamental design flaw that will have to be addressed before work can continue. If the application was not tested early it may have been too late into the development cycle to find out that there is a serious design flaw and there is a possibility that nothing could be done.

Listed below are some best practices for testing your application:

Test Often

As stated above, the more often you test, the better the possibility of success. However, this does not mean just keep testing the same thing. You must test often, but you must test everything and even things you don't even think are possible. As well as testing often, you must keep testing; once it is working, it must stay working. When a developer does anything with the functionality in the system, even if it is to fix one bug that the quality assurance team reported, you must retest everything. I bet every developer has said "well that should not have happened" or "that is impossible, they are not related". After any change throughout the life cycle of the application, you must keep testing.

Test Functionality with No Data

This best practice seems to get missed more often than not. The first thing you do with any application is make sure that it takes the inputted data and returns the correct data. What happens when you don't put in any data at all? The application should be able to handle this use case gracefully, informing the user or the calling application that it failed due to missing data.

Test with Real User Data

This best practice usually gets dealt with near the end of the development cycle. One scenario of this would be if you have to transfer data from an old legacy system to SQL Server 2000 and that data must be used in the new application. Do all the fields appear correctly? Does the data change upon resaving the information? Unless a very thorough analysis is done at the beginning, you may receive a value or range of data that you thought was not possible. This may require you to change your validation routines, or even change the entire structure of an entity. The earlier you test with real user data, the less chance of errors when you have to deliver the application.

Test with Extremely Strange Data

This may sound a little strange in itself, but how often have you looked at the data in a customer database and say "how did that get in there?" So, how did that data get in there and since it did what is it going to do to the rest of the application? Test with the strangest data possible and make sure that all validation routines and constraints are working correctly based on your use cases. It is amazing what a person, who is computer illiterate, will enter in a textbox. Several good items to try are `null` values from a database, different language characters, words with apostrophes and quotes (O'Brien), characters in a numeric field, as well as trying to enter more than the maximum allowed value for range as well as length.

Test with Different People

Every human being is different and they do things slightly differently. Make sure that you rotate the quality assurance staff to different areas of the application to test. This rotation of staff will provide a fresh outlook on that area of the application and they may find or think of something different to the person before. Depending on the size of the team, areas of the application that are being tested and the time that is left, you will want to have a rotation schedule that makes sure that every member is allowed to test and retest each area of the application. This may be very difficult, but it will help ensure that the broadest range of people test the application.

Another best practice that works well in this area is, if possible, to have the customer or audience of the application test it for you. It has become the de facto standard in today's development environment that beta versions of the software are distributed through different means to the intended customer base. Microsoft is not alone in this area. Visual Studio .NET Beta 1 and Beta 2 are Microsoft's largest releases to date of a pre-production development tool. With the diversity of running environments, especially in the Internet arena, it is to your benefit to have as many people as possible test your application before it is complete. If they know it is beta they won't complain (too much), but if the application goes to production and it is full of bugs your customers will complain very loudly.

Test with More Data than you have Planned

As discussed previously, what is the capacity of the application? You will have planned for growth of users and resources, but what levels can the application really function efficiently at? Develop scripts to generate data to fill the database beyond capacity if you have to. You may find that the application works fine if you have 100 orders in the system at any one time, but what if the company grows and you end up with 1,000 or 10,000 orders at any one time, how will the application cope with this? Will it crash or will it become so slow that your search routine takes ten minutes to return? The sooner you test the capacity of the application, the sooner you will be able to fix or re-evaluate your code.

Create Test Scripts to Automate All Use Cases

As mentioned above, the best test scripts are well written automatic scripts. No matter how well you write a test script on paper, it has to be executed by a human and no human is perfect (as much as we think we are). Every human will also find some way of following a test script differently. Also mentioned above is that you want to test as often as possible and as reliably as possible. It is very difficult for a human to do the same task the same way over and over again, but of course this is exactly what computers are for. Using scripts to automate your testing is a great way to regression test any changes made to your application. If you make a change in one area of your application it is very difficult to test the entire application manually to make sure that that change does not have any adverse affects. By using scripts to automate the testing process, any change can be regression tested for effects on the application in less time and with greater confidence that nothing was missed.

There are many automated testing applications (for example Rational Visual Test, Mercury Interactive Winrunner) out on the market, from simple to very complicated ones where you almost need a developer to write the script testing code to test the application. The very best ones tend to be expensive (in the tens of thousands of dollars), but once set up they will be able to automatically test your latest version of code without any human interaction. You can have your automated build process place your latest compiled code on a test server, where at a certain time your automated test scripts activate. Once you return to work in the morning you will be provided with a print out of just what errors have occurred. Now if only it could write the code...

Stress Testing and Total Cost Analysis

In the world of client server and monolithic applications using Microsoft development tools, you may have had a large install base of users (up to hundreds, possibly a thousand users) and these generally were not accessing your application all at one time. Welcome to the world of the Internet. With the ease of development of .NET, just about anyone can create a web application that can be used by thousands, or tens of thousands of users (this was possible with Visual Studio 6 with very carefully constructed applications). The problem is that you only have a team of twenty developers and five quality assurance people – how do you test your application for one thousand users? This is where stress-testing tools can be used to simulate load on a server so you see how your application behaves, as well as capacity planning your web server farm.

For the first time Microsoft has included a web stress tool in Visual Studio, it is called Microsoft Application Center Test.

You could download from Microsoft their previous web stress tool called Microsoft Web Application Stress tool from the following location: http://webtool.rte.microsoft.com. Microsoft does not officially support this tool so it is entirely possible that once Application Center Test goes to production it will be pulled from their site.

There are two versions of Application Center Test, the Developer and Enterprise Edition. The two main differences are that the Enterprise Edition can Replay Tests and duplicate realistic network traffic and errors. The Developer edition is also limited to using a single test client in a test run.

Application Center Test is a tool for stress testing web servers, as well as analyzing scalability, reliability and performance. By using dynamic tests, Application Center Test provides some means to also test application functionality. Application Center Test is compatible with any server that adheres to the HTTP protocol.

You should include stress testing in the beginning of your development and continue to do it for every major change in code and design.

Conduct Stress Testing on Debug Versions of Code as well as Production Code

The main purpose of stress testing is to know how your application will behave in a production environment. However, a secondary test that comes in very handy is to run your development code in a debug mode under the same stress conditions. This test is not for performance or planning the capacity of a web farm, but to see if any errors occur under load that don't show up when tested in a local environment. These errors could be thread locking, deadlocks when accessing the cache, database transaction errors, and so on. If you don't turn on your error-handling debug version of your code, you may never know just what your code is doing.

When creating a large web-based e-commerce system it is a great idea to have compile flags that will turn on writing extra debug information to the event viewer or special logs. This may not be just for error descriptions, but for informational messages that help in the debug process. It will help you 'see' what the certain values are when needed, but not waste performance when running in production.

Include Database Profiling as part of your Stress Tests

When you run your initial stress testing and your application uses a database it is a good idea to run that database's profiling tool (SQL Server Profile if you are using SQL Server) to monitor what calls are being made to the database. You may find that under stress accessing the same data, your application may not be working as effectively. A potential scenario is you may find that you are accessing the same data over and over, whereas if you implemented some type of data cache those database calls could almost be eliminated.

Include Event Viewer Results

When using Application Center Test 2000, you will have access to all the system performance counters; the logs include any errors that may have occurred (for example, 404 Page Not Found errors under web site testing) once the test has completed. You should also clear all event viewer logs before you start a stress test, as this will allow you to see other areas of your application and areas that your application affects. Check the System log for errors in services, the security log for errors in accessing files and objects, and the application log for errors caused by your program or its interaction with the operating system.

Include Other Application Logs

Application Center Test 2000 does provide you with result codes of how many Internet Information Server errors occurred (total number of 404 File Not Found during the duration of the test), but it does not tell you on exactly what page that error occurred and with what data. By isolating the Internet Information Server logs for the time period of the stress test, you will be able to find what pages may be causing errors and what data it involves. Hopefully by running the page manually you will be able to track down the problem.

Use Performance Logs and Alert Utility to Monitor Real Time Activity

Application Center Test 2000 stores all performance counter information that it collects during the test, but does not show you what it is doing and the results in real time. You can set up Performance Logs and Alert Utility in Windows 2000 to display on your client machine just what the stress testing is doing in real time. Just set up the same performance counters that you have in Application Center Test in Performance Logs and Alert Utility. It is possible that this may cause problems, as you will be trying to get the same information twice from the server you are testing. There may even be a small hit on the server by this duplicate action depending on the load that the server being tested is under. Also, if your stress client is all ready running near 100% capacity before you set up the Performance Logs and Alert Utility, it may cause the stress client to run at its maximum and therefore not stress the server to the best of its ability.

Isolate the Network as much as Possible

If your stress test hardware is on your regular work network, you will not be isolating a possible area of contention, which is the network. The stress client will be writing packets as fast as it can, but if the rest of the traffic on the network interrupts those packets you will not be able to get a correct representation of the performance of your application. If the server has to wait for any information it will cause the test to be unrepresentative. Set up your stress test lab in its own local network that is either completely separate or on a network switch that can isolate packet travel.

Summary

Hopefully you have learned from this chapter that there are many aspects of best practices for developing an application with the .NET framework. It takes more than just the fastest code to make sure that your application will perform to its wanted expectations. Due to the size of today's .NET applications you need to plan for the continued availability of the application, its reliability, the security of data and infrastructure and the manageability of its sheer size and complexity. Also, if you don't create the code in a reliable, well documented, and easy to understand manner, no one person will ever know how the entire application works. Once you have accomplished all of the above tasks, including exhaustive testing that will have found all the possible issues that you may have missed, you will have one of the best engineered .NET framework applications available.

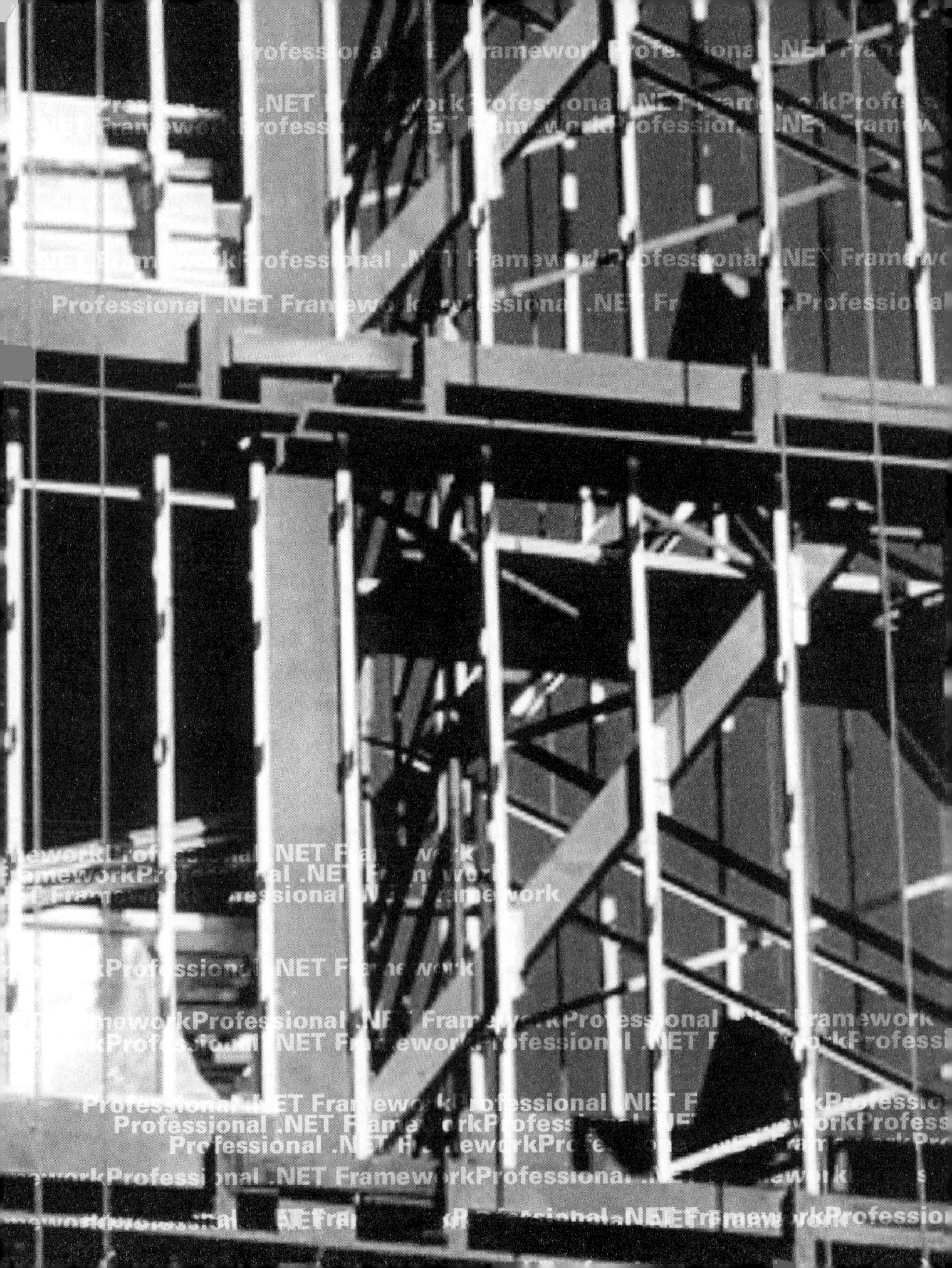

Professional .NET Framework

13

Migrating to .NET

So far, this book has provided you with a wealth of information on how to produce high-quality, professional applications built on Microsoft's new .NET Framework. While it is essential that you know how to build .NET applications from the ground up, it isn't practical to assume that that's what you're going to be doing. Chances are, your first foray into using the .NET framework is going to be in order to migrate code or reuse existing code via COM InterOp.

The truth is, most of you reading this book have been programming for quite a while, and have a lot of time invested in classic COM and Windows development. It will be a very small minority of companies that have the time, resources, and bravery to drop all of their old code and rewrite everything from scratch.

One of the greatest features of the .NET framework is its flexibility and power. For any given problem, there are dozens of solutions in dozens of different languages, using different base classes and features of the framework. If you ask ten programmers how to do something in .NET that they all know how to do in Windows, you will invariably get ten different solutions.

How do you tell which solution is the right solution? The unfortunate answer to that question is that *you can't*. There is no such thing as a single correct solution. The nature of the framework takes much of the hard work out of the implementation portion of the software life cycle and places it where it should always have been – the *design*.

This chapter will *not* tell you the single cure-all method for migration to the .NET framework. However, it will give you enough information about the pros and cons of various methods to help you reach your own decision. In addition, it may provide you with enough information to spot the *wrong* solutions to your migration needs.

After completing this chapter, you should be able to answer the following questions:

❑   Should you migrate to .NET?

❑   Why should you migrate to .NET?

❑   Which components of your existing application do you need to migrate?

❑   What goals and tasks do you have for your migration?

❑   Which migration path should you take?

❑   Which .NET features should you try to take advantage of?

❑   What migration tools are available to help the process?

Project Evaluation

If you've been following the progress of .NET, you've no doubt seen the multitude of web sites appearing dedicated to sharing code samples, custom ASP.NET web controls, custom Windows Forms controls, tutorials, and much more. All of those things are important to know, but in a complex development process such as enterprise development, large applications, or large-team development, they typically fall into the low-priority category of tools.

All truly successful software development projects are successful because of one factor: good design. Development efforts like CORBA, technologies like COM, and productivity suites like Office and Works would never have succeeded without an incredibly extensive design and architecture. If all the programmers on a project are absolute geniuses, it won't save the project if it has poor and inconsistent design. The same holds true for a migration project.

The first question you need to ask yourself is: *Should I migrate to .NET?* You're reading this chapter either because you've already decided that you want to migrate to .NET, or you're interested in finding out if you should. It is our firm belief that the .NET framework is going to be an extremely important and groundbreaking technology on which to build the next generation of applications and "software as a service". As much as we would all love to admit that decisions are made based on the code, that just isn't true. You're only going to want to migrate to the .NET framework if you can make a business case for it, and you've decided that you or your business will profit by taking the risk to embrace this new technology.

Once you've decided that you want to migrate, you need to make some more decisions about your project. This next section will give you some information to help you come to a conclusion.

Define Project Need

The first thing you should be thinking about is whether or not you truly do need to migrate your code to .NET. Examine your application's features and functionality in its current version, and then detail what features you have planned for your application over the next year or so. If you've determined that you do indeed need to migrate to .NET, you should determine how much of your application and functionality you *need* to move to the framework.

Some applications are in maintenance mode. The publisher of the application may not have any more features planned for it, and they're simply maintaining it and publishing patches containing bug fixes and minor changes. In a case like this, the application probably doesn't need to be migrated to .NET. Examples of applications that might be in this mode are applications that were written in 16-bit Windows (VB3, etc), applications a company no longer has any plan of upgrading, or applications where the intended target audience of the application won't benefit from any of the new features available in .NET-based applications. Converting all the previous code for a stale application that will continue to work for years on backwards-compatible operating systems isn't worth the time or effort of the development team.

The majority of applications, however, have a near infinite list of features that the consumers, designers, architects (and don't forget salespeople!) want to have implemented. In this case, the application should be migrated to .NET. Many companies have decided to either support both their current versions and new .NET versions simultaneously, while others are freezing the feature lists for their current versions and only adding new features to their .NET applications.

After deciding that the application is going to be migrated, the development team needs to define when the actual migration will take place. As you'll see later in this chapter, there are ways of migrating some of the application at a time or migrating it all at once. I shouldn't have to get into an explanation of software development management here, but the very least you'll need to consider is at what point the developers stop working on the "classic" code and start working on .NET. The majority of projects will probably have some developers move on to .NET while others remain on the classic code, providing a nearly seamless transition for the customers.

Obviously, if you're running an e-Commerce or large web site, your transition might simply be upgrading all the code onto a new farm of servers, and at some pre-determined time simply switching the old site to the new.

Justifying the Migration

Before we get into the mechanics of migrating and the technical details of migrating to the .NET framework, you need to know why you should even bother migrating. In order to be able to make the most use of the information contained in this book and this chapter, you need to be convinced that migrating to the .NET framework is the best track for your product, and you need to be able to convince your employer or your co-workers.

The short story is that the .NET framework will reduce time to market, it will ease maintenance of existing code (written for .NET), and it will radically change and improve connectivity of peer applications and client applications with vendor servers, as well as introduce new ways of extending the reach of applications that people haven't even thought of yet. In particular, the Web Services aspect of the .NET framework is going to literally wipe away a huge portion of the Business-to-Business headaches that plague today's e-Commerce web sites.

A lot of the hype and publicity surrounding the framework is actually pretty inaccurate. On the other hand, a good portion of the inaccuracy is in *understating* many of the benefits of this framework. The true beauty of the framework's benefits is that the benefits have not yet all been realized. As people continue to use the framework and grow in their knowledge and creativity, they will come up with new and exciting ways to use these tools and this infrastructure.

The bottom line is that everyone is hopping on this bandwagon, whether or not we agree with them. Customers are going to see all kinds of enhanced functionality offered by next-generation web applications, incredible connectivity offered by services like Microsoft's *Hailstorm* initiative (a push toward maintaining your information such as address book, contacts, favorites, etc. in a central location accessible from anywhere), and dramatically improved user interfaces. Once they've been given a taste of this, they're going to demand it from all of their software. The question then becomes one of whether you're going to provide them that functionality before or after they realize how much they want it.

Benefits of the .NET Framework

Even if you're already convinced that the .NET framework is the way to go, chances are you're not the only one involved in the decision to migrate. What you need is a quick and straightforward list of some of the things about the framework that stand out as tremendous benefits over your existing code.

❑ **Source Code Bulk**

This goes to the issue of avoiding the re-invention of the wheel (discussed later). Microsoft has done an extremely good job of providing a base set of classes that move the largest bottleneck away from the actual typing of the code to where it belongs – architecture and design. Unless you're actually trying to be inefficient, the source code generated in most .NET applications (web or desktop) is going to be smaller, easier to read, and more concise than in traditional applications.

❑ **Binary Bulk**

Because the Common Language Runtime (CLR) is just that – a runtime – the Assemblies and executables produced by your code will be far smaller than those produced by traditional Windows compilers. The reason for this is that no execution headers or logic needs to be placed into your compiled IL (Intermediate Language) code. The runtime knows exactly what to do with IL and doesn't need archaic things like VBRUN600.DLL to be in the system directory or bloated headers at the top of .EXE files that actually contain a separate copy of the runtime (I'm referring to building an MFC app with the MFC libraries statically linked, or languages like Delphi which allow you to compile standalone executables that contain their own execution environment). However, even though the size of your binaries may be smaller, don't be fooled by thinking that there isn't a large amount of DLLs that are supporting your code. The Runtime itself has an extensive set of DLLs that must be available in order for your code to execute. The size of the binaries your application distributes will be smaller, but keep in mind that the binaries for the CLR must already be on the client system for them to work.

❑ **Speed and Execution**

Many people claim that interpreted code is slower than compiled code. Well, byte-for-byte, compiled code does execute faster than interpreted code. A standard Java applet is not going to be able to outperform a compiled C application. However, the CLR is actually executing interpreted, Just In Time (JIT)-compiled code. When a JIT request is made for your IL code, it is compiled into machine code and cached for later use. Once compiled into machine code, the CLR can execute your code with comparable speed to any compiled application.

The IL code contained in your application's Assemblies can be cached. Once cached, the entire compiled form of your Assembly is available in memory. Once in memory, the load time of a managed code application can actually be *faster* than a traditional COM component or Windows executable.

❑ **Deployment**

While I continue my elusive search for the bumper sticker that contains the phrase, "I brake for Xcopy Deployment", I will have to be content with preaching that phrase to everyone I come in contact with. It has become a habit. Every time I am asked what the benefits of the .NET framework are, I respond with the following: Xcopy deployment, no GUIDs, and did I mention Xcopy deployment?

The incredibly thoughtful way in which the framework is organized allows you to avoid all of the headaches previously caused by "DLL Hell". You do not need to register in the registry an Assembly that your application is using. The process of using an Assembly is actually extremely simple.

Don't be fooled into thinking that it is all a complete GUID-free DLL nirvana, however. You can still get into versioning conflicts where your classes might not be able to find other classes because they've been rebuilt as new versions. This is typically solved with a simple re-compile or some thoughtful use of Visual Studio features – still no need to use the registry.

As an example, if you want to reference the `CarDealershipUtilities` Assembly, in VB6, you would go to your Project menu, then choose References, then find the appropriately registered class. Then, to deploy your application, you had to modify your installation routine to copy the file, *and* make sure that it was properly registered, either by using `regsvr32.exe`, or by calling `DllRegisterServer` in the component DLL itself.

In the realm of .NET, you simply add a reference to the Assembly by browsing for it. When you deploy your application, the CLR will look in your application's current directory for references specified by the project. If it doesn't find the Assembly in the application's directory, it will look in something called the *Global Assembly Cache*. This approach to finding required and supported Assemblies or DLLs is a far smoother, more elegant approach than trudging through the registry and opening applications to horrible, GUID-related mishaps.

Another beneficial side effect of this approach is that it allows multiple versions of the same Assembly (DLL) to exist on the same machine at the same time. In fact, assuming your application is designed that way, it could be written to dynamically choose which version of an Assembly it needs.

Examine Resources – Can You Migrate?

Many programmers who have worked with the .NET framework will tell you that the move to it is as welcome as an ice-cold glass of water on a hot day. That doesn't change the fact that implementing and planning a large-scale migration of code that is firmly entrenched in the legacy world is not an easy task. It is not an inexpensive task, either. The cost of development time, tools, resources, and the ability to maintain the current application during the migration period needs to be taken into account. In addition, if your time frame is too narrow, then the same programmers who thought the move to .NET was a welcome one will be sharing a different story. No matter which method you choose for migration, the migration will consume time and resources for which you need to plan extensively.

In order to successfully upgrade your application to .NET, you will need some time. Granted, the architecture of the .NET framework actually speeds up most development tasks; however, depending on the size of your application you could still be looking at a considerable time investment. The amount of time you have available may impact your choice of migration paths (discussed later).

Every application needs programmers. If you don't have enough manpower to dedicate a programmer (including yourself) to the migration project, obviously you're not going to be able to migrate. Some companies are going as far as hiring completely new programmers who started working on .NET with Beta 1 or Beta 2 to do the majority of the development work for their upgrade.

Depending on the backgrounds of your current developers, or your background if you're the only one doing the upgrade, the learning curve may be significant. The syntax of C# is an absolute breeze, and should only take someone familiar with C or Java a week or so to get the hang of the basic syntax. The learning curve comes from mastering the .NET framework class library. In it are 99% of all the functions you're going to need to do things that previous languages allowed you to do (beyond basic calculations, class and data definitions, etc). The programmer(s) working on the migration will need time to explore and experiment with the .NET base class library. Most poor algorithm decisions come not from stupidity or lack of ability, but instead from lack of knowledge of a better algorithm or function.

Training is another facet of the migration that should not be underestimated. At the time of this writing, there are some training programs available, and some of the conferences have been providing .NET-based sessions. However, the availability of "experts" on the .NET framework is still not as widespread as it is for many other technologies. That should change drastically by the time this book is released. Very soon there should be dozens of week-long .NET training classes ranging from architecture to advanced C# and VB.NET programming up to full training sessions on enterprise ASP.NET web sites.

If formal training isn't available at the time, or isn't enough, there are still other options. There are dozens of web sites dedicated to hosting programming examples, FAQs and other useful information on the .NET framework. In addition to these independent web sites, never underestimate the usefulness of MSDN. During the early stages of Beta 1, MSDN was my sole source of information. Microsoft has actually done a remarkable job in documenting the framework and the class library. The exception to that is with managed VC++ and to some extent VB.NET. The Beta 1 MSDN documentation for VB.NET was non-existent, and the Beta 2 documentation still needs serious work. Another excellent source of training and documentation on the .NET framework is Wrox's extensive series of .NET-based Professional and Programmer's Reference books.

To access Microsoft's on-line documentation on the framework, including samples, tutorials, and full-scale enterprise example applications, click over to http://msdn.microsoft.com/net. Microsoft has also recently converted its streaming media talk show "The MSDN Show" into "The .NET Show". Every show contains about an hour of informative video content. To access "The .NET Show", click to http://msdn.microsoft.com/theshow.

As a supplement to formal training, your own experimentation with your own code, and on-line documentation, I strongly recommend getting yourself and any other developers on your team into some .NET newsgroups or mailing lists. Wrox's P2P lists and detailed books are an exceptional source of useful information. No matter how much formal training you've had, or reading you've done, there's no substitute for personal experience. Get into the framework, experiment, try things. It's all well and good to know what a certain function does, but it's far more important to find out how that function fits into the big picture of accomplishing a larger task.

So, before you decide for sure if you want to migrate, or how you're planning on migrating, you should first determine if you have the time, manpower, and training/knowledge to do the migration in the first place.

Implications of Migration

As fun as it may be to program for the .NET framework, there is a bottom line. The customers buying your application (this may not necessarily apply to a web site/e-Commerce implementation) need to accept the platform on which your application runs. This one fact has been a constant thorn in my side, and the side of programmers worldwide since the dawn of time. Back in the good old days of Windows 3.1, thousands of customers refused to run Windows, and so businesses that depended on those customers were forced to either delay migration, or to maintain two separate and parallel development paths (yes, we all have flashbacks of this particular nightmare). Even though Windows 2000 has been available for retail purchase for some time now, and two service packs released, many consumers are still hesitant to even adopt this extremely solid operating system.

The same might be true of Microsoft's .NET framework. The .NET framework's CLR will be available as a separately installable re-distributable file that can either be downloaded from Microsoft or installed with .NET applications. Microsoft has announced that in addition to its full line of Windows XP servers, they are going to release a Windows.NET server that will ship with the .NET framework already on it. This means that .NET client applications are going to have to re-distribute and install the CLR and related files. Some customers might actually refuse to purchase the product if it contains the .NET framework on it before the framework has been released for over a year. It is actually a pretty common policy among large corporations to not adopt a new software product from Microsoft until a year after its initial public release or until a service pack or two have been released.

Therefore, you need to evaluate the mindset of your customers. If they are not going to accept .NET/CLR-based programs until a year after the .NET framework is released, obviously that is going to impact your decision as to when or if you migrate your existing code base. If customer acceptance of the .NET framework (and Windows 2000) is going to be delayed, it might actually buy you some extra time to fully flesh out the design and implementation of your .NET solution.

Reduce, Reuse, Recycle – Migration for the Environmentally Conscious

One of the golden rules of many programmers (immediately following *He who finishes the coffee pot must start a new one*) is to *Never re-invent the wheel.* The last thing any programmer should want to do is rewrite something that has already been written. It's a really bad scene when you've rewritten your own customized version of the wheel, and someone releases *Wheel v2.0*, complete with all the features you've spent the last eight months coding, and some that'll take you another year to add.

When you migrate your code to .NET, you want to make sure to keep in mind the Reduce, Reuse, and Recycle ideas. This should hopefully keep the amount of redundant code you have to write to a minimum, and should ease the task of maintaining the code.

Reduce

One of the hardest parts of migrating any application to any new format is determining what *doesn't* need to be converted. If you keep the following items in mind when migrating your code, and try to adhere to these guidelines as much as possible, you will find that the resulting code and architecture will be far more elegant and scalable as an end result:

Determine which features you don't need to migrate to .NET

Take a long look at the features your application provides. Make sure that you still want to be providing that functionality in the .NET version. Weed out functionality that newer operating systems/environments might provide natively that your application used to provide. Also take this opportunity to get rid of features that the consumers of your application are not using (many programmers call this "trimming the fat"). Even if there are informational screens, dialogs, or reports that people haven't been using for some time, get rid of them in your new migrated version.

Take a critical look at your application relative to your current business environment. Determine how your business has changed, or how the needs of your customers might have changed since the application was originally designed and implemented.

Many times features make it into an application without being designed first. Take a look at the features in your application and see which ones were added haphazardly or with poor design and take the time to re-work them.

An application that does exactly what it was designed to do, and does it extremely well, is a far better application (and used more often) than one that does a few hundred things moderately well. List the "defining" features of your application, then list the rest of the features it supplies and determine which ones are still applicable given the current state of affairs at your company and with technology as it is today.

Eliminate the duct tape.

You have a really good opportunity here to "clean" up the code. Over a long period of time, as features are added to an application, it changes in appearance from an elegant solution to a bloated solution with features glued, stapled, and duct-taped to the surface. Sit down and list all your features and make sure that the new design for your .NET application takes those all into account natively.

This duct-tape feature phenomenon is very common in the User Interface. As time goes by and features are added, menus, buttons, icons, and other eye candy are thrown haphazard onto the application, generating a confusing interface. This 'duct taping' of features into the user interface generally creates a lot of "spaghetti code", especially in event handling. Take advantage of new flexibility in user interface and re-integrate all your features into logical menu structures, appropriate icons and positions, etc. The new flexibility in user interface and language features will be especially evident in VB.NET as there are some substantial changes in the language and the language's capabilities.

Eliminate home-grown features that are now natively part of the framework class library.

Many applications, including web sites, have hundreds of thousands of lines of code to implement custom features that were not available as basic parts of whatever programming language was used originally.

For example, I recently completed a project where I had to completely re-invent the wheel that has now become **web services**. I had to have a client application communicating to the database that my web server was utilizing. The client would never be on the same Windows network, and could conceivably be behind a firewall. What I ended up doing was using the XMLHTTP component to transmit proprietary streams of XML to a **listener** ASP page that I had created. The first migration I do on this application will be to convert that scenario to Web Services.

I've selected a couple of really quick examples to illustrate my point. The .NET framework class library is ripe with native functionality that programmers have previously had to "roll" on their own or purchase from third party developers. You can get plenty of examples on *how* to do things in the rest of this book. The purpose of these examples is to show you that with the .NET framework, you can easily and quickly accomplish many complex tasks that previously may have only been possible through the use of third party components and software.

❑ **Cryptography**

What used to be the source of incredible headaches for Windows and Web programmers alike is now a simple matter of creating an object, getting a Hash, and that's it. Encryption of anything, including files, strings, etc, is now a snap.

The first few lines of this example all begin with the keyword using. Many people get confused and think that this is like adding a reference or using an #include in C. It actually works much more like a with statement. Each using statement allows you to reference classes, enumerations, and other types within that namespace without having to preface that reference with the name of the namespace. For example, I can refer to a SHA1CryptoServiceProvider class without a namespace identifier if I have a using System.Security.Cryptography; statement at the top of my file. However, without that using statement, all references to SHA1CryptoServiceProvider would need to be converted to System.Security.Cryptography.SHA1CryptoServiceProvider. This example and the others in this section are all written in C#.

```
using System;
using System.IO;
using System.Security;
```

```
using System.Security.Cryptography;

// every application is a class.
public class SampleEncryption {

    // every Console application has a static Main(), much
    // like C programs have a void main()
    public static void Main()
    {
        byte[] data = new byte[3];
        byte[] result;


        data[0] = 65;
        data[1] = 65;
        data[2] = 65;

        SHA1 sha = new SHA1CryptoServiceProvider();

        result = sha.ComputeHash(data);

        Console.WriteLine("result has been encrypted.");
    }
}
```

The point of this sample and the others in this section is to bring to your attention the fact that many things that used to require either complex, time-consuming programming or purchase of third party components is now easy. The above sample consumes about 3,000 lines of VB6 code when the SHA1 algorithm is implemented "by hand".

❑ **Hash Tables**

Anyone accustomed to the `Scripting.Dictionary` object (or `Commerce.Dictionary` for you Commerce Server programmers) will love the new `Hashtable` class. Hash Tables are specialized classes that store name/value pairs. Aside from the basic types provided with languages, Dictionaries are one of the most often used classes. In VB6, you had to either get an early-bound Dictionary by referencing the Visual Basic Scripting Runtime, or you had to create an instance of it late by using `CreateObject`. With .NET, all you have to do is make sure you're using `System.Collections` and you have full access to all kinds of classes useful for storing complex data and lists.

```
using System;
using System.Collections;

public class SampleHash {

    public static void Main() {
        // Create a new Hashtable instance. You can optionally
        // specify the capacity(size) of the Hashtable in the
        // constructor.
        Hashtable htMovieRatings = new Hashtable();

        // Add a name/value pair. The first argument is the "key"
        // while the second is the value.
        htMovieRatings.Add( "Pulp Fiction", "***");
        htMovieRatings.Add( "Star Wars: Episode One", "****");
        htMovieRatings.Add( "Big Trouble In Little China", "*****");

        Console.WriteLine( "{0} movie picks for you:", htMovieRatings.Count );
```

```
        // We know that a Hashtable supports the
        // IDictionaryEnumerator interface,
        // so we can set a variable to that Interface from
        // our Hash Table variable, allowing us to iterate
        // through its Dictionary items.
        IDictionaryEnumerator myEnum = htMovieRatings.GetEnumerator();
        while (myEnum.MoveNext()) {
            Console.WriteLine( "{0}:{1}", myEnum.Key, myEnum.Value );
        }
        Console.WriteLine();
    }
}
```

Many programmers concerned about migrating to a new platform are wary of losing their tools and some of their favorite programming constructs. One of the constructs used all the time is the Scripting Dictionary. The above sample is designed to assure you that with the .NET framework, your dictionary functionality (and much, much more) is built into the system without you having to worry about distributing the scripting runtime.

❑   **Array Sorting**

Anyone who's ever had to implement a lot of array sorting code knows exactly how much fun it is. Needless to say, there are tons of things you can do to an Array, beyond the scope of this chapter. The point being is that Arrays are now one of the many things that the class library has completely done for you, so you won't need to re-invent that wheel.

```
using System;
using System.Collections;

class SortSample
{
    public static void Main()
    {
        // this construct may look odd to C programmers. The []
        // array indicator is in front of the variable name, not
        // after.
        string []strArray={"Pulp Fiction", "Star Wars: Episode One",
                        "Big Trouble in Little China"};

        // Look how easy this is!
        // By default, the array will sort elements alphabetically. You
        // can provide your own comparison function to customize the
        // sorting behavior yourself.
        Array.Sort(strArray);

        Console.WriteLine("Sorted Array:");

        // The "foreach" keyword allows you to iterate through any
        // class that supports the IEnumerator interface. This allows
        // you to create your own Collection-type classes or make your
        // own custom array class, etc.
        foreach (object o in strArray)
        {
```

```
            // All objects in C# support the "ToString()" method. This
            // will be called on each object to obtain something that
            // can be printed to the console.
            Console.Write("{0},", o);
        }
        Console.WriteLine();

    }
}
```

Stay as high-level as possible

One of the big trends that you can see in Microsoft development, if you look at how the System namespace is structured, is to encapsulate a lot of previously hard-to-reach functionality. For example, Microsoft now supplies some really easy-to-use Sockets components that make implementing TCP/IP communication a breeze.

A good rule of thumb to keep in mind is to utilize the highest level of abstraction available to you. For example, if you are trying to read an XML file from disk, you have many options available. You can open it as a text file and read it character by character, or you can open it as a text stream and read it in that way. However, if you're working with an XML file, chances are you want the full DOM Level 2 functionality. For this, you can use the XmlDocument class, which not only provides all of the file I/O functions you need, but exposes the text file as an XML DOM. A quiz you can take is to ask yourself what steps are required to achieve your end result. If there is anything in the .NET class libraries that can reduce those steps, then you should consider using it.

Another example of using the highest possible level of abstraction is Queued Components. Through the use of COM+, you can actually create COM+ components that have delayed method call operations. Instead of remotely invoking a method call for a remote component immediately, the client proxy for a queued component will place the request for the method call in a Message Queue. A process on the server with the COM+ application listens on the queue for requests, turns the stored requests back into method calls, and executes them. All of this is now possible in the .NET framework through the use of custom Assembly Attributes and COM+ configuration. Assembly attributes, as you know from other portions of this book, are ways of supplying meta data to be stored in the Assembly itself (.DLL or .EXE). This meta data can then be read by the COM+ services so it can automatically determine how to host a particular component.

The moral of the story is that if you want to implement a Queued Component, use the highest possible level of abstraction available. This would be using custom attributes that indicate in the Assembly's meta data that it is a Queued Component. By doing this instead of implementing your own send and receive methods on a Message Queue, your component will still continue to function, even if Microsoft decides to change the underlying communication protocol used for Queued Components.

By utilizing the highest possible level of abstraction available for the task you're trying to accomplish, you insulate yourself from the underpinnings of the implementation. One caveat, however, is that you also don't want to insulate yourself more than you need. It is possible to use too high a level of abstraction that you end up doing more work than required to accomplish your task, or worse, you end up rewriting existing and tested code. By utilizing the appropriate abstractions, you don't need to worry about network protocols and TCP/IP to obtain a stream of text from a web server, nor do you need to worry about how pixels get transmitted to the video card's memory to utilize the features in GDI+. Using higher-level abstractions allows implementation and core changes to the implementations in the framework to take place with little or no effect on how your code functions.

Reuse

If there is one thing I have heard more technology educators preach than anything else, it is *Code Reuse*. When you are migrating your code to the .NET framework, you should be thinking about how you can get the most out of your old code. Also, you should be considering how to implement your new code to eliminate as much redundancy as possible, and position your new application so that it can be easily expanded and upgraded.

Never re-invent the wheel. If someone else has already done something for you, and it's accepted as solid code, then by all means, don't rewrite your own wheel. Well, in a sense, the .NET framework is Microsoft Wheel v1.0. Years of research (and listening to complaining and whining programmers) has led Microsoft to a comprehensive library of classes and tools that it feels will satisfy the core needs of most programmers. If there is something in that core library of classes that duplicates functionality you have, *seriously* consider rewriting that portion of your code to use the functionality from the class library rather than your own proprietary component.

Rewrite or Repackage?

One major decision in upgrading your project to .NET is deciding whether to rewrite your existing classes, or to simply leave them as COM objects and invoke them from your .NET front-end via a COM wrapper that is part of the class library. Whenever you invoke a framework method from a COM component, via a Type Library and the COM wrapper, you incur a loss in performance. However, for many projects, this loss in performance may be acceptable compared to the time it might take to convert that COM object into an Assembly of C# or VB.NET classes.

Wherever possible, create new classes in your .NET application that are designed from the ground up to take advantage of the rich feature set of the .NET framework. In many cases, such as DLLs containing nothing but business rules, many programmers choose to leave the components in the legacy COM DLL. However, DLLs that you should probably give serious thought to rewriting completely are data-tier components that use ADO. ADO.NET provides an incredibly rich (not to mention extremely fast, especially for SQL Server) set of classes for accessing, manipulating, and analyzing data. The `DataSet` class and its native support of XML are absolutely invaluable in enterprise applications.

MTS deserves some special consideration. There are many programmers who have invested literally years of programming time writing components in MTS. Fortunately, COM+ under Windows 2000 allows most of those old components to reside in COM+ Applications just as easily as they existed in MTS Packages in legacy systems. There are a few exceptions to this for components that utilized some very MTS-specific functionality. In general, however, most MTS components can be hosted in COM+ without any code changes. In addition, classic COM+ components can access .NET components hosted in COM+ natively (as far as what the programmer and calling component see).

Therefore, if you have a lot of COM+ components that don't do data access, there's no need for you to migrate them right now. Spend your time migrating the portions of your application that need it the most and go back for the COM+/MTS components later. This of course is assuming that these old COM+ components are not VB components. VB6 (and earlier) components are single-threaded, and performance nightmares on large-scale servers. If you need performance in your upgrade, get rid of VB components in critical paths.

Sustainability

Sustainability is the ability of your application to last for a very long time. A highly sustainable application can maintain its usefulness, ease of use, functionality, and customer demand as technology and business models change.

When you migrate your software to .NET, you want to position your application for scalability, growth, and future expansion. Identify areas of often-used functionality in your application to see if they can be conglomerated into new, more appropriate classes. The functionality of your application should be modularized into *Assemblies* that contain classes that all serve a common purpose.

For example, if you have twenty classes that deal with parts and labor in an auto shop, and another twenty that deal with accounting, pricing and finances, you might want to create two assemblies: `PartsLabor.DLL` and `Accounting.DLL`

Note: a practice that you will find many application developers and web site architects have is prefacing the Assembly filename with the *Namespace* that the assembly belongs to. In the new (and old, for those who remember DOS programming) paradigm of *Xcopy Deployment* it makes things easier to see and organize. So, the above two assemblies might be renamed to: `AutoManager.PartsLabor.DLL` and `AutoManager.Accounting.DLL`.

Grouping related classes into large DLLs in legacy situations would be cause for concern. If you're from an MTS background, you know that you should never have transactional and non-transactional classes in the same DLL. It is worth mentioning here that DLLs built under .NET are not necessarily the same as legacy DLLs. In fact, .NET DLLs can actually house the functionality of multiple legacy DLLs through the use of modules and command-line compilers (discussed in Chapter 8 on .NET components).

One of the "rules to live by" in DLL creation under VB6 was to avoid having a DLL that contained functionality to be used by different portions of your application at different times. For example, you have components driving your web site, and a DLL that houses a class for the shopping cart, and a class for the wish list. Under the Single-Threaded model of VB6, you might encounter wait times in the shopping cart due to heavy activity in the wish list. This is no longer an issue in .NET. The Assembly is managed far more efficiently, and VB.NET can now generate multi-threaded code, allowing more than one request for the same method at the same time to occur.

Jump on the XML Bandwagon

If there is one thing that you can do to your application that might prepare it for upgrades in the future, expansion, and scalability, it is the embracing and acceptance of XML. I'm sure some of you are sick and tired of hearing how XML is the next big thing, that it will fix all your problems, make your coffee in the morning, and cure the common cold. Take some of the advice in this section seriously, but at all costs avoid using XML for the sake of using XML. You should only use it where appropriate.

There is, however, quite a bit of truth to the part about it fixing a lot of your problems. The use of XML for as much of your native data handling as possible will *absolutely* position your application for scalability and expansion in the future. Not only that, but it will make such scaling and expansion far easier than if you had not decided to use XML. How exactly do you use XML in your application?

If you are working with an enterprise, n-tier application, you should consider using XML for the exchange of information between tiers, not only as arguments to methods, but as return values from methods and properties. When sending XML between tiers, what is often done is a DOM document (XmlDocument) is built containing all of the data and parameters to be sent to the next tier, and then the string representation of that XML is sent. Even though the programmer has to do some initial work, when sending large amounts of data this method is actually faster than traditional COM marshaling. In addition to using XML for transmission between tiers, you can use XML for transmitting data between any two entities that can work in HTTP via SOAP. In classic VB, doing this gets you out of a lot of problems spawned from DLL Hell, and makes revisions and GUID management a bit easier as well. In .NET, it allows for greater modularity of individual portions of your application, and allows "snap-in" future functionality between two modules at a later date.

Recently I decided to write a Windows Forms application to try out some features in .NET and to toy around with creating my own custom controls. For this test application, I needed to store some data, and didn't have SQL Server loaded on the test machine. I didn't want to mess with Access (didn't have that loaded either!), so I decided to use XML as the format for my desktop database. It was an absolutely joyful experience – the program was blazingly fast, I could use style sheets (declared as string constants!) to sort my elements, I used XPath to allow the user to search through the desktop database, and because it was XML, I could use more style sheets to export it into readable text files as well as HTML. Inserts, Updates, and Deletes were a breeze, and future versions of the application would have no problem using the data, as I could tag the file itself with a "version" attribute on the DocumentElement Node. This model of using XML text files as your local database is great, but it isn't practical for applications that need to scale well or take advantage of other data sources. It should really be reserved for applications that only need to store small amounts of local information.

Some people still haven't found a use for XML, as their applications might not benefit from it (though thinking of anything that couldn't benefit from XML seems alien to me…). Even I was an XML critic, thinking that it wouldn't do anything useful for me. However, as soon as I found that I needed what XML was good for, I found it an absolutely invaluable programming tool. I now worship the ground that XML can describe.

For the truly motivated, you should consider defining an XML dialect specific to your business. You may even find that there is already a dialect for your particular type of business transactions. Search the Internet for schemas that might be appropriate for your tasks and use ones already in existence to make your application compliant to tried and true standards. Take a look at the data entities that your application (or suite of applications) uses. Is there any set of information that other applications in your suite might want to share? Is there information that you think would be good for other, third party applications to have?

There are already hundreds of dialects springing up to describe everything from AI character behavior in video games to entire sets of medical information. There are also dialects to describe chemical information, environmental, and more. There is a user group currently under way to create a single standardized dialect of XML to describe an MSDS (Material Safety Data Sheet), a collection of information required for safety compliance.

Standardizing information in this manner not only allows various components within your application to operate on the same common formatted data, but it allows any third party to interact with your application using the dialect you have defined in your XML data. For example, using XML, various buildings within an organization could exchange chemical use information, games could reuse the same user information, and so on. Adopting XML in your application is an excellent way of "learning to share".

XML standardization and dialect user groups are everywhere, and they're easier to find. The more widely your application accepts and supports global standards, the more people will be able to use your application, and the more third party interaction you will be able to take advantage of.

A few pointers for code reuse in .NET

Obviously we don't have enough pages in this book to go over everything you can do to maximize your code reuse in the .NET framework. Most of the concepts behind good reuse of code apply equally well to classic COM and .NET alike. What I would like to do is give a couple of examples of ways that I've found can really maximize code reuse that have applications to the .NET framework as well as to development in general.

❑ **Code Librarian**

One of the best things you can do for yourself and the success of your project is to designate an official *Code Librarian*. The primary duty of this person is to maintain a library of common code, utilities and tools. By having a single point of contact (either a single person or a team of librarians) for all code reuse, the amount of redundant code in any large application is drastically reduced. This approach also produces some very good internal documentation and increases productive communication among programmers.

I'm sure we all have flashbacks from time to time of looking through a drawer of disks, frantically searching for a program we wrote a couple of months back because we knew it had that great binary-tree class implementation that took us three weeks to perfect. For projects where you are the only programmer, and you only have to contend with your own memory, you can get away without a librarian. However, when the development project involves multiple applications, dozens of developers, and dozens of shared components, classes and data structures, a librarian is a necessity.

Ever since seeing my first namespace, I've been a huge fan of using namespaces in creative and organized ways to organize your code in such a way that it looks almost like an extension of the .NET framework itself. One practice that I highly recommend is giving your librarian an entire namespace beneath your company's root namespace to organize as he or she sees fit.

Later in the chapter I discuss some good uses for namespaces, including a Common namespace, which is an ideal candidate for being managed by a code librarian.

If everyone on your project is using Visual Studio.NET, it might be a good idea for the Code Librarian to regularly build the Code Reports from the XML source documentation and the solution structure that VS.NET supports via the triple-slash (///) comment code. This triple-slash comment is only available in C#, and can be applied to class definitions, properties, and methods. There is currently no equivalent code documentation facility in VB.NET.

VS.NET allows you to simply pick an item from a drop-down menu and it will automatically generate HTML reports that document the structure and parameters of your code. If you are using C# and the "///" comment character, all of those comments will be built into the web reports. This is an absolutely invaluable tool for team programming with .NET as you can have the code librarian regularly publish the solution documentation to an intranet web site for all of the programmers to examine.

❑ **Separate User Interface from Business and Data Code**
One of the most important things that you can do when you're upgrading is make sure that
you have a clear separation of UI and underlying process. If you have ever tried to maintain
code for an application that had tons of data access routines embedded in an
`OKbutton_Click()` event, you've seen this problem before. To prepare yourself not only for
ASP.NET and WebForms, but Windows Forms as well, before you write a line of .NET code,
decide to separate the interface from the underlying functionality of the application. The more
intertwined your business and data code is with your interface code, the harder it will be to
read, upgrade, maintain and debug. The last thing you want to do is propagate a design flaw
like that to your new application.

❑ **Strongly Typed DataSets**
One tip that I've found really works well is to strongly type commonly used `DataSets`. One
thing that you'll find when using ADO.NET is that the `DataSet` is an incredibly versatile and
useful class. If you supply an XSD schema to the `XSD.EXE` tool supplied in the SDK, you can
create a class that derives from a `DataSet`, but contains member definitions from your
schema. VS.NET allows you to do all of this automatically by simply adding a "`DataSet`" to
your project. VS.NET will then add an XSD file to your project, and then behind the scenes
execute the following command line to convert your schema into a class. The command-line
for this tool looks as follows:

```
xsd.exe /d /l:C# {filename.xsd} /n:(namespace)
```

where the /d signifies that you want it to create a `DataSet` class. This tool will create as
output a C# class (indicated by the /l:C# portion of the command-line) that derives from a
`DataSet` and defines strongly-typed members that correspond with the data from your XSD
schema. You can also produce VB.NET `DataSet` classes by specifying /l:VB or Jscript by
specifying /l:JS. The tool does not provide any mechanism for creating C++ managed
classes deriving from the `DataSet`. The /n flag indicates into which namespace to place the
newly created class.

Just to review, an XSD schema is an XML file that contains a particular dialect of XML (XSD)
that lays out data validation rules for XML data. If you have ever seen the top of an ADO
Recordset persisted into XML, you will see text that looks very much like the XSD schemas
that Visual Studio .NET produces.

One of my personal favorite features of Visual Studio .NET is the ability to visually create a
database design, including tables, relationships and data types. From this visual diagram of a
`DataSet`, you can examine the actual XSD source code. This XSD source code is what you
can use to create a strongly-typed `DataSet` that represents the data in your diagram.

Here's an example of what a design of an XSD element looks like in VS.NET:

E	Customers	(Customers)
A	CustomerID	int
A	Name	string

❑   That same design produces the following XSD source code:

```xml
<?xml version="1.0" encoding="utf-8" ?>
<xsd:schema targetNamespace="http://tempuri.org/XMLSchema.xsd"
elementFormDefault="qualified" xmlns="http://tempuri.org/XMLSchema.xsd"
xmlns:xsd="http://www.w3.org/2001/XMLSchema">
    <xsd:element name="Customers">
        <xsd:complexType>
            <xsd:sequence />
            <xsd:attribute name="CustomerID" type="xsd:int" />
            <xsd:attribute name="Name" type="xsd:string" />
        </xsd:complexType>
    </xsd:element>
</xsd:schema>
```

You can then access fields from the table in the same manner that you would access members of a value-type struct. Not only does this allow you to access the data within the DataSet in a faster, more efficient manner, but it will actually allow the Visual Studio compiler to generate compile-time type mismatch errors when a field is being misused. In this next code example, we're illustrating how to utilize a strongly-typed DataSet. The code generated for that class is quite large, so for clarity's sake we'll just assume that it was defined elsewhere. The following section of code demonstrates how a strongly-typed DataSet can be accessed and instantiated:

```csharp
// Create a new instance of the movieDataSet strongly-typed class.
movieDataSet dsMovies = new movieDataSet();
// Create a new instance of a SqlDataAdapter, supplying a select
// query and a connection string.
SqlDataAdapter movieDA = new SqlDataAdapter("SELECT Title, Rating FROM Movies",
    "server=localhost;uid=sa;pwd=;database=Movies;");

// DataSets can actually contain multiple linked tables. The
// Fill method will place the results from a SqlDataAdapter
// into a named table in a DataSet.
movieDA.Fill (dsMovies, "Movies");

Console.WriteLine("A few movie picks for you:");

// Just like we saw earlier, anything that implements an enumerator
// interface can be iterated through using the foreach keyword.
// moviesRow is a class defined by the .cs file created by the XSD tool.
foreach(moviesRow movieRow in dsMovies.movies)
{
    Console.WriteLine("{0}:{1}", movieRow.Title, movieRow.Rating);
}
```

❑   **Real-World Class Structure Modeling**
    One thing that I have seen destroy program after program, and cause massive hair loss among apparently healthy programmers, is poor object-oriented design. Everything in the .NET framework is object oriented. The entire structure of the class library is structured with a rigid class hierarchy and meaningful namespace separation.

It is entirely too easy to fall into the bad habit of using a class simply as a warehouse of procedural functionality. What happens far too often is that, in a rush to meet a deadline or provide some essential functionality, a programmer will create a class that initially looks as though it meets most OOP guidelines fairly well. Then, as more and more features need to be added to the application, the programmer starts stuffing features into the original class because there isn't enough time to redesign the class structure. You end up with a bloated, slow, inefficient, and pretty homely-looking class.

To avoid the pitfall of bloating your classes, you should make sure that they are designed thoroughly to begin with. The problem of becoming a warehouse of functionality occurs when features are added without enough design time. Each and every time a property or method is added to your class to support a new feature, refer to the original design guidelines of that class. If the new method or property violates that design, you need to go back and refactor your classes to make room for the new feature.

As I've said before, you have a rare opportunity here to re-architect your classes. You're going to be migrating from classic COM (or Windows, etc.) to the .NET framework. You don't have to map your classes 1:1 from old to new. The following two guidelines should ease this step in your migration, hopefully preventing you from falling victim to B.C.S. (*Bloated Class Syndrome*).

❑ **Model Real-World Entities**
When designing your new class structure, try as hard as possible to make each class as atomic as possible, representing as closely as possible singular entities relevant to your application. Try to avoid creating useless abstracts that could actually be multiple separate classes. Modeling classes in this way increases your chances of successful code reuse without any adverse side effects.

❑ **Never Model Singular and Plural in the Same Class**
Far more programmers than are willing to admit it violate this rule everyday. As the demand for rapid introduction of new features and bug fixes grows, programmers simply don't have the time or the resources to create new classes, redesign previous classes, or worry about how to upgrade a single DLL in an old version that really ought to be three different DLLs. Violating this rule is a basic violation of all the other rules: it's basically the "Do it all wrong in one shot" method.

A real-world entity model should never model its counterpart and a plural of its counterpart in the same class. For example, you shouldn't have a class that represents a Car and have that same class, depending on strange circumstances or configuration switches, represent a list of Car objects. Most fundamentalist OOP designers would pass out from agony if they saw a class designed this way. It might work for a small project, for a short period of time. However, as the class grows in functionality, so too does the need for list-producing functionality, and soon you find yourself coding into the Car object the ability to search the Car database and retrieve results, also stored in a Car object. Then you end up coding operations into the Car object that perform manipulation of data on lists of Car objects (parking lot assignments, etc.). Pretty soon, you find that the Car class is now a warehouse for procedural functionality for the entire car dealership management system, and as an aside it also can function as a single Car representation.

The bottom line is that if you make a drastic mistake in your class design, no amount of tricky code in C# or VB.NET can save you from the inevitable crash and complete redesign of your application once its needs outgrow the restricting harness that poor design placed around it.

The following diagram illustrates the Object-Oriented Design of a single scenario, an automobile dealership management system. This approach is a poor design. The Car object is completely overburdened, modeling both singular and plural real-world counterparts, and containing far too much procedural functionality, turning the class into a function warehouse.

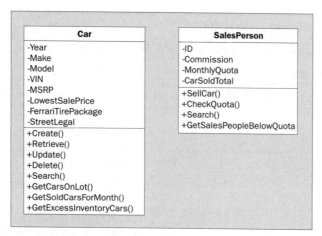

The next diagram illustrates a better approach, using inheritance and multiple classes to properly model the real-world problem that the application is designed to solve:

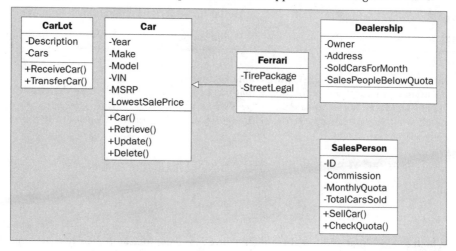

As you can see from the above example, the second method is a far more realistic and easy to understand modeling approach. You can see that the Ferrari class inherits from the Car class. This removes the need to have code specific to only one type of car in the car base class, and moves that code to the class where it is truly appropriate. All operations that work on Cars can simply create a Car variable from either a Car or a *Ferrari*, where Ferrari-specific operations can ignore classes that are not Ferraris. The key is to avoid bloating classes with code that is only going to be used in a small percentage of the instances of that class (in this case, placing Ferrari code in the generic Car class). Code that more closely resembles the real-world entity you are modeling will invariably scale more efficiently, as it will be able to adapt to any changes that its real-world counterpart can experience.

Because SQL Server isn't inherently an object-oriented database system, we need some kind of flat, non-hierarchical way to represent the data that populates the inherited functionality of our new class design. The following two tables show the Cars and Ferrari tables as a sample of one of the many ways to represent this. Keep in mind that there are always more options for data structures in SQL:

Ferraris Table

Column	Type	Description
CarID	Int	Unique ID for the information in the Car table
TirePackage	Int	ID indicating which tire package Ferrari has
StreetLegal	Bit	Boolean indicating whether Ferrari is street legal

Cars Table

Column	Type	Description
CarID	Int	Unique ID representing a particular car
Year	Int	4-digit number indicating car's model year
Make	Int	ID of the make of the car, related to "Makes" table.
VIN	VarChar(13)	Unique VIN of vehicle
MSRP	Real	Dollar amount of Manufacturer recommended price
LowestSalePrice	Real	Dollar amount of dealerhip's bottom line on the car

❑ **Inheritance versus Multiple Configurable Instances**
It's an age-old question, perhaps one that has boggled more people than the classic "Chicken versus The Road" case: *Should you create multiple classes that inherit from the base, or simply instantiate the base and set properties to distinguish multiple instances?* Consider the following two code snippets:

```
if (oCar.CarType == Cars.cartypeFerrari) { … }
```

and

```
if (oCar is Cars.Ferrari) { … }
```

Which one, without additional comments or documentation, most clearly represents the intent of the Boolean evaluation? Hands down, I would have to say that the second code sample is far more readable, and requires far less explanation in a comment section. In addition, the second example has the added benefit of not confusing operators. Just about every C programmer has written code that accidentally used the assignment operator (=) to test for equality (==). The second option uses the is operator, preventing the ability to confuse operators and reducing the chance of hard-to-track bugs.

The first sample uses a member property of the *instance* of the Car class to store what kind of car it is. Therefore, to access any property of that instance that might only have meaning when the instance is of the Ferrari persuasion, the first conditional statement needs to be placed redundantly in the code.

The second sample, however, is far more powerful. What it does is ask the C# compiler if the oCar instance can be resolved down to an instance of the Ferrari class in the namespace Cars. The immediate benefit of this may not be that obvious. However, if you use the as operator to actually cast a variable to the Ferrari class, you can then perform Ferrari-specific operations on the class without having to worry if they are available or not. The following code sample expands on this:

```
oCar = oTestCar as Cars.Ferrari;
if (oCar != null) {
    Console.WriteLine(oCar.StreetLegal);
}
```

For those who like to keep their code short, the above example can be rewritten as:

```
if ( (oCar = oTestCar as Cars.Ferrari)!= null )
    Console.WriteLine(oCar.StreetLegal);
```

The above code sample casts the oCar object to the Ferrari base class within oTestCar. If this cast is successful, then the code assumes that oCar is a Ferrari, and proceeds to print out the Ferrari-only property StreetLegal.

❑ **Inheritance Caveats**

As your migration progresses into the coding stage, you are going to realize that the entire .NET framework seems to have been designed entirely with the idea of supporting and encouraging object-oriented programming. It makes inheritance and use of base classes and interfaces extremely easy. VB programmers may feel a bit overwhelmed when looking at the inheritance structure of the .NET class libraries, but the language makes using inheritance easy enough so that most programmers should pick up the concepts fairly easily.

You can even inherit classes written in other programming languages as if they were part of your own project, even if all you have at your disposal is the compiled Assembly. .NET makes inheriting from and encapsulating other people's classes extremely easy. Therein lies the problem: unless you take appropriate precautions, you could be opening your application to all kinds of unintended activity. As the format of an Assembly is the same, no matter which language created it, any language can inherit from and extend any class contained in that Assembly.

Let's say your application contains a Car class. Your Car class restricted member data that indicates the make and model of that car. This way, you can control what kinds of cars can be stored in your data. This is all fine, until some adventurous programmer creates a new class, Junker, that inherits from your Car class. As a child class, it has access to data that external classes don't, so it can then modify its make and model, circumventing your business logic and allowing storage of non-existent makes and models.

To secure your application from unintended functionality like this, you need to make sure that all of the classes that you do not want anyone to derive from are coded as *sealed*. Sealed is a keyword in C# that you can place in front of your class name declaration that tells the compiler not to allow any code from any language to use that class as a base class. VB.NET uses the keyword NotInheritable.

❑ **Assembly Security**
One of the things that makes it so easy for people to inherit from classes contained in Assemblies is that, by default, the Assemblies are basically public information. Anyone using the `ILDASM.EXE` tool can examine in excruciating detail your Assembly's manifest, `meta data`, and even the IL code for all of your methods and classes. IL code is remarkably easy to read, and wouldn't take long for anyone to figure out any proprietary algorithms you have contained in your DLL.

In Beta 1, there was a concept of an assembly "owner". If someone compiled an Assembly with an owner, then only the same owner could disassemble that Assembly using the `ILDASM.EXE` tool. However, in Beta 2 the entire notion of ownership in Assemblies has disappeared. Once the full public release of the .NET framework is out, you should make it a very strong personal goal to determine the best way to secure your DLLs against prying eyes.

The reason I'm mentioning all this in a chapter on migration is that in the world of VB6, you weren't accustomed to the concept of people prying into your code. Your DLL contained code that no one could see, and that was the end of it. Due to the nature of COM and VB6, no one could use classes in your DLLs as base classes; all they could do was instantiate classes from within your DLL. Now, the .NET framework's open and flexible cross-language inheritance ability requires that you pay closer attention to which classes you leave open for inheritance, and which classes you make sure you *seal* to prevent abuse of your application and methods. In addition, you now need to be aware that the code contained within is basically an open book for anyone with the time or energy to look.

The reason why I'm going over good OOP design here in a chapter on .NET migration is that one of the largest keys to migrating code to .NET is adopting a very good, very controlled, and organized object-oriented programming model. You will find that the better your object model, the more easily your code will adapt to .NET. On the other hand, the looser, less-structured (procedure warehouse) object models will not adapt well to use in the .NET framework.

Recycle

In the hey-day of COM, the idea was to write COM components so that you could replace individual components with new and improved functionality as needed without having to re-install an entire application (or rebuild an entire web server). Application vendors wrote secure, licensed COM components for use by other programmers so they could avoid re-inventing the wheel. It was a beautiful and wonderful system, and all was good in the world.

Then people tried to implement it. DLL versioning ruined the stomachs of millions of programmers world-wide, and raised the stock value of Pepto Bismol by many points. People decided to use scriptlets, Beans, and other packaged components to distribute compartmentalized functionality across an enterprise application or to individual customer desktops.

Now we have the .NET framework. The boundary between your application and other applications on the customer's computer is a hazy, barely visible line. The boundary between the customer's computer, the Internet, and millions of services and web sites is just as hazy and transparent. You could write your upgraded .NET application to exist in a sealed box on the customer's desktop, or on a lonely web server – but why would you?

This may sound like marketing talk, but it's the truth as we see it. .NET is going to blur all of the lines of the Internet and applications. Personal finance programs are going to be consuming web services to grab stock quotes, and grab bank balances from ten different banks in five different countries. Document and file sharing is going to become an immense, far-reaching, global operation. Your computer is going to show you "your" files, even though they could be on twenty different web sites around the world. You're going to order an item from an e-Commerce site using your PDA (your PalmPilot or iPAQ, etc.), check the shipping status with it from your PC, and confirm delivery from your cell phone. Like it or not, everything is about to get a *lot* more connected.

The question is – with all of this incredible functionality being placed at the fingertips of *your* customer, are you going to be happy with providing them a stale, unconnected, isolated program that knows nothing about any other services, and provides no services of its own? Obviously not.

Web Services

When you are examining the functionality and services provided by your application, you should be looking at everything your application does very carefully. Take a second look at any functionality that you think can be packaged for reuse by other programs your company is working on, or by third party programs that haven't even been designed yet.

Find out what you can expose as a web service (if that paradigm applies to your application). If your application is currently an enterprise web application, see what you can expose as a service to allow other web sites to integrate with yours, sharing content and information. If you're upgrading a standard Windows application, consider making it a combination application, such as one that incorporates any combination of desktop interface, web pages, or web services.

A really good example of a combination application is a collection manager. In its simplest form, all it does is track your CDs, or your DVDs, or whatever. In its .NET form, it could do the same, but also allow you to look at other people's DVD lists, to see how much they paid for them, what kind of audio encoding people buy most often, etc. This could all be accomplished by having a web site host a hobby list service. The following figures illustrate the architecture of an isolated Windows hobby manager, contrasted with the same hobby manager upgraded to take advantage of .NET and web services.

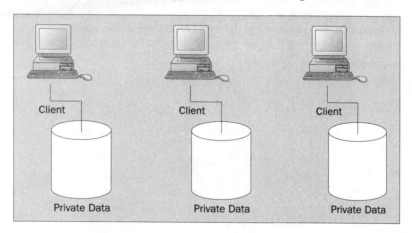

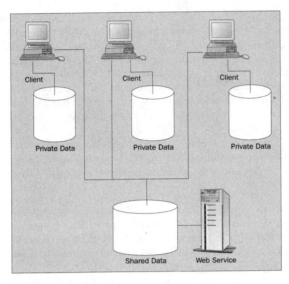

An example of a web site that might benefit from exposing some of its functionality as a service is a video game's fan site. There are several 'massively multiplayer' role-playing games on the market today that have cult-like followings. Included in these followings are web sites that devote massive time and effort to compiling lists of items, monsters, areas, and quests that are available in the game. The problem is that many of them are duplicating effort. Many different sites, each sharing a portion of their viewers, will be compiling distinct (and probably redundant) databases. What could be done to alleviate this problem, and take advantage of .NET code recycling in the form of Web Services, is to provide the central database as a web service. Affiliated sites (*extremely common* in gaming web sites) could simply subscribe to the service to allow their database to mirror the central. When new items or creatures are logged from an affiliated site, they're actually logged into the central site via the web service.

A design like this is definitely not restricted to the gaming community. Content like this can be shared via Web Services for any number of web sites, including news, forums & newsgroups, programming sites (several .NET programming sites share code examples and news via Web Services), and many more, limited only by the imagination of the site architects. The following diagram illustrates the simple architecture of a new, .NET gaming site that is exposing its database as a subscription-based web service.

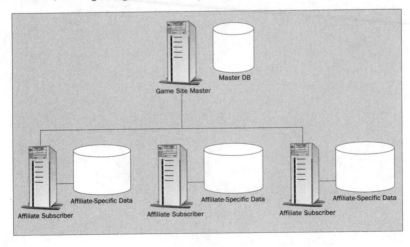

Getting into the .NET Framework

This following section of the chapter gets into detail about the various aspects of the .NET framework that you need to be aware of when migrating. No matter how fast you can write code for the .NET framework, if you're writing that code without being aware of the consequences, your entire application is going to fall apart quickly.

The following section gives you some useful information on Namespaces, a contrast of Inheritance with Interfaces, and a quick primer on writing code for a garbage-collected environment.

Namespaces

There's been some discussion on the technical aspect of namespaces and how they affect .NET applications. Even though the framework is still in beta, I have seen code that horribly abuses the concept of namespaces. Namespaces are a layer of organization on top of classes. They are a way of logically grouping classes into a container. This container, or *namespace*, is not necessarily one single DLL; in fact, a namespace can actually span multiple DLLs.

What I've done is come up with a sample namespace usage that might help you get your new, upgraded application running in an enterprise environment. You might be wondering why you want to use namespaces – after all, Visual Studio automatically gives you one namespace per project, why would you need to change it?

In some really large enterprise applications, I've seen hundreds of Business Logic Layer (BLL) components, hundreds of Data Access Layer (DAL) components in several COM+ Applications, and dozens more UI/Front-end components. To prevent conflicts, people had to use odd and confusing-looking naming conventions.

Let's take the Car and Ferrari example. Assuming that application has become a large, n-tier application, and it has followed all of the "rules" about statelessness and atomicity, then it probably has a read-only DAL component, a transactional DAL component, a BLL component, and probably a UI component for formatting Car data in either HTML or some portable format like XML.

How do you distinguish between layers, and still have the component have a meaningful name? Even worse, how do you guarantee that your CLSID of Car.Car (or something equally vague) isn't going to be used by some other application installed on the system?

This is where the dreaded "naming convention" comes in. In legacy COM code, you would've had to modify your CLSIDs so that they reflected not only the layer in which the class resided, but the application identity as well to prevent naming conflicts. So, because you couldn't early-bind to an MTS/COM+ component, you had to late-bind, using CreateObject to obtain your objects. So, a typical call to create an object from a tier of your application might have looked like this:

```
Set tCar = CreateObject("MYAPP_tCar.tCar")
```

Now, in .NET, with the use of namespaces, you don't need to do anything near so confusing. A class that represents a Car should be called a Car, regardless of whether it represents transactional processing for a car, read-only data access for a car, or business logic for a car. An early-bound instantiation of a Car using namespaces might look like the following:

```
CarApplication.DAL.Car tCar = new CarApplication.DAL.Car();
```

My recommendation for a "best practice" for using namespaces in n-tier, enterprise applications is to nest the namespaces as follows:

```
namespace Company
{
    namespace Application
    {
        namespace Tier
        {
            public class YourClass
            {
            }
        }
    }
}
```

The Company outer namespace may not be necessary, but it comes in handy if your company has separately bundled utilities or support components that are shared among many applications. To add further granularity so that you can distinguish between the read-only Car class and the transactional *Car* class, both within the same tier, you might want to implement something like this:

```
namespace Company
{
    namespace Application
    {
        namespace Tier
        {
            namespace Transactional
            {
                public class YourClass
                {
                }
            }
        }
    }
}
```

As a shorthand, instead of trying to nest things so deep, you can actually separate your nested namespace declarations with periods rather than nesting them within a code block:

```
namespace Company.Application.Tier.Transactional
{
    class MyClass
    {
    }
}
```

The following figure shows a graphical representation of a good use of namespaces as containers in an enterprise application. Each of the traditional tiers of an n-tier application are separate namespaces, with extra namespaces provided for shared or common functionality, and an additional level of namespace to house the transactional COM+ components. Both the Company and the Application namespace contain a nested namespace called "Common". This namespace would be reserved for utilities, tools, and support code that doesn't particularly belong to a given tier. You might place registration key encoding and decoding tools into the application's Common namespace, and you might place code that your company has written that is to be shared across all of its applications into the company's Common namespace.

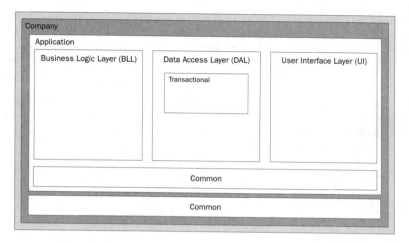

Based on the above example, a sample header of `using` statements might look like this:

```
using Company;
using Company.Application;
using Company.Application.BLL;
using Company.Application.DAL;
using Company.Application.UI;
using Company.Common;
using Company.Application.Common;
```

The only caveat you need to be aware of by using namespaces to distinguish between various tiers where classes have the same name is when multiple tiers contain a class with the same name. In such a case, you would need to prefix the class name with its tier to distinguish one class from another, in other words, referencing classes as `BLL.Car` or `DAL.Car` or `UI.Car`, etc. Generally this isn't too much of an issue because any given tier only typically has access to the tier immediately "below" it.

With a well-organized namespace structure, your physical deployment can be a snap, mimicking in directory structure what you have coded in logical structure. In addition, a well-organized namespace structure like the one above completely prevents the need for obscure, confusing naming conventions.

Inheritance or Interfaces

One thing that many people found surprising was the .NET framework's strong support of the concept of an Interface. Some people who thought that .NET was replacing COM couldn't quite figure out why Microsoft would've kept the Interface concept around. Needless to say, the concept of the Interface remains, and will continue to be a large part of the core of the .NET framework.

The simplest way to distinguish between Inheritance and Interfaces is this:

- ❑ A class that *inherits* another class is said to demonstrate an "is a" relationship.

- ❑ A class that implements an *Interface* is merely stating that it conforms to a previously stated contract of functionality.

For example, the class `Ferrari` inherits from the base class `Car`. Thus, the statement "A Ferrari is a Car" is a real-world modeling scenario that should give you a clue that Inheritance would be the way to go.

533

However, having doors that open and shut is not something limited only to automobiles. Houses, planes, windows, and thousands more things all have doors that open and shut, but are not cars. For the sake of example, everything that has a door supports the ability to open and close it. This is a prime example of where you would use an interface. A vast variety of dissimilar objects all support a common set of methods.

In this case, a Car can be said to implement an interface, IDoor. The IDoor interface could then implement two methods, OpenDoor and CloseDoor. The code and nature of Interfaces guarantee (hence the commonly used term "contract") that anything implementing the IDoor interface *must* provide both the OpenDoor and CloseDoor methods.

The following example shows briefly how the Car class can be modified to support the IDoor interface:

```
interface IDoor
{
    void OpenDoor();
    void CloseDoor();
}

public class Car: IDoor
{
    // because we're implementing the IDoor interface,
    // must implement OpenDoor and CloseDoor()

    public void OpenDoor()
    {
    }

    public void CloseDoor()
    {
    }
}
```

What does all this have to do with migration? It simply cannot be stressed enough that knowledge of the framework to which you are migrating is absolutely essential to creating a good design on the new platform. If you don't know the capabilities of your destination platform, you cannot effectively design your application to take advantage of those capabilities. In any decision, computer-related or not, if you don't know all of the available options, you can't possibly make the best possible informed decision. This is definitely the case with inheritance and Interfaces: knowing when to use them and when not to use them can mean the difference between a solid, scalable, sustainable solution and a solution that will grind to a halt as technology improves.

Writing Code in a Garbage-Collected Environment

This is always a controversial topic. Some programmers complain that they can manage their own memory far better than a Garbage Collector can, whereas some programmers feel that programming in a GC environment inspires lazy and sloppy coding. Whether you like it or not, if you're going to be upgrading your code to the .NET framework, your code is going to be garbage collected.

The Garbage Collector (GC) is a process within the Runtime that handles all of the memory management for all of the programs it is executing. When you create new instances and new value-types in your code, the Runtime allocates some space for the objects you requested. At some point in the future, the GC will come around and reclaim the memory that you used. The memory being reclaimed by the garbage collector is only memory that is not currently in use by your application.

The most important thing to keep in mind, especially when migrating code from a non-GC environment, is that the time when your memory is reclaimed is *not necessarily* the time when your code is done using that memory. The cardinal rule for object management in VB6 is to *always* set your variants to `nothing` when you're done with them. When you set a VB6 variant to nothing, you actually reclaim the memory used by that variant. When you dispose of variables within the .NET framework, the GC may or may not reclaim the memory for that variable at that time. The fact that the time at which memory is reclaimed is not necessarily the time at which you stop using that variable (either by disposing it, setting it to nothing or some other method) is referred to as **non-deterministic finalization**.

The real impact of this is that you absolutely *cannot* count on being able to port class code that relies on *Destructors* for critical behavior. In C++, if you dispose of a pointer to a class, you know that *at that exact moment*, the Destructor for that class will fire, and any code within it will execute. In the .NET framework, it is very possible, in fact very likely, that when you dispose of a class, the destructor for that class might not get called until much later.

The framework actually refers to destructors as *Finalizers*, the reason being that the code executed in it is executed when the GC removes it from memory, not necessarily when the code explicitly indicates that it is done with it.

To convert a class with critical code in a Destructor, move the code from the Destructor into a separate function. Then, instead of explicitly disposing of the variable, simply call the new function and leave the GC to reclaim the memory. For example:

```
myClass myVar = new myClass();

// … Do something with myVar …

// classic C++: delete myVar;
myVar.DoDestruct(); //release resources
```

There is actually a destructor method called `Finalize` that all objects support. However, you should only use a finalizer when you know that what you need to be done actually needs to be done at the time of garbage collection, as classes with finalizers take up slightly more overhead in memory than classes without.

The Migration Design How-To

Even though there are a multitude of issues relating specifically to the migration of legacy code to the .NET framework, the fact still remains that you are migrating. No matter what you are migrating, or for what reasons, there is still a common set of guidelines and procedures that you can follow to ensure that your migration goes as smoothly as possible. It cannot be stressed enough times that the key to a successful migration or implementation of a .NET application is thorough preparation and good design. The four key steps in creating a migration design are described below. Each step needs to be completed before the next step can begin. If you reach the final step and the system is not ready, you will need to go through the steps in order again. The following flowchart illustrates the flow of the steps for implementing a migration.

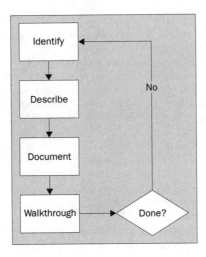

Identify

The first step in any migration should be to identify the objects, relationships, etc. that should be migrated, as well as identify coding standards, design and implementation standards, and the core business rules and features that your migrated application will support.

At this point, you may not want to take a linear approach. One approach that I've found to be very effective is a corkboard and 3x5 index cards. Every single entity, entity relationship, feature and business rule should be placed on a business card. Scatter them out on a table and then start pinning them up. You'll find yourself pulling down and re-pinning often, grouping things logically and by related functionality.

One thing that should become fairly clear during this process is where inheritance might be useful and where Interfaces might be created. Remember that any time you have some common functionality that might need to be placed in varying, dissimilar objects you may want to consider the use of interfaces.

Describe

Describe in detail the entities that you identified in the previous step. The purpose of this step is a forced mental exercise. Once you get into the process of describing in lengthy detail all of the entities, relationships, rules, and features that are going to be migrated, patterns of potential code reuse, inheritance and object classification should begin to appear. This step is essential to determining the best potential places for code reuse.

If you were using index cards to identify each individual entity that needs to be upgraded to the .NET framework for your new application, you might want to consider attaching a piece of paper to each of the components or writing a quick, one-paragraph text file for each index card you have identified.

Document

Document in lengthy detail the things that you described in the previous step. The result of this step should actually provide the team with a preliminary plan of attack for migrating your application, including plenty of details about everything that is going to be included in the migration.

The results of this step can be a single word document, or a folder of word documents corresponding to the individual items that were identified and described above. If you have someone on your team skilled in producing Windows Help files, you might want to consider creating one of these as your internal document. Windows Help files have nice tree views for easy navigation, as well as searching and bookmarking capabilities.

Walkthrough

Walk through your design with users and the designers. Use your original design and specifications as an aid to walk through the flow and functionality of your application. At this point you should be looking at putting together a test plan and development and rollout schedules. Once this step is complete, more than likely the design will fall short. At some point, someone is going to bring up something that will put a gaping hole in your design. Don't worry about it, that gaping hole is part of the plan. When this happens, pack up all your work and head back to Step 1. Continue to rework and revise your identifications, descriptions, and documentation until you can complete the walkthrough to the satisfaction of all your testers, designers, and programmers.

Implementing a .NET Migration

So far we've talked about why you should migrate. We've talked about how you might decide what you should migrate, and we've talked about code reuse, recycling and reduction. After that we talked about the procedures involved in actually carrying out a migration. Now it's finally time to get down to business and get into the actual implementation of your migration plan. By the time you get around to implementation, you should have a well-rounded, fully-designed object model for your new application. This section of the chapter will cover some of the goals you should be keeping in mind, a few possible migration paths your project can take, and some tools that might help you in your migration.

Goals and Issues

Whenever you're working on a large project, it is always helpful to keep in mind your main goal. It keeps the line you travel from start to finish straight, and helps keep your efforts and the efforts of everyone else on your team more focused.

When you're working on a migration of an existing project, one of the things you might want to be concerned with is achieving the quickest time to market as possible. That's obviously something that you'll have to figure out on your own, dividing your resources between the migration and other current projects. Another thing to keep in mind as you're migrating and writing code is that your ultimate goal is to create an extremely extensible, scalable, and sustainable solution. Sustainability, as we covered earlier, includes adoption of standards (not just XML) and writing code in a flexible enough structure to allow your application to grow and change as the market grows and changes. Also keep in mind that you may not only be migrating architectures, but programming languages as well. Make sure that you've found all the references you can on migrating specific languages to .NET (such as VB6 to VB.NET, etc.)

The issues you need to concern yourself with when migrating to .NET currently start with the Beta. The .NET framework is in Beta 2 at the time of the release of this book. Once the beta is done, and the CLR is available as a public redistributable installation, then you have to worry about *customer acceptance*. You need to keep in mind what platform you're writing your application for (client and server), and make sure that the infrastructure of your customers can support that. In addition to dealing with the .NET framework and your general migration, you need to create fall-back plans to handle the worst-case scenarios. You may want to have some discussion on what you might do if unexpected delays occur during your .NET migration, or you run into a hard stopping-point, etc.

Migration Paths

One of the great things about the .NET framework is that because of its incredible flexibility, there are dozens of possible ways of migrating your existing applications to the .NET framework. Almost all migration paths eventually boil down to two different ways of migrating: a progressive upgrade, or a complete upgrade.

Baby Steps to .NET

The *Baby Steps* approach to .NET migration is a progressive or partial approach. If the driving force behind your migration is the absolute need to get something out the door that you can market as new, fresh, and being written for .NET, then this is the approach for you. This type of migration usually takes place in three stages, which can be broken down into smaller stages as the need arises.

❑ **Stage One** – Rebuild your User Interface
As the driving force behind your migration is the need to get something out the door as soon as possible, and it needs to be using .NET, the first changes you want to make are changes that you're going to want the consumers of your application to see.

.NET makes creating custom Windows Forms and WebForms controls much easier than doing the same thing, even in Visual Basic 6. Rewriting the User Interface of a large application can be a daunting task. The key is not to get yourself stuck in the "port" mentality. Take the class structure and design that you have in mind for your new .NET application and try to build the user interface up from there, rather than limit yourself by trying to upgrade what might already be a 'kludgy' interface.

If you've been a good programmer, and encapsulated your business and data logic in COM objects (or at the very least, separate modules) rather than loaded your UI with bloated logic, then converting your interface should be fairly straightforward. Using the COM-Callable Wrapper and Reflection, you can invoke COM methods and objects from within managed code. This will allow you to create a very flexible, modern user interface that has access to all of the functionality of the .NET framework, but you will still be able to call your existing business code in legacy VB6 or VC++ DLLs.

❑ **Stage Two** – Complete .NET Application
After you have released a version of your application that has the .NET framework available to it, the front-end should be far easier to maintain until your next release. The next release of your application will be a full-blown implementation of a native .NET application.

Once your .NET UI has left the building, you can then get to work on converting your business logic and data access to use the .NET framework, the class library, ADO.NET, etc. This release of your application should contain all of the core functionality of your application rewritten in the .NET framework. This stage will also have to include some touch-ups to the recently upgraded user interface, as code that returns a `DataSet` requires a different UI wrapper to code that returns a `RecordSet`.

❑ **Stage Three** – To Infinity and Beyond
This is where the fun part begins. You've built and released a .NET front-end user interface. You then constructed and released a well-planned, extensible and flexible object model business and data layer in .NET. Now, your entire application from end to end is running in managed code. The sky is now the limit.

At this point, your application is limited only by the imagination, time, and resources of its programmers. Try to capitalize on the idea of Software as a Service. If there is any way at all that you can use the Internet, Web Services, or Remoting to connect your application to a server, or your web application to other servers, or your client application to other clients, you should consider taking that opportunity. That is the direction of the Internet, and it would greatly enhance the marketability of any application to be involved in that revolution.

The following figure is a timeline that demonstrates a sample development rollout schedule of a partial integration of the .NET framework into an application. It shows how the development process continues in maintenance mode on the "legacy" version of the application while additional resources are dedicated to creating the initial user interface "port". Once the port of the UI is done, developers from both teams begin work on porting the business and data tiers and continue on from there.

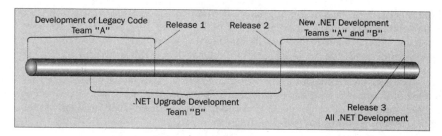

While there is no reliable way to estimate how long it will take any migration without actually being involved in the specific migration, I have seen a trend in migration times. Assuming the learning curve has been crested, I've noticed that each .NET component takes roughly half the time of its predecessor in VB6. For web-based applications, the user interface (WebForms) can take as little as one tenth of the time of a classic page (bound, colored, and styled DataGrids are a good example of this), or it can take twice as long, depending on what you need to do.

The only time-related information I can give you is that when estimating the time to migrate to .NET, you should completely ignore the time it took to you get to your current position. You've had months or years of customer feedback, upgrades, improvements, overhauls and more. What you're doing is rolling all of that knowledge into a single upgrade that has its own time estimate, based on .NET coding time and the ability of your team to create a versatile, sustainable and extensible design.

The "Full Monty" Migration

The "Full Monty" migration is a complete and total rewrite of all existing code. When you are done migrating using this approach, nothing that you release to your customers will be in classic VB6 or any other non-.NET language. Everything from the ground up, including your core design, will be based on the .NET framework.

The "Full Monty" approach to migration is the most straightforward. The new, .NET-based code is written entirely from scratch. Depending on how good the previous code is, much of it should be able to be reused in essence, but the code base will be completely original. The benefit of this approach is that the new application will not be slowed or hindered by old conventions, or hacks that may have been in the old code to provide support for something that the .NET framework now supports natively. The downside is that the "Full Monty" approach takes considerably more time, effort and money than the previous. This initial cost is only for the initial release. Maintaining a .NET application has a much smaller cost than the "Full Monty" migration. There is a lot of merit to this approach, and if you or your company has the time and resources to accomplish this migration path, there will be plenty of rewards later.

As has been mentioned before, when rewriting your code for .NET, take the time to re-evaluate the class structure and hierarchy. Make sure that the classes appropriately model their namesakes rather than just implement a warehouse of procedural functionality. As always, when working with .NET, utilize the built-in functionality of the framework and the classes already written for you in the .NET framework class library (such as the `XmlDocument`, `HashTable`, `Array`, `Collection`, `DataSet`, SQL/ADO connections, etc.).

When you migrate using the "Full Monty" philosophy, you have a key opportunity to re-evaluate the core design of your application. Keep in the back of your mind at all times the question: *Can I repackage any of the functionality of my application as a service?* Remember that services don't have to be things that anyone but your own internal applications consume. However, the use of services can facilitate things like splitting a Windows interface into a Windows Forms and WebForms (ASP.NET) interface without much hassle at all.

Throughout the entire process of the migration, the ability to communicate with the other members of the migration team is absolutely essential. Each developer and designer has a unique set of experiences, even though you may all have been working on the same project. The more you communicate throughout the entire process, the less chance there is of overlooking an important feature.

Part of the process of increasing communication and avoiding disparate efforts is designating an overall librarian. One of the pointers for code reuse that I mentioned earlier was to have a designated librarian in charge of maintaining common and shared code. This also holds true for documentation, specifications, and migration plans during a migration project.

Embrace the idea that the users of your application are not just individuals sitting at their own completely disconnected desktops without any contact to the outside world. The users of your new .NET application are consumers of a service that you are providing. Your customers form a community of knowledge, skills, and common interest that your application can not only facilitate, but foster and stimulate.

Many programs have fan communities, or newsgroups, dedicated to helpful hints and FAQs regarding the use of that software. With .NET, you could very easily provide a web service that facilitated that community, actually building into your own application chats and newsgroups/forums for communicating with other users of your application. A strong fan base, or strong and well-informed user base has always been a major factor in repeat business and the length of time people use an application.

Picture this: a user in Texas turns on their laptop, completely disconnected from the Internet, without a phone line or any other form of connectivity. This user opens up your application, finds a feature they would like to see included, and logs that into a forum interface. Two weeks later, that user connects to the Internet with their 56k modem, the request for the new feature is unobtrusively sent off to your company's website. At the same time, active content is pulled from your web site. The user runs your application and is greeted with news about an upcoming release of your application, and other company news.

What was just described is the difference between a *port* application and a *native* application. A port application blindly takes Windows functionality and reproduces it. The chapters prior to this one all give you great information on how to reproduce old functionality in the new framework. However, they also give you the knowledge you need to produce amazing, new, original features that no one has ever seen before. The ability to design your application beyond the constraints that once held it chained down is what is going to make your new application an absolute joy to use, and foster a community of enthusiastic, knowledgeable customers.

A very well known saying is that *a platform is only as good as the applications running on it*. This holds true for .NET as well. It is very possible for a vast array of horrible software to flood the market for the .NET platform, giving it a horrible reputation. However, it is also possible to introduce to the market a large amount of really beautiful applications, with robust, connected paradigms and features people have never seen before on Windows.

.NET Framework Design and Style Guidelines

Earlier in this chapter, I mentioned that if you are migrating code written by programmers with good programming habits (or if you possess them yourself), then the migration to the .NET framework will be a smoother transition. While this may be true, it does not mean that the framework will compensate for bad habits developed while learning C# or VB.NET. This next section should give you a good overview of some of the recommended Do's and Don'ts of .NET development and programming style. Essentially, it is a list of really good habits to pick up as early as possible so that you won't have to un-learn more bad habits later.

When programming for the .NET framework, the environment is drastically different from that of legacy applications. Picture each application or class library (.DLL) that you create as an extension of the framework itself; a particular encapsulation of functionality that is added on or snapped into the core framework.

With this concept in mind, you should keep in mind the following goals when producing your libraries, namespaces, and applications:

❑ **Consistency**
You should implement similar styles and design patterns throughout your libraries and applications. If one transactional component has a particular feature, consider making that feature available on all of your transactional components. The classes, methods, and properties should all conform to a strong naming and case convention.

❑ **Web centered (or at least aware)**
Your code should not code you into a box. It should be flexible enough to be able to be executed locally, or expanded to run remotely. If your application makes use of another of your libraries, consider making it an option to invoke that library remotely or locally.

❑ **Predictable**
Programmers experienced in using the .NET framework's core functionality should have an easy time discovering the functionality of your library. Don't provide five different methods that all accomplish the same thing. Each atomic action should have one and only one way of accomplishing it (this doesn't mean you can't shroud that one method in different overloads to allow for greater flexibility).

Class Names

Your class names should all be meaningful representations of the entity for which they are abstractions. Class names should either be nouns or noun phrases, and not verbs or descriptions of provided functionality. Many ex-MFC programmers, myself included, have a tendency to prefix class names with a capital C. When digging deep into the bowels of your legacy C++ code, it was infinitely handy to know when you were dealing with a class or an instance of it with the C prefix, and many other useful things. However, there is absolutely no need to preface your class names in the .NET framework. Below are listed a couple of good class names, as well as a couple of bad names. Despite the Microsoft-sponsored trend toward not prefixing your classes with the capital "C", they are actually recommending for clarity the prefix of the "I" for interface definitions.

```
public class Car
{
}
public class SpinningButton
{
}
```

```
// Now for the poorly named classes.
public class ObtainCar
{
}
public class CMyclass
{
}
```

Just as your class names and property names should indicate nouns or noun phrases, method names within those classes should be verbs or verb phrases. In general, your code should be as close to self-documenting as possible. It should be easy to read. Class and data-type prefixes before variable names tend to confuse things (all classes look the same).

Enumerations

Not only should you follow a strict naming convention for your enumerations (especially considering how easily enumerations are made visible to the rest of the world in the .NET framework), but you should use them wherever appropriate. Any time you are sending numeric information as a method argument that can be considered part of enumeration (an option, a flag, debug level, etc.), use an enumeration to strongly type that argument. This will not only allow the compiler to weed out out-of-range arguments, but will allow IntelliSense to populate a handy drop-down of useful information.

Do *not* prefix your enumerations with abbreviations. I'm sure there are at least a dozen VB books that preach a two-letter application prefix code for all enumerations to avoid duplication when being used in COM, etc. With the .NET framework, you can prefix the enumeration value with the enumeration name, if further clarification is necessary. For example, below are two enumeration references: one for VB 6 and one for C#:

```
'VB6

myValue = myAppCarColorRed;
```

```
//C#
myValue = CarColors.Red;
```

Here's what the enumeration definitions look like for both the VB6 and C# versions:

```
Public Enum myAppCarColors
    myAppCarColorRed = 1
    myAppCarColorBlue = 2
    myAppCarColorWhite = 3
End Enum
```

And now the C# enumeration:

```
enum CarColors
{
    Red,
    Blue,
    White
}
```

You are not Alone

You need to remember that, with the increasing complexity and modularity of high-end applications these days, you are almost never the sole programmer on a project anymore (ah, those were the good old days). Unfortunately, you now have to deal with multiple teams working on various modules of one or more applications, all destined for the same installation CD and the same customer's PC or Web Server.

The flexibility of the framework allows all of those teams to work in the languages they all prefer, and interact with the programs and libraries developed by the other programming teams. Essentially, this is true – but there are a few catches. There are some things that some languages can do that others cannot. The most prominent is that C# will consider two methods with the same name differing only by case to be two different methods. If such methods are implemented in a .NET class library, VB.NET will have a terrible time executing the appropriate method, since it doesn't use case as a distinguishing characteristic.

You should also keep in mind the concept of operator overloading. There are many languages within the .NET framework that do not support operator overloading. With that in mind, if you provide an overload to the "+" operator for a class, also consider providing a method called Add to provide some access to that functionality for languages that don't support operator overloading.

There are many more detailed examples of things that can interfere with language interoperability. It should be your responsibility (or your team's) to make sure that if language interoperability is one of your design goals, then steps should be taken to conform to the Common Type System as closely as possible, and keep in mind the limitations (or enhancements) of other languages when programming.

Properties or Methods?

A common design problem (certainly not specific to the .NET framework) among object-oriented programming languages is deciding when a class should implement a method or expose data as a property.

In general, you should use properties to expose the natural attributes of the entity which the class models. For example, the wingspan of a bird would be a likely candidate for a property in a class modeling a bird.

You should *not* use properties when obtaining the data for a property is expensive (such as retrieving the entire flight path of that bird for a period of six months). In addition, if the data that supports the property is not consistent, that is, it may not be the same the next time you request the property, it should be exposed as a method. Also, don't use properties to return arrays, as this will truly confuse you and anyone attempting to use your class. It is also fairly difficult to implement this efficiently.

Nested Types

One of the language features that don't seem to get too much publicity on the sample sites and public .NET discussion sites is *Nested Types*. This allows you to nest the definition of a class or type within another class. At first glance that might not appear all that useful, but it actually has quite a few benefits.

Consider an example where you're providing a very large *Flags* type numeration (items are bitwise compared to test and set). That enumeration is only supplied to properties and methods for one of your classes. Rather than clutter up the global namespace with an enumeration only used once, you can define it within the class that requires it. In the example below, assume that the Car class defines a CarColors enumeration inside its own definition:

```
myCar.Color = Car.CarColors.Red;
```

In the above example, `Car` is the static reference to the class itself, `CarColors` is a reference to the nested enumeration, and `Red` is an individual item in that enumeration. With *Nested Types*, a class requiring an enumeration or class type can supply its own definition without worrying about external dependencies.

Multi-Threading

Those of you "crossing over" from VB6 may not be all that familiar with code that supports true multi-threaded execution. With VB.NET and C#, the languages support execution in a threaded environment automatically. If your code is going to be run anywhere but on a low-end, disconnected PC (not exactly the target we're aiming at), you should be aware of the consequences of multi-threading. For more detail on how to implement multi-threading control in your applications, consult the Wrox books *Professional C#* or *Professional VB.NET*.

It is up to you and your programming team how much threading to support. You can do as little as simply acknowledge that it exists (a popular choice), all the way up to making almost everything your application does happen in a background processing thread. Threads may seem daunting and intimidating at first, but they are simply tools there to help you and your application achieve the performance it is capable of. Things like locks, race conditions, thread safety, and static state should be researched carefully before implementing any truly multi-threaded solution.

Asynchronous Execution

Taking some of the ideas brought up by the multi-threading topic, we need to bring up a little about Asynchronous Execution. In a classic, legacy application, a user clicks a button, some processing takes place while the user watches, and then a message comes back indicating that the processing has completed. If you're lucky, you might even get a progress bar, or even some fancy graphics indicating that some processing is taking place.

The world of Web Services, Remoting, the Internet, and broadband simply won't settle for that kind of behavior. Let's say that the processing taking place by clicking that button was actually being executed remotely on a server. That server is extremely taxed (due to millions of people clicking that button) and the process takes ten minutes to complete. Do you really want to relinquish control of your entire Windows experience for 10 minutes? I didn't think so.

A truly elegant solution to this problem would allow for asynchronous communication with a Web Service. The user clicks the button, and all related menu items gray out. A subtle, animated reminder that the remote server is doing something appears while you can then go about your business. Then, a nice audio cue plays to indicate that the entire conversation between client proxy and Web Service has completed.

Once users get a taste of this type of functionality, they're going to demand it from everything they use. When building your new .NET application, take a look at the distributed and disconnected functionality that it provides. If any of that can be done asynchronously via callbacks, delegates, etc., then your users will certainly thank you for it.

Don't think that it is all a fancy interface, however. Implementing a reliable and sturdy asynchronous set of functionality is difficult and requires meticulous attention to detail. Each time a new asynchronous process begins, all functionality in your program that depends on the result of that process must be disabled until the process has completed successfully, and remain disabled if the process completes with an error or doesn't complete at all.

Attribute Classes

Attribute Classes are one of those features where using them feels like opening a new toy at Christmas. Using *Reflection*, an application can inspect all of its own meta data at run-time and display that information to users, or use it in some meaningful way. Reflection allows virtually limitless introspection and inspection of other assemblies at run-time.

One type of meta data that are stored in an assembly is the attributes. These attributes can apply to virtually anything. Attributes are used to indicate COM+ Application membership, transactional requirements, the name and version of an Assembly, and much more.

The great thing about these classes is that you can define your own. In other words, you can self-document your classes at run-time with meaningful information that can be extracted. One sample implementation of this was a team of developers stamping each Assembly in their project with the name and e-mail address of the programmer. They used a custom attribute class to store that information in the DLL. At run-time, anytime an Exception occurred, they used a custom event class to send a notification to that programmer that a problem had occurred in their Assembly.

The possibilities are limited only by your imagination. Again, it is a case of knowing what features are available to you when you migrate in order to determine what features you want to implement. You could easily implement some kind of context-sensitive, XML-based Help system that keyed itself on attributes built directly into the DLL by the programmers. Another implement I've seen is using attributes to store unique serial numbers for customers/licensees of a particular assembly. If the combination of a code entered by the customer, and the code stored in the Assembly doesn't mesh the way it should, then the Assembly isn't licensed for use and can refuse to execute.

Custom Exception Classes

As with Attribute Classes, these are things that you can take advantage of to add robust functionality and style to your applications. For the most part, you should use the standard exception types that are provided for you, as these cover most of the basic, general failures that you can trap.

You might want to derive a subclassed Exception when you expect users of your library to be specifically expecting a custom Exception to be thrown in certain circumstances. For example, you might want to specifically trap a Primary Key violation from SQL Server. This may not be something you want to terminate your program, but it is information you want to trap. However, you want the standard SqlException to generate an error. In this case, you would derive an SqlPrimaryKeyException (this is just an example) that code could specifically look for in a catch statement, allowing the more generalized SqlException to halt program execution.

As with all of the other features of the .NET framework, use your good judgment on when to implement those features, and avoid implementing them simply because they're available. There should be a specific, driven need for your implementations beyond the simple fact that some of these features are downright *cool*.

Migration Tools

The tools you use to migrate from your legacy Windows code to your new .NET framework code are basically going to be the same tools you would use for any programming project. Visual Studio .NET, which supports plug-in functionality for dozens of languages, as well as a marvelous XML schema editor, will play a pretty key role.

A tool that I've found to be invaluable is a UML modeling tool. UML may take some time to get used to for some, but I've found that the ability to point to a box or a line and know immediately how to implement that design to be an incredible time- (and stress-) saving asset to any programming project.

At a recent software development conference, I had the opportunity to look at a tool that converted legacy VB code to the new VB.NET. I was a bit skeptical, but it did do a fairly good job of performing pure syntactical translations. For those doing a *Baby Steps* migration, it might be a helpful tool for converting some user-interface-based modules, but all the Forms code will be different. In addition, in order to truly take advantage of .NET, there's no direct syntax conversion that can be done for you that will make the change.

Summary

This chapter should have given you a thorough, solid foundation of knowledge that you can use to help plan and implement your migration to the .NET framework.

We looked at what things you need to examine in detail when evaluating a potential migration project. It is important to remember that even if you think migration is the right thing to do, your customers need to agree with you, and you need to have the manpower, training, and time to implement a proper migration.

In addition, we looked at ways in which you can reduce excess code, promote the reuse of common code, and prepare your application and services for recycling and repackaging. Beyond that you got a review of some of the key points of programming for the .NET framework that you'll need to keep in mind when writing and designing your migration.

If you keep in mind the general procedure outlined in this chapter for creating a migration plan, and all the points brought up for making your actual code implementation easier, more scalable, and more robust, your migration should be an enjoyable experience.

You should now be able to easily answer the questions posed at the beginning of the chapter, as well as have a mind full of other ideas and questions that you know are relevant to your migration.

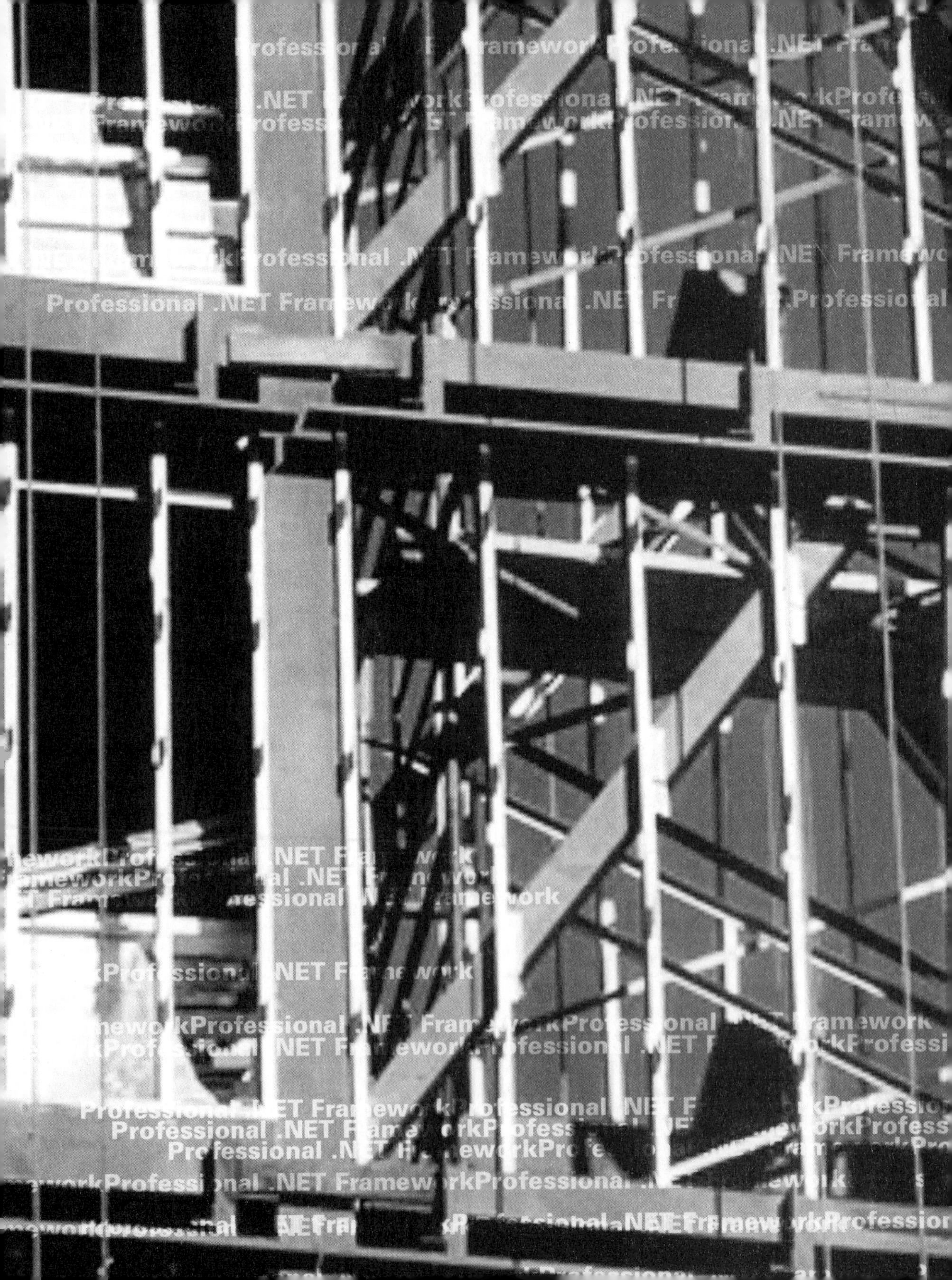
Professional .NET Framework

14

Migrating a VB 6 Application to VB.NET

This book has gone into great detail on many individual pieces of the .NET framework and how each individual piece works. While it is certainly useful to spend a lot of time learning each and every component of the framework, not much of it will seem practical or useful to you unless you see how it all melds together into a single cohesive application.

The purpose of this case study is to walk you through the migration of a classic VB6 application to the .NET framework. Not only will you be able to experience hands-on the implementation of many of the things this book has taught you, but you will also be able to draw some clear parallels between the .NET framework and the classic programming environments you're working in now.

At the end of this chapter, you should have a very good idea of what a complete, Internet-enabled .NET application looks like and how you go about building it. Also, you should have some very useful and pertinent knowledge of some best practices for taking your existing legacy code and not just *porting* it to .NET, but truly *upgrading* it to the .NET framework and allowing it to take advantage of the framework's wide variety of useful new features.

Our finished .NET application will demonstrate many features of the framework, including, but not limited to:

- ❑ Web Services
- ❑ .NET Data Access Components hosted in COM+
- ❑ Enterprise-class development

Introducing UFixIT Software

The case study in this chapter is based on a defect tracking system created by a fictitious company called *UFixIT Software* (*UFIX*). UFIX started out writing software for Windows 3.1, and they eventually got around to migrating their software into the 32-bit world of Windows 95.

Now, they are faced with migrating to the .NET framework. They are constantly losing money to competitors who can offer web-based, enterprise-class solutions. They feel that if they migrate to the .NET framework, and take the migration a bit further, their application might be ready to compete in the enterprise-class defect tracking software market.

Their software as it is now allows users to log into the system with a username/password combination. From there, they can enter issues into the system, add comments to existing issues, and browse a tree of applications and releases.

Migration Scenario

After reading Chapter 15, UFIX decided to go with the "Full Monty" migration approach. They are going to make the investment of creating a brand-new .NET application based on the VB6 application that they have been maintaining for a few years.

In order to attract a wider customer base, and make their application far more useful in the process, UFIX has decided to bring their application onto the Internet/Intranet market. Instead of simply migrating their standalone client application to .NET, they are going to convert the stand-alone client into a thin, Internet client. All of the data access and business rules will then be housed on a web server, and exposed via Web Services, which will then be rendered by a WinForms user interface.

We'll walk you through each step of the migration process, from examining the current code and architecture, all the way to implementing the new code for this application.

Language Choice

The language to be used in a .NET application is actually a far more pleasant choice than it has been in the past. In the good ol' days, the goals and tasks that your application needed to accomplish dictated the language in which it was implemented. For example, for those that had the skill, and needed to implement very fast COM objects in a multi-threaded environment, there was no real choice; C++ and the ATL were the only options. However, if the application was to sport a very pretty user interface laden with bells and whistles and not too much quick horsepower, then VB was the obvious choice. These are, of course, generalizations. There are many VB applications that have both a pretty interface and a very fast operating speed, and depending on the programmer, there are also quite a few slow C++ programs. One of the main advantages of Visual Basic, even before code compilation, is the ability to rapidly put together prototypes and applications.

Now the choice has become one of preference. Asking a programmer which language they like using for the .NET framework now is like asking someone their favorite color. Every .NET language has to guarantee you a minimum amount of access to the .NET framework class library, and the framework itself defines all of the native data types (see *CTS, Common Type System*, in Chapter 2). With all the worries about type compatibility, method argument passing, and common functionality removed, the choice of language boils down to which set of syntax you like working with more. Of course, some languages support features that others don't, such as operator overloading, class indexers, etc. The choice of language will be based on which language-specific features you want, especially since the IDE (VS.NET) will remain the same no matter which language you choose.

This case study is written in two languages. The classic application that we will be migrating is written in Visual Basic 6.0. The new, .NET application will be written in C#. It is a very powerful language, but also easy to read. Make no mistake however, that all of the code in this chapter could easily be written in VB.NET if we so chose.

Installing the Samples

Before getting started describing the VB6 and the .NET application in more detail, let's go through installing the samples so that you can have them on your machine to play with while reading the rest of this chapter.

In order to make quick access to the source code of the samples simple and easy, I didn't bundle anything in an installation module. As I can't guarantee that a deployment module created on my version of Visual Studio.NET will work with one on a newer version, I've opted for simple bundles.

That fact is also a pretty good testament to the *Xcopy Deployment* theory behind some of the structure of the framework. There are four bundles for the samples:

❑ **BugScope_VB6**
This bundle contains all the source code and files you need to load the "classic", pre-migration projects up in Visual Basic 6 and start playing. You can unzip this anywhere you like as it's a stand-alone set of projects. Make sure that you build and register the support component DLL before building and running the actual VB6 application.

❑ **BugScopeDotNet_InetPub**
This bundle contains all the files that are placed in the \inetpub\wwwroot\BugServices directory. This includes the .asmx files and the \bin directory with the pre-compiled DLLs from the last time the sample was built.

❑ **BugScopeDotNet_BugScope**
This is the big solution that contains all of the projects for the Common, DAL, BLL, and BugServices. Unzip this anywhere on your test machine preserving the directory structure. One thing you'll need to keep in mind is that all the DLLs are strong-named. Each time you rebuild this package, you will need to take BugScope.DAL.dll and BugScope.Common.dll out of the Global Assembly Cache (via gacutil or c:\winnt\assembly) and place the new builds back in. Also, each time DAL is rebuilt, you'll need to destroy the COM+ Application to get it to load the new version by opening up the Component Services control panel in Windows 2000 and removing the "BugScope DAL" package that is created the first time the sample application is executed..

Make sure that when you're adding the assemblies to the global assembly cache, you add the assemblies from your VS.NET project path, and not the assemblies from the \inetpub\wwwroot\BugServices\bin directory. A perfectly valid location for the DLLs from the BugScope solution would be in your ~My Documents\Visual Studio Projects\BugScope directory. This way, it'll be nearby all your other test and experimentation code from VS.NET on your machine, though you can place the files wherever you like.

❑ **BugScopeDotNet_Client**
This bundle is the Visual Studio.NET solution and all related support files required to build the client Windows Forms application. Just unzip this into an appropriate directory and you should be able to get it to work. It contains the client proxy for the web service ready to compile.

You will also find two .SQL files in the download packages. These files are SQL scripts that will automatically generate all of the data structures and stored procedures you need to set up an empty database for both samples. These scripts were generated from SQL 2000 Server.

BugScope Classic

Before moving on to creating our .NET application, we need to examine the current application in detail in order to figure out *how* we're going to migrate it, what our new design and architecture will be, and *why*. Actually typing in the C# code will be the last and least important thing we do.

BugScope is a defect tracking system that runs on Windows95, 98, Me, and 2000. It was written in Visual Basic 6.0. It is an example of a classic data-driven client (or *desktop*) application that maintains all of its persistent data in a server database.

BugScope Classic was written to work with Oracle, SQL Server, or any other RDBMS that provides an ODBC or OLEDB connection via Microsoft ADO. Its only dependencies, aside from the VB Runtime, are Microsoft XML 2.0 and Microsoft ActiveX Data Objects (ADO) v2.5.

It is a secure system that presents users with a login screen when they start the application. After successfully logging into the system, end users can then maintain the application and release hierarchy as well as enter in issues and log activity on existing issues. The security here is nothing more than validating a username/password combination against the information stored in the database. There is no encryption on the password or the request for data from the database.

There is no current administration system; all changes to the core tables must be done through whatever database management tool the customer has. The folks at UFIX had planned on adding that functionality in an upcoming release. They're now planning on putting that functionality in the first .NET release of their application.

Architectural Overview

The BugScope application, as it stands in its VB6 form, is by no means a production-level quality application. It is a stand-alone desktop application that has obviously been contrived for the purpose of this demonstration. However, the functionality it provides is still representative of an application that could easily be available on store shelves right now.

The architecture of the application is quite simple. It is intended to be a stand-alone application used by multiple users all on the same Intranet connection to a central database server. It is a classic example of a *fat client* client/server application where the server is simply the data store. A few years ago, this type of application was all the rage and is still extremely common.

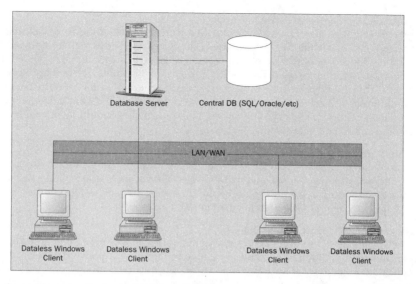

The figure above illustrates the basic architecture of the current version of BugScope. Multiple machines all have client-installed copies of the entire application. The application then communicates with the database server to perform all of its persistence operations. It doesn't maintain any local data, nor does it use any DCOM objects, MTS, or any other server components.

Functional Requirements

Now that we've seen the basic architecture of the legacy application, it's time to analyze what its core functionality is. Because this is an existing application, it should be pretty easy to take a look at the code and the existing user interface and find out what the core functional requirements of the application are. Let's assume that the folks at our fictitious UFIX company have done this and that they've come up with the following:

❑ **Authenticate users of the application**
Before anyone can view, change or create any data within the system, we need to authenticate them. Users must supply a username and a password in order to log into the system. This username and password is then compared against values in the database.

There is no encryption on the password or the username. The folks at UFIX have been meaning to get around to adding encryption, so they're thinking about doing it for their .NET release. At the moment, encrypting the passwords in VB6 seems to be a big hassle to the development team there. Of course, programmers and companies can simply buy or lease third-party libraries that contain code for encryption, but that introduces dependencies and costs that our fictional company felt was unacceptable.

There is no administrative way to create new users. As we said earlier, there's no administration module in BugScope Classic. All users are created manually by entering their information into the SQL Server database. As this application was originally designed to fill an in-house problem, and UFIX is only now considering upgrading to enterprise-scale functionality, this lack of functionality isn't surprising. Again, the lack of an administration module (and many other useful features) in the VB6 application is due to the fact that, for this sample, the application used to be an in-house tool where the programmers did all the administration via SQL Server's Enterprise Manager.

❑   **Browse the Application/Release hierarchy**
The application needs to provide users with a tree-like view of the Application hierarchy. Each application is composed of Releases. The Release is the actual entity that all Issues in the system are logged against. The reason for this is that UFIX found that, even for the same version number, there were actual multiple Releases (or builds) for that application. For example, they found that some of their customers would release v1.0 of their application on three different sets of media, or, more commonly, for three different customers with customized configurations. Having an Application consist of multiple releases, each with their own description and version number, seemed to solve this problem.

❑   **Create/Retrieve/Update/Delete Applications**
The application needs to provide some method for adding Applications into the database. As well, users need to be able to rename or delete existing applications. The requirement for this version does not specify who should or should not be allowed to modify the Application data. UFIX is planning on looking at this for the .NET release.

❑   **Create/Retrieve/Update/Delete Releases**
As well as applications, users need to have the ability to add new Release profiles to a given Application. In addition, they need to be able to modify or remove that release. As with the Application data, there is no secured access to this information; any user who can log into the system can delete Releases.

❑   **Create/Retrieve/Update/Delete Issues**
All users must have the ability to create new Issues against any given Release. As well, users can update and delete Issues in the system. There is no planned restriction as to who can modify Issue data.

❑   **Create Activity for existing Issues**
All users must have the ability to log a new Activity for Issues. Once an Activity has been logged onto an Issue, it cannot be removed. To correct for an error in time reporting, users can add more activity to the Issue with the appropriately positive or negative hours of adjustment.

❑   **Supply comments on existing activity**
All users must have the ability to comment on Activities in the system. Users cannot modify existing comments, as comments should be simple text additions to the actual text stored for a given Issue.

Database Schema

Now that we have defined the core functionality that the BugScope VB6 application provides, we can now proceed to mapping out the data that will support the application. It is often helpful to categorize the types of data that your application supports. It may not seem like it's worth the effort for such a small application, but it will become useful when we get around to working on the .NET application. Always remember that the more effort you spend designing and planning, the fewer headaches you'll have when it comes to coding time. The following is a list of the data categories that BugScope Classic uses:

❑   User Data

❑   Application Data

❑   Release Data

❑   Issue Data

User Data

This is a pretty simple category. There is only one table, the bsUsers table. The bsUsers table stores the basic information about the users of the application. If you're wondering about the naming convention bs in front of the table name, it's a habit I picked up from an Oracle DBA a while back. The bs doesn't stand for what you might think. Instead it is just a two-letter abbreviation of the application's name (BugScope). We had all kinds of reports that ran showing table utilization and the reports didn't distinguish which Tablespace (an Oracle term) the tables came from. One fix for this was to preface the tables with a two-letter application abbreviation. It stuck, and I like organization, so I've been doing it ever since. Many times multiple applications will share the same database, but use their own set of tables. Prefixing the table name with the application makes it easy for DBAs and programmers to determine to which application any given table belongs in a situation like that. In most other cases, there is no real need to prefix table names, especially when even Microsoft is discouraging doing things like prefixing class names with a capital "C".

bsUsers

Column Name	Data Type	Nullable	Description
UserID	Int Identity	N	This is the primary key. Used to identify the user in various related tables/fields.
UserName	Varchar	N	Name of the user. Used at login and in comment descriptions.
Password	Varchar	N	User's password. Stored un-encrypted
FirstName	Varchar	N	First name of the user.
LastName	Varchar	N	Last name of the user.
JobTitle	Varchar	N	Job Title of the user. Used in comments.

Application Data

Again, there's only one table in this category as well, bsApplications, the table that serves as the toplevel of the product tree.

bsApplications

Column Name	Data Type	Nullable	Description
ApplicationID	Int Identity	N	This is the primary key. Used to identify the application in related tables.
ApplicationName	Varchar	N	Name of the application.

Release Data

This category also has only one table. It contains the `bsReleases` table, which is considered a child table of `bsApplications`.

`bsReleases`

Column Name	Data Type	Nullable	Description
ReleaseID	Int Identity	N	This is the primary key. Used to identify this release in related tables.
ApplicationID	Int	N	This is a foreign key. Indicates the Application to which this Release belongs.
Description	Varchar	N	Description of the application.

Issue Data

There are several tables in this category. Issues are essentially the main type of data that BugScope deals with. All of the support tables in the application support the Issue category of data.

`bsIssues`

Column Name	Data Type	Nullable	Description
IssueID	Int Identity	N	This is the primary key. Identifies this issue in related tables.
IssueType	Int	N	Foreign key indicating the record in the `bsIssueTypes` table that corresponds to this issue.
SubmitterID	Int	N	Foreign key indicating the `UserID` that submitted this issue.
AssignedToID	Int	N	Foreign key indicating the `UserID` that the issue is currently assigned to.
ReleaseID	Int	N	Foreign key indicating which Release this issue was logged against.
Description	Varchar	N	Initial description of the issue.
IssueStatusID	Int	N	Foreign key indicating the status of the issue as described in `bsIssueStatus`.
IssueDate	Datetime	N	Date that the issue was submitted.

`bsIssueType`

Column Name	Data Type	Nullable	Description
IssueTypeID	Int Identity	N	This is the primary key. Used to identify this Issue type in other tables.
Description	Varchar	N	Description of the Issue Type.

`bsIssueStatus`

Column Name	Data Type	Nullable	Description
IssueStatusID	Int Identity	N	This is the primary key. Used to identify this Issue Status in other related tables.
Description	Varchar	N	Description of the Issue Status.
Priority	Int	N	Priority associated with this Issue status.

`bsIssueActivity`

Column Name	Data Type	Nullable	Description
ActivityID	Int Identity	N	This is the primary key. This is used to identify this Issue Activity in other related tables.
IssueID	Int	N	Foreign key. Indicates which Issue this Activity has been logged against.
Notes	Text	N	Extended text description of the Activity. User comments are also appended to this field.
UserID	Int	N	Foreign key. Indicates the User that logged this Activity.
ActivityTypeID	Int	N	Foreign key. Indicates the type of this Activity (bsActivityTypes).
HoursLogged	Int	N	Hours logged for this particular Activity.
ActivityDate	Datetime	N	Date/Time the Issue Activity took place.

bsActivityTypes

Column Name	Data Type	Nullable	Description
ActivityTypeID	Int Identity	N	Primary key. Used to identify this activity type to related tables.
Description	Varchar	N	Description of the Activity Type.

The following diagram illustrates the relationships of all of the tables described above.

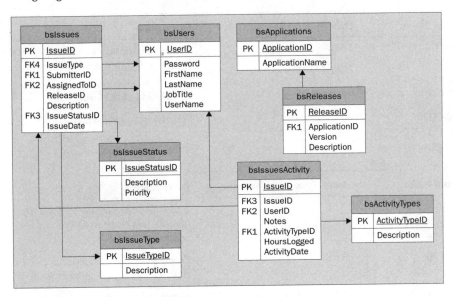

Stored Procedures

BugScope Classic only uses Stored Procedures to create new records in the database. It uses the return value of the stored procedure to indicate the Identity/ID of the new record. Because most of the stored procedures look alike, we'll just show one of them. The rest are available with all of the sample code for this book.

Here is the code used to generate the sp_CreateIssue procedure. It utilizes the SQL built-in global @@IDENTITY to retrieve the newly generated ID column. This is the best way to keep a multi-user system from returning stale identities or identities from another user's insert (very common when VB does the insert and then uses a MAX() query to retrieve the new identity).

```
CREATE PROCEDURE sp_CreateIssue
@IssueType int,
@SubmitterID int,
@AssignedToID int,
@ReleaseID int,
@Description varchar(255),
@IssueStatusID int
```

```
        AS

            INSERT INTO bsIssues(IssueType, SubmitterID, AssignedToID, ReleaseID,
                     Description, IssueStatusID)
            VALUES(@IssueType, @SubmitterID, @AssignedToID, @ReleaseID,
                     @Description, @IssueStatusID)

            RETURN @@IDENTITY
        GO
```

Support DLL Classes

The developers at UFIX may have cut a few corners in the implementation of some features of the BugScope application, but they actually did a pretty good job of creating a good object model to work from. The following is a diagram of the class structure that supports the BugScope application for VB6:

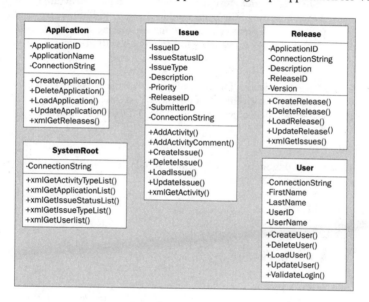

Application

The Application class supports the basic Create, Retrieve, Update, and Delete routines. As with all of the classes in this application, it accesses the database directly. In addition to the standard functionality, it provides an XML routine that retrieves a list of associated Releases.

Issue

The Issue class is the most complex of the classes in the support DLL. It supports the usual Create, Retrieve, Update, and Delete. In addition, it contains methods for adding Activity and Activity Comment data. It also contains an XML routine to retrieve the associated Activity for that Issue.

Release

The Release object is pretty straightforward. In addition to the usual functionality, it also contains an XML routine to retrieve the list of associated Issues with that Release.

User

The `User` class represents a user of the application capable of logging into the software. It allows the calling interface code to Create, Retrieve, Update and Delete users. In addition, it contains a function, `ValidateLogin`, that authorizes a given username and password combination for logging into the system.

SystemRoot

The `SystemRoot` class is the catch-all utility class. It is responsible for allowing read access to the system tables. The system tables are those tables that are used to populate the dropdown lists like Issue Activity, Issue Type, etc.

The Code

Now that we've fully examined the layout, design, architecture and class structure of the BugScope Classic application, we can take a look at some of the code used to produce it. Because we're interested in upgrading the application rather than writing it from scratch, we won't be looking at all of the code. The remainder of the code that isn't shown in this chapter is available for download with the source materials for this book from Wrox Press.

What we will look at are a few representative functions of how BugScope accomplished certain tasks in VB6, as well as a couple of sections of code that drive the user interface. You can take it as a more than subtle hint that the code shown here will be referenced often when we're upgrading UFIX's flagship product to the .NET framework.

Creating an Issue

The following code is from the BugScope Classic application. It demonstrates the `CreateIssue` method of the `Issue` class in the `BugScope_VB6Support.DLL` library.

```
Public Function CreateIssue() As Long
    Dim oCMD As ADODB.Command
    Dim oRetVal As ADODB.Parameter

    Set oCMD = New ADODB.Command
```

The `m_Connection` object is a private variable (of type `ADODB.Connection`) that is created when the class is instantiated. Each of the data operations will open and close the connection for the short time that it will be in communication with the database.

```
    m_Connection.Open

    oCMD.CommandText = "sp_CreateIssue"
    oCMD.CommandType = adCmdStoredProc
    Set oCMD.ActiveConnection = m_Connection
```

The SQL Server keyword `RETURN_VALUE` allows us to declare a command parameter that will, upon successful execution of the stored procedure, contain the return value of that procedure.

```
    Set oRetVal = oCMD.CreateParameter("RETURN_VALUE", adInteger, _
        adParamReturnValue)
    oCMD.Parameters.Append oRetVal
    oCMD.Parameters.Append oCMD.CreateParameter("IssueType", adInteger, _
        adParamInput, , m_Data.IssueType)
```

```
        oCMD.Parameters.Append oCMD.CreateParameter("SubmitterID", adInteger,
            adParamInput, , m_Data.SubmitterID)
        oCMD.Parameters.Append oCMD.CreateParameter("AssignedToID", adInteger,
            adParamInput, , m_Data.AssignedToID)
        oCMD.Parameters.Append oCMD.CreateParameter("ReleaseID", adInteger,
            adParamInput, , m_Data.ReleaseID)
        oCMD.Parameters.Append oCMD.CreateParameter("Description", adVarChar,
            adParamInput, 255, m_Data.Description)
        oCMD.Parameters.Append oCMD.CreateParameter("IssueStatusID", adInteger,
            adParamInput, , m_Data.IssueStatusID)

        oCMD.Execute

        CreateIssue = oRetVal.Value
        Set oCMD = Nothing
        Set oRetVal = Nothing
        m_Connection.Close
    End Function
```

The first section of importance in this code is the use of the return value in the stored procedure. All of BugScope's stored procedures are designed to return the identity of the newly inserted record so that, in case the interface wanted to, it could do some work based on the new id without having to reload anything from the database.

```
        Set oRetVal = oCMD.CreateParameter("RETURN_VALUE", adInteger,
            adParamReturnValue)
```

Even though the code that calls this method doesn't use that identity, if upgrades were made to the user interface requiring it, the component wouldn't have to be modified. The m_Data variable is a private member variable that is used as a container for all of the internal state variables of that class. This paradigm is used throughout the support DLL for all classes. It is defined for the Issue class as follows:

```
'** struct to maintain internal state
Private Type m_DataType
    IssueID As Long
    IssueType As Long
    SubmitterID As Long
    AssignedToID As Long
    ReleaseID As Long
    Description As String
    IssueStatusID As Long
    Priority As Long
End Type
```

Logging In

Admittedly, the security system in BugScope Classic is pretty lax. The password isn't encrypted, so anyone with database reading privileges can easily go and grab everyone's passwords.

When the start-up form (frmMain) first loads, it will then load the frmLogin form. This form asks for a username and password combination, and will then verify the account information as shown in the code below:

```
Private Sub cmdOK_Click()
    Dim oUser As BugScope_VB6Support.User
    Dim lUserID As Long
    Set oUser = New BugScope_VB6Support.User
    oUser.ConnectionString = dbConnStr
```

```
lUserID = oUser.ValidateLogin(txtUserName.Text, txtPassword.Text)
If lUserID > -1 Then
    LoginSucceeded = True
    Set gUser = New BugScope_VB6Support.User
    gUser.ConnectionString = dbConnStr
    gUser.LoadUser (lUserID)
Else
    LoginSucceeded = False
End If
Set oUser = Nothing

If Not LoginSucceeded Then
    MsgBox "Invalid Password, try again!", , "Login"
    txtPassword.SetFocus
    SendKeys "{Home}+{End}"
Else
    Me.Hide
End If

End Sub
```

The above code is executed in response to clicking the **OK** button on the login screen. First, a reference to the User object in the `BugScope_VB6Support` DLL is created.

```
Dim oUser As BugScope_VB6Support.User
Dim lUserID As Long
Set oUser = New BugScope_VB6Support.User
oUser.ConnectionString = dbConnStr
```

After that, the `ValidateLogin` method is invoked. It returns the identity of a user that matches the supplied username and password. If no such user and password combination exists, that method returns a -1, indicating either an unknown user or a password failure. If everything goes well, the form disappears, returning control to the calling form. When the login form disappears, the calling form (`frmMain`) checks the `LoginSucceeded` member variable. If it was `false`, the entire application will quit, otherwise the application will retain the information on the user in the `gUser` global variable initialized during the login form's **OK** button handler event.

```
Private Sub MDIForm_Load()
    Load frmLogin
    frmLogin.Show vbModal
    If frmLogin.LoginSucceeded = False Then
        Unload Me
        End
    End If
    Unload frmLogin
    StatusBar1.Panels(1).Text = "User " & gUser.UserName & " Logged into
                                                BugScope."
End Sub
```

Retrieving the Product Tree

If you've tried to load data into a TreeView control before, you're probably thinking that BugScope either used a Recordset that utilized DataShaping, or you might be thinking that it embedded some ugly-looking parent/child searching logic directly into the loading code. Another thing that we've seen often is that the TreeView is built in two passes: the first pass builds all of the parent or root nodes, and the second pass runs a chain of subqueries, one for each parent node. This method is obviously ridiculously slow and inefficient.

Actually, none of the above are true. BugScope actually uses a remarkably elegant solution and takes full advantage of the power of the DOM object and some XPath to pull off a fast TreeView load in a single pass using only features available with XML. That code is listed below.

```
Private Sub Form_Activate()
    Dim oSystemRoot As BugScope_VB6Support.SystemRoot
    Dim strXML As String
    Dim oDom As MSXML.DOMDocument
    Dim oRoot As IXMLDOMElement
    Dim oAppNode As IXMLDOMElement
    Dim oRelNode As IXMLDOMElement
    Dim appIDX As Long
    Dim relIDX As Long
    Dim nodApp As Node
    Dim nodRel As Node
    Dim nodRoot As Node
    Dim strAppKey As String

    Set oDom = New MSXML.DOMDocument

    Set oSystemRoot = New BugScope_VB6Support.SystemRoot
    oSystemRoot.ConnectionString = dbConnStr
    strXML = oSystemRoot.xmlGetApplicationList

    oDom.loadXML strXML
    Set oRoot = oDom.documentElement

    trvApplications.Nodes.Clear
    Set nodRoot = trvApplications.Nodes.Add(, , "ROOT", "Product Tree", 0, 0)
    For appIDX = 0 To oRoot.childNodes.length - 1
       Set oAppNode = oRoot.childNodes.Item(appIDX)
       strAppKey = "APP" & oAppNode.getAttribute("applicationid")
       Set nodApp = trvApplications.Nodes.Add("ROOT", tvwChild, strAppKey,_
                oAppNode.getAttribute("description"), 2, 2)
       For relIDX = 0 To oAppNode.childNodes.length - 1
          Set oRelNode = oAppNode.childNodes.Item(relIDX)
          Set nodRel = trvApplications.Nodes.Add(strAppKey, tvwChild, "REL" _
                & oRelNode.getAttribute("releaseid"), _
                oRelNode.getAttribute("description") & " v" &_
                oRelNode.getAttribute("version"), 1, 1)
       Next relIDX
    Next appIDX

    Set oSystemRoot = Nothing
    Set oDom = Nothing
End Sub
```

The really key thing to look at here is how short the above code is. It's actually pretty straightforward. The code loads the result of the xmlGetApplicationList (code shown below) method into a DOM object. This DOM object actually does represent a hierarchical tree structure. Each Application element contains a list of Release subelements. At this point, the task of the code is merely to move the XML tree structure into the TreeView control.

The xmlGetApplicationList method, where the really interesting XML manipulation actually takes place, is shown below:

```
Public Function xmlGetApplicationList() As String
    Dim oDom As MSXML.DOMDocument
    Dim oRoot As IXMLDOMElement
    Dim oAppNode As IXMLDOMElement
    Dim oRelNode As IXMLDOMElement
    Dim oRS As ADODB.Recordset
    Dim strSQL As String

    m_Connection.Open
    strSQL = "SELECT ap.ApplicationID, ap.ApplicationName, r.ReleaseID,_
            r.Version, r.Description " & "FROM bsApplications ap LEFT_
            JOIN bsReleases r ON ap.ApplicationID = r.ApplicationID " & "_
            ORDER BY ap.ApplicationName, r.Version"

    Set oDom = New MSXML.DOMDocument
    Set oRoot = oDom.createElement("APPLICATIONLIST")
    Set oDom.documentElement = oRoot

    Set oRS = New ADODB.Recordset
    oRS.Open strSQL, m_Connection, adOpenForwardOnly, adLockReadOnly
    Do While Not oRS.EOF
        '** select the node in the XML document that represents the root of
        '** the current application
        '** The XPath statement here, in English says: Select the APPLICATION
        '** node whose applicationid attribute is equal to
        '** ors("ApplicationID").value if SelectSingleNode fails,
        '** it returns "nothing"
        Set oAppNode = oDom.documentElement.selectSingleNode("APPLICATION[@_
                    applicationid=" & oRS("ApplicationID").Value & "]")
        If oAppNode Is Nothing Then
            '** if the application hasn't yet made it into the document,
            '** put it there.
            Set oAppNode = oDom.createElement("APPLICATION")
            oAppNode.setAttribute "applicationid", oRS("ApplicationID").Value
            oAppNode.setAttribute "description", oRS("ApplicationName").Value
            oRoot.appendChild oAppNode
        End If
        '** add the release to the current application node
        If Not IsNull(oRS("ReleaseID")) Then
            Set oRelNode = oDom.createElement("RELEASE")
            oRelNode.setAttribute "releaseid", oRS("ReleaseID").Value
            oRelNode.setAttribute "description", oRS("Description").Value
            oRelNode.setAttribute "version", oRS("Version").Value
            oAppNode.appendChild oRelNode
        End If
        oRS.MoveNext
    Loop
```

```
    Set oRS = Nothing
    m_Connection.Close
    xmlGetApplicationList = oDom.xml
    Set oDom = Nothing
    Set oRoot = Nothing
    Set oRelNode = Nothing
    Set oAppNode = Nothing
End Function
```

The above code uses a standard SQL join to create a Recordset that contains `Application/Release` pairs, representing a flattened, non-normalized view of our tree structure. Then, iterating through the list, it creates a new `Application` element in the top of the XML hierarchy for each new `Application` element it encounters. Immediately after that, it attaches the `Release` side of the `Application/Release` pair to the `Application` element that was either just located or just created. The result is XML that appears in the following format, just ripe for transfer to a TreeView control:

```xml
<APPLICATIONLIST>
    <APPLICATION applicationid="1" description="BugScope">
        <RELEASE releaseid="4" description="Public Release" version="1.0"/>
        <RELEASE releaseid="1" description="Alpha Release (private)"
                                            version="1.0a"/>
    </APPLICATION>
    <APPLICATION applicationid="2" description="RoachScope">
        <RELEASE releaseid="3" description="Public Beta" version="2.0"/>
    </APPLICATION>
</APPLICATIONLIST>
```

As you can see, the root element of this XML is the `APPLICATIONLIST` element. From there, the tree goes to `Applications` and then `Releases`. This mirrors the output of the TreeView in the BugScope application almost identically.

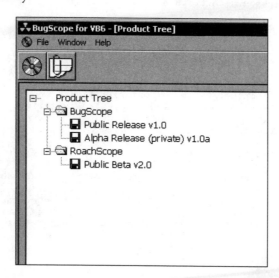

Retrieving the Issue List

Another control that is the bane of many programmers is the ListView. On the surface, it can seem easy to use and easy to populate with data. However, to populate it with data meaningfully, and with a visually pleasing result, is not always as easy as it looks. BugScope does a pretty good job of populating a ListView control in retrieving a list of Issues. It utilizes the Report view form of the ListView to display special icons in the list representing Issues that the user owns and Issues that have a status that contains a high priority.

The following code is invoked whenever the **Refresh** button is clicked from the Issue's MDI child form. It will reload the list of Issues in the ListView control. It pulls an XML representation of the Issue list from the Release object's xmlGetIssues method.

```
Public Sub Refresh_IssueList()
   Dim ReleaseID As Long
   Dim oRelease As BugScope_VB6Support.Release
   Dim strXML As String
   Dim oDom As MSXML.DOMDocument
   Dim oNode As IXMLDOMElement
   Dim issueIDX As Long
   Dim newItem As ListItem
   Dim newIcon As Integer

   If cbRelease.ListCount > 0 Then
       Set oDom = New MSXML.DOMDocument
       lvIssues.ListItems.Clear
       ReleaseID = cbRelease.ItemData(cbRelease.ListIndex)
       Set oRelease = New BugScope_VB6Support.Release
       oRelease.ConnectionString = dbConnStr
       oRelease.ReleaseID = ReleaseID
       strXML = oRelease.xmlGetIssues
       Set oRelease = nothing
       oDom.loadXML strXML
       For issueIDX = 0 To oDom.documentElement.childNodes.length - 1
           Set oNode = oDom.documentElement.childNodes.Item(issueIDX)
           If CLng(oNode.getAttribute("assignedtoid")) = CLng(gUser.UserID)
           Then
               Set newItem = lvIssues.ListItems.Add(, "ISS" &
                       oNode.getAttribute("issueid"), , 1, 1)
           Else
               Set newItem = lvIssues.ListItems.Add(, "ISS" &
                       oNode.getAttribute("issueid"), , 0, 0)
           End If
           If CLng(oNode.getAttribute("priority")) = 1 Then
               newItem.ListSubItems.Add , , , 2, "High Priority"
           Else
               newItem.ListSubItems.Add , , , 0
           End If
           newItem.ListSubItems.Add , , oNode.getAttribute("issuetypedesc")_
                   , 0
           newItem.ListSubItems.Add , , oNode.getAttribute("issuestatusdesc")_
                   , 0
           newItem.ListSubItems.Add , , oNode.getAttribute("submittername"), 0
           newItem.ListSubItems.Add , , oNode.getAttribute("priority"), 0
           newItem.ListSubItems.Add , , oNode.getAttribute("description"), 0

       Next issueIDX
       Set oNode = Nothing
       Set oDom = Nothing

   End If
End Sub
```

The code will set the icon of the first column in the Listview to a yellow exclamation point (Index 1 in the associated `ImageList` control) if the user is assigned to that `Issue`. If the `Issue` is high priority, then an image of a red light will appear in the second column. The user-interface code above is driven by the DLL support function `xmlGetIssues` shown in the code below:

```
Public Function xmlGetIssues() As String
    Dim oDom As MSXML.DOMDocument
    Dim oRoot As IXMLDOMElement
    Dim oElem As IXMLDOMElement
    Dim oRS As ADODB.Recordset
    Dim strSQL As String

    m_Connection.Open
    Set oDom = New MSXML.DOMDocument
    Set oRoot = oDom.createElement("RELEASEISSUES")
    Set oRS = New ADODB.Recordset
    Set oDom.documentElement = oRoot
    strSQL = "SELECT i.IssueID, i.IssueType, i.SubmitterID, i.AssignedToID,_
            i.ReleaseID, i.Description, i.IssueStatusID, " & _
            "iss.Description IssueStatusDesc, iss.Priority, _
            bsUsers.UserName AS SubmitterName, b2.UserName As _
            AssignedToName, " & "it.Description AS IssueTypeDesc " & _
            "FROM bsIssues i INNER JOIN bsIssueStatus iss ON _
            i.IssueStatusID = iss.IssueStatusID " & _
            "INNER JOIN bsIssueType it ON i.IssueType = it.IssueTypeID " & _
            "INNER JOIN bsUsers ON i.SubmitterID = bsUsers.UserID " & _
            "INNER JOIN bsUsers b2 ON i.AssignedToID = b2.UserID " & _
            "WHERE i.ReleaseID = " & m_Data.ReleaseID & " ORDER BY _
            i.IssueDate DESC, iss.Priority DESC"
    oRS.Open strSQL, m_Connection, adOpenForwardOnly, adLockReadOnly
    Do While Not oRS.EOF
        Set oElem = oDom.createElement("ISSUE")
        oRoot.appendChild oElem
        oElem.setAttribute "issueid", oRS("IssueID").Value
        oElem.setAttribute "issuetype", oRS("IssueType").Value
        oElem.setAttribute "submitterid", oRS("SubmitterID").Value
        oElem.setAttribute "assignedtoid", oRS("AssignedToID").Value
        oElem.setAttribute "releaseid", oRS("ReleaseID").Value
        oElem.setAttribute "description", oRS("Description").Value
        oElem.setAttribute "issuestatusid", oRS("IssueStatusID").Value
        oElem.setAttribute "issuestatusdesc", oRS("IssueStatusDesc").Value
        oElem.setAttribute "priority", oRS("Priority").Value
        oElem.setAttribute "submittername", oRS("SubmitterName").Value
        oElem.setAttribute "assignedtoname", oRS("AssignedToName").Value
        oElem.setAttribute "issuetypedesc", oRS("IssueTypeDesc").Value
        oRS.MoveNext
    Loop
    oRS.Close
    Set oRS = Nothing
    xmlGetIssues = oDom.xml
    Set oDom = Nothing
    Set oRoot = Nothing
    Set oElem = Nothing
End Function
```

It's worth pointing out that all of the XML returned by all of the methods in the support DLLs is well-formed XML. The elements themselves contain no text, except possible subelements. Each element then consists of 0 or more attributes indicating properties of an element. This commonly used form of well-formed XML is industry accepted as a very good way to represent data, and positions BugScope for interaction with third party programs in the future if they choose to go in that direction.

Also, you can probably tell that the developers of BugScope are paranoid about wasting memory. All of the forms are unloaded immediately after they're needed, all the object references are set to nothing before a function exits, and none of the code in the support DLL returns anything other than intrinsic types. This means that absolutely nothing has to be marshaled (even though the object references are contained in the same process space as the main application).

Populating Data Controls

All of us, at some point or another, if we've done any data-driven Windows programming, have had to populate controls on a form with information stored in a database. Way back when I first got a hold of VB, I databound a control to a datasource and thought it was the coolest thing since sliced bread; everything was done for me.

Then, I actually sat down and watched how that databinding performance fared. It was actually pretty horrible. Every time I clicked the down-arrow on a databound combobox, it would requery the database for the contents of the dropdown list, even if that information hadn't changed. Shortly after that I decided that automatic databinding (at least in the languages that I'd tried it with, including VB and Delphi) was for the birds.

It appears as though the developers of BugScope Classic feel the same way. In addition to being concerned about databinding performance, it is impossible in VB6 to natively databind a control to an XML document. All of the components in the support DLLs return lists in the form of XML documents.

The following is an example of a `Form_Activate` event, which shows the drudgery that the developers had to go through to populate the form controls with preloaded data from the support components. While the code is pretty clean as a result of the XML, the developers still think that databinding would look cleaner, if only they could get good performance out of it.

```
Private Sub Form_Activate()
    Dim oDom As MSXML.DOMDocument
    Dim oNode As IXMLDOMElement
    Dim nodeIDX As Long
    Dim strXML As String
    Dim oSystemRoot As BugScope_VB6Support.SystemRoot
    Dim newItem As ListItem

    oIssue.LoadIssue (IssueID)
    oSubmitter.LoadUser (oIssue.SubmitterID)
    Caption = "Issue Details - " & oIssue.Description
    lblSubmittedBy.Caption = oSubmitter.FirstName & " " & oSubmitter.LastName
    lblPriority.Caption = oIssue.Priority
    txtDescription.Text = oIssue.Description

    '** populate the dropdown lists with lists from systemroot.
    Set oSystemRoot = New BugScope_VB6Support.SystemRoot
    oSystemRoot.ConnectionString = dbConnStr
    Set oDom = New MSXML.DOMDocument

    strXML = oSystemRoot.xmlGetIssueTypeList
```

```
        oDom.loadXML strXML
        For nodeIDX = 0 To oDom.documentElement.childNodes.length - 1
            Set oNode = oDom.documentElement.childNodes.Item(nodeIDX)
            cboIssueType.AddItem oNode.getAttribute("description")
            cboIssueType.ItemData(cboIssueType.NewIndex) =
                        CLng(oNode.getAttribute("issuetypeid"))
        Next nodeIDX
        cboIssueType.ListIndex = cboIndexOf(cboIssueType, oIssue.IssueType)

        strXML = oSystemRoot.xmlGetUserList
        oDom.loadXML strXML
        For nodeIDX = 0 To oDom.documentElement.childNodes.length - 1
            Set oNode = oDom.documentElement.childNodes.Item(nodeIDX)
            cboAssignedTo.AddItem oNode.getAttribute("firstname") & " " &
                        oNode.getAttribute("lastname")
            cboAssignedTo.ItemData(cboAssignedTo.NewIndex) =
                        CLng(oNode.getAttribute("userid"))
        Next nodeIDX
        cboAssignedTo.ListIndex = cboIndexOf(cboAssignedTo, oIssue.AssignedToID)

        strXML = oSystemRoot.xmlGetIssueStatusList
        oDom.loadXML strXML
        For nodeIDX = 0 To oDom.documentElement.childNodes.length - 1
            Set oNode = oDom.documentElement.childNodes.Item(nodeIDX)
            cboStatus.AddItem oNode.getAttribute("description")
            cboStatus.ItemData(cboStatus.NewIndex) =
                    CLng(oNode.getAttribute("issuestatusid"))
        Next nodeIDX
        cboStatus.ListIndex = cboIndexOf(cboStatus, oIssue.IssueStatusID)

        strXML = oIssue.xmlGetActivity
        lvHistory.ListItems.Clear
        oHistoryDom.loadXML strXML
        For nodeIDX = 0 To oHistoryDom.documentElement.childNodes.length - 1
            Set oNode = oHistoryDom.documentElement.childNodes.Item(nodeIDX)
            Set newItem = lvHistory.ListItems.Add(, "HIS" &
                oNode.getAttribute("activityid"), FormatDateTime_
                (oNode.getAttribute("activitydate"), vbShortDate), 0, 0)
            newItem.ListSubItems.Add , , oNode.getAttribute("username")
            newItem.ListSubItems.Add , , oNode.getAttribute("activitytypedesc")
            newItem.ListSubItems.Add , , oNode.getAttribute("hourslogged")
        Next nodeIDX


        Set oDom = Nothing
        Set oNode = Nothing
    End Sub
```

The first thing we should look at in detail is populating the first ComboBox control. Here, the control containing the list of available `IssueTypes` that the user can select is populated. First, a reference to the `SystemRoot` object is obtained, then a new DOM (as in, Microsoft XML Document Object Model component, `MSXML.DOMDocument`) is created. This DOM will serve as a single placeholder for all of the XML that's going to be retrieved throughout the course of this `Form_Activate` event.

```
'** populate the dropdown lists with lists from systemroot.
Set oSystemRoot = New BugScope_VB6Support.SystemRoot
oSystemRoot.ConnectionString = dbConnStr
Set oDom = New MSXML.DOMDocument

strXML = oSystemRoot.xmlGetIssueTypeList
```

```
oDom.loadXML strXML
For nodeIDX = 0 To oDom.documentElement.childNodes.length - 1
    Set oNode = oDom.documentElement.childNodes.Item(nodeIDX)
    cboIssueType.AddItem oNode.getAttribute("description")
    cboIssueType.ItemData(cboIssueType.NewIndex) =
                CLng(oNode.getAttribute("issuetypeid"))
Next nodeIDX
cboIssueType.ListIndex = cboIndexOf(cboIssueType, oIssue.IssueType)
```

Once the DOM has been populated with the XML results from the SystemRoot object, we see that the code then iterates through all of the child nodes of the documentElement. The last line of the above code bears some further inspection.

```
cboIssueType.ListIndex = cboIndexOf(cboIssueType, oIssue.IssueType)
```

Because VB6's ComboBox control doesn't natively support any IndexOf method, the BugScope developers had to write their own, shown below. When asked what they disliked most about BugScope development, the developers unanimously agreed that it was populating the ComboBoxes and ListViews with data to emulate databinding behavior manually.

```
Public Function cboIndexOf(ByVal inCBO As ComboBox, ByVal SearchData As Long) As
Long
    Dim X As Long

    cboIndexOf = 0
    For X = 0 To inCBO.ListCount - 1
        If inCBO.ItemData(X) = SearchData Then
            cboIndexOf = X
        End If
    Next X
End Function
```

Now that we've taken a thorough look at the design, code, architecture, and layout of the existing BugScope Classic application, let's move on to the good part – it's time to migrate this application to the .NET framework.

BugScope .NET

BugScope.NET is going to be an application that will hopefully bring UFixIT's defect tracking system onto the Internet and into the realm of truly enterprise-class applications. When we decided to migrate the application to the .NET framework, we decided to take the "Full Monty" approach and completely rewrite everything.

Once we decided to rewrite the whole thing, we followed some of the advice laid out in Chapter 13 of this book and examined what things we could improve on to fully take advantage of the .NET framework. The main thing we decided to do was modify the application's core architecture so that it was dependent on a Web Service for all of its information, rather than a direct SQL Connection.

BugScope.NET is a distributed, enterprise scale, n-tier application. It consists of a Windows client application that will be the user interface for all users of the application. The users will log in to the secure application from the Windows interface.

Once authenticated against the BugScope server, users will be able to use the application in a manner that will look very much like the Classic version of BugScope. The key difference is that instead of communicating with a local intranet SQL server for all of its data, BugScope.NET will be communicating via HTTP and Web Services with a Web Service on the Internet. There are issues with communicating with a server in this way. For example, if you are not careful, you might make your web service available for anyone on the Internet to use (or abuse, as the case may be). When implementing a Web Service as a back-end to a user interface, validations need to take place that allow only valid front-ends to communicate with the service.

BugScope.NET will also incorporate some new functionality that the previous version of the application simply couldn't do (or couldn't do easily).

Architectural Overview

BugScope.NET's architecture is radically different to the previous version: it is essentially two programs instead of one. The structure of BugScope.NET consists of many levels. The base level is the WinForms client application. Beyond that is the Web Service. The Web Service is driven by a collection of components in the Business Tier, which are in turn driven by components in the Data Access Tier residing in a COM+ application for scalability and performance.

The following is a diagram of the basic structure of the BugScope.NET application.

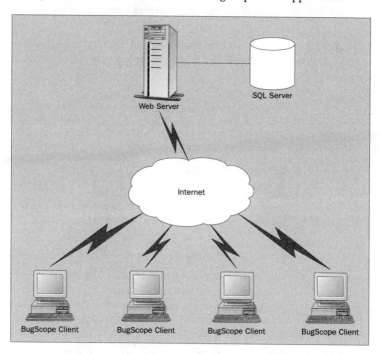

Functional Requirements

The functional requirements of the .NET application should be fairly close to the Classic VB6 application. During the initial design phase of the .NET portion of the product, the designers decided that they should maintain the core functionality of the previous application while adding a few features that they believed should be included. The following is a list of the .NET application's functional requirements after designing the upgrade. In keeping with good guidelines about requirements documents, we won't go into any detail on how the application actually might meet the requirements laid out. That level of detail won't be reached until after the requirements have been agreed on. After spending some time examining their previous application, and the features and functionality provided in the .NET framework, the UFIX software team has come up with the following list of requirements that they want their .NET application to meet:

❑ **Authenticate users of the application**
Just like the Classic application, the .NET application should be secure. Each user should have their own password and means for identifying themselves to the system. No data should be able to be modified or viewed by any unauthenticated user. The passwords in the system must also be stored and transmitted in an encrypted form in order to allow for greater security and less chance of unwanted intrusion.

❑ **Browse the Application/Release hierarchy**
Just like the classic application, the .NET application needs to provide some method for users to browse the entire tree of applications and releases beneath each application.

❑ **Manage Applications**
The .NET application must allow users to manage all aspects of Applications. This includes allowing them to create new Applications, modify existing Applications, and delete existing Applications.

❑ **Manage Releases**
BugScope .NET must allow users to manage all aspects of Releases. This includes allowing them to create new Releases, modify existing Releases, and delete existing Releases.

❑ **Manage Issues**
Just as with Applications and Releases, BugScope.NET must allow users to create, retrieve, update, and delete Issues.

❑ **Create Activity for existing Issues**
Just like the classic VB6 application, BugScope.NET must allow users to log new Activity against an existing Issue. The business rule that no Activity can be deleted once created still remains.

❑ **Supply comments on existing activity**
All users must have the ability to log additional comments against any given Activity.

❑ **Administer the application core data and configuration**
Classic BugScope didn't have any application administration features. BugScope.NET should allow appropriate users to edit the core data (such as Issue Types, Issue Status lists, and users). Of the application as well as the configuration of the client application. The configuration of the client application should only include the configuration of the URL for the Web Service.

❑ **Properly detect and handle communication failures to/from the Web Service.**
The application should detect when it cannot communicate with the Web Service, or when some other communication failure across the network has taken place. These errors should be trapped and displayed to the users in a friendly format, allowing them to exit the client application gracefully.

❑ **Prevent unauthorized use of the Web Service**
Because all of the functionality of this application is now exposed as a Web Service, the Web Service must provide some method by which client applications indicate that they are indeed valid client applications, preventing the unauthorized use of the application by programmers with discovery tools, etc. This authorization may be limited to the username/password combination, or may be as complicated as authenticating the actual client software. When a Web Service is exposed, it can be used by anyone who has the appropriate tools. Because of the nature of this application, we don't want it to be used by anyone except customers running a valid client application, to avoid abusive users damaging sensitive data.

❑ **Allow entry of "external" issues into the system from third-party software**
The new BugScope.NET application should provide some method by which third-party applications, such as Help Desk applications, can enter "external" issues into the system. This feature will give the third-party application some external ID by which it can link its own database to the BugScope information. BugScope must then also provide the ability for valid external applications to query the system for all issues in the system that originated from that valid external application. For example, a valid external help desk/support application must be able to not only convert support concerns into defect tracking issues, but be able to, at a later point, retrieve a list of all items that it has created, including all updated Activity for those items.

Database Schema

For the most part, the database schema for BugScope.NET should look pretty similar to the database schema from the original application. A few tables have been added to support the notion of externally-supplied Issues, and a new table has been added to support ActivityComments. The designers weren't pleased with the text-only commenting feature and want to add some robust Issue and Activity manipulation functionality.

❑ User Data
❑ Application Data
❑ Release Data
❑ Issue Data

User Data

Not much has changed here since the original application. Users must still have a username and password. One additional table has been added that is related to users of the application. The `bsExternalSources` table is a list of valid external sources for externally submitted Issues.

`bsUsers`

Column Name	Data Type	Nullable	Description
UserID	Int Identity	N	This is the primary key. Used to identify the user in various related tables/fields.
UserName	Varchar	N	Name of the user. Used at login and in comment descriptions.
Password	Binary	N	User's password. Stored encrypted to avoid tampering and snooping.
FirstName	Varchar	N	First name of the user.
LastName	Varchar	N	Last name of the user.
JobTitle	Varchar	N	Job Title of the user. Used in comments.

`bsExternalSources`

Column Name	Data Type	Nullable	Description
SourceID	Int Identity	N	This is the primary key. This is used to identify the external source in related tables.
Description	Varchar	N	Name of the external source.
ClientCode	Varchar	N	Valid client code. All clients that wish to use the Web Service must have a valid client code. A string that is sent when a client UI connects to the service as an authorization code. Anyone attempting to abuse the Web Service will not be able to without a valid `ClientCode`. This feature is not fully implemented in this example, though the data structure exists to support it.

Application Data

The database schema for application-related data has not changed since classic BugScope for VB6. The following is the definition of the `Application` table in BugScope.NET

`BsApplications`

Column Name	Data Type	Nullable	Description
ApplicationID	Int Identity	N	This is the primary key. Used to identify the application in related tables.
Description	Varchar	N	Description of the application.

Release Data

There is also only one table in this category, the `bsReleases` table.

bsReleases

Column Name	Data Type	Nullable	Description
ReleaseID	Int Identity	N	This is the primary key. Used to identify this release in related tables.
ApplicationID	Int	N	This is a foreign key. Indicates the Application to which this Release belongs.
Description	Varchar	N	Description of the application.

Issue Data

With Issues being the main type of data this application was designed to manipulate, this category is obviously the largest. Some changes from the previous version of BugScope include the addition of the `ExternalSourceID` field to the `bsIssues` table, the addition of the `bsActivityComments` table, and the allowing of `nulls` in the `SubmitterID` field for Issues.

bsIssues

Column Name	Data Type	Nullable	Description
IssueID	Int Identity	N	This is the primary key. Identifies this issue in related tables.
IssueType	Int	N	Foreign key indicating the record in the `bsIssueTypes` table that corresponds to this issue.
SubmitterID	Int	Y	Foreign key indicating the `UserID` that submitted this Issue. Will be `Null` for externally submitted Issues.
AssignedToID	Int	N	Foreign key indicating the `UserID` that the issue is currently assigned to.
ReleaseID	Int	N	Foreign key indicating which Release this Issue was logged against.
Description	Varchar	N	Initial description of the Issue.
IssueStatusID	Int	N	Foreign key indicating the status of the Issue as described in `bsIssueStatus`.
IssueDate	Datetime	N	Date that the Issue was submitted.
ExternalSourceID	Int	Y	ID indicating the external application source that submitted this Issue. Relates to the `bsExternalSources` table.

bsIssueType

Column Name	Data Type	Nullable	Description
IssueTypeID	Int Identity	N	This is the primary key. Used to identify this Issue type in other tables.
Description	Varchar	N	Description of the Issue Type.

bsIssueStatus

Column Name	Data Type	Nullable	Description
IssueStatusID	Int Identity	N	This is the primary key. Used to identify this Issue Status in other related tables.
Description	Varchar	N	Description of the Issue Status.
Priority	Int	N	Priority associated with this Issue status.

bsIssueActivity

Column Name	Data Type	Nullable	Description
ActivityID	Int Identity	N	This is the primary key. This is used to identify this Issue Activity in other related tables.
IssueID	Int	N	Foreign key. Indicates which Issue this Activity has been logged against.
Notes	Text	N	Extended text description of the Activity. User comments are also appended to this field.
UserID	Int	N	Foreign key. Indicates the User that logged this Activity.
ActivityTypeID	Int	N	Foreign key. Indicates the type of this Activity (bsActivityTypes).
HoursLogged	Int	N	Hours logged for this particular Activity.
ActivityDate	Datetime	N	Date/Time the Issue Activity took place.

bsActivityComments

Column Name	Data Type	Nullable	Description
CommentID	Int Identity	N	Primary key. Used to identify this comment in other related tables (if any).
Notes	Text	N	Notes of the comment.
SubmitterID	Int	N	User ID of the submitter of the comment.
CommentDate	Datetime	N	Date/time stamp of when the comment was created.
ActivityID	Int	N	ID of the Activity for which this comment was logged.

bsActivityTypes

Column Name	Data Type	Nullable	Description
ActivityTypeID	Int Identity	N	Primary key. Used to identify this activity type to related tables.
Description	Varchar	N	Description of the Activity Type.

The following diagram illustrates the relationship among the various tables required for the .NET version of the BugScope application. There are a few new tables and relationships, but things should look pretty familiar.

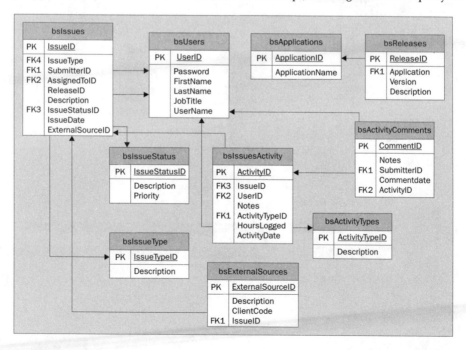

Server-Side Classes

Because of the new requirement that the majority of the processing in the application take place behind a Web Service, everyone knew that they would have to be designing classes for implementation on a server. As such, these classes should also follow a robust n-tier model, increasing the sustainability and scalability of the new application.

The following is a component diagram showing all of the puzzle pieces that the designers of BugScope.NET have come up with.

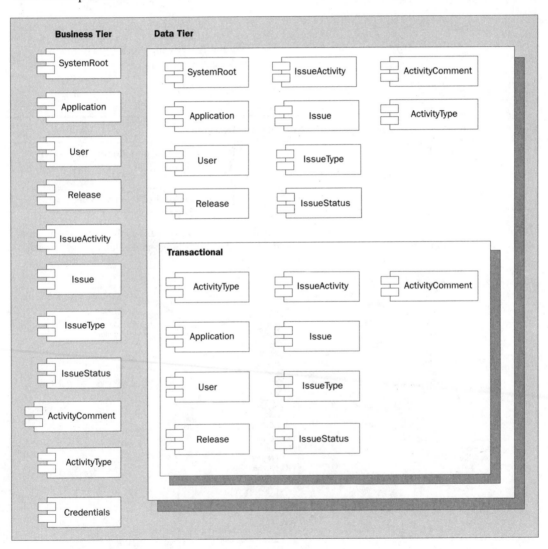

There are a couple of things worth noticing about this diagram. The class design of this new application is far more robust than the old BugScope VB6 application. The first thing that we see is a new business-tier class called `Credentials`. Also, you'll notice that `SystemRoot` does not have a transactional component. The other thing worth pointing out is that all of these classes have the same name as their other-tiered counterparts, such as `SystemRoot` and `Application`, etc. In classic COM days, this would have been impossible, which is why so many DLLs ended up with odd naming conventions like `bsBusIssue.DLL` and `bsDatIssueTrx.DLL`.

All of the above components will be discussed in the following section. One thing that is not visible from the component diagram is that the design of BugScope.NET will make good use of inheritance and base classes. For example, all Data-Tier classes will inherit from a single class common to all Data-Tier classes. The same will go for the Business-Tier classes. The above diagram is more of a packaging diagram, and doesn't show class inheritance and structure.

Business Tier

In BugScope Classic, all of the components were entirely self-contained. The `Application` object handled all operations that could be done on an Application. The same holds true for the Business-Tier classes in BugScope.NET, with one exception. In BugScope.NET, the Business Tier delegates the tasks of reading from and writing to the database to components being hosted in a COM+ Application.

This decision allows for greater scalability, reliability, and overall application performance. By placing all of the data access components in COM+, those components can then be pooled and cached, removing instantiation overhead and allowing multiple instances of the same class to be loaded in memory at the same time. Until the advent of the .NET framework, the only objects that could take advantage of pooling and caching were C++ components. The fact that .NET components host in COM+ without regard to language, allows VB, C# and C++ programmers alike to take full advantage of the rich feature set of COM+ services.

The other noticeable change over the previous version is the format of list-type data. In the previous application, all operations that returned more than one row of data returned that information to the calling function in the form of persisted, well-formed XML.

For example, in the VB6 application, the code would load information from the database into a `RecordSet` object, and then from there convert it into a well-formed XML document/stream. That XML looked like this:

```xml
<APPLICATIONLIST>
   <APPLICATION applicationid="1" description="BugScope">
      <RELEASE releaseid="4" description="Public Release" version="1.0"/>
      <RELEASE releaseid="1" description="Alpha Release (private)"
            version="1.0a"/>
   </APPLICATION>
   <APPLICATION applicationid="2" description="RoachScope">
      <RELEASE releaseid="3" description="Public Beta" version="2.0"/>
   </APPLICATION>
</APPLICATIONLIST>
```

The .NET version of the application needs to perform no such conversion. The DataSet stores the data internally as XML, which looks like this:

```xml
<ApplicationDataSet>
   <Application>
      <ApplicationID="1"/>
```

```
        <Description="BugScope"/>
        <Releases>
           <Release>
               <ReleaseID="1"/>
               <Description="Alpha Release (private)"/>
           </Release>
        </Releases>
     </Application>
  . . .
  </ApplicationDataSet>
```

There is a lot more to the internal storage of the DataSet, but you can see that the XML elements correspond exactly to the table and column names within the database (as defined by the strongly-typed DataSet's internal schema).

The Business Tier in BugScope.NET makes extensive use of **Strongly-Typed DataSets**. In all list-returning functions, the Business Tier components will return strongly-typed DataSets. These DataSets are designed specifically for the exchange of data between tiers and between disparate applications or components. They are also designed specifically for XML serialization, allowing them to be easily transmitted across process boundaries or the Internet as the result of a Web Service call.

By using these DataSets, more relevant data and related tables can be stored along with the requested information. This allows an application querying for a list to obtain all the relevant details about each individual row without having to perform separate instantiations of classes whenever more detail is required.

One other thing you may notice is that more functionality is provided by the Business Tier than is strictly required by the Web Service it is supporting. The reason for this is that a great rule of thumb in component design is that you can *assume absolutely nothing.* Just because we're demonstrating a Web Service for the purpose of this chapter doesn't mean that a couple of weeks from now the same components won't be used to build an ASP.NET application or a fat WinForms client with all three tiers residing locally, etc. By providing a strong standard set of across-the-board functionality now, the designers of the BugScope.NET application are allowing for sustainability and scalability, two major goals when migrating.

Data Access Tier

For obvious reasons, the BugScope.NET Data Tier is more complicated than that of the previous application. This probably has something to do with the fact that the old version of the application didn't *have* a Data Tier.

As with many enterprise-scale applications, the Data Tier is divided into two categories. These categories are Transactional and Non-Transactional. Anyone familiar with MTS or COM+ programming will recognize the need for this separation.

By separating the non-transactional components from the transactional components, we can avoid incurring the overhead of involving the distributed transaction coordinator for read-only operations that simply require no coordination. Even though we want the two types of data components separated, we still want them hosted in COM+ to give us the benefits of object pooling, and in some cases, automatic interoperability with legacy COM+ components.

The read-only type data components all return strongly-typed DataSets to the calling component or application. This provides an easy way for the calling component to populate its internal data for providing a property list, and an extremely easy way of making changes to single fields. This advantage will become extremely apparent once we get to covering the actual code of the application.

Common Classes

The common classes in BugScope.NET are those classes that are shared by both the server components and any client application, including our sample WinForms application. The sharing is accomplished by having these classes be the return values of various functions called at the Web Service level.

The Web Services system and the .NET framework are extremely adept at quickly serializing a class into XML. This is how these classes are transmitted from server to client. The class is serialized to XML, stored in a SOAP envelope, and then transferred. At the receiving end, the SOAP envelope is opened, the XML persistence of the class is then "run", building a brand new instance of that class and handing a reference to that class to the calling function.

The following diagram illustrates how class instances are serialized, placed in SOAP envelopes, and then reconstructed on the client side for use as a proxy.

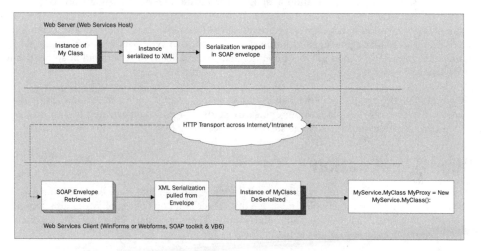

All of the following classes have something in common at a much lower level than the concept of shared data between client and server. All of the following classes are defined solely by their public properties. In order for XML serialization of a class instance to take place without unexpected errors, that class must not maintain any private data. Private member variables are inaccessible to a serializer, and therefore would not be transmitted across the "wire", causing inconsistent data at both ends of the transmission.

- ❑ Credentials
- ❑ ApplicationDataSet
- ❑ ReleaseDataSet
- ❑ IssueDataSet

The Credentials Class

The Credentials class is a special class that deserves some extra discussion. This class is essentially a container for authentication information. Think of it as our own custom "Passport". Because the requirements of the application don't specify that the client or server have actual Internet access, the BugScope.NET designers ruled out using MS Passport as an authentication scheme.

However, the concept of a token of some kind that is passed around for every method call really appealed to the designers. Halfway through the design process, the designers decided that they didn't want to deal with maintaining the traffic of an authentication token. So, they decided that if a request for credentials verification passed, then an encrypted hash of some kind would be stored in the ASP.NET `Session` object. This way, any time a request is made of a WebMethod through the actual management service, all it needs to do is see if the encrypted hash is in the `Session` object. This not only cleared up a little bit of redundant traffic but also added the security of preventing savvy programmers from spoofing the authenticated encryption code from their client programs.

The Web Service

The "Web Service", as such, is actually a combination of two services. The first of the two services does nothing but validate credentials. If a calling client application wants to use the main application service, the calling client must strike up a conversation with the authentication service that BugScope.NET provides.

The result of this conversation is either a disappointing cold shoulder, or a modified `Session` object that can then be utilized by the management service (the second of our two Web Services in this example). This allows the management service to prevent unauthorized use and keeps the overhead of authentication in its own self-contained service.

We will go into lengthy detail on the mechanics of this system and the code that supports those mechanics when we come to the code sample portion of this case study. For now, you can simply stew on the number of applications that an authentication scheme such as this can apply to.

The Client Application

The client application for BugScope.NET is actually nothing but user interface. Interface purists and n-tier design supporters will be extremely pleased to see this. The client application provides an interactive interface to the BugScope web service, and nothing more. There is no data stored locally, no calculations are done locally, and no business rules are enforced locally.

You might actually be wondering what the benefit of something like this might be. This discussion could get quite lengthy – in fact, I've seen discussions like these last weeks on message boards and newsgroups.

The first true benefit to the total and complete separation of user interface from implementation and business logic is a true benefit to large, multi-team development environments. Many web-based e-commerce sites have a multi-team setup. They may have a crew of designers who spend their days whipping out fancy graphics and churning out page layouts that are designed to grab the user's attention, to sell a particular product, and many more marketing-type things. This same company also might have a crew of programmers who spend their days writing low-level code. However, when the art team comes up with a new page layout, it is up to the programmers to spend their days tweaking tables, cells, divs, spans, and other such HTML drudgery.

What the separation of UI from the business implementation code affords us is the ability to dedicate two entirely different skillsets to their own respective specialties. The people who know how to design user interfaces to be pleasing, easy to use, simple, and visually stunning can spend their days actually building the user interfaces. Those programmers who specialize in producing well-designed, object-oriented, data-driven code can spend their days producing that code.

The beauty of the Microsoft Web Service implementation is that it is self-documenting. Simply by hitting the latest version of the service's `.asmx` page, the User Interface team can see the contract they need to abide by in order to connect their interface to the back-end server code. The prospect for peace, unity and an all-out cease-fire between the "UI guys" and the "server geeks" is truly attainable with Web Services, ASP.NET, and the .NET framework.

The other benefit of the separation of code logic and data access from UI implementation is maintenance. It is far easier to debug a user-interface problem (be it Windows or Web) if there is no data access or business logic code cluttering up the innards of the interface.

The Code

The following section will walk you through how we built some of the more important portions of BugScope.NET. Coupled with the architecture and design descriptions above, it should hopefully complete the experience of going from VB6 design, to VB6 code, then on to .NET design, and finally to .NET code. One of the things we hope you take away from this is that with any really strong design, the code simply falls into place, and is easier and faster to create.

The other thing worth mentioning is that even with the new, Internet-enabled architecture, the Web Services, advanced authentication model, and the addition of the ability to administer core tables, BugScope.NET didn't take much longer to develop from the ground up than BugScope Classic did.

This should bring to light one of the great benefits of the framework. That benefit is that the .NET framework allows programmers today to quickly and elegantly create data-driven, super-connected enterprise solutions in the same way that tools like Visual Basic 3 and Delphi 1 introduced rapid development of standardized Windows user interfaces.

We are going to walk through the following usage scenarios from end-to-end, showing the control flow and code involved in accomplishing each task:

- Logging in
- Populating the Product Tree
- Logging a new Issue
- Viewing Issue Activity
- Logging new Issue Activity
- Creating a new User

As with all of the samples in this book, the entire source code to both BugScope.NET and BugScope Classic is available for download from Wrox Press.

Base Classes

All of the classes in the Data Access Layer (DAL) Assembly (`BugScope.DAL.dll`) inherit from the same base class. This base class provides two standardized methods for running stored procedures, as well as the Instantiation and disposal of the `SqlConnection` object and configuration of the connection string. By providing a base class from which all classes in the tier derive, it will be extremely easy to either modify the core database behavior of all classes, or add more functionality later.

Below is the C# source code for the DAO object, a base class from which all data-tier classes inherit. Note the XML comments after the / / / comment character. This is used to dynamically build XML and/or HTML source documentation.

```csharp
/*
 * DAO.cs
 * This file houses the DAO class, the base class from which all data-tier
 * classes inherit.
 */

using System;
using System.EnterpriseServices;
using System.Data;
using System.Data.SqlClient;
using System.Diagnostics;
using System.Runtime.InteropServices;

namespace BugScope.DAL
{
    /// <summary>
    /// DAO is a ServicedComponent class, meaning that it runs natively
    /// within the context of a COM+ Application. It provides standard,
    /// low-level data access functionality that the data classes will use.
    /// The DAO base class concept is extremely prevalent in Microsoft
    /// ASP.NET enterprise-class examples and tutorials. It is used here
    /// for its usefulness, not its acceptance within Microsoft.
    /// This class is abstract, as such it can only be inherited, not
    /// instantiated.
    /// </summary>
    abstract public class DAO: ServicedComponent
    {
        protected SqlConnection Connection;
        private string m_DSN;

        /// <summary>
        /// This method creates a SqlCommand object designed to execute a
        /// stored procedure.
        /// </summary>
        /// <param name="sprocName">String representing the name of the
        /// stored procedure to execute</param>
        /// <param name="parameters">SqlParameter[] array of arguments
        /// (not including argument for return value)</param>
        /// <returns>Newly instantiated SqlCommand object</returns>
        private SqlCommand CreateCommand(string sprocName, IDataParameter[]
                parameters)
        {
            SqlCommand command = new SqlCommand( sprocName, Connection );
            command.CommandType = CommandType.StoredProcedure;

            // Populate the Sql Command's parameter array.
            foreach (SqlParameter parameter in parameters)
            {
                command.Parameters.Add( parameter );
            }

            // Add a SqlParameter representing the return value from the
```

```
      // stored procedure.
      command.Parameters.Add( new SqlParameter ( "ReturnValue",
            SqlDbType.Int,
            4, /* Size */
            ParameterDirection.ReturnValue,
            false, /* is nullable */
            0, /* byte precision */
            0, /* byte scale */
            string.Empty,
            DataRowVersion.Default,
            null ));

      return command;
}

protected string DSN
{
   get
   {
      return m_DSN;
   }
}


/// <summary>
/// Executes a stored procedure within the database
/// </summary>
/// <param name="sprocName">String representing the name of the
/// stored procedure to execute</param>
/// <param name="parameters">SqlParameter[] array of arguments to
/// the stored procedure</param>
/// <returns>Integer representing the integer value returned from
/// the stored procedure</returns>
protected int RunSP( string sprocName, IDataParameter[] parameters )
{
   Connection.Open();
   SqlCommand command = CreateCommand( sprocName, parameters );
   command.ExecuteNonQuery();
   Connection.Close();
   return (int)command.Parameters[ "ReturnValue" ].Value;
}


/// <summary>
/// Executes a stored procedure, placing results in a DataSet.
/// </summary>
/// <param name="sprocName">String representing the name of the
/// stored procedure to execute.</param>
/// <param name="parameters">SqlParameter[] array of arguments to
/// the stored procedure.</param>
/// <param name="dataSet">DataSet into which to place return results
/// from stored procedure</param>
/// <returns></returns>
protected int RunSP( string sprocName, IDataParameter[] parameters,
         DataSet dataSet )
{
   SqlDataAdapter sqlDA = new SqlDataAdapter();
   Connection.Open();
```

```
            sqlDA.SelectCommand = CreateCommand( sprocName, parameters );
            sqlDA.Fill( dataSet, "SourceTable" );
            Connection.Close();
            return (int)sqlDA.SelectCommand.Parameters[ "ReturnValue" ].Value;
        }

        /// <summary>
        /// Overridden ServicedComponent method. Takes the ConstructionString
        /// (found by right-clicking the component
        /// in COM+ console, getting properties) and stores it privately as
        /// the DB connection string (DSN)
        /// </summary>
        /// <param name="ConstructString">String sent to the object as a
        ///construction string from COM+</param>
        public override void Construct(string ConstructString)
        {
            m_DSN = ConstructString;
        }


        /// <summary>
        /// Overridden ServicedComponent method. Called when COM+
        /// JIT-activates this component. Used to instantiate the
        /// database connection.
        /// </summary>
        public override void Activate()
        {
            Connection = new SqlConnection(m_DSN);
        }


        /// <summary>
        /// Overridden ServicedComponent method. Called when COM+
        /// JIT-deactivates this component. Used to dispose of the Sql
        /// Connection object.
        /// </summary>
        public override void Deactivate()
        {
            Connection.Dispose();
        }

    }
}
```

The base class for the business tier is basically empty. At the moment, there is no special functionality required for the business tier. However, in the future that might not be the case, so all of the middle/business-tier components inherit from a base class called BLO (Business Logic Object).

Execution Flow

Once we've all agreed that the server is going to be a multi-tiered enterprise configuration with a set of Web Services serving up functionality to clients, we need to be aware of how the execution of tasks will flow. The Windows client in this application may appear much like most Windows 95/98 clients on the surface, but beneath it has very little in common. The biggest difference is that all of its functionality is being performed remotely via SOAP, XML, and the Web Services architecture.

The following diagram illustrates the flow of process and execution control in response to a simple request for data from the Windows Client. After looking at this diagram, you should be extremely thankful for how much of the process Microsoft automates and shields from you.

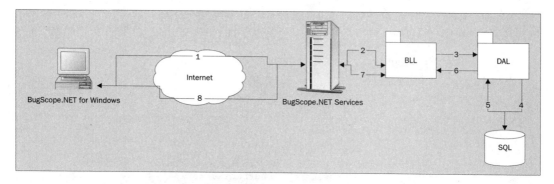

As you can tell, there is an incredibly large amount of processing going on in the above diagram. For example, the Windows client doesn't even see its requested data until after Step 8. Microsoft's Web Services architecture and the use of SOAP and XML allows a complicated process like the one above to be executed simply without much knowledge by the end user (the client programmer, in this case). For example, all eight steps above can actually take place in the following line of code:

```
StrongDataSet sds = oServiceClient.GetStrongDataSet();
```

Even though there is an incredibly large amount of processing going on when you make this request, the client programmer doesn't need to know about any of it. All they need to know is that they can obtain an instance of an object from a Web Service using the same language syntax they use to create an instance of a local class.

Logging In

Now that we know the basic traffic route of information in the BugScope.NET architecture, we can start examining its key portions of code. Obviously, in any secure application, one of the most important pieces of functionality is securing access to the system. In BugScope.NET, this is done through the use of one of its two Web Services (bsAuthenticator).

When the client application first starts, its main form (frmMain) is loaded. While loading, and before actually displaying, the main form pops up the login dialog box. This dialog box asks the user for their Username, their Password, and the base URL of the BugScope web server. This is an HTTP URI for the hostname of the BugScope Web Services. By default, it uses the hostname for my laptop (mephisto), but this functionality could easily be upgraded to provide a dropdown list of available servers.

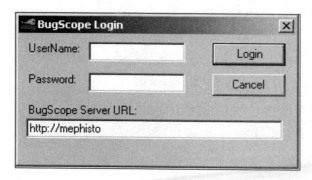

The following is the `try`/`finally` block that actually uses the Web Service client to verify the credentials of the application user. The rest of the form's `load` event has been snipped out for clarity, as it will be discussed later:

```
if (loginForm.DialogResult == DialogResult.OK)
{
    int result;
    int x;

    // Attempt to establish communication with the BugScope Authentication
    // service (bsAuthenticator.asmx)
    try
    {
        bsAuthenticator.bsAuthenticator myAuth = new
                        bsAuthenticator.bsAuthenticator();
        // Yes! Beta 2 finally lets us change the URL of web service clients
        // programmatically.
        myAuth.Url = loginForm.txtURL.Text +
                    object"/BugServices/bsAuthenticator.asmx";
        if (myAuth == null)
        {
            MessageBox.Show(this, "Failed to Instantiate Authentication
                            Service", "Big Trouble");
            this.Close();
            Dispose();
        }
        result = myAuth.VerifyCredentials(loginForm.txtUserName.Text,
                loginForm.txtPassword.Text, "BUGSCOPECLIENT", out AccessCode);
        if (result == -1)
        {
            MessageBox.Show(this, "Username/Password Invalid.");
            this.Close();
            Dispose();
        }
    }
    catch (Exception myException)
    {
        MessageBox.Show(this, myException.Message, "Communication Failure");
        this.Close();
        Dispose();
    }

    // ... Removed for clarity ...

}
```

That's what happens on the client side. Once the client issues a request to the Web Service, the service (running on the remote machine) then instantiates the BLL User object and invokes the `ValidateLogin` method in the BLL object. The BLL method then instantiates a DAL object that actually executes a stored procedure that makes the final determination if the credentials match.

The **BLL** `ValidateLogin` method in the `User` class.

```
public int ValidateLogin( Credentials creds )
{
    DAL.User oUser = new DAL.User();

    return oUser.ValidateLogin( creds );
}
```

The **DAL** `ValidateLogin` method in the `User` class.

```
/// <summary>
/// Validates the credentials class (encrypted password, username, etc) against
/// the database.
/// </summary>
/// <param name="creds">Valid instances of a Credentials class</param>
/// <returns>-1 if no valid match occurred for the credentials. Otherwise, the
UserID (key) of the user that obtained the match is returned.</returns>
public int ValidateLogin(Credentials creds)
{
    SqlParameter[] parameters =
    {
        new SqlParameter( "@UserName", SqlDbType.VarChar, 20 ), // 0
        new SqlParameter( "@Password", SqlDbType.Binary, 20 ) // 1
    };

    parameters[0].Value = creds.UserName;
    parameters[1].Value = creds.Password;

    return RunSP( "sp_ValidateLogin", parameters );

}
```

Populating the Product Tree

Populating the product tree is done immediately after logging in. If you'll remember, in the VB6 version of BugScope you actually had to click the appropriate icon to bring up the product tree window. In BugScope.NET, the default view as soon as you've logged in is that of the product tree. This is because most work done against the system has to start with an `Application` or a `Release`, so it made sense to make those two things available immediately.

This section of code is important for several reasons. The first reason is that it is the first time in the BugScope.NET application that a non-primitive data type is being transmitted from server to client. The other reason is that this non-primitive data type is actually a strongly-typed DataSet, generated automatically at compile-time by reading a `.xsd` (XML Schema Definition) file.

Sometimes it's worth just sitting back and pondering the impact of this for a minute. The server has a data structure definition of a hierarchical DataSet, strongly typed through the use of a `.xsd` file. Not only can the server use that definition, but when Visual Studio.NET grabs a reference to that service, it creates nested classes within that service proxy class that represents the data structures defined by the server-side strongly-typed DataSet derivation class. Chapter 13 mentioned briefly that nested classes were an important concept to understand and think about when migrating to the .NET framework. Strongly-typed DataSets are the classes that you might see most often taking advantage of nested classes.

Let's take a look at the Windows client code for this first:

```
// If execution gets this far, the user is authenticated and we can proceed
// to load the application hierarchy.
statusBar1.Text = "User " + loginForm.txtUserName.Text + " Logged in.";

// keep the tree from flickering during updates.
trvProducts.BeginUpdate();

nodRoot = new TreeNode("Product Tree");
trvProducts.Nodes.Add(new TreeNode("Product Tree"));
```

```
myClient = new bsManager.bsManager();
myClient.Url = loginForm.txtURL.Text + "/BugServices/bsManager.asmx";

// appDS is a variable of type bsManager.ApplicationDataSet
appDS = myClient.GetApplications();

// Because its a strongly-typed dataSet, we can grab an enumerator and loop
// through strongly-typed rows.
foreach ( bsManager.ApplicationDataSet.bsApplicationsRow appRow in
appDS.bsApplications.Rows )
{
    // appRow.ApplicationName is much more self-documenting than
    // an equivalent rs.Fields("ApplicationName").Value in classic ADO
    newNode = new TreeNode( appRow.ApplicationName );
    newNode.ImageIndex = 1;
    trvProducts.Nodes[0].Nodes.Add( newNode );

    // because the dataset knows about the hierarchy, we can iterate
    // through the children of the current row. This massive methodname
    // for obtaining child rows is the "poster boy" for using "annotation"
    // to name your own children-obtaining methods rather than using the
    // defaults like I did.
    foreach (bsManager.ApplicationDataSet.bsReleasesRow relRow in
            appRow.GetbsReleasesRowsBybsApplicationsbsReleases() )
    {
        newNode.Nodes.Add( new TreeNode( relRow.Description, 2, 0 ) );
    }
}
```

Now let's examine the BLL code behind the Web Service for the GetApplications method in the SystemRoot class.

```
public ApplicationDataSet GetApplications()
{
    ApplicationDataSet apDS;

    BugScope.DAL.SystemRoot rSystemRoot = new BugScope.DAL.SystemRoot();
    apDS = rSystemRoot.GetApplications();
    rSystemRoot.Dispose();
    return apDS;
}
```

And now for the actual population of the two-table, hierarchical DataSet:

```
public ApplicationDataSet GetApplications()
{
```

First, we'll use a DataAdapter to load the Application information.

```
SqlDataAdapter appDA = new SqlDataAdapter("SELECT ApplicationID,
            ApplicationName FROM bsApplications ORDER BY
            ApplicationName", Connection);
```

Secondly, we need another `DataAdapter` to load Release information.

```
SqlDataAdapter relDA = new SqlDataAdapter("SELECT ReleaseID, Description,
            Version, ApplicationID FROM bsReleases ORDER BY
            Version", Connection);

Connection.Open();
ApplicationDataSet appDS = new ApplicationDataSet();
```

Because our `ApplicationDataSet` is a typed DataSet with a hierarchical relationship defined between the `bsApplications` and `bsReleases` tables, all we need to do is simply fill the tables, and the DataSet does all the work. Note, however, that we can't fill the `Releases` table first, or we'll violate the foreign key constraint that defines the hierarchical relationship.

```
appDA.Fill(appDS, "bsApplications");
relDA.Fill(appDS, "bsReleases");

Connection.Close();

return appDS;
}
```

The first thing that might be confusing is that the second `SqlDataAdapter` and query seems to be missing a `WHERE` clause. The first query doesn't have a filter condition because it represents the top level of the hierarchy. The reason for the second query's missing filter condition is that the schema of the DataSet is actually defining a parent-child relationship, so all hierarchical filtering is done by the DataSet on your behalf.

And finally, let's take a look at the Visual Studio generated schema for the `ApplicationDataSet` strong DataSet type. Keep in mind that the version of Visual Studio.NET I was using kept randomly inserting and removing keys, so the format of the schema may not match 100% the format of the schemas your copy of VS.NET is producing:

```
<?xml version="1.0" encoding="utf-8" ?>
<xsd:schema id="ApplicationDataSet"
targetNamespace="http://tempuri.org/ApplicationDataSet.xsd" elementFormDefault="qualified"
xmlns="http://tempuri.org/ApplicationDataSet.xsd"
xmlns:xsd="http://www.w3.org/2001/XMLSchema" xmlns:msdata="urn:schemas-microsoft-com:xml-
msdata">
    <xsd:element name="ApplicationDataSet" msdata:IsDataSet="true">
      <xsd:complexType>
        <xsd:choice maxOccurs="unbounded">
          <xsd:element name="bsApplications">
            <xsd:complexType>
              <xsd:sequence>
                <xsd:element name="ApplicationID" msdata:ReadOnly="true"
                            msdata:AutoIncrement="true" type="xsd:int" />
                <xsd:element name="ApplicationName" type="xsd:string" />
                <xsd:element name="bsReleases">
                  <xsd:complexType>
                    <xsd:sequence>
                      <xsd:element name="ReleaseID" msdata:ReadOnly="true"
                                  msdata:AutoIncrement="true" type="xsd:int" />
                      <xsd:element name="ApplicationID" type="xsd:int" />
                      <xsd:element name="Version" type="xsd:string" />
```

```
                    <xsd:element name="Description" type="xsd:string" />
               </xsd:sequence>
            </xsd:complexType>
         </xsd:element>
      </xsd:sequence>
   </xsd:complexType>
</xsd:element>
   </xsd:choice>
</xsd:complexType>
<xsd:key name="ApplicationDataSetKey1">
   <xsd:selector xpath=".//bsApplications" />
   <xsd:field xpath="ApplicationID" />
</xsd:key>
<xsd:keyref name="bsApplicationsbsReleases" refer="ApplicationDataSetKey1">
   <xsd:selector xpath=".//bsReleases" />
   <xsd:field xpath="ApplicationID" />
</xsd:keyref>
   </xsd:element>
</xsd:schema>
```

Logging a New Issue

The interface of the BugScope.NET client is structured pretty uniformly. In order to create any new item, you must first navigate to the editor/details screen of that item's parent (if there is one). So, to create a new issue, you must navigate to the release on which the issue is to be logged. You do this by double-clicking the release name in the product tree.

Underneath the `DataGrid` containing the current list of Issues logged against the current release there is a button labeled **New Issue**. Clicking that button invokes the following event handler. Pay close attention to the code that sets the `DataSource` of the ComboBoxes and modifies the `DataBindings` property of the priority label. Allowing free binding of controls to DataSets allows you to bind to XML created on the fly, XML retrieved from a file or from SQL or from data retrieved using a `DataAdapter`.

```
private void btnNew_Click(object sender, System.EventArgs e)
{
    frmIssue oIssueForm = new frmIssue();
    int NewIssueID;

    // Its now extremely easy to grab a dataset from anywhere (memory,
    // xml, Sql, etc) and just map it to any kind of list control. Then
    // simply define the field to be used to display in the list and you're
    // done. No more need to maintain arrays or dictionaries of list keys.
    bsManager.UserDataSet uDS = MainForm.myClient.GetUsers();
    oIssueForm.cbAssignedTo.DataSource = uDS.bsUsers;
    oIssueForm.cbAssignedTo.DisplayMember = "UserName";

    bsManager.IssueStatusDataSet isDS =
            MainForm.myClient.GetIssueStatusList();
    oIssueForm.cbStatus.DataSource = isDS.bsIssueStatus;
    oIssueForm.cbStatus.DisplayMember = "Description";

    bsManager.IssueTypeDataSet itDS = MainForm.myClient.GetIssueTypes();
    oIssueForm.cbIssueType.DataSource = itDS.bsIssueType;
    oIssueForm.cbIssueType.DisplayMember = "Description";
```

```
// How cool is this?? All we have to do is bind the text of the label
// to the Priority field in the dataset. As the user manipulates the
// bound dropdown, they move the currentrow on the dataset,
// automatically changing the label text. We don't have to write a
// single line of the typical "OnClick" event handler we would've had
// to use in VB6. Since the DataSet is completely offline and
// disconnected, there's no round-trip performance penalty for binding
// to it.
oIssueForm.lblPriority.DataBindings.Add( new Binding("Text",
        isDS.bsIssueStatus, "Priority"));

oIssueForm.lblSubmittedBy.Text = MainForm.UserName;

oIssueForm.Text = "New Issue";
oIssueForm.ShowDialog();
if ( oIssueForm.DialogResult == DialogResult.OK )
{
    bsManager.GenericInsertStatus result;
    result = MainForm.myClient.CreateIssue( itDS.bsIssueType[_
            oIssueForm.cbIssueType.SelectedIndex ].IssueTypeID,_
            MainForm.UserID,_
            uDS.bsUsers[ oIssueForm.cbAssignedTo.SelectedIndex ].UserID,_
            ReleaseID, oIssueForm.txtDescription.Text,_
            isDS.bsIssueStatus[ oIssueForm.cbStatus.SelectedIndex_
            ].IssueStatusID, 0, out NewIssueID );

}

uDS.Dispose();
isDS.Dispose();
itDS.Dispose();
oIssueForm.Dispose();

// Good potential spot for calling function to reload form data
// from Web Service.
Close();
}
```

The above code actually performs quite a few extremely complex operations. However, thanks to the wonder of Strongly-Typed DataSets and Web Services, SOAP, and all the other acronyms, it becomes much less of a chore for the programmer. The code above actually calls three different DataSet-loading operations, all of which communicate with the Web Service.

Once the DataSet has been populated, it is then bound to a ComboBox control. The binding to the control is actually a very easy process. In class VB6 applications, if you had any more complex data beyond a simple integer you could load in the control's ItemData collection, you had to create a structure that would maintain data alongside the control, making sure the indexes matched in some way. Now all you have to do is bind the DataSet to the control, and you instantly have access to a wealth of information about the items in the ComboBox.

Once the form is populated with all of the selection lists it needs, we call ShowDialog, which runs the form modally. If the user clicked OK, then the Web Service is again invoked, this time to create a new Issue record in the database.

The Business Layer Create method on the Issue class.

```
public GenericInsertStatus Create()
{
    GenericInsertStatus result;
    BugScope.DAL.Transactional.Issue tIssue = new _
            BugScope.DAL.Transactional.Issue();

    result = tIssue.Create( _IssueType, _SubmitterID, _AssignedToID,
            _ReleaseID, _Description, _IssueStatusID, _ExternalSourceID,
            out _IssueID );

    tIssue = null;
    return result;
}
```

As you can see, it creates an instance of the Transactional Data-Tier `Issue` class and invokes the `Create` method with the private member variables that were set when the Web Service set this class' properties.

The Data Layer Create method on the Issue class.

```
[Transaction( TransactionOption.RequiresNew )]
[ConstructionEnabled( Default = "Data Source=localhost; Initial
Catalog=BugScope_DotNet; User id=sa; Password=;" )]
public sealed class Issue: DAO
{
    /// <summary>
    /// Creates a new Issue in the database based on the information
    /// provided in the argument list.
    /// </summary>
    /// <param name="IssueType">ID into the bsIssueType table</param>
    /// <param name="SubmitterID">User who submitted this Issue, a UserID
    /// in the bsUsers table</param>
    /// <param name="AssignedToID">User to whom this Issue is to be assigned.
    /// Also a USerID in the bsUsers table</param>
    /// <param name="ReleaseID">Release to which this new Issue belongs.
    /// A ReleaseID in the bsReleases table</param>
    /// <param name="Description">Description (short) of the new Issue.
    /// Further information should be recorded by adding activity</param>
    /// <param name="IssueStatusID">Status of the new issue. An IssueStatusID
    /// in the bsIssueStatus table</param>
    /// <param name="ExternalSourceID">0 if internal. >1 - an
    /// ExternalSourceID in the bsExternalSources table
    /// representing a third-party application that is creating this new
    /// issue. The BugScope client shouldn't allow creation of external
    /// issues.
    /// </param>
    /// <param name="IssueID">Upon successful completion, this is the
    /// IssueID of the new Issue</param>
    /// <returns>GenericInsertStatus, indicating success, failure, or
    /// PK/Unique violation</returns>
    public GenericInsertStatus Create( int IssueType, int SubmitterID,
            int AssignedToID, int ReleaseID, string Description,
            int IssueStatusID, int ExternalSourceID, out int IssueID )
    {
```

```
        GenericInsertStatus result;

        SqlParameter[] parameters =
        {
           new SqlParameter( "@IssueType", SqlDbType.Int, 4),
           new SqlParameter( "@SubmitterID", SqlDbType.Int, 4),
           new SqlParameter( "@AssignedToID", SqlDbType.Int, 4),
           new SqlParameter( "@ReleaseID", SqlDbType.Int, 4),
           new SqlParameter( "@Description", SqlDbType.VarChar, 255),
           new SqlParameter( "@IssueStatusID", SqlDbType.Int, 4),
           new SqlParameter( "@ExternalSourceID", SqlDbType.Int, 4),
           new SqlParameter( "@IssueID", SqlDbType.Int, 4)
        };

        parameters[0].Value = IssueType;
        parameters[1].Value = SubmitterID;
        parameters[2].Value = AssignedToID;
        parameters[3].Value = ReleaseID;
        parameters[4].Value = Description;
        parameters[5].Value = IssueStatusID;
        parameters[6].Value = ExternalSourceID;
        parameters[7].Direction = ParameterDirection.Output;

        try
        {
           RunSP( "sp_CreateIssue", parameters );
           IssueID = (int)parameters[6].Value;
           result = GenericInsertStatus.Success;
           ContextUtil.SetComplete();
        }
        catch (SqlException e)
        {
           IssueID = 0;
           ContextUtil.SetAbort();
           if ( (e.Errors[0].Number != 0xA43) && (e.Errors[0].Number
                 != 2601) )
           {
              throw e;
           }
           result = GenericInsertStatus.ItemAlreadyExists;
        }

        return result;
}
```

Viewing Issue Activity

As with the rest of the user interface, to get to a list interface, you need to first reach the details/editor form of the parent item. For Issue Activity, the parent is obviously an Issue. To get to the Issue Activity view, double-click a release. Then, select one of the Issue rows in the DataGrid and click Edit Issue. This will take you to the Issue Editor screen, which has a DataGrid displaying Issue Activity.

This is where things get *really* nice. Chapter 13 made a point of stressing that, wherever possible, you should avoid re-inventing the wheel. Microsoft's DataGrid control is an amazing tool. By simply binding it to a hierarchical DataSet, the grid actually places "+" tree-expansion symbols next to each row, allowing you to view that row's children. This can continue through more than one level of nesting as well. In addition, little navigation controls appear allowing you to hide/reveal the parent row, navigate up to the parent row, and scroll the columns left/right if there isn't enough room on the form for them all. All of that functionality is out of the box, and you don't have to write any code to enable it.

BugScope.NET client code to retrieve Issue details and bind the Activity list to the DataGrid.

```
private void btnEdit_Click(object sender, System.EventArgs e)
{
    int rowNumber;
    rowNumber = dgIssues.CurrentCell.RowNumber;
    frmIssueEdit oIssueForm = new frmIssueEdit();
    oIssueForm.Text = "Issue Editor - " +
            _issDS.bsIssues[rowNumber].Description;

    bsManager.UserDataSet uDS = MainForm.myClient.GetUsers();
    oIssueForm.cbAssignedTo.DataSource = uDS.bsUsers;
    oIssueForm.cbAssignedTo.DisplayMember = "UserName";

    bsManager.IssueStatusDataSet isDS =
            MainForm.myClient.GetIssueStatusList();
    oIssueForm.cbStatus.DataSource = isDS.bsIssueStatus;
    oIssueForm.cbStatus.DisplayMember = "Description";

    bsManager.IssueTypeDataSet itDS = MainForm.myClient.GetIssueTypes();
    oIssueForm.cbIssueType.DataSource = itDS.bsIssueType;
    oIssueForm.cbIssueType.DisplayMember = "Description";

    bsManager.IssueActivityDataSet iaDS = MainForm.myClient.
            GetIssueActivity( _issDS.bsIssues[rowNumber].IssueID );
    oIssueForm.dgActivity.DataSource = iaDS.bsIssueActivity;
    oIssueForm.dgActivity.Refresh();

    oIssueForm.ShowDialog();
    oIssueForm.Dispose();
}
```

The only thing new in this particular event handler is the use of the GetIssueActivity method. We'll show all of the steps involved in retrieving the Issue Activity list, including the method definition in the Web Service.

Web Service method GetIssueActivity

```
[WebMethod(true)]
public IssueActivityDataSet GetIssueActivity( int IssueID )
{
    IssueActivityDataSet issDS;
    BugScope.BLL.Issue oIssue = new BugScope.BLL.Issue( IssueID );

    issDS = oIssue.GetActivity();
    oIssue = null;
    return issDS;
}
```

This is a standard class method, except that it is sporting the WebMethod Attribute. This tells the compiler that the method will be exposed publicly for Web Service consumption. The true is a Boolean indicating that Session state should be supplied and preserved for the duration of the method call. This allows you to do things like enforce security checks based on the encryption code stored in the session by the Authenticator service. Since both services are on the same machine, in the same directory, they share the same state when Session state has been enabled, allowing the Authenticator to pass information along to the Manager.

BLL GetActivity method in the Issue class.

```
public IssueActivityDataSet GetActivity()
{
    IssueActivityDataSet issDS;
    BugScope.DAL.Issue oIssue = new BugScope.DAL.Issue();

    issDS = oIssue.GetActivity( _IssueID );

    oIssue.Dispose();
    return issDS;
}
```

DAL GetActivity method in the Issue class.

```
public IssueActivityDataSet GetActivity( int IssueID )
{
    SqlDataAdapter actDA = new SqlDataAdapter("SELECT IssueID, ActivityID,
        UserID, Notes, bsIssueActivity.ActivityTypeID, HoursLogged, "+
        "ActivityDate, ats.Description as ActivityTypeDescription FROM "+
        "bsIssueActivity INNER JOIN bsActivityTypes ats ON "+
        "bsIssueActivity.ActivityTypeID = ats.ActivityTypeID WHERE IssueID
        = " + IssueID + " ORDER BY ActivityDate DESC", Connection);
    SqlDataAdapter comDA = new SqlDataAdapter("SELECT CommentID, Notes,
        SubmitterID, CommentDate, ActivityID FROM bsActivityComments "+
        "ORDER BY CommentDate DESC", Connection);

    Connection.Open();
    IssueActivityDataSet issDS = new IssueActivityDataSet();
    actDA.Fill(issDS, "bsIssueActivity");
    comDA.Fill(issDS, "bsActivityComments");
    Connection.Close();
    actDA = null;
    comDA = null;

    return issDS;
}
```

Again, take special note of the fact that the child table, bsActivityComments is completely unfiltered. Assuming that the schema that generated the Strong DataSet IssueActivityDataSet contains a valid parent/child relationship on the ActivityID column, the DataSet will build the hierarchical structure internally.

By deliberately avoiding recoding the wheel, and allowing as many precoded tools to work for you instead of against you, you'll find that a lot of functionality that used to be extremely hard to implement is now simply automatic (such as implementing a clickable hierarchy in a DataGrid).

Logging New Issue Activity

Logging new Issue Activity against an existing Issue works much like any other data operation in BugScope.NET. Double-click the Release in question, find an Issue in the list, and click the Edit Issue button. This will bring up the Issue details screen, showing all of the activity for that Issue, and the New Activity button.

New Activity event handler in the BugScope.NET client application.

```
private void btnNewActivity_Click(object sender, System.EventArgs e)
{
    frmActivity oActivityForm = new frmActivity();
    int NewActivityID;
    bsManager.ActivityTypeDataSet atDS;

    atDS = MainForm.myClient.GetActivityTypes();
    oActivityForm.cbActivityType.DataSource = atDS.bsActivityTypes;
    oActivityForm.cbActivityType.DisplayMember = "Description";

    oActivityForm.ShowDialog();
    if ( oActivityForm.DialogResult == DialogResult.OK )
    {
        bsManager.GenericInsertStatus result;

        result = MainForm.myClient.LogActivity( _IssueID, MainForm.UserID,
            oActivityForm.txtNotes.Text, atDS.bsActivityTypes[
            oActivityForm.cbActivityType.SelectedIndex ].ActivityTypeID,
            Convert.ToInt32(oActivityForm.txtHours.Text), out NewActivityID );

        if (result == bsManager.GenericInsertStatus.ItemAlreadyExists )
        {
            MessageBox.Show(this, "That Activity already exists.");
        }

        Close();
    }
    oActivityForm.Dispose();
}
```

As you can see, the `ActivityForm` is instantiated and the Activity Type ComboBox is bound to the `ActivityTypeDataSet`. If the user clicks the **OK** button, the `DialogResult` indicates that, and the code then invokes the Web Service to perform the creation of the Issue Activity.

Web Service LogActivity method.

```
[WebMethod(true)]
public GenericInsertStatus LogActivity( int IssueID, int UserID, string Notes, int
ActivityTypeID,
    int HoursLogged, out int ActivityID )
{
    GenericInsertStatus result;
    BugScope.BLL.IssueActivity oActivity = new BugScope.BLL.IssueActivity();

    oActivity.IssueID = IssueID;
    oActivity.UserID = UserID;
    oActivity.Notes = Notes;
    oActivity.ActivityTypeID = ActivityTypeID;
    oActivity.HoursLogged = HoursLogged;

    result = oActivity.Create();
    ActivityID = oActivity.ActivityID;

    return result;
}
```

The above code creates an instance of a Business-Layer object, populates that object with the intended properties of the new Issue Activity, and then invokes the `Create()` method on that BLL object, shown hereafter:

```
public GenericInsertStatus Create()
{
    GenericInsertStatus result;
    TransDAL.IssueActivity tActivity = new TransDAL.IssueActivity();

    result = tActivity.Create( _IssueID, _UserID, _Notes, _ActivityTypeID,
            _HoursLogged, out _ActivityID );
    tActivity = null;
    return result;
}
```

The above code is not much more than a simple relay between the Web Service and the data layer. However, keeping the relay in place in the n-tier architecture allows the scalability of making it easy to plug in business rules and/or further data validation before being transferred to the COM+/Data Layer. Once at the Data Tier, the code looks as follows:

```
public GenericInsertStatus Create( int IssueID, int UserID, string Notes, int
ActivityTypeID, int HoursLogged, out int ActivityID)
{
    GenericInsertStatus result;

    SqlParameter[] parameters =
    {
        new SqlParameter( "@IssueID", SqlDbType.Int, 4),
        new SqlParameter( "@UserID", SqlDbType.Int, 4),
        new SqlParameter( "@Notes", SqlDbType.Text),
        new SqlParameter( "@ActivityTypeID", SqlDbType.Int, 4),
        new SqlParameter( "@HoursLogged", SqlDbType.Int, 4),
        new SqlParameter( "@ActivityID", SqlDbType.Int, 4)
    };

    parameters[0].Value = IssueID;
    parameters[1].Value = UserID;
    parameters[2].Value = Notes;
    parameters[3].Value = ActivityTypeID;
    parameters[4].Value = HoursLogged;
    parameters[5].Direction = ParameterDirection.Output;

    try
    {
        RunSP( "sp_CreateIssueActivity", parameters );
        result = GenericInsertStatus.Success;
        ActivityID = (int)parameters[5].Value;
        ContextUtil.SetComplete();
    }
    catch (SqlException e)
    {
        ActivityID = 0;
        ContextUtil.SetAbort();
        if ( (e.Errors[0].Number != 0xA43) && (e.Errors[0].Number != 0xA29) )
        {
            throw e;
        }
        result = GenericInsertStatus.ItemAlreadyExists;
    }

    return result;

}
```

The Data Tier method builds the parameter array to use in calling the stored procedure. The stored procedure is invoked and the new ID of the Activity just created is returned via an *out* parameter while an arbitrary error or status code is returned by the actual return value of the function. BugScope.NET doesn't actually make use of those, but the structure is there to add finer-grained results detail by having the stored procedures return meaningful result codes.

Creating a User

The last usage scenario we're going to look at for BugScope.NET is creating a User. This is done slightly different to the other scenarios in that to create a user you don't have to navigate to the parent of a User (since there is no logical parent). Instead, you simply click on the Administration menu and choose Users. A simple dialog will appear with a list of the users in the system with buttons to create, edit, and delete Users. There is nothing dynamic that needs to change on this form as a result of a change in the current row of the DataSet, so we didn't bother with any DataBinding. Instead, we simply populated the list items.

Event handler for the menu item click in the Windows client application.

```
private void menuItem10_Click(object sender, System.EventArgs e)
{
    frmUsers oUserForm = new frmUsers();
    bsManager.UserDataSet uDS;
    ListViewItem lvItem;

    uDS = myClient.GetUsers();
    oUserForm.MainForm = this;

    foreach (bsManager.UserDataSet.bsUsersRow userRow in uDS.bsUsers)
    {
        lvItem = new ListViewItem( userRow.UserName );
        lvItem.SubItems.Add( userRow.FirstName );
        lvItem.SubItems.Add( userRow.LastName );
        lvItem.SubItems.Add( userRow.JobTitle );

        oUserForm.lvUsers.Items.Add( lvItem );
    }

    oUserForm.ShowDialog();
    oUserForm.Dispose();
}
```

On the user form (frmUsers), there is a button labeled New User. The following code is the event handler for clicking that button.

```
private void btnNewUser_Click(object sender, System.EventArgs e)
{
    frmUser UserForm = new frmUser();
    UserForm.ShowDialog();
    if ( UserForm.DialogResult == DialogResult.OK )
    {
        MainForm.myClient.CreateUser( UserForm.txtUserName.Text,
            UserForm.txtPassword.Text, UserForm.txtFirstName.Text,
            UserForm.txtLastName.Text, UserForm.txtJobTitle.Text );
    }
    Close();
}
```

The code for the `CreateUser` method on the BugScope server is as follows:

```
[WebMethod(true)]
public int CreateUser( string UserName, string Password, string FirstName,
          string LastName, string JobTitle )
{
   int result;
   Credentials creds = new Credentials(UserName, Password);
   BugScope.BLL.User oUser = new BugScope.BLL.User();

   result = oUser.Create(creds, FirstName, LastName, JobTitle);

   return result;
}
```

There's something in the above code that we haven't seen yet in this application: we're actually passing an instance of a class into the Business Layer. In order for this to work, the class must be marked with the `Serializeable()` class attribute. Note that you can also mark a class as Serializable by adding the `ISerializable` interface to its inheritance list.

When this class is serialized, all of its public members are placed in an XML stream and then sent as XML to the receiving class. The framework will actually then "replay" the XML into a newly created instance of that class. When allowing your classes to be serialized, you need to take care into which members you make private. If a class depends on private members, it may not function properly or even cause an exception when used after being deserialized. The `Credentials` class is instantiated here because the constructor for the class automatically encrypts the password.

The Business Layer User class' Create method.

```
public int Create(Credentials creds, string FirstName, string LastName, string
JobTitle)
{
   DAL.Transactional.User oUser = new DAL.Transactional.User();
   _UserID = oUser.Create( creds, FirstName, LastName, JobTitle);
   _creds.UserName = creds.UserName;
   _creds.Password = creds.Password;
   _FirstName = FirstName;
   _LastName = LastName;
   _JobTitle = JobTitle;

   oUser = null;
   return _UserID;
}
```

As with many of our sample methods, the Business Layer simply transfers information from the Web Service to the Data Layer. Having intermediary methods like this is a great preparation for scaling the application and allowing enforcement of more strict business rules.

```
public int Create(Credentials creds, string FirstName, string LastName, string
JobTitle)
{
   int result;

   SqlParameter[] parameters =
   {
      new SqlParameter( "@UserName", SqlDbType.VarChar, 20),
```

```
        new SqlParameter( "@Password", SqlDbType.Binary, 20),
        new SqlParameter( "@FirstName", SqlDbType.VarChar, 40),
        new SqlParameter( "@LastName", SqlDbType.VarChar, 40),
        new SqlParameter( "@JobTitle", SqlDbType.VarChar, 255)
    };

    parameters[0].Value = creds.UserName;
    parameters[1].Value = creds.Password;
    parameters[2].Value = FirstName;
    parameters[3].Value = LastName;
    parameters[4].Value = JobTitle;

    try
    {
        result = RunSP( "sp_CreateUser", parameters );
        ContextUtil.SetComplete();
    }
    catch (SqlException e)
    {
        ContextUtil.SetAbort();
        throw e;
    }

    return result;
}
```

As you can see, it's just a simple matter of obtaining the encrypted binary password from the Credentials instance and supplying it to the stored procedure. From there, the password is stored in the database encrypted and should be safe from tampering and prying eyes with SQL privileges.

Extending the Sample Application

You've just experienced the basics of what it is like to go from a stand-alone, fat-client Windows application to a distributed, thin-client, Windows program that gets all of its information and does all of its processing through a Web Service.

The best way to firmly cement the learning of a new technology is to use it. It is always helpful and informative to look at how someone else implemented a solution that you were interested in. However, you learn far more and far more quickly when you are the one typing in the code. We've come up with a couple of exercise suggestions to help you learn and extend your knowledge of the .NET framework by extending the functionality of this sample application.

If the architecture of your original application was designed for scalability and reliability, then you should be able to extend the features and functionality of the application without doing any harm. However, it is very possible to cause problems by extending your application beyond the boundaries of its original design. Whenever you are extending an existing application, be aware of its original design and how well that design will support the new feature you're planning on creating.

Asynchronous Operation

One of the incredibly useful features of Web Services is that the client proxy classes that interact with them support asynchronous execution. Basically, you register a delegate method that will be invoked when the execution of a certain method on the Web Service has completed.

What this affords you is the ability to graphically indicate to your users that something is going on. One of my favorite implementations of asynchronous service operation was one that had an AVI file (much like the file copy or paper recycling AVIs that come with Windows) that played a spinning globe. Every time a request was made of the service, the globe started spinning. Once the service had completed the request, the globe stopped. An error in communication caused the globe to stop spinning with a red circle and slash through it.

Experiment with logging in asynchronously. Display the login dialog, get the user's information and then invoke the web service. However, instead of waiting for the service to come back, bring up the main form with all the controls disabled and a StatusBar message indicating communication. Once the verification of login comes back, either activate all the controls or bring up the dialog indicating a username/password failure.

As with all technologies, you should be aware of its limitations. Asynchronous execution should only be done to perform tasks in the background when your application's structure is designed to receive responses from function calls asynchronously, and where the user isn't expecting a response to their actions. Modifying the BugScope.NET application to log in asynchronously would require modifying the login form to display some kind of message that it was awaiting a reply from the service and not close until the response had been received. In a case like this, the overhead isn't worth it since the user is still sitting around, waiting for a response – which defeats the purpose of Asynchronous execution.

True Security

Make use of the currently unused Session state structure for storing the encrypted password. Make the method calls to the service actually check for valid credentials in the session before allowing access to the core functionality of the service. This would also be a good spot to experiment with throwing exceptions on the server and having them caught and handled gracefully on the client. For any of you used to MTS and n-Tier programming, the idea of propagating a true exception (especially one you derived on your own) across a wire in the form of a SOAP envelope is a dream come true. This is especially handy since you don't have to do anything other than wrap your Service call in a try/catch block in order to make use of that functionality.

Referential Integrity

Because this is a sample application not intended for commercial use, we cut a few corners. One of them was not enforcing referential integrity. If you try out the application, you'll find that you can delete ActivityTypes that are currently in use by Activities in the system.

One way to deal with this is to create another enumeration in the Common assembly, possibly `GenericDeleteStatus`. You could then have the stored procedures return appropriate codes indicating whether referential integrity would be broken by the delete, and if so, how, etc.

Most database administrators will tell you that you can have the database enforce such constraints. This is true, and the databases do a really good job of enforcing it, but users don't typically know how to interpret raw SQL error messages with strange numbers and codes and things. Either do pre-checks before deletion and prevent integrity failures that way, or trap the appropriate error numbers produced when SQL throws constraint restriction exceptions.

Form Handling Standards

As you went through the source code of the BugScope.NET application, you may have noticed that form handling is done in an inconsistent manner. This is actually done deliberately. It was done to demonstrate that even though we're using Windows Forms, a library provided by Microsoft, there's an enormous variety in the way in which we handle those forms.

There are a wide variety of opinions on the best way to handle forms. BugScope.NET shows two extremes, and we'll suggest that for your forms, you use something somewhere in the middle. One extreme sets all of the controls on a form to be public, where the calling form is completely responsible for populating and selecting all data on that form. The second extreme is where all of the data is private, special properties are provided to allow the calling/invoking form to access the member controls, and all of the data for that form is loaded and populated in an event or method on that form.

What I would like to suggest is a happy medium. There is a lot to be said for leaving the controls of a form private, and only allowing the setting of their values via properties. However, instead of having the calling form populate *all* of the data, I would suggest that the calling form only populate the data that it's directly concerned with editing.

For example, to edit an Issue in BugScope.NET, the invoking form retrieves a few DataSets from the Web Service, binds them to ComboBoxes, and then sets the specific index of the combo box. One thing that would be far easier and far more scalable would be to simply hand off a `bsIssuesRow` to the Issue Editor. If the row is populated with an existing row, the form is in edit mode and handles itself accordingly, whereas if the row is new, the form can also deal with that.

Essentially the bottom line is that even if you spend countless hours building code reuse into your server code and your Data-Tier classes, it won't be worth much if your client-side code is sloppy and redundant. The BugScope.NET code has some examples of good reuse, and some examples of bad reuse. Look at them closely and look at how your forms need to be generated, and hopefully you'll glean from the example an efficient, reusable and fast method of navigating through your application.

Offline Operation and Concurrency

Because BugScope.NET operates in an offline and disconnected model, there are some caveats that need to be brought up. Much of this can be handled by properly handling referential integrity. However, there might be cases in the application where the problem isn't referential integrity, but synchronization of activities between various disconnected users of the same service.

For example, if someone deletes an Issue from one client a split second (or longer depending on connection speed over the Internet and other factors) before you click the Edit button on that Issue, obviously your client (in its current form) is going to crash by attempting to edit a non-existent Issue. One way of handling this is to build into the system some more meaningful error enumerations, allowing your result codes to properly trap "missing" records so that the display can be updated and the user can be notified about the issue while the application synchronizes.

There are hundreds of other ways of dealing with this problem. The point here is not to tell you how to solve it, but hopefully this chapter has given you enough information so that you can develop your own solution. In any offline, quick-burst connection scenario where multiple users are working with an application offline, you need to make sure that nothing anyone does without knowledge of the other clients can cause any of the other clients to crash. It is a simple sentence but if implemented poorly can be a nightmare for ongoing application support.

External Issue Sources

Extend the current application to make good use of the `ExternalSourceID` field on the Issues. The Web Service and related data structures are all set up to allow for this expansion to take place.

ASP.NET

As an exercise for your ASP.NET skills, you could extend this application by creating a web-based front end. You could either create a very distributed system whereby the ASP.NET server contacted a remote server (our original BugServices Web Service) for all of its data, or use a Business Layer locally to manage its information.

Because the design of BugScope.NET favors strongly the separation of User Interface from the actual underlying code, you should find that adding an ASP.NET interface to the existing application will be relatively easy and quite enjoyable. The end result will be a widely distributed application that not only has a Windows interface, but a Web/browser interface as well.

Essentially, all you would need to do is create a new ASP.NET solution in VS.NET and add a reference to the BLL tier of the BugScope.NET application. In fact, in the samples, the web services are actually sitting in an ASP.NET application, so you could simply right-click the BugServices solution and add a new web page, which would immediately have access to the business tier of BugScope.NET.

For more information on creating ASP.NET web sites, pages, and how to utilize the features of ASP.NET to their fullest extent, you should consult the *Professional ASP.NET* book already available from Wrox Press.

Summary

Let's take a step back and look at what's been accomplished. Our fictitious sample company, UFixIT Software, started out with a standalone, fat-client Windows program written in Microsoft Visual Basic 6. It used a library DLL to house a collection of supporting classes to manage all of the interaction between the interface and the back-end database.

That was actually a fairly good architecture, and the use of XML to pass information from the support classes to the user interface was an excellent idea that would have held the application together for some time.

What we've discovered is that by embracing the new features of the .NET framework, rather than trying a simple port "just to get it to compile", we've achieved great things. The simple, standalone application is now an application that supports being run by hundreds of people from hundreds of locations throughout the world, behind firewalls and private networks and more. In addition, it is poised to have an enhanced Web front-end placed on it, turning it into an incredibly useful and versatile tool.

In about the same amount of time as it took to design and develop the limited, small and disconnected VB6 application, we created a far-reaching, connected, Internet-enabled enterprise-class application for the .NET framework. That alone should be enough to make people sit up and take notice.

Again, the absolute bottom line is that you should never think about simply migrating to .NET. Instead, you should be thinking about how your application can *embrace* it, and upgrade and *expand* its functionality using the myriad of new features and tools available with .NET. If the final result of your migration has only the same functionality of your original application, you have truly missed the entire purpose and scope of the .NET framework.

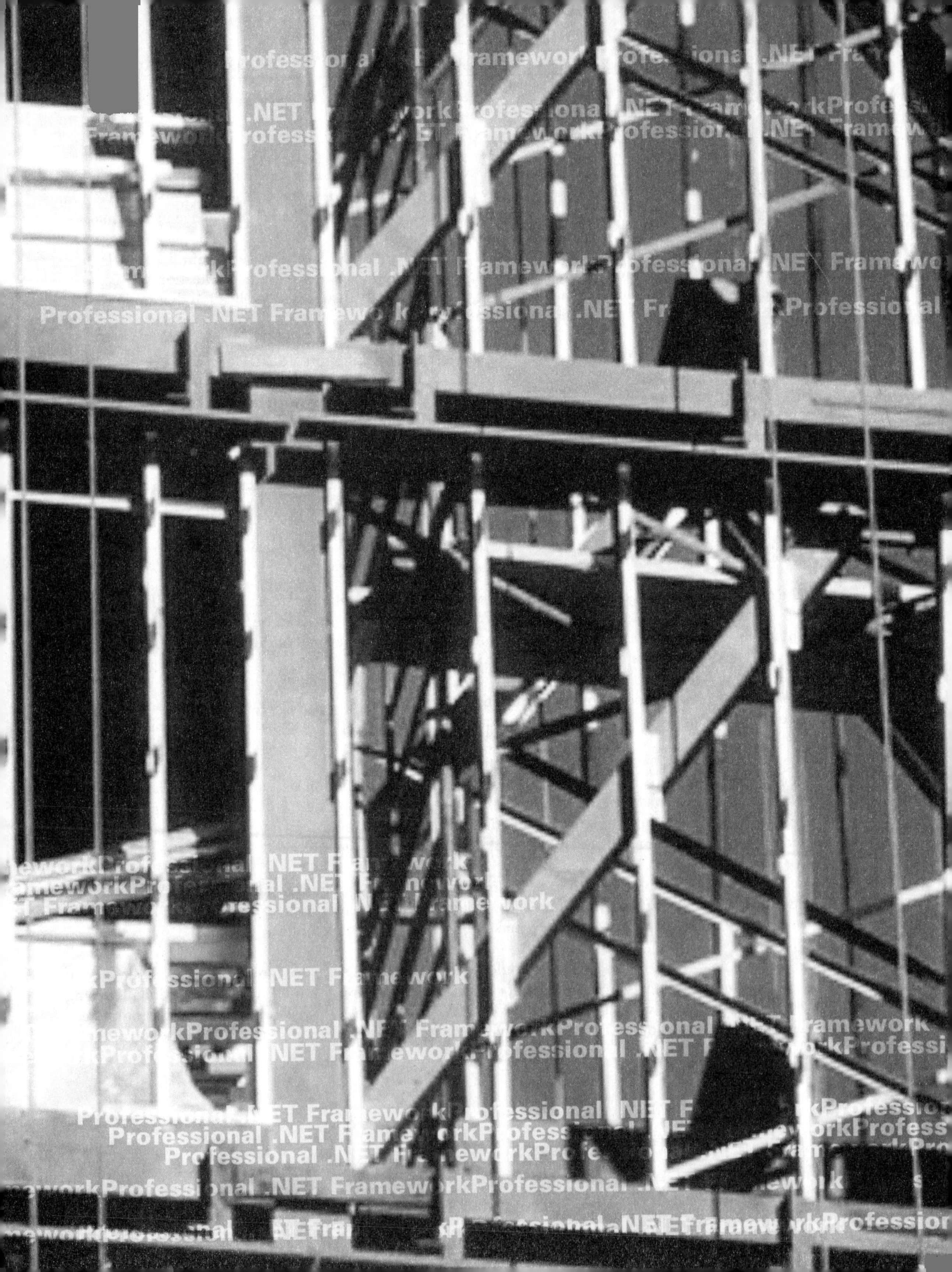
Professional .NET Framework

15

Building a Web Application that Consumes the Functionality of a Web Service

In Chapter 10, we discussed the powerful features offered by the XML-based web services in the .NET framework and we were also provided with an overview of the web services. In this case study, we are going to implement our knowledge of web services and see for ourselves how this revolutionary concept can be used to engineer practical, extensible, maintainable, flexible, and easy-to-implement solutions for many real world problems. Let us consider the following business problems and see how web services can address them.

❑ Many companies have already made significant investments in automating their business processes on back-end systems. One of the most important things that these companies might want to pursue is making these processes available to the business partners, vendors, and customers on the Internet. Web services can be easily used to make these processes available on the Internet with minimal changes to the existing infrastructure.

❑ In this fast growing world of e-commerce and web application development, one of the big challenges faced by Internet developers has been not only to create scalable and extensible web sites, but also to create sites that are intelligent and smart enough to accomplish the requirements that arise from the amount of 'Business To Business' communication that occurs on the Internet these days. Web services can be a perfect fit in that environment due to its platform-independent nature and ease of consumption. For example, consider the B2B scenario where suppliers and customers want to exchange information through the Internet. To address this problem, we can create a routing service that serves as the point of integration between customers and suppliers. First, the seller takes an order from a customer. Then the seller sends the order to the supplier, who finally sends it to the customer. The seller doesn't want to handle the communication, routing, and error handling between each of the suppliers. Instead, they send the order to the integration Service that communicates with each supplier and performs the following: tracking failure to respond, delivering notifications when problems arise, and performing necessary document translations. As we can see, a system of this kind developed using web services delivers value by providing custom connectivity, store and forward, and custom transformations.

Introduction to the Case Study

The great thing about the Internet is that it is a wide-open network where anyone can connect to any Internet site, anywhere, at any time, to get any information. However, today's web sites provide only limited behavior in the sense that they provide services only to the end users. With web services, we can also provide services to other applications. For example, web services can be used to enable peer-to-peer scenarios such as the one provided by Napster. In this case study, we will see how web services can be employed to make these Internet sites talk to each other and exchange information in a seamless and integrated way.

Definition of our Business Problem

This case study is based on a web site called ShoppingLegend.com, which provides a one-stop shop for consumers that want to find out information, such as the products that are on sale, availability of products in different stores, or comparison of the price of the product across different stores. It also provides consumers with the product attributes and reviews and then highlights stores that feature the item within a specified mileage radius. ShoppingLegend.com also supplies the consumers with access to the online guide that provides the best local values and product information.

Currently, ShoppingLegend.com gets all the required information from its content provider partners in the form of an XML feed. It accomplishes this by making a remote request to the ASP file, or any other server-side scripting file, receiving the response in the form of XML and converting the response back to the form that is usable in the site. For example, we could implement a simple ASP file that can accept the required parameters in the form of a querystring or form values. We can use these parameters to query a database, or any other storage mechanism, and generate a XML document, which is returned to the requestor. As we can clearly see, this requires a lot of plumbing and infrastructure code for achieving this functionality. And also due to the tightly-coupled nature of the design, even minor changes in the logic that is used to generate the XML document might end up breaking the client-side implementation of the application. It is needless to mention that maintaining this kind of application is a nightmare due to the complexity of the code.

Proposed Solution

The above problem can easily be addressed by implementing web services in the content provider site. This solution requires that the content provider channels expose their data through the use of web services. Our ShoppingLegend.com application can consume this data in an easier, effective, and transparent fashion using protocols such as XML, HTTP and SOAP.

Goals of Application Design

The architecture of the application we propose to implement is shown in the following diagram.

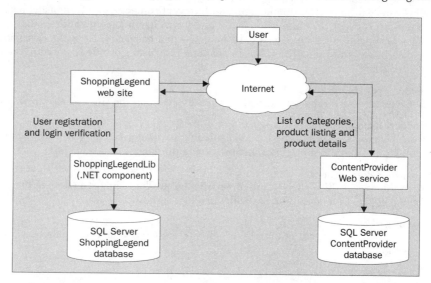

When the user comes to the site and performs operations such as registration and login verification, the ShoppingLegend web application invokes the methods of the .NET component ShoppingLegendLib to carry out those tasks.

The ShoppingLegend web application connects to the remote web service across the Internet to fetch information whenever the user performs any of the following actions:

❏   Browsing the categories page

❏   Browsing the product listing page

❏   Navigating to the product details page

Business Processes

Clearly the scope of the case study is to show how to use web services in implementing solutions for a web application. Since it is not our intention to learn e-commerce development through this case study, we will restrict ourselves to discussing only the following processes of the solution:

❏   **Login Process**
Registered users are given the option to log in to our site and retrieve their personal profile. The login system allows the users to identify themselves to the system. The user must provide an existing user id and a valid password to be allowed to enter the system. Once the user is logged in to the system, he can proceed to the site and look up information about all products on the site.

❑ **New user Registration process**
New users are given the opportunity to become members of the site by filling out our online form and selecting their preferences. In this step, the user is asked to create a unique user id, which is used to identify the user in the system. The user is also required to choose a password of his choice to protect his membership and prevent someone else from using his account without his consent. The user also can fill out details like name and address that can be used by the system administrator to contact the user when necessary. After the user has entered all the details, and once the data has been validated, the user's profile is stored in the database for later retrieval.

❑ **Catalog browsing process**
Users can browse through the list of products available in the site and also their prices.

❑ **Products listing process**
In this process, the list of products available in a particular category is shown with a hyperlink that takes the users to more information about a product.

❑ **Products details process**
When the user clicks the hyperlink of a particular product, they are taken to the page where detailed explanation about the particular product is shown.

❑ **Logout process**
Allows the user to log out of the site, which internally nulls the cookie, thereby terminating the session.

Implementation

Now that we have understood the business processes involved, let us construct the building blocks that are required for implementing this solution. We will split our discussion of the remaining part of the case study into five parts.

❑ Database Design

❑ Implementation of the `ContentProvider` web service

❑ Implementation of the `Proxy` class library for accessing the web service

❑ Implementation of the .NET component `ShoppingLegendLib`

❑ Implementation of the `ShoppingLegend` web application

We will start our discussion of the implementation by looking at the database design that is required to support our application.

Database Design

As we can see from the architecture of our system, two data stores are used to store and provide information to our application. Since the main aim of the case study is to lay emphasis on .NET web application development using web services, the database we are going to use will have the minimum number of tables required to implement this solution.

Firstly, we will consider the design of the ShoppingLegend database.

ShoppingLegend Database Design

This database is basically used to store and retrieve information about the list of users registered in our site.

Name	DataType	Length	AllowNull	Description
UserID	varchar	20	No	Represents the user id
Password	char	10	No	Indicates the password
Name	varchar	128	Yes	Name of the user
Address	varchar	128	Yes	Address of the user
City	varchar	50	Yes	City of the user
State	char	2	Yes	State of the user
Zip	char	9	Yes	Zip code of the user's area

The following stored procedures are used in our application.

The `UserLogIn` stored procedure returns 1 if a record with the supplied username and password is found in the `Users` table, otherwise it returns –1. It uses output parameters to pass the results back to the caller.

```
CREATE Procedure UserLogin
    (
        @UserID varchar(20),
        @Password varchar(10),
        @RetValue int OUTPUT
    )
As
    SELECT * FROM Users WHERE UserID = @UserID AND Password = @Password
    IF @@Rowcount < 1
        SELECT @RetValue = -1
    ELSE
        SELECT @RetValue = 1
```

As the name suggests, the `InsertUser` procedure inserts a record into the `Users` table based on the supplied parameters.

```
CREATE Procedure InsertUser
(
    @UserID char(20),
    @Password char(10),
    @Name varchar(128),
    @Address varchar(128),
    @City varchar(50),
    @State char(2),
    @Zip char(9))
AS

    Insert into Users(UserID,Password,Name,Address,City,State,Zip)
    Values(@UserID,@Password,@Name,@Address,@City,@State,@Zip)

GO
```

ContentProvider Database Design

This consists of the `Categories` and `Products` tables. The entity relationship diagram for `ContentProvider` is as follows:

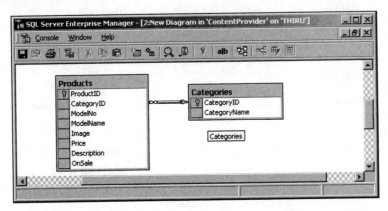

The above diagram shows that the `ProductID` column acts as the primary key for the `Products` table and the `CategoryID` column is used as the primary key for the `Categories` table. It also shows that the referential integrity is enforced between the `Products` and `Categories` tables through the use of the `CategoryID` column.

The `Categories` table contains the following:

Name	DataType	Length	AllowNull	Description
CategoryID	int	4	No	Indicates the category id
CategoryName	varchar	50	No	Represents the category name

The table design for the `Products` table is:

Name	DataType	Length	AllowNull	Description
ProductID	int	4	No	Represents the product id
CategoryID	int	4	No	Indicates the category id
ModelNo	varchar	50	Yes	Model number of the product
ModelName	varchar	50	Yes	Model name of the product
Image	varchar	50	Yes	Image name of the product
Price	money	8	No	Price of the product
Description	varchar	2000	Yes	Description of the product
OnSale	char	1	No	Specifies whether the product is on sale

Let us consider the stored procedures in the `ContentProvider` database that we will be using in our application. The stored procedure `CategoriesGet` returns all the categories present in the `Categories` table.

```
CREATE Procedure CategoriesGet
As
    SELECT *  FROM Categories
GO
```

The `ProductsGet` stored procedure is used to return all the products that belong to a particular category.

```
CREATE Procedure ProductsGet

    (
        @CategoryID int
    )
As
    SELECT *  FROM Products
    WHERE CategoryID = @CategoryID
GO
```

As the name suggests, the `ProductDetailsGet` procedure returns the details of a particular product based on the passed `productid`.

```
CREATE Procedure ProductDetailsGet

    (
        @ProductID int
    )
As
    SELECT *  FROM Products
    WHERE ProductID = @ProductID
GO
```

Implementation of Web Service

In this section, we will create a web service called `ContentProviderService`, which contains methods that are used to expose information to its consumers. Through its methods, the web service provides information such as a list of product categories available in the site, a list of products in a particular category, and the details of a specific product in the form of a dataset.

Even though we are going to use Visual Studio.NET to develop the web service, it is also important to realize that the following web service can also be developed using the command line compilers that are supplied with the Microsoft.NET SDK, or simple text editors like Notepad.

Now let us get started by creating the web service project using Visual Studio.NET. We create the web service by going through the following steps.

- ❏ In the **New Project** dialog box, we select **Visual Basic Projects** from the left-hand side, selecting **ASP.NET Web Service** from the right side.

- ❏ We will name this web service project **ContentProviderService**.

- ❏ We will also change the name of the default class from **service1** to **ProductService**.

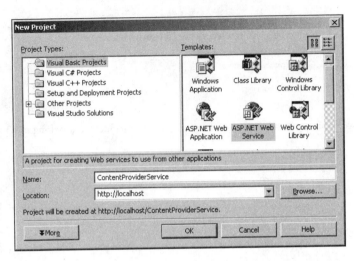

After the project is created, we import the `System.Data.SqlClient` namespace into our project by selecting **Project | Properties** and adding the namespace in the Imports tab of the property page dialog box. This is done to have access to a set of high-performance classes contained in the `System.Data.SqlClient` namespace that expose functionality to access the SQL Server database in the managed environment.

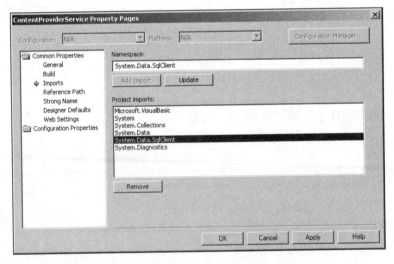

Let us look at the code that is required for implementing the web service. We will start our explanation by examining the `ProductDetails` class, which is used to represent a single instance of a product in our site. As we can see from the following, the `ProductDetails` class contains protected member variables that are used to hold information about a product. We will expose these member variables in the form of properties, since it allows us to exercise a greater degree of control over the values that can be assigned to the member variables. It also permits us to execute a set of statements when values are assigned to the member variables.

```
Public Class ProductDetails
    Protected m_ProductID As Integer
    Protected m_CategoryID As Integer
```

```vb
Protected m_ModelNo As String
Protected m_ModelName As String
Protected m_Image As String
Protected m_Price As String
Protected m_Description As String

Public Property ProductID()
    Get
        Return m_ProductID
    End Get
    Set(ByVal Value)
        m_ProductID = Value
    End Set
End Property

Public Property CategoryID()
    Get
        Return m_CategoryID
    End Get
    Set(ByVal Value)
        m_CategoryID = Value
    End Set
End Property

Public Property ModelNo()
    Get
        Return m_ModelNo
    End Get
    Set(ByVal Value)
        m_ModelNo = Value
    End Set
End Property

Public Property ModelName()
    Get
        Return m_ModelName
    End Get
    Set(ByVal Value)
        m_ModelName = Value
    End Set
End Property

Public Property Image()
    Get
        Return m_Image
    End Get
    Set(ByVal Value)
        m_Image = Value
    End Set
End Property

Public Property Price()
    Get
        Return m_Price
    End Get
```

```
        Set(ByVal Value)
            m_Price = Value
        End Set
    End Property

    Public Property Description()
        Get
            Return m_Description
        End Get
        Set(ByVal Value)
            m_Description = Value
        End Set
    End Property
End Class
```

How to Return a DataSet from a Web Service Method

In this section, we will list the procedures to be followed to return a dataset from a web service, and in the later part of this case study we will see how a client application can consume this returned dataset in a seamless fashion. When we create an ASP.NET web service project using Visual Studio.NET, by default it creates a class named Service1. We rename this class to ProductService to reflect on the functionalities that we are trying to achieve using this.

As you can see from the following declaration, the ProductService class is derived from the class System.Web.Services.WebService. When we inherit a class from the WebService class, our class will have access to the common ASP.NET objects such as Application, Session, User and Context. Application and Session objects can be used to store and retrieve state across the lifetime of the web application or a particular session. The User property gives us information about the identity of the caller, if authentication is turned on for the web service.

```
Public Class ProductService
    Inherits System.Web.Services.WebService

<WebMethod(Description:="The ProductDetailsGetDataSet method allows a remote
client to retrieve the details of a product based on the product id in the form of
a Dataset.", EnableSession:=False)>

Public Function ProductDetailsGetDataSet(ByVal iProductID As Integer)_
        As DataSet

    Dim oDataSet As DataSet
    Dim oSQLConnection As SqlConnection
    Dim oSQLCommand As SqlDataAdapter

    Try
        oSQLConnection = New SqlConnection(ConfigurationSettings._
                    AppSettings("connectionString"))
        oSQLCommand = New SqlDataAdapter("ProductDetailsGet",_
                    oSQLConnection)
        oSQLCommand.SelectCommand.CommandType = CommandType.StoredProcedure
        oSQLCommand.SelectCommand.Parameters.Add(New _
                    SqlParameter("@ProductID", SqlDbType.Int))
        oSQLCommand.SelectCommand.Parameters("@ProductID").Value =_
                    iProductID
```

```
            oDataSet = New DataSet()
            oSQLCommand.Fill(oDataSet, "Products")
            Return oDataSet

        Catch ex As Exception
            Throw ex

        Finally
            'Close the connection if it is still open
            If oSQLConnection.State = ConnectionState.Open Then
                oSQLConnection.Close()
            End If
        End Try

    End Function
```

As we can see, the `ProductDetailsGetDataSet` method returns a dataset to the caller of the web service. Returning a dataset from a web service is an extremely powerful feature of web services, as datasets can be used to store complex information and relationships in an intelligent XML-based schema. Also by exposing datasets through a web service, we can limit the number of database connections in the database server.

In the code shown below, the attribute `WebMethod` indicates that the method is to be exposed as a web-callable method and when it is deployed, the ASP.NET runtime provides all the plumbing required to make this method callable across the Internet using protocols like XML and SOAP. We also specify a brief description of the functionality of our web method by using the named parameter `Description`. If we want to store the session state in the `HttpSessionState` object, we need to set the `EnableSession` property to `True`. In our case, since we do not want to store session state for our method, we set it to `False`. Setting `EnableSession` to `False` allows us to indicate to the ASP.NET runtime that we do not want the session-specific data to be stored, thereby eliminating the performance overheads that may be caused due to the amount of resources required for storing the session state. This reduction in overhead helps in improving the performance of the application.

```
<WebMethod(Description:="The ProductDetailsGetDataSet method allows a remote
client to retrieve the details of a product based on the product id in the form of
a Dataset.", EnableSession:=False)>
```

As the name of the method suggests, it returns a `DataSet` as the return value of the method. This method takes a `ProductID` as an argument and returns the details of that product in the form of a dataset.

```
Public Function ProductDetailsGetDataSet(ByVal iProductID As Integer)_
        As DataSet
```

Next we declare objects that are required for connecting to the database, executing a stored procedure command against the database, and returning the result set in the form of a dataset.

```
Dim oDataSet As DataSet
Dim oSQLConnection As SqlConnection
Dim oSQLCommand As SqlDataAdapter
```

Then we enclose all the executable statements in a `try...catch` block to handle any errors that may occur during the execution of the following statements.

In this line, we create an instance of the `SqlConnection` object, passing to it the connection string that is required for establishing a connection to the database.

```
oSQLConnection = New SqlConnection(ConfigurationSettings._
            AppSettings("connectionString"))
```

In the above line, we get the connection string from the `<appsettings>` section of the `web.config` file, using the `AppSettings` property of the `ConfigurationSettings` class. The connection string is defined as follows in the `web.config` file:

```
<appSettings>
    <add key="connectionString" value="server=localhost;uid=sa;_
            pwd=;database=ContentProvider" />
</appSettings>
```

The `web.config` file is used to store all the configuration information for an ASP.NET application and it essentially replaces the IIS Metabase that was used to store the configuration settings for a traditional ASP application. `Web.config` is located in the root directory of the web application. This file is made up of nested hierarchial XML tags that are utilized to store information, such as type of authentication, debugging settings, handling of sessions, and many more. And also, as we can see from the above, it can be used as a placeholder to store settings that are specific to the application. The practice of storing configuration settings in the `web.config` file permits administrators to change the configuration settings without having to touch the application code.

Next, we create an instance of the `SqlDataAdapter` class, passing to its constructor the name of the stored procedure we want to execute and the `Sqlconnection` object that we created in the previous step.

```
oSQLCommand = New SqlDataAdapter("ProductDetailsGet",_
            oSQLConnection)
```

Since stored procedures are compiled and cached for subsequent executions, we get a tremendous performance boost by implementing stored procedures in our application. Hence it is needless to mention that using stored procedures is the recommended choice for building high-performance and scalable web applications.

We then set the `SelectCommand` property to an appropriate value to indicate that we want to execute a stored procedure.

```
oSQLCommand.SelectCommand.CommandType = CommandType.StoredProcedure
```

Once we set the `CommandType` to `StoredProcedure`, we can then add parameters to the command object by invoking the `Add` method of the `Parameters` collection of the `SelectCommand` property.

```
oSQLCommand.SelectCommand.Parameters.Add(New _
            SqlParameter("@ProductID", SqlDbType.Int))
oSQLCommand.SelectCommand.Parameters("@ProductID").Value =_
            iProductID
```

Now we use the `Fill` method to retrieve the data from the data source by executing the previously assigned stored procedure against the data source.

```
oSQLCommand.Fill(oDataSet, "Products")
```

Finally we return the dataset to the caller of the method using the keyword `return`.

```
Return oDataSet
```

If any error occurs during the execution of the above statements, control will be automatically transferred to the `catch` block, where the error is raised back to the clients.

```
Catch ex As Exception
    Throw ex
```

The statements in the `Finally` block are executed regardless of whether the statements in the `try` block are executed successfully or not. Here we inspect the `State` property to verify whether the connection is still open. If the connection is still open, we close it by calling the `Close` method of the `Connection` object.

```
Finally
    'Close the connection if it is still open
    If oSQLConnection.State = ConnectionState.Open Then
        oSQLConnection.Close()
    End If
End Try
End Function
```

How to Return a User-Defined Object from the Web Service

As the name suggests, the method `ProductDetailsGetObject` returns a user-defined object called `ProductDetails` to the caller of the method. This method is similar to the above method, except that it encapsulates the return value in the form of a `ProductDetails` object, which allows clients to consume the web service in a truly object-oriented fashion. The code for the `ProductDetailsGetObject` is as follows:

```
<WebMethod(Description:="The ProductDetailsGetObject method allows a remote client
to retrieve the details of a product based on the product id in the form of a
ProductDetails object.", EnableSession:=False)>

Public Function ProductDetailsGetObject(ByVal iProductID As Integer)_
        As ProductDetails
    Dim oDataSet As DataSet
    Dim oSQLConnection As SqlConnection
    Dim oSQLCommand As SqlDataAdapter
    Dim dtProdTable As DataTable
    Dim oProdDetails As ProductDetails

    Try
        oProdDetails = New ProductDetails()
        oSQLConnection = New SqlConnection(ConfigurationSettings._
            AppSettings("connectionString"))
```

```
            oSQLCommand = New SqlDataAdapter("ProductDetailsGet", oSQLConnection)
            oSQLCommand.SelectCommand.CommandType = CommandType.StoredProcedure
            oSQLCommand.SelectCommand.Parameters.Add(New_
                SqlParameter("@ProductID", SqlDbType.Int))
            oSQLCommand.SelectCommand.Parameters("@ProductID").Value = iProductID
            oDataSet = New DataSet()
            oSQLCommand.Fill(oDataSet, "Products")
            'Assign the table to the DataTable object variable
            dtProdTable = oDataSet.Tables("Products")
            'Assign the column values to the ProdDetails object
            oProdDetails.ProductID = CType((dtProdTable.Rows.Item(0))_
                ("ProductID").ToString, Integer)
            oProdDetails.CategoryID = CType((dtProdTable.Rows.Item(0))_
                ("CategoryID").ToString, Integer)
            oProdDetails.ModelNo = (dtProdTable.Rows.Item(0))("ModelNo").ToString
            oProdDetails.ModelName = (dtProdTable.Rows.Item(0))_
                ("ModelName").ToString
            oProdDetails.Image = (dtProdTable.Rows.Item(0))("Image").ToString
            oProdDetails.Price = (dtProdTable.Rows.Item(0))("Price").ToString
            oProdDetails.Description = (dtProdTable.Rows.Item(0))_
                ("Description").ToString
            Return oProdDetails

        Catch ex As Exception
            Throw ex

        Finally
            'Close the connection if it is still open
            If oSQLConnection.State = ConnectionState.Open Then
                oSQLConnection.Close()
            End If
        End Try
    End Function
```

Similar to the previous method, this method also indicates that it can be called across the Internet by
specifying the attribute WebMethod.

```
<WebMethod(Description:="The ProductDetailsGetObject method allows a remote client
to retrieve the details of a product based on the product id in the form of a
ProductDetails object.", EnableSession:=False)>
```

As we can see from the declaration, the scope of the method is public and the return value of the method is a
ProductDetails object that represents the details of a particular product.

```
Public Function ProductDetailsGetObject(ByVal iProductID As Integer)_
        As ProductDetails
```

Here, we declare the objects that are required for retrieving details from the data store.

```
Dim oDataSet As DataSet
Dim oSQLConnection As SqlConnection
Dim oSQLCommand As SqlDataAdapter
Dim dtProdTable As DataTable
Dim oProdDetails As ProductDetails

Try
```

The following lines of code are used to perform operations such as setting the command type, adding parameters to the command object, and finally filling the dataset with data from the data source.

```
oProdDetails = New ProductDetails()
oSQLConnection = New SqlConnection(ConfigurationSettings._
      AppSettings("connectionString"))
oSQLCommand = New SqlDataAdapter("ProductDetailsGet", oSQLConnection)
oSQLCommand.SelectCommand.CommandType = CommandType.StoredProcedure
oSQLCommand.SelectCommand.Parameters.Add(New_
      SqlParameter("@ProductID", SqlDbType.Int))
oSQLCommand.SelectCommand.Parameters("@ProductID").Value = iProductID
oDataSet = New DataSet()
oSQLCommand.Fill(oDataSet, "Products")
'Assign the table to the DataTable object variable
```

After we fill the dataset with the data from the data store, we use the `Tables` collection property to get the `Products` table from the dataset in the form of a `DataTable` object. The `DataTable` object represents an instance of a table that is present in memory.

```
dtProdTable = oDataSet.Tables("Products")
```

Once we get the `DataTable` object, we can then loop through all the columns in the first row of the `DataTable` object to get the details of the product.

```
'Assign the column values to the ProdDetails object
oProdDetails.ProductID = CType((dtProdTable.Rows.Item(0))_
      ("ProductID").ToString, Integer)
oProdDetails.CategoryID = CType((dtProdTable.Rows.Item(0))_
      ("CategoryID").ToString, Integer)
oProdDetails.ModelNo = (dtProdTable.Rows.Item(0))("ModelNo").ToString
oProdDetails.ModelName = (dtProdTable.Rows.Item(0))_
      ("ModelName").ToString
oProdDetails.Image = (dtProdTable.Rows.Item(0))("Image").ToString
oProdDetails.Price = (dtProdTable.Rows.Item(0))("Price").ToString
oProdDetails.Description = (dtProdTable.Rows.Item(0))_
      ("Description").ToString
```

Finally we return the Product Details object to the caller of this web service.

```
Return oProdDetails
```

As before, we handle the errors by implementing a `Catch` block and we perform clean-up activities in the `Finally` block.

```
Catch ex As Exception
   Throw ex

Finally
   'Close the connection if it is still open
   If oSQLConnection.State = ConnectionState.Open Then
      oSQLConnection.Close()
   End If
End Try
End Function
```

ProductsGet Method

In this method, we return the list of products that are present in a particular category. It takes a `CategoryID` as an argument and the return value of the method is `Dataset`. This method is also similar to the `ProductDetailsGetDataSet` method, except for the change in the arguments and the name of the stored procedure to be executed.

```
<WebMethod(Description:="The ProductsGet method allows a remote client to retrieve
all the products based on the category id.", EnableSession:=False)>

Public Function ProductsGet(ByVal iCategoryID As Integer) As DataSet
    Dim oDataSet As DataSet
    Dim oSQLConnection As SqlConnection
    Dim oSQLCommand As SqlDataAdapter

    Try
        oSQLConnection = New SqlConnection(ConfigurationSettings._
            AppSettings("connectionString"))
        oSQLCommand = New SqlDataAdapter("ProductsGet", oSQLConnection)
        oSQLCommand.SelectCommand.CommandType = CommandType.StoredProcedure
        oSQLCommand.SelectCommand.Parameters.Add(New _
            SqlParameter("@CategoryID", SqlDbType.Int))
        oSQLCommand.SelectCommand.Parameters("@CategoryID").Value = _
            iCategoryID
        oDataSet = New DataSet()
        oSQLCommand.Fill(oDataSet, "Products")
        Return oDataSet

    Catch ex As Exception
        Throw ex

    Finally
        'Close the connection if it is still open
        If oSQLConnection.State = ConnectionState.Open Then
            oSQLConnection.Close()
        End If
    End Try
End Function
```

CategoriesGet Method

The `CategoriesGet` method returns the list of categories available in the `ContentProvider` database. The return value of this method is `Dataset`. This method executes a stored procedure called `CategoriesGet` and returns the list of all categories present in the `ContentProvider` database.

```
<WebMethod(Description:="The CategoriesGet method allows a remote client to
retrieve all the categories available in the site.", EnableSession:=False)>

Public Function CategoriesGet() As DataSet
    Dim oDataSet As DataSet
    Dim oSQLConnection As SqlConnection
    Dim oSQLCommand As SqlDataAdapter

    Try
```

```
          oSQLConnection = New SqlConnection(ConfigurationSettings._
              AppSettings("connectionString"))
          oSQLCommand = New SqlDataAdapter("CategoriesGet", oSQLConnection)
          'Set the CommandType to indicate that we want to execute a
          'stored procedure
          oSQLCommand.SelectCommand.CommandType = CommandType.StoredProcedure
          oDataSet = New DataSet()
          oSQLCommand.Fill(oDataSet, "Categories")
          'Return the DataSet to the caller of the web service
          Return oDataSet

      Catch ex As Exception
          Throw ex

      Finally
          'Close the connection if it is still open
          If oSQLConnection.State = ConnectionState.Open Then
              oSQLConnection.Close()
          End If
      End Try
  End Function
```

Implementation of the Proxy class

The important step in consuming web services is creating a proxy class that mediates between the client and the actual web service, which might be present anywhere in the Internet. When we invoke a method of a remote web service, the proxy receives the requests and wires the details of the request to the remote method, gets the results back from the remote server, and finally passes the result of the execution back to the client. It is important to note that the proxy class provides an abstraction for the underlying plumbing required for communicating with the web service. However, if required, we can use custom SOAP packets created using raw formatted XML to communicate with the web services.

There are three different approaches to creating a proxy class:

❑ Using the Web Services Description Language (WSDL) Utility tool that is supplied with the Microsoft.NET Framework SDK.

❑ Using the Add Web Reference option and letting Visual Studio.NET create the proxy class for us.

❑ Using the soapsuds utility that is part of the Microsoft.NET framework SDK.

In this case study, we will discuss the first two approaches in detail.

WSDL Utility

As we already said, the WSDL utility is used to generate a web service client proxy class. When we use WSDL to generate the proxy class, we generate a single source file that is based on the language that we specified. The generated file contains a proxy class for exposing both synchronous and asynchronous methods for each web service method of the web service. Each method of the proxy class contains the appropriate network invocation and marshaling code to invoke and receive a response from the remote web service method.

For example, to generate a proxy class for our web service, we specify the following command at the prompt:

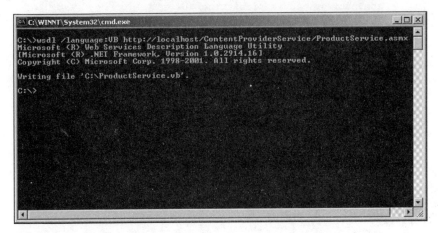

In the above command, since we did not specify the name of the proxy file to be created, it created a proxy class file called `ProductService.vb`.

The language switch is used to specify the name of the language in which the proxy class should be created. If no language is specified, the proxy class is generated in C#.

To create a proxy class with a different name to that of the web service, we use the `/out:` option.

Typing **wsdl /?** at the command prompt allows us to have a look at all the options available while creating the proxy class. For more descriptive information of the list of options available, please consult the .NET framework SDK documentation.

Once we create the proxy class, the next step is to create a class library that will be referenced by the clients of the web service. We can create the proxy class library using any one of the following methods:

❑ Using the class library template of Visual Studio.NET

❑ Using the appropriate command line language compilers. This will be useful if you are dependent on Microsoft.NET SDK for the creation of web services.

Before we go ahead and create the proxy library, let us try to understand the role of the proxy in the web services technology. Any time a client makes a request to the web service, the proxy class receives the request, packages the requests, and marshals it across the Internet to the actual web service. Once the method is finished executing, the proxy receives the results back from the web service and finally passes the results back to the caller of the web service.

Now we will create the proxy library using Visual Studio.NET.

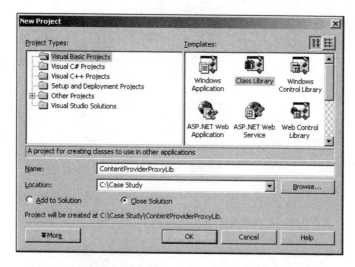

Here we create a new project using the New Project wizard and select the options as shown above. We then add the previously created proxy class to the project. We also add a reference to the `System.Web.Services` assembly in our application by choosing the Project | Add Reference option from the Solution Explorer. Now by building the project, we can create a proxy class library that can be used by the clients of the web services to connect to the web service and invoke its methods. As we mentioned, we can also create a proxy library using the respective command line compilers that are supplied with the Microsoft.NET SDK. This is very useful if you do not have a copy of Visual Studio.NET. For example, to compile the above created proxy class into a proxy class library, we need to use the following command:

```
vbc /t:library  /r:System.dll /r:System.Web.dll /r:System.Web.Services.dll
/r:System.Xml.dll /r:System.Data.dll ProductService.vb
```

Using the Add Web Reference Option

One of the benefits of using Visual Studio.NET to consume a web service is the Add Web Reference option, which allows us to generate the proxy class for any web service that might be present elsewhere on the Internet. This option automates all the plumbing that is required for creating the proxy class. When we add a web reference of the web service to our project, Visual Studio.NET automatically generates a proxy class that interfaces with the web, and the proxy class is used to provide the local representation of the web service.

To add the web reference, we select Project | Add Web Reference. In the Add Web Reference dialog box, we need to specify the path of the `.disco` file of the web service.

For example, to add web reference to our `ContentProviderService` web service, we need to enter the following URL in the address bar of the Add Web Reference prompt. The `ContentProviderService.vsdisco` file was auto-generated by Visual Studio.NET when we created the web service project and it contains information to identify the details of the web services exposed by the application.

http://localhost/ContentProviderService/ContentProviderService.vsdisco

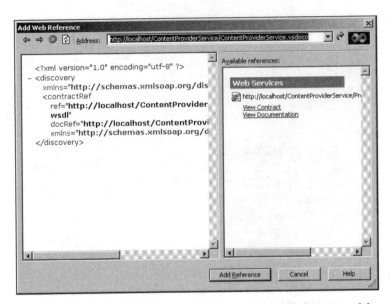

When we click **Add Reference**, Visual Studio.NET creates a folder with the name of the server name under the **Web References** folder. By default, the name of the server is considered as the root namespace for the local Proxy class. To assign a different namespace for the proxy, we need to rename the server name folder with the new name.

Once we add reference to a web service in this manner, we can treat the web service as if it is present in the local machine and invoke its methods to accomplish the desired functionalities.

Implementation of .NET Component

In this section, we will implement the .NET component that will be used by our ShoppingLegend application. We will start by creating a new Visual Basic Class library project as shown in the following figure. We will call the project `ShoppingLegendLib`. After the project is created, we will change the name of the default class to `User`.

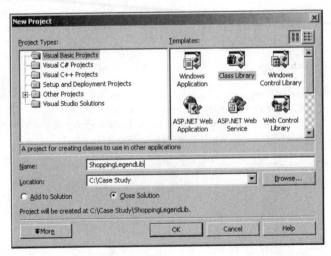

The User class contains the following methods: CheckLogIn and SaveUserDetails. We will shortly discuss both of these methods in detail. At the top of the User.vb file, we write the following line of code to import the System.Data.SqlClient namespace.

```
Imports System.Data.SqlClient
```

We also import the System.Configuration namespace to make use of the ConfigurationSettings class to have access to the connection string that is stored in the web.config file of the ShoppingLegend application.

```
Imports System.Configuration
```

We add a new class called UserDetails, which provides the data structure for storing the necessary details of a specific user. An instance of this class will represent a user in our Users table. This time we will expose all the member variables of the UserDetails class to the outside world by means of public properties.

```
Public Class UserDetails
    Protected m_UserID As String
    Protected m_Password As String
    Protected m_Name As String
    Protected m_Address As String
    Protected m_City As String
    Protected m_State As String
    Protected m_Zip As String

    Public Property UserID()
        Get
            Return m_UserID
        End Get
        Set(ByVal Value)
            m_UserID = Value
        End Set
    End Property

    Public Property Password()
        Get
            Return m_Password
        End Get
        Set(ByVal Value)
            m_Password = Value
        End Set
    End Property

    Public Property Name()
        Get
            Return m_Name
        End Get
        Set(ByVal Value)
            m_Name = Value
        End Set
    End Property

    Public Property Address()
        Get
            Return m_Address
```

```
                End Get
                Set(ByVal Value)
                    m_Address = Value
                End Set
            End Property

            Public Property City()
                Get
                    Return m_City
                End Get
                Set(ByVal Value)
                    m_City = Value
                End Set
            End Property

            Public Property State()
                Get
                    Return m_State
                End Get
                Set(ByVal Value)
                    m_State = Value
                End Set
            End Property

            Public Property Zip()
                Get
                    Return m_Zip
                End Get
                Set(ByVal Value)
                    m_Zip = Value
                End Set
            End Property

    End Class
```

Now, let us discuss the implementation of the user-defined exception class `InValidCredentialsException`. By employing user-defined exception classes, we can publish to the clients that we will only be raising exceptions of a predetermined type. It also allows us to implement custom exception processing logic, like logging the errors to event log and sending e-mail to the administrator any time an error occurs. In the constructor of the `InValidCredentialsException` class, we invoke the constructor of the base exception class and store the exception message for later retrieval.

```
    Public Class InValidCredentialsException
        Inherits Exception
        Public Sub New(ByVal sMessage As String)
            MyBase.New(sMessage)
        End Sub
    End Class
```

CheckLogIn

The `CheckLogIn` method authenticates a customer's username and password against the `ShoppingLegend` database. It returns `True` if the username and password match up against a record in the `Users` table: otherwise it raises an exception of type `InValidCredentialsException`. The `CheckLogIn` method invokes the stored procedure `UserLogIn`. The `UserLogIn` stored procedure returns 1 if a record with the specified username and password is found, else it returns −1.

Now let us consider the CheckLogIn method that encapsulates the code that does the stored procedure invocation.

```vb
Public Function CheckLogIn(ByVal sUserName As String, ByVal sPassWord_
        As String) As Boolean
    Dim oSQLConnection As SqlConnection
    Dim oSQLCommand As SqlCommand

    Try
        oSQLConnection = New SqlConnection(ConfigurationSettings._
            AppSettings("connectionString"))
        oSQLCommand = New SqlCommand("UserLogIn", oSQLConnection)

        'Set the Command type to Stored procedure
        oSQLCommand.CommandType = CommandType.StoredProcedure

        'Add the User name parameter
        Dim oSQLUserNameParam As SqlParameter = New SqlParameter("@UserID",_
            SqlDbType.VarChar, 20)
        oSQLUserNameParam.Value = sUserName
        oSQLCommand.Parameters.Add(oSQLUserNameParam)
        'Add the password parameter
        Dim oSQLPassWordParam As SqlParameter = New SqlParameter("@Password",_
            SqlDbType.VarChar, 10)
        oSQLPassWordParam.Value = sPassWord
        oSQLCommand.Parameters.Add(oSQLPassWordParam)

        'Add the return value parameter
        Dim oSQLRetValueParam As SqlParameter = New SqlParameter("@RetValue",_
            SqlDbType.Int, 4)
        oSQLRetValueParam.Direction = ParameterDirection.Output
        oSQLCommand.Parameters.Add(oSQLRetValueParam)

        'Execute the command
        oSQLConnection.Open()
        oSQLCommand.ExecuteNonQuery()
        oSQLConnection.Close()

        'Obtain the return value of the stored procedure into a variable
        Dim iRetValue As Integer = CInt(oSQLRetValueParam.Value)
        If iRetValue = -1 Then
            Throw New InValidCredentialsException("InValid Login")
        Else
            'Return true to indicate that the login is successful
            Return True
        End If

    Catch ex As Exception
        Throw ex

    Finally
        If oSQLConnection.State = ConnectionState.Open Then
            oSQLConnection.Close()
        End If
    End Try
End Function
```

We start by declaring the `SqlConnection` object and the `SqlCommand` object.

```
Dim oSQLConnection As SqlConnection
Dim oSQLCommand As SqlCommand

Try
```

Here, we instantiate the `SqlConnection` object and pass the connection string to its constructor.

```
oSQLConnection = New SqlConnection(ConfigurationSettings._
        AppSettings("connectionString"))
```

At the time of instantiating the `SqlCommand` object, we pass the name of the stored procedure that we want to execute and an instance of the `SqlConnection` object. We also set the `CommandType` property to `StoredProcedure` to indicate that we want to execute a stored procedure.

```
oSQLCommand = New SqlCommand("UserLogIn", oSQLConnection)

'Set the Command type to Stored procedure
oSQLCommand.CommandType = CommandType.StoredProcedure
```

Then we add the input parameters `UserID` and `Password` to the `SqlCommand` object by executing the following lines of code:

```
'Add the User name parameter
Dim oSQLUserNameParam As SqlParameter = New SqlParameter("@UserID",_
        SqlDbType.VarChar, 20)
oSQLUserNameParam.Value = sUserName
oSQLCommand.Parameters.Add(oSQLUserNameParam)
'Add the password parameter
Dim oSQLPassWordParam As SqlParameter = New SqlParameter("@Password",_
        SqlDbType.VarChar, 10)
oSQLPassWordParam.Value = sPassWord
oSQLCommand.Parameters.Add(oSQLPassWordParam)
```

Since the `RetValue` parameter is an output parameter, we set the `Direction` of that to the value `ParameterDirection.Output`.

```
'Add the return value parameter
Dim oSQLRetValueParam As SqlParameter = New SqlParameter("@RetValue",_
        SqlDbType.Int, 4)
oSQLRetValueParam.Direction = ParameterDirection.Output
oSQLCommand.Parameters.Add(oSQLRetValueParam)
```

Once all the parameters are added and set to proper values, we can execute the stored procedure by invoking the `ExecuteNonQuery` method of the `SqlCommand` object.

```
'Execute the command
oSQLConnection.Open()
oSQLCommand.ExecuteNonQuery()
oSQLConnection.Close()
```

After the stored procedure is executed, we can get the value returned from the stored procedure using the
`SqlParameter` object that we created above.

```
'Obtain the return value of the stored procedure into a variable
Dim iRetValue As Integer = CInt(oSQLRetValueParam.Value)
```

If the return value is –1, we throw an exception of type `InValidCredentialsException` to indicate that
the supplied credentials are invalid.

```
If iRetValue = -1 Then
    Throw New InValidCredentialsException("InValid Login")
Else
    'Return true to indicate that the login is successful
    Return True
End If

Catch ex As Exception
    Throw ex

Finally
    If oSQLConnection.State = ConnectionState.Open Then
        oSQLConnection.Close()
    End If
End Try
```

SaveUserDetails

This method is used to save the details of a user to the `ShoppingLegend` database. It takes a `UserDetails`
object as an argument and returns `True` or `False` depending on the result of its execution. This method is
similar to the previous method `CheckLogIn` except that it executes a different stored procedure. For this
case study, we are storing the password as plain text in the password column of the `Users` table – in a real
world application, the password has to be encrypted before it is stored in the database.

```
Public Function SaveUserDetails(ByVal oUserDetails As UserDetails)_
    As Boolean
Dim oSQLConnection As SqlConnection
Dim oSQLCommand As SqlCommand

Try
    oSQLConnection = New SqlConnection(ConfigurationSettings._
        AppSettings("connectionString"))
    oSQLCommand = New SqlCommand("InsertUser", oSQLConnection)
    oSQLCommand.CommandType = CommandType.StoredProcedure
    oSQLCommand.Parameters.Add(New SqlParameter("@UserID",_
        SqlDbType.Char, 20))
    oSQLCommand.Parameters("@UserID").Value = oUserDetails.UserID
    oSQLCommand.Parameters.Add(New SqlParameter("@Password",_
        SqlDbType.Char, 10))
    oSQLCommand.Parameters("@Password").Value = oUserDetails.Password
    oSQLCommand.Parameters.Add(New SqlParameter("@Name",_
        SqlDbType.VarChar, 128))
    oSQLCommand.Parameters("@Name").Value = oUserDetails.Name
    oSQLCommand.Parameters.Add(New SqlParameter("@Address",_
```

```
            SqlDbType.VarChar, 128))
    oSQLCommand.Parameters("@Address").Value = oUserDetails.Address
    oSQLCommand.Parameters.Add(New SqlParameter("@City", _
            SqlDbType.VarChar, 50))
    oSQLCommand.Parameters("@City").Value = oUserDetails.City
    oSQLCommand.Parameters.Add(New SqlParameter("@State",_
            SqlDbType.Char, 2))
    oSQLCommand.Parameters("@State").Value = oUserDetails.State
    oSQLCommand.Parameters.Add(New SqlParameter("@Zip",_
            SqlDbType.Char, 5))
    oSQLCommand.Parameters("@Zip").Value = oUserDetails.Zip
    oSQLConnection.Open()
    oSQLCommand.ExecuteNonQuery()
    oSQLConnection.Close()
    Return True

  Catch ex As Exception
     Throw ex

  Finally
     If oSQLConnection.State = ConnectionState.Open Then
        oSQLConnection.Close()
     End If
  End Try
End Function
End Class
```

Implementation of ShoppingLegend Web Application

In this part of the case study, we will discuss the implementation of the ShoppingLegend web application that uses the following building blocks that we have already created:

❑ **ContentProviderService – ASP.NET Web service**
Provides information such as list of categories available, products present in each category and the details of the product. We add reference to this web service by selecting the Add Web Reference option.

❑ **ShoppingLegendLib – VB.NET Class library**
Exposes a method that allows the ShoppingLegend application to create new users in the ShoppingLegend database. It also provides for validation of a particular user's credentials against the database. We add reference to this library by using the Add Reference option.

We will start with our discussion of the web application by considering the login process.

Login Process

In our site, the user must be logged in to perform tasks such as browsing through the site and adding a new product to the database. As we already discussed, the login page authenticates the customer's username and password against the ShoppingLegend database. After the user is validated, he is redirected to the categories listing page. If the user does not have a valid login, he can opt to create one by clicking the hyperlink New Users Click here in the login page. Clicking the hyperlink takes the user to the registration page where the user provides all the necessary details for completing the registration.

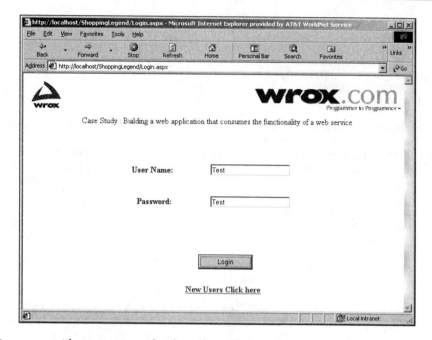

The Login page provides customers with a forms-based login authentication mechanism through which they can authenticate themselves in the ShoppingLegend application. This form-based authentication technology depends on cookies to store the authentication information for the current user. Cookies are just simple text files that can be written to the user's hard drive and they are mainly employed to personalize the user's experience in the site. Once the user is authenticated using the information present in the Users table, cookies are used to store and maintain session information thereby allowing us to identify the current user.

We enable forms-based authentication in our application by making the following entry in the web.config file:

```
<authentication mode="Forms">
    <forms name="ShoppingLegendAuth"
           loginUrl="Login.aspx"
           path="/">
    </forms>
</authentication>
```

The loginUrl attribute specifies the name of the login page that we want the users to be redirected to any time they access a resource that does not allow anonymous access.

In our application, since we do not want to allow anonymous users to browse the site, we need to secure the following pages using entries in the web.config file:

❑ Categories listing page (CategoryListing.aspx)

❑ Product listing page (ProductListing.aspx)

❑ Product Details page (ProductDetails.aspx)

For example, to set the restrictions of authenticated user access for a page called ProductListing.aspx, we need to set the following entry directly under the configuration tag of the web.config file:

```
    <location path="ProductListing.aspx">
        <system.web>
            <authorization>
                <deny users="?" />
            </authorization>
        </system.web>
    </location>
```

When a user attempts to access the `ProductListing.aspx` page, the ASP.NET forms-based security system will automatically redirect them to the `Login.aspx` page, and will continue to prevent them from accessing it until they have successfully validated their username and password credentials to the ShoppingLegend application. Similarly, we protect the other above-mentioned pages, such as `ProductListing.aspx` and `ProductDetails.aspx`, using the entries in the `web.config` file.

Before we start discussing the login page, let us go over the code of the `_Header.ascx` user control file that provides the standard header for our site that is used across all the pages in our web application. User controls are very powerful and flexible in that they allow us to define our own controls using the same programming techniques that we use for writing web forms.

To create a user control, the following steps are to be followed:

❑ Create a user control and save it with the extension `.ascx`. A file with the extension `.ascx` is identified as a user control and it cannot be executed independently as a stand-alone web page.

❑ Include the user control in the container web form page using the `Register` directive.

```
<%@ Register TagPrefix="ShoppingLegend" TagName="Header" Src="_Header.ascx" %>
```

In the above directive, the `TagPrefix` indicates the unique namespace for the user control and the `TagName` is used to give a unique name for the control. The `Src` attribute is used to identify the virtual path to the user control.

❑ Finally place the user control in a web forms page using the following line of code:

```
<ShoppingLegend:Header id="HeaderControl" runat="server" />
```

Once we place the control using the above directive, we can invoke its properties and methods using the name that is provided in the `id` attribute of the above line.

Now that we have understood the concepts involved in creating a user control, let us create a user control that encapsulates the header information for every page in our site. This reusable user control is embedded in all the pages of the ShoppingLegend application. The code of the user control `_Header.ascx` looks like the following.

```
<%@ Control Language="vb" AutoEventWireup="false" Codebehind="_Header.ascx.vb"
            Inherits="ShoppingLegend.C_Header" %>

<asp:Table id=tblTop style="Z-INDEX: 101; LEFT: 12px; POSITION: absolute; TOP:
            11px" runat="server" Width="735px" Height="55px" ForeColor="Blue"
            tabIndex=6>
    <asp:TableRow>
        <asp:TableCell>
```

```
        <img src="newwroxlogo.gif">
    </asp:TableCell>
    <asp:TableCell>
        <img  align="right" src="newwroxhead.gif">
    </asp:TableCell>
  </asp:TableRow>
  <asp:TableRow HorizontalAlign="Center">
    <asp:TableCell ColumnSpan="2" class="largeRed">
        Case Study : Building a web application that consumes the
        functionality of a web service
    </asp:TableCell>
  </asp:TableRow>
</asp:Table>
```

Now we will turn our attention back to the code that is needed for implementing the login functionality in our application.

The code-behind file of the login page `login.aspx.vb` contains the following lines of code.

Firstly, we import the `ShoppingLegendLib` namespace into our application.

```
Imports ShoppingLegendLib
```

```
Private Sub btnLogin_Click(ByVal sender As System.Object, ByVal e As_
        System.EventArgs) Handles btnLogin.Click

    Try
    Dim oUserLogIn As New User()
    'CheckLogIn returns true to indicate that the login is successful
    If oUserLogIn.CheckLogIn(txtUserName.Text, txtPassword.Text) = True Then
        FormsAuthentication.SetAuthCookie(txtUserName.Text, True)
        Response.Redirect("ProductListing.aspx")
    End If

    Catch ex As InValidCredentialsException
        lblMessage.Visible = True
        lblMessage.Text = ex.Message()
    End Try
End Sub
```

When the user enters the user id and password and then clicks Login, we execute the above lines of code. Here, we instantiate an object of type `User` and assign its reference to the `oUserLogIn` variable. As we already discussed, the `CheckLogin` method returns `True` if the login is successful, else it throws an exception of type `InvalidCredentialsException`.

```
Dim oUserLogIn As New User()
'CheckLogIn returns true to indicate that the login is successful
If oUserLogIn.CheckLogIn(txtUserName.Text, txtPassword.Text) = True Then
```

If the login is successful, we then invoke the `SetAuthCookie` method to generate an authentication ticket for the authenticated username and password and attach it to the cookies collection of the outgoing response. Once the cookie is generated, it is used to maintain information about the session information for every user that logs in to our site. In the next line, we perform a redirect to the `CategoryListing.aspx` page that displays information about the categories available in the site.

```
FormsAuthentication.SetAuthCookie(txtUserName.Text, True)
```

```
            Response.Redirect("ProductListing.aspx")
      End If
```

Whenever the exception `InValidCredentialsException` occurs, we catch that in the `catch` block and show the exception message in the label called `lblMessage`. The label control named `lblMessage`, by default, has its visibility set to `False` and is used as a placeholder to display custom messages to the user. In the following lines of code, we set its visibility to `True` and use it to show the error messages that are raised from the component.

```
      Catch ex As InValidCredentialsException
          lblMessage.Visible = True
          lblMessage.Text = ex.Message()
      End Try
```

Registration Process

The registration page `Registration.aspx` allows users browsing the ShoppingLegend application to register themselves as customers. The registration page is as follows:

To perform validations, we use the `asp:RequiredFieldValidator` server control to validate the input entry of a particular field. For example, to ensure that the user enters values for the input field `txtUserName`, we need to perform the following.

First, we declare a server-side validation control and then we associate that with the control to be validated by using the `ControlToValidate` property. If the input validation fails, the error message set in the `ErrorMessage` is displayed.

```
<asp:RequiredFieldValidator id=RequiredFieldValidator1 style="Z-INDEX: 120; LEFT:
518px; POSITION: absolute; TOP: 178px" ControlToValidate="txtUserName"
runat="server" ErrorMessage="*"></asp:RequiredFieldValidator>
```

To check whether the user enters the same value for the **Password** and **Confirm** password textboxes, we use the built-in server-side validation control `asp:CompareValidator`. As we can see from the properties, the combination of `ControlToValidate` and `ControlToCompare` are used to do the trick.

```
<asp:CompareValidator id=CompareValidator1 style="Z-INDEX: 128; LEFT: 544px;
POSITION: absolute; TOP: 218px" runat="server" Height="20px" Width="203px"
ErrorMessage="Please enter same value for Password and Confirm Password"
ControlToValidate="txtPassWord"
ControlToCompare="txtConfirmPassword"></asp:CompareValidator>
```

The entire page logic for the registration page is encapsulated in the `btnSave_Click` event handler.

```
Private Sub btnSave_Click(ByVal sender As System.Object, ByVal e As_
        System.EventArgs) Handles btnSave.Click

    'This code invokes the ShoppingLegendLib's SaveUserDetail method to save
    'the user details to the database
    Dim oUserRegister As New User()
    Dim oUserDetails As New UserDetails()

    'Assign values to the UserDetails object
    oUserDetails.UserID = txtUserName.Text
    oUserDetails.Password = txtPassWord.Text
    oUserDetails.Name = txtName.Text
    oUserDetails.Address = txtAddress.Text
    oUserDetails.City = txtCity.Text
    oUserDetails.State = txtState.Text
    oUserDetails.Zip = txtZip.Text

    'Invoke the SaveUserDetails method to save the user details to the
    'database
    oUserRegister.SaveUserDetails(oUserDetails)

    'Redirect the user to the Confirmation page
    Server.Transfer("Confirmation.aspx")

End Sub
```

We start the implementation of the registration process by declaring and instantiating an instance of type `User` and assign it to the variable `oUserRegister`.

```
Dim oUserRegister As New User()
```

In this line, we create an instance of object type `UserDetails`. As we already mentioned, the `UserDetails` class is used to represent a user in our site.

```
Dim oUserDetails As New UserDetails()
```

Once we create the `UserDetails` object, we can set its public member variables to appropriate values.

```
'Assign values to the UserDetails object
oUserDetails.UserID = txtUserName.Text
oUserDetails.Password = txtPassWord.Text
oUserDetails.Name = txtName.Text
oUserDetails.Address = txtAddress.Text
oUserDetails.City = txtCity.Text
oUserDetails.State = txtState.Text
oUserDetails.Zip = txtZip.Text
```

Here, we invoke the `SaveUserDetails` method of the `User` class and pass the `UserDetails` object as an argument.

```
'Invoke the SaveUserDetails method to save the user details to the
'database
oUserRegister.SaveUserDetails(oUserDetails)
```

Finally we redirect the users to the confirmation page to provide the users with the confirmation that they have been successfully registered.

```
'Redirect the user to the Confirmation page
Server.Transfer("Confirmation.aspx")
```

The confirmation page, to which the users are redirected, looks like the following:

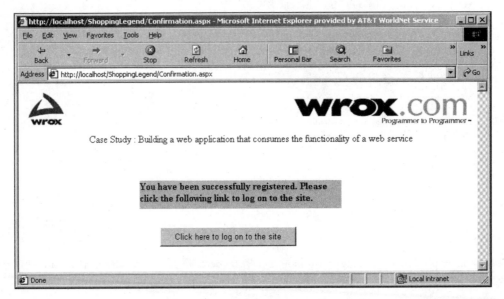

When the user clicks the Click here to log on to the site button, we invoke the `Transfer` method of the `Server` object to redirect the user back to the login page.

CategoriesListing Process

All the categories present in the site are displayed through the `CategoryListing.aspx` page. In the categories listing page, we use an `asp:DataGrid` to display the categories. We bind this control directly to the value returned by the web service in the `Page_Load` event.

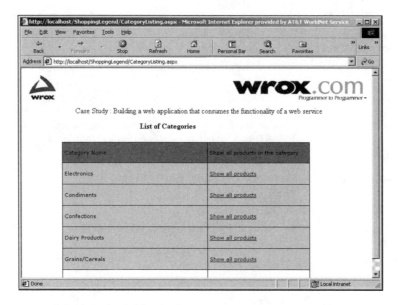

The DataGrid control displays the fields of a data source as columns in a table. The nice thing about DataGrid is it provides for customization of appearance by allowing us to set various style properties such as HeaderStyle, ItemStyle, AlternatingItemStyle, FooterStyle and SelectedItemStyle.

In the code shown below, we use the declarative directive OutputCache to cache the output of this page for 60 seconds. Since the list of categories in our site is not dependent on any parameters, we set the VaryByParam attribute to 'None' to indicate that we want to cache the page for 60 seconds regardless of the supplied parameters. As the name suggests, the Duration attribute allows us to specify the time, in terms of seconds, that the page is cached.

The usage of output caching improves the performance of the application to a great degree, especially when invoking the methods of a web service, which might be present anywhere on the Internet. When we implement output caching, the results of the previously requested pages are stored in the output cache and if a similar request is made, the cached pages can be used to service the request instead of recreating the entire response from the scratch.

```
<%@ OutputCache Duration="60" VaryByParam="None" %>
<%@ Page Language="vb" AutoEventWireup="false"
Codebehind="CategoryListing.aspx.vb" Inherits="ShoppingLegend.CategoryListing"%>
<%@ Register TagPrefix="ShoppingLegend" TagName="Header" Src="_Header.ascx" %>

<HTML>
<HEAD>
<title></title>
<!DOCTYPE HTML PUBLIC "-//W3C//DTD HTML 4.0 Transitional//EN">
<meta name="GENERATOR" content="Microsoft Visual Studio.NET 7.0">
<meta name="CODE_LANGUAGE" content="Visual Basic 7.0">
<meta name=vs_defaultClientScript content="JavaScript">
<meta name=vs_targetSchema content="Internet Explorer 5.0">
</HEAD>
<body MS_POSITIONING="GridLayout">

<form id="Form1" method="post" runat="server">
```

```
<ShoppingLegend:Header id="HeaderControl" runat="server" />
<asp:Label id=lblCategories style="Z-INDEX: 101; LEFT: 252px; POSITION: absolute;
TOP: 115px" runat="server" Width="220px" Height="19px" Font-Bold="True">List of
Categories</asp:Label>

<asp:DataGrid id=gridCategories style="Z-INDEX: 102; LEFT: 87px; POSITION:
absolute; TOP: 159px" runat="server" Height="321px" width="529px"
BorderColor="Black" cellpadding="4" Font-Name="Verdana" Font-Size="8pt"
HeaderStyle-CssClass="CartListHead" FooterStyle-CssClass="cartlistfooter"
ItemStyle-CssClass="CartListItem" AlternatingItemStyle-CssClass="CartListItemAlt"
AutoGenerateColumns="False" ShowFooter="True" Font-Names="Verdana">

<FooterStyle ForeColor="Control" CssClass="cartlistfooter"
BackColor="ActiveCaptionText">
</FooterStyle>

<HeaderStyle CssClass="CartListHead" BackColor="#00AAAA">
</HeaderStyle>

<AlternatingItemStyle CssClass="CartListItemAlt">
</AlternatingItemStyle>

<ItemStyle CssClass="CartListItem" BackColor="Control">
</ItemStyle>

<Columns>
<asp:BoundColumn DataField="CategoryName" HeaderText="Category Name">
<HeaderStyle Width="300px">
</HeaderStyle>
</asp:BoundColumn>
<asp:HyperLinkColumn Text="Show all products" DataNavigateUrlField="CategoryID"
DataNavigateUrlFormatString="productlisting.aspx?CategoryID={0}" HeaderText="Show
all products in the category"></asp:HyperLinkColumn>
</Columns>
</asp:DataGrid>
</form>
</body>
</HTML>
```

The hyperlink for navigating to the list of products is displayed using one of the column type
HyperLinkColumn that is contained in the Columns tag. As we can see from the following line of code, the
data field CategoryID is bound to the hyperlink column by means of the property
DataNavigateUrlField and this CategoryID is also passed as a querystring parameter to the
product-listing page.

```
<asp:HyperLinkColumn Text="Show all products" DataNavigateUrlField="CategoryID"
DataNavigateUrlFormatString="productlisting.aspx?CategoryID={0}" HeaderText="Show
all products in the category"></asp:HyperLinkColumn>
```

ProductListing Process

The `ProductListing.aspx` page shows the list of products available on the site; the list shown is based on the category the user has selected in the categories listing page. The screenshot of the `ProductListing` page is as follows:

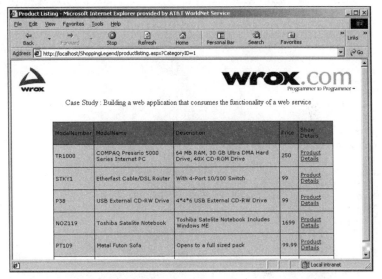

As we can see from the above figure, the list of products shown in the product-listing page is dependent on the category id that is passed via the querystring. In the following line of code, we set the `VaryByParam` to `'*'` to indicate that we want multiple versions of the page to be stored in the cache. These multiple versions of the page are determined by the different parameters that are passed through the querystring. Since the only parameter that is passed to this page is `categoryid`, the different versions stored in the cache will vary based on the values of the `categoryid`.

```
<%@ OutputCache Duration="60" VaryByParam="*" %>
```

Now we will see the code that needs to be written to bind the data grid control to the dataview.

```
<asp:DataGrid id="gridProducts" width="602px" BorderColor="black"
cellpadding="4" cellspacing="0" Font-Name="Verdana" Font-Size="8pt" HeaderStyle-
CssClass="CartListHead" FooterStyle-CssClass="cartlistfooter" ItemStyle-
CssClass="CartListItem" AlternatingItemStyle-CssClass="CartListItemAlt"
AutoGenerateColumns="false" runat="server" style="Z-INDEX: 101; LEFT: 77px;
POSITION: absolute; TOP: 110px" Height="321px" ShowFooter=true>
<FooterStyle ForeColor="Control" CssClass="cartlistfooter"
BackColor="ActiveCaptionText">
</FooterStyle>

<HeaderStyle CssClass="CartListHead" BackColor="#00AAAA">
</HeaderStyle>

<AlternatingItemStyle CssClass="CartListItemAlt">
</AlternatingItemStyle>

<ItemStyle CssClass="CartListItem" BackColor="Control">
</ItemStyle>
```

The number of columns that we specify between the opening and closing <Columns> tags determines the number of columns that appear in the data grid control. The DataField property of the BoundColumn allows us to specify the name of the column in the data view that we want to bind to.

```
<Columns>
<asp:BoundColumn DataField="ModelNo" HeaderText="ModelNumber"></asp:BoundColumn>
<asp:BoundColumn DataField="ModelName" HeaderText="ModelName"></asp:BoundColumn>
<asp:BoundColumn DataField="Description"
HeaderText="Description"></asp:BoundColumn>
<asp:BoundColumn DataField="Price" HeaderText="Price"></asp:BoundColumn>
<asp:HyperLinkColumn Text="Product Details" DataNavigateUrlField="ProductID"
DataNavigateUrlFormatString="productdetails.aspx?ProductID={0}" HeaderText="Show
Details"></asp:HyperLinkColumn>
</Columns>
</asp:DataGrid>
```

The Page_Load event handler contains the code to invoke the web service, retrieve data from it, and then display its contents in a data grid control.

```
Private Sub Page_Load(ByVal sender As System.Object, ByVal e As _
        System.EventArgs) Handles MyBase.Load
   Dim oService As New localhost.ProductService()
   Dim oDataSet As DataSet
   Dim iCategoryID As Integer
iCategoryID = CType(Request.Params("CategoryID"), Integer)
   oDataSet = oService.ProductsGet(iCategoryID)
   gridProducts.DataSource = oDataSet.Tables("Products").DefaultView
   gridProducts.DataBind()
End Sub
```

First we declare a variable of type ProductService that is part of the namespace localhost. This namespace localhost was created as a result of adding web reference to the ContentProviderService using the **Add Web Reference** option.

```
Dim oService As New localhost.ProductService()
Dim oDataSet As DataSet
Dim iCategoryID As Integer
```

In this line, we convert the CategoryID that is passed in the query string to an integer variable by using the CType function.

```
iCategoryID = CType(Request.Params("CategoryID"), Integer)
```

Now we invoke the ProductsGet method of the web service passing in the CategoryID as an argument.

```
oDataSet = oService.ProductsGet(iCategoryID)
```

Once we get reference to the dataset, we can then obtain a single table in the dataset in the form of a DataView by using the DefaultView property of the DataTable class.

```
gridProducts.DataSource = oDataSet.Tables("Products").DefaultView
```

Finally we bind the grid to the Products table of the data set.

```
gridProducts.DataBind()
```

Product Details Listing Process

When the user selects a particular product from the list of products, the user is taken to the product details page where details about the product are shown. For showing the product details we will create a reusable user control named `ProductDetailControl.ascx` that encapsulates all the code required for retrieving the details of the product from the web service. It exposes a public property called `ProductID`. By setting the `ProductID` property to an appropriate value, we can determine the product whose details are to be shown.

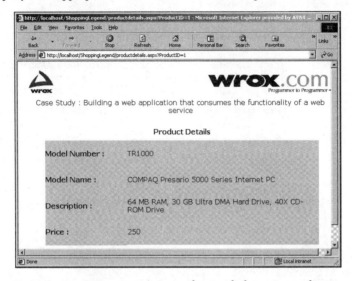

The code for the `ProductDetailControl.ascx`, along with the entire application, can be downloaded from the Wrox web site. The user control uses an `asp:Repeater` control to display the information about the product. The repeater control is a server-side control whose appearance can be customized by associating them with predefined HTML templates such as header templates, item templates, and footer templates. Now we will explore the code behind the user control (`ProductDetailControl.ascx.vb`) to understand the implementation of the user control.

First we declare the `ProductID` member with `Public` scope to allow the clients to set its value directly.

```
Public ProductID As Integer
```

The `Page_Load` event handler contains all the code required for connecting up to the web service and retrieving the product details.

```
Private Sub Page_Load(ByVal sender As System.Object, ByVal e As_
        System.EventArgs) Handles MyBase.Load
    Dim oService As New localhost.ProductService()
    Dim oDataSet As DataSet
    oDataSet = oService.ProductDetailsGetDataSet(ProductID)
    'Bind the Control to the DataView returned by the method
    prodDetailControl.DataSource = oDataSet.Tables("Products").DefaultView
    prodDetailControl.DataBind()

    'Hide the list if no items are in it
    If prodDetailControl.Items.Count = 0 Then
        prodDetailControl.Visible = False
    End If
End Sub
```

643

As before, we create an instance of type `ProductService` using the following line of code:

```
Dim oService As New localhost.ProductService()
Dim oDataSet As DataSet
```

Now, we invoke the `ProductDetailsGetDataSet` method of the web service to get the details of the product based on the product id that is passed in.

```
oDataSet = oService.ProductDetailsGetDataSet(ProductID)
```

Then we set the `DataSource` property of the `asp:Repeater` control to the DataView that is obtained by calling the `DefaultView` property of the `DataTable` class.

```
prodDetailControl.DataSource = oDataSet.Tables("Products").DefaultView
```

Finally, we bind the repeater control to the dataview by invoking the `DataBind` method of the repeater control.

```
prodDetailControl.DataBind()
```

We also check to see whether the repeater has any items in it by examining the `Count` property. If the count returns 0, then we set the `Visible` property to `False`.

```
'Hide the list if no items are in it
If prodDetailControl.Items.Count = 0 Then
    prodDetailControl.Visible = False
End If
```

Now that we have seen the steps involved in creating the user control, let us turn our attention to see what it takes to embed and use this user control in our product details page.

The code of the `ProductDetails.aspx` page is as follows:

```
<%@ OutputCache Duration="60" VaryByParam="*" %>
<%@ Page Language="vb" AutoEventWireup="false" Codebehind="ProductDetails.aspx.vb"
Inherits="ShoppingLegend.ProductDetails"%>
<%@ Register TagPrefix="ShoppingLegend" TagName="Header" Src="_Header.ascx" %>
<%@ Register TagPrefix="ShoppingLegend" TagName="ProductDetails"
Src="ProductDetailControl.ascx" %>

<HTML>
<HEAD>
<title>Product Details </title>

<script runat="server">
Sub Page_Load(ByVal sender As System.Object, ByVal e As System.EventArgs) Handles
MyBase.Load
    'Put user code to initialize the page here
    Dim iProductID as integer
    iProductID = CType(Request.Params("ProductID"),Integer)
    prodDetailControl.ProductID = iProductID
End Sub
```

```
</script>

<!DOCTYPE HTML PUBLIC "-//W3C//DTD HTML 4.0 Transitional//EN">
<meta content="Microsoft Visual Studio.NET 7.0" name=GENERATOR>
<meta content="Visual Basic 7.0" name=CODE_LANGUAGE>
<meta content=JavaScript name=vs_defaultClientScript>
<meta content="Internet Explorer 5.0" name=vs_targetSchema>
<link rel="stylesheet" type="text/css" href="Styles.css">
</HEAD>
<BODY MS_POSITIONING="GridLayout">
<FORM id=Form1 method=post runat="server">
<ShoppingLegend:Header id="HeaderControl" runat="server" />
<asp:Table id=Table1 style="Z-INDEX: 111; LEFT: 61px; POSITION: absolute; TOP:
112px" runat="server" Width="678px" Height="366px">
    <asp:TableRow>
        <asp:TableCell>
            <ShoppingLegend:ProductDetails id="prodDetailControl"
            runat="server" />
        </asp:TableCell>
    </asp:TableRow>
    <asp:TableRow>
        <asp:TableCell>
             
        </asp:TableCell>
    </asp:TableRow>
</asp:Table>
</FORM>
</BODY>
</HTML>
```

We start by importing the user-defined controls by using a Register directive.

```
<%@ Register TagPrefix="ShoppingLegend" TagName="Header" Src="_Header.ascx" %>
<%@ Register TagPrefix="ShoppingLegend" TagName="ProductDetails"
Src="ProductDetailControl.ascx" %>
```

In the Page_Load event, we set the ProductID property of the user control to the value that is passed in the query string parameter.

```
Sub Page_Load(ByVal sender As System.Object, ByVal e As System.EventArgs) Handles
MyBase.Load
    'Put user code to initialize the page here
    Dim iProductID as integer
    iProductID = CType(Request.Params("ProductID"),Integer)
```

In our code, we refer to the product details control by the name prodDetailControl. This is due to the fact that at the time of defining the control we set the id attribute to the value prodDetailControl.

```
    prodDetailControl.ProductID = iProductID
End Sub
```

645

How the Exceptions are Handled

As we all know, in an ideal world, all the code we write would always run without error. But the reality is, no matter how careful we are in writing the code, errors can and will occur especially due to the high level of dependency on public networks and the other machines that are beyond our control. For that reason, it is good to have an efficient error-handling routine in place that may handle the errors in a graceful manner. For our ShoppingLegend application, we will take advantage of the excellent in-built exception handling mechanism that the ASP.NET runtime provides.

To take advantage of this exception handling plumbing that is provided by ASP.NET, we need to add the following entry in the `web.config` file:

```
<customErrors defaultRedirect="ErrorPage.aspx"
      mode="RemoteOnly">
</customErrors>
```

The `defaultRedirect` attribute allows us to specify the URL to direct the browser to, any time an error occurs in our site. The attribute mode indicates whether custom errors are enabled, disabled or displayed only to remote clients. It can take any one of the following values:

❑ On – indicates that custom errors are enabled

❑ Off – specifies that custom errors are disabled

❑ RemoteOnly – indicates that the custom errors are shown only to the remote clients

The above entry in the `web.config` file indicates that we want the remote users to be redirected to the page `ErrorPage.aspx` any time an error occurs in our ShoppingLegend application.

Whenever an error occurs in our site, users will see the following generic error message page:

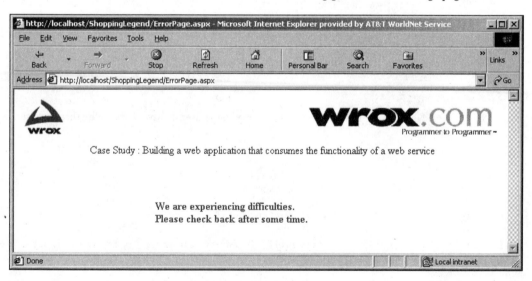

Putting it all Together

Now that we have constructed the different parts of the application, let us test it by navigating to the login page of our site. If we choose to enter a valid user id and password and click login, we will be directed to the categories listing page where all the categories in the site are displayed. Clicking the hyperlink Show all Products takes us to the product listing page where we can see all the products that belong to the selected category. If we click the hyperlink Product Details in the product listing page, we should be able to see the details of the specific product. If you are a new user and you choose to create a new registration account for yourself, you can opt to do that in the login page where there is a hyperlink for creating a new account.

Prerequisites and Deployment

Before we explore the steps to be followed in deploying this application, let us take a look at the prerequisites required for running this application.

Prerequisites

To execute the code that is available for download, you need to have the following software installed on your machine.

- ❑ Microsoft.NET SDK Beta 2 and above or Visual Studio.NET Beta 2 and above
- ❑ ASP.NET Premium edition (for testing the output caching features)
- ❑ SQL Server 2000 Release Version

Deployment

To deploy the entire application, the following steps are to be followed:

- ❑ Create the database objects by executing the SQL script files that are supplied along with the download material of the case study. This script will create all the necessary databases, tables and stored procedures and it will also insert the minimum data that is required for running the application.

- ❑ Copy the web application directories ContentProviderService and ShoppingLegend to your local folder.

- ❑ Create two virtual directories called ContentProviderService and ShoppingLegend through the Internet Services Manager. While creating the directories ensure that you specify the local folders, to which we copied the web applications in the previous step, as the content directory.

- ❑ Modify the connection string that is present in the web.config (present in the root web directory) file in both web applications to a value that suits your machine settings. The connection string is stored as a subelement in the appSettings section of the web.config file.

Summary

In this case study, we have seen how to design and develop next-generation web services using the Microsoft.NET platform. We have also seen how to consume them from a client application that is created using web forms technology. Specifically, we covered:

❑ The steps involved in creating a web service. Towards this end, we have seen what are the prerequisites for exposing a method as a web method. We also talked about returning values that belong to different data types such as a dataset and a user-defined object from a web service.

❑ Two ways of creating a proxy class, which serves to mediate between the web service and the client application. Towards this end, we also discussed the importance of the WSDL utility and saw an example of this utility in action.

❑ How to consume the web service from the client application. Towards this end, we considered different ways through which a client application can discover information (for example, Add Web Reference) about a web service.

❑ While creating the client application, we have understood the steps involved in creating a user-defined server control that can be used across all the pages.

❑ In this step, we have also understood how to improve the performance and throughput of the application by incorporating output caching policy features.

We also discussed the implementation of a .NET component and understood how to access it from our web application.

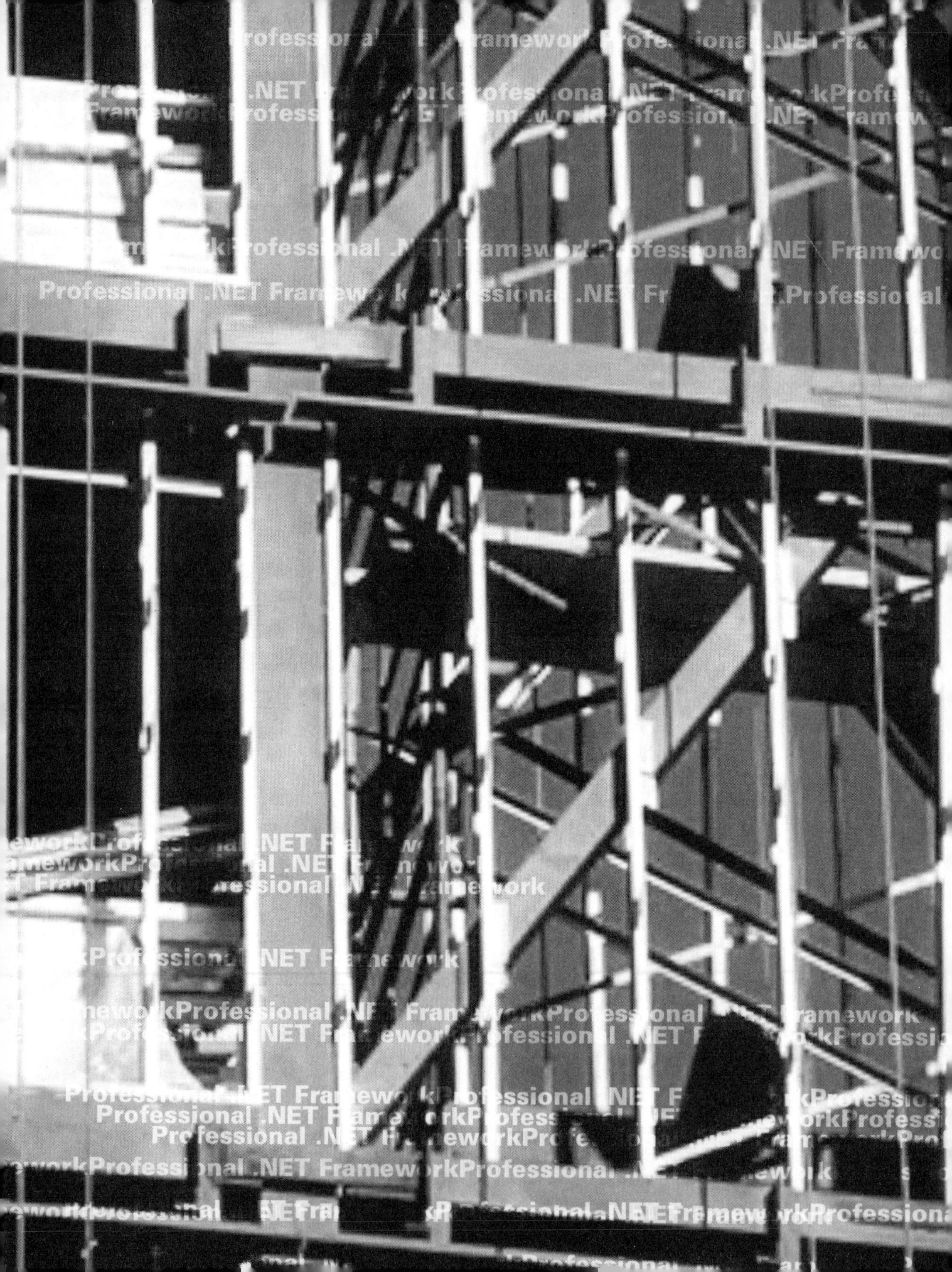
Professional .NET Framework

The .NET Class Library
Namespaces

As you have seen elsewhere in this book, namespaces provide a way to organize large amounts of classes, structs, enumerations and other definitions so that we can find what we want as quickly as possible.

The .NET framework classes that provide functionality for .NET applications are organized in namespaces which are stored under two 'roots' – Microsoft and System. Each namespace contains a specific set of functionality within it. The System.Web namespace, for example, contains functionality for developing web application and web-ready services. System.XML contains parsing, editing, and viewing objects for XML.

A namespace is not limited to just two levels – each namespace is capable of storing various lower levels of namespaces within themselves, adding to the overall organization of the namespace system and allowing us to use simple English to find and remember what we need. As you may have noticed from the two previous examples, the namespaces are usually self-explanatory in name.

A typical namespace has the following format:

```
System.Namespace
```

or

```
System.Namespace.Namespace
```

To reference a class within a namespace, we use the following format:

```
System.Namespace.Class
```

This appendix will provide an overview of the namespaces that organize the class library.

The Microsoft Namespace

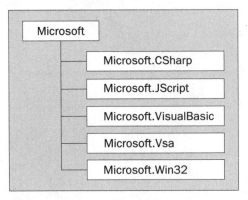

We are just going to briefly glance at the Microsoft namespace. `Microsoft.CSharp`, and `Microsoft.JScript` both contain classes that allow for language-specific compilation and on-the-fly code generation. `Microsoft.VisualBasic` provides the same function but also contains the VB.NET runtime, which allows you to basically create an on-the-fly Visual Basic compiler or runtime. So if you are coding in Visual Basic import `Microsoft.VisualBasic`.

`Microsoft.Win32` and `Microsoft.VSA` are the only namespaces that do not provide some type of language-specific interaction, `Microsoft.Win32` provides the user with a way to manipulate windows events and work with the system registry and `Microsoft.VSA` provides a way to embed VSA apps into .NET.

The System Namespace

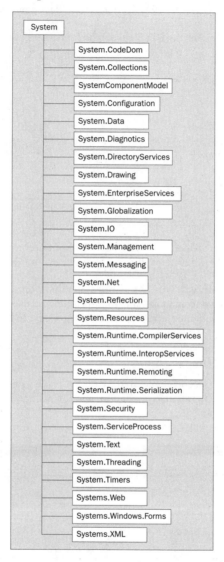

System is the base namespace for the .NET framework; you can think of it as the "mother of all namespaces". All of the other base classes within .NET derive a lot of their functionality from the classes within the System namespace; you don't have to worry about calling the System namespace explicitly since the application will do it for you.

This root namespace is very important; as previously stated the System namespace is the root namespace of the .NET namespace structure. The System namespace is also important in its own right – it contains lots of fundamental classes that are very commonly used. Every single .NET class is ultimately derived from the class System.Object

The basic data types, such as `Boolean` and `Int32`, are in the `System` namespace, as is the `String` class and the `Array` class. All .NET languages use these data types, regardless of what they call them internally. (For instance, VB.NET uses the name `Integer` to refer to the data type `Int32`.)

The `System` namespace also contains the `Math` class, which provides commonly used mathematical constants and functions.

The `Console` class provides basic console interaction.

System.CodeDom

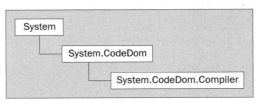

`CodeDom` is the Document Object Model for .NET code. We can use `CodeDom` to generate code that creates a programming structure of the various items that can be found within .NET.

For instance you can use `CodeDom` as a type of security system for your application; if you think someone has hacked a small assembly within your multi-assembly application you can use `CodeDom` to dynamically generate new code and use its subnamespace, `CodeDom.Compiler`, to compile the code properly and replace the damaged / altered assembly.

System.CodeDom.Compiler

`CodeDom.Compiler` compiles the code generated by `CodeDom`. It's pretty nifty in the sense that you can create a virtual compiler, error generation, compilation, and it can compile your `CodeDom`-generated code as either VB.NET Code or C# Code.

System.Collections

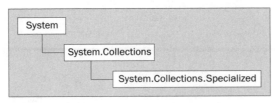

All of the basic collections, such as `Arrays` and `Hashes` are defined or expanded here.
The basic manipulations of collections, such as the ability to compare two objects (within the `Comparer` class) are also found here.

Arrays, although technically collections (they implement the `ICollection` interface) are defined in the `System` root namespace. `System.Collections` does provide the `ArrayList` class, which defines an array whose size can be dynamically increased by adding items, or decreased by calling the `TrimToSize` method.

`Queue` and `Stack` are also defined here. `Queue` provides a first in, first out (FIFO) collection while `Stack` provides a first in, last out collection (FILO).

System.Collections.Specialized

This namespace contains the base classes used to create strong type collections of objects; this is useful for dealing with objects in an abstract manner and also allows us to create specialized lists, such as a linked-list dictionary.

The `System.Collections.Specialized` namespace contains some strongly-typed collections, such as `StringDictionary` and `NameObjectCollection`.

System.ComponentModel

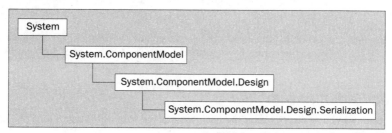

Arguably one of the most heavily used namespaces, `System.ComponentModel` contains (almost) everything you can think of to create components and controls at runtime.

Namespaces that deal with creating windowed applications, such as `System.WinForms`, inherit many of their classes from `ComponentModel` (specifically the `Component` class). You will probably reference this class directly if you are planning on working directly with the design / runtime behavior of objects and controls.

Every single class needed to convert a file type from its present type to another type is found within this namespace. They all have the word "Converter" at the end, such as `StringConverter` or `CharConverter`.

The `ReadOnlyAttribute` can be used to effectively lock down the property of an attribute this is bound to as "read-only". This is extremely useful if you want to keep a value or property locked until a specific event is triggered or a clause is met, which means you can use this for security algorithms.

Be wary of the `GUIDConverter`, unless its current ability to change a GUID object to and from a string is either changed or improved. It can cause headaches if improperly used.

System.ComponentModel.Design

This namespace provides classes that will allow you to provide the same design-time facilities for your classes as is already available for the components included in the .NET class library.

An interface, `IDesigner` is provided which can be implemented to create custom design-time tools. A class, `ComponentDesigner`, is provided that implements `IDesigner`. `ComponentDesigner` can be used as a parent class for custom designers.

System.ComponentModel.Design.Serialization

Serialization, the process of writing the state of an object to a data stream or other type of persistence storage, is controlled through this namespace. Use this when you need to restore an object's state at a later time, whether in a different process, a remote machine or simply after a restart. This can be very useful when combined with XML to span persistence over various servers.

System.Configuration

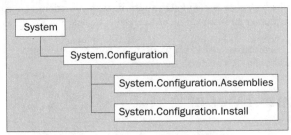

`System.Configuration` contains the classes needed to create an "on-the-fly" configuration file or point to the AppDomain / HTTP where the config file is located, as well as troubleshoot and handle errors raised by the config file.

System.Configuration.Assemblies

This namespace allows you to directly alter the hash table of an Assembly's manifest. You can change values, types and other settings on-the-fly using this namespace.

System.Configuration.Install

As the name implies, this namespace allows you to create a custom installer for your .NET application / assembly that contains the "full" suite expected from an installer: `Install`, `Commit`, `Rollback`, and `Uninstall`. All of the activity in this namespace can be controlled using the `Installer` class. You can, of course, set the actions that you want the installer to take during these steps.

System.Data

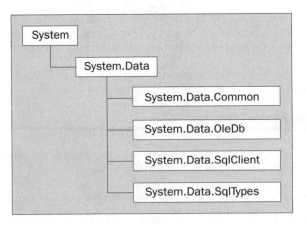

ADO.NET is encapsulated within this namespace. The gem of all database programmers lies right here, folks! Database connection, functionality, parsing, and error handling are taken care of through the various classes, interfaces, and enumerations this very rich package provides.

Using the classes in the System.Data namespace you can create complex SQL / SQL Compliant database connections; Beta 2 has basic read/write XML support as well. The majority of your connectivity and basic database classes can be found within the System.Data.Common namespace and are implemented in the System.Data.OleDb namespace. SQL Server specific interaction can be found within the System.Data.SqlClient, and System.Data.SqlTypes namespace.

System.Data.Common

This namespace contains classes that handle the "low-level" database functions; all other classes in other System.Data namespaces share or inherit classes from this namespace to provide their functionality. You will rarely have to use this one namespace directly unless you need to write some type of raw database connection.

System.Data.OleDb

All of the basic OLEDB classes are stored within this namespace.

System.Data.SqlClient

SQL Client interaction is handled through this namespace. Referred to as a "data provider" by Microsoft, System.Data.SqlClient not only provides the classes to interact with an SQL data source but also work with SQL permissions through the SqlClientPermission and SqlClientPermissionAttribute class. It is very neat not to have to rely on several DLL files to provide these services.

System.Data.SqlTypes

This namespace provides classes to handle the native data types of SQL Server.

System.Diagnostics

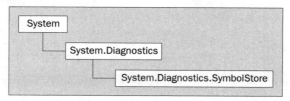

Troubleshooting, anyone? Diagnostics provides a very full set of debugging tools that allow users to trace code execution even along the stack. The key classes are Trace and Debug, which both provide the same set of functionality outputting.

System.Diagnostics.SymbolStore

This namespace allows you to go a bit deeper into the debugging process by allowing you to read and write debug symbol information.

System.DirectoryServices

Talk about a misleading name! This namespace should perhaps have been called System.ActiveDirectoryServices since that's all this applies to. This namespace provides interaction to any Active Directory provider, such as IIS (Internet Information Services) or LDAP (Lightweight Directory Access Protocol).

The Active Directory is navigated as a tree, going through nodes and child nodes. Full functionality, such as reading and writing, is provided through this namespace.

System.Drawing

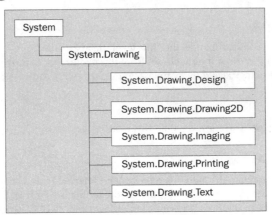

This namespace contains all the basic GDI+ functionality and a couple of new tricks, such as custom `Brush`, cursor manipulation through `Cursor`, and `Icon` for full icon editing. Just the basic 2D bitmap routines are in the main namespace but for greater control you can also use `System.Drawing.Imaging`, `System.Drawing.Design` or `System.Drawing.Drawing2D` namespaces.

System.Drawing.Design

This particular namespace allows you to "draw" custom toolboxes and other types of graphical UI tools. You control every aspect of the toolbox, from the shape to the font it uses.

System.Drawing.Drawing2D

An enhancement to the standard `Drawing` namespace, 2D adds specialized classes such as `ColorBlend` for gradients and `HatchBrush` to create rectangular brushes.

System.Drawing.Imaging

This namespace provides some low-level access when saving and recording image files, such as setting the codec and encoding of an image. This namespace also brings support for common file types, such as JPG and GIF.

System.Drawing.Printing

This namespace allows you to set settings commonly used in printing, such as margins and resolution.

System.Drawing.Text

`System.Drawing.Text` provides font support for listing and displaying fonts; it can also be used to set font rendering quality separate from the rendering quality of other items.

System.EnterpriseServices

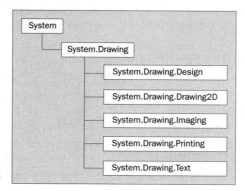

`System.EnterpriseService` contains the classes that allow interaction with Enterprise-level services. Security and interaction are also encapsulated within this namespace.

System.EnterpriseServices.CompensatingResourceManager

Allows you to enable and control a Compensating Resource Manager within .NET.

System.Globalization

All the items to determine or define specific region information, such as language or calendar type, can be found here. `Calendar` is the main class for the date; `CultureInfo` contains the more social aspects, such as language and writing format. `DateTimeFormatInfo` is a very nice addition as well; it allows us to set how date and time values are formatted on-screen.

System.IO

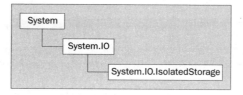

Console, file, and directory manipulation is found in this namespace. The pure goodness that can be found here, while nothing new for all of the C/C++ people, will amaze and astound traditional Visual Basic programmers – finally they can also create true console applications that run from the command line!

The really neat thing about this particular namespace is its flexibility and how well it's logically packaged. It contains, true to its name, all of the basic input and output classes and methods you'll ever need.

System.IO.IsolatedStorage

This namespace allows for the creation of an isolated area that can store information that can not be accessed by code which either does not have the proper security settings or is not very high on the trust area. The area is isolated by the current user and the assembly that created the space. If it's needed the data can be further separated by domain.

System.Management

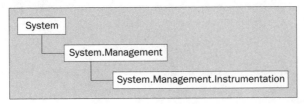

The System.Management namespace manipulates Windows Management Instrumentation.

System.Management.Instrumentation

This namespace provides classes which allow you to expose your .NET applications through Windows Management Instrumentation.

System.Messaging

System.Messaging provides .NET users with access to the Microsoft Message Queue (MSMQ). We can build a very robust messaging system, such as an internal instant message system or a "page" e-mail system. If you plan on using this namespace, install MSMQ before attempting to use it or it won't work.

In a very basic view, System.Messaging allows us to reference MSMQ, and use MSMQ to send a message (which is usually wrapped by XML and SOAP) by placing it on the queue; once the message is on the queue we can then read it and format it appropriately. Visual Basic programmers may recognize this as the Message object.

System.Net

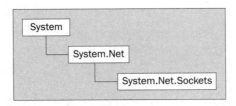

Browsing the Internet is a lot of fun using System.Net. It contains the basic files that are needed in order to create an Internet connection. Full HTTP support is included, as well as authorization protocols, DNS resolution, and basic socket support.

System.Net.Sockets

This namespace contains a specialized namespace control structure for dealing with raw connections. Protocols, sockets, data streams and TCP controls are very precise, allowing for users to define how a connection is created, answered, replied, and closed. Higher-level protocols, such as HTTP, can be found in the System.Web namespace.

System.Reflection

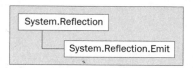

Reflection provides the programmer with the ability to view, depending on permissions available, the information that is available within an application's meta data at runtime. This type of interaction is generally not allowed by .NET due to the obvious security and application integrity issues but sometimes it can be useful for determining and verifying data types or even as a security measure. It can even be used to generate MSIL code on-the-fly at runtime.

System.Reflection.Emit

You can emulate (that is, emit) the meta data or MSIL from an assembly. This is useful if you want to emit an assembly and check a setting / value that's hard-coded against the setting / value in an assembly that may have been tampered with. You can even use the meta data and MSIL information that is emitted to create a new executable file.

System.Resources

If you need to create a deployable application for .NET you will want to include `System.Resources` in your plans. Using this namespace you can create a file for each localization (culture-specific setting) your application will deploy to, which stores the internal localization information.

Each resource file will have the same name used when created; the only exception is that it will have an extension to it, such as "`Resource.es - AR.resources`"; the only part that really matters in this naming convention is the middle identifier, "`es - AR`". This is exactly like the HTTP language reference used by browsers to identify primary and secondary language / text for a web page. In this example we're using `es` (Spanish) from `AR` (Argentina).

> *A word of caution: if you plan on using stand alone* `.resource` *files in .NET you can't use XCOPY (in other words, just copying the assembly to your hard drive) deployment unless you compile the files as a 'satellite assembly'.*

System.Runtime

There is no actual `System.Runtime` namespace but a number of other namespaces use it as their root. They provide a diverse range of functionality from COM interoperability to remoting for distributed applications.

System.Runtime.CompilerServices

This namespace is for programmers writing compilers only; it allows the programmer to control meta data attributes that affect the runtime behavior of the common language runtime.

System.Runtime.InteropServices

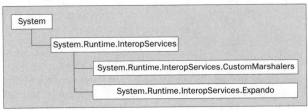

The classes within this namespace can be used to access COM and native APIs. Of special note within this namespace is DllImportAttribute, which can be used to define methods to access native system APIs.

System.Runtime.Remoting

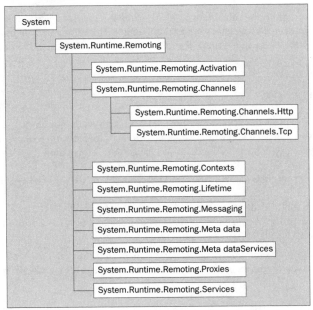

System.Runtime.Remoting provides a way for programmers to work with and configure distributed applications. You can interface with configuration settings, edit the configuration files, client-end and server-end registration as well as publishing remote objects.

System.Runtime.Remoting.Activation

This namespace allows for the server and client activation of remote objects.

System.Runtime.Remoting.Channels

Channels, which are the transport medium for a client call to a remote object, are handled through this namespace. It includes built-in support for channel sinks as well.

System.Runtime.Remoting.Channels.HTTP

Uses the SOAP protocol for HTTP channels in order to transport messages from and to remote objects.

System.Runtime.Remoting.Channels.TCP

Uses the channels to transport the objects themselves in binary format to and from a remote location.

System.Runtime.Remoting.Contexts

Contexts are created during remote object activation and handle automatic services like security or synchronization. This namespace allows the programmer to define the environments for a context.

System.Runtime.Remoting.Lifetime

This namespace provides classes that manage the lifetime of remote objects.

System.Runtime.Remoting.Messaging

This namespace provides classes that handle message passing through message sinks.

System.Runtime.Remoting.Meta data

This namespace can be used to customize the HTTP `SoapAction` type output and XML Namespace URI.

System.Runtime.Remoting.Meta dataServices

The classes in this namespace are used by SOAPSUDS to convert meta data to and from XML Schema.

System.Runtime.Remoting.Proxies

This namespace provides classes that handle the control and functionality of proxies; in this case a proxy is a local object that is an exact image of a remote object.

System.Runtime.Remoting.Services

This namespace provides the classes that give functionality to the whole `System.Runtime.Remoting` namespace.

System.Runtime.Serialization

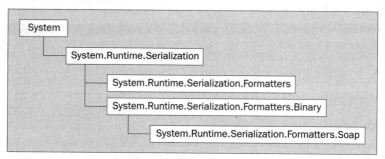

The classes and interfaces in this namespace can be used to serialize and deserialize objects as well as provide classes with a way to control their own serialization behavior.

System.Runtime.Serialization.Formatters

This namespace provides classes that support functions used by serialization formatters

System.Runtime.Serialization.Formatters.Binary

This namespace allows for the serialization and deserializaton of objects in binary format.

System.Runtime.Serialization.Formatters.Soap

This namespace allows for the serialization and deserialization of objects in SOAP format.

System.Security

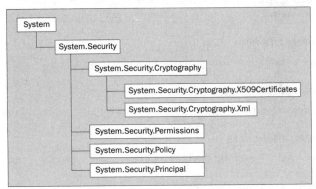

.NET has a very good security system in place, both in the runtime and, for our use, in this namespace. Covering everything from cryptography to code-base security this namespace has it all.

System.Security.Cryptography

This namespace provides cryptographic tools, such as hash, random numbers, and encoding / decoding of files using any of the built-in cryptographic algorithms. There are two types of algorithms supported: Symmetric and Asymmetric.

The symmetric algorithms consist of the popular DES (both in normal single-crypt form and triple-crypt form) and RC2. Both of these algorithms have a strong following and have been used for quite some time now and are freely available online.

Asymmetric algorithms consist of publicly available key encoding / decoding, such as RSA. These algorithms are publicly available and consist of two keys – one public key that is used for encrypting messages and a private key for decrypting them. The usual situation is that a message is encrypted from someone using the public key while the owner of the key decrypts the message using the private key.

This namespace is completely new to Windows development; usually we would have to depend on third-party plug-ins or products in order to have the functionality that is now provided through .NET.

System.Security.Cryptography.X509Certificates

X.509 Certificates are the some of the standard certificates found on various sites online. This namespace creates (or inserts) the meta data from a certificate for deployment usage. All of the basic functions available for use with X.509 Certificates, such as getting the public key (GetPublicKey) or viewing the serial number (GetSerialNumber) are here.

System.Security.Cryptography.XML

This namespace allows XML documents to be digitally signed; this model is apparently only for use within the .NET framework according to Microsoft.

At first glance, and due to the warning from Microsoft that it should not be used for general purposes, it may have some usefulness as an intranet certification system that can be used to keep track of who's going where within the intranet. DES and RC2 encryption are supported as well as the Base64 and C14N transform.

System.Security.Permissions

Permissions are a security system used by .NET to check to see if the referrer can access the information it's requesting.

Using a reflection request as an example, `assembly1` is receiving a request by `assembly2` that it wants to reflect some of its information. `Assembly1` assesses the permissions required to provide such a service and compares it to the permissions that `assembly2` has. If the permissions match then access is granted; otherwise no access will be given. This is similar to basic authentication.

System.Security.Policy

A policy contains the actual privileges that the code contains. The information is contained as membership conditions, evidence, and code groups. Usually when using this namespace, having prior knowledge of the system and permissions really make things a lot easier for the programmer since the policies can be specifically written to what's needed.

Policies are used with Code-access security (or Code-based security, as some refer to it as) where the code itself provides the needed requirements that allow it to access the needed services and / or information requested or needed.

System.Security.Principal

The principal system can save you the trouble of having to track down every single needed security. The principal, in essence, acts as an in-between for the code that's making a request and the code is to grant the request by passing along the needed requirements that may not be internally coded. Even if your user account may not have the proper rights the principal, which has the proper rights, will step in and let you through.

Imagine that you need access to a database solution stored within another assembly. You have already written your assembly and don't want to redo the whole code just to add a whole new set of principals, so you may just choose to change a couple of lines and reference a principal that contains the requirements needed to access the database. All your new code does is just make a call to the principal and then the principal does the rest of the work to get the correct access.

System.ServiceProcess

Windows always lacked a proper system to run background processes that were "self-aware"; that is to say that they knew at what timed intervals to perform certain tasks and jobs. Startup programs, while created to do this, aren't really the best things on the planet. A lot of times they wind up taking too much memory and remove overhead away from the user.

`System.ServiceProcess` allows .NET programmers to create an assembly that can run by itself in the background performing tasks as simple or as complex as you need them to be, while the Framework continues to provide it with its built-in memory management tools and clean-up routines.

The assembly(ies) created through the `System.ServiceProcess` classes are referred to as **Services**. Any service has to be installed via `InstallUtil.exe`.

System.Text

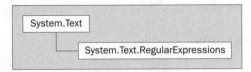

System.Text contains basic classes implement string conversion routines, such as ASCII to UTF8 conversion. It also includes two abstract classes, Encode and Decode, that you may not find much use for except for buffering purposes.

System.Text.RegularExpressions

All Regular Expression fans rejoice! All the needs (well, base needs at least) for working with Regular Expressions are found within this namespace. There have been improvements to Regular Expression matching within .NET as well as the other standard Regular Expression routines.

A regular expression is a text string that describes a set of strings. REGEX is usually used for searching for specified patterns. Through this namespace you can create groups of regular expressions for sorting or create, a group of captures.

System.Threading

Multi-threading takes on a new look in .NET (but maybe an old one to experienced JAVA programmers). In .NET, multithreading can be as simple as importing and using the System.Threading namespace, declaring the thread object, filling in the code, starting the thread, and stopping / killing the thread.

System.Timers

The System.Timers namespace contains a more powerful version of the Timer object used by Visual Basic programmers. The System.Timers classes let a programmer fire off events at certain intervals based on the internal server time. A definite advantage to this namespace when compared to its VB predecessor is its ability to schedule itself and fire an event daily, weekly, or monthly; the schedule component is so flexible you can tell it to fire on extremely specific periods, such as the 4th of every month!

System.Web

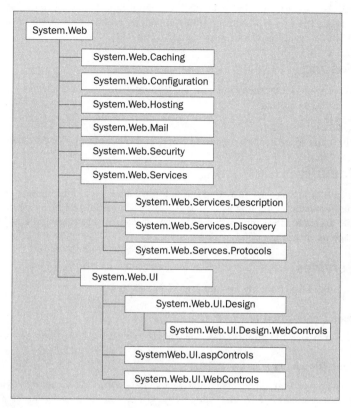

This is .NET's specialist area – Internet applications and Internet deployment. Before we can even get that far we need a concise set of classes that we can use to create the connection to the Internet and begin to apply at least basic and generic settings. System.Web provides us with all of the above.

Many of the System.Web classes are best used within an ASP.NET application but they can be turned to good use outside of ASP.NET.

Of special note are HTTPDebugHandler and HTTPException; these two classes simplify error identification. HTTPDebugHandler allows for online debug assistance and HTTPException allows ASP.NET to provide more thorough exception information. Exception methods supported include displaying the error code, help file link, message accompanying the error, and a full stack trace.

System.Web.Caching

This namespace provides ASP.NET with a method to pass information through the cache object that's available to every user on the site. Only one instance of the Cache object is available per application domain and it's alive while the app domain is still active. The minute the app domain is killed the object will automatically enter garbage collection.

An object that is passed through the cache is tracked immediately to see if there's any changes to it and any of its dependencies through CacheDependency.

System.Web.Configuration

This namespace can be used to configure your ASP.NET application via the remote `Config.web` file of your choosing. This can be used as a security setting as well by requiring an application to connect to the Internet and verify its own settings via a central `Config.web` file.

System.Web.Hosting

The classes in this namespace communicate with the Windows IIS host and ISAPI runtime.

System.Web.Mail

Just like it reads, this namespace provides access to e-mail capabilities using Windows 2000 SMTP mail service.

System.Web.Security

ASP.NET authentication services are provided through this namespace. This namespace provides basic cookie and web authentication handling as well as two IIS / Microsoft-specific authentication resources – Passport cookie file access to allow integration of Microsoft Password settings and IIS/ Windows authentication usage permission.

System.Web.Services

This namespace provides functionality for building Web Services.

System.Web.Services.Description

The classes in this namespace can publicly describe a web service using Microsoft's service description language.

System.Web.Services.Discovery

This namespace is a companion to `System.Web.Services.Description`; it provides functionality that allows consumers to locate all publicly broadcast web services running on a server.

System.Web.Services.Protocol

This namespace provides ASP.NET with a set of protocols that it can use to communicate between itself and any web service clients or providers. Currently the set of supported protocols are HTTP requests and SOAP requests.

System.Web.SessionState

This namespace contains classes which allow ASP.NET web applications to maintain session state between page requests.

System.Web.UI

ASP programmers suffered from having to deal with poor user interfaces due to HTML's lack of proper form objects. Now through the `System.Web.UI` namespace you can use Web Form components within your ASP code in the same way as you might use Windows Forms components for a Windows application.

`System.Web.UI` itself contains only the base classes and two text editing classes for HTML: `HtmlTextWriter` and `Html32TextWriter`. `HtmlTextWriter` has basic text capabilities that are primarily geared towards inserting basic string characters into an ASP file. `Html32TextWriter` is an extension of `HtmlTextWriter` and it can add various other styles to the text, including CSS.

System.Web.UI.Design

This namespace contains the majority of the data-binding resources you are going to need when working with your web UI.

System.Web.UI.Design.WebControls

The properties and methods for the ASP web form objects, such as the label, can be modified through this namespace. There is also support for using Regular Expressions within this namespace for use with your web UI!

System.Web.UI.aspControls

The classes in this namespace allow you to create (a better way to look at it is "generate") HTML code on the server for displaying to a client browser. Every HTML tag is represented here, from the <IMG> tag to the <TABLE> tag with all their options.

System.Web.UI.WebControls

The form objects that can be displayed on the web page are stored within this namespace. Don't confuse `System.Web.UI.WebControls` with `System.Web.UI.Design.WebControls` though; `System.Web.UI.Design.WebControls` provide the properties and methods that can be used to change the properties of the objects located in `System.Web.UI.WebControls`.

System.Windows.Forms

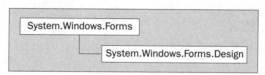

Need to create a Win32 form? This is the namespace that provides all of your objects for creating a GUI. The standard set of items that is available for use through Visual Basic is here, such as the ComboBox and the Clipboard. In fact, Visual Basic programmers will probably have a faster time realizing the power behind this namespace in its .NET form.

System.Windows.Forms.Design

Most of the menu items, such as Tabs or MenuCommands, can be altered during run time and design time through this namespace.

System.Xml

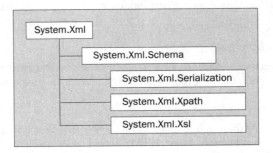

This namespace provides all the base functions for using XML. It can work with XML 1.0, XML Namespaces, XML Schemas, Xpath Expressions, XSL/T Transformations, DOM Level 2, and SOAP1.1 XML standards. A very verbose namespace indeed but it should not come as a surprise that there is no support for XML DTD's; remember that Microsoft is pushing for Schemas to be the web XML standard through the W3C.

System.Xml.Schema

This namespace contains classes that allow the creation and usage of XML Schemas based on the W3C standard. Contains every single possible supported facet, attribute, and classification for Schemas.

System.Xml.Serialization

Allows for the serialization of objects and data structures within applications into XML.

System.Xml.XPath

This namespace provides the functionality needed to traverse through an XSL/T document.

System.Xml.Xsl

This namespace provides the functionality needed to transform XML based on the XSL/T document as well as handle XSL/T exceptions and context resolution

Summary

Namespaces in .NET give us, the everyday code-warriors, a way to easily find and locate the classes and functionality that we need from .NET when we need it. If it's not there or maybe not to our liking we can even create brand-new namespaces to pass around and share with friends.

We have learned that namespaces follow a hierarchal pattern with the System namespace as its root. As other namespaces appear under the System namespace they can use the System classes and add their own functionality.

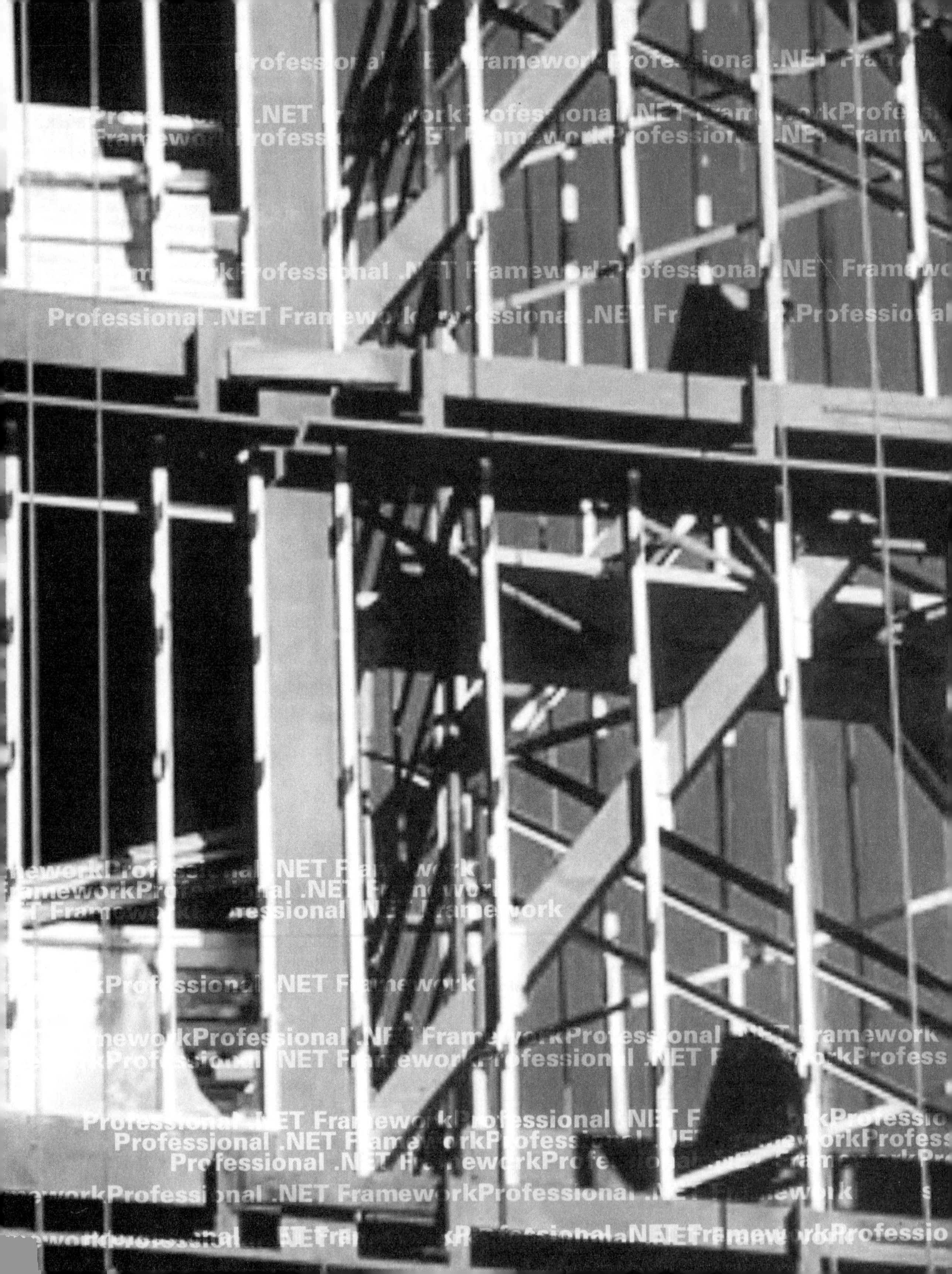
Professional .NET Framework

Object Oriented-Programming

The .NET Framework is based on object-oriented programming (OOP) principles. Every time you write applications that are based on the .NET Framework, you will have to program with OOP concepts.

In this appendix, we will look at the following topics:

- ❑ Key concepts of Object-Orientation
- ❑ What benefits can be gained by using OOP
- ❑ How OOP concepts apply to .NET

The first sections of this appendix outline the major concepts of object-oriented programming in a theoretical manner. Although object-oriented programming could easily take up a whole book, these sections aim to provide you with the basic underpinnings or a chance to refresh your knowledge.

After the theory we discuss how to incorporate the object-oriented programming style into your everyday work of creating .NET applications. If you are already comfortable with object orientation, this part of the appendix will show you how the .NET languages support the key concepts.

Concepts of Object-Oriented Programming

Programs using an object-oriented design differ greatly from the old fashioned, procedure-based style. Using the procedural approach, the entire functionality is often stored in one single file. The functionality is described step-by-step like an algorithm, where the operations are separated from the data structures. Object orientation takes a different approach. Here the code is split into stand-alone modules called classes. A class resembles a "blueprint" that is later used to create instances of an object. This blueprint defines data structures and the necessary functions that process the data structure to fulfill the application's objective.

You, as a programmer, write classes, and objects do the work at run-time – but what exactly are objects? Objects are in-memory manifestations of a class. The state of an object is determined by the data structures and the behavior defined in the class. As there is usually more than one object, these objects can interact with each other.

There are a number of key concepts in object-orientated programming.

❑ Abstraction

❑ Encapsulation

❑ Inheritance

❑ Polymorphism

We will now take a look at each of these concepts in turn.

Abstraction

Abstraction provides the ability for programmers to concentrate on what their code is doing, rather than how the results are achieved. Obviously, a good programmer *should* have some understanding of the underlying system that executes their code, but this does not mean that they *need* to.

For instance, imagine you want to write a program that sums two variables. To accomplish this simple task you have a choice of programming languages, ranging from assembly language to higher-level languages such as VB.NET and C#. While the assembly language contains a detailed set of instructions for the CPU, the readability of the source code for "average" people is low.

Low-level languages generally provide better performance, but, as programming projects become more complex, development costs become more important. Higher-level, more abstracted languages facilitate faster development and minimize the problems that come with complexity.

Encapsulation and Data Hiding

Encapsulation is the ability to embed and hide the internal object data or implementation details. You determine which elements are to be exposed to the outside of the object and which are to remain hidden. The idiom 'hidden' denotes that these members of an object are inaccessible and therefore protected from access or alteration. This principle is called data hiding.

A key practice in encapsulation is to deny direct access to the data members of the class. By forcing users of your class to access data members through methods, rather than directly, you retain the freedom to change your implementation without breaking any other code that relies on it.

Inheritance

Inheritance refers to the ability to derive functionality from a base class. This means that, rather than constructing a class from scratch, you can base it on an existing class. This feature is of great importance and it allows you to reuse common functionality for free, just by inheriting from a base class.

To get a picture of inheritance, think of the following example. Assume a base class called mammal. A mammal can, for example, drink. Drinking would be one of its basic abilities. A subclass derived from the base class mammal could be called 'Human'. As mentioned before, when inheriting from a base class the subclass has the same functionality as the base class – and in our case a human is able to drink too.

In .NET, a class can only inherit functionality from a single parent class. When more flexibility is required, interfaces can be used. An interface, as the name implies, defines an interface for functionality, but not the functionality itself. A class can implement as many interfaces as required. Interfaces can inherit from other interfaces.

Polymorphism

Inheritance provides the ability to derive functionality from a base class, but sometimes it can be limiting – what if our 'Human' class needs to implement the drinking action in a different way to the general Mammal class? Polymorphism lets you alter (redefine) the methods of a base class. You are now able to override the exposed methods of the base class and fit them to your needs.

Another example of polymorphism is known as 'overloading'. This refers to methods of a class that have the same name, but take different types of parameters or return a different type of result. The combination of parameter types and return types is known as the signature. Overloading allows a class to provide any number of methods with the same name, providing their signatures are different.

Benefits of Using Object-Orientation

Writing applications based on object-oriented principles can be cumbersome at first, because you have to abide to several rules to unlock the full potential of object orientation – so why bother? The more complex your software gets, the more you profit from object orientation, because using object-orientated principles makes your software:

❑ Robust – encapsulation protects the inner workings of your classes from outside influence. If you change these inner workings, it doesn't have an effect on the outside world, because other programmers or users always interact with the same interface. The source code has a clear and easy to read structure, in contrast to the spaghetti-like code of procedural-programming style.

❑ Modular and reusable: – large software projects almost always require more than one programmer. Programmers can work together on the same project without conflicting or overwriting the code, because they work on independent modules of the software. Inheritance lets you reuse basic functionality, or even alter it when needed.

❑ Simple and Flexible: – as your software consists of independent modules you can easily apply changes to the source code without rewriting it.

Object Orientation in .NET

.NET is firmly built around object-orientated principals. Intermediate Language, which all .NET languages are compiled to, is itself object orientated. This means that even a program written in a non-object-orientated .NET language will be object orientated once compiled.

The two main .NET languages, VB.NET and C#, provide a number of features to support object orientation.

Classes

Classes are the building blocks of every .NET application. A class is defined with the following syntax:

```
'VB.NET
Public Class Person
    ' class members
End Class
```

```
//C#
public class Person
{
    // class members
}
```

'public' in these examples can be any of the following:

❑ Public – the class can be used by any other class or application.

❑ Protected – the class can be used by its containing class or classes derived from it.

❑ Internal (Friend in VB.NET) – the class is only accessible within its own assembly.

❑ Private – the class is only accessible within its containing type.

The following modifiers can be used in addition to the accessibility modifier.

❑ Sealed (NotInheritable in VB.NET) – the class cannot be used as a parent for derived classes.

❑ Abstract (MustInherit in VB.NET) – the class cannot itself be instantiated. This is used for classes that are designed to act only as parents for derived classes.

Data Members

Each class contains its own data. Each data member has their accessibility defined using the same modifiers as were used for classes. Data members are usually protected or private, in order to maintain encapsulation.

Here is the Person class with some data members:

```
'VB.NET
Public Class Person
    Protected Dim age As Integer
    Private Dim privateThoughts As String
End Class
```

```
//C#
public class Person
{
    protected int age;
    private String privateThoughts;
}
```

Methods

The behavior of a class is defined by its methods. The accessibility of methods is defined in the same way as for data members.

In VB.NET, methods are defined using the Sub keyword (for methods that do not return a result) or the Function keyword (for methods that do return a result).

```
'VB.NET
Public Class Person
    Protected Dim age As Integer
    Private Dim privateThoughts As String

    Public Sub HaveBirthday()
        age++
    End Sub

    Public Function TellUsYourThoughts() As String
        Return privateThoughts
    End Function

End Class
```

In C#, methods are defined in the same way whether or not they return a result (those that do not return a value have the return type void).

```
//C#
public class Person
{
    protected int age;
    private String privateThoughts;

    public void HaveBirthday()
    {
        age++;
    }

    public String TellUsYourThoughts()
    {
        return privateThoughts;
    }
}
```

Constructors

Constructors are the first statements of a class that are executed automatically whenever an instance of your class is created. They give you control over the initialization process of your object's data members.

If you don't write a constructor yourself, a default constructor is created for you. This process avoids errors from using any variables that have not been initialized.

Constructors are not inherited, cannot be directly invoked, and don't have a return type declared. Constructors are set to `public` by default. You can use any other access modifier to prohibit access to it from outside the class.

C# and VB.NET take different approaches to defining constructors. Whereas C# requires you to use the class name for the constructor, VB.NET requires you to state a subprocedure with the `New()` keyword.

Consider the following snippets using C# and VB.NET:

C#:

```
class Person
{
    public Person()
    {
        age = 0;
    }
}
```

A VB.NET constructor would look like this:

```
Class Person
    Public Sub Person()
            age = 0
    End Sub
End Class
```

A note to VB programmers: the `Class_Initialize` event is no longer supported in VB.NET since VB.NET now utilizes constructors.

If required you can pass additional arguments to initialize members:

```
//C#
class Person
{
    public Person(int a)
    {
        age = a;
    }
}
```

```
'VB.NET
Class Test
    Public Sub New(a As Integer)
        age = a
    End Sub
End Class
```

But you have to explicitly call this new constructor (otherwise, the default constructor with no parameters is used):

```
//C#
Test myPerson = new Person(23);
```

```
'VB.NET
Dim myPerson As Person = new Person(23)
```

Properties

Properties appear to the outside world as data members, but allow processing when their values are retrieved or set. Properties are defined with property declarations. The basic syntax for a property declaration that is accessible from outside (using the Public access modifier) looks like this:

VB.NET:

```
Public Property myAge As Integer
    Get
        myAge = age
    End Get

    Set
        age = value
    End Set
End Property
```

C#:

```
public int myAge
{
    get {return age}
    set {age = value}
}
```

Properties are good for providing access to private data members.

Operator Overloading

Operator overloading is a neat feature: it allows you to redefine operators to fit your needs. Using C# you can utilize the `operator` keyword to define a static member function of the overloaded operator. Overloadable operators are the unary (for example, +, -, ++, etc.), binary (for example, +, -, *, /, etc.), and comparison operators (for example, ==, !=, <, >, etc.). All others can't be overloaded.

> The plus (+) and minus (-) operator can function as either unary or binary operator.

The next code listing shows an example where operator overloading is a useful feature. Assume you have to sum two complex numbers. As you know, a complex number has a real and an imaginary part. Of course, you can sum each part in an extra pass, but once you overload the + operator you need just a single line. I admit that operator overloading does make even more sense the more complex the program becomes.

We create a new console application and type in the following source code:

```
//C#
using System;

class ComplexNumber
{
    public int real, imaginary;

    public ComplexNumber (int real, int imaginary)
    {
        this.real = real;
        this.imaginary = imaginary;
    }

    public static ComplexNumber operator +( ComplexNumber compl1,
            ComplexNumber compl2)
    {
        return new ComplexNumber (compl1.real + compl2.real, compl1.imaginary
            + compl2.imaginary);
    }

    public static void Main()
    {
        ComplexNumber Complex1 = new ComplexNumber (5,7);
        ComplexNumber Complex2 = new ComplexNumber (1,3);

        ComplexNumber Sum = Complex1 + Complex2;

        Console.WriteLine("First complex number:  {0} + {1}i", Complex1.real,
                Complex1.imaginary);
        Console.WriteLine("Second complex number: {0} + {1}i", Complex2.real,
                Complex2.imaginary);
        Console.WriteLine("The sum of the two numbers: {0} + {1}i", Sum.real,
                Sum.imaginary);

    }
}
```

In this example we declare the + operator to be overloaded by means of the `operator` keyword. Then we declare the two objects, `compl1` and `compl2`, that have to be added, and the new return type (`SumComplex`). In the `Main` method, we create a new object for each complex number and then easily add the two complex numbers.

To compile this example save it as `OverloadingCs.cs` and issue the following compiler statement at the command prompt:

```
csc.exe OverloadingCs.cs
```

Executing the example, displays the following output:

```
First complex number:  5 + 7i
Second complex number: 1 + 3i
The sum of the two numbers: 6 + 10i
```

Interfaces

An Interface declares a reference type, which has abstract members. Therefore, you can declare methods, properties, and so on in an interface. Multiple Interfaces can be implemented by classes, solving the problem that classes can only derive from a single parent class.

An interface resembles a contract between the caller and the actual implementation. If you implement an interface, the caller can expect the object to obey the interface specification. This specification represents a strict definition of the interface members, such as properties, methods, and so on.

VB.NET:

```
Interface IDraw
    Sub Draw()
End Interface
```

C#:

```
Interface IDraw
{
    void Draw() {}
}
```

Inheritance

As mentioned before, inheritance is the ability to reuse source code from an existing (base) class. This section discusses this ability applied to classes and additionally shows how in can be applied to interfaces.

The following snippets show a basic class written in VB.NET and C#. Though they don't inherit explicitly from a base class, they inherit from the "mother of all classes": `System.Object`.

```
'VB.NET
Class TestClass

    Sub TheMethod()
            System.Console.WriteLine("This is TestClass.ItsMethod")
    End Sub
End Class
```

```
//C#
class TestClass
{
    void ItsMethod()
    {
            System.Console.WriteLine("This is TestClass.ItsMethod");
    }
}
```

These two snippets show a class called `TestClass` that implicitly derives from `System.Object`, the ultimate base class of the .NET Framework. The next snippet shows a slightly more advanced sample using inheritance:

```
'VB.NET
Class Class_A

    Public Sub Method_A()
            System.Console.WriteLine("This is Class_A.Method_A")
    End Sub
End Class

Class Class_B
    Inherits Class_A

    Public Sub Method_B()
            System.Console.WriteLine("This is Class_B.Method_B")
    End Sub

End Class

Class MainApp

    Shared Sub Main()

            Dim MyClass_B As New Class_B()

            MyClass_B.Method_A()
            MyClass_B.Method_B()

    End Sub
End Class
```

This little command line program sports a class called `Class_A` that has a method called `Method_A`. This method displays a simple message, informing the reader where it comes from, to the command line. `Class_B` inherits from `Class_A` using the `Inherits` keyword and introduces a new method called `Method_B`. The `Method_B` writes another message to the command line.

In the `MainApp` class we instantiate a new object called `MyClass_B` created from the "blueprint" class `Class_B`. `Class_B` contains both methods, `Method_A` and `Method_B`, and they are accessible from outside the class, because we applied the access modifier keyword `Public`. Therefore, we can now invoke them to display:

```
This is Class_A.Method_A
This is Class_B.Method_B
```

at the command prompt.

C# uses a colon (:) to signal that a subclass is inheriting from a parent class. Consider the following C# example that represents the previous VB.NET one:

```csharp
//C#
class Class_A
{
    public void Method_A()
    {
        System.Console.WriteLine("This is Class_A.Method_A");
    }
}

class Class_B:Class_A
{
    public void Method_B()
    {
        System.Console.WriteLine("This is Class_B.Method_B");
    }
}

class MainApp
{
    static void Main()
    {
        Class_B MyClass_B = new Class_B();

        MyClass_B.Method_A();
        MyClass_B.Method_B();
    }
}
```

Interface Inheritance

As you can inherit from classes, you can inherit from interfaces, too. But why would you do that? As mentioned earlier in this chapter, the .NET Framework supports single inheritance from base classes only. However, interfaces introduce the ability to inherit from multiple base interfaces. Therefore, you can inherit an identically named type member from different base interfaces. However, you must reference the type members through their base interface names to avoid ambiguity.

Another important aspect to mention is that if you inherit from an interface you only get a set of specifications, not the actual blueprints, as it would be with implementation inheritance.

Consider the following VB.NET example that has two different interfaces, one with a property and the other with a method. Assume that the property and the method have an identical name (`Sum`). This would cause an ambiguity and the source code won't compile. Instead you code the following to avoid conflicts:

```
'VB.NET
Interface ISumStorage
     Property Sum() As Double
End Interface

Interface ISumIt

    Sub Sum(nVar As Integer)

End Interface

Interface ICalculation
    Inherits ISumStorage, ISumIt
End Interface

Class MainApp

    Public Sub CastIt(sum As ICalculation)

    CType(sum, ISumStorage).Sum = 12
    CType(sum, ISumIt).Sum(2)

    End Sub
End Class
```

Interfaces are inherited using the Inherits keyword (see interface Icalculation). As shown by the example above, the ambiguity is avoided by casting sum located in the Main procedure (using CType()) to the appropriate base interface (Interface IsumStorage and IsumIt respectively).

As with classes, C# uses the colon (:) to inherit from base interfaces:

```
//C#
interface ISumStorage
{
    double Sum
    {
        get;
        set;
    }
}

interface ISumIt
{
    void Sum(int nVar);
}

interface ICalculation: ISumStorage, ISumIt {}

class MainApp
{
    void CastIt(ICalculation sum)
    {
        ((ISumStorage)sum).Sum = 12;
        ((ISumIt)sum).Sum(2);
    }
}
```

Using Abstract and Base Classes

Base classes can be instantiated. If you want to inhibit this option you must use the `MustInherit` option in VB.NET (or `abstract` in C#). The inherited class of the abstract (base) class must then implement all its members.

The following example shows such an abstract class (`Test`). Then another class (`DerivedAbstract`) is derived from the abstract `Test` class. The derived class can be instantiated later at the entry point of the VB.NET example.

```
MustInherit Public Class Test

    Public MustOverride Sub MyAbstract()

End Class

Public Class DerivedAbstract
    Inherits Test

    Public Overrides Sub MyAbstract()

        System.Console.WriteLine("Derived Abstract Class Method")

    End Sub
End Class

Class MainApp

    Public Shared Sub Main()
        Dim MyDerivedAbstract As DerivedAbstract = New _
                    DerivedAbstract()
        MyDerivedAbstract.MyAbstract()
    End Sub
End Class
```

To derive the abstract base class, `Test`, we use the `Inherits` statement. Then, as mentioned before, we have to override all its members (`MyAbstract` method). By using the `override` statement we can add additional functionality to the derived method `MyAbstract`. From now on we deal with the derived class only. Because it can be instantiated again, we can create a new instance in `Main()`.

Here is the equivalent source code written in C#. Note that we use `override` rather than `overrides`.

```
abstract class Test
{
    abstract public void MyAbstract();

}

class DerivedAbstract: Test
{
    public override void MyAbstract()
```

```
    {
        System.Console.WriteLine("Derived Abstract Class Method");
    }

}
class MainApp
{
    public static void Main()
    {
    DerivedAbstract MyTest = new DerivedAbstract();
    MyTest.MyAbstract();
    }
}
```

The .NET Framework doesn't allow us to override interface member implementations. A work around is to call a method of the interface implementation that is declared with the virtual keyword.

More information

This appendix has taken a very brief look at how VB.NET and C# support object orientation concepts. A lot more information on both of the languages can be found in the books *Beginning VB.NET*, *Professional VB.NET*, *Beginning C#*, and *Professional C#*, all published by Wrox.

Index

A Guide to the Index

The index is arranged hierarchically, in alphabetical order, with symbols preceding the letter A. Most second-level entries and many third-level entries also occur as first-level entries. This is to ensure that users will find the information they require however they choose to search for it.

S

Z

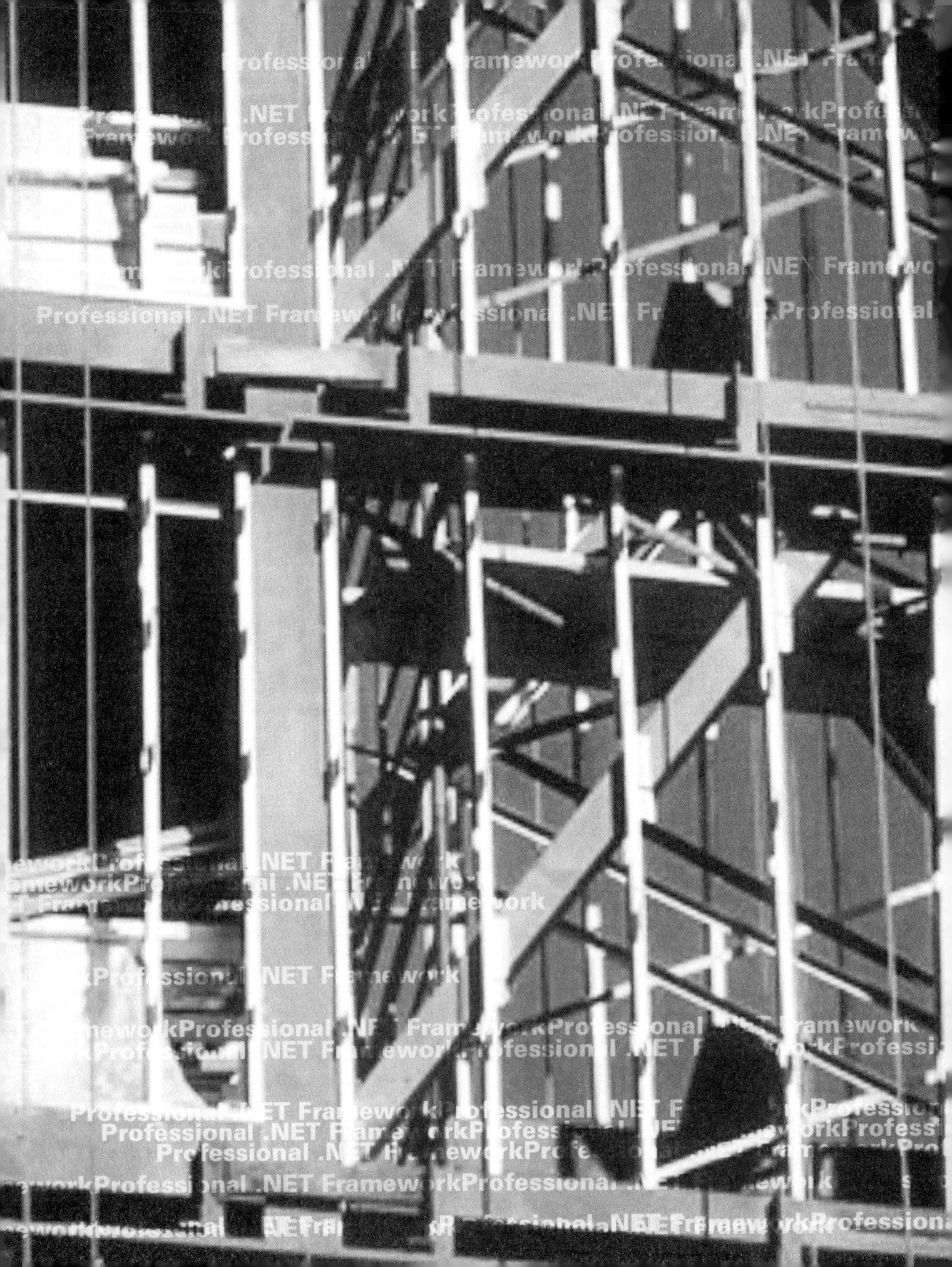
Professional .NET Framework

Notes

Notes

Notes

Notes

Notes

wrox

Programmer to Programmer™

Wrox writes books for you. Any suggestions, or ideas about how you want information given in your ideal book will be studied by our team.
Your comments are always valued at Wrox.

Free phone in USA 800-USE-WROX
Fax (312) 893 8001

UK Tel.: (0121) 687 4100   Fax: (0121) 687 4101

Professional .NET Framework – Registration Card

Name _____

Address _____

_____

_____

_____

City _____ State/Region _____

Country _____ Postcode/Zip _____

E-Mail _____

Occupation _____

How did you hear about this book?

☐ Book review (name) _____

☐ Advertisement (name) _____

☐ Recommendation _____

☐ Catalog _____

☐ Other _____

Where did you buy this book?

☐ Bookstore (name) _____ City _____

☐ Computer store (name) _____

☐ Mail order _____

☐ Other _____

What influenced you in the purchase of this book?

☐ Cover Design ☐ Contents ☐ Other (please specify):

_____

How did you rate the overall content of this book?

☐ Excellent ☐ Good ☐ Average ☐ Poor

What did you find most useful about this book? _____

_____

What did you find least useful about this book? _____

_____

Please add any additional comments. _____

_____

What other subjects will you buy a computer book on soon?

_____

What is the best computer book you have used this year?

_____

wrox

Programmer to Programmer™

Note: If you post the bounce back card below in the UK, please send it to:

Wrox Press Limited, Arden House, 1102 Warwick Road,
Acocks Green, Birmingham B27 6HB. UK.

Computer Book Publishers

NO POSTAGE
NECESSARY
IF MAILED
IN THE
UNITED STATES

BUSINESS REPLY MAIL

FIRST CLASS MAIL   PERMIT#64   CHICAGO, IL

POSTAGE WILL BE PAID BY ADDRESSEE

WROX PRESS INC.
29 S. LA SALLE ST.
SUITE 520
CHICAGO IL 60603-USA